BUGS BRITANNICA

BUGS
BRITANNICA

PETER MARREN

AND

RICHARD MABEY

Chatto & Windus
LONDON

Published by Chatto & Windus 2010

2 4 6 8 10 9 7 5 3 1

Copyright © Peter Marren 2010

Peter Marren has asserted his right under the Copyright,
Designs and Patents Act 1988 to be identified as the author
of this work

First published in Great Britain in 2010 by
Chatto & Windus
Random House, 20 Vauxhall Bridge Road,
London SW1V 2SA
www.rbooks.co.uk

Addresses for companies within The Random House Group
Limited can be found at: www.randomhouse.co.uk/offices.
htm

The Random House Group Limited Reg. No. 954009

A CIP catalogue record for this book
is available from the British Library

ISBN 9780701181802

The Random House Group Limited supports The Forest
Stewardship Council (FSC), the leading international forest
certification organisation. All our titles that are printed on
Greenpeace approved FSC certified paper carry the FSC logo.
Our paper procurement policy can be found at www.rbooks.
co.uk/environment

Printed and bound by C&C Offset Printing Co., Ltd., China
Design: Peter Ward

For Sue, from Peter

CONTENTS

INTRODUCTION

This is a book about insects. It is also about spiders, snails, worms, crabs and starfish – in other words, about all forms of animals without a backbone. Together they make up 98 per cent of all animal life on the planet. They teem and swarm over the globe, on the land, in rivers and oceans and in the air. Like stars in the Milky Way, their numbers defy our imaginations. A single wood-ant nest lodges the equivalent of the population of a large market town. A termite mound encloses that of a capital city. And the astronomical figures extend to species. A single, ordinary suburban garden in Leicestershire was found to contain 8000 species of insects alone (though it took 18 years to find them all). We all have such insect rainforests on our doorsteps.

Small as they are, 'bugs' are life-sustaining, and we would not survive long without them. They are the cornerstones of ecosystems, the creatures that generate the cycles and food-webs of the living earth. They pollinate our flowers and crops, recycle waste into fertile soil and help to maintain clear, clean water. But our relationship is not all positive. Bugs suck our blood and spread typhoid and malaria. They compete with us as crop pests and seek their share of our stores, gardens and kitchens. Bugs enter our lives as heroes and villains: bug-bears and bug-delights. For better or worse, the lives of the British and their bugs are entangled and thereby enriched.

We have called our book *Bugs Britannica*. Its subject is the small life of Britain. It ranges from the tiny amoeba, which might be described as 'nearly an animal', to the amphioxus, or lancelet, which is 'nearly a fish'. In between are all the bugs that make a profound impact on our lives and thoughts: earthworms, house and garden spiders, butterflies and moths, bees and wasps, winkles and shrimps.

The Reconciliation of Oberon and Titania, 1847, by Sir Joseph Noel Paton, shows an imaginary scene from Shakespeare's A Midsummer Night's Dream *in which the artist's fancy roams free among the miniature world of insects. Among the fairy queen's attendants are identifiable butterflies, moths, glow-worms and snails.*

They act as ambassadors for the estimated 40,000 species of bug that live on or around Britain.

This is not a book of entomology, or an identification guide, or a biological textbook. Rather, like its companion volumes, *Birds Britannica* and *Flora Britannica*, *Bugs Britannica* is concerned with the cultural story of the British and their wildlife, with what Mark Cocker termed 'our shared ecological history'. We are interested primarily in the places where bug lives and human experience meet, with what we see, think and feel about insects and other small life. We are not exclusively concerned, like scientists, with what is objectively true. *Bugs Britannica* is more of a record of what we *believe*. Artists, poets and advertisers are interested not in the humdrum facts of invertebrate anatomy but in the bug's popular *image*. Hence the moths of *Bugs Britannica* are not only nocturnal insects with dusty wings and feathered antennae but also the ghosts of departed souls or metaphors for the rusting away of human aspirations or furry-winged teddy-bears beloved by wide-eyed children. They are not only hawkmoths and silkmoths but also 'witches', 'millers', 'buzzards' and 'bob-owlers'.

Even in a book of this size it is impossible to mention, let alone describe, every species of British invertebrate. Fortunately this doesn't matter because the majority of them are unknown except to a few experts, and they have no cultural profile whatever. In terms of their image, most of our bugs are collective beings. For example, what we say and think about grasshoppers is common to the whole group and not to any particular species, with the possible exception of the supposedly all-devouring locust (whose 'lore' comes from the Bible, not from the British countryside). We have set out our pages in rough evolutionary order, starting with primitive life and then ranging through progressively more advanced forms. This inevitably produces a formidable parade of worms near the start, but don't let that put you off. *Bugs Britannica* is designed for pleasurable dipping and dabbling, not for a marathon swim, and you can read it in any order you like. We have a lot to say about bees, ants and butterflies, rather less about hydroids, flatworms and bryozoa.

We have tried as far as possible to produce a genuinely grassroots portrait of our small life. *Bugs Britannica*, like its predecessors, is an interactive project in which the British public was invited to take part. Using an online blog, together with appeals and publicity in a range of newspapers, magazines and journals, we advertised the project and urged people to send us stories and anecdotes of personal encounters. Hundreds of contributions came in over the two-and-a-half-year lifetime of the project, and with their colours of amusement, wonder, fear, insight and sympathy, we have included many of them here. In their totality they suggest that our links with bug life are still reasonably strong and informed by our concern for our common future. We are, many of our contributors seemed to feel, all in this together.

Some wonderful stories, modern reworkings of ancient beliefs, took shape in front of our eyes. In the autumn of 2006, there had been a memorable and, to some, slightly unsettling explosion of craneflies or, as we all insist on calling them, daddy-longlegs. In former times it would have been called a plague. The event became a hot topic on internet blogs and talkshops. A rumour spread that the insects were deadly poisonous; not only that, but there seemed to be a real danger of the fly creeping from its lair in the corner of the bedroom to take up new quarters inside the sleeper's open, snoring mouth. In a glorious moment at the fag-end of the silly season, we had collectively produced a new myth, as potent and ridiculous as any from a medieval bestiary. A few months later, the Nottinghamshire Wildlife Trust made a touching gesture of reparation. Going into partnership with a local brewery, they marketed Cranefly Ale, with a homily about our much maligned and misunderstood insects on the back of each bottle.

Similar but older myths and stories about insects and spiders survive in the forms of children's stories and games. As part of that sudden, intense interest in the world around them, young children will still make a wish to the ladybird perched on the tip of a finger. They still watch intently as a slug or snail traces mysterious initials in the dust of an upturned dustbin lid or will entice a garden snail to put out its 'horns'. Their parents, meanwhile, compete to 'charm' the most worms from the ground, organise wacky snail races with tipsters and stopwatches or take part in competitions to see who can down the largest number of raw, live oysters in a minute. In May 2009, someone visiting the war cemeteries of the Western Front noticed a large number of Painted Lady butterflies flying over the graves, as though, as some still believe, they were the souls of the soldiers killed at Ypres and the Somme. Apparently we still believe, with at least half our minds, that bees are virtuous and perpetually busy, that crabs are sour-natured and duplicitous, and that snails are prudent and thrifty – notions that have been held dear since the time of Aristotle.

And the stories, like the species, evolve over time, mirroring contemporary concerns and finding their ways into the most rarified technologies. A few years ago, the hottest Christmas toy was a remote-controlled dragonfly with shimmering wings that wonderfully matched the motions of the real thing (and whose green-glowing eyes seemed to magnify its innate bugginess). But the model was merely the play form of a serious project to implant microengineered systems into real insects to produce living cyborgs that carry miniature microphones, video cameras or gas detectors. Perhaps some of the nature films of the near future will be shot by the insects themselves through sensors embedded harmlessly in their enormous eyes. Meanwhile, ant behaviour is being studied by mathematicians seeking hidden numerical patterns in apparently random actions. The results may contribute to the design of that half-feared object, the intelligent robot, the 'Hal' of *2001: A Space Odyssey*. Our own world and that of bugs continue to collide in ways previous generations could not have imagined.

We have deliberately avoided overburdening the book with relatively familiar material about collecting and conservation. Collecting and rearing invertebrate life were among the grand passions of the Victorians. It remained popular throughout much of the twentieth century, especially in the form of butterfly-collecting. But collecting is essentially the study of dead, inert insects or live ones about to become specimens. The passion today, which can be seen in the eyes of children at the popular insect fairs around the country, is for *living* bugs: stick insects, caterpillars, cockroaches, scorpions and spiders. Creatures that once made most of us recoil in fear have become much-loved pets. We have opted, unashamedly, for life.

Conservation, many would argue, is the most urgent meeting ground of humans and nature today. How we accommodate our shrinking wildlife on an ever more crowded planet is a concern that unites us all. British bugs are certainly in decline. Almost any measure of insect biodiversity has shown worrying falls in both numbers and species. Formerly common and familiar things such as bees or the Garden Tiger Moth, with its 'woolly bear' caterpillar, are slipping away. We do not need science to notice that there are fewer insects in the car headlights or splodged on the windscreen, or settled on the windowpanes in the morning or the bedroom ceiling at night. The reasons – declining habitats, insecticides, street lights, competition from invasive species – may be complex, but the consequence is not in doubt (and it is hard not to suspect a link with a similar decline in insect-eating birds such as the cuckoo).

But conservation, like collecting, is a large subject and addressed in the main to habitats and more familiar wildlife (there are no meaningful conservation plans for the vast majority of invertebrate species). We do include conservation stories, and though we have not wandered far into its generalities, we have, we hope, suggested reasons why we should care. It would be a tragedy if our children never saw a stag beetle, reared a woolly bear in a jam-jar or experienced wonder and discovery in a single scoop of the pond net.

We hope you enjoy this nationwide record of the British and their bugs. Putting it all together – continually marrying timeless lore, art and literature with contemporary passions for technology, advertising and conservation – felt at times like a long voyage of discovery. There were familiar shorelines and ports, sure enough, but also unexpected and fascinating new islands and rivers to explore. Along the way, the bugs themselves took on new clothes; they became to us, as to many before us, not mere biological entities but beings with character – mirrors of human existence. They are, for all the ways they bother and disturb us, fellow citizens of a teeming and troubled world.

Peter Marren
Ramsbury, Wiltshire
2009

A NOTE ON THE TEXT

Bugs Britannica is about the native and naturalised insects and other invertebrates of Britain, including indoor ones and some that are traded or kept as pets. The cultural context is British (and Irish), but we have included some aspects of folklore from North America and Western Europe where it is relevant. Since the availability of instant global communications, it is becoming increasingly hard to draw the line between Britain and the rest of the world.

For the names of species, we have generally followed the most recent field guides (which are based in turn on the most up-to-date check-lists). We took the decision to omit scientific names from the main body of the text, except where they are necessary for identification or are in some way interesting and part of the profile. But they are all listed in Appendix I at the end of the book.

As in *Flora Britannica* and *Birds Britannica*, we have begun each entry with a list of the vernacular names – that is, their unofficial country names, past and present. These are prefixed as VN and are presented in alphabetical order. We have made an effort to gather as many country names as possible. Many were sent to us by members of the public,

while others may have passed out of the spoken language but are preserved in rhymes, dictionaries and songs – wonderful old country names such as zow-pigs, nimble dicks, clock-ladies and whame-flies.

We found it necessary to invent a second category, 'alternative names' (AN), for book names that were used in the past before English names became standardised. For example, our butterflies have long enjoyed English names (some of them pre-date their scientific ones), but they used to vary from one book to another before the turn of the twentieth century. Even today, the Hedge Brown is often known as the Gatekeeper, and the Short-tailed Blue as the Bloxworth Blue.

We have confined text references in the main to direct quotations and list the sources at the end of the book, unless they are necessary to the context. In each case we have included the title, author, date, publisher and page number. For quotations taken from the internet, we have listed the appropriate website. The literature of the folklore and symbolism of British bugs is scattered far and wide, but the sources that were particularly valuable are listed with the references.

BUGS BRITANNICA

SIMPLE LIFE

Single cells

Amoebas

An amoeba is perhaps the simplest form of life that we would recognise as a fellow animal. Though little more than an animated cell, a morsel of living protoplasm, an amoeba moves in a chosen direction, catches and digests its food, breathes air and has senses of a sort that enable it to react to light and physical changes in the water. And, of course, it has a sex life – indeed, an arresting choice of reproductive techniques, choosing either to exchange genes with a partner or, if it feels like it, just splitting in half to form two identical selves.

To the Victorians, this was where life began, with energetic blobs of self-contained life at the bottom of the pond. Modern biologists would demur and point out that an amoeba has various advanced features that rule it out as an ancestor. They would even hesitate to call it an animal, being reluctant to afford that status to any being with only one cell. Yet even if an amoeba is not an animal in the strict zoological sense, it certainly has the appearance of one. It may not be a molecular biologist's idea of a fully developed being but, to borrow Galileo's dying words, 'yet it moves'.

Poo-Bah, wrote W. S. Gilbert in the libretto of *The Mikado*, was a 'particularly haughty and exclusive person'. He could trace his ancestry all the way back 'to a protoplasmal atomic globule'. At that time, in 1884, protoplasm was believed to be the 'vital force' behind all life, a mysterious fluid with the magical ability to self-replicate and so multiply without external aid. Pooh-Bah could imagine his distant ancestor to be part of the primordial slime that coated the seabed of the ancient seas at the dawn of time. In theory, at least, the genes of his

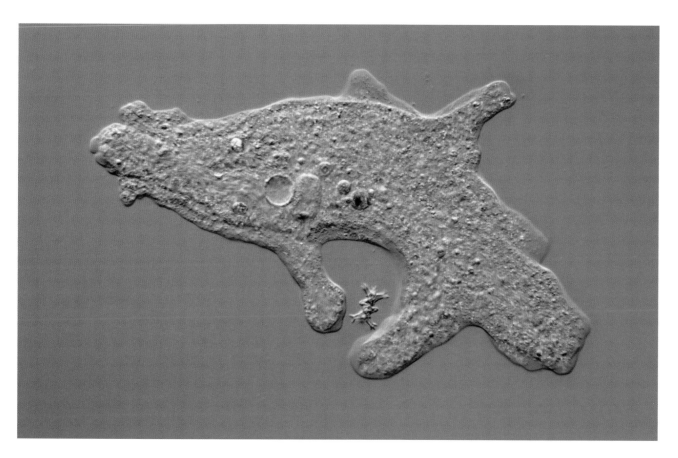

An amoeba engulfing a desmid (a tiny green plant).

3

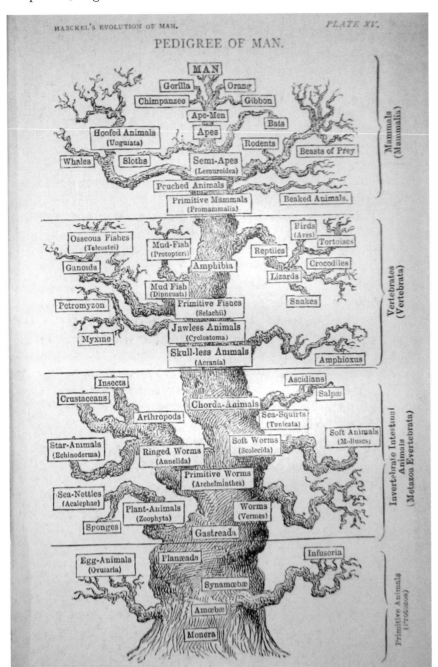

HAECKEL'S EVOLUTION OF MAN.   PLATE XV.

PEDIGREE OF MAN.

A nineteenth-century 'Tree of Life' inspired by Darwin's The Origin of Species, *with amoeba at the bottom and man at the top. On a modern evolutionary tree, amoeba would be further from the starting point, and man would be far less significant.*

distant ancestor could be still alive and well today. As the writer Tom Robbins reminds us in his novel *Even Cowgirls Get the Blues* (1976), since the amoeba can multiply indefinitely by binary fission, the original 'protoplasmal globule' should be with us still, infinitely multiplied, 'the coolest animal on the planet'.

They took these things seriously in the mid-nineteenth century. Charles Darwin's theory of evolution by natural selection seemed to turn the world order on its head. Instead of an ordered universe created by God in six days only a few thousand years ago, Darwin postulated an extraordinary, almost unimaginable vision of gradual change over fathomless depths of time. In *Genesis*, God made man 'in his own image' (and woman from Adam's rib), but Darwin asserted that mankind descended from upright walking apes. The effect was to undermine the church's traditional view of a man-centred natural world. Hence Pooh-Bah's claimed ancestry, not merely from apes but from the original 'blob', was a typical piece of Gilbertian irony. By claiming so much, Pooh-Bah was only trivialising his origins.

For a long time amoebas were considered to belong to the protozoa, in a class known as the rhizopoda, or 'root-feet'. Today the new wisdom is that the protozoa is an artificial assemblage of different, unrelated single-cells, and that 'amoeboid' organisms deserve a little kingdom of their own, the Amoebozoa. Nor are they any longer seen as especially primitive: amoebas, too, have ancestors. Their distinguishing feature, those mobile, oozing pseudopodia (false feet) are, in fact, rather complicated and specialised, with their complex chemistry of nucleic acids, lipids, proteins, carbohydrates and salts, not to mention internal organelles. Life on earth probably existed for a billion years or more before it progressed sufficiently far to produce an amoeba.

The amoeba was discovered in 1755 by the German naturalist Johann Roessel, while examining a sample of pond slime under his simple microscope. Struck by the way the creature constantly changed its shape, he dubbed it the Proteus Animalcule, after a character from Greek myth with similar powers (hence the term 'protean', meaning versatile). The name amoeba comes from the Greek word *amoibe*, 'to change', and was given to it later by the French naturalist Jean Baptiste de St Vincent. Both names survive in the best-known type, *Amoeba proteus*, the blob on the slide beneath the microscope lens in the school biology lab.

Understandably, since they had just endured a shaky journey in the post within their glass tube, my school's consignment of O-Level slimeballs were reluctant to do their stuff. I remember staring at various scraps of dirt under the microscope and wondering which one was an amoeba. When I finally tracked one down, it was in a sulk, a barely animate lump, not at all like the splendidly protean amoeba of textbooks.

But a wide-awake amoeba in full flow, extending its pseudopodia in all directions, with its various 'vacuoles' pumping away in lively manner, is unforgettable. Under contrast illumination that allows it to be seen in three dimensions, it seems to roll along, its body fluids circulating and flowing smoothly like the ocean currents. You watch, spellbound, as the amoeba catches up with some nameless microbe and envelopes it, extending false feet in a clammy embrace and forming a little temporary stomach in its middle. You think of the white blood corpuscles coursing through your arteries doing much the same thing with, you hope, remorseless efficiency.

No one has watched more amoebae in action than the American scientist H. S. Jennings (1868

–1947). Maybe it was only his fancy, but it seemed to Jennings that, even at this seemingly lowly level, life was not a game of chance. He was impressed by the amoeba's appearance of purposeful activity, proceeding by trial and error and making apparently conscious choices about what to eat and what to reject, where to go and how to get there. As he saw it, the blob was a patient and tenacious life-form, which exhibited states of desire and fruition:

'One seems to see that the Amoeba is trying to obtain this [animal] for food, that it shows remarkable pertinacity in continuing its attempts to put forth efforts to accomplish this in various ways, and in continuing its attempts to ingest the food when it meets with difficulties. Indeed the scene could be described in a much more vivid and interesting way by the use of terms still more anthropomorphic in tendency.' If the Amoeba was a large animal, he concluded, its behaviour 'would call forth to its states of pleasure and pain, of hunger and desire, and the like, on precisely the same basis as we attribute these things to the dog.'[1]

The comic possibilities of an intelligent blob have been explored by Paul Tye in his original cartoon series, 'The Amoeba', about the school-life observations of a friendly microscopic globule and his eternal-youth-seeking human friend, 'Doc'. As a shape-shifting, pale blue blob, Tye's amoeba is nothing if not versatile, a bit of living Blu-tack capable of doing most things we do and, in this case, often rather better.

Amoebae are just visible to the naked eye as whitish specks. They live on mud and detritus, especially in clear, well-aerated ponds and in places where debris collects along the margins and around tree roots. One way to collect them is to hold a jam-jar just above the bottom and then slowly tilt the jar so that some of the air escapes, thus sucking in the top layer of pond mud. Once the mud has settled, any amoebas present should be visible on the surface, and perhaps also the larger *Pelomyxa*, a spherical, grayish globule about the size of an 'o' on this page. Amoebas can be persuaded to multiply by placing them in an infusion of rainwater and boiled wheat grains.

Shelled amoebas

Some amoebas live inside hard shells, or 'tests', and so look like tiny molluscs. *Difflugia* builds a shell out of grains of silt, sometimes adorned with little horns, while *Arcella* secretes a saucer-like construct

Glass models of a shelled amoeba (Difflugia pyriformis) *created by Leopold and Rudolf Blaschka in the late nineteenth century.*

with a circular aperture for its long, narrow false feet to protrude. Both were great favourites when amateur microscopy was popular. They could even perform 'tricks'. Small-life enthusiasts would offer them coloured grains to build garish, psychedelic shells. Some museums display beautiful glass models of them, the product of a specialised nineteenth-century craft industry (see Sea Anemones). *Difflugia* and co. are common in ponds, but the easiest way to find them is to squeeze moss from a bog-pool over a microscope slide.

Heliozoans

The 'sun animalcule', *Actinophrys sol*, resembles a blob of froth with radiating tendrils like a child's drawing of the sun. These rays are sticky, and the animal uses them to capture prey (effectively, anything that moves, so long as it is small enough) and deliver it to the body. Sometimes two sun animalcules team up to share a prey item. These

A glass model of a 'sun animalcule', Actinophrys sol, *by Leopold and Rudolf Blaschka.*

6

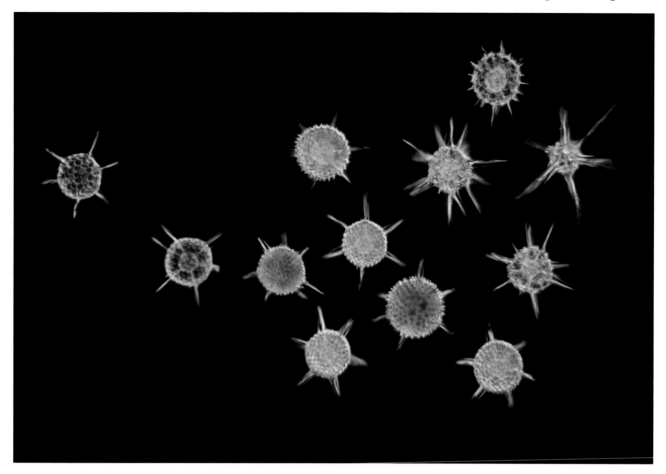

Skeletons of long-dead radiolarians from the ocean bottom, like stars in space.

strange creatures used to be classed as a subset among the amoebae, the Heliozoa ('sun-life'). Today, some scientists place them in another little supergroup of their own, the Chromalveolata, primitive single cells that evolved from specialised algae. Whether we call them animals or plants seems to hang on an obscure dispute about biochemistry.

Radiolarians

These exquisitely shaped life-forms are heliozoans with an internal skeleton made mainly of silica (though one group has weird skeletons made of strontium sulphate). Their name, meaning 'little radius', refers to their regular geometry, appearing more like crystals than life-forms (one species is an almost perfect icosahedron). Living radiolarians occur in the marine plankton. Their dead silica skeletons accumulate at the bottom of the sea and, over time, fossilise as flint and chert (so the arrowheads of our Stone Age ancestors were made of hundred-million-year-old plankton). Identifiable remains of radiolarians are found in the full sequence of rocks more than 600 million years old, and since many of them are confined to particular strata, they can be used to sequence and date the rocks as well as cast light on ancient climates and sediment processes. Radiolarians fascinated Ernst Haeckel, the man who coined the word 'ecology', and he devoted much of his time to drawing them in exquisite, if slightly formalised, detail. They have also inspired craftsmen to recreate their intricate patterns in gold and silver, in ceramics and in quilt designs.

Foraminiferans

The word foraminifera means 'hole bearers'. Mostly measuring less than a millimetre, foraminiferans are shelled amoebas that have lived in the seas of the world for more than 500 million years. Known in the trade as forams, they come in various shapes,

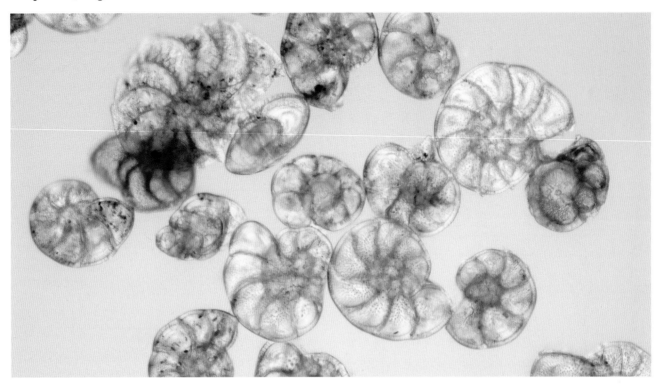

The building blocks of chalk: shells of foraminifera – each would fit comfortably on a pin head.

some coiled, some knobbly and others like shelly bubbles. The larger forams live on the seabed, while others float among the plankton, with little keels to keep them in position. Their remains are found in clay, marl, shell sand and limestone but most abundantly in chalk; the White Cliffs of Dover and the Seven Sisters of Sussex are essentially pure, deep foram beds, offering a wonderful example of a landscape formed by single-celled animals. Even today, forams generate an estimated 43 million tonnes of calcium carbonate per year, destined to form the chalk downs and cliffs of the distant future.

The unlikely hero of foram studies is Edward Heron-Allen, violin virtuoso, translator of Persian classics and friend of Oscar Wilde. In the course of his polymathic career, he managed to collect 4 million specimens of foram, many of them new to science (in 2000, the Heron-Allen Society was dedicated to the study of his life and interests).

About a quarter of a million species of foram have been described, and they are used by the oil industry to identify strata and predict where reservoirs of oil lie, far beneath the surface. The construction industry also needs foram experts when appraising the rock sequence for tunnelling purposes, not least when the Channel Tunnel was under construction. The fossil remains of forams are also used to reconstruct past climates and levels of ocean productivity, and by archaeologists needing fossil signatures to match against samples of stone. There cannot be many life-forms on earth that have proved so useful to us and yet are so little known, except to the few people who devote their professional lives to them.

Nummulites

These now-extinct organisms are exceptionally large single-celled organisms that form distinct oval or disc-like fossils – nummulite means 'stone coin'. They lived on the seabed in the early Tertiary between about 23 to 55 million years ago and are among the largest single-celled organisms known, some of them reaching six centimetres in diameter. When packed together, these fossils produce a distinctive yellowish limestone – which, among other things, formed the building blocks of the Great Pyramids of Egypt (leading the ancient-Greek geographer Strabo to speculate that they were the fossilised food of the slaves who built them). They were known in Britain as 'angel's money' – small change from heaven.

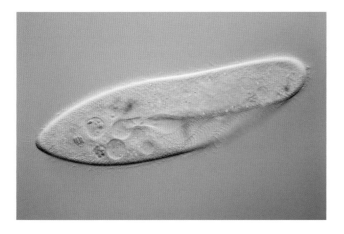

Above: *Early users of the microscope were struck by the similarity between certain 'animalcules' and everyday objects. This* Paramecium *(x250) reminded them of a slipper.*

Right: *The 'bell animalcule'* Vorticella *(x250), another well-known microscopic object that has entertained generations of pondwater-watchers with its flickering bells and spiralling stalks.*

Ciliates

What must it have been like to be the first person to witness living, swimming forms of life in a drop of water? It was the moment when the inner dimension of the planet was revealed for the first time – worlds within worlds, predators and prey, an entire ecosystem in a drop of water.

It took a surprisingly long time, long after the invention of the compound microscope in about 1590, for anyone to notice them. The person who drew back the curtain came in the unlikely form of a dry-goods tradesman and minor official in the Dutch town of Delft – Antonie van Leeuwenhoek (1632–1723), who had perfected a superior type of microscope capable of magnifying 250 times.

'In the year 1675, about halfway through September', wrote Leeuwenhoek, 'I discovered living creatures in rain.'[2] It must have been like finding life on the moon. No one believed a word of it, but the newly formed Royal Society was sufficiently intrigued to send an investigatory team to Delft. Leeuwenhoek was vindicated, and he was made a Fellow of the Royal Society, whose members soon discovered that microscopic life was not confined to Delft. Meanwhile, Leeuwenhoek moved from studying rainwater to gruesome experiments with his own body fluids. He found minute life-forms shaped like pills and squiggles behind his teeth, described disc-like 'corpuscles' in his blood, strange hairy creatures swimming around in his faeces, and noted with interest the tadpole-like 'homunculi' in his sperm. To his embarrassment, his fellow townsfolk hailed Leeuwenhoek as a magician.

Before 1675, the smallest known animals were water fleas. Now microscopes were revealing oval or top-shaped creatures 'a thousand times less than the eye of a louse'. In his first paper, Leeuwenhoek described several different kinds, one with two 'horns' and a tail and swimming with the aid of numerous little 'feet', another oval with a number of intriguing internal globules, a third even smaller with 'very quick' motion 'both round-about and in a straight line', and a fourth that spun like a top. One particularly engaging little beast was 'fashioned like a bell' and attached to a long 'tail' that could stretch and contract at will, a sight Leeuwenhoek found 'mightily diverting'.

Such finds created a fashion for microscopy in

9

Britain that lasted until the mid-twentieth century (when microscopes were eclipsed by binoculars). The most influential enthusiast after Leeuwenhoek was Henry Baker FRS, author of *The Microscope Made Easy* (1742), in which he coined the word 'animalcule' (little animal) for the minute creatures that 'swim about with as much Freedom as Whales do in the Ocean'. To him, they were 'breathing atoms' – clockwork mechanisms come to life, 'so small they are almost all Workmanship'.[3]

The majority of 'animalcules' he described are now known as ciliates, active single cells distinguished by rows of fine hairs that propel them through the water and set up currents to draw food into what could loosely be called their mouths. Ciliates come in many shapes and sizes, some like sausages or beans, with various distinguishing spines and projections, others shaped like bells, slippers or trumpets. They occur in every garden pond and can be cultured in infusions by simply adding straw or hay to a jar of boiled water, to which, after a day or two, a drop or two of pond water is added. Other tried-and-tested infusions include brews of rotting fish, cabbage or lettuce leaves, or boiled rice and wheat grains. In this food-rich medium, the ciliates multiply rapidly by binary fission to the point where any drop placed on a microscope slide will be alive with them.

Today, the fascination that earlier generations found in such things has waned, and university courses specialising in ciliates and other free-living protozoa have declined to vanishing point. A recent survey found only 17 academics able to name species of ciliates, and only eight who felt reasonably conversant with amoebas (and most of those have since retired).[4]

Ciliates are among the few forms of animal life in Britain that lack a mapping scheme. There is a good reason for this, quite apart from the absence of potential mappers. Unlike most forms of life, ciliates are truly cosmopolitan and not bounded by geographical boundaries. Their extraordinary powers of dispersal mean that, if the habitat is right, they will find it, wherever it is. A single well-studied pond in the Lake District turned out to contain a quarter of the world's freshwater species of ciliates (equivalent to having 3000 species of birds on your doorstep). Wherever you travel, to Norway or Turkey or even Australia, the ciliates are more or less the same. A British expert is also a world expert.

Sponges *Porifera*

Ever since ancient times, we have used sponges to wash ourselves. Their familiarity has spawned many terms and sayings: a sponge-bag; a sponge cake; to throw in the sponge (i.e. to give up) – a metaphor borrowed from the boxing ring. A sponge is also someone who drinks to excess, probably using money he sponged off someone else.

Until it became possible to manufacture artificial ones from softened wood-pulp or polyurethane, all sponges came from nature. They were the remains of primitive sea animals that, in life, look more like plants: greenish and anchored to the seabed. The commercial sponge, known as the Bath Sponge, is made up of tough, absorbent fibres that, after suitable processing – cleaning, drying and bleaching – would last for months or even years of use. In ancient Rome, people entering the public *lavatorium* were handed pieces of sponge attached to sticks for swabbing down the body – the customers must have hoped they were fresh ones. Everyone thinks of these natural washcloths as the archetypal sponge, but they are in fact untypical. Of the 8000-odd species of sponge in the world, only seven have been gathered and traded for washing purposes. Most of the others are held together not by natural fibres but by a spiky internal scaffolding known as spicules. A rub-down with one of these would be like polishing your skin with emery paper.

The ancient Greeks had to invent a special category for sponges: 'zoofitans', half animal and half plant. Sponges are not plants, but they are only just animals. They have no guts, no blood, no heart or brain and hardly anything one could even describe as an organ. They lack arms, legs or wings, and for their whole adult lives remain motionless, feeding by passively sifting the water. Sponges are, in fact, little more than loose aggregates of cells that have got together to feed and reproduce socially. A rather cruel trick you can do with a sponge is to push it through a sieve into a bowl of fresh seawater. After a while the bits begin to cleave together again, like the bad alien in the *Terminator* films, perhaps each seeking its old place in the sponge's geography.

Sponges feed by inhaling water, extracting edible titbits of detritus and blowing the water out again. It is this ability to soak up liquid that makes them so useful in the bathroom. A good-quality natural

*Low-life: the finger-like projections of a pond sponge (*Spongilla lacustris*) encrusting a rock.*

sponge can absorb 30 times its own weight of water, far more than cheaper synthetic copies can. Today, the best-quality Mediterranean sponges have been reduced to a fraction of their former abundance by overfishing; Bath Sponges can take 20 years to grow to marketable size, and they are impossible to farm. The best retail sponges are now more likely to be the products of second-best species such as the Honeycomb Sponge. The leading sponge-exporting nation is now Tunisia, and the main market is France, followed by the United States. Genuine sponges are now luxury goods; a good-sized 'silk' quality natural sea sponge costs around £30. The British market increased slightly around 2000 through the fashion for 'marbled' walls, an effect produced by assiduous polishing with natural sponges.

There are nearly 400 species of marine sponges in UK waters (though only 30 or so occur in rock pools) but only five species that live in fresh water. None of them looks like a bathroom sponge and most form carpets or lumps on hard surfaces. A few are sufficiently familiar to have acquired English names. The Purse Sponge is shaped like a hot-water bottle or old-fashioned belt-purse, with a narrow opening at the top. Diagrams of sponges in school textbooks borrow the classic features of the Purse Sponge to show water flowing in and out again, running over the rapids of thousands of little flickering cells within. The common Breadcrumb Sponge comes in various shades of orange and green, with a vaguely crumbly texture that reminded Victorian rock-pool watchers of toasted breadcrumbs. It is a 'keystone' species that binds together gravel, sand and shell debris to form fragile reefs, used for shelter and food by many marine animals. Touch a Breadcrumb Sponge, and its sickly sweet-sour smell will cling to your skin. A third type, the Mermaid's Glove, lives in deeper water, but after death, its detached fibrous, finger-like branches are sometimes washed up on to the strandline. Another is known, without conscious irony, as the Boring Sponge. The Elephant's-hide Sponge is lobed, greyish and flat. Related species, known as elephant's-ear sponges, have a rough side and a smooth side when dried and are used by potters to moisten and smooth their vessels.

Britain's two common freshwater sponges are the

The Elephant's-hide Sponge, one of the largest British marine sponges, with a Painted Topshell as a companion.

Pond Sponge (poorly named, for it is just as likely to be found in slow rivers) and the River Sponge. Both form a crust over rocks or submerged stumps, but the Pond Sponge also projects elegant finger-like growths resembling tiny underwater cacti. By constantly filtering the water, they help to keep it clean and clear; silt in dirty water clogs up their delicate pores and eventually kills them. To the disappointment of many young pond-dippers, they rarely stay alive for long in a jar or small tank. A healthy sponge needs to filter large quantities of water to survive.

The spicules of sponges make excellent itching powder. Duly dried and ground up, they also produce a warming effect when rubbed on the skin. An extract of sponge spicules, known as Russian Fleas, was formerly used as an embrocation for rheumatism and related disorders. The association with Russia is mysterious, but they say Russian girls used it on their cheeks to create the illusion of perfect health and vitality.

Fossil sponges are fairly frequent in the chalk and greensand of southern England. A form shaped like a goblet with perforated holes at the top was known by quarrymen as 'petrified salt-cellars'.

The study of sponges is, you might think, an acquired taste, and one who acquired it was Maurice Burton, who wrote nature notes for the *Daily Telegraph* over 40 years; his day job was the curator of sponges at the Natural History Museum, London. Another was Professor Isao Iijima of Tokyo University, whose hobby was preparing sponges for museums, especially the beautiful glass sponges of tropical seas, whose skeletons resemble natural chandeliers or lace petrified into crystal. His work can be found in museums and collections around the world (the Natural History Museum has some of the best). Unfortunately much of his life's work was shattered into pieces by the Tokyo earthquake of 1923.

How bored do you have to be to keep a sponge as a pet? The author Gerald Durrell once received a fan letter from a teenage girl who lived in Sofia: 'I love animals very much,' she told him, 'and I am terribly sorry that in our house there is no room to turn, let alone for domestic animals. But I have a sponge. His name is Klavdy. He live in one jar and eat only sea salt. He has four/five children. Sponge, pitiful sponge . . .'[5]

Hydras and sea-firs
Hydrozoa

Cnidarians

Cnidarians (pronounced 'kinnidarians') are animals with stinging tentacles, named from the Greek word for nettle, *knide*. They were formerly known as Coelenterates and include the well-known jellyfish, sea anemones and corals, as well as lesser-known groups such as sea-pens and hydroids. Unlike more advanced animals with recognisable bodies, heads and legs, their body symmetry is radial, based on a ring of tentacles with a mouth (doubling as an anus) in the middle. Nearly all British Cnidarians are marine; in fresh water we have only a few species of hydra and a little-known miniature jellyfish.

Hydra and its relatives *Hydrozoa*

The Green Hydra is the pond's modest answer to a sea anemone, a flower-like animal whose body cavity forms the stalk and its spreading tentacles the petals. It was originally known as the freshwater polyp but later renamed after the Hydra of legend, whose many heads were like snakes. Though of miniature size, the freshwater hydra shared with its monstrous namesake a capacity to regenerate new 'snake heads' after being beheaded. It could even recover its original form after being turned inside out. Another monster-like quality was the tiny hydra's insatiable appetite. It will swallow a water flea whole, nearly burst with the effort of digesting it and then instantly seem just as hungry as before.

Seven species of freshwater hydra occur in Britain, including the Brown Hydra, which has very long, dangling tentacles that trail in the water and function like the stinging tendrils of a jellyfish. Hydras are intriguing to watch and make an attractive addition to a freshwater aquarium. But be alert: they are fully capable of catching and swallowing small fish, while bigger fish are equally keen to swallow the hydra. My infant school kept a few hydras in a weedy tank. I remember staring at them through the glass wall, gazing at their bending green bodies and their tentacles flexing and twisting in the water, and reflecting for a moment how rich and wonderful life is, before abruptly losing interest and shooting out to play football.

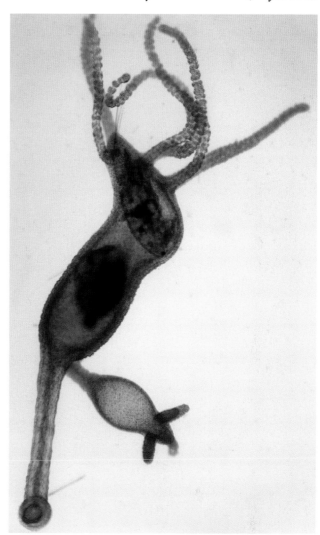

A hydra digests two water fleas. The baby hydra at the base was produced without sex by simple 'budding'.

Sea-firs

The animals known as hydras are confined to fresh water. Their more numerous relatives in the sea are conventionally known as hydroids or polyps. They begin their life in the plankton as microscopic jellyfish-like creatures known as medusas, but later settle down on the seabed, sometimes singly, more often as colonies of tiny plant-like animals shaped like feathers, tufts of hair or tiny fir trees. Like coral, hydroid colonies are often stiffened by internal skeletons, generally made of chitin, which remain long after the little animals have died and are often washed ashore.

Identifying marine hydroids is specialist work, but some of the larger ones have familiar names. Sea Beard is an orange-buff species; its wisps of stiff,

An Obelia, *a common colonial hydroid that clings to seaweeds and rocks along the shore. The name derives from a Greek word for a toasting fork*

A related species of sea-fir is sometimes sold alive for aquaculture but more often is displayed in a pot as an 'air fern' or 'Neptune plant'. 'Air fern' came on the market as a novelty, a supposed 'wonder of nature'. 'Unable to be classified in any botanical category,' its advertisers claimed, the mysterious plant 'retains its luminous green hue without watering.'[6] Moreover it emits 'fragrant secretions' which, in a reversal of the usual function of natural scents, drive away insects. The 'plant' is, in fact, the skeleton of a long-dead hydroid dyed with luminous paint to give the impression of a living water-world weed.

This drove a member of the Botanical Society of the British Isles to complain to the Advertising Standards Agency. Telling a botanist that he couldn't classify a fake plant was absurd, he pointed out. You might as well tell a geologist he couldn't classify a rock bun. In the fullness of time, the agency replied, admitting that the Neptune plant is not, strictly speaking, a plant, but insisting, by apparent contradiction, that it was nonetheless 'a type of air fern unknown to botanical science'.[7] In advertising brochures, therefore, the hydroid remains, officially, a plant.

Sea-pens *Pennatulacea*

Sea-pens are soft corals made up of numerous tiny polyps that resemble antique quill pens (when they first received this name, quill pens were on every desk). They live on the seabed in deep water and so are accessible only to divers. When touched, a sea-pen has an unexpected defence: it emits a pulse of energy in the form of a flash of bright greenish light.

Sea-pens are among the oldest animals on earth. Similar animals have been found in Cambrian rocks, and some believe that the mysterious fossils known as the Ediacaran fauna, the oldest fossil multicelled animals in the world, were relatives of sea-pens. As fragile and sedentary animals, sea-pens are frequent victims of deep-sea trawling.

Sea-fans *Gorgonacea*

Hydroids resemble tiny fir trees, and sea-pens quill pens, but the colonial animals known as sea-fans spread themselves into semicircles of colourful branches up to a metre across like ladies' fans. Related to coral, a sea-fan orientates itself across the prevailing current so that its tiny polyps net

unbranched stems attached to stones resemble a traditional mandarin's thin beard. Sea Oak grows on brown seaweed at low tide and is easily recognised from its finely notched stems, reminiscent of the outline of an oak leaf. The Oaten Pipes Hydroid grows to 18 centimetres or more and can clog the nets of moored fish cages, when it is known as 'bull's wool'.

Plant-like hydroids are often included as background material in saltwater aquariums, but it is the larger sea-fan-like forms that have grabbed most of the attention in recent years. The bleached and dyed skeletons of Sea Fir, whose scales are like the leaves of cypress trees, are popular with florists and flower arrangers, and many of us must have bought them without realising what they were. Known in the trade as 'whiteweed', they are fished from muddy estuaries by the thousands and make a useful income supplement for small fishing trawlers.

The Pink Sea-fan, a frequent victim of seabed trawlers and scallop dredgers. It is now a protected species.

A glass model of the Portuguese Man-o'-War, by Leopold and Rudolf Blaschka, late nineteenth century.

edible titbits as they sweep past. In parts of the coast of south-west England and South Wales, the very attractive Pink Sea-fan grows in reef-like 'forests', which were pillaged by divers in the 1960s for the souvenir trade. Today's divers are much more conservation-minded, but sea-fans are slow-growing organisms and, ominously, most of those in British waters seem to be mature. An action plan, led by the Wildlife Trusts, aims to find out what has gone wrong with sea-fan regeneration and to preserve as far as possible what remains.

Men-o'-war *Siphonophora*

Siphonophores look superficially like jellyfish, but their body plan is quite different. While jellyfish are individual organisms, siphonophores are technically colonies of individual 'polyps'. The members of the colony are of common genetic origin, developing from the same larva, but they develop specialised tasks: some become hollow tentacles, others (gastrozoids) form parts of the mouth, and yet others are set aside for reproductive purposes. The best-known siphonophore, the Portuguese Man-o'-war, shares with a jellyfish the same basic shape and long tentacles, but with a crucial difference: a jellyfish can swim, but a man-o'-war, lacking any means of propulsion, simply bobs on the ocean, like a ghost ship, with the help of an inflated airbag and sail.

The Portuguese Man-o'-war and its diminutive relative, the By-the-wind-sailor, are the only

15

Bright blue floats of By-the-wind-sailors washed ashore after a storm.

siphonophores that regularly visit British shores. The man-o'-war acquired its name from its transparent sail, which resembled the billowing sails of Portuguese fighting ships known as caravels. It is perhaps the most feared 'jellyfish' in the sea, and with reason. Its long, coiled, blue tentacles cause an intense burning pain akin to an electric shock. Most of its few British victims have been bare-armed fishermen who came into contact with tentacles caught around a rope or tangled in a net. The traditional standby, when stung by a jellyfish, is to pee on the sting, but with the Portuguese Man-o'-war, that makes it worse. Some say the terrible pain can be relieved by hot water or ice cubes, but otherwise there is little option but to wait patiently until it goes away.

Belying its fearsome reputation, the Portuguese Man-o'-war is a beautiful animal. Its glossy, gas-filled float shines among the dark rocks like a pink and blue party balloon. In the sunlight, it 'is of an almost iridescent blue merging into mauve and pink at the top of the crest where there is a touch of orange'.[8] In Australia and the Pacific, where men-o'-war are much more familiar, they are called 'bluebottles' or 'bluebubbles'.

The wet summer of 2007 was a vintage season for 'bluebottles'; more than a hundred were reported from beaches in Cornwall and the Isles of Scilly, one of which was taken alive and displayed in a tank at the Blue Reef Aquarium in Newquay. Perhaps it shows a very British caution in our dealings with the natural world that no one was stung.

The quaintly named By-the-wind-sailor – sailors also knew them as 'Jack-sail-by-the-wind' – does not sting. It is best known to beachcombers, who pick up the stiff 'backbone', like an oval of clear plastic – all that is left after the soft parts have rotted away. Live 'sailors' are coloured a deep blue like the ocean itself, on which they float like flotillas of toy boats. They resemble small jellyfish with short tentacles, but instead of a bell, each has a flattish float, or bubble-raft, which projects in the middle to form a little sail. They must be present in enormous numbers in the open sea, for every so often a westerly gale blows millions of them ashore, and for a day or two their glistening, iridescent bodies pile up on the strand, especially after a late summer storm on the west coast. By-the-wind-sailors can be 'right-handed', with the sail orientated north-west/south-east or 'left-handed' and pointing north-east/south-west. The curious consequence is that, caught together in the same wind, one lot heads one way and the other in the opposite direction. Since currents in the northern hemisphere turn clockwise, one would expect the left-sailing ones to predominate in British waters, and this does seem to be the case.

Sea Anemones *Actiniaria*

VN: actinia, blood-sucker (Cornwall), herring-shine (Yorks.), jilly (NE Eng.), paps, paup, sea nettles, sea paps (Scot.), selkie paps (Orkney), sookers

L. P. Hartley's novel about an Edwardian childhood, *The Shrimp and the Anemone* (1944), opens with an ethical dilemma familiar to many children. While playing on the beach, nine-year-old Eustace spots a sea anemone in the process of swallowing a shrimp. Should he intervene and try to save the shrimp or let nature take its course? His sensitive heart bleeds for the unfortunate shrimp, but could he rob the anemone of its dinner? And would the latter die of hunger if he did? The well-being of one seemed to depend on the misfortune of the other. To make the choice even more difficult, the anemone was clearly more beautiful than the shrimp, as well as rarer and more interesting (it was of the feathery 'plumose' kind).

Eustace made his choice and pulled the shrimp out by the tail, only to find that the shrimp was already past saving and that he had tugged out the guts of the anemone in doing so. His older sister, Hilda, set about 'the distasteful task of replacing the anemone's insides where they belonged, but her amateur surgery failed to restore its appetite, and it took no interest in the proffered shrimp.' Eustace now wished he had left the animals alone. But his sister argued that they had to do something, for 'we couldn't let them go on like that'.[9] Since this is Hartley country, the seemingly trivial incident at the rock pool prefigures the boy's relationship with and dependence on his tougher sister that leads, over three novels, to ultimate tragedy.

Like the hydra, sea anemones seem to possess an unbridled appetite and will swallow anything of a suitable size that gets within touching distance of their stinging tentacles. Many species are beautifully coloured, and their circles of bright tentacles reminded their admirers of the petals of a garden flower or, in the old name of 'actinia', the radiations of a star. The Victorian writers who first introduced the beauties of rock pools to a popular readership described massed anemones as 'living flower beds' or, aptly enough, as 'flowers of flesh'. The Dahlia Anemone and the Daisy Anemone were named after flowers twice over. Certain sea caves lined with anemones and exposed only at spring tides were also

Ocean flowers: Beadlet Anemones coat the walls of the Gouliot Caves on Sark.

compared with Aladdin-like grottos glistening with jewels. The names of common rock-pool anemones capture this earthy combination of flesh, flower and gemstone: Beadlet, Opelet or Snakelocks Anemone, Wartlet, Gem Anemone, Jewel Anemone.

Despite their beauty, sea anemones could not be casually collected like seashells or mounted in an album like seaweeds. Their colours fade after death, and a pallid, bleached sea anemone in a bottle of spirit is a sad ghost of the living animal. Hence the vogue for sea anemones only began after the discovery, in the 1850s, that marine life could be kept alive in a tank simply by supplying sufficient weed to maintain oxygen levels. At the same time, advances in sheet-glass production brought the cost of aquariums within reach of the average country doctor or jobbing writer. The poet laureate himself,

Robert Southey, was caught up in new-found wonder for 'coral-bowers, And grots of madrepores':

> Here too were living flowers
> Which like a bud compacted,
> Their purple cups contracted.
> And now, in open blossom spread,
> Stretch'd like green anthers many a seeking head.[10]

No one did more to study and popularise 'actinias' than Philip Gosse. He is remembered now as the terrifying religious zealot in his son Edmund's memoir, *Father and Son*, but Gosse was also a great naturalist, a gifted artist and writer, and a patient and curious observer with a sympathy for life that was ahead of his time. His books on aquariums and shore-life introduced the masses to the then little-known natural wonders of the coast, with the help of forgotten invented names such as 'tintlet', 'muzzlet', 'pintlet' and 'pufflet'.[11] Contemporaries recalled Gosse clambering over the rocks near Ilfracombe 'in full sacerdotal black' before stripping off, wading waist-deep into a likely pool and emerging 'dazzled'. He collected sea anemones for study and painting by chiselling the tight, retracted blobs from the rocks and then 'plunging them in jars of saltwater, carried in an immense square basket'. At that time, remembered Edmund Gosse, the coast was still pristine; father and son roamed the shore together as 'if the Garden of Eden had been situate in Devonshire'.

'These pools were our mirrors, in which, reflected in the dark hyaline and framed by the sleek and shining fronds of oar-weed, there used to appear the shapes of a middle-aged man and a funny little boy, equally eager . . . [There were] submarine gardens of a beauty that seemed often to be fabulous . . . if we delicately lifted the weedcurtains of a windless pool, [though] we might for a moment see its sides and floor paven with living blossoms, ivory-white, rosy-red, grange and amethyst, yet all that panoply would melt away, furled into the hollow rock, if we so much as dropped a pebble in to disturb the magic dream.'[12]

Though the son's outlook soon diverged sharply from his father's, the 'eager, funny little boy' was an adept at anemone-spotting; the first step in the glittering career of Sir Edmund Gosse, man of letters, was the discovery of a new species known as the Walled Corklet, or '*Phellia murocincta* E. Gosse, 1858'.

The English names of sea anemones had been invented in the previous century by Thomas Pennant, but it was Gosse who familiarised them to a mass audience. Sea anemone itself is a much older word, whose origin is obscure. Though many are flower-like, none look like actual anemones – dahlias or chrysanthemums would be nearer the mark. But anemone means 'wind flower', and the sea anemone's tentacles wave in the tide as though fluttered by a breeze. The anemone was also the flower of Aphrodite, who first arose from the sea in a scallop shell and retained her marine associations ever afterwards. Perhaps sea anemones were originally seen as her flowers.

Even Rick Stein has yet to extol the pleasures of steamed sea anemone, but they have been eaten in parts of Italy for at least 2000 years. As 'sea nettles', they appear on a recipe for 'fish custard' attributed to Apicius, a first-century Roman gourmet. Chop up the fish, mash it up with some eggs and lay the sea nettles gently on top. Steam for a few minutes, and there it is: ancestral seafood with a difference. Today sea anemones tend to be eaten simply, fried or boiled in seawater, spiced to taste.

In William Golding's novel *Pincher Martin* about a sea-wrecked sailor marooned on a rock in the mid-Atlantic, the desperate Martin is reduced to eating the red blobs of jelly, the 'beadlets', 'dotted like sucked sweets' in the rock pools. 'Under water they opened their mouths in a circle of petals but up by his face, waiting for the increase of the tide, they were pursed up and slumped like breasts when the milk has been drawn from them.' Unwisely, Martin forces down some of the raw jellies and suffers for it afterwards, though not as much as he would do in real life – for, like jellyfish, sea anemones go on stinging after death.

Since sea anemones cannot be preserved in lifelike condition, museums went for the next-best thing, models made from glass and enamel. The best of these are the work of a father-and-son partnership, Leopold and Rudolf Blaschka – who, between them, produced museum models from their workshop in Dresden for more than 50 years. Leopold Blaschka, who described himself as a 'natural history artisan', came from a background of Venetian glass-making, though he was apprenticed as a gemcutter and goldsmith. Caught up in the craze for natural history and aquariums in the 1850s, he began to fashion models of water life and flowers from glass. Fine glasswork was perfect for capturing the translucent, shimmering colours of the living anemones. Some he designed with tentacles extended, others withdrawn, and all resting on a realistic piece of rock or section of sandy seafloor. They are almost more art objects than museum specimens, combining the anatomical knowledge of a zoologist with the craftsmanship of a Fabergé.

A curator at Dresden Museum, noticing that his collection of sea anemones, imprisoned in their jars of formalin, was dismally failing to attract attention, commissioned a set of models from Leopold Blaschka. The word got round, and soon Blaschka was making models for aquariums and museums around the world, including an order for 68 sea anemones from the South Kensington Museum (now the Natural History Museum) in 1876. Joined that year by his son Rudolf, they also 'lampworked' models of other translucent marine animals, including protozoa, corals, sea-slugs, sea cucumbers, cephalopods and, above all, jellyfish. A visitor from Harvard watched Leopold produce three beautiful glass flowers in less than three hours using nothing more complex than a solid-fuel paraffin lamp, a pair of bellows and a glass blast-tube. Realistic translucency was achieved by a method of speckling fine layers of paint on the underside of the glass, while a more opaque effect was obtained by mixing paint with powdered glass. Fiddly tentacles were attached with well-disguised copper wires. There were no patents or craft secrets involved – just rare natural dexterity.

A Dahlia Anemone half-buried in the sand at low tide.

Anemone species

The Beadlet is the commonest intertidal sea anemone and one that is instantly recognisable. In Philip Gosse's words, it stands 'glossy and plump, like some ripe, pulpy fruit'[13], with a distinctive row of peacock-blue warts or 'beads' circling the red tentacles. It is an amazingly resilient animal, occurring not only on almost every rocky shore but also all the way down it, from the puddles of seawater on the middle shore to the deep pools at low tide. Despite its flower-like appearance, the Beadlet is a surprisingly lively, if slow-moving, animal, capable of roaming around its rocky lair, advancing and retreating and occasionally bumping into fellow anemones, with which it instantly locks tentacles (for some reason, the intruder always loses; in seemingly dejected condition, it lets go and allows itself to be washed away by the tide from the scene of its defeat). Beadlets are immensely hardy. Though mortality during winter storms is high, especially among young anemones, and though they face predation by starfish and sea-slugs, Beadlets are capable of outliving most invertebrates. Sir John Dalyell kept a sturdy Beadlet called 'Granny' in a tank in Edinburgh for more than 50 years; in fact, it outlived him.

A common and attractive form of Beadlet with small yellow spots looks like a strawberry, and is often called the Strawberry Beadlet. Once regarded as a variety, it is now believed to be a separate species. There is also a green variety that favours deep pools on the lower shore.

The Dahlia Anemone, also known as the 'wartlet' or, in Yorkshire, as the 'scaurcock', is the largest of our intertidal sea anemones, and a big one can be 10 cm across. It has short tentacles that are reminiscent of dahlia petals, and a squat, warty trunk often disguised with small pebbles and shell fragments. Like most anemones, except the Beadlet and the Snakelocks, it does not like direct light and is commonest in weedy, shaded pools beneath rock underhangs at low water. The crimson and grey Dahlia Anemone, with its pale, stumpy tentacles, is a popular highlight on seashore forays – once seen, never forgotten.

The Snakelocks Anemone is common in rock pools on the lower shore on south-western coasts. Its long, green tentacles reminded classically educated zoologists of the Medusa's head, in which hair is replaced by hissing snakes. Unlike other anemones, it does not retract when touched; this permanently 'open' appearance is the reason for its alternate name of 'opelet'. The Snakelocks is a favourite aquarium animal: put several in at once, and each will use its purple-tipped tentacles in a slow-motion duel to gain sufficient feeding space.

Alone among the common anemones, this one feels sticky when touched, the result of stinging cells embedding themselves in our skin. The stings are unable to penetrate the tough skin of our fingers and toes, but if they come into contact with tender places, it can be a different story. A baby's accidental dip in a bed of Snakelocks on Guernsey in 1999 resulted in a blistered leg. A man swimming in the Fleet on the Dorset coast felt a tingling sensation as the anemones brushed his belly, which was soon bubbling with nasty-looking welts. Though anemone stings are relatively mild, they can leave a long-lasting brown mark on the skin, the result of anemone venom interacting with human blood to form iron oxide – that is, rust. The toxin in Snakelocks stings has been isolated and is of potential use in the treatment of heart disease.

The Plumose Anemone has dense, creamy and seemingly fluffy tentacles adapted for sieving animal plankton from the incoming tides. Though among the commonest and most beautiful of sea anemones, it is rarely seen at its best except by divers. It is a characteristic sight on wrecks, including ropes and anchor chains. Out of water, the Plumose Anemone is a sorry sight, its beautiful tentacles withdrawn and the trunk loose and floppy, like deflated balloons the morning after the party.

The Daisy Anemone, or Sand Anemone, was one of several sea anemones (the Gem Anemone is another) discovered by a British naturalist, Thomas Pennant, in the 1770s. The fancied resemblance to a daisy comes from the shape of the crown – circular with short radiating tentacles – more than the colour, which is variable but often shot with interesting purplish iridescence. The Daisy Anemone is less often seen than other intertidal anemones, since the animal is normally buried in a rock crevice or attached to a pebble deep in the sand or mud, with just its tentacles showing (and withdrawn at the slightest touch or disturbance). But it is one of the easiest species to keep in an aquarium, and it often multiplies by budding to cover the floor with a carpet of iridescent sea daisies.

Corals *Alcyonaria*

Corals are not confined to the tropics. In Britain's warmer waters, there are banks of stony coral, like miniature sea anemones encased in limestone. These are the cup corals. The commonest is the Devonshire Cup Coral, discovered by the novelist Charles Kingsley on the island of Lundy. At a time when tropical reefs were barely known, these exquisite little cup corals sent Kingsley into raptures: 'bright little buds, like salmon-coloured Banksia roses, half expanded, sitting closely on the stone. Touch them; the soft part is retracted, and the orange flower of flesh is transformed into a pale pink flower of stone.' Gosse, too, was deeply impressed; in Ilfracombe's deepest pools, perhaps immersed up to his neck, he saw coral 'lips' of 'fawn or chestnut-brown; the star or vandyked circle rich red, pale vermilion, and sometimes the most brilliant green, as brilliant as the gorget of a hummingbird.'[14]

Gosse himself discovered the most colourful species of all, aptly, if rather prosaically, known as the Scarlet-and-gold Cup Coral. He described his good fortune in one of his seaside potboilers, *Devonshire Coast* (1852):

'It was a spring-tide, and the water receded lower than I have seen it . . . I was searching among the extremely rugged rocks that run out from the Tunnels, forming walls and pinnacles of dangerous abruptness, with deep, almost inaccessible cavities between . . . At last I fairly stripped, though it was blowing very cold, and jumped in. I had examined a good many things . . . and was just about to come out, when my eye rested on what I saw at once to be a Madrepore, but of an unusual colour, a most refulgent orange . . . The whole body and disc, exclusive of the tentacles, is of a rich orange, yellower in young specimens, almost approaching to vivid scarlet in adults . . . The tentacles, about fifty in number, in my largest specimen, are of a fine gamboges-yellow.'

Gosse was soon at work detaching them with his hammer, filling his jars with 'madrepores'. 'I left a good many remaining,' he added, 'for which I was afterwards very sorry.'[15]

There are also soft corals, colonial animals made up of hundreds of tiny polyps embedded in jelly and strengthened, like sponges, with 'spicules' of lime. Out of water they seem no more than bobbles of slime, but when the polyps are feeding, the animal is

Sunset Cup-coral or Yellow Cave Coral: one of the cold-water corals found round Britain. 'A Madrepore of a most refulgent orange.'

covered by the soft fuzz of its feeding tentacles and is delightful to watch. The best-known species is Dead Man's Fingers, an orange- or yellowish-white coral, which grows as thick, fleshy lobes that diverge like the fingers of a hand. The effect is accentuated when the polyps are extended, giving the impression of mouldy, decomposing digits. It shares its ghoulish name with a seaweed, *Codium fragile*, and a fungus, *Xylaria polymorpha*.

In recent years, ship-borne cameras that penetrate the deep sea have revealed extensive cold-water reefs running along the continental shelf from western Ireland to northern Scotland and on to Norway. They are dominated by pink or creamy growths of *Lophelia* coral – which, despite the low temperatures, grows faster than most stony corals in tropical reefs. The diversity of life among these inaccessible reefs, beyond even the reach of divers (but not, unfortunately, beyond that of trawlers or oil prospectors), has been a revelation: so far, some 1300 species have been found living among the cauliflower-like growths of *Lophelia*, including beautiful growths of crinoids, known as feather-stars or sea-lilies, primitive relatives of the starfish. Many of these species are new to science.

Jellyfish *Scyphozoa*

VN: blubber, blue-slutter (Kent), galls (Kent), jenny-nettle (Isle of Man), jilly (NE Eng.), klanker (Orkney), loch-liver (Scot.), lubbertie (Scot.), mallygolder (Cornwall), medusa, miller's-eyes (Kent), scaler or scowder (Scot.), scouther (Scot.), sea starch (Kent), skate bubble, slouree (Isle of Man), slum, swatter (NE Eng.), swither or switheral (Scot.), tonie (Scot.), whaal-bubble (Scot.)

Jellyfish are seldom seen singly. Large numbers bobbing on the ocean are called drifts, shoals or swarms. Fishermen will refer to a 'fluther' or a 'smack' of jellyfish, onomatopoeic words that match their wobble or the sound a big jellyfish makes as it slips from the net and hits the deck (a small-decked fishing boat shares the same name: a smack). Steve Palin (2000) suggested that 'smack' is 'the noise made when one inadvertently steps upon a stranded jellyfish on the beach, or perhaps the sound made when one might prod and lift it with a stick and part-suck its body like a plastic bag full of water

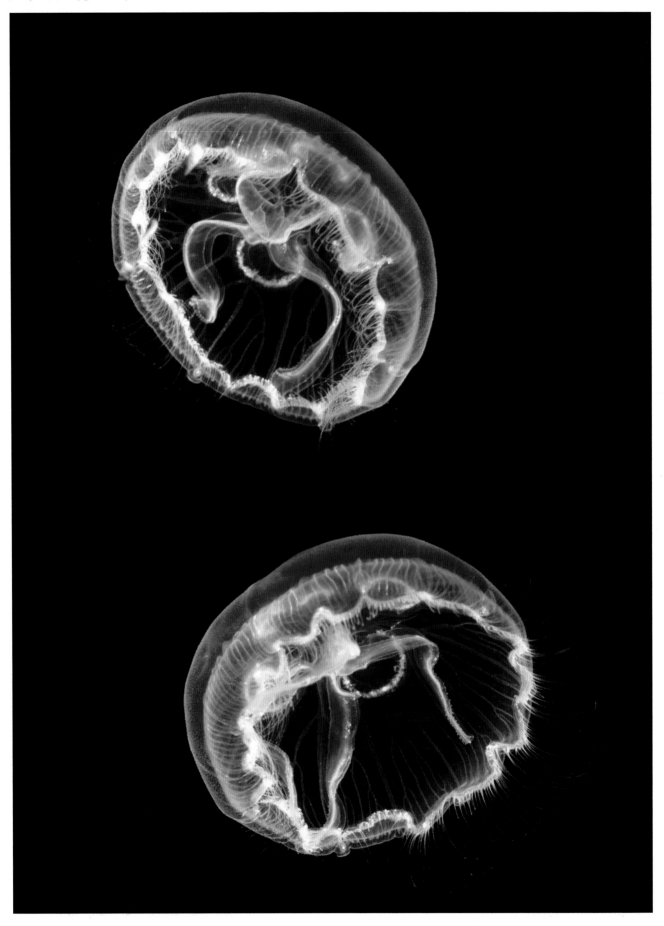

from the wet sand – smmmuck! – like a noisy kiss.' In support of this contention, 'smack' is also spelt as 'smuck' or, weirdly, as 'stuck'.

Jellyfish is a relatively recent name coined in the nineteenth century; the older name was 'medusa' (plural medusae), named after the snake-haired monster of legend. Some point out that jellyfish are not fish and prefer to call them jellies or sea-jellies. The Cornish folk-name, 'mallygolder', is reserved for a big jellyfish, such as the golden Compass Jellyfish. The Scots names 'scowder' and 'scalder', refer to the hot (scalding) sensation of a jellyfish sting.

Jellyfish have a trembling, evanescent quality that embodies a fairly minimalist conception of life. They lack not only bones but also brains, hearts, eyes, ears, legs and most other prerequisites of an interesting life; evolved along radial lines, they lack even a left and a right. Though recent films of captive jellyfish point to a certain sentient awareness that enables them to sense and move towards objects of interest, jellyfish are normally perceived as passive creatures, at the mercy of the winds and tides. They can swim, after a fashion, by pulsating water in and out of their hemispherical bells (they can also use the sun as a compass), but essentially they are a giant form of plankton. With their body cavities full of water, live jellyfish can be surprisingly heavy: one with a diameter of a metre might weigh 50–100 kilos.

When their glistening lampshade forms wobble and flutter into view, large jellyfish can strike terror into swimmers – though, in British waters, there is no reason to fear them, for most forms encountered by the casual sea bather are harmless. By far the commonest is the Moon Jellyfish, which washes ashore by the hundred after storms. In spring 2002, a raft of Moon Jellyfish 12 metres long by 90 centimetres thick, resembling a huge mass of floating bubblewrap, was spotted in Loch Nevis on the west coast of Scotland. Moon Jellyfish, which look like living glass paperweights, are so named from the four pink crescents (the animal's gonads) on the transparent bell. They live on plankton and smaller jellyfish, and their stinging cells are far too feeble to break human skin. Another common one, the Barrel Jellyfish, is rubbery and grey and has been nicknamed 'the blubber', or the 'dustbin-

lid jellyfish'. As its scientific name *Rhizostoma octopus* implies, it has eight 'arms' and in the water can resemble the shape of a swimming octopus. *Rhizostoma* is the favourite food of the leatherback turtle, which visits bays on the west coast of Wales, and so helps the tourist industry in a small way.

The colourful, streaked bells of the beautiful Compass Jellyfish look curiously like Tiffany lampshades (the radiating streaks form the points of the 'compass'). I once broke into a flailing retreat when I bumped into a large one while swimming off the coast of Ireland (the frightening thing about big jellyfish is that they seem to follow you). There are, in fact, few records of it stinging bathers, though a warm-water relative, the Sea Nettle, inflicts a painful lash with its trailing tentacles.

Jellyfish that sting are seen most often by divers, though they occasionally wash up on the beach, often in pieces. The Lion's-mane Jellyfish, one of the world's largest, looks like a floating Christmas decoration, with its disconcertingly long frills and tendrils. Stranded on the shore, its brownish-red mass resembles a mane removed from a lion by some reckless barber. British specimens are normally less than a quarter the size of the two-metre giants that occur in the Arctic (where, perhaps fortunately, few of us choose to swim), but even small ones contain a powerful venom with a potency somewhere between a bee sting and an electric shock. Broken up bits of mane on shore or stuck to a buoy rope retain their power to sting for hours or even days.

This species was the subject of one of the classic Sherlock Holmes stories, *The Adventure of the Lion's Mane*. It is one of the few narrated by Holmes himself, rather than Dr Watson (who does not appear). The great detective is enjoying a day at the seaside when a man staggers up, obviously in agony, and gasping something about 'a lion's mane' before dying. Holmes observes that he has red welts all over his back. Later the man's dog is also found dead near the same spot. The police, never very bright in a Holmes story, suspect foul play, possibly involving torture by a red-hot wire or a cat-o'-nine-tails. Suspicion points to the dead man's rival in love. Holmes solves the mystery in the nick of time by wandering down to the pool where the victim had been bathing, spotting the guilty jellyfish and beating the life out of it with a rock. Any student of shore-life would have seen that coming from the start.

No one in real life has been killed by a Lion's-mane in British waters. Divers say the worst

Left: *Moon Jellyfish illuminated against a dark background – objects of delicate, alien beauty.*

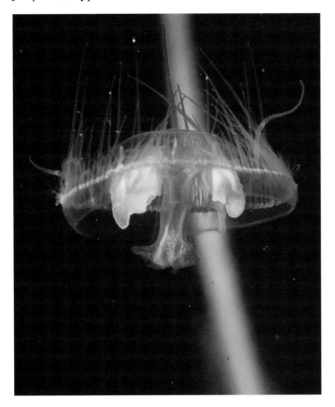

The coin-sized Freshwater Jellyfish, now established in warm waters in Britain.

British jellyfish is not this one but the smaller and sinisterly beautiful Bluefire Jellyfish. One diver unlucky enough to be stung on the wrist spent three uncomfortable days in hospital. The Bluefire Jellyfish is uncommon in British waters, though some Mediterranean beaches have recently suffered a plague of them (almost certainly because we have overfished their main predator, Bluefin Tuna).

A new word has recently entered the lexicon of marine biology: jellyplankton. For reasons that remain obscure (but which are almost certainly man-made and probably due to overfishing of predatory fish), jellyfish are appearing in enormous numbers along the Atlantic fringe of Europe, and they represent a serious threat to fish farms. Shetland experienced three 'invasions' in 2004, and other farms on the west coast are reporting huge rafts of jellyfish that pile up against the nets and sometimes overwhelm them. Even small jellyfish can harm fish by blocking their gills or passing through the gills and stinging them from the inside. Massed together and resembling floating sheets of plastic, they are capable of lifting salmon nets and reducing the flow of clean water and oxygen into the cages, at which point the unfortunate fish face a triple whammy

of foodlessness, stress and oxygen starvation. European jellyfish specialists have clubbed together to find out what is causing these mass outbreaks. They call themselves Eurogel.

In November 2007, Northern Ireland's one and only fish farm lost its entire stock to a jellyfish known as the Mauve Stinger. This handsome purple drifter, which ranges in size from a ten-pence piece to a bunched fist, is familiar to swimmers in the Mediterranean but not, until recently, in British waters. The uncountable billions of them that flooded into the sheltered waters at Glenarm Bay in County Antrim came as a complete surprise. John Russell, who had become the fish farm's managing director three days before, described the onslaught as 'unprecedented, absolutely amazing. The sea was red with them, and there was nothing we could do about it, absolutely nothing.' The sheer mass of jellyfish prevented the boats from reaching the cages, situated a mile offshore, until it was too late. The damage was estimated at a million pounds, and the fish farm now faces closure.[16] A second moving mass of Mauve Stingers was spotted off Scotland, but chance and offshore currents prevented further damage.

The Natural Environment Research Council hastily provided funds to find out more about the jellyfish and their movements in the Irish Sea and North Atlantic. One curious aspect that may help them is that the Mauve Stinger is visible in the dark. The animal is faintly luminescent and, en masse, emits an eerie purple radiance at night that, in 2007, lit up the entire beach.

We associate jellyfish with the seaside, but there is a little-known species that lives in lakes and has colonised parts of Britain. A pulsating, transparent creature about the size of a five-pence coin, the Freshwater Jellyfish, sometimes known as the Amazonian Jellyfish, first turned up in the water-lily tanks at Kew, where it was thought to have hitch-hiked on roots brought back from an expedition to the jungles of South America. Later it was found in the ship canal at Exeter, where it presumably lay low for a while until it was refound in the 1970s. Most spectacularly, it appeared in a flooded sandpit at Doncaster's Hatfield Water Park during the warm summer of 2002. First seen in ones and twos, there were scores after a few weeks of warm sunshine, and thousands by August, pulsating gently in the shallows. In places, there were up to 45 per square metre, fascinating, harmless but slightly eerie.[17]

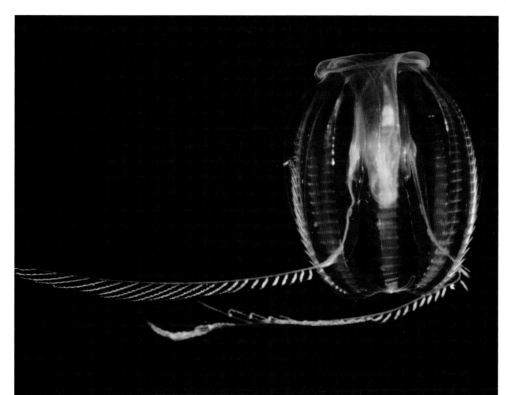

The Sea Gooseberry, shimmering as it swims.

Comb jellies *Ctenophora*

Comb jellies have been called 'glowing ghosts of the sea'. They are transparent and shine with an eerie phosphorescence, producing fantastical displays of light, accentuated by the shimmering effect of their flickering tentacles. Occasionally one gets trapped in a rock pool to produce what Rachel Carson called its 'elusive moonbeam flashes'.[18] They would make wonderful inhabitants of a dimly lit aquarium but for the unfortunate fact that comb jellies are fragile and rarely live long in captivity.

Though they resemble jellyfish, comb jellies are in a class of their own, known as the Ctenophores (from the Greek, meaning 'comb-bearer'). The most familiar one is the Sea Gooseberry, whose oval body, as transparent as crystal glass, is roughly the size and shape of a hairy berry, with gooseberry-like bristles arranged in four paired rows along its round body. Behind trail two long, sticky but non-stinging tentacles, which are effectively fishing lines and which also deliver food to the animal's mouth like an alien hand. Sea Gooseberries are most often seen stranded along the shoreline after a storm, when we can briefly experience something of their beauty by placing one in a jar of fresh seawater.

Several other comb jellies have attracted English names. The graceful, ribbon-like Venus's Girdle is a reference to the birth of Venus in ocean foam. An East Atlantic species, *Mnemiopsis leidyi*, known from its two-halved shape as the Sea Walnut, has recently begun to appear in British waters. This species was accidentally introduced into the Black Sea in ship's ballast water and, lacking natural predators, rapidly multiplied. At one point, there were an estimated million tonnes of Sea Walnut, like phosphorescent bubble-wrap, enough to wipe out the local anchovy fishery. The balance was eventually restored by introducing another species of comb jelly that preyed on Sea Walnuts.

Comb jellies look as simple and primitive as jellyfish, but recent genetic studies suggest otherwise. They possess more of a group of genes known as SOX genes, which regulate development, than any other invertebrate. This raises questions about our understanding of the evolution of life and whether we are right to place comb jellies somewhere near the bottom. Partly because of their unexpected complexity, they are of current interest in medical research; in the future, 'essence of comb jelly' could be used to enhance drug-delivery systems and other cutting-edge medical technologies.

Rotifers *Rotifera*

AN: rotatoria, wheel animalcule

To the true enthusiast, rotifers are 'jewels of nature',[19] exquisite life-forms of astonishing shapes and beautiful colours. Some look like urns or jars, others like little pigs or mice or flowers in a vase, while some free-swimming ones are more like little coracles or wide-beamed boats. One admirer referred to their 'lively and amusing mannerisms' that never fail to entertain.[20] Unfortunately, rotifers are all invisibly small, and so their charm and amusement value is wasted, except to the few who enjoy watching pond water through a microscope.

Rotifers are named from a characteristic circle of bristle-like hairs (cilia), which from their constant motion give the impression of a rotating wheel, hence their older name of 'wheel animalcules'. Despite being no bigger than protozoa, a rotifer is a multicellular wonder of miniaturisation: it has a nervous system as well as a digestive gut, sex organs, a heart and a brain, all packed into a space smaller than a full stop.

The first rotifer-watcher was Henry Baker (1698–1774), the man who, through his writings, opened a new world to anyone who could afford an eighteenth-century brass microscope: 'I call it a Water Animal . . .' he wrote, but 'I give it also for Distinction sake the Name of Wheeler, Wheel Insect or Animal; from its being furnished with a Pair of Instruments, which in Figure and Motion, appear much to resemble Wheels . . . They have very much the Similitude of Wheels, and seem to turn round with a considerable Degree of Velocity, by which means a pretty rapid Current of Water is brought from a great Distance to the very Mouth of the Creature, who is thereby supplied with as many little Animalcules and various Particles of Matter that the waters are furnished with . . .'[21]

As Baker's fellow enthusiasts soon discovered, rotifers swarm in such homely places as water butts, roof gutters and even birdbaths, as well as garden ponds. One species, *Philodina roseola*, sometimes called the Birdbath Rotifer, becomes visible when the water dries out as a reddish stain – a sediment made up of innumerable cysts of sleeping rotifers patiently waiting for the rain. It can be persuaded to wake by scraping up some of the deposit and mounting it on a slide with a drop of rainwater.

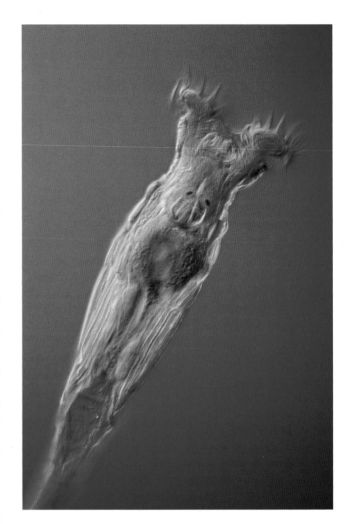

The Birdbath Rotifer, an everyday garden alien.

There, before your eyes, each dried-out rotifer swells up into a plump, pinkish, pig-like animal that stretches itself and moves groggily out of view in a methodical, stop-go manner.

Not all rotifers bear obvious head 'wheels', and if Baker had begun with some other kind, he might have given them a different name. *Diurella porcellus* resembles a plump porker, though it rolls through the water like a barrel. *Trichocerca* has a whiskery head and long tail-bristle suggesting a budgerigar. *Pleurotrocha daphnicola* sticks by its toes to the body of a water flea and feeds on the crumbs that fall from its mouth, while a related species lives inside worms at the bottom of deep lakes. *Testudinella* lives on the tummy of a water hog-louse, wafted by currents from the louse's frantically thrashing feet.

No rotifer impressed naturalists more than a tube-dweller called *Floscularia ringens*, better known by its former name of *Mellicerta*. *Floscularia* means 'little flowers', and the animal protruding from

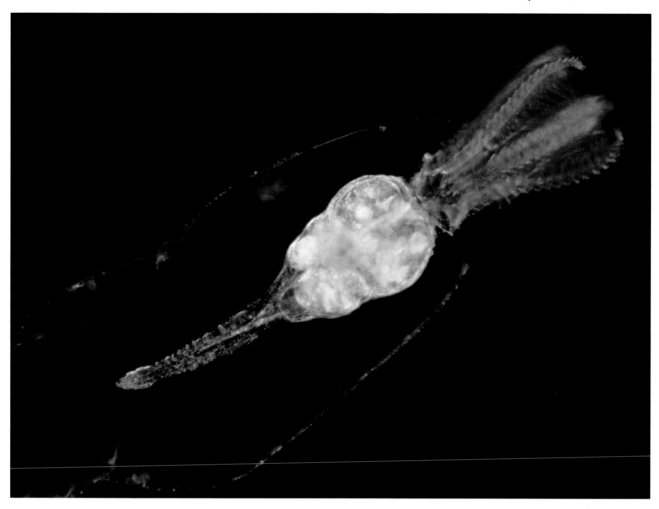

The transparent rotifer Stephanoceros, *known as the Queen of the Pond from its thorny crown.*

its tube to filter-feed in a self-created whirlpool is indeed flower-like, with delicate petalloid 'wheels'. But it was the wonderfully neat 'vase' made from pellets of silt and rotifer-glue that drew the gasps. In his *Marvels of Pond Life* (*c.*1900), H. J. Slack described the animal as 'at once brickmaker, mason and architect. [It] fabricates as pretty a tower as is easy to conceive . . . Pellet by pellet, or brick by brick, does the Mellicerta build her home, which widens gradually from the foundation to the summit, and every layer is placed with admirable regularity.' Particularly pretty towers could be created by feeding the animal with coloured sand or glass.

There have been periodic attempts to dignify this and other rotifers with English names; in 1926, F. J. Plaskett suggested the Bricklayer for *Mellicerta*, while another, *Stephanoceros*, was dubbed the Queen of the Pond. But rotifer enthusiasts are few and scientifically minded, and the descriptive vernacular names never caught on.

Hairybacks *Gastrotricha*

AN: gastrotriches, scaly-backs

Hairybacks, or gastrotriches (meaning hairy tummy), have been called the forgotten phylum. Only a dozen species have been recorded from Britain, almost certainly a vast underestimate. Yet there is a growing interest in them by developmental evolutionists, for hairybacks seem to be an evolutionary throwback or blind alley. One study suggests a distant link with rotifers, another with flatworms and yet another with moulting animals such as crabs and insects.

A typical hairyback is transparent and worm-like, with a body covered with distinctive bristles (or, in some species, with scales, like tiny fish); at one end is a rounded head, sometimes with spreading whiskers

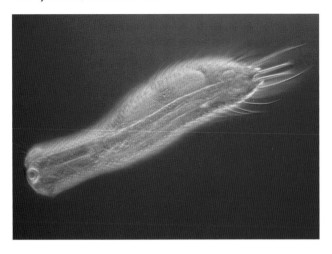

A 'hairy back', Chaetonotus, *'like a chip of glass'*.

like a cat, and at the other, a pair of adhesive 'toes' that anchor the animal to a stone or water plant. Richard Fitter described them as looking 'like chips of glass' from the way the light is refracted through their spines and scales.[22]

Hairybacks can be extremely numerous among vegetation on the quiet margins of ponds, in bogs or among the sand-grains on the lower part of the beach, but being microscopic, they go unnoticed. They must play a key ecological role in aquatic food-chains, bridging the gap between protozoa and bacteria and larger forms such as flatworms. Like rotifers, they can be surprisingly lively. F. J. Plaskitt described how their bodies make 'sudden leaps forwards or sideways, or instantly reverse their courses . . . All movements, in earnest, are done in a smart decisive manner.'[23] They seemed to him to bite chunks out of passing ciliates 'with a vicious snap' (though hairybacks in fact have no jaws to snap with and swallow their prey whole).

Hairybacks compound their other oddities by being entirely female (at least in fresh water): they reproduce, without sex, by parthenogenesis. They seem to have pathetically short lives: captive hairybacks live for no more than a few days. As microscopic objects, they are considered to be 'not quite as entertaining as rotifers and tardigrades [water-bears]' . . . 'but nearly'.[24]

Sea-mats and moss animals
Bryozoa

AN: lace coral, moss animalcule, sea mat

Bryozoa means 'moss animal'. These are tiny aquatic life-forms, which to the naked eye look like fuzzy moss or lichen and so, not unnaturally, were at first assumed to be plants (the freshwater ones even reproduce from little 'seeds' called statoblasts). Under a microscope, they are quite different: circles of tentacles, like tiny feather-dusters, emerge from a transparent tube or jelly-like mass, and it becomes obvious that they are animals similar to (but not necessarily related to) corals and hydroids. Some bryozoans are even capable of slow movement, sliding over a water-lily leaf or along a submerged stem.

It was not until 1825 that the full distinctiveness of 'moss animals' was recognised and a new phylum, the Bryozoa, formed to accommodate them. Until the mid-twentieth century, they were often known as polyzoans (meaning 'many animals'). One internet site also calls them 'homozoa' (gay animals), though this is probably a joke. There are around 300 British species, the majority marine. The most familiar are the white, net-like constructions known as 'sea-mats', commonly found attached to seaweeds. Each white 'cell' is made of calcium carbonate, inside which lives a minute animal consisting mostly of tentacles. A common find along the strandline is Hornwrack, which looks exactly like a flat piece of bleached seaweed ('wrack' is an old name for seaweed) but which, under a lens, looks more like a honeycomb and is the dried remains of a colony of bryozoans. When alive and attached to a sand-scoured rock in the shallows, Hornwrack is said to smell delightfully of lemons.

Scents and smells imply interesting body chemistry, and many marine sea-mats do indeed contain compounds of potential interest to pharmacists. One common species, *Bugula neritina*, contains bryostatin 1, a potential anti-cancer drug. Yet before its useful chemicals were identified and extracted, *Bugula* was nothing but a nuisance. It is found in ports and harbours, where it forms an encrusting layer over piers, buoys and ships' hulls, seeming to prefer man-made structures to natural rocks. Too much *Bugula* can increase drag and reduce a ship's performance.

The bryozoan Cristatella mucedo. *It resembles a slowly moving caterpillar but under a microscope, its shimmering tentacle 'flowers' are revealed.*

Bugula's freshwater equivalents are softer, jelly-like animals that lack the hard calcium cell of sea-mats. They are often common on canal locks, wooden piers and landing stages for boats, but since they resemble nothing so much as fuzzy brown moss, they are usually overlooked. When freshwater microscopy was popular, they were favourite subjects for study as, under low power, they project flower-like crowns of tentacles, transforming the 'moss' into a garden of semi-transparent anemones flickering in the lamplight. They were accordingly given unusually flowery Latin names, such as *Fredericella* and *Plumatella*. One of the most sought-after was *Cristatella mucedo,* which forms oval patches on the underside of lily pads, easily mistaken for the egg-masses of pond snails. *Cristatella* is not only pretty but also exceptionally active, a crystal-like bed of miniature anemones sliding along like a hover-caterpillar. It ought to be a well-known pond animal, but unfortunately it lacks an English name; in the era when such things were popular, common names were thought to be, well, common.

Moss animals used to cause trouble by encrusting water pipes. Their feathery mats could restrict the water supply, and when the animals died back in the autumn, they gave the water a fishy taste. This is rarely a problem today, partly because water-treatment works are so much more effective. One species has also been fingered as the intermediate host of a parasite that causes kidney disease in salmon.

The first British moss animal to be described and illustrated, in 1753, is now, 250 years later, the subject of a Biodiversity Action Plan. This is *Lophopus cristallina*, which, as 'the bell-flower animal', was one of the stars of a remarkably early popular book on the use of the microscope. Despite its familiarity from pictures in books, *Lophopus* has been quietly disappearing. In 1911 it was common enough in the once crystal-clear waters of the Norfolk Broads for someone to fill a bucket with a single haul of the net. But there have been no more than four records since 1970. *Lophopus*-watchers may be almost equally rare today, but the animal has certainly declined drastically, probably through water pollution.

Another rare species, *Victorella pavida*, has become known in conservation circles chiefly because of its silly name, 'Trembling Sea Mat'. Its Latin name *Victorella* commemorates the Victoria Docks in London, where the animal was first found in 1870. Today it is seemingly confined to the waters of Swanpool Lagoon near Falmouth, but though apparently trembling on the brink of extinction in Britain, it is elsewhere a widespread and successful species in warmer waters, from North America to India.

Brush-heads *Loricifera*

Brush-head is a recently minted term for an obscure group of marine organisms first discovered in 1983. They are microscopic worm-like animals, mostly less than half a millimetre long, which live in shelly sediment at the bottom of the sea. Consisting mainly of a collection of organs inside a transparent shell, or lorica, they resemble nothing so much as a vase of withered flowers. Very little is known about brush-head habits, but since they possess a gut and a sharp beak, or stylet, they are assumed to feed by piercing animals or plants like a bug and sucking their fluids. With a unique set of attributes unlike any other animal, they are placed in a phylum of their own, the Loricifera, from the Greek word *lorica*, meaning a corselet or breastplate. Of the 20-odd species described so far, three are British.

WORMS

Flatworms, flukes and tapeworms *Platyhelminthes*

Flatworms *Platyhelminthes*

Unlike sponges or sea anemones, it is obvious at first glance that flatworms are animals. The free-living forms are long and narrow, with a head at one end and a tail at the other. They move under their own volition, they feed and they mate. They have a simple gut but no lungs or gills, which is why they are flat: the worm simply absorbs oxygen through its skin, and for this to work, no part of the body must be far from the surface (the parasitic

flatworms known as tapeworms also manage to feed by absorption). The scientific name for flatworms, Platyhelminth, is simply Greek for flat worm. They are traditionally divided into the free-living forms, the Turbellaria, and the less appealing parasitic flukes and tapeworms.

Free-living flatworms *Turbellaria*

Flatworms were the first beneficiaries of one of life's really good ideas: bilateral symmetry. We share with them bodies in which one side is the mirror image of the other. Perhaps because of this we can appreciate worms as fellow mortals more easily than jellyfish, sponges or hydroids. Worms hunt gliding gracefully along with the help of a film of mucus and rows of

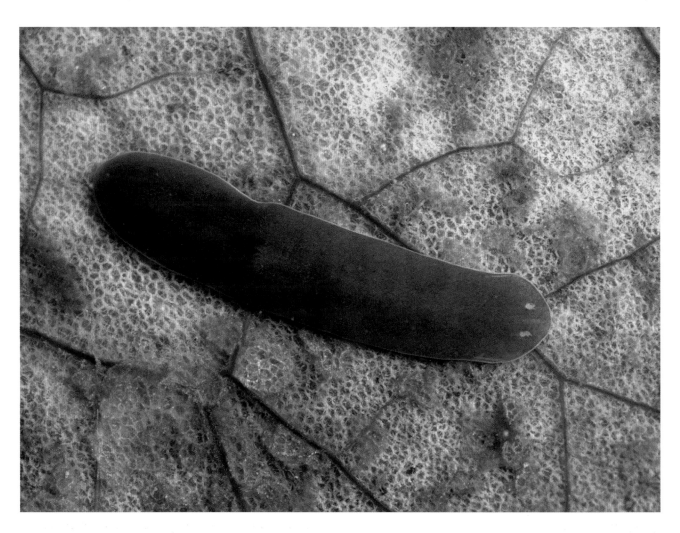

The planarian flatworm Dugesia lugubris, *so-named for the doleful expression of its simple eyes.*

tiny, endlessly beating hairs on their underbellies. They flee from predators, and they search for good-looking (or, more likely, good-smelling) worms to mate with and safe places to deposit their eggs. In short, they behave as animals.

On the other hand, a flatworm is undeniably a very basic animal. It has eyes of a sort, but they are no more than light-sensitive pits in the skin: a flatworm can distinguish between light and dark but probably cannot see images. It has a gut, but only one opening – so, thriftily, the waste goes out where the food came in. The brain is not so much an organ of thought and reflection as a couple of nerve ganglions at the forward end. Yet flatworms do have interesting sex lives. They are hermaphrodite, possessing both testes and ovaries and retaining the option of reproducing asexually or persuading another flatworm to exchange sperm. They also share with amoebas the ability simply to split in half, after which the tail end wiggles away and duly develops into another flatworm. All in all, the flatworm shows how far you can go on very little.

Flatworms live in fresh water, in the sea and in the soil. The best known are the freshwater forms, referred to as triclads (from their triple-branched gut), planarians or, mainly in America, detritus worms. In Britain, some 59 species have been found and can be distinguished at least to the right genus with no more than a hand lens. Unfortunately, few of us have ever bothered with them, and so they lack English names. Planarians range in size from the chunky, 2.5-centimetre-long *Bdellocephala punctata* to the trim little *Planaria torva,* which measures barely a centimetre. Anyone who has been pond-dipping will probably know the white flatworm *Dendrocoelum lacteum,* whose semi-transparent skin allows the sight of its greenish food sliding down its gut, or *Dugesia,* which possess a delightfully clownish triangular head with a pair of boss eyes, as though the worm is suffering appalling bellyache – a state summed up in the scientific name *Dugesia lugubris.*

Planarians are normally found on stones or the leaves of pond plants. The larger ones can also be caught like a fish with a bit of liver or dog meat attached to the end of a string. They are environmentally sensitive and, because they breathe through their skin, need clean water with a high percentage of dissolved oxygen. This confines some species to ultra-clear cold water in springs and spring-fed pools.

Flatworms are used the world over in school and college laboratories to demonstrate some of the fundamentals of life. These animals are cheap to acquire and easy to keep. They respond obligingly to a variety of stimuli, including bright lights or puffs of air, and their behaviour, though hardly sophisticated, is sufficient to demonstrate animals interacting with each other, consuming and digesting a meal or getting from A to B (navigating a simple maze is within their powers). Planarians are also of interest to molecular geneticists. Recent genetic screening using double-stranded RNA has revealed that flatworms and humans have many genes in common, especially those which govern the regeneration of tissues.

Planarians are famous for their seemingly miraculous powers of regeneration. Chop one in half, either lengthways or crossways, and each bit will grow into a complete flatworm. Bisect the head, and the animal will grow two heads. It used to amuse cruel-minded child biologists to see just how many heads they could 'make' on a single flatworm.

Though there is currently no society dedicated to flatworms alone, there are such things as flatworm enthusiasts. Planarians have a fan-base with a website selling T-shirts, coffee mugs, fridge magnets and other eye-catching items of flatworm memorabilia, each with a *Dugesia* sprouting a pair of understandably doleful-looking heads. Flatworm fans collect and keep freshwater ones in clean pond water away from bright lights, feeding them on hard-boiled egg-yolk. 'It is fun to see their gastro-vascular cavity fill with egg-yolk after a big meal,' enthused one proud owner.[1] In the wild, where egg-yolk must be a luxury few worms ever encounter, they live on algae, even smaller worms and detritus.

As well as the relatively large planaria, there are small, more cylindrical species ranging downwards from five millimetres to microscopic size. They are known as Microturbellarians. Many live head-to-tail in chains, while others are coloured yellow or green by algae living lichen-like within their tiny bodies. They seldom come to our attention, but they are abundant enough to play a key role in freshwater ecosystems as predators of small life and food for small fish.

Marine flatworms are larger and often very colourful (their bright colours are a warning – they are poisonous). Referred to as polyclads from their multi-branched gut, they are best known from tropical coral reefs, where they grow to the size of a human hand. British polyclads are more modestly sized and coloured. They are occasionally found in rock pools, like wavy-sided wisps of living muslin. Polyclads should be handled considerately, as they literally go to pieces under stress. Because of their capacity for almost instant regeneration, they have been studied by neurologists interested in their potential application to damaged nerve tissue in accident victims or paraplegia sufferers.

Land flatworms

Land flatworms are smooth and slimy; when at rest they look like small slugs (but lack a slug's 'horns' and textured body). When moving, they slither along like little snakes with the pointed head end raised up and questing from side to side. They live in the soil and in odd, damp, shaded corners, and often lurk inconspicuously in gardens. To see if you have any, squash a slug and cover the remains with a stone. After a day or so, the flatworms, attracted by the smell, will be feeding on the corpse.

Some 14 species have been found in Britain, though all but four are probably introductions. Unfortunately their good reputation has been ruined by an exotic species that feeds on earthworms, the New Zealand flatworm (its lengthy generic name, *Arthurdendylus*, commemorates a Professor Arthur Dendy of Canterbury, New Zealand, who discovered the worm in 1897). At a centimetre broad and up to 12 or more centimetres long when outstretched and moving, purple-brown on top with a paler buff underbelly, *Arthurdendylus* is an exotic-looking worm. In its native haunts, it does no harm, but in Britain, it has no natural enemies. Since its discovery in Northern Ireland in 1963, and in Edinburgh two years later, it has turned up in many places across northern Britain. The invasion of the worm and its blackcurrant-like eggs is unwittingly being aided by the nursery trade, carried with imported plants. Many suspected New Zealand flatworms sent to specialists for identification have, however, turned out to be harmless native flatworms, leeches or even slugs.

The New Zealand flatworm is formidably hardy: it can reproduce without mating and live for a year or more without feeding. The problem, though, is its appetite for earthworms. It hunts them by gliding nightmarishly through their burrows. Lacking teeth or jaws, the flatworm slithers alongside its prey in a clammy embrace and pumps out a lethal, earthworm-dissolving enzyme. Once the earthworm's innards have been sufficiently liquidised, the flatworm simply wallows in the worm soup and soaks it up through its skin. Under certain conditions, whole earthworm populations have been wiped out in this way. Then the knock-on effects begin. Without earthworms to turn over and aerate the soil, it becomes sour and ill-drained. This is now a problem on grass leys in Ireland, where flooding and the loss of sown grass has been blamed on the flatworm. A recent survey discovered that, while the flatworm was detected in only 4 per cent of grass fields in 1991, the proportion had risen to 70 per cent by the end of the decade.[2] The loss of earthworms has meant a corresponding diminution in the numbers of wild birds and mammals, notably moles and hedgehogs.

In Scotland, the worm has been found mainly in gardens; it is, for some reason, particularly common in Orkney. The damage there is not so much ecological as economic: our European partners have become understandably anxious about importing pot-plants from Scotland. There are no chemical controls available nor, so far, bio-controls, though there is current interest in a gnat that parasitises the worm in its native New Zealand. Fortunately it is possible to trap the worms by spreading sheets of black polystyrene or dustbin bags and searching for the coiled worms the next morning. Then the gardener is faced with the interesting problem of what to do with them. Handling New Zealand flatworms is not advised since their slime irritates the skin. And, as they lack vital organs, they are curiously hard to destroy. One gardener tried chopping them up, only to watch aghast as some of the pieces started to crawl away. One recommendation is to grind them up between two stones and then pour boiling water on the remains. Commercial nurseries are advised to expose plant containers to temperature-controlled hot water for ten minutes or to keep them in a room heated to not less than 26°C for 24 hours.

A related species, a bright orange Australian flatworm, has become established in places after forming a bridgehead on the Isles of Scilly in 1980. It, too, feeds on earthworms, but so far there is no evidence of a similar malign impact.

Flukes *Trematoda*

AN: fleuk (Lancs), fluke-worm, milt (Glos.)

Flukes are parasitic flatworms that live inside the bodies of their hosts for the whole of their adult lives. Consequently, few of us will have seen a

An eerily beautiful pair of mating blood flukes (Schistosoma), *transmitters of the sometimes fatal tropical disaease bilharzia.*

fluke. We know them instead by their reputation. The name fluke derives from the adult worm's rhomboidal shape, which reminded people of the flounder, a flatfish of estuaries whose Old English name was the *floke* (the flounder is still known as the fluke in America). The same name is used for the rhomboidal barbs of ships' anchors and the lobed tails of large whales. Paradoxically, it seems to have nothing to do with the more common use of the word as an accidental success, though 'fluky' is exactly the right word to describe this worm's unlikely parasite's progress through one animal to another.

In her book, *Fleas, Flukes and Cuckoos*, Miriam Rothschild presents a remarkable rogue's gallery of flukes. One of the most unbelievable is the species which passes 'from freedom in pond water to the liver of snails, to the body cavity of a shrimp, to the guts of a dragonfly larva, finally to end its peregrinations and live happily ever after under the tongue of a frog.'[3] Another depends on being eaten by the right kind of snail, then of finding a goby fish for a mid-career move, and finally of coming across

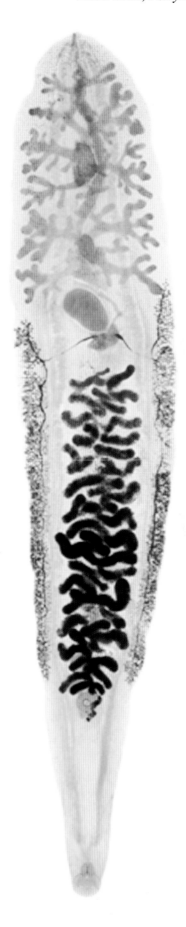

Right: *The liver fluke* Clonorchis sinensis, *its body organs scattered 'like currants in a cake'. An estimated 30 million people, mainly in the Far East, act as unwitting hosts for this species.*

an obliging redshank to swallow the goby and so allow the fluke to enjoy a well-earned retirement inside its stomach. Apparently no other kind of waterbird will do. It has to be a redshank.

Flukes live by attaching themselves to the internal tissues of their host and feeding on blood, lymph and other body fluids. Their bodies are pared down for an event-free life of passive gorging; the fluke's organs are scattered about its body, in Miriam Rothschild's words, 'like currants in a cake'. On the other hand, they have the most fantastically complicated reproductive system, which when stained and mounted on a microscope slide, reveals intricate and attractive patterns – the hidden inner beauty of the parasite. The necessarily hermaphroditic fluke devotes most of its energy to producing its eggs. It needs a lot of them, for the odds against any of its hatchlings finding the right host to continue the fluke's baroque lifecycle are daunting. One species, the Common, or Sheep, Liver Fluke, can lay around 25,000 eggs per day or up to half a million over its brief adult life.

I remember being entranced by the story of the liver fluke as it was outlined in the Puffin picture book *Pond Life*: the sliver of transparent flesh browsing on the animal's liver before slithering instinctively towards the bile duct to lay its eggs; the eggs that pass out of the sheep into the grass and hatch into thousands of microscopic, furry little beasts called miracidia, which then somehow track down a snail and worm their way into its breathing tubes; the new, non-motile form, the redia, which is what a miracidium becomes once snug and safe inside the snail; then, after turning restless and burrowing its way out again, reproducing without sex into yet another form, the tadpole-like cercaria, which swims around for a while before wriggling up a blade of wet grass, losing its tail in the process and turning into a cyst. Finally, when a cyst is swallowed by that unwitting sheep, it changes its skin one last time, turning into a fluke. The whole cycle takes a year or more.

These flukes cause 'liver rot', or fasciolosis, in infected animals. In one year, 1862, some 60 per cent of Ireland's sheep flocks caught fasciolosis, becoming listless, with shrunken bellies and swollen jaws. The destructiveness of the fluke was a great incentive to farmers to drain their wet fields and to treat their water courses with toxic compounds, which killed the water snails but unfortunately killed nearly everything else, too. The sheep, meanwhile, were treated with carcinogenic chemicals such as carbon tetrachloride. The fluke and the anti-fluke poisons are the twin reasons why we are earnestly warned not to eat unwashed wild watercress. Today, flukes can easily be knocked on the head by less environmentally damaging proprietary drugs (though they do have a habit of developing resistance to each one in turn).

Flukes are still a health hazard in countries where human waste is used to fertilise the ground. Bilharzia, caught by wading or swimming in infected water, is caused by the *Schistosoma* flukes and afflicts an estimated 200 million people in Africa, South America and South-east Asia. It is probably the most devastating disease in the world after malaria.

Another fluke in the news today is the Bile Fluke, which reached Britain inside imported fish and is now established in the wild on the Somerset Levels and other places. It is no threat to us, but it can be fatal to wild animals, especially otters; in 2008, the Somerset Wildlife Trust found several dead otter cubs with fluke in their livers.

Flukes have had surprisingly little impact on our imaginations. *Fluke*, the 1977 novel by James Herbert, later made into a film, is simply the name of a dog. Another novel with the same name is about a whale. Fluke Incorporation makes and tests electronic equipment. Perhaps Fluke, the 1980s electronic band that produced such albums as *Bubble*, *Squirt* and *Tosh*, comes a little closer to the spirit of real flukes.

Tapeworms *Cestoda*

It used to be said that if you were eating a lot without putting on weight you must have a tapeworm. Tapeworms were indeed once marketed in America and, to a smaller extent in Britain, in pill form as an aid to dieting. An advertisement dating from about 1900 has a fashionably dressed woman eying a vast pile of fattening foods against an inviting caption urging her to 'Eat, eat, EAT!' Unfortunately this form of slimming came at a price. If the pills worked and resulted in a tapeworm coiled up in the gut, the unwanted side-effects might include flatulence, diarrhoea or constipation, and what is described as 'rectal fluttering'. Tapeworm pills have long since been withdrawn from the market and become part of urban legend, but there is a resurgence of interest in them on the internet by people seeking ingenious ways of piling up the plate without piling on the pounds.

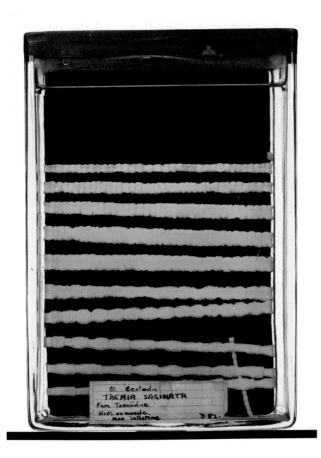

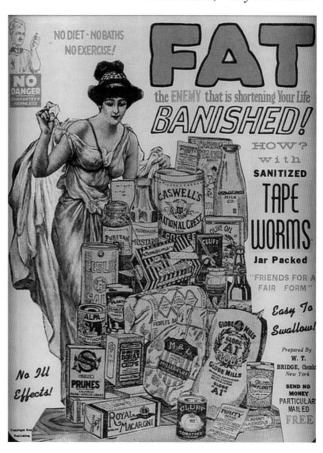

*A giant tapeworm (*Taenia saginata*) in a spirit jar, wound around like tape.*

Tapeworm eggs as slimming pills, from a magazine advertisement around 1900.

A big tapeworm resembles a roll of tape or, even more, a coil of perforated postage stamps. Its body is long and flat, with a pin-like head armed with hooks and adhesive suckers. Each segment of its body is a self-contained survival package, with a set of vital organs and, crucially, a bag of ripe eggs. The segments tear off, one by one, passing out of its host in its droppings. By the standards of intestinal parasites, tapeworms are fairly benign; you can have a tapeworm in your tummy without knowing it is there. The horrified realisation that a tapeworm is sharing your dinner comes only after you notice something white and suspicious in the toilet bowl or, perhaps worse, spot what appear to be flattened grains of rice in your undergarments and suddenly seeing them flex or wriggle.

There are three sources of human tapeworms: in pork, beef and fish. The beef tapeworm is a monster that just grows and grows, looping repeatedly back on itself, to a maximum of 25 metres or so. But tapeworm cysts and eggs are killed by cooking, and so the greatest risk of being infected comes from raw food such as sushi (though strenuous attempts are made to minimise this risk). Food hygiene laws have reduced tapeworm infections to vanishing point. Any bits of rice-like tapeworm seen in the home are likely to be from a dog or cat which has accidentally ingested the worm's eggs inside dead fleas. Standard vet's worming products easily get rid of tapeworms. The hardest part (since dogs are always swallowing dead fleas) is to prevent a recurrence.

Another group of people who will be familiar with tapeworms is grouse beaters. 'As young grouse take flight, lengths of creamy-white worm spurt from their backsides to dangle grotesquely before breaking off into egg-laden segments,' say Adam Watson and Robert Moss.[4] To try to get rid of them, many grouse-moor owners sprinkle their shoots with medicated grit.

One of the longest tapeworms ever found is coiled up inside a large jar at the Natural History Museum, where it makes a popular travelling exhibit. Dr Eileen Harris recalled how 'it was brought to me in a bucket after being found in a killer whale stranded off the coast of Cornwall in 1978. It was only the second tapeworm of that species ever to have been found. We've grown close over the years. That worm and I have been everywhere together – even to Buckingham Palace. We went to a science fair for the Queen's eightieth birthday . . . The royals were very interested in the worms.'[5]

The sociopathic police sergeant in Irvine Welsh's 1998 novel *Filth* has a talking tapeworm, which in many ways is the most attractive character in the novel. Initially simply an embodiment of appetite, Welsh's worm later becomes the repellent leading character's alter-ego, his better self, lamenting that its simple construction leaves no mechanism for translating its thoughts into action. Instead it soaks up details of the policeman's life, providing a new perspective on the experiences that have made him what he is.[6] On the same lines, Avus, aka Scott Edwards, released a 2006 EP of dance music titled *Tapeworm*, which includes 'Me and my Tapeworm'.

It is possible to discern a kind of beauty in a tapeworm. One of Miriam Rothschild's favourite animals was the tapeworm *Schistocephalus*, which hitchhikes its way through the carousel of life, from water fleas to sticklebacks and then on to kingfishers. *Prochristianella* lives in the stomachs of sharks and has long spiny tentacles instead of hooks. It 'is a real beauty,' says Eileen Harris. 'The longer you work with worms, the more you love them.'

Ribbon worms *Nemertea*

Also known as proboscis worms, these little-known, mostly marine creatures include the world's longest worm, the Bootlace Worm (it has an entirely appropriate scientific name: *Lineus longissimum*, 'the longest of lines'). In Britain, modest-sized specimens can be found in rock pools, generally under a stone, as slimy coils of narrow, purple-brown loops. These normally measure only a metre or two at most and would fit into a soup spoon. In deeper waters, the worms can grow to enormous lengths, and one celebrated specimen when fully uncoiled stretched 30 metres – longer than a blue whale. There are unconfirmed reports of even more monstrous worms 50 or 60 metres long. Accurate measurement is difficult, as the worms have a distressing habit of breaking up when handled.

Zoologists once believed that ribbon worms were the ancestors of all vertebrate animals, including man. This happy thought was based on the worm's internal structure, particularly the extensible proboscis, with which the worm impales and devours its prey. It was this organ, they believed, that turned by gradual degrees into a notochord and thence into a backbone, enabling animals to colonise the land and conquer the world. Molecular science has, however, killed that old idea stone dead: we are not descended from ribbon worms. In fact they have no close relatives and occupy a phylum of their own, the Nemertea, meaning sea-nymph.

For what ribbon worms get up to down on the seafloor, it is hard to improve on Charles Kingsley's gruesome account of the antics of a pet one he kept in a tank:

'There are animals in which results so strange, fantastic, even seemingly horrible, are produced, that fallen man may be pardoned, if he shrinks from them in disgust . . . It hangs, helpless and motionless, a mere velvet string across the hand … trailing itself among the gravel; you cannot tell where it begins or ends; it may be a dead strip of seaweed or even a tarred string. So thinks the little fish that plays over and over it, till he touches at last what is too surely a head. In an instant, a bell-shaped sucker mouth has fastened to his side. In another instant, from one lip, a concave double proboscis, just like a tapir's, has clasped him like a finger; and now begins the struggle: but in vain. He is being "played" with such a fishing line as the skill of a Wilson or a Stoddart never could invent; a living line, with elasticity beyond that of the most delicate fly-rod, which follows every lunge, shortening and lengthening, slipping and twining round every piece of gravel and stem of sea-weed, with a tiring drag . . . The victim is tired now; and slowly, and yet dexterously, his blind assailant is feeling and shifting along his side, till he reaches one end of him; and then the black lips expand, and slowly and surely the curved finger begins packing him end-foremost into the gullet, where he sinks, inch by inch, till the swelling which marks his place is lost among the coils, and he is probably macerated to a pulp long before he has reached the opposite extremity of his cave of doom. Once safe down, the black murderer slowly contracts again into a knotted heap, and lies, like a boa with a stag inside him, motionless and blest.'[7]

Ribbon worms have a nasty surprise for predators, too: 'On a field course I was helping to run back in 1984, we found a ribbon worm – not the classic

30-feet-long one but a respectable size nonetheless – and a student offered our young helper Rosie five pounds if she would swallow it. Which she promptly did, whole, and said it tasted remarkably nasty. She spent her fiver (they went further then) on cream teas for all. Rosie was lucky. Had I known then what toxins lay in a ribbon worm's epidermis . . .'[8]

Roundworms *Nematoda*

AN: bookworm, eelworm, hookworm, lungworm, nematode, pinworm, seat-worm, threadworm, thunderworm, whipworm

Though we barely notice them, nematodes, or roundworms, are our teeming neighbours. Every acre of fertile soil, every patch of leafmould or compost, contains tens of millions of them. An American agriculturalist, Nathan A. Cobb, once suggested that 'if all matter in the universe except the nematodes were swept away, our world would still be dimly recognizable, and if, as disembodied spirits, we could then investigate it, we should find its mountains, hills, vales, rivers, lakes and oceans represented by a thin film of nematodes. The locations of towns would be decipherable, since for every massing of human beings there would be a corresponding massing of certain nematodes. Trees would still stand in ghostly rows representing our streets and highways. The location of the various plants and animals would still be decipherable, and, had we sufficient knowledge, in many cases even their species could be determined by an examination of their erstwhile nematode parasites.'[9] He might have added that we could probably still find our way to the pub. When I was at school, the one thing I knew about nematodes was that one kind lives only inside beer mats.

Nematode means 'thread-like'. The average nematode is tiny, often microscopic, pointed at both ends and whitish (or, under the microscope, semi-transparent). Since only an expert can tell one nematode from another, this is one phylum where every species could be said to be average. Some 20,000 species have been scientifically described, of which around 3270 are British; estimates of how many species may exist range from hundreds of thousands

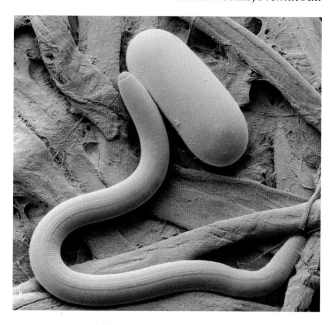

Electron micrograph of a soybean nematode worm with its egg sac.

to many millions. Nematodes even have their own particular science: nematology. Amateur naturalists have generally left them alone, though the standard Victorian text, *Monograph of the Anguillulidae,* was written by a Cornish physiologist, Henry Bastian. Under the microscope, they can be unexpectedly beautiful: 'Most nematodes are really quite nice and you can get some attractive ones with rows of spines, frills or intricate teeth,' says Eileen Harris, expert on parasitic worms at the Natural History Museum.

As their name implies, roundworms are roughly circular in section. They are effectively living tubes of chitin, with a proboscis at one end and an anus at the other. About half live freely in the soil and, to a lesser extent, in the water (including the ocean floor), where they play a fundamental role in decomposition and recycling, feeding on bacteria, single-celled life and fungi (though certain fungi get their own back and trap nematodes). The other half live as parasites in plants and animals, and it is these, of course, that attract most attention.

Nematode parasites are no longer serious problems in Europe, though pinworms are still the cause of itchy bottoms in children. In parts of Europe and America, more than half of the youngsters whose bottoms were examined showed signs of the worm. It is easily banished with a chemical agent, but the problem is the ease with which children can be reinfected. There is some evidence of a linkage

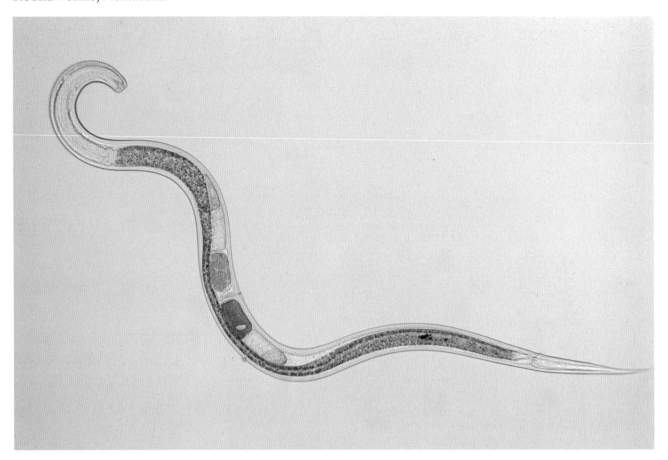

A nematode worm (x100), transparent under a light microscope but white to the naked eye.

between pinworms and a deficiency of zinc in the body; concerned parents should feed their infants with food rich in zinc, such as dairy food, steak and shellfish.

Chickens seem to have the record number of nematodes. One form lives in a chicken's wind-pipe and is the cause a disease known as 'gapes'. Another lives inside the chicken's gut, a third in its crop, while a fourth ekes out its existence inside the unfortunate bird's eyeball. *Ascardia*, a comparative giant that can grow up to the size of a drinking straw, finds its way into the hen's eggs by way of its oviducts. This weakness of nematodes for chickens means, of course, that it is important to buy live birds from a reputable source.

Gardeners know nematodes as eelworms. They are vectors for several commercially important plant diseases including potato cyst, raspberry ringspot and chrysanthemum mosaic. Other eelworms damage onions, leeks and sugar beets or the roots of cereals. Once established, there is no easy way of getting rid of them; hygiene (including the burning of infected plants) and resistant varieties are the solution.

On the basis of using a sprat to catch a mackerel, certain nematodes are now being reared as bio-control agents against such everyday garden pests as slugs and vine weevil. Unlike most bugs used for biological control, nematodes can survive British winters outdoors. The worms casually wipe out their victims by infecting them with lethal bacteria. So far, 30 species of nematode have been identified as potential bio-control agents; others are sure to follow.

The roundworm *Caenorhabditis elegans* is one of the world's most intensively studied animals. Chosen as a 'model organism', it has had its entire genome mapped and sequenced, and the developmental fate of every single cell determined.

Nematodes are robust animals. Hundreds of them survived the Space Shuttle Columbia disaster in 2003 and were later recovered alive inside their scorched canister.

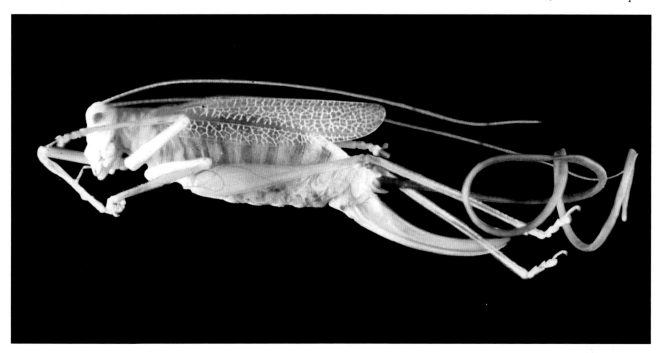

A hairworm (Spinochordodes sp.) exiting from a now dead bush-cricket.

Horsehair worms
Nematomorpha

AN: cabbage-hairs, Gordian worms, hair-worms

Horsehair worms are the world's slenderest worms; stiff and blackish and between a centimetre and a metre in length, they look like horsehair come to life (the name of their phylum, Nematomorpha, means 'thread-shaped'). Though common in freshwater and nearby damp places, they seldom come to notice except on the infrequent occasions when one turns up in a pet dish, or squirming and twisting in the toilet bowl. On the latter occasion, it would be natural to assume that the worms came from inside us, but they are, in fact, not parasites of humans or dogs but of insects, especially cockroaches and crickets (they occasionally wriggle nightmarishly out when someone crushes a roach). One species that infects grasshoppers sends a message to its brain that orders the insect to find the nearest puddle and drown itself, thus enabling the worm to swim away to its next victim.

Groups of horsehair worms found tangled into a wriggling ball have been called Gordian worms, from the legend of the impossibly intricate 'Gordian knot' (which Alexander the Great 'undid' by cutting it in half with his horse). Horsehair worms found among growing vegetables after rain have been called 'cabbage-hairs'.

Spiny-headed worms *Acanthocephala*

AN: thorny-headed worms

These parasitic worms are named from the heavily barbed proboscis that they use to hook themselves to the gut lining of waterbirds and other hosts. Spiny-headed worms are seldom noticed except as curious orange blobs visible in the translucent bodies of freshwater shrimps, which act as intermediate hosts. The name of their phylum, Acanthocephala, means 'thorn-head'.

Segmented worms *Annelida*

In days gone by, a 'worm' could mean any long, thin animal, big or small, including snakes, centipedes, lizards or even dragons. It was also another word for an insect grub or maggot, as in 'woodworm' or 'wireworm' or 'food for worms', which we become after we die. Worms represent the convergence of a useful shape. Long and thin is simply the best form for burrowing, whether the medium is wood, vegetation, mud, soil or the innards of another animal. Biologically, worms include many unrelated groups, from simple flatworms to comparatively complex ragworms and leeches. But when we speak of worms, we tend to have one form in mind over all others: that worm of worms, the earthworm.

'Worm' is an Old English word of uncertain meaning, probably related to the Latin word for worm, *vermis*. Worms were traditionally regarded, wrongly, as the lowest, most humble form of life. This is still reflected in everyday sayings such as 'Even a worm will turn', that is, even the most abject of creatures will turn on its tormentors if driven to the extremity.

Other worm sayings stress the creature's wriggliness or appetite:

Worm-eaten can refer to timbers, where the 'worms' are beetle larvae, or as a metaphor for old, shabby and generally worn-out, where it means the same thing as 'moth-eaten'.

A *worm-hole* in space is a hypothetical tunnel in space-time, taking us from one place to another distant one in the blinking of a cosmic eye.

To have a worm in one's tongue is to be cantankerous, or, as *Brewer's Dictionary of Phrase and Fable* puts it, 'to snarl and bite like a mad dog'. This saying is often applied to critics.

The early bird gets the worm means that success comes to those who prepare well and put in the effort. The phrase first appears in print around 1670, though it was probably in use long before that.

A *worm's-eye view* means a view of events as seen from a low or humble position. Earthworms, of course, do not have a view, being blind or virtually so.

To satisfy the worm is to appease your hunger, an allusion to the tapeworm, which supposedly keeps its host in a constant state of keen appetite.

To worm oneself into favour means to insinuate yourself into another's good graces by appropriate wriggling and slithering.

To worm out information means to extract useful information piecemeal or indirectly.

It was once believed that tiny worms appeared spontaneously in the fingers of idle servants. Shakespeare was referring to this when, in *Romeo and Juliet*, someone happened to mention 'A round little worm/Pricked from the lazy finger of a maid.'

To a child, a worm is above all wriggly and probably slimy (the collective name is a *knot* of worms). 'Wiggly Woo' is a cheerful, bounce-along nursery song about a worm that does nothing but wriggle:

There's a worm at the bottom of the garden
And his name is Wiggly Woo
There's a worm at the bottom of the garden
And all that he can do
Is wiggle all night
And wiggle all day
Whatever else the people do say
There's a worm at the bottom of the garden
And his name is Wiggly Woo.

One of the persistent myths about earthworms is that, if you cut one in half, the result will be two new worms. It would, in fact, be a single, mutilated and probably fatally injured worm, though earthworms can, up to a point, regenerate lost segments. It is flatworms that have powers of regeneration (see page 31).

The most familiar worms, including earthworms, lugworms and leeches, are members of the phylum Annelida, or segmented worms. They are more advanced in their construction than flatworms, with a digestive gut running the length of their bodies, from mouth to anus, a circulatory system with a heart to pump their either colourless or red blood and another to rid them of the unwanted byproducts of breathing. They have simple eyes, move along with surprising efficiency and even possess a brain of sorts. Earthworms, or Oligochaetes ('few bristles'), have sparse, short bristles and live in fresh water as well as in the soil. Bristleworms, or polychaetes ('many bristles'), are mainly marine, while leeches are well-known bloodsucking worms that live in ponds and rivers, with a few that live in the sea.

The early bird gets the worm.

Earthworms *Lumbricidae*

VN: angle-dutch (Cornwall), angle touch (S. Wales), angleworm, dew-worm, eace (Isle of Wight), fish-worm, lob, lobworm, night crawler, rainworm, yeth-worrm (Yorks.), woggams (Lincs.)

Earthworms were one of Charles Darwin's passions, and the subject of his last book, that quiet epic *Formation of Vegetable Mould Through the Action of Worms* (1881). He had, over more than 40 years, conducted innumerable experiments in his home-made wormeries to prove what every farmer knew by intuition, that earthworms are nature's ploughmen (and also nature's fertilisers, in the sense that their droppings assist the germination of seeds). 'It may be doubted whether there are many other animals which have played so important a part in the history of the world, as have these lowly organised creatures,' he concluded. Darwin effectively changed their image from slithering nullities, even pests, to benevolent animals of great benefit to mankind.

Long before Darwin, gardeners were vaguely aware that earthworms devoured and recycled dead vegetation in the soil. Aristotle described them aptly and succinctly as 'the intestines of the soil'. Gilbert White devoted a whole letter (on 20 May 1777) to this 'small and despicable link in the Chain of Nature', which if lost, would open up a 'lamentable chasm'. By boring into the soil, perforating and loosening it, and 'drawing straws and stalks of leaves and twigs into it', the worm quietly aerates and replenishes the land. 'The earth without worms', wrote White, 'would soon become cold, hard-bound and void of fermentation, and consequently sterile.'[10] The Irish government calculated that earthworms are worth 723 million euros a year to local agriculture. For Britain, the figure may be close to £16 billion.[11]

PUNCH'S FANCY PORTRAITS.—NO. 54.

CHARLES ROBERT DARWIN, LL.D., F.R.S.

IN HIS *DESCENT OF MAN* HE BROUGHT HIS OWN SPECIES DOWN AS LOW AS POSSIBLE—*I.E.*, TO "A HAIRY QUADRUPED FURNISHED WITH A TAIL AND POINTED EARS, AND PROBABLY *ARBOREAL* IN ITS HABITS"—WHICH IS A REASON FOR THE VERY GENERAL INTEREST IN A "FAMILY TREE." HE HAS LATELY BEEN TURNING HIS ATTENTION TO THE "POLITIC WORM."

A 'fancy portrait' of Charles Darwin from Punch, *1881, noting that he had turned his attention from evolution to 'the Politic Worm' (in the shape of a question mark).*

The richer the soil, the more earthworms there are likely to be, and the richest place of all is often under the garden compost heap. Large populations are also found in long-established grassland and in orchards, wherever the soil has lain undisturbed for years. Wormcasts are disliked by many gardeners because they spoil the neat look of cut grass, but they are an ecological compliment, and the casts are themselves rich in minerals. Without worms to pull dead plant material into the soil, a fibrous layer will build up, and the finer grasses will lose out to coarser ones.

Earthworms move with the aid of short, stiff bristles. Though the bristles are barely visible, you can feel them by running a finger along an earthworm's belly. The pulling power of a large worm is remarkable. You can test its strength by holding one in your closed fist: it is hard to prevent it from nosing out between your fingers. The natural state of a healthy, active earthworm is to be slimy and pinkish-grey. Their pinkness is produced by red blood flowing just beneath the skin; earthworms have no lungs and absorb oxygen through the skin straight into the bloodstream.

Earthworms have surprisingly few local names. 'Angleworm' ('angle-dutches' in Cornwall) and 'fishworm' reflect their use as wriggling live-bait on a fisherman's hook or bent pin. Worms are often found on the surface after a night of rain, hence their redundant name 'rainworm' or 'night crawler'. 'Dew-worm' is another name used in the past by anglers who collected worms in the evening or early morning, without the need to dig for them, and kept them alive in damp newspaper or sawdust until needed.

The impalement of earthworms on hooks as angling bait begs the question of whether they feel pain as we do. Worms lack the part of the brain that registers pain, and their simple nervous system cannot process emotional information. Hence they cannot be said to suffer as we do. On the other hand, worms certainly react to unpleasant stimuli, and wriggling on a hook indicates a desire to escape. So, if by pain we mean a reaction followed by an instinctive will to flee from danger, then earthworms certainly experience something analogous to it.

At one time, earthworms were used to alleviate various *human* pains. Pharmaceutical worms were prepared by first wrapping them in moss to get rid of their slime, and then pressing them to expel the digested earth. They were then washed in white wine with a little salt, and finally dried to a powder in an oven. At this point, the earthworms apparently smell rather pleasant, like rennet or soft cheese. Powdered earthworm was considered to be a cure-all, and the worm powder could be adapted to a variety of maladies by mixing it with different liquids. For example, added to marigold juice, it had the power to cure epilepsy. With the juice of comfrey, it was effective 'against endless pissing'. Mixed with honey and fine-powdered alum, it had the power to heal wounds. The versatile worm could also be mixed with mead to cure the dropsy, with wine and myrrh for jaundice or with boiled wine for the stone or bladder ailments. Worms could be boiled

The earthworm Allobophora longa *and its cast.*

Below: *Worms for garden wormeries: the Brandling, otherwise known as redworm, wriggler or stripey.*

in goose-fat for dealing with earache. Boiled worms on their own were said to be good for the stomach. If you cared to carry one around in your mouth, it might help to relieve toothache. Earthworms have probably never been collected for food, but many children have swallowed one for a dare. Few of us risked a chew to see what they tasted like.

Mary Beith picked up an old Highland story that worms could even be used as a truth test: 'A stranger who claimed to be a seventh son of a seventh son was tested by an earthworm put in the palm of his hand. If the man was telling the truth, it was believed the worm would die at once.'[12]

There are 25 species of earthworms in Britain, though only four or five are found regularly in gardens. The Lobworm is the largest and most often seen. It is normally pink with a bluish tinge and has characteristically blunt ends, with a noticeably broad, flattened tail (the head is the narrow, pointed end). It mates on the surface on warm, humid nights, when pairs can be found by torchlight lying head to tail (earthworms are hermaphrodite, but need a little help from a mate to get things going; each fertilises the other).

The lengths to which Lobworms will go to find a mate are surprising. Caroline Searle witnessed hundreds of worms 'migrating' across the fields in late winter, even negotiating cattle grids. 'At one point I found it difficult to drive my vehicle or walk across the fields without squashing amorous earthworms!'

Lobworms can be found in some unlikely places such as damp, rotting leaf litter in the cracks

and hollows high up in the trees. The worms are evidently able to climb, using their short bristles to grip the fissures of the bark, and presumably they live out their lives high above the ground. Their favourite trees are beech, lime and sycamore.

The Longworm, or Blackhead, is the one that makes casts on the surface of clipped lawns and bowling greens. Longworms are slim and brownish, and live in deep, vertical burrows. During the hottest part of the summer, they take a siesta, tied up in a knot, which is why wormcasts are commonest in spring and autumn. Longworms can be enticed to wriggle to the surface and peer out of their burrows if you vibrate the soil with a tuning fork. Another, smaller species is pale blue-grey with an orange 'saddle' and is often dug up when working a flower bed or vegetable plot.

The Brandling or Tiger Worm (so-named because it has orange bands, like a tiger) is another common garden earthworm that feeds on organic waste in rich soil, often close to garden compost or a heap of manure. It is a distinctive, reddish worm familiar to gardeners, who also know it as redworm, 'red wriggler' or, especially in the north, as 'bramlin', 'brammel' or simply 'stripey'. The Brandling and its close relatives have long been bred commercially as a source of high-protein feed for fish and livestock or as angling bait. More recently, they have become the stars of the garden wormery, a popular feature of eco-friendly gardens since their invention as a commercial product in the late 1980s.

A wormery is simply a bin or set of shallow shelves containing the worms (which are hardy enough to dispatch through the post in packets) and some start-up cereal-based worm food. The worms happily devour most kinds of domestic rubbish, from scraps and left-overs to toilet rolls and egg boxes. There is even a wormery that can deal with dog poo. Over weeks and months, the worms recycle the waste, producing a useful reward in the form of nutrient-rich 'vermicompost' and liquid plant feed, as well as reducing the environmental burden of landfill and its harmful methane emissions. Wormeries are also educational. Some children love watching and playing with worms, and commercial wormeries come with a cheerful booklet illustrated with friendly worms wearing glasses or brandishing knives and forks.

Less fortunate bred worms are destined for angling suppliers. The most popular is the Dendrobaena worm, a close relative of the Brandling worm, which is reddish and suitably tough and wriggly. It is marketed in large numbers with worm-food inside plastic bait containers as an all-purpose bait for coarse fishing. The success of these small, manically wriggling red worms has cast more traditional baits, such as 'blackworms' or the garden lobworm, into the shade. The very small kind of angling worm known as bloodworms or Tubifex worms retain their popularity for those targeting small species of fish, and rolled up into to a ball they can also be a magnet for hungry carp.

Worm-charming – that is, persuading the worms to leave the ground – is an age-old way of collecting angling bait. Homegrown methods include vibrating the tines of a fork or rubbing a wooden stake, or 'stob', with an iron, a method known as worm-grunting. Others use a method called worm-fiddling, by dragging a blunt saw over the stob. A few swear by the merits of tap-dancing, meditation or playing music. The best time to practise worm-charming is in wet weather when the soil is already saturated, but in dry seasons the worms can be softened up by watering. How it all works is disputed. Some say the vibration simulates rainfall, others that it sounds to the worm like the approach of a hungry mole. Either way, it seems, the worm is not so much charmed as trying to escape.

The village of Willaston near Nantwich in Cheshire is the venue for the annual World Worm Charming Championships, originally devised in 1980 by John Bailey, deputy head of the local primary school. Each competitor is allotted three square metres of turf in the 'worm arena' and, after the ringing of a handbell at two o'clock prompt, the charming begins. The

The worm-charming championship in full swing at Willaston, Cheshire. Contestants are allotted three metres of turf in which to coax as many worms as possible to the surface without chemical aids.

winner is the person with the most worms after half an hour; an additional prize is given to the contestant with the heaviest worm. Digging and the use of fluids or chemicals is banned.[13]

The record was established early in the championships by a teenage farmer's son, Tom Shufflebotham, whose artful twanging of his garden fork – the favoured method in South Cheshire – was found irresistible by no fewer than 511 worms. The coveted Golden Worm Trophy was invariably won by the local villagers, until 1996, when the title was snatched by visitors Phil and David Williams from Wiltshire, who managed to charm 157 worms during a difficult dry season. The television presenter Ben Fogle, on the other hand, attracted only seven worms with his preferred tin whistle. Many contestants like to work in pairs with a 'ghillie' to second the charmer and corral the worms once they have been enticed to the surface. The worms are later released in the evening after the local sparrows have gone to bed.

A growing threat to the championships at Willaston is the predatory New Zealand Flatworm (q.v.). This alien is suspected of having done away with 'Willie Worm', a large and popular worm that disappeared from the arena in suspicious circumstances. Nowadays the turf is inspected closely before the competition for any signs of the intruder.

'OK, here's an embarrassing story. As a child of about five, my love of bugs combined with my hoarding instincts. It seemed such a shame to throw away the empty box of After Eight mints, with all those neat little packets … so: I put tiny amounts of soil in each one, then caught the smallest worms I could find, and kept them in the box – like a filing cabinet.'[14]

Tubifex worms *Tubificidae*

AN: bloodworms, sewage worms, sludge worms

Tubifex worms, better known as bloodworms (they share the name with the smaller larvae of Chironomid midges), live in the sediment of pools and lakes and are among the handful of animals that thrive in sewage-polluted water. The worm lives and feeds head-down in the mud inside a protective tube, with its signature red tail endlessly wriggling in the water. The red haemoglobin in its body enables the worm to breathe in putrid water all but starved of oxygen.

Bloodworms make excellent fish-food and can be bought from pet shops as dry pellets or wormy freeze-dried blocks cut like ice cream. They are also handy for feeding tadpoles in the garden pond. The worms are easy to culture, but are not easy neighbours to have in a fish-tank. Apart from contaminating the water, they can carry and transmit disease; the potential danger to trout in fish farms is one good reason for maintaining strict water-quality standards.

Potworms *Enchytraeidae*

AN: enchytraeid worms, whiteworms

Potworms are small worms, rarely more than a centimetre long, which often turn up in plant pots, especially when natural peat has been used. They can also appear in wriggling clusters when you are digging compost or well-rotted manure. Potworms are whitish or grayish in colour, hence their alternative name of whiteworms. They are harmless, and even beneficial. Effectively, they are small earthworms, maintaining the soil's fertility with their nutrient-rich droppings. They can, however, be enticed to leave a plant pot by offering them a piece of bread soaked in milk; once the bread is fully loaded with worms, it can be dropped into the compost. Potworms are sensitive to toxic heavy metals such as copper and lead and have been used as biological indicators of unpolluted soil. They are also a welcome treat for tropical fish.

Leeches *Hirudinea*

VN: bloodsuckers, gell or gellie (Scot.), horse gellie, loch-leech

Leech is an Old English word for cure or healing. In pre-scientific times, someone skilled in healing was known as a 'leech' (or 'leach'), and his or her calling as leechcraft. The name was shared with that of a bloodsucking worm, which was once as central to the healing trade as pills and injections are to a modern healthcare centre. In the TV comedy *Blackadder*, the Tudor clinic was full of leeches: pictures of leeches on the wall, jars of leeches everywhere, even a blackboard with a large leech drawn on it. It was presided over by a Dr Leech, whose answer to every ailment, including Blackadder's worrying fascination for his page, was another 'course of leeches'.

The leech in question was the Medicinal Leech, the largest of the 15 or so British species of freshwater leech and the only one capable of penetrating human skin. Medicinal Leeches live in warm, shallow ponds, usually near the coast, where they feed mainly on the blood of amphibians and fish, though they will also attach themselves to cattle, sheep and, given a chance, humans. A single leech can part us, quite painlessly, with between five and ten cubic centimetres of blood – around five times the leech's body weight. Such an appetite for blood made leeches extremely useful in the days when the solution for many ailments, from fevers to piles, was to stick on a few of them to relieve the blood pressure. 'It were too tedious to reckon up all the melancholique and mad people that have been cured by applying leeches to the hemarrods (sic) in their fundaments,' wrote Blackadder's Tudor contemporary, Dr Thomas Muffet. But it was easy to overdo it: George Washington is said to have expired after an over-zealous application of leeches as he lay weak and helpless.

After a blood meal, a leech does not need to feed again for weeks or even months and so becomes medically useless. For this reason, hospitals always needed fresh supplies. Collecting leeches for the medical profession became a useful pursuit for the rural poor, and some institutions, such as monasteries, would keep a supply in special ponds. Inglemire, near Hull, is believed to come from Old Norse words meaning 'leech-pond'.

Leech finders, from The Costume of Yorkshire *(1814), by George Walker.*

In George Walker's *The Costume of Yorkshire* (1814), there is a drawing of women collecting leeches. Two are wading bare-legged, their skirts rucked up around their hips. One uses a pole to stir up the mud, while the other daintily picks out the worms between finger and thumb and drops them through a hole into a little barrel she carries on a sling. A third woman sits on the bank with a spare barrel, her ankles splashing in the water to disturb the leeches.

The catching of wild leeches, together with land drainage, led to a severe decline in British Medicinal Leeches. Long before the mid-nineteenth-century peak in the trade, leeches were not as easy to find as they had been. In his poem 'Resolution and Independence' (1802), William Wordsworth recalled an elderly leech-gatherer who wandered the moors, sleeping rough:

> . . . gathering Leeches, far and wide
> He travelled; stirring thus about his feet
> The waters of the Ponds where they abide.

> 'Once I could meet with them on every side:
> But they have dwindled long by slow decay;
> Yet still I persevere, and find them where I
> may.'[15]

Wordsworth's leech-gatherer was probably among the last. By the mid-nineteenth century, hospitals were turning to Eastern Europe or even America (which has a closely related species) for supplies. Some 7 million leeches were imported by London hospitals in 1863, and even that figure pales in comparison with the 42 million leeches imported to France in 1832 or the 30 million per year from America to Germany.[16] Leeches were kept ready for use in glazed earthenware jars. Perhaps to reassure the sweating, wide-eyed patient, these jars were often ornamental and attractive, made of marble with gilt decoration and the word LEECHES in large, friendly capital letters. Such 'medical ceramics' are highly collectible today (so much so that modern replica leech jars are now available at around £50 each).

A Medicinal Leech and a nineteenth-century leech jar. Leeches were kept in marble jars to ensure that they were cool and healthy.

Today the Medicinal Leech is found mainly in ditches on coastal 'levels'. Their last great stronghold is Romney Marsh and the nearby gravel pits at Dungeness. Though local boys had long known about them, the leeches came to the attention of the wider world as recently as 1978 after a dog had gone on an ill-advised swim there: what appeared to be part of the animal's gut hanging out of its side turned out to be an unusually large and well-fed leech. A survey carried out for conservation purposes estimated that more than 10,000 adult leeches were living in the gravel pits, making it possibly the largest population of Medicinal Leeches left in Western Europe. When not feeding, the leeches live quietly in the mud. No one had noticed them because conservationists had taken little interest in humble, worm-like creatures in ponds.

The best way to attract a Medicinal Leech, says Owen Leyshon, who is studying their biology, is to take a tip from the leech-gatherers of old and make a gentle splashing motion. If the water is reasonably warm and the leeches in the right mood,

they will wake up and head, with disconcerting speed, towards the source of the commotion, which they instinctively associate with animals drinking. Leeches are 'very temperamental', says Leyshon. On a perfect evening, you may find up to 30 of them circling round your legs like hungry sharks, but the next day it may be hard to attract more than one or two.

'The leeches stick to your wellies, and you can peel them off and put them in a jar. But if you miss them, they can crawl up and disappear down your welly boot.' Leyshon knows at least one leech surveyor who pulled off his boot to find his sock soaked in blood and a big leech feeding on his ankle. 'Most people who work with this species have been bitten,' adds Leyshon. 'They leave a mark on the skin like a three-pronged triangle – the shape of their jaws – which looks a bit like the Mercedes-Benz symbol.'[17]

The traditional way of persuading a leech to let go, learned in tropical forests rather than British gravel pits, is to apply some salt or to touch it with the glowing tip of a cigarette. Such methods can, however, make the leech regurgitate into the wound and so increase the risk of infection. The best way is simply to break the leech's suction with a long finger-nail. Leeches do not transmit diseases, and have often fed and fallen off before they are noticed.

Local children at Dungeness and Lydd used to swim across one of the gravel pits for a dare. The trick was to make as little splashing as possible, for the more you splashed the more likely a leech would get you before you arrived at the far bank. Sheep also attract leeches. Leyshon has seen animals pulled out from one of the ditches that run across Romney Marsh with up to ten of them clinging to their udders. He has also seen apparently suicidal swans wandering along the road at Dungeness with leeches stuck to their ankles – which must be one way that leeches manage to travel from pond to pond.

The Romney leeches have acquired local celebrity status. Owen Leyshon tours the village fetes and carnivals with his prize leeches inside glass pickled-egg jars (he gave up using old-fashioned sweet jars with plastic lids when the leeches found a way out by somehow squeezing past the gap between the glass thread and the lid). 'We describe them as Worms with Character,' he says.

'Leech therapy' is now back in medical fashion. Specimens mass-reared in the laboratory rather than wild-gathered are used to restore circulation to grafted tissues and to surgically reattach fingers and toes, noses and ears. They apparently apply just the right amount of gentle suction to restore the flow of blood. Leech saliva contains substances that anaesthetise a wounded area while dilating the blood vessels, so allowing the blood to flow more easily.

Most leeches bred for medicine today come from a single place, Biopharm near Swansea, whose slogan is 'the biting edge of science'. Biopharm now supplies 50,000 Medicinal Leeches to hospitals and research laboratories each year. To breed leeches of the highest clinical standard, their environment is made as sterile and pure as possible. The leeches are themselves sterile, and helped on their way with such technological investments as 'ultra-violet light sterilization, reverse osmosis, activated carbon absorption and foam fractionating'. Even the water they live in is artificially distilled with added 'hirudosalt' from a jar.[18]

Perhaps these medical leeches are only fractionally luckier than those used as catfish bait. There are apparently a growing number of fishermen anxious to try their luck with these monstrous fish, and even a catfish society for swapping yarns and displaying photographs of triumphant anglers holding the hideous, 'grinning' fish like babes in arms.

Leeches have two non-medicinal connotations. To call someone a leech is to deplore the way they cling or prey on another person – financially, emotionally or in some other way. The fabled bloodthirstiness of leeches also provided one of the Biblical proverbs: 'The horse leach hath two daughters, Crying, Give, give. There are three things that are never satisfied, yea, four that say not, Enough.' (*Proverbs*, 30:15) [English revised version]. The leech, it was believed, will drink and drink until it bursts.

The Biblical horse leech is a semi-mythical worm that was supposed to attach itself to the lips and mouths of horses as they came to the pool to drink. It was said that the worms were born spontaneously from the dung of cattle and horses as it fell into the water; hence the animals were authors of their own misfortune. Elephants too, wrote Pliny, would be driven mad by leeches sticking to their trunks as they drank and slithering into their nasal cavities, 'tickling and sucking'. This showed 'the wonderful power of Insects. For what is there greater than an Elephant?' asked Pliny, 'and what is more contemptible than a Horse Leech? Yet the greatness and wit of the Elephant must give way and yield to this Worm.'

The 'horse leech' of Proverbs and Pliny is the Medicinal Leech or one of its relatives. The species known today as the Horse Leech is a large, dark green leech that is common in small water bodies but, despite its name (including its bloodcurdling scientific name *Haemopsis sanguisuga*, or 'little bloodsucker that sucks blood'), feeds only on small life such as snails and tadpoles which it swallows whole. Its name may derive not from an appetite for horses but through the use of 'horse' to mean 'coarse', as in 'horseradish' or 'horse mussel'.

A smaller leech resembling a matchstick in size and shape is the Fish Leech, which sometimes makes a nuisance of itself in garden fish ponds. The Bird Leech is a larger, fatter leech that attaches itself to the beaks or respiratory passage of waterbirds.

Bristleworms *Polychaeta*

Though the bristleworms are by far the largest group of segmented worms, and some are much larger than earthworms, they are almost exclusively marine and so little known, except to fishermen. Many use their bristles as swimming aids, while others, such as the beautiful fan worms, employ them as filters to sieve the water for edible matter. Among the most familiar bristleworms are the ragworms and lugworms. The most abundant are tiny tubeworms that live inside protective burrows of lime, 'paper' or sand.

Ragworms *Nereidae*

VN: clamworm, maddies, mussel worm, raggies, rags, rigger-worm (Scot.), rockbait (Guernsey), sandworm, worrurns (NE Eng.)

Ragworms are well known to sea anglers and almost unknown to everyone else. Their bodies have pinched segments with ragged outlines, but this is obvious only when they are swimming with a wriggling side-to-side action. Ragworms spend most of the time buried in the mud of estuaries and soft shores, often lying up in mussel-beds with just their heads poking up. The commonest species is

The King Rag, among the largest and most attractive marine worms, with a beautiful, flickering iridescence when swimming.

49

the Estuary (or Harbour) Ragworm, which comes in green, orange or yellow colour-forms, each with a prominent red blood vessel running down its back. The most impressive is the green, iridescent King Ragworm, or King Rag, which can grow to be as thick as a finger and at least half a metre long. Smaller species include the Red Ragworm and the Herringbone Ragworm. All of them have jaws, and big King Rags in particular can deliver a nasty nip if handled carelessly. The exceptionally lucky ragworm that is not eaten by a fish or a seabird, or used to bait a hook, can expect to live for up to three years.

They say that everything that swims loves a ragworm. Known by anglers as 'maddies' or, in the Channel Islands, as 'rockbait', they are generally hooked up with other bait, such as a cockle or a piece of squid. The smaller ones are used alive and whole to provide the electric wriggle so irresistible to bass, sole and plaice. Hardcore anglers collect them by digging along the beach at low tide. The worms can be kept alive and fresh in a bucket or, at least in worm-tolerant homes, tucked up among layers of damp newspaper at the bottom of the fridge (they are said to be a useful way of discouraging hungry teenagers). Spoilsports unwilling to spend back-breaking hours shovelling trenches through the mud can order bred ragworms by post. One firm of suppliers, Seabait Ltd of Ashington, Northumberland, has found a way of improving on nature and offers a year-round supply of them.[19]

Catworms *Nephtyidae*

VN: silvers, white cat

Catworms are pearly white bristleworms about ten centimetres long and known to anglers as 'silvers' or 'white cat'. They earn their feline name from their round, vaguely cat-like head and slender, ever-flickering tail. Catworms live in shallow water on clean sandy shores, mainly on the east coast. It is hard work digging them out at low tide, but the worms repay the effort by being magnets for codfish. Bait-diggers risk their fingers – for, like cats, cat-worms react to adverse circumstances with a sharp nip.

Paddleworms *Phyllodicidae*

Paddleworms are thin, green and very active. A well-grown one displays a beautiful bluish iridescence as it swims with elegant loops of its long, flexible body. The scientific name *Phyllodoce*, or 'assertive leaf' (which the paddleworm shares with a group of alpine heathers), comes from a fancied resemblance between the flaps running along the length of its body and the way leaves tremble in the wind. The 'leaves' serve both to propel the animal forward and to stabilise it as it swims. Paddleworms lurk under rocks at low tide and are always exciting to find. They are too rare to be worth searching for as bait, but dealers do supply the next best thing – wriggly plastic paddleworms in a variety of colours that are seemingly realistic enough to fool the fish.

Sea mouse *Aphroditidae*

AN: scaleworm

At first sight, few would identify this strange and beautiful creature as a worm. For hundreds of years it has been known as 'Aphrodite's mouse', and its plump, oval body, covered with a dense felt of 'hair' (chaetae), flashes with a red-and-blue iridescence under water. At the front end, a pair of horn-like palps look a little like whiskers, while the underside is ridged like the soles of a shoe. The sea mouse is occasionally seen in the shallows, trundling sedately over the sand, but it is never more mouse-like than when it is freshly dead, cast on the shore, with its 'fur' clogged with silt. Not surprisingly, it is a popular choice in aquariums, and also as angling bait for fishermen with no heart.

Lugworms *Arenicolidae*

VN: Blackpool black, blowlug, gulley-worm, gullies, king-lug, lob-worm, lug, runny-downs, sewie-lug, yellow-tails

Lugworms are the earthworms of the seashore, long pinkish or blackish bristleworms that live in U-shaped burrows near the tide line. The worm gives away its presence by its casts of silt, the size and shape of a Walnut Whip. These mark one end of the burrow, after which the other can be traced as a dimple in the sand; the worm will be

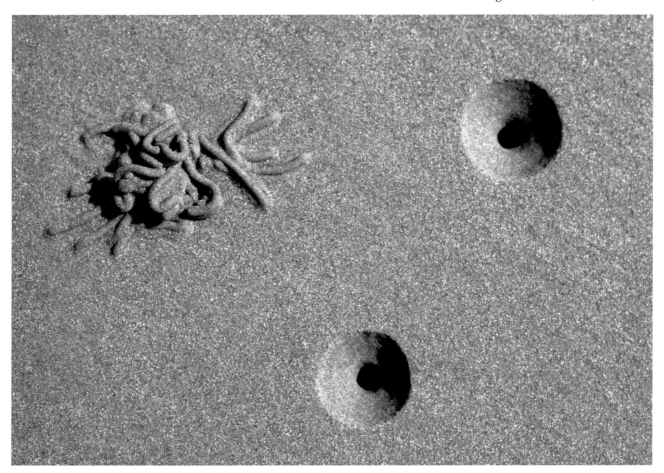

Lugworm cast and burrows on the shoreline.

lurking somewhere between the two, roughly 30 centimetres below the surface. Lugworms, which can occur in vast numbers on the right beach, are in great demand as general-purpose angling bait. To obtain their day's supply, anglers work along the tideline digging out a trench with a broad-tined fork, or 'draining spade', and cleaning the worms in a bucket of clean saltwater. In loose silt, some resort to a bait pump. Handled as little as possible, lugworms can be kept alive for up to a week, 'bedded down' between layers of damp newspaper in a cool place (usually the fridge). Some preserve them for even longer by freezing the worms in layers of salt. Failing that, you can buy fresh lugworms from a tackle shop.

The species most in demand are the Blow Lug and the larger Black Lug. They can be told apart without looking at the animal, for they have differently shaped casts: the Blow Lug leaves an untidy heap like an earthworm, while the Black Lug somehow manages to produce a tidy, almost elegant, cast shaped like a Catherine wheel. They are known locally by a variety of names. Black Lugs leave a nicotine-like stain on the fingers when handled, and so are called 'yellow tails'. Other nicknames include 'runny-downs', 'sewie-lugs' and 'Blackpool blacks'.

From time to time conservationists worry about the overexploitation of lugworms by anglers, not so much out of sympathy for the worms but because it denies top-quality protein to large wading birds such as godwit and curlew. During the miner's strike in 1984, the rich worm-shores of Budle Bay in Northumberland were riddled with trenches. Anglers claim that they have the eternal right to dig for worms on the public foreshore under the Magna Carta, and retort that more lugworms are washed ashore in a single storm than they can ever dig up with spades.

In 2002, the cartoonist Piers Baker created a strip called 'Ollie and Quentin' about the unlikely friendship between a gull (Ollie) and a lugworm (Quentin). The strip, he says, is 'a homage to all the poor lugworms I used as bait while sea fishing in my youth.'

Sand mason worms *Terebellidae*

AN: sand worm, spaghetti worm, terebellid worm, tube worm

A sand mason is a fragile, soft-bodied worm that constructs a branched tube of sand grains anchored to a buried shell or pebble (the tangled coils of its tentacles provide its alternative name of 'spaghetti worm'). The tubes are easily spotted when paddling, but they are vulnerable to disturbance and hence not found in heavily used bays. A related family that builds paper-like tubes is known as parchment worms. Another group, the bamboo worms, have jointed, blunt-ended bodies that resemble twigs or miniature bamboos.

Fan worms *Sabellidae*

AN: Christmas worm, feather-duster worm, medusa worm

The beautiful, feathery crowns of fan worms are more often seen in aquariums or by divers than by the shore-bound walker, and at the least sign of disturbance, they are withdrawn into the animal's rubbery tube in a twinkling. Fan worms need super-clean water to thrive. The commonest species is the Feather Duster, or Feather-duster Worm, so-called because of its multiple rays of yellowish-brown 'feathers'. The Peacock Worm is even more beautiful, with a single set of blue and yellow feathers arranged in a crown, suggestive of a peacock's tail. Most television documentaries of sunken ships show a few Peacock Worms, which could perhaps be regarded, along with sea anemones, as sea-grave flowers. Certain aquarium species are called 'Christmas worms' from a fancied resemblance to tiny Christmas trees lit up by coloured lights.

Tubeworms *Serpulidae* and *Spirorbidae*

Tubeworms live inside hard limy tubes attached to objects. The tiny but extremely common *Spirorbis* worms make circular or spiral tubes attached to seaweed that look like miniature seashells. Larger species, such as the Keelworm, live inside sinuous

Peacock worms on the seabed of Loch Duich, Scotland.

tunnels of lime, often on the hulls of ships, where they can foul the propellers and reduce performance by increasing the drag.

Honeycomb worms are colonial worms which form comb-like masses or even small reefs on rocks half-buried in the sand. They are the basis of a declining cold-water reef system, which is now protected under European law. Efforts are being made to locate as many honeycomb reefs as possible to try to protect them from trawling and dredging.

Penis worms *Priapulida*

AN: priapulid worms

Penis worms, or priapulids, are bizarre, worm-like evolutionary throwbacks, which last held centre stage in the Cambrian, half a billion years ago. A fossil penis worm called *Ottoia*, preserved in miraculous detail in the Burgess Shales of Canada, looks almost identical to living species.

Priapus was the Roman god of fertility. He is commonly represented with an enormous penis, and 'priapulid' is a polite way of expressing what this fat, pink worm most resembles. It has a swollen 'head' – in fact, the animal's large and active proboscis – attached to a wrinkled trunk, with tassels of short, tentacle-like 'hair' at the far end. The Cambrian, it seems, was full of such phallic creatures lolling in the mud. Surprisingly, they may have been among the top predators of the time. Penis worms feed by using their extensible proboscis to snap at smaller, soft-bodied prey, into which they sink a hidden row of teeth. Once secured, the victim is drawn whole into the worm's guts. It worked half a billion years ago, and it still works now, though only up to a point. Only 16 species are known worldwide, of which just one, *Priapulis caudatus* ('tailed penis'), pink and about three inches long, is found regularly in British waters. Some marvellously preserved fossil ones occur in Silurian rocks in Wales.

Spoon worms *Echiura*

AN: burrow worm, echiuran worm, innkeeper worm

Spoon worms have plump, pear-shaped bodies and a long extensible proboscis, which in some species exceeds the length of the body and looks like the handle of a spoon. Their scientific name, *Echiura*, means 'spiny-tail' and refers to a set of small hooks on the worm's posterior that anchor it to the sea bottom. All spoon worms are marine. One is known as the Innkeeper Worm because of the motley crew of marine life, including small fish and crabs, that share its capacious home. The deep burrowings of another spoon worm, *Maxmuelleria lankesteri*, are reported to have stirred up radionucleotides from Sellafield's nuclear reprocessing plant.

The most remarkable British species is the Green Spoon Worm, whose bright green, gherkin-like body is normally hidden beneath a stone, leaving its proboscis, which ends in a pair of flukes like the tail of a whale, to creep and probe the bed like the hose of a vacuum cleaner. It contains a unique pigment, bonellin, which is toxic enough to kill bacteria and has medical potential as a model for a new generation of antibiotics. It has other, seemingly magical qualities: any spoon worm larva touching the worm's skin will turn into a male. This is not a desirable fate, since male spoon worms are parasitic creatures only a few millimetres long that live by attaching themselves to the vast, whale-like body of a female, and are later swallowed by her.

A Green Spoon Worm showing its characteristic tail flukes (right).

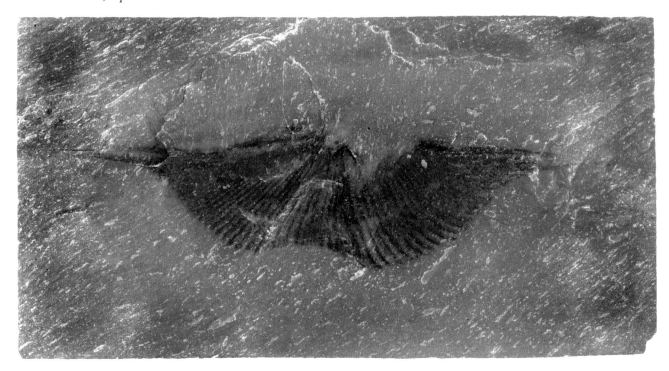

A 'Delabole butterfly' from Devonian rocks at Delabole Quarry in Cornwall. This fossil, some 350 million years old, bears an uncanny resemblance to RAF pilot's wings.

Peanut worms *Sipuncula*

AN: sipunculids

Peanut worms are an evolutionary oddity. Their plump bodies, known, with unintentional appropriateness, as introverts, resemble raw sausages or, for the more warty ones, gherkins. The front end has a mouth surrounded by tufts of tentacles, which retract into the body at the first sign of danger. The name peanut worm seems to have originated in Australia and comes from the hard, oval form into which the worm shrinks when thoroughly alarmed. Peanut worms live in burrows on the seafloor, where they filter-feed detritus in the sand. At Xiamen in China, they make a kind of butter out of peanut worms; apparently you simply boil a cleaned-up worm and it obligingly turns into jelly; it is served in a traditional handleless cup.

The commonest British peanut worm, *Golfingia vulgaris*, owes its unusual name to a golfing holiday at St Andrews in Scotland. The biologist Sir Ray Lankester was enjoying a day on the links in summer 1885 when a bad miss sent his ball spinning over the dunes and rolling on towards the tide. Retrieving the ball, the great naturalist spotted a hole in the muddy sand and, investigating, unearthed the first specimen of what he decided to call *Golfingia*.

That exhausts the fund of stories about British peanut worms. As one expert rather unkindly put it, 'these warty little hole-dwellers really are as uninteresting as their appearance suggests'.[20]

Horseshoe worms *Phoronida*

AN: phoronid worms

Horseshoe worms are an obscure group of marine worms with no close relatives; hence they have been given a phylum to themselves: the Phoronida. They are another ancient group, and burrows attributed to them have been found in Cambrian rocks half a billion years old. The 'horseshoe' is, in fact, their gut, which doubles around into a distinctive U-shape, with the result that the worm's anus sits alongside its mouth, a no-doubt convenient arrangement for an animal that lives inside a closed tube. Horseshoe worms live massed together on the seabed or in chinks in the rock. Some species have the mysterious ability to drill into oyster shells, limestone or even concrete piers, where their borings are known as bio-erosion.

Brachiopods *Brachiopoda*

AN: brach, brachiopod, Delabole butterfly, lamp shell

Brachiopods are better known as fossils than as living animals, for 99 per cent of all described species are extinct. Just a few live on or around our shore, attached to rocks and seaweeds and easily passed over as small limpets or clams. Brachiopod shells have a socket-like extension to hold a short stalk, which gives them a resemblance to an old-fashioned Aladdin's lamp – hence their alternative name of lamp shell. But they are not ancestral clams so much as shelled worms.

In Cornwall, where some fossil 'brachs' have shells like angel's wings, they were known as 'Delabole butterflies'.

Mud dragons *Kinorhyncha*

AN: kinorhynchan worms, spiny-crown worms, thorn-skins

Mud dragons, or kinorhynchans (from Greek words meaning 'movable snout'), are another group of bizarre, microscopic, worm-like animals found in ocean sediments. Looking roughly like a cross between a prawn and a worm, they seem to have no close relatives. Their main characteristic is a blunt, spiny head, with which they draw themselves through the mud. Very little is known about them, but mud dragons are thought to feed on diatoms and other small life in the sediment. About 150 species have been described, a few of which have turned up in British waters. Three new species were described recently from the stomach contents of a shrimp.

CRUSTACEANS

Crustaceans *Arthropoda*

Thus far, every bug in this book has been either aquatic or confined to damp environments. We have now reached the arthropods ('joint-feet'), which include the insects and spiders, animals completely adapted to life on land and in the air. Arthropods have evolved the most versatile and in some ways the most simple body-plan on earth, consisting of repeated segments, each one with a pair of appendages. Most of these appendages function as legs, but they may be modified to form wings, antennae or feeding apparatus such as 'palps' (effectively, tiny arms) or jaws. Arthropods have been compared with Swiss army knives: among the phalanx of appendages, there is a tool for every purpose. It has enabled them to diversify far beyond the boundaries of any other invertebrate phylum, to the point where it is impossible to describe a typical arthropod. Yet 80 per cent of all described invertebrate species are arthropods. In other words, everything that is not an arthropod falls within a minority group.

There are well over a million species of Arthropoda out there (and, probably, many more millions that have not yet been described). Some 35,000 species occur in Britain alone. Yet few of us, even entomologists, use the word arthropod very often. Rather, we call shelly creatures, such as crabs and shrimps, crustaceans – an older, pre-scientific word for a animal with a shell-like skin. For other arthropods it is a matter of counting the legs. Those with eight legs are classed as spiders or their relatives, multi-legged ones millipedes or centipedes, and six-legged ones insects. It is the insects and their predators the spiders that, long ago, broke free of the shackles that wedded their ancestors to watery environments and became fully land animals. It is because they share our world that we know them better than other invertebrates. We feel empathy for butterflies, bees, flies, ants and spiders that we are unlikely to feel (or not to the same degree) for jellyfish, flatworms, sea urchins or even snails. The Bible exhorts good Christians to learn from the ant and the bee. We, have, it seems, less to learn from worms.

Acorn barnacles, sharp-edged filter-feeders of the upper shore.

Right: Semibalanus balanoides, *by Anna Kirk-Smith (mixed media, 16 'tiles' in frame). 'The infant barnacle is released into the water as a free-swimming "naupilus" and moults into a "cypris", which sticks to a suitable substrate and becomes stationary for the rest of its life, apart from its still-mobile legs. A fascinating process!'*

Barnacles *Cirripedia*

VN: barnitickle (NE Eng.), claik (Scot.), gwyrain (Wales), klecks (Orkney), scaw (Scot.), slykee (Orkney)

Barnacles are a byword for toughness and resilience. High up on the rocky shore, their small, sharp shells encrust the rocks and challenge our barefoot walk to the beach. In winter they face the full rigour of ocean storms, in summer the bleaching sun and drying wind. Encased inside their plates of lime, the tiny, stripped-down animals emerge for just a few hours per day, or for those near the top of the shore, just a few days per month (of course, we never witness their underwater emergence except in aquariums or on film). The reward for such austerity is freedom from competition and unlimited food in the form of small organic particles brought in on each tide.

Barnacles are the most abundant shore animals. An estimated 1000 million of them are found on an average kilometre of rocky shoreline, and they consume about 600 kilograms (dry weight) of plankton per day. A well-barnacled shore is equivalent to a small herd of cows consuming a daily half tonne of hay.

Though they share the rocks with limpets and look like tiny shells, barnacles are not molluscs but arthropods. Unlike limpets, they have modified legs called cirri (hence their group name of 'cirripede', meaning 'curl-foot'), which are used to kick food into their mouths. At the height of his career, Charles Darwin became entranced by the underwater transformation of these seemingly passive, limy plates into dynamic and strangely beautiful organisms. With characteristic meticulousness, he spent several years staring patiently through his brass microscope at barnacle larvae, noting the ways in which they had diverged from their crabby ancestors and adapted to a sedentary life, and how an organ such as a leg could be turned into a kind of food basket. Over seven years, Darwin produced four densely written volumes about barnacles; perhaps unsurprisingly, the work made him ill.[1] Nevertheless, the insights provided by these humble animals sharpened his nascent theory of evolution, and shortly after finishing his work on barnacles, he turned to writing *The Origin of Species*.

The commonest group of barnacles are the pyramid-shaped acorn barnacles, named after their faint resemblance to a budding acorn in its cup. To attach themselves to rocks and floating objects, barnacles use one of the strongest natural cements known. Experiments revealed that a thin layer of barnacle-glue spread over a square inch will support a three-tonne weight. Furthermore, the glue will stay solid and fast in temperatures up to 3315°C (after which it will soften but not actually melt). It is also impervious to most acids and organic solvents and altogether makes better super-glue than Superglue. If we could find a way of manufacturing barnacle-glue, broken bones could be mended without splints, fillings would last a lifetime and someone would be as rich as Bill Gates.

Thanks to their tenacious hold on rock, barnacles encrust the shores of the world and, unless prevented, would line the bottom of every boat and ship on the sea, as well as the pipes of every desalination plant. A thickly barnacled hull reduces a ship's performance, slowing its speed and increasing its fuel consumption. The world's fishing fleets spend more than £5 billion a year dealing with the problem. The Romans found that toxic copper nails were a partial solution, and the Royal Navy later took to sheathing the hulls of its warships with copper rather than face weeks of scraping in a dry or freshwater dock.

Today, most boat owners use chemical anti-fouling paints, of which the most successful (that is, the most toxic) was one based on tributyl-tin, known as TBT. Unfortunately TBT kills not only barnacles but shorelife in general, especially shellfish, and accumulates in the food-chain. The effect on marine ecosystems in places where large numbers of boats were moored was devastating. Today, the use of TBT paint is restricted, and more eco-friendly ways of keeping boats barnacle-free have been introduced. One is a less lethal copper-based paint – though, almost by definition, it is less efficient at getting rid of barnacles. The alternative is to use materials that prevent barnacles from sticking in the first place. Silicone paints have had a limited success, but nanotechnology can engineer a kind of anti-barnacle Teflon by incorporating tiny cylinders of carbon, each a thousand times thinner than a human hair, on which even the barnacle's powerful glue fails to find a purchase.

Barnacles are a metaphor for the type of rough, nautical individual represented by Barnacle Bill the Sailor, who features in a well-known rugby song, returning to port bristle-chinned, thirsty and slavering with lust after a long sea voyage. Originally 'Bollicking Bill', he is said to be based on a nineteenth century San Francisco character, Bill Bayle Bernard, a hard-drinking ex-miner. *Barnacle Bill* was also the name of a non-bawdy 1957 Ealing comedy starring Alec Guinness as an ironically named seasick sea-dog, who comes closest to the derring-do of his nautical ancestors when he tries to turn the pier into an entertainment centre. Barnacle Bill has lent his name to numerous seafood restaurants. It is also the name for a boulder on Mars.

The Tite Barnacles, father and son, in Charles Dickens' novel *Little Dorrit* are senior civil servants who ensure that the system grinds on as slowly as possible and without ever changing. Tite senior, 'who had only one idea in his head and that was a wrong one', is the archetype of the obstructive official, clinging rigidly to his rock of forms and procedures. We have all banged heads in vain with bureaucratic Barnacles, who endure the wind and tide of circumstance with unmoving certainty.

Goose barnacles *Lepadidae*

VN: bernacle, bernekke, bernicle (medieval names)

What came first, the goose barnacle or the barnacle goose? According to one of the most persistent myths of the animal world, certain kinds of geese hatch not from eggs but from seashells. The barnacle goose, the 'bernekke' of the medieval world, arrived in vast flocks along the west coasts of Britain and Ireland from where no one knew. The logical conclusion was that the birds had emerged from the sea. There was, in fact, a sea animal that looked a little like a tiny 'bernekke', with a long, black 'neck', a goose-shaped body and even internal growths that seemed to be feathers. This was named the goose barnacle. The twelfth-century chronicler Giraldus Cambrensis (Gerald of Wales) claimed to have personally witnessed this miraculous transformation from shell to bird during a tour of Ireland:

'They are produced from fir timber tossed along the sea and are at first like gum. Afterwards they hang down by their beaks as if they were seaweed attached to the timber, and are surrounded by shells in order to grow more freely. Having thus in the process of time been clothed with a strong coat of feathers, they either fall into the water or fly freely away into the air. I have frequently seen, with my own eyes, more than a thousand of these small birds, hanging down on the sea-shore from one piece of timber, enclosed in their shells and already formed.'[2]

The myth had its uses. In Gerald's world, up to four days per week were set aside as 'fast days', on which flesh was forbidden. But animals born in the water were classed as fish, so Gerald and his fellows were allowed to serve roast geese for dinner on such days, on the grounds that 'they are not flesh nor born of flesh'. This convenient belief survived in rural parts of Ireland until the twentieth century, long after the true nature of both barnacles and geese had been determined.

Another story claimed that the goose barnacle was also a vegetable shell, the product not of animal reproduction but of a seed. The myth of 'the barnacle tree' took root in Gerard's famous *Herbal* of 1597. He, too, claimed to have witnessed the wonder. 'What our eies have seene and hands have touched, we shall declare . . .' On an island called the Pile of Foulders off the coast of Lancashire, the timbers of wrecked ships had bred a strange shell 'which in time commeth to the shape and forme of a Bird'.

A Goose barnacle (Lepas sp.) with extended 'cirri', the feeding structures that were once mistaken for goose quills. Note the baby barnacle attached to its 'parent'.

Once ripe, the seed-shell gaped open, bringing forth the bird's legs, followed in due course by the rest of it, "til at length it is all come foorth, and hangeth onely by the bill; in short space after it cometh to full maturitie and falleth into the sea, where it gathereth feathers, and growth to a fowle, bigger than a Mallard and lesser than a Goose, having blacke legs and bill or beake.' Gerard thought the discovery important enough to illustrate with a specially commissioned woodcut, portentously titled '*Britannica concha anatifera*'.[3]

One can sympathise with Gerald and Gerard, for the goose barnacle baffled even zoologists. Its true identity was not revealed until 1830, when John Thompson, an army surgeon based in County Cork, was whiling away his plentiful spare time by studying marine life. He was the first to take a close look at the barnacle's strange, free-swimming larva, a tiny legged creature like a water flea. He identified it correctly as a segmented animal, more akin to a crab than a mollusc.

Goose barnacles mass together on floating material of every imaginable kind: chunks of polystyrene, trawler balls, milk crates, fish boxes, even whales. If there is no flotsam to cling to, they can club together and form their own raft, a mutually dependent community of barnacles stuck together like bits of an Airfix model. By far the commonest goose barnacle, hence *the* Goose Barnacle is *Lepas anatifera* (*anatifera* means 'duck-made'). A related species, the Buoy Barnacle, prepares for life on the choppy ocean waves by secreting frothy bubbles that harden into a substance the colour and texture of expanded polystyrene. On these home-made life-rafts, looking like misshapen tennis balls, clusters of pale, grayish barnacles ride the seas, filter-feeding as they go. After a storm in July 1986, Inch Beach in County Kerry was covered in white lumps of 'natural polystyrene' – shipwrecked barnacle crews.

In Spain a related species, the Goose-neck Barnacle *Pollicipes,* is sold in streets and quaysides or tapas bars as *percebes*, a popular snack. The edible bit is the pinkish-white, tube-like 'neck'; briefly steamed, it tastes like crab or shrimp and goes well with a cold beer. Though prized as food, the *percebe* is not rated as an intelligent animal. The Spanish have a saying: '*tienes cara de percebe*', best translated as 'you're a bit of a dork'. Recently, specimens of *Pollicipes* have been found on the Cornish coast, and since the species is potentially invasive, they may be here to stay. Perhaps *percebes* and chips will be on our menus soon.

Water bears *Tardigrada*

AN: moss piglets, tardigrades

In his book *Microscopic Fresh Water Life* (which has a water bear embossed on the cover), F. J. Plaskitt described the water bear's rather pathetic habit of endlessly 'trying to catch hold of objects that are not there.' The microscopic beast appeared quite unable to profit by experience, continuing blindly to claw its way about, unable to obtain a foothold until, with 'a literal shrug of the head and an expressive turn of the body', it turned away in apparent despair and an 'evident disgust of things, and probably of a Water Bear's life in general.'[4]

Water bears are one of the lesser-known delights of microscope-watching. Under low power, the semi-transparent creatures clamber about among wet moss on their stumpy legs in an undeniably bear-like manner. No one is sure where water bears fit into the evolutionary tree: they share the segmented body of an arthropod and have eight legs like a spider, but their piercing mouthparts are more like those of a nematode worm. Their legs are unique: stubby balloons of transparent flesh ending in little tufts of claws. Johann Goeze, the first to observe them in 1773, named them 'little water bears'. Their scientific name, tardigrade, means 'slow walker'. One water bear, known only as a fossil in amber, has been called *Beorn leggi*; Beorn was a character in *The Hobbit,* who turned into a bear at night.

Water bears are best known for their tenacity of life. Living in shallow water or among damp moss, they are obliged to survive periods of drought. They achieve this by curling up and encysting into a tough-skinned, roundish shape known as a tun (an old name for a barrel). In this state, the water bear's life processes come to a complete stop, and so long as its tissues are not crushed, it can survive almost any conditions.

It became something of a challenge to scientists to subject dormant water bears to increasingly extreme conditions to find out just how tough they are. So far, they have survived heating well above the boiling point of water, being subjected to pressures greater than the deepest ocean, irradiation worse than a microwave oven, total asphyxiation, freezing in liquid nitrogen and immersion in toxic chemicals. Having endured all this, the animal is brought back to life by a single drop of water. In an experiment

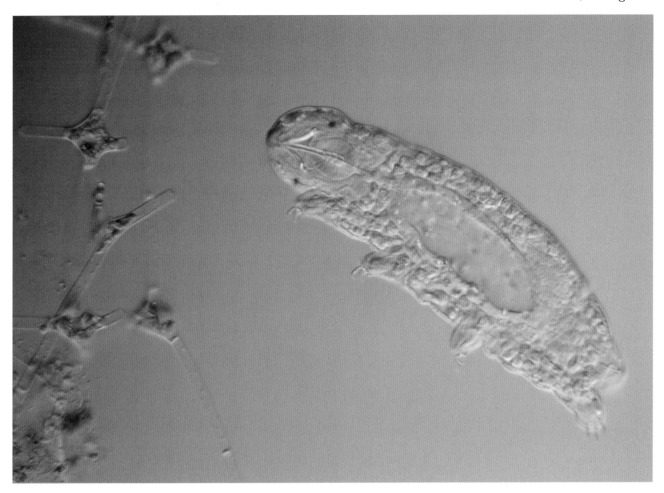

*A water bear (*Macrobiotus *sp.): like a microscopic airship coming in to land.*

to test the ultimate endurance of water bears, the European Space Agency sent a batch of them into space. Those that eventually returned to earth were the first animals to have been exposed to the vacuum of space and unprotected solar radiation – and lived.[5]

For some reason, water bears are more popular in Germany and Italy than in Britain, where they seldom merit more than a footnote in field guides. But a small group of enthusiasts has determined that there are 74 species in Britain (68 terrestrial and 6 marine) and has started to map their distribution. So far, these maps suggest a total absence of water bears in eastern England, probably not because there are none but because, by chance, most tardigrade enthusiasts live in the north or west.[6]

There are probably fewer than a hundred water bear experts in the world, but international interest in them is growing. In 1997, American scientists working on the DNA sequences of invertebrates discovered that all species which periodically shed their skins are genetically related. Hence, counter-intuitively, roundworms (nematodes) must be more closely related to crabs and insects, than, say, to earthworms or flatworms. Water bears shed their skins, which places them in a newly minted super-phylum, the Ecdysozoa, whose members must all have had a common ancestor. Might it have been a water bear that has attributes of insects, crabs *and* roundworms? A tardigrade genome project has been set up to try to find out.

Water bears have made little, if any, impact on the wider consciousness of mankind. One exception is *Dark Space* (2007), a science-fiction novel by the Australian writer Marianne de Pierres. In it, the heroine comes to the rescue of 'a planet torn apart by the invasion of a race of giant tardigrades', an undoubtedly disturbing, if rather unlikely, scenario.

A dense swarm of daphnia water fleas.

Water fleas *Cladocera*

Water fleas have nothing in common with true fleas apart from their small size and habit of jerking through the water in a way that reminded people of jumping fleas. They are not insects, as true fleas are, but tiny crustaceans that teem in fresh water and are of fundamental importance to ecology (without water fleas there would be no fish). Most feed on microscopic algae and bacteria (a few are active hunters) and are eaten in turn by fish fry, small insects and many other aquatic animals. There are around 80 species in Britain, all but five occurring in fresh water, from ponds and drinking troughs to ditches and canals.

Though no water flea has an accepted common name, they are often collectively referred to as 'daphnia', meaning 'water nymph'. *Daphnia*, in the biological sense, is a genus of common, relatively large, water fleas, which are easy to culture and so favourites in school and university biology labs. The

water flea is an open demonstration of how bodies work. Beneath its transparent carapace, everything is on display, and you can see the creature's heart pumping its blood, food moving through the gut, and even its young wriggling about inside the brood pouch. You can watch its reaction to alcohol (swimming drunkenly round in circles) and its manic reaction to stimulants such as caffeine or nicotine. Daphnia are also bred in vast quantities as fish-food.

Water fleas are popular microscopic objects. They look especially beautiful under dark-field illumination, in which the animal gains definition and depth, appearing pearly white against the dark-toned background. Many are roundish with bristly 'arms', but a few species break the mould and are much odder. *Leptodora kindtii*, the Giant Water

Right: A single daphnia with its organs visible as if through glass (which makes daphnia useful for physiology demonstrations).

Flea is as transparent as a sliver of glass and difficult to spot until you see its enormous single beady eye staring back at you. *Polyphemus* is another one-eyed water flea, named after the giant in Homer's Odyssey. It is a hunter, using the spines on its 'feet' to grip its prey. *Chydorus*, the smallest and perhaps commonest water flea, is round and tubby, looking to the naked eye like a tiny, white, animated dot. Along with the similarly diminutive *Bosmina* and *Moinia*, it is available commercially for feeding fish fry.

Water fleas are most abundant during the twin peaks of water 'blooms' in late spring and early autumn. At such times, one can often scoop up enough of them to feed a tank-full of fish simply by dipping a jam-jar into the shallows. Where they are less plentiful, they can be swept up in a home-made net of muslin or net-curtain arranged round a bent coathanger and attached to a broom handle. The trick is to pass the net through the water in gentle figure-of-eight fashion and not too quickly, since too much pressure can damage the fleas.

Water fleas can be cultured in any tank or jar or even a children's paddling pool; old-fashioned sweet jars are perfect. Pond water usually has enough algae as food, but a top-up of yeast or fish pellets often helps. Some advocate wrapping a lump of dried-out horse dung in muslin and hanging it in the water: this generates a lot of bacteria, which are eagerly devoured. Water fleas reproduce without sex and so multiply with incredible speed. Most of their modest store of energy is spent on reproduction; to put it another way, they don't do much except feed and ripen eggs.

Seed shrimps *Ostracoda*

AN: bean animalcules, ostracods

Seed shrimps are the size of water fleas (averaging a millimetre across) but live within a pair of plates, like a tiny bivalve mollusc or the halves of a seed. Their scientific name, Ostracod, means, simply, 'shell'. They are common in both fresh and saltwater, and are an ancient life-form that evolved more than 500 million years ago. With their hard plates they fossilise well and are of interest to micropaleontologists for elucidating ancient environments and bygone climates. The more recent fossil seed shrimps are also studied as indicators of 'biozones' in marine sediments.

Cyclops, the one-eyed giant of Greek myth, from the 'Myths and Monsters' exhibition at the Natural History Museum, 1998.

Copepods *Copepoda*

Copepods are small, transparent crustaceans that abound in both freshwater and in seawater in the plankton: only one or two millimetres long, they have been called the 'insects of the sea'. Though rarely noticed, they are among the most abundant animals on earth: copepods may be the world's largest source of animal protein. Without these barely visible animals to feed the oceans there would be no whales and probably no marine fish, either. 'Copepod' is Greek, meaning 'oar-foot', a reference to the way some species swim with the help of fringed, scull-like legs.

The best-known copepod is a freshwater genus, *Cyclops*, so named because, like the giant of myth,

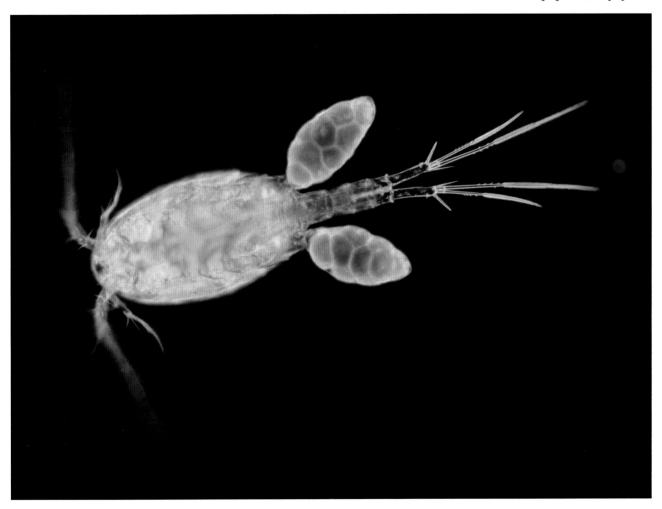

The giant's alter ego: the one-eyed copepod Cyclops. *This is a female carrying its eggs in a pair of sacks.*

it has a single eye in the middle of its head (so, for that matter, does nearly every other copepod, but *Cyclops* was discovered first). Practically every permanent water body – even puddles in hollow trees – will have *Cyclops*-like copepods. In a jar, its paired egg sacs are more easily spotted than the semi-transparent animal carrying them. Like water fleas, they are wonderful to watch under a low-power binocular microscope as they propel themselves along with kicks of their legs and powerful beats of their long antennae.

A few copepods are parasites. Those known as anchor worms (*Lernea* species) – they look more like small leeches than crustaceans – can be a nuisance in fish tanks and fish farms since a bad infestation may weaken the fish and make them prone to secondary infections. The gill maggot *Salminicola* attaches itself to the gills of a salmon and sucks its blood. Since the 'maggot' changes its form after the salmon returns to the sea, it can indicate whether the fish is

a first- or second-time spawner (though, with far fewer salmon now returning to spawn for a second time, the lot of a gill-maggot may not be a happy one).

The Salmon Louse, better known as the sea-louse *Lepeophtheirus salmonis*, is a larger parasite, which attaches itself to a salmon's scales. Anglers greet them with delight, as they are a sign of a 'fresh run' fish. Fish farmers are less delighted, since in the confines of the cages, they can multiply and cost the farmer dear in terms of treatment and lost production. Worse, sea-lice from fish farms are suspected to be the cause of lethal louse-loads on wild salmon and sea trout.

Leptodora kindtii, a giant among water fleas – a grasping yet nearly transparent predator up to two centimetres long.

Fairy shrimps *Anostraca*

Britain has only one true fairy shrimp, *Chirocephalus diaphanus*, a graceful, transparent creature about 2.5 centimetres long that swims on its back. The shrimp is defenceless against predators and so is confined to fishless pools, even puddles and water-filled ruts. It must have been common once in the ruts made by horse-drawn wagons and coaches on the muddy lanes of southern England. Today the shrimp is confined to tracks, mainly in chalk or limestone districts. The late Max Walters once bred them from mud scraped off his wellies after a visit to one of its puddle-haunts near Cambridge. The fairy shrimp is still quite common on Salisbury Plain, where it does well in the deep ruts created by army vehicles and tanks. Fairy shrimp eggs are available commercially (from America), though the favoured species is a marine relative, the Brine Shrimp (*see below*).

Its distant relative the Tadpole Shrimp is a wonderful-looking crustacean resembling a miniature horseshoe crab, with red legs and a pair of woeful-looking eyes protruding from its oval shell. It has been called the oldest species on earth and is marketed and sold as 'a prehistoric monster from the time of the dinosaurs'.[7] Its tough, drought-resistant eggs (they can survive a journey through the bowels of a duck) are sold in toyshops as 'Triop World', and can be induced to hatch into Tadpole Shrimps inside a plastic tank. Children love them as a sort of instant 'monster': just add water and 'Triops food' and watch them grow.[8] As a nod to their popularity, the American alternative rock band They Might Be Giants sang 'Triops has Three Eyes' on their children's album, *Here Come the 123s* (2008). 'Triops' is rare in Britain and currently known only from a fish-free pool opposite a pub in the New Forest, though it is the sort of animal that could turn up anywhere.

The Brine Shrimp is found in salt lakes and brine pools around the world, including a handful of places in Britain. It, too, is marketed as a kind of pet-in-a-packet as 'sea monkeys' or 'sea dragons' or, in the 1970s, as 'artful arties', after its scientific name *Artemia*.[9] It has to be said that this pale pinkish shrimp, 15 millimetres or so when fully grown, makes a rather disappointing monkey, bearing little resemblance to the smiling and playful, or alternatively fierce and toothy, creature on the packet. Perhaps the mystique of such pets lies not in themselves so much as the god-like sense of creating life from apparent dust.

Sand-hoppers and freshwater shrimps *Amphipoda*

Amphipods ('both-feet', meaning some of their feet are adapted for swimming and some for walking) are shrimp-like crustaceans whose bodies are compressed from side to side. Most amphipods are marine, but one is a common species in well-oxygenated streams in Britain.

(from the Old Norse, *hlaupa*, to leap), which also refer to their jumping feats. In Orkney dialect, the sand-hopper is a 'sholtie', a word it shares with the Shetland pony. The name sand-hopper has been borrowed for the name of a shallow-drafted sailing boat and, in another sense, a machine that fills sand-bags.

Shallow-water relatives of the sand-hopper include ghost, or skeleton, shrimps – slow-moving, skeletally thin shrimps with lobster-like claws.

Sand-hoppers *Talitridae*

VN: beach flea, *jiargan-traie* (strand-flea) (Isle of Man), jumpan jecks, loopacks (Orkney), sand-flea, sand-lowper or sand-jumper (Scot.), sea-flechs (Scot.), sholties (Orkney)

Go out on a warm night and walk along the strandline with a torch and you will almost certainly find countless small hopping creatures feeding on the washed-up weed and other rotting debris. These are sand-hoppers, also known as beach fleas or jumping jacks. Other local names are 'lowper' or 'loopacks'

Freshwater shrimps *Gammaridae*

VN: gammarus, river shrimp, screw or scrow (Scot.), scud, side-swimmer

The freshwater shrimp *Gammarus pulex* looks rather like a giant flea (*pulex* is, in fact, the Latin word for flea), and swims on its side in a characteristic way, hence its nickname 'side-swimmer'. It is important food for waterbirds and fish, especially trout and grayling. The shrimps themselves are scavengers and, by nibbling away any organic debris such as rotting leaves, help to keep the water clear and

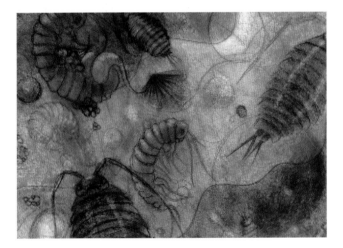

Sea slaters and sand-hoppers, *by Annabel Harris, who attempts to capture in art 'the immediacy of nature' – that fleeting moment of contact with an insect. 'When exploring the representation of insects in art, I begin with the environment they live in. A day out at the beach, for example, can throw up surprises in nature, like watching these quirky little creatures rattling and crawling out of the way of the incoming tide from their pebbly homes on the shore.'*

The Freshwater Shrimp swimming upside down, flattened from side to side like a flea.

bubbly. They are also the reason why the flesh of wild-caught trout is a wholesome salmon-pink. Like true shrimps, freshwater shrimps contain the pink or orange pigment carotene, which they pass on to the animals that eat them. Farmed salmon and trout need artificial or processed additives to achieve the same effect.

Despite its ecological benefits, *G. pulex* is regarded in Northern Ireland as an unwanted alien. There the native freshwater shrimp is a different species, *Gammarus duebeni*, which has larger, kidney-shaped eyes and prefers brackish water near the coast. When fishermen released the non-native *G. pulex* into Irish loughs and streams, with blithe disregard for the consequences, it quickly multiplied and muscled into the territory of its native cousin. The replacement of one shrimp by another may not sound important, but *G. pulex* now stands accused of gobbling up good Irish mayflies as well as carrying a nasty worm in its gut that infects fish and wild ducks.

In North America, the creature known as a freshwater shrimp is a different crustacean, related to true, marine shrimps. The British species is referred to there as a Gammarus shrimp or a freshwater amphipod.

A mysterious jumping land shrimp, which is increasing on lawns and in gardens near the south coast of England and Wales and sometimes strays indoors, is the Lawn Shrimp, a native of North America and Australia, where it is also known as land hopper, shrimp bug or house hopper. Unlike its freshwater relatives, it is a land animal – though, at least in its native Florida, the shrimp has been known to hop from the lawn into the outdoor pool, occasionally in large enough numbers to clog the filters. One well-meaning householder in Kent, mistaking these shrimps for freshwater ones, painstakingly and kindly gathered them all up and released them into the nearest stream – where they probably drowned.[10]

Shrimps and prawns
Decapoda

Shrimps *Crangonidae*

VN: bunting (Kent), pandle (Kent), strimp (Isle of Man)

A human shrimp is small and skinny, a meaning that probably dates back centuries to the Old English *scrimman*, meaning to shrink. Biological shrimps are small decapod ('ten-foot') crustaceans, with small pincers and long antennae. Alive they are brownish and speckled to match the sandy bottom; shrimps turn pink only when boiled. The commercial shrimp, the one most often caught and eaten fresh-boiled or potted, is the Brown, or Common, Shrimp, which has a rich, sweet flavour. Being smaller than prawns, they are fiddly to peel, and many are destined to be mixed with butter and bottled as potted shrimps. Shrimping boats use a scaled-up version of a child's shrimping net to catch them: a crossbar agitates the sand while a trailing net scoops up the shrimps as they swim up from the bottom. The British eat a lot of them: Baxter's, who has sold potted shrimps from Morecambe Bay since 1799, sells around 13 million jars a year, mostly by mail-order.[11]

There is no close season for shrimps, but they say it is a waste of time fishing for them until the water has turned warmer and a bit murky. The best shrimping grounds are broad, shallow bays over mud or sand. Morecambe Bay has had a profitable shrimp fishery since the eighteenth century. Traditional netting was done by custom-built, shallow-drafted boats known as 'nobbies' or 'prawners', with nets attached to the stern. They have a sharp bow for negotiating the shifting sands and often carry a stove behind the galley for boiling the catch. Today, though, wooden, carvel-built nobbies earn as much from taking tourists round the harbour as from the sale of shrimps.

More often, shrimps are caught by tractor-drawn trawl nets strung out on booms (formerly it was done more picturesquely using horses to draw the nets). At Formby they have even experimented with army-surplus amphibious vehicles. A few shrimpers trawled their nets by manpower alone, by tying the ends to their waists. On the banks of the Severn, they used to catch them in wickerwork baskets or staked nets, which strain out the shrimps

The Common Prawn, one of several species of decapods (meaning ten-feet) targeted by fisheries.

as the water rises – a simple but effective method that is mentioned in the Domesday Book and might date back to prehistoric times. Another method used by the Severn shrimpers was the 'mud horse', which looks like an inverted ironing board and was paddled or pushed along the shallows, putting up the shrimps as it went. The lost way of life of the shrimpers of old is recounted in Brian Waters' book, *Severn Tide* (1947).

Shrimps are extraordinarily resilient. In 2008, a scientist put a shrimp on a tiny treadmill to see how far it was prepared to travel in search of food. The 10-centimetre crustacean paddled away for hours at an average speed of 20 metres per minute before pausing to rest. The loop was posted on the internet with a backing track from *Chariots of Fire*.[12]

Prawns *Palaemonidae*

VN: beetle (Northumb.), Billy Winters (Dorset), clonker (Northumb.), wasp (NE Eng.)

Prawns are often confused with shrimps – and Americans call them all shrimps – but the true prawn is larger and flattened from side to side rather than from top to bottom. Unlike shrimps they are migratory and come close to the shore only in summer and autumn; autumn is the peak season for prawn fishing, since they are then well fed and at their plumpest. The British eat them in vast numbers, boiled in their shells until they have turned pink and then served straight away, often by the 'pint', with or without garlic butter, though they are even better grilled or fried. A smaller number are dunked in seafood sauce for that classic seventies retro-dish, the prawn cocktail.

British prawns are wild-caught by trawling, but the regulations do not require fishermen to identify the exact species (to do so would need a course in decapod anatomy). Probably most of those we eat are the large and nutritious Common Prawn, though a growing number are the misnamed Pink Shrimp. A smaller species, *Pandalus elegans*, fished for late in the year, is sometimes known by its Dorset name of Billy Winters. Our cold-water prawns are said to have a better flavour than the bigger king prawns and tiger prawns imported from shellfish farms in Asia.

Britain consumes more prawns than any other EU country, but nowadays most of those that we eat are imported. In 2000 we caught just 2100 tonnes of prawns in home waters, but imported 77,900 tonnes. In 2003, the Environmental Justice Foundation claimed that prawn-fishing is extremely wasteful to ocean life. For every kilogram of prawns, some 20 kilograms of other sea life is scooped up, including marine turtles and seahorses, most of which perish in the nets before they can be returned to the sea.[13]

Prawn is an old word, originally pronounced 'prane', of uncertain meaning. It is easy to recognise a prawn – it is a long crustacean, with a pair of long antennae, a toothed, nose-like rostrum between the eyes and a downward-curving body ending in a characteristic tail-fan known as a telson. Prawns are related to crabs and lobsters; most are free-swimming scavengers but a few, the burrowing prawns, live in the sediment.

The prawn crackers of Chinese cuisine are featherweight, deep-fried crisps, lightly flavoured with a seafood essence that may or may not have included prawn. The Australian expression 'don't come the raw prawn' became well known in Britain in the sixties through the *Private Eye* cartoon series 'Barry McKenzie', about the adventures of an Aussie innocent abroad in Earl's Court. It means, 'don't mess with me, mate' or, according to the more po-faced dictionaries, 'do not make an attempt to deceive'.

'A couple of years ago I was on holiday with a friend on the coast of mid-Wales, and we found some common prawns while wading in the rock pools. We were mesmerised by the creatures, and found that if we stood still they would come very close. They were trimming the skin round the cuticles on our toenails with their pincers and eating it: a prawn pedicure!'[14]

Opossum shrimps, or mysids, are small, transparent shrimp-like animals that are active mainly at night in sheltered bays and water bodies in sea caves. The shrimp is so named because, like the opossum, it carries its young in a brood pouch.

Lobsters and crayfish
Astacidea

Lobsters *Nephropidae*

VN: gimmagh (Isle of Man), parick or perrick (Isle of Man)

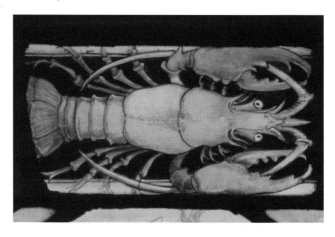

A representation of a lobster forming part of an early-twentieth-century stained-glass window at St Mary's Church at Bolton-on-Swale, North Yorks.

The lobster is a noble animal, handsome, powerful, long-lived and, of course, delicious. Its name derives from the Old English *lopustre*, based in turn on the Latin *locusta*, a segmented or armoured 'insect'. Hence, locusts and lobsters come from the same word. Live lobsters are deep blue, with stiff, red antennae, their eyes swivelling on moveable stalks. Boiled ones turn bright red, and in this guise, the lobster has sometimes appeared in still-life paintings as a stand-in for the devil. Lobster also became a nickname for red-coated British soldiers and puffing, red-faced men generally. The helmets of soldiers in the English Civil War were known as 'lobster tails' from the resemblance of their neck plates to the body plates of a lobster.

Lobsters grow throughout their lives and live for up to 30 years or even longer. The biggest one ever caught in British waters was a 9.3 kg, 1.26-metre-long leviathan cornered during the construction of a jetty at Fowey, Cornwall, in 1931. Monsters nearly as big are still occasionally caught; one weighing more than 6 kilograms was found growling inside a creel in 2001. Nicknamed Barney, it was bought

A mature lobster showing its formidable claws.

by Mayfair's Kaspia restaurant, but when it came to the point, the chef lacked the heart to kill such a splendid animal. He passed it on to an aquarium, which released it back into Plymouth Sound – where, perhaps, it is none the worse after its adventure and is still growing.[15] Another monster weighing nearly 8 kg was caught off the coast of Devon in July 2008. Fishing lore insists that lobsters this size can be a hundred years old. Whether or not this is so, in Japan lobsters are considered to be emblems of longevity.

Along the North Sea coast of northern England, fishermen have a set of dialect terms to describe lobsters with reduced or no commercial value. A lobster with a claw missing is a 'limmitter', one with small claws is a 'miffy', and one without claws a 'pistil'. Undersized lobsters were described in different places as 'jinnies', 'linties', 'pawks' or 'nannycocks'. Even the traps in which they are caught have their own terminology. The standard pot or basket is a 'creel'. A type with a soft flap entrance is a 'Bob an' Wully'. A dead-end trap is a 'parlour pot'.

Lobsters have always been an expensive luxury food and, until recent times, they were largely restricted to the tables of the rich. Even today, all table lobsters on this side of the Atlantic are wild-caught in creels or lobster pots baited with scraps of oily fish. The fishery is largely unregulated, and there are concerns that lobsters are being overfished, especially in near-shore waters. Farmed lobster may be the answer, but so far it is only a tantalising dream. Lobsters are aggressive, solitary creatures and potential cannibals; even young, pencil-sized ones will attack and kill one another and have to be separated. On experimental farms, they have also proved stubbornly slow-growing and so economically unviable. The nearest thing to a lobster farm in Britain is the National Lobster Hatchery at Padstow, where young lobsters are collected for fattening up in a predator-free environment before being released back into the sea.[16]

In 2002, work began on what could be the next best thing, a man-made 'fish ranch'. In a partnership between the Scottish Association for Marine Science and the owner of a local quarry in Loch Linnhe, on the west coast of Scotland, and based on experience from such artificial reefs in Japan, thousands of tonnes of concrete blocks were unloaded onto the seabed in the hope of attracting fish, prawns and crabs, as well as lobsters. Unlike in fish farms, the marine life should colonise the 'reef' naturally and will not be supplied with food pellets.[17] If all goes well with this experiment, there are plans for a second reef in Nigg Bay, near Aberdeen. There is also optimistic talk of using the superstructure of offshore windfarms as the basis for lobster ranches.

Do lobsters feel pain? What lobsters, prawns and crabs might sense as they are boiled alive has worried the RSPCA and other animal-health bodies. Yet a court case held in Scotland decided that cruelty against invertebrates such as crustaceans has no force in law. A scientific team report commissioned by the Norwegian government in 2005 concluded that lobsters probably do not experience what we would call pain, despite their violent reaction to being plunged into hot water. But a more recent study at Queen's University in Belfast came to the opposite conclusion after measuring their reaction to drops of acetic acid on their antennae.[18] Pain is a necessary adjunct to the life of any animal as part of its conditioning to avoid harmful and unpleasant sensations. Though no one knows what a lobster feels as its life drains away in the boiling water, it shows every sign of objecting strongly to the experience. A device now available, called with grim kitchen humour the Crustastun, kills lobsters instantly by electrocution. Though pricy, it is apparently now being used by many seafood chefs.

The orange, slim-clawed Norway Lobster lives in burrows on the seabed, where it can occur in enormous numbers, scavenging worms and fish eggs. It is better known from its menu names, Dublin Bay prawn or langoustine. The tails of small-fry Norway Lobsters, covered in breadcrumbs and deep-fried, also make scampi (from the plural of the lobster's Italian name *scampo*). The species supports a large and important fishery in Britain and Ireland; some 25,000 tonnes of langoustine worth £85 million was trawled in British waters in 2002, and it offers hope to Scotland's beleaguered small-boat fishing fleet. There are concerns that such a catch-level may not be sustainable, and EU quotas have been introduced in Ireland. 'Dublin Bay prawn' is a misnomer; the Norway Lobster is more common on the Irish west coast.

A colourful Squat Lobster, or 'sixpenny man'– its Latin name, Galathea, *is that of a classical sea-nymph.*

Squat lobsters *Galatheidae*

VN: gowdie (Northumb.), mud shrimp, nancy (NE Eng.), sixpenny man (NE Eng.), wiggy (NE Eng.)

Squat lobsters are shorter, flatter and stouter than true lobsters. They have impressive defensive pincers but eke out a low-key existence among submerged rocks and on the seabed scavenging detritus. In Scotland, there is a small commercial fishery for the largest of them, *Munida rugosa*, which is occasionally seen on supermarket counters. Its rich, sweet meat is confined to the claws and the tail.

Above: *Our native Freshwater Crayfish. Its survival is threatened by a more powerful incomer from America, the Signal Crayfish with its enormous claws (shown here,* left, *cooked and red).*

Spiny lobsters *Palinuridae*

VN: crawfish, rock lobster, swap lobster (NE Eng.)

Spiny lobsters, or *longouste*, have a stout, spiny and heavily armoured carapace. Unlike the true lobster they are naturally reddish and are sometimes known as the 'red lobster'. There is a small, west-coast rock-lobster fishery, though the animals are reluctant to enter lobster pots and are obtained mainly as a bycatch in 'cray nets'. The rock lobster's generic name *Palinurus* is taken from the helmsman of Aeneas' ship in *The Aenied*; it was borrowed by Sir Thomas More in his *Utopia* as the archetype of a careless traveller and thence lent the writer Cyril Connolly his pseudonym of Palinurus for his book *The Unquiet Grave*.

Freshwater crayfish *Astacidae*

VN: crawdad, crawfish, gaver (Cornwall), *gimmagh awin* (Isle of Man), penprock or pimprock (Isle of Man)

The crayfish is the 'freshwater lobster', a retiring creature, most active at night and, despite its formidable pincers, easily handled. Like all crayfish, it is delicious to eat, especially its claw-meat, and is trapped for the occasional crayfish supper, especially in early autumn when the water is at its warmest. In 1688, Samuel Pepys noted that The Bear in Hungerford offered 'very good trouts, eels and crayfish'. Villages, especially in the Thames catchment, held jolly crayfish parties, and manor houses once stocked them in moats and ponds, perhaps for fish-days when flesh was forbidden.

Britain has only one native species of freshwater crayfish, known internationally as the White-clawed, or Atlantic Stream, Crayfish (though at home it was simply *the* freshwater crayfish). Until the 1980s, it was common in clean, well-oxygenated streams and rivers and, less often, in lakes and reservoirs up to the Scottish border. It is a scavenger, hiding by day in crevices or sheltered places among the tree roots and, as scavengers do, performing a key ecological service in maintaining the water quality of the stream.

Unfortunately, the freshwater lobster in most rivers today is not our native crayfish but the Signal Crayfish, an interloper from North America. This larger species was chosen for crayfish farms because it yields more meat and is easier to keep than the native species. From 1976, crayfish farms, which were often no more than a pond behind a chicken-wire fence, were supported by government set-up grants, despite the knowledge that the Signal Crayfish carries a fungal disease that is fatal to European crayfish and had wiped out the native Noble Crayfish in parts of Europe. So it proved in Britain, too. One by one, the main crayfish rivers in England succumbed to 'plague' carried by escaped farmed crayfish. The symptoms begin with odd behaviour: the stricken crayfish emerges from the water, often in broad daylight, and totters about on stiff joints, as if on stilts. Later it falls over on its back, legs wriggling helplessly, and as it dies, nasty puffs of mildew appear through its joints.

Dead and dying crayfish were an everyday sight on chalk streams and rivers in the 1980s.[19] The Signals, which seem immune to the disease, expanded into the ecological gap left by an important scavenger and have now largely replaced the native crayfish throughout its range. Desperate attempts to repair the damage by poisoning the water or fishing the Signals out proved an expensive waste of time; Scottish Natural Heritage alone spent more than £100,000 combating the invader in the Scottish Borders before giving up.[20] The only hope left for the native species is in isolated streams and reservoirs, but the number of remaining refuges is steadily decreasing. The Signal Crayfish occurs in much higher densities than the native crayfish, and has a catholic diet that may even include smaller crayfish. River-keepers blame it for the low fly-hatches on many trout streams in recent years, and anglers claim the Signals pull bait off their hooks and even cut fishing lines.

The only positive aspect to this sorry tale is a revival of crayfish parties. The Signal is large and meaty, with fat, lobster-like claws, and is ridiculously easy to catch once the water is sufficiently warm.

The Edible Crab, or ponger, with its pie-crust armour.

One way is simply to lower a net wash-bag baited with scraps of fish or catfood into a weir pool: you can pull them out two or three at a time, and the bucket is soon filled. Some people enjoy a plateful plain-boiled, but young specimens make a delicious crayfish bisque. Many restaurants in the Thames area now include locally caught Signals on the menu. Newbury Manor even adds them to the list of attractions as a waterside spectacular: 'See the crayfish climb out of the rushing white waters of the sluice in the evening light!'[21] Dining out on Signal Crayfish may have no impact on their numbers, but we can at least knock them back with a clear green conscience.

Crabs *Brachyura*

vn: cruban (Scot.), dogger (NE Eng.), flaish crab (Shore Crab, Isle of Man), gilly or gillie (Norfolk), Harry Norris (Velvet Crab, Isle of Man), hever or heaver (Kent), keavie (Scot.), mettick (Scot.), pallawa (N Eng. & Scot.), partan (Isle of Man & Scot.), peeler, pillan (Scot.), ponger or pung (Kent), poo (Scot.), rothick (Scot.), sclunhach (Scot.), softie

We have probably called them crabs for as long as we have eaten them. The word comes from the Old English *crabba*, which seems to have meant 'a crawling creature'. The Latin name for a crab, *cancer*, has given us not only the sign of the zodiac but also a name for a malignant disease of the body cells,

which causes about 13 per cent of all human deaths. It was Hippocrates who first fancied a resemblance between a tumour and the oval body of a crab, with radiating veins representing the animal's feet.

Given how delicious they are, we are surprisingly negative about crabs. Crabbed handwriting is cramped and hard to decipher, and in former days 'to crab' meant to criticise, decry, obstruct, wreck, frustrate and be generally very annoying. A crabby person is someone with a grumpy, bad-tempered personality. To be crab-faced is to have a sour, peevish expression. Crab apples are hard, sour and inedible. This malign reputation is probably linked to the unusual way a crab moves, scurrying along on the tips of its toes, with a stiff, cramped gait (forced on it by the crab's simple peg-in-socket joints). They were said to walk backwards (in fact they move sidewise), and so it stood to reason that they were dishonest creatures. They are also said to be bad-tempered, and even today, the French refer to '*le crabe enragé*'.

We have inherited much of this slander from the Middle Ages, when the crab was seen as the embodiment of treachery, inconstancy and greed. The Cambridge *Bestiary* records how the crab tricks the oyster by lobbing a stone into its shell. Unable to close its shell, the oyster is thereupon torn to pieces and eaten. This is a warning against being lured into sin by deceit and cunning: 'Let it be left to us to make use of the marine example, in perfecting our own well-being, not in the undoing of our neighbour.'[22]

Its image as a crusty, aggressive character is the basis for the crab's occasional cultural outings. For example, 'Shore Crab', by the contemporary Scots poet Gerry Cambridge, imagines it as Chug the Claw, a tough-talking Glaswegian hard man: 'Haw, Jimmy, dinnae mess wi' me/ Fancy yer chances, eh? Eh? We'll see.' Popular with children, the Shore Crab's aggressive banter was put into music for acoustic guitar and harmonica by folk-musician Neil Thomson.[23]

Among Rudyard Kipling's *Just So* stories, first published in 1902, was 'The Crab that Played with the Sea'. It is one of the oddest of his tales, a dense, oriental creation myth in which the crab plays the part of a rebel, a kind of fallen animal-angel. Kipling evidently associated in his mind the zodiac constellation Cancer the Crab with cancer, of which he had an irrational dread. In the tale, the crab is gigantic, 'as tall as the smoke of three volcanoes'. His illustrator showed it as a king, or horseshoe,

A haul of crabs from Weybourne, Norfolk.

The pier at Cromer, the crab capital of Norfolk, with an incoming crab boat.

crab (strictly speaking, this is not a crab but a distant relative of spiders), but in the final part of the story, it seems to transmute into a tree-climbing land crab. Tricked into losing its shell, the fearful crab is forced to agree to become a small, scuttling creature that hides its puny body under stone and weed. A kindly disposed little girl hands it 'a pair of scissors' to defend itself. And so, to this day, concludes Kipling, crabs are not on friendly terms with mankind, and if annoyed they will nip you with their scissors. The Post Office used an image of this story (along with 'The Butterfly that Stamped', q.v.) for a first-class stamp to commemorate the centenary of Rudyard Kipling's *Just So* stories in January 2002.

Andrew Young's short and deceptively simple poem 'The Dead Crab' is a reflection on a paradox of nature: that which protects you can also destroy you. Crabs are tough; of all creatures they seem the best-protected – robotic, scuttling creatures, all sown up inside their shell of natural armour:

'A rosy shield upon its back/That not the hardest storm could crack.' Yet something had killed it. 'I cannot think this creature died/By storm or fish or sea-fowl harmed/ Walking the sea so heavily armed', he muses, but 'to be/ Oneself a living armoury?' is itself a kind of living death.[24]

The crab's chitin shell is hardened by calcium carbonate and is too inflexible to allow much growth. Instead it is cast regularly, and the crab retires to a hiding place in a rock crevice to wait until the new one has hardened. The old (and false) belief that crabs moult only at full moon is the reason why, in some cultures, the crab is a lunar symbol. Christianity borrowed it as a symbol of rebirth or resurrection, a role curiously at odds with the crab's truculent reputation.

Anglers see crabs in terms of their use as bait, which is reflected in their terminology, based not on species but on states of growth. A crab which is about to moult and whose body has turned soft

The Shore Crab, the commonest British crab, though rarely gathered for food in Britain.

and soapy is known as a 'peeler'; immediately after moulting, the crab becomes a 'jellyback' (or 'shucker' or 'softback'). In parts of northern England and Scotland, such a crab is known as a 'pillan', a 'mettick' or a 'softie'. The favourite bait species is the Shore Crab, or 'gilly', simply because it is by far the easiest crab to find and occurs further up the shore than other species.

Lone, wandering peeler crabs are known as 'walkers', while a male mating crab is a 'carrier', since it walks or swims with the female slung underneath. Hard-shelled crabs, meanwhile, are called 'greenbacks' or 'hardbacks'. Welsh peeler crabs have been called 'weelers'. A 'pallawa' is a small crab not worth eating but still handy as bait. In the crab-fishing villages on the north-east coast of Scotland, hard-shelled edible crabs are 'partans', while a full-sized one is a 'poo' and a young one a 'rothick'.

The Shore, or Green, Crab (or Green Shore Crab) is the commonest large crab on British shores, and our idea of what a crab looks like is generally based either on this species or the Edible Crab. As children, many of us caught them with a net or a baited crab-

line or, perhaps for a dare, gingerly with our fingers. In some popular coves, Shore Crabs must have got used to being collected, kept in a bucket for a while and then released back into the rock pool. It rarely occurs to us that we might eat them (they are, in fact, perfectly edible, though scant of meat). The Shore Crab's tolerance to exposure and low salinity enables it to survive out of water for some hours and also to live in estuaries and salt-marshes.

'We once found the mouth of a small river where Shore Crabs had gathered in large numbers, and we joined other children in fishing for them. All we needed was a small pebble tied to the end of a length of string. When a crab was teased into grabbing the pebble, it was flicked out of the water before it had time to let go'.[25]

The Velvet Swimming Crab, also called the Velvet Fiddler Crab, is a lively, dark, red-eyed crab whose carapace is covered in short, fine hairs. It is much more aggressive than the Shore Crab, with a feisty come-and-get-me attitude, and its sharp claws can draw blood. A beachcomber jumping up and down with a crab clamped to his finger has most likely found a Velvet Crab, whose alternate name is 'devil's crab'. Few eat them in Britain, but since the 1980s, a small Velvet Crab fishery has grown up on the west coast of Scotland for export, either live or frozen, to France and Spain, where they are the centerpiece of a rich seafood stew. In the Isle of Man this crab is known as Harry Norris.

Edible crab

VN: brown crab, chancre (Channel Islands), Cromer crab, partan

In Britain, the crab on our plate, whether dressed or undressed, potted or mashed into mousse, is almost invariably the Edible Crab, also known (since most big crabs are edible) as the Brown Crab. By good fortune, there are probably more of them in British and Irish waters than anywhere on earth; nearly half of the world catch is from UK waters. It is easily the largest common crab, and much the most wholesome-looking, with its pie-crust shell and plump black-tipped claws. It is rarely found in rock pools (and then only small ones), and is traditionally caught in baited creels or crab pots anchored with a marker buoy and serviced by local crab boats. A law in the 1870s introduced a minimum size for sale, to prevent the taking of immature crabs. Some places also forbid the catching of egg-carrying ('berried') female crabs. By custom, Edible Crabs are never used as bait.

The crab capital is the Norfolk town of Cromer, where top-quality crabs grow fat and sweet on the offshore reefs of chalk. Since the 1960s, the inshore crab fishery has declined, and most crabs are now caught with mobile pots in deeper water. Doubts have been raised about whether the present fishery of around 20,000 tonnes per year is sustainable, but female Edible Crabs lay around 3 million eggs, and the recruitment rate seems to be holding up.

Purists like their crabs as fresh as possible, straight from the boil. But picking crabmeat from the shell is something of an art, and so it is often sold 'dressed', that is, picked off and then stuffed back into the shell. Cromer crab is often potted with butter, shallots and a little sherry. A traditional dish from the Isle of Skye called 'partan pie' is a mixture of crabmeat, butter, vinegar and mustard baked in the shell and served hot. But many crabs today end up ignominiously torn from any recognisable shape, as processed crab sticks.

Spider crabs *Majidae*

VN: paddy (NE Eng.), piper (NE Eng.), runch (NE Eng.), tyed (NE Eng.), tyellier (NE Eng.)

Spider crabs have long, spidery legs and thin, attenuated claws. There are about 20 species in European waters but only the Common Spider Crab is commercially fished, mainly for export. Its Latin name *Maja* refers to the month of May, when the crabs come inshore to moult and are most easily caught. Their meat is sweet but awkward to extract from their narrow claws, and despite the best efforts of Rick Stein, spider crabs have never been popular in Britain. Perhaps their resemblance to a giant marine spider puts off many people (and the memory of something similar clamped tight to John Hurt's face in *Alien* cannot have helped).

The Red King Crab, or Stalin's Crab, one of the world's largest crabs (or invertebrates, for that matter), made the headlines in 2007 after claims that it was marauding along the Norwegian seabed and damaging the fisheries (though local fishermen

The Spider Crab, *a characteristically lively collage by the Orkney-based artist John Wallington.*

responded by establishing another fishery and selling the crabs at up to $60 a kilo).[26] Stalin's Crab, a native of the Far East, was experimentally introduced to Murmansk Fjord in the 1960s and has since spread west into the North Sea. Speculations, whipped up by the media, that it would soon invade British waters and gobble up our remaining fish have not yet been borne out.

Mitten crabs *Grapsidae*

The claws of mitten crabs are covered in soft bristles; their generic name, *Eriocheir*, means 'wool-hand'. Only one species, an unwelcome introduction from the Far East, is found in Britain. This is the Chinese Mitten Crab, and unlike most crabs, it lives in large rivers and lakes, though it has to return to the estuary to breed. In its native China, the crab is a delicacy, believed to have a 'cooling' ('yin') effect on the body when steamed and cooked with soya sauce.

The mitten crab has hitchhiked around the world in the ballast tanks of ships and colonised North America and parts of Europe, where there are no native freshwater crabs to compete with it. It is tolerant of at least mildly polluted conditions, and thrives in the Thames estuary, where its burrows

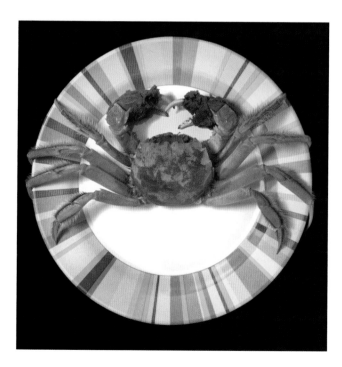

A mature Chinese Mitten Crab, anticipating its likely fate.

damage embankments and clog drainage systems. Little known in Britain before the 1990s, it sprang into prominence in 1995, when the *London Evening Standard* reported large crabs emerging from the Thames at Greenwich and heading towards the High Street. Others were also spotted in car headlights on damp country lanes, waving their furry claws. There was talk of saucer-sized crabs taking up residence in swimming pools and garden ponds. In 2007, the residents of Twickenham were seriously advised to keep their toilet lids closed after reports that mitten crabs had been spotted in the sewage tunnels.

Though no friend to flood-defence engineers, the crab's tunnelling activities do at least provide a habitat for other invertebrates and small fish, including small eels, and are helping to 'renaturalise' steep engineered banks. In 1997, John Prescott was filmed with a particularly mean-looking mitten crab which, with apparent reference to his cabinet colleague Peter Mandelson, he addressed as Peter.[27] Government media advisers decided to make use of 'Peter the Crab' as a prop for a news story about improved flood defence on the Thames. The Environment Agency explained afterwards that the crab was actually called Dennis, and that 'he' was, in fact, a 'she'.

Hermit crabs *Paguridae*

VN: craaler, craalin boockie (NE Eng.), dols or dolpaw (Isle of Man), kleppispur (Orkney), soldier crab

Just as the holy men of old would seek a remote hut or cave for their private devotions, so the hermit crab lives alone inside a borrowed seashell. It is skilled at finding exactly the right-sized shell to house its soft body and regularly upgrades to larger shells as it grows; the size of its shell is, therefore, a good guide to a hermit crab's age. The largest species is the Common Hermit Crab, also known as the soldier crab. Those found in rock pools are normally quite small and occupy empty winkles or topshells. Bigger ones in deeper water often choose whelk shells. As scavengers of the seafloor, hermit crabs are among the few marine animals that do well out of modern fishing methods. They have been spotted by divers prowling happily among the carnage: broken clams, shattered sea urchins, disinterred worms . . .

Their clean-up habits. and their attractive appearance, make hermit crabs popular additions to

A hermit crab with a hitch-hiking sea anemone.

the saltwater aquarium. They can live for up to ten years in a tank, though many die from the shock of being introduced to a new environment (it is known in the crab trade as the 'post-purchase syndrome'). Some stockists attempt to gild the lily by painting the crabs' shells, an operation that the crab strongly dislikes (especially when the paint turns out to be toxic). The most desirable kind of hermit crab is one with a sea anemone on its shell; the Cloak Anemone wraps around the shell and lives off titbits left by the crab, while offering it the protection of its stinging tentacles. The association of this pink-spotted anemone and the crab is sometimes called 'the strawberry crab'.

Other crabs

Pea Crabs are tiny, soft-shelled crabs that live inside mussel shells. Any gathering of mussels is likely to contain one or two of them – pale, pea-sized creatures that scuttle about sideways when exposed to the light. They are not only harmless but said to give a pleasant crunchy texture to the mussel when cooked together. The slightly larger Porcelain Crab has a thin, flat, pearly white shell, which enables this five-pence-sized miniature crab to eke out a modest living under stones.

The Sponge Crab builds a home-grown camouflage out of bits of sponge, which it delicately nips off the rocks, and with infinite care, like a gardener putting in bedding plants, attaches to its shell. After the gardening is complete, the crab is all but invisible beneath its floppy beret of inedible sponge.

The Masked Crab tunnels into the sand, where it maintains contact with the watery world above by means of what looks like a remarkably long 'nose' (it is, in fact, a fused pair of antennae that prop up a breathing tube). Its carapace has markings that resemble a cartoonish mask or, some thought, an ancient helmet. The scientific name *cassivelaunus* commemorates an ancient British leader, who was thought to have worn such a helmet with a long spike on top.

Dudley bugs (fossil trilobites)

AN: Dudley locusts, stone butterflies

Trilobites have been extinct for 200 million years, but their well-preserved fossils look as though they might wake up and crawl out of the rock. They are marine animals, with a distinctive threefold body topped by an armoured carapace somewhat like a crab (their nearest living relatives are probably horseshoe crabs, though they look more like giant woodlice). Trilobites must have been abundant in the distant seas, and never more so than in the reef of limestone that is now the rocky hill known as the Wren's Nest in Dudley. It fittingly became Britain's first geological nature reserve in 1956. The area of crumbling limestone called the Reef Mound is known by local kids as 'fossil pizza' for its masses of petrified seafood: shells, corals and other animals, all tumbled together. The star of the show is Dudley's signature fossil, the trilobite. It appeared on the town's coat-of-arms until recently as an exact heraldic rendition of a Silurian species *Calymene blumenbachi*. Before they were identified as ancient fossils, these stone impressions were collected and sold by quarrymen as 'Dudley bugs' or 'Dudley locusts'. Later, fossil collectors flocked to Dudley, and their specimens are found in museums the world over. Some especially nice ones were preserved in a glass case in Dudley's own museum until someone stole them. In South Wales, meanwhile, trilobites were known as 'stone butterflies', in the belief that they had been living insects turned to stone by the magician, Merlin.

Sea spiders *Pycnogonida*

Its old name, 'pantopod', meaning 'all legs', is not a bad description of a sea spider. The creature's eight legs meet in the middle, leaving little space for a body (in America they are called 'no-body crabs'), and most of the head is taken up by an intricate set of mouthparts, which it uses to pierce sea anemones and hydroids. The modern name, *Pycnogonid*, means 'thick knee'. Small sea spiders live in rock pools but are difficult to spot in the field. The best way to detect them is to place a mass of red seaweed in a dish and wait for them to emerge – ponderously, as if in slow motion – on their long, spindly legs. Larger sea spiders live in deeper water, and relative monsters the size of dinner plates have been found in Antarctic waters. Sea spiders are an ancient group, more closely related to crabs than true spiders. Some of the world's oldest have been preserved by volcanic ash in rocks of Silurian age in Herefordshire.

Woodlice and hoglice
Isopoda

Isopods ('equal-legs') are crustaceans with flattened bodies and seven pairs of legs born on a similar number of body segments (plus another five, legless segments projecting beyond). The best-known isopods are woodlice, which have mastered the art of living on land. Other isopods live in fresh water (the 'hoglice', or 'water slaters'), on shores ('slaters') or in the sea, including the deep sea. They are an ancient group, little changed since the Carboniferous; one can find very similar bugs petrified into immortality inside lumps of coal. Most of the 'lore' is about woodlice, our familiars in house and garden.

Woodlice *Oniscidea*

VN: baker, bibble-bug, Billy button, carpenter (West Midlands), carpenter's flea, cheese-bug, cheese-log (Bucks), cheesy-bob, cherbug, chesbug, chisel-bob, chisleps, chisel-pig (Berkshire), chizzle-ball (Devon), chiggy-pig (Devon), chooky or chucky-pig, chuggy-pig, church pigs (Glos.), cob, cobber, coffin-cutter, crawlers, crawly pig, crilly-greens, crockies (Manchester), cruller, cudworm, curly-button, doodly-bug, elephant, fairy pig (Isle of Man), fairy's pig, flat-back, fuzzy-pig, gammer-louse, God Almighty's pig (Oxon), God's little pig, gramfer (Somerset), gramfer-grig or granfer-grey (Devon), grammar-zow (SW England), grampus wood-bug, grandfathers (Bristol area), granny picker, granny grey (Wales), grumpy-gravie (Suffolk), guinea-pig, hobby horses (Dorset), hardyback, hog-louse, hog-thrush-louse, horace, jacky-pig, Jacobites (Bristol), Johnny bug, journey-pig, jovial louse, lockchest (Oxon), millacreen (Isle of Man), monkey-peas or mankie-peas or monkeypede (Kent), parson's pig (Isle of Man), pea-bug, penny mouse, penny pig (Ireland), pig, pig's buttons, pig's louse, piggy-wiggy, pill bug, pill pig, pissibeds, potato bug, roll-in-balls, roly-poly, St Anthony's pig or Anthony's pig, sclater (Northumb.), sheel-back, shoemaker, sink louse, slaitero or slatroo (Orkney), slater (N England & Scotland), slaterworm (Orkney), snot, sour-bug, sow (Norfolk), sow-bug, sow-pig, Susie pig, tank, thrush-louse, tiddy-hog or tiggy-hog, trilobite, William button, wood-bug, wood-pig (Lincs), woozy pug, zowey pig (Devon)

Woodlice are the sort of animals that acquire nicknames; we have found more than 80, past and present, 34 of them gathered from Devon alone during the 1960s. Familiar and yet rather odd, with their armoured bodies, rows of spiky legs and a pair of 'feelers' upfront, woodlice have great character and do little harm. Hence most of their nicknames appear rather affectionate. We see them as little round objects – buttons, pills or peas – or as unrelated insects, whether lice, bugs or worms, or in anthropomorphic terms, as shoemakers, carpenters or slaters. Above all, we see them as little pigs, as in 'sow-bug' or 'chucky-pig'.

Woodlouse names go back a long way. As early as the fifteenth century, they were known as 'chestlockes', 'lockdors', 'chisleps' or 'monk's peas'. There was even an Anglo-Saxon name: *eselchans*, which meant ass-coloured. Today many names are confined to a particular part of the country, and an expert would probably be able to tell roughly where he was from the name the locals give to a woodlouse. In the north, they are 'slaters', in the Midlands 'sow-pigs' or 'chucky-pigs', in the south 'gramfer grigs' or 'sow pigs', in the south-east, 'monkey-peas', while in the east they are known, perhaps less affectionately, as 'pig's-lice' or, simply, 'pigs'.

Why did woodlice attract such linguistic invention? Their distinctiveness and familiarity was obviously one reason, but another was that they were useful. When curled up they were the size and shape of an apothecary's pills, which in the days when people were looking for natural 'signatures', was a heaven-sent hint that they had medicinal properties. They seem to have been a widely used peasant medicine: you ground up their dried bodies into powder or simply swallowed them whole. 'Mother's better – I gave her three sowpigs last night,' said one believer. In Sabine Baring-Gould's Devon-based novel *Furze Bloom*, a character recalls that 'nothing ekals a sow-pig' for 'indiagestion (sic)'.[28] The habit of swallowing woodlice every time you experienced a tummy ache survived well into modern times: 'A Mr Albert Golding told me how his grandfather had treated him for jaundice whilst a baby by grinding up woodlice in a mill and then feeding it to him. This was in the 1930s, in the Bristol area.'[29]

The round shape of rolled-up woodlice also provided the cue for the 'button' and 'cob' names, while round Dutch cheeses probably lie behind names such as 'cheese-bob' or 'chizzle-bob'. The old

A Common, or Rough, Woodlouse changing its skin. Its scientific name, Porcellio scaber, *means 'rough little pig'.*

name 'chisleps' seems to come from an Old English word *ceselyb* for a natural agent, such as rennet, that helped to turn sour milk into cheese. Were woodlice also once used for that purpose? 'Monkey-peas' is another name with a long pedigree. It dates from the Middle Ages, when the name was 'monk's peason' or monk's peas, but by 1682, monks had already turned into monkeys.

Certain trades were particularly familiar with woodlice. The name 'shoemaker' is probably linked to the shoe-shape of a woodlouse on its back. Woodlice are often found hiding under loose roof slates, hence their name 'slaters', though the overlapping segments of common grey woodlice also recall the way stone roof slates are fitted. Because woodlice feed on rotting wood, they were also regular companions of carpenters, hence 'carpenter's flea'. This predilection for damp, crumbling timber also lies behind their macabre name of 'coffin-cutters'.

Woodlouse itself seems to be a nickname that stuck. Though not remotely related to lice, they bear a passing resemblance to a once familiar large louse that lives on pigs (the same mistake lies behind the commonest woodlouse's scientific name, *porcellio*, or little pig). The pig association is deepened by the vaguely pig-like shape of woodlice when seen from above and the way they aggregate like piglets around a farrowing sow. 'Chucky' or 'choogey' is a West Country name for a piglet. The same idea lies behind 'granfer': though granfer means grandfather, it is also a Hampshire name for the smallest pig in the litter, the one that was often rescued and brought up by hand. A 'tiddy-hog' is simply a small (tiddley) pig. The name 'Anthony's pig', used in nineteenth century Devon and perhaps elsewhere, recalls that St Anthony is the patron saint of swineherds. Another old Devon name, 'fuzzy-pig' was shared with the hedgehog. Both curl up defensively, and though the woodlouse lacks the latter's 'furzey' (gorse-like) prickles, it does at least present a well-armoured carapace to the world. Yorkshire's 'thrush-louse', by contrast, has nothing to do with thrushes. The word is believed to come from 'thurs', an old name for a sprite.

Children still make up names for woodlice. Sue Everett's son David called them 'wigglemice'. Three-year-old Louisa Marshall from Kintbury, Berkshire, found another name, 'Dougal spiders', because they move about like Dougal, the dog with the hidden feet in the BBC series *The Magic Roundabout*.

Here is a sample of the woodlouse names our contributors have sent us:

'"Chuggy pig" in Cornwall, "granny grey" in Wales, "monkeypede" in Kent.' (Andrew Whitehouse)

'"Cheesy bugs", "pillbugs" (especially the harder ones which roll up into a ball), even "guinea pigs".' (Jonathan Rye)

'As a kid in North Lincolnshire, we knew woodlice as "pigs", except for one type, which I'm pretty sure was *Porcellio scaber*, which was an "elephant".' (Roger Key, Lincolnshire)

'When we were young my sister and I called them "granferdigs" – but that was probably a word we invented.' (Jo Dunn)

'My father, who grew up in Woodbridge, Suffolk, used the name "grumpy-gravies". I've asked people over the years and no one seems to have heard of it before.' (Johnny Birks)

'I call woodlice "Johnny Crumps" as my grandparents, and then my mum, always have. My gran, who is Spanish, once called them "Jenny crumpets".' (Penny Green, Sussex)

'I have been trying to find out where the name "bakers" for woodlice came from. I can't find this name anywhere and yet me and my peers always called them that.' (Sara Reading)

'In the Isle of Man, we called them "parsons pigs".' (Gwen Walker)

'As a child in North Yorkshire, I was familiar with the term "slater", meaning a woodlouse. A colleague from Glasgow also used this word. He had an expression, "Well, it's better than a slater up your nose." He said it was an old Glaswegian expression.' (John Showers)

Woodlouse remedies

In former times, woodlice were thought to need only 'warm moisture' or dew to survive. They smelt faintly of ammonia or urine (hence their Dutch name, *pissebed*), which, along with their rolled-up pill shape, was a cue that they were at our disposal for the treatment of diseases of the bladder or urinary tract. Woodlice appear in medical tracts from the Middle Ages onwards for the treatment of disorders such as jaundice or kidney stones, and few apothecaries would have been without their jar of dried woodlice, supplied by one of those long-lost country trades, the 'chisleps' gatherer.

Their smell, more obvious in confined spaces than in the wild, comes from the woodlouse's excretory products, which are solid in order to conserve water. One might expect woodlice to taste horribly bitter, and by all accounts they do. Young birds, even spiders (with the exception of the specialist Woodlouse Spider), spit them out. Doctors tried to disguise their bitterness with wine or, more interestingly, with mouse or pigeon droppings. Thomas Muffet preserved an Elizabethan recipe for dispensing crushed woodlice mixed in wine for patients suffering from 'the Stone and difficulty of urine'. 'Drink it,' he urged his struggling patient, 'and the pain will cease, and you shall void either the Stone, or much small sand.'[30] Perhaps it is just coincidence, but live woodlice do, indeed, contain medically nitrogenous compounds that make them useful today in certain kinds of treatment.

An example of a woodlouse recipe, which he called 'Expression of millipedes', is in the herbalist Nicholas Culpeper's *Dispensatory* of 1649:

Take of live millipedes (commonly called woodlice) three ounces; simple fennel water, one pint; compound horse-radish water, half a pint. Bruise the millipedes, gradually adding to them the distilled waters; and afterwards press out the liquor. This is an excellent diuretic, sweetener and cleanser of the blood and a most efficacious medicine in all chronic cases that are to be relieved by promoting the urinary discharges, as are many inveterate ulcers, strumas and scrophulous disorders.[31]

When, around 1700, the great naturalist John Ray lay sick with the colic, he was treated by his physician with a decoction of crushed woodlice, though, according to Anna Pavord, the treatment 'exacerbated rather than cured his complaints.'[32] For poor Ray's recurring epilepsy, the good doctor turned to another surefire cure, peacock dung.

Such was the power of woodlice that even a bagful of 'sow-bugs' worn around the neck could help with a cough or sores in the mouth. Some said that the cure worked best if there were exactly 13 woodlice in the bag.

All this handed the satirist Jonathan Swift a weapon in his campaign against an unpopular local official named William Wood:

> The louse of the wood for a Med'cine is us'd,
> Or swallow'd alive, or skillfully bruis'd.
> And, let but our mother Hibernia contrive
> To swallow Will Wood, either bruis'd or alive,
> She need be no more with the jaundice possest,
> Or sick of obstructions, and pains in her chest.[33]

Woodlice as literary symbols

In keeping with their status as medical curiosities, woodlice have occasionally been elevated as art. St Mary's Church in Shrewsbury has the third-highest spire in England. It is noted for its beautiful stained glass, and among its gems, on the west wall of the south porch, is a plump little animal in a roundel of glass. It is unmistakably a woodlouse, for it is shown accurately with seven legs running along the visible side, two bulging eyes and a pair of short antennae; its warty back indicates it is the Common Woodlouse, *Porcellio scaber* (meaning 'scaly pig'). The inscription '*Sol in cancro*' suggests that it stands in lieu of a crab for the zodiac. This ancient woodlouse was chosen as the cover illustration for the first issue of the scientific journal *Isopoda*.

In literature, woodlice are sometimes symbols of decay. Halfway through his gigantic *History of Frederick the Great*, Thomas Carlyle had a moment of doubt. What is the use of it, he groaned. 'Sticking like a woodlouse to an old bedpost and boring one more hole in it?'[34] He was wrong about woodlice, which do not bore holes, but possibly right about lengthy biographies (not that it stopped him writing several more).

More often, woodlice evoke a damp, musty atmosphere. In *Madame Bovary*, Gustave Flaubert had the idea of 'expressing a tone, this colouration of mustiness in the state of being a woodlouse.' As the trapped, bored Emma Bovary wanders past the coping of the vineyard wall with the dew on the cabbages, 'many-legged woodlice' scuttle away. Late in life, Flaubert toyed with the idea of calling his last, unfinished novel *Les Deux Cloportes* (The Two Woodlice), envisaging his two heroes as representatives of contemptible bourgeois stupidity, which, for reasons of his own, he associated with isopods.[35]

In France, *cloporte* is a term of abuse; it means

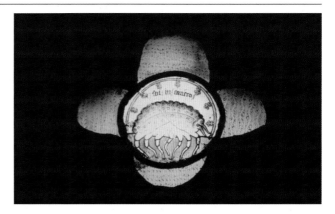

An endearing representation of a woodlouse on a stained glass oval at St Mary's Church, Shrewbury. The legend 'sol in cancro' – 'the sun in Cancer' – suggests it is a stand-in for the crab as a sign of the zodiac.

'closed-door' and is similar to the old English names of 'chestlockes' or 'lockdors' for rolled-up woodlice. The nineteenth-century writer Edmond de Goncourt refers to a '*vie de cloporte*', meaning a self-centred life, totally turned in on itself. Joris-Karl Huysmans speaks of 'an art so groveling and so flat that I shall willingly call it "*cloportisme*"' – that is, essence of woodlouse.

In Britain, their image is much milder, and in literature they tend to retain their biological identity. In her first novel, *Under the Net* (1954), Iris Murdoch compared the policemen appearing from beneath pieces of boarding with 'a nest of disquieted woodlice'. In T. F. Powys's novel *Unclay* (1931), the prevailing sense of mortality is given emphasis by the 'tiny pigs-louse that lived in the grass upon Madder Hill', which ate its unspecified 'prey', then 'rolled up into a ball to sleep near an anthill, and was eaten itself.' A more exalted role was offered to the woodlouse by Algernon Charles Swinburne (1837–1909), who enrolled it as fellow narrator in his 'The Poet and the Woodlouse'. 'Thou art certainly my brother,' says poet to woodlouse, 'I discern in thee the markings of the fingers of the Whole.' Had the dice rolled the other way, he implied, it might have been Swinburne who was the 'insect'.[36]

In his poem 'Winter' (1866), later set to music by Arthur Sullivan, Alfred Tennyson coupled the woodlouse with the dormouse as a symbol of contentment in adversity:

> Bite, frost, bite!
> You roll up away from the light
> The blue wood-louse, and the plump dormouse,
> And the bees are still'd, and the flies are kill'd,
> And you bite far into the heart of the house,
> But not into mine.[37]

The most sympathetic woodlouse poet is Jean Kenward, who pities its vulnerability to what most animals welcome – the return of the sun in the 'the bird-invested morning':

> Deep in a crumbling
> darkness, crisply armoured
> against attack,
> grey woodlice are assembled, dry and silent,
> cushioned in cleft and crack.
>
> Cold, spherical,
> steelhard, they fold their tiny
> bodies so tight
> as to allow
> no entry to the summer's
> pervasive light;
>
> Only – at a brief
> raising of the curtain –
> in sudden, wild hysteria, they run
> this way and that,
> unrolling, unprotected,
> unloosed, undone,
>
> Certain that without
> any word or warning,
> each one must brace
> himself to bear
> the bird-invested morning,
> and the sun's face.[38]

In Wiltshire children had a chant which they said to a woodlouse held in the hand and could make the creature suddenly curl up:

> 'Granfer Grig killed a pig
> Hing un up in corners
> Granfer cried and piggy died
> And all the fun was over'.[39]

It is the sort of nonsensical rhyme children recite to other 'insects', especially ladybirds, but it is a reminder of the links between 'granfer' and 'piggy'; both are 'little pigs'.

In children's books, woodlice tend to be presented, by contrast, as tough, even resourceful creatures. In *A House Inside Out* (1987), Penelope Lively has a woodlouse hero called Nat, a rather broad-bodied, bug-eyed one, possessing considerable spirit and tact. Nat is three weeks old – just entering his adulthood, in woodlouse terms. His extended family is governed by 'stern and ancient creatures with whiskers of immense length', for no one counts for much in this woodlouse world until their whiskers have grown sufficiently impressive.

Censorship rears its ugly head in Beatrix Potter's story *The Tale of Mrs Tittlemouse* (1909). In the original version, Mr Jackson, an odious and unwelcome frog, paid a visit to Mrs Tittlemouse's pantry in search of honey: 'There were three wood-lice hiding in the plate-rack. Two of them got away; but the littlest one he caught.' For some reason her publisher Harold Warne objected to the word 'wood-louse' in a children's book, and Potter was obliged to change it to 'creepy-crawly'. Fortunately three panic-stricken woodlice survive in the accompanying picture.

Woodlouse lives

Students of woodlice call themselves oniscologists, after the name of the latter's sub-order, Oniscidea. There are about 40 native (outdoor) British species and another 12 that inhabit heated greenhouses. Only nine are common and only five, known among the *cognoscenti* as 'the famous five', are *really* common and live in gardens. A habitat that includes 'all five, plus another one' is likely to be reasonably rich in invertebrates.[40] Woodlice are conventionally divided by their habits as 'runners', 'clampers', 'rollers' and 'creepers', plus a single non-conformist one that lives inside ants' nests.[41] While the commonest woodlice are grey, many others are surprisingly colourful, in mottled browns and yellows, purples or off-whites. The prettiest is perhaps the Rosy Woodlouse, which has a pair of bright yellow stripes running down its back.

Woodlice need to eat 5–10 per cent of their body weight every day, but fortunately they are not fussy

The Common Pill Woodlouse, also known as 'curly button' or 'monkey-peas'.

eaters. They munch methodically through masses of rotten wood and detritus, including their own droppings. Such thrifty habits make them useful decomposers and recyclers. Though woodlice on the carpet may be seen as worrying signs of damp, it could be that they just got lost during the night.

Woodlice can be a nuisance in glasshouses, where they nibble seedlings. Suggested ways of getting rid of them included some spectacular examples of overkill. In the 1930s, gardeners were advised to sprinkle 'phospho nicotyl' at a rate of about half an ounce per square yard. As late as 1979, the Ministry of Agriculture was advising glasshouse owners to 'drench' the soil of affected plants in DDT. A kinder and much safer solution is to keep a tidy greenhouse and so remove their potential refuges.

At Maidstone in Kent, the woodlouse has entered local folklore. The Council had hoped to sell some of their open land at Vinter's Park for development, but the locals, understandably less keen on seeing cherished and historic parkland turned into the headquarters of some multinational company, mounted a campaign to overturn the decision. Enter an unlikely local hero in the form of *Eluma caelatum*, a dowdy little woodlouse, whose one redeeming feature is a single, mauve-coloured Cyclopean eye. The turning point in the Vinter's Park affair arrived during the inspector's tour of the park, pursued by the customary swarms of advocates and protesters. He paused by a quaint, tumbledown barrel-bridge and, as if on cue, the one-eyed mauve woodlouse chose that moment to trundle across the stonework. A local entomologist pounced, the inspector's attention was drawn to its beauty and rarity, and in the fullness of time he decided in favour of conserving the site.[42]

Pill woodlice *Armadillidae*

VN: armadillo, billy button, curly button, monkey peas or mankie peas (Kent), pea bug, peasie bug, pill bugs, roly-poly

Pill woodlice, or pill bugs, are compact woodlice that roll up into a tight ball when threatened. Their thick shell allows them to live in drier habitats, such as crumbling walls. The scientific name of the Common Pill Woodlouse, *Armadillidium vulgare*, means 'common little armadillo'. Their tight, round balls are commonly known as 'monkey peas' (q.v.) or 'roly-polies'.

Water hoglice *Asellidae*

AN: hog-louse, water louse, water slater

Water hoglice are rather unkindly named after a large louse that lives on pigs (scientists have been equally unkind: their scientific group name, *Asellus*, means

The Water hoglouse, the woodlouse of ponds and streams.

'little ass' or donkey). They are, in fact, relatives of woodlice that live in fresh water, and like them, live by scavenging whatever rotting matter they can find. There are two common British species; a third species lives in caves, while a fourth is naturalised in a lake in northern England.

Slaters *Ligiidae*

'Slater' is a nickname for woodlice, especially in the north, but the 'true' slater is a seaside species, the Sea Slater. At up to three centimetres long, it is impressively large and normally lurks in rock crevices by day, emerging only in the evening. Slaters are particularly common among the rocks used as tidal defences along the Thames estuary as far upstream as Gravesend. They perform a useful service in stripping the beach of edible rubbish after the crowds have gone home. 'All the summer ice cream sticks left on the beach at La Valette on Guernsey's east coast after a hot summer's day have been well cleaned by an army of Sea Slaters who descend at night from their crevices in the granite revetment at the top of the shore. They also clean out crisp packets and sugary drink bottles.'[43]

'The wonder in the face of a child on discovering a fully grown Sea Slater is a joy. Even the most worldly-wise and hard-to-impress seven-year-old is a little in awe of a woodlouse that fills their palm. They are further impressed by the fact that the slater, confronted by a limited time-window to scavenge the moon-lit strand, gulps down its food so fast that its droppings contain undigested shreds of seaweed and carrion.'[44]

Gribbles *Limnoriidae*

The Gribble is a pale marine isopod that bores into wood. It has been called the termite of the sea for its propensity to attack soft, wet wood of all kinds – pier pilings, jetties, groynes, lobster pots, neglected wooden boats and submerged wrecks – giving it a reputation second only to the shipworm. Though small – a full-size gribble measures only 4 millimetres long – it occurs in vast numbers. Four hundred of them have been collected from a single cubic inch of rotten timber. A gribble has asymmetric jaws that act like a rasp and file, enabling the animal to chew its way through the wood, generally with the grain and just beneath the surface. Though it can

digest wood cellulose, it lives mainly on algae and bacteria within the rotting wood. Gribble-infested wood becomes spongy and friable and gradually crumbles away, much as timber and furniture does when attacked by termites. In the past, wooden piers were accordingly safeguarded with creosote, metal sheathing or head-to-head beds of nails. After the Second World War, when there were large stockpiles of explosives, it was found that detonating a charge close to a pier would shock-blast the gribbles stone dead, at some risk to the pier. Today it is easier in the long run to build them out of more durable materials.

From our perspective, the Gribble is a nuisance, but it plays a key role in recycling driftwood and kelp stems. How the gribble came by its funny name is uncertain; perhaps there was an association in someone's mind with a little grub, hence 'gribble'.

a centipede in having not one but two pairs of legs per segment, hence the name of its class, Diplopoda ('twin feet'). Millipedes and centipedes together are known as myriapods ('many-feet').

At one time, millipedes were known as 'galley-worms', from the resemblance of their many legs to the oars of a ship. There was also a small, dark one that lived in the soil and was known as 'earth-bowels'. Both kinds had their uses. Rubbing yourself with millipede powder helped to get rid of unwanted body hair. And millipedes were also a useful diuretic: 'galley-worms found in cellars, burnt to a powder, doth wonderfully provoke Urine', noted Muffet. Specimens needed for this purpose could be trapped with a bait of 'St Thomas Sugar'; they were drawn to the finest sugar 'as Mice do to the best Cheese'.[46]

Unlike the carnivorous centipedes, millipedes feed on decaying plant matter and so are important recyclers, converting fallen leaves and other dead vegetation into soil by way of their bacteria-rich droppings. Since their chosen food is not especially nutritious, they need to eat vast quantities of it, and a millipede is one of those animals that spends most of its life eating. Some consume 10 per cent of their body weight every day of their life – and they can live a long time, up to 11 years in captivity.

Living among swarms of potential predators, millipedes rely on passive defence. Their battery of caustic or noxious chemicals, created by a complex biochemistry, is secreted as caustic vapour or glues. It doesn't always work. While some predators cannot abide them, others manage to eat millipedes without any trouble. Some of these chemicals are potentially useful. For example, glomerin, which is secreted by the Pill Millipede, is chemically similar to the synthetic chemical quaalude, used in hospitals as a sedative.

The 64 species of millipede known in Britain and Ireland are comparatively well-studied and recorded thanks to the activities of the small but busy British Myriapod and Isopod Study Group. It has even published a millipede atlas. Many species are widespread, but a few are unaccountably rare. The unlovely sounding *Unciger foetidus*, for example, is 'still known only from Dick Jones's garden in Norfolk'. *Anthogona brittanica*, found at Slapton

Millipedes *Diplopoda*

VN: coach and horses (Yorks), galley-worm, pill, pill bulldozer, thrush-lice (Yorkshire), two-heads

Millipedes fascinate us with their countless legs, wormy bodies and ability to curl up tight in a second. They move with a wonderful wave-motion of their short legs, and as with worms, it can be hard to tell their heads from their tails (even when moving, for millipedes can walk backwards as well as forwards): one of their old names was 'two-heads'. 'They far surpass all kindes of insects in the number of their feet', claimed Thomas Muffet, and were called 'many-feet, hundred-feet or thousand feet'.[45] Millipede means 'thousand-feet', though no living millipede has that many legs. The champion boasts an impressive 750 legs (i.e., 375 pairs), but most possess fewer than 50. A millipede differs from

Roly-polies: the pill millipede is able to curl up tight and resembles a woodlouse.

Ley in Devon in 1993, has been found nowhere else in the world. Another tiny, soil-living species, *Adenomeris gibbosa*, was thought to be confined to Dublin until it turned up in the Chilterns.[47]

Pill millipedes, known also as 'rollers', are relatively short, fat and well-armoured and resemble pill woodlice in their ability to curl up tight (though the millipedes have many more segments – 17 or 19 compared with only 7). A modern nickname for them is 'pill bulldozers', because of their notion of going forward to push at something until it gives.[48] They can also squeeze themselves into narrow crannies, with the help of their rows of pushing, shoving legs.

Millipedes of the order Julida are what most of us would regard as typical millipedes, being long, dark and wormy, with their numerous legs well tucked in underneath. Their name comes from '*Juli*', the word used by Aristotle for this kind of tough, wormy animal, while millipede enthusiasts call them 'bulldozers' or 'rammers'. Most live in the soil, pushing their way through self-made tunnels. They have a lot of legs. One species, the Blunt-tailed Snake Millipede, has around 200, though even so, it cannot move very fast: short legs are built for shoving, not running.

A third group is the flat-backed millipedes of the order Polydesmida, which live in soil or compacted layers of dead leaves. They use their flat bodies as wedges to lift open cracks and then work in their bodies using their relatively long legs to push

themselves forward, rather like a rugby fullback. Hence they are known as 'wedgers'. When held in the hand, some species will release a pungent whiff of bitter almonds, the smell of raw cyanide. It is said that, if you put a flat-backed millipede in a jar with beetles and other bugs, the whole lot of them will be dead within the hour, apart from the millipede, which will be, as it were, whistling innocently in the corner.

In conservation circles, perhaps the best-known species is the Boring Millipede, a name bestowed on it by the charity Buglife (reflecting its burrowing abilities), to the dismay of most millipede enthusiasts, who prefer 'the Pin-head Millipede'. It is one of three rare millipedes with their own 'biodiversity action plan'.

Just a few species of millipedes are considered to be pests. In 1984, the Ministry of Agriculture thought it was worth drenching the soil with expensive and lethally toxic carbamates to get rid of them. In the days of coal fires, soot from the chimneys was used for the same purpose. The main target species is the yellow, semi-translucent Spotted-snake Millipede, which has rows of crimson glands on either side of its body. It has a taste for stored potatoes, and swarms of wireworm-like spotted creatures on the pile of half-rotten spuds in the garden will probably be this one.

Millipedes normally become a nuisance only when they enter an artificial environment, such as a heated greenhouse, which has ideal breeding conditions and few predators. Even then, it is not the native species that cause trouble so much as introduced ones, such as the flat-backed Greenhouse Millipede. On the whole, our native millipedes tend to keep a low profile, unlike the one in Japan known as the Train Millipede, which has been known to swarm on railway tracks in such numbers that locomotives slip and slide on the squashed remains. There have been reports of occasional millipede swarms in Britain, mainly in upland areas (where they have not yet been known to delay a train). A walker in Wharfedale found 'myriads' of small millipedes with a bronze-green iridescence on a hilltop, so packed together that it was impossible to make a step without crushing 'dozens' of them.[49] The cause of such occasional 'millipede plagues' is unknown.

Jack-o'-the-knives, the large, foxy-red centipede Lithobius variegatus.

Millipede relatives

Colourless creatures, no more than a centimetre long, can be common in glasshouses, as well as in the soil. They are known as 'garden centipedes' or 'greenhouse symphylans'. Technically, they are not centipedes but members of the class Symphyla, more closely related to millipedes. With their dozen or so pairs of legs (they put on an extra pair each time they moult), they move rapidly through the pores in the soil, where they feed on rotting vegetation. Symphylans can damage cultivated plants by chewing their way through rootlets and root hairs. The worst offender is *Scutigerella immaculata*, which can be a serious pest of vegetable crops and tree seedlings.

Pauropods ('small feet') are another group of tiny soil animals, no more than a millimetre long, which under a lens look like small, squat centipedes. Most have nine pairs of legs and long sensory hairs that make up for their lack of eyes; they rush around in loose soil and among rotting leaves like tiny white mice, with their antennae whirring. Because they can be extremely numerous, they are important recyclers. There may be several thousand of them living in a square metre of fertile soil, but being so tiny, they escape our notice completely.

Centipedes *Chilopoda*

VN: forty-feeter (Orkney), forty-legs (E England), Jecky forty-feet (Scot.), Jennie-hunder-feet (or legs) (Scot.), Jock wi' the monyfeet (Scot.), lad o' the knives, Maggie hunder-legs (Orkney), Maggie monny-feet, Martin o' the knives, Meg-monny-legs (N England), red fox

The extravagant legginess of centipedes is their chief distinguishing feature. Centipede means 'hundred legs', yet no species ever found has exactly that many. Arranged in pairs, at two legs per segment, their number varies from between 15 and 101 leg-pairs (though foreign centipedes can have as many as 181 pairs). Their shape and means of locomotion allow centipedes to creep through the crevices of the soil, under bark and stones and, in the case of the smaller ones, through the pores in the soil. All true centipedes are carnivores that hunt and kill their prey with poison claws. Though the largest ones can give a nip and moments of mild pain, our few cases of serious centipede bites are from foreign species lurking in imported fruit or timber or, in the recent case of a woman nipped by a 10-centimetre-long tiger centipede, in holiday luggage.

91

Centipedes attract nicknames, though these seem to be used mostly in the north. In Scotland, the centipede may be 'Maggie monny-feet' or 'Meg-monny-legs' (the names are shared with the equally multi-legged millipedes). Such names tend to characterise centipedes as feminine, as Maggie or Jenny, though in the Hebrides, they were considered male, as in 'lad o' the knives' or 'Martin of the knives', presumably a reference to the blade-like legs of the larger species. Another Hebridean name, perhaps reserved for big, coppery-brown centipedes, is 'red fox'. To some, centipedes were scary-looking creatures, whose imagined dangers could be invoked, like dragonflies, to keep children in line. In the days when children ran around all day in bare feet, they were warned to wash their toes before coming in to supper and bed, for 'otherwise the centipede will get you.'[50]

The more legs an animal has, the more co-ordination is required. Centipedes move by instinct, and, we say, if they stopped for a moment to consider how they did it, they would be unable to move. The following anonymous rhyme was quoted by Professor Ray Lankester, who had been studying centipede locomotion, in a letter to the journal *Nature* in 1889:

> The centipede was happy quite
> Until a toad in fun
> Said, 'Pray, which leg moves after which?'
> This raised its doubts to such a pitch
> It fell exhausted in a ditch,
> Not knowing how to run.[51]

The same disastrous consequences are retailed in the Scottish folk-song, 'The Wee Kirkcudbright Centipede'. The centipede, justifiably proud of her dexterity, entertains her insect neighbours with a 'beautiful little dance', which she performs without fault until a jealous spider innocently asks her how she did it. Humiliation follows:

> As legs number one and two
> Were tied to three and four,
> Legs number five and six
> Were trampled on the floor,
> Leg number fifteen
> Was attacked by number ten,
> Ninety seven and ninety eight
> Will never dance again.[52]

The moral is: never try to explain what comes naturally.

As carnivores, and hence devourers of pests,

A centipede with an animal's face doing duty as a misericord support at Winchester College, Hampshire. Late-fourteenth-century wood carving.

centipedes have a positive image. Thomas Muffet praised them for hunting down 'that most stinking creature, the wig louse' (that is, the head louse), which Muffet thought they killed with their breath. The larger sorts, thought Muffet, were of uncertain temper and were said to be venomous. One had sunk its fangs through the kid gloves of a friend and hung on his hand like a bulldog.[53]

Centipede is a collective common name for a variety of different animals. Those that conform most closely with the notion of a leggy, scurrying animal are the stone centipedes. One group has glossy, flattened bodies and 15 pairs of longish legs; these are the ones that scuttle away as you lift a stone or a piece of loose bark. The other, with 21 leg-pairs, is even faster-running and related to the giant centipedes of the tropics.

The earth centipedes, by contrast, are slender, pale and worm-like, with short legs. They are slow-moving and live among leaf litter, under the bark of dead wood and in the soil, where they are sometimes

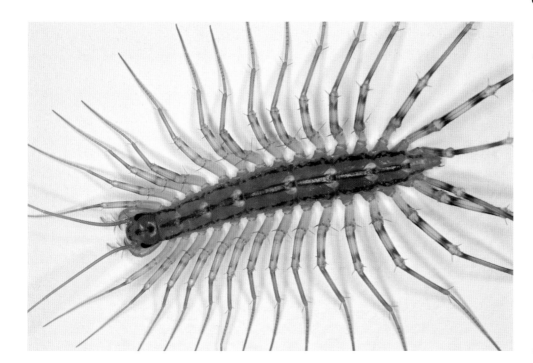

Soon to be with us? The super-leggy House Centipede.

known as 'wireworms' (a name that confuses them with certain insect larvae).

Some that cast a faint luminescence have been called 'glow-worms'. This phenomenon, which has been known since ancient times, forcibly struck the seventeenth-century naturalist William Brewer, who, wiping his face on a towel one hot night, saw it suddenly flame into phosphorescence. The source of the 'shining vapour' was a centipede, which had curled up unnoticed inside the cloth.[54] Their eerie shine suggests, wrongly, that the creatures are hot to touch, as in Michael Jackson's song, 'Centipede': '. . . when the centipede is hot/ you're bound to feel the fire'.[55]

Perhaps the most alarming-looking species found in Britain (but only just) is the House Centipede, a very long-legged centipede up to 5 centimetres long. It haunts cellars and dark, dank corners. As an outdoor animal, it is restricted to the Channel Islands, but it turns up periodically in buildings on the mainland and also in cases of imported fruit and vegetables. It will probably one day establish itself in the warmer parts of the south. House centipedes prey on small insects, including bedbugs, but their size and dramatic legginess makes them seem scary, and they can certainly bite if mishandled.

Centipedes have not made much cultural impact on our lives, though a piece of medieval stained glass at West Hallam, Derbyshire, mysteriously shows a bird with a centipede in its beak. A centipede is, however, a leading character in Roald Dahl's story *James and the Giant Peach* (1967). This story of an orphan who lives with his unpleasant aunts (his parents having been eaten by a rhinoceros) is markedly sympathetic to invertebrate-kind. A giant peach appears in the garden, enclosing a gang of well-disposed and unnaturally large 'insects'. In each case, they embody elements of folklore: the grasshopper is not only old and wise but also plays the fiddle; the ladybird is kind and motherly; the glow-worm is a living lighting-system. The odd one out is the centipede, which lacks a well-defined folk-reputation in Britain. Perhaps Dahl borrowed aspects of native American myth (the book was written and first published in America) to present the beast as an extrovert, rascally but good-natured, fond of singing and eating. Together they briskly wipe out the dreadful aunts and set off for America for fun and adventure. Rarely have invertebrates been presented in such a generous spirit: they charm the young reader without losing a millimetre of their bugginess.

The Water Springtail (Podura aquatica) *scavenges on the surface of sheltered ponds but can also leap to safety.*

Springtails *Collembola*

Springtails are tiny and hardly noticed by most people, but they occur in vast numbers in the soil, among rotting wood and leaves and in debris around the edge of ponds. The not particularly fertile soil around tussocks of grass at the edge of Irish peat bogs supports up to 64,000 springtails per square metre.[56] They are among nature's most important recyclers, releasing nutrients from rotting matter and helping to maintain the fertility of the soil (one of whose main ingredients must be springtail droppings). Without springtails, there would be very little and much less fertile soil, not much greenery and certainly not pastures and woods. We owe the British countryside to an abundance of these largely invisible and surprisingly little-known wingless creatures.

Springtails are named after their ability to bound effortlessly into the air like fleas. Their secret is a long 'spring' kept tucked under the body and used only in emergencies. Scientifically, they are known as Collembola or Collemboles, a combination of Greek words meaning 'piston glue'. It refers to a tube filled with sticky fluid on their undersides enabling them to stick to surfaces without getting stuck and to land the right way up after springing into the unknown. Experts disagree about whether springtails are insects. They have six legs but also specialised features that set them apart from other six-legged arthropods. They appear very early in the fossil record and were among the first animals to colonise the land. Four-hundred-million-year-old springtails occur together with some of the world's oldest land plants in the celebrated Rhynie Chert of Scotland, and they look remarkably similar to those you find today in the compost heap. Appropriately for such a 'living fossil', springtails are remarkably hardy. They have been recovered alive from jet-aircraft air intakes at 9245 metres.

There are around 250 species in Britain.[57] None is familiar enough to have an English name, but at least two are easy to spot and recognise. *Podura aquatica* lives around pond margins and has mastered the art of walking on water. It is bluish-grey and sausage-shaped, with a pair of stumpy antennae at the head end. Being touched with the shadow of your fingertip is all it needs to coax it to take a spring onto the safety of the bank. *Tomocerus longicornis* is, at up to six millimetres, a giant among springtails and has extravagantly long antennae, which curl up into spirals if you gently blow on them. It is common in gardens, under stones and among compost.

ARACHNIDS

Spiders *Arachnida*

VN: arran or aren (N Eng.), attercob (Cheshire), attercop or attercap (N Eng.), cob, granfer-long-legs, jinny-spinner (Isle of Man), kirstie kringlick (Orkney), meggie-spinnie (Scot.), nettercap, netterie (Scot.), speeder, spider webster (Scot.), spinnin Maggie (Scot.), wabster (Scot.), waever, weaver

Spiders – you love them or you hate them. Or perhaps you both love *and* hate them. On the one hand, you may admire them for their industry and skill at weaving complex webs and tolerate or even encourage them, since they feed on flies and other noxious insects. But on the other hand, you may not appreciate their leggy forms running over the carpet or jumping out of a box of bananas. Even if you are ambivalent about spiders, it is hard to ignore them.

The oldest invertebrate names are usually based on what a creature does. Spider means 'spinner'. It came from the Old English word *spinnan* and gradually turned into spider via the Middle English 'spither'. Spinster is effectively the same root; folk tales are full of passive heroines such as Sleeping Beauty who come to grief while spinning. Perhaps Marvel Comics' Spider Woman was invented as a feminist counterblast: Spider Woman not only sticks usefully to walls and converts bioelectric energy into 'venom blasts' but can actually time-travel (she prefers the sixth century).

Spiders were thought to be poisonous, not just in the biologically accurate sense of their toxic bites but, literally, as living bags of poison. The Saxons called them 'attercops', or 'poison heads', a name that, with variant spelling, is still sometimes used in the north. 'Cop' means head and forms the word cobweb. The name appears in *The Hobbit*, when Bilbo attempts to divert the giant spiders from eating the dwarfs by calling them insulting folk-names. No spider, explains J. R. R. Tolkien, ever likes being called 'Attercop'. There is an even more horrible spider in *The Lord of the Rings*, Shelob; 'lob' is another spider nickname, and the biggest, baddest spiders of legend are nearly always female. Tolkien, it seems safe to suggest, did not like spiders.

The folklore of spiders begins with an ancient Greek legend, told by Ovid but already old when

A watercolour of a house spider and other species by Eleazar Albin, from his Natural History of Spiders & other Curious Insects *(1736). Taking his cue from Dutch masters, he was among the first English artists to paint insects and spiders, and in exquisite detail.*

he was writing in the first century AD. The original Spider Woman, Arachne, became renowned for her skill at spinning and weaving, for she had been taught by the best in the business, the divine Athene. But Arachne made the mistake of outweaving the goddess herself, and this did not go down well. In a contest between them, Athene wove a tapestry in which the vengeful goddess Nemesis carries away those who dare to challenge the Immortals. Arachne was too absorbed in her own design to take the hint and, most unwisely, her tapestry showed the gods misbehaving like jealous children.

Understandably irritated by this impertinence, Athene tore Arachne's tapestry to shreds and beat her rival about the head with the shuttle. Arachne ran for her life and decided to end it all on a silken rope hung from the branch of a tree. Athene caught up, saw the unfortunate girl dangling there at her last gasp and turned her into a spider. 'Live on, wicked one,' said the goddess, 'but you must be suspended in the air like this, all the time. Do not hope for any respite for in the future this same condition is imposed on your race, for ever.' At this, Arachne's hair fell out, followed by her pretty nose and ears. Her head shrank almost to nothing and 'her slender fingers were fastened to her sides to serve as legs, and all the rest of her was belly; from that belly she yet spins her thread, and as a spider is busy, she yet spins her thread, and as a spider is bust with her web as of old.'

Rough justice, you might think, but the theme of Ovid's *Metamorphoses* is of the gods turning people into creatures or objects at a whim. Arachne, the champion weaver, became the prototype spider, dispensing good fortune through her spinning and fear through her ugliness and monstrous appetite.

Spiders are the most numerous members of the Arachnida, or arachnids, which also include harvestmen, scorpions, mites and ticks. They all possess eight legs, unlike insects, which have six. Spiders are solitary animals, and yet the collective name for them is a cluster. This refers not to adult spiders but to the baby spiderlings of the Garden Spider and its relatives, which cling together in a tight ball. All spiders are carnivores; they possess sharp fangs and kill their prey with a venomous bite. Another asset is a set of spinning glands, or spinnerets, which produce fine lines of silk from an internal syrup of liquid protein that instantly sets solid and waterproof on contact with the air. The female spider uses her silk to protect her young as well as to build a web, and some small species also use strands of silk to 'balloon' through the air like dandelion seeds. Not all spiders build webs, but those that do create a wide range of different types, from densely woven structures shaped like socks or purses to flimsy structures based on trip-wires. The best known are the beautiful cross-hatched thread-wheels of the Garden Spider family, which lends them the name of orb spiders.

Spider's webs are best seen shortly after dawn on a misty autumn morning, when each strand glistens with tiny beads of water. A web is usually constructed at night, and so we miss seeing the spider at work, casting its first line like a fisherman, tightening its mooring lines and finally constructing the fine mesh working from the middle outwards. Many species, including the Garden Spider, finish the whole process inside an hour. A typical orb web will contain between 20 and 60 metres of silk and yet weigh no more than a milligram and is capable of being rolled into a ball no larger than a grain of rice.

In folklore, spiders are charms that can bring good luck or, in some equally mysterious way, bestow protection. The twentieth-century authority on British spiders William Bristowe gave three instances from personal experience of people who believed passionately in the benign power of spiders. The first was a gambler he met in Monte Carlo in 1924, who always carried a spider to the casino. He kept it in a glass-topped box, half red and half black. Before a game of roulette, he rolled the box like dice to decide on which colour to place his money. Another was a well-known London tattoo artist, who on several occasions had etched a lucky spider onto the backs of young women. The third 'was a burglar with whom I came in contact in 1933. He had several small spiders tattooed on his forehead in the belief that they would bring him success in his profession.'[1]

To bring good luck, a spider must cross your path. A spider running across a wall may bring luck of a modest kind, but it is better if an airborne spider lands on your clothes. Since spiders are associated with weaving, the idea is that the spider has come to make you a new jacket or, perhaps, to mend a hole in your old one. It is only a small imaginative skip from new clothes to a gift and from a gift to cash – hence 'money spider'. 'Even timid ladies, who would faint were any creeping thing to touch them, will allow the money spider to crawl upon them with impunity, hoping that by permitting it to do so, some form of good luck will ensue', wrote Frank Gibson, the author of *Superstitions About Animals* (1904).[2]

The spider specialist Paul Hillyard has drawn on the lore of different countries, including Britain, to reveal a kind of spider code of fortune. In China, for example, a spider on the length of a long thread means that you should expect to meet a friend from far away; the longer the thread, the farther the friend. If its legs are drawn in like a clenched hand, say the

Japanese, this friend will bring a nice present, but if they are outstretched, he will arrive empty-handed. In Puerto Rico, it is lucky to see a spider climbing up a thread but unlucky to see one climbing down. If a spider crawls on to your bed, a stranger is coming. Kill the spider and he will not come (so what you do presumably depends on whether or not you want to meet this stranger). If you accidentally walk into a spider's web and it breaks across your face, it might not be a pleasant experience but it *is* lucky, at least in Kentucky. As for the bride who finds a spider on her wedding dress, she can consider herself blessed (though a spider on her neck suggests a secret lover). In Egypt, a spider is placed in the bed of a newly married couple for extra luck.[3]

None of this convinced the vengeful arachnophobes of New England, who claimed that, with every spider you killed, you killed an enemy. More level-headed folk, such as the eighteenth-century poet laureate Robert Southey, argued that spiders are our friends, if only because they trap flies:

> Spider! Thou need'st not run in fear about
> To shun my curious eyes,
> I won't humanely crush thy bowels out,
> Lest thou should'st eat the flies.[4]

'If you wish to live and thrive,' it is said, 'let a spider run alive.' Some have gone to extreme lengths to avoid hurting them. Bristowe cited a correspondent in the *Daily Express* who called on an old lady in Worthing twice a week to search her house for spiders. 'If I find any,' he said, 'I have to pick them up without harming them and deposit them in a field, some distance from her house. I am paid five shillings a visit.'[5]

In the north of England, they said:

> Kill a spider, bad luck yours will be
> Until of flies you've swatted fifty-three.

In other words, if you kill a spider, you'll need to swat your own flies. It was the same in Canada, where they say that, if you step on a spider, trouble will follow as night follows day, perhaps bad weather, perhaps a swarm of flies.

Of all people who had cause to thank the spider, none was luckier than King Frederick the Great of Prussia. The story goes that the king was making his way to the room in the Sanssouci Palace in Potsdam, where it was his custom to drink a fortifying cup of hot chocolate. He left it to cool for a moment as he visited the royal loo and, returning, found a spider floating in the cup. The king called for a fresh cup

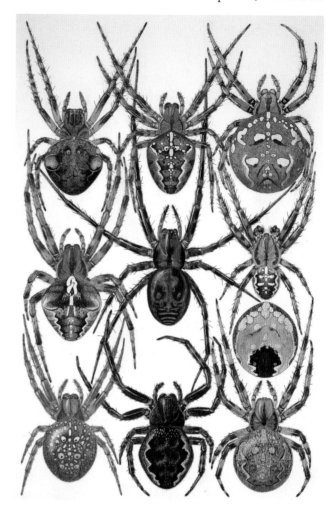

A coloured ink drawing of British orb spiders by Michael J. Roberts, a medical practitioner and the finest illustrator of spiders in our own time.

and, the next moment, heard the report of a pistol. The cook had just shot himself. It transpired that the cook had been bribed to poison the drink and, supposing his treachery to have been detected, had done away with himself. Whether or not the story is true, there is a painted spider on the ceiling of the room where King Frederick had his lucky escape.

Spiders also foretell the weather. Gabriel Oak, the shepherd in Thomas Hardy's novel *Far from the Madding Crowd*, was adept at picking up clues from nature. The 'serpentine sheen' left by a large garden slug on the kitchen table suggested stormy weather ahead, but what made it certain was 'two black spiders, of the kind common in thatched houses, promenading the ceiling, ultimately dropping to the floor'.[6] The best weather forecasters are garden spiders, and a contented spider sitting in the middle of its web is as good as a barometer for stable, sunny

A lesson in patience: Robert the Bruce and the spider, imagined by Angus McBride in 1973.

weather. But if the spider is busy like a seasoned mariner, shortening its stay-lines, bad weather is approaching. The appearance of a large number of spiders indoors means rain. Once the spider has recommenced its spinning, no more rain is likely. An abundance of webs in the grass is a sign of a fine day. In Scandinavia, they say that the height at which spiders spin their webs in the corn indicates the depth of snow in the forthcoming winter.

The spider is a maker of matchstick houses in a land of giants. Its lot is a hard one: the web that may have taken hours to construct is all too easily torn apart by a passing animal or a flick of a feather duster. Hence it is hardly surprising that the spider has been held up by many cultures as an emblem of patience and persistence. The folk-tale of Robert the Bruce and the spider is so well known that, in *1066 and All That*, the spider becomes the king's key ally at the Battle of Bannockburn. When he encountered the spider, the great Scottish leader was at the low point in his fortunes, on the run from his enemies and taking refuge in a cave. As he sat there despondently weighing his options, Bruce spotted the spider trying to spin a web across the entrance. Time after time it failed to connect with the far side, but with the persistence of its kind, it finally succeeded on the seventh try. Duly inspired, the future hero took heart, decided to have one more go at defeating the English and strode off to

glory (inevitably breaking the spider's web in the process). The legend is, of course, an object lesson along the lines of 'If at first you don't succeed, try, try and try again.'

There are several 'King's Caves' where Bruce is supposed to have met his spider. In one of them, on the Isle of Arran, William Bristowe watched the faltering steps of an orb spider, *Zygiella x-notata* on the roof of the cave.[7] Sir Walter Scott, who perpetuated the tale and made it famous, claimed that no one by the name of Bruce would ever intentionally injure a spider – and, he added, it would be a foul crime if he did.

The Bruce legend may be based on a Biblical folk-legend about David and Saul. David had fallen out with King Saul and, being pursued and in fear of his life, took refuge in a cave. There God sent a spider to spin a web over the cave's mouth. When Saul and his soldiers came up to search the cave, Saul saw the web and, reasoning that its intact state proved that no one could have entered the cave recently, called off his men. The moral is that tiny, apparently feeble creatures nevertheless have their uses.

The dark side of spiders is expressed through arachnophobia – one of the commonest of human fears, and perhaps most of us have at least a little of it. Many would think twice before handling a house spider, not to mention a big hairy tarantula. Charles Kingsley knew a naturalist who, after 'petting and admiring all day long every uncouth and venomous beast', could not avoid 'a paroxysm of horror at the sight of a common house spider.'[8] The wildlife photographer Stephen Dalton had a lifelong fear of them, having been bitten at the age of four. He eventually overcame his phobia by enrolling on a field course on spiders.[9]

The true arachnophobe, however, is one who is absolutely terrified of spiders, big or small. Paul Hillyard, former curator of arachnids at the Natural History Museum, London, knew of a sufferer who could not even write the word 'spider': 'I daren't put my handbag on the floor in case a spider crawled into it . . . I could never go into a room until someone else had made sure there were no spiders inside.'[10]

Of course, there is no rational ground for such fear, least of all in Britain, where far more people have been stung by wasps or bees or pricked by mosquitoes or horseflies than have been bitten by spiders (and the bite of even the largest native spiders is not dangerous). In places such as Papua New Guinea or the Amazon, where there are big, frightening spiders, the native people have no fear of them; on the contrary, they catch and eat spiders.

Extreme arachnophobia is often associated with a nasty incident in childhood, such as that of Aunt Ada Doom in *Cold Comfort Farm,* who had once 'seen something nasty in the woodshed' (we never find out what, but no doubt it was a spider). Parents would discourage children from going to forbidden places on the grounds that there might be spiders lurking there. Hillyard suggested there were three reasons why people fear spiders, none of which have anything to do with legs, hairiness or toxicity. One may be an inherited tendency within a family to be anxious or nervous. Another is that some have been conditioned to fear spiders through an unpleasant experience, especially in childhood, such as a spider being dropped inside a shirt. Finally, Hillyard suggests that people may associate spiders with dirt, along with creatures such as slugs, cockroaches and maggots. Spiders are in fact clean and fastidious animals, but folk-memories of spiders as dark, malign 'insects' still run deep.

One of our contributors admitted that she was terrified of spiders. 'I am not in the least afraid of their bite. Nor does size have anything to do with it, for I'm just as frightened of tiny spiders as large ones. It's the legs: eight legs. I can tell if it's an insect, such as a daddy-longlegs, in a split second, and then I'm fine. But I'm equally frightened of crabs with eight legs. I will not set a foot on the grass if I spot a spider there.'

Perhaps our most arachnophobic poet was John Byrne Leicester Warren, a clergyman who was knowledgeable about insects and flowers (he compiled a *Flora* of his native Cheshire) but was more concerned with the revealed 'theology' of insects than their biological role. Hence Warren saw angelic beauty in the wings of a housefly and bees as little elves, but regarded the spider as demonic, an 'insect ghoul', with its 'venom mouth' and 'paunch grown sleek with sacrifice'. In 'The Study of a Spider', the creature is accused of most of the deadly sins, including drunkenness and gluttony (the 'glutton of creation's sighs', the 'toper' in his 'lonely feasting chair'), avarice ('miser of many miseries'), lust ('thou type of selfish lechery') and cruelty ('thy felon anchorite of pain').[11]

The innate wickedness of spiders was indicated by the venom they carry. They were considered to be deadly poisonous, like a toxic berry; a Professor Ross of Aberdeen is said to have died from the effects of swallowing a spider floating in his glass of claret. To Thomas Wyatt, the one-time lover of Anne Boleyn, the spider was a kind of anti-bee, a dark bug that turned the natural order on its head by gathering poison from a flower:

> Nature, that gave the bee so feat a grace
> To find honey of so wondrous fashion,
> Hath taught the spider out of the same place
> To fetch poison, by strange alteration.[12]

In 1616, there was a celebrated trial in which the Earl and Countess of Somerset were accused of procuring the death of a royal favourite, Sir Thomas Overbury, with the help of seven deadly spiders (the mystic number seven deepened the toxicity of the dose). In reality, as it transpired during the course of the trial, the unfortunate Sir Thomas had been murdered with seven different kinds of poison, among them arsenic, powdered diamonds and nitric acid. Four suspects, including the apothecary from whom these substances were obtained, were condemned and hanged, but the Somersets, being of a higher order, were merely imprisoned and eventually pardoned. The murderers, whoever they were, presumably took it for granted that spiders are every bit as dangerous as nitric acid or rat poison.

St Patrick, it is said, used his influence with God to banish all noxious beasts from the Emerald Isle. These included venomous spiders. Apparently the ban was so successful that spiders fear the very earth and timbers of Ireland. The roof timbers of Westminster Hall are said to have come from Ireland, and according to one Matthew Hanmer, writing in 1633, 'no English spider webbeth or breedeth [there] to this day':

> Happy Ierne, whose most wholesome air
> Poisons envenomed spiders, and forbids
> The baleful toad and viper from her share.

A venomous spider appears in the life of St Norbert, an eleventh-century German-born priest and preacher, whose emblem is a chalice, or 'monstrance'. According to the story, the holy man spotted a spider floating in a cup of sacramental wine as it was passed to him at Communion. Since pausing to evict the creature would be sacrilegious, he courageously drank the wine, along with the spider, and by a miracle remained unharmed. Perhaps Shakespeare had the tale in mind when he gave these lines to Leontes in *The Winter's Tale*:

> There may be in the cup
> A spider steeped, and one may drink, depart,
> And yet partake no venom.[13]

There are now gadgets available for those who want to evict spiders without harming them. One is the Bug Vacuum. Basically a low-power vacuum cleaner, it gently sucks the spider into a tube and releases it unharmed at the flick of a button. Another device works on the principle of ultrasound, a sonic pitch that cannot be heard by humans or their pets but is said to be unbearable to spiders. You plug one of these into the mains and, so claim the makers, your home life will be spider free.

Among the traditional spider repellents are conkers, which contain soap-like chemicals that deter clothes moths and, evidently, do the same for spiders. Helpfully, the conker season coincides with the time (their mating season) when house spiders are most likely to be seen running along the floor. The conkers are placed along their runs and in the corners of the room; old copper pennies were also said to do the trick.

In America, some use the fruit of the Osage orange tree, also called 'hedge apples' or 'monkey balls', to ward off spiders. The fruit is aromatic, and spiders supposedly dislike the smell and so keep away. Hanging Osage oranges on your walls is also said to work with other unwanted invertebrates, such as cockroaches, mosquitoes and mites.

The spider and the fly

> 'Will you walk into my parlour?' said the spider
>   to the fly;
> ''Tis the prettiest little parlour that ever you did
>   spy.
> The way into my parlour is up a winding stair,
> And I have many curious things to show you
>   when you're there.'
> 'Oh no, no,' said the little fly, 'to ask me is in
>   vain,
> For who goes up your winding stair can ne'er
>   come down again.'
> Mary Howitt, *The Spider and the Fly* (1821)

In folklore, the spider conveys the spirit of wiliness, but a spider with a fly embodies something different: covetousness. Much as people admired the energy and artistry that spiders devote to their webs, weaving a trap and waiting for victims seems to us a sinister way of life. Just as bad is the spider's use of

The spider and the fly, *by Arthur Rackham, from a 1912 edition of* Aesop's Fables.

poison to subdue its prey. But the final ingredient in the devil's cocktail is sex. In rhymes about the spider and the fly, it is implied, if not explicitly stated, that the spider is female and the fly male. The one thing everyone knows about female spiders is that they are apt to eat their mates during what Victorians called 'the act of love'.

For all these reasons, spiders were the stuff of nightmares. Carl Jung claimed that the appearance of spiders in dreams is a sign of an unconscious obsession with suicide. For Freud, however, dream-spiders symbolise the Mother and, more generally, a feeling of inferiority to women. The writer Primo Levi put it this way:

'The capturing technique of the spider who covers with filaments the prey caught in a web supposedly turns it into a maternal symbol: the spider is the enemy-mother who envelops and encompasses, who wants to make us re-enter the womb from which we have issued, bind us tightly to take us back to the impotence of infancy, subject us again to her power; and there are those who remember that in almost all languages the spider's name is feminine, that the larger and more beautiful webs are those of female spiders.'[14]

A Common House Spider in the bath – a male, as is usually the case.

The spider in the bath

Many of us are familiar with the spider in the bath that leers at us first thing in the morning (it seems even larger than normal when outlined against clean white enamel – on which the spider may have left some unpleasant excretory spots). Flanders and Swann mocked the moment when our bleary eyes make contact with our nemesis:

> What a frightful looking beast –
> Half an inch across at least –
> It would frighten even Superman or Garth.
> There's contempt it can't disguise
> In the little beady eyes
> Of the spider glowering in the bath.[15]

What is so awful about the spider in the bath? Perhaps it is knowing we are going to have to fish it out (is it too big to wash down the plughole, and if we did, would it come back?). Perhaps there is a sense that it is waiting there for us, as though we were the fly and the bath its ambitious web. It turns a place of comfort and security into a hostile zone. Yet we are reluctant to squash it.

How does the spider get there? House spiders tend to like dark, secluded corners, not the brightest room in the house. Yet, despite their skill as silk-spinners and trapeze artists, spiders have accidents like the rest of us. Male spiders may wander into the

bathroom under cover of darkness, perhaps looking for a mate or attracted by the insects drawn by the bathroom light, and slip helplessly down the steep, smooth-sided surface. Possibly they may also be enticed there by moisture, for even house spiders sometimes get thirsty in the desert-dry environment of the home. But it is unlikely that the spider got there by crawling out of the plughole or overflow. Modern drains contain a liquid-filled sediment trap through which spiders cannot penetrate. And few spiders can swim.

Despite the unlikelihood of spiders living in water pipes, it has become one of the accepted idioms of spider lore. Many small children perhaps first learn about spiders from 'Incy wincy spider', the unfrightening but ticklish spider in the drainpipe. As you chant the words, you make a creepy-crawly spider motion up the child's arm:

> Incy wincy spider
> Crawled up the water spout.
> Down came the rain
> And washed the spider out.
> Out came the sun
> And dried up all the rain
> And incy wincy spider
> Crawled up the spout again.

'Itsy bitsy spider' is the American version, which is starting to sweep 'incy wincy' under the carpet. Other versions of the rhyme are closer to the unsentimental realities of spider life, such as:

> Incy wincy spider was looking for his lunch.
> Along came a wasp, he was eaten with a munch.
> Then came a bluebottle and landed in the thread,
> So incy wincy spider bit off his head.[16]

A spider that lives in a water pipe is the star of the children's animated series *Spider*, following the fortunes of a simple spider whose slogan is 'I'm only scary 'cos I'm hairy.' First broadcast in 13 five-minute episodes on BBC in 1991, it became a cult hit from the beauty of its drawings and the poignancy of its storylines. The spider, which lives in a water pipe in the bathroom, wants only a quiet life but is constantly being pestered by a mischievous small boy, who eventually becomes its friend. The spider's world is presented as vignettes from a picture book using soft-crayoned colours against white backgrounds. Its soliloquies are vocalised through music by Rick Cassman to suit the occasion, sometimes rock 'n' roll, sometimes haunting and full of melancholy.

Little Miss Muffet, *by a playful Rex Whistler. As the spider drops down, the eyes snap open.*

Little Miss Muffet and her dad

> Little Miss Muffet sat on a tuffet
> Eating her curds and whey.
> Along came a spider and sat down beside her
> And frightened Miss Muffet *away.*

A tuffet is either a small stool with a cushion or just a grassy mound. We are not told what kind of spider it was that sat down beside Miss Muffet, though clearly it was a large one. In the pictures it is usually at least the size of a cat.

The rhyme first appeared in print in 1805 in *Songs for the Nursery*, but it is probably much older. There was a real Miss Muffet in an appropriate context: Patience Muffet, the step-daughter of Thomas Muffet, the Elizabethan physician and proto-entomologist. Did little Patience have a reason to be wary of spiders? As his great book, *The Theatre of Insects*, reveals, Muffet senior was not simply tolerant of the spidery 'tapestry and hangings' in his half-timbered home but felt an affinity with them that borders on the sensual: 'The skin [of the spider] is so soft,' he wrote, 'so smooth, polished and neat, that she precedes the softest skin'd Mayds, and the daintiest and most beautiful Strumpets … she hath fingers that the most gallant Virgins desire to have theirs like them, long, slender, round, of exact feeling, that there is no man, nor any creature, that can compare with her.'

In praise of the spider, Muffet proceeded, systematically, to set before his readers 'the riches of its body, then of its fortunes, [and] lastly of its mind'.[17] To Muffet, the spider was a treasure chest of cures and remedies. Whatever the malady, he had a spider cure to match it:

1. Wrapped in a linen cloth and hung from the left arm, the 'flie-catching spider' drives away Quotidian fevers. The cure is even more effective when the spider is boiled in oil of bay to the consistency of a liniment and spread onto the arteries of wrists, arms and temples.

2. If you suffer from earache, boil three more spiders alive in whatever oil is leftover from the fever-cure and use it, warm, as eardrops.

3. If you 'bruise' a spider (i.e., mash it to a pulp), then spread it onto a cloth and apply to the temples, you can say goodbye to headaches.

4. Stuffing a dead house spider inside a nutshell or piece of leather and hanging it around your neck or arm is a sensible precaution against the onslaughts of the tertiary fever.

5. The running of the eyes can be prevented with eyedrops made from the dung or urine of spiders mixed with oil of roses, 'whereby you may know there is nothing so filthy in a spider that is not good for something'.

6. Gout sufferers can be helped by the 'laying on' of spiders. You must take good care to ensure that neither the sun nor the moon are shining at the time, and that you have first ripped off the 'hinder pair legs' of the spider. Those who preserve spider's webs at home, observed Muffet, rarely catch the gout.

7. Fresh wounds should be plastered with spider's webs 'for it binds, cools, dries, glutinates, and will let no putrefaction continue there'. Also, applied to 'the swellings of the fundament, it consumes them without pain'.

8. Failing all that, one should try mashing up some spiders and eating them with a spoon.

'O the wonderful virtue of a poor contemptible creature', concluded Muffet. It is in this context that we should consider why Little Miss Muffet was so frightened by the spider. The rhyme may have originated as a well-aimed satirical swipe at the good doctor.

Spider 'factoids'

Oliver Rackham defined a 'factoid' as something that is widely regarded as a fact and resembles a fact in every way except one: that it isn't true. There are more 'urban legends' about spiders than any other group of animals. Here is a selection. We repeat: everything that follows is untrue.

1. *You unknowingly swallow up to four live spiders in your sleep each year.* Others say you swallow 20 live spiders over a lifetime – which, at four per year, would imply a tragically short life. The most alarming version of the myth claims that we may swallow as much as a pound of spiders – at least 20,000 of them – over a lifetime, which would imply a veritable army of spiders marching regularly into your open, snoring mouth. In fact, there does not seem to be a foundation for swallowing even one spider while asleep (a spider hiding in your ear or up your nose is marginally more likely). Unconscious spider-swallowing is a myth.

2. *Spiders drink moisture from your mouth or lips or possibly your eyes, as you sleep.* Spiders, like bogeymen, are scarier in the dark. As they used to say in New York City, 'A spider by day is quite okay/ but a spider at night should cause you flight.'

3. *The average person sees 50 species of spiders in a lifetime.* One wonders how such statistics are arrived at. The number of people who could identify 50 different kinds of spider must be fairly limited. For the record, 81 species of spiders and harvestmen were found in urban gardens in Sheffield.[18]

4. *In June 2001, telephone engineers found 'swarms' of spiders in utility tunnels beneath the Queen's apartments at Windsor Castle.* They were told to stop working until the beasts could be identified, but before that could happen 'an expert entomologist' was wheeled out to assert that the spiders were probably a new species or at least one

that had been extinct for thousands of years. The tabloids presented them as 'giant', 'aggressive' and 'venomous'. One suggested that their lairs should be sought out 'by electronic mole cameras' and the spiders transported, one by one, to a 'safer' location, since they obviously posed a real danger not only to BT engineers but perhaps also to the royal family.[19] It was a great fuss about very little. The spiders were real but they were a known species, the European Cave Spider, a plain brown orb-spinner that has never bitten anything larger than a fly. Perhaps they looked bigger in the dark.

5. *The Daddy-longlegs Spider has the world's most powerful venom. Fortunately it cannot bite you because its jaws are too small.* This nonsense was reported as fact by several national newspapers as well as the television news. The alleged toxicity of the spider was transferred in people's minds to the Daddy-longlegs cranefly. There was talk of the terrible consequences of accidentally swallowing one while asleep. The Daddy-longlegs spider, like all spiders, uses venom to subdue its prey, but the truth is that its poison is weaker than that of the average spider. The jaws of a large one could, in theory, pierce human skin, though the sensation would be no worse than a pin-prick.

6. *Tarantula spiders can jump three to four feet.* Tarantulas can lunge at their prey in an eye-blink, but only from a few centimetres, and they cannot jump. A large spider that fell or was dropped from a metre or so would be at risk of serious injury. This is chiefly of interest to anyone keeping a large, hairy spider as a pet.

7. *Soft bubble gum contains spider legs.* In the mid-seventies, a kind of gum came onto the market that produced a satisfactory bubble after only a languid chew or two. Called Bubble Yum, it was a spectacular commercial success. Then word went round that the gum was soft because it used spider parts, possibly the legs or, alternatively, spider 'eggs'. There were playground horror stories about gum-chewing youngsters waking up in the morning with spider's webs all over their faces. Another, less well-circulated rumour claimed that the gum caused cancer. This proved more than enough for the sales to crash. The company had no choice but to try to counter the rumours with an expensive advertising campaign, under the tagline: 'Someone is telling very bad lies about a very good product.' It worked, and sales crept up again. How did spiders ever come into it? Probably because children asked themselves: 'Why is it so chewy, why does it feel so slippery in the mouth?' and came up with a scary solution that brought a delicious tingle down the spine. What could be more slippery than spider's eggs?

8. *Deadly poisonous spiders lurk beneath toilet seats in airports. According to a widespread rumour, three women were hospitalised and later died. All of them had visited the same restaurant at Chicago Airport, and all were reported to have a puncture wound on the right buttock.* In true Sherlock Holmes fashion, a toxicologist, remembering an article he had read, investigated the restaurant and found a small spider, later identified as a 'South American Blush Spider, *Arachnius gluteus*', hiding in the loo. The case became famous through the internet, and airport users were warned: 'Please, before you use a public toilet, lift the seat to check for spiders. It could save your life!' The story was a hoax that exploited our feelings of vulnerability. There is no such thing as a South American Blush Spider.[20]

9. *Spiders can lay eggs in your body.* A person, usually a woman, is bitten on the cheek by a spider. Some time later, she develops a swelling from which, in due course, baby spiders emerge. In his book *Dancing Naked in the Mind Field*, the Nobel Prize-winning chemist Kary Mullis claimed that a certain kind of spider bites its human victim and then brings along its babies to feed on the wound. Proof of this biologically unlikely story is still lacking.

10. *Spiders love music.* Bristowe dismissed such sentimentality as 'cupboard love', but spiders are undoubtedly sensitive to vibrations. Orb spiders are thrown into excitement if their webs are touched with a tuning fork, and it is said that a violinist can draw the same response. But what the spiders 'love' is not music but the prospect of another meal.

Maman, *Louise Bourgeois's towering maternal arachnid, 'like a creature escaped from a dream.'*

Spiders in art and literature

To occupy the spaces of the Tate Modern's vast hall in the former power station on London's Bankside, the gallery commissioned a suitably eye-catching piece of art: a spider more than 10 metres high. It had a short, round body and vast, spindly legs straddling the hall. Called *Maman*, it is the work of the French-born artist Louise Bourgeois. At first sight, it has a fearsome, Black Widow-like presence, 'like a creature escaped from a dream', the very embodiment of secret childhood terrors. Then one notices the counterintuitive details, the pure white marble eggs protected by the monster's cage-like body and the way that the spider's body conveys a poignant sense of motherhood and surprising vulnerability. *Maman* means 'mummy'. Louise Bourgeois's own mother, a talented spinner and weaver, had run a tapestry restoration business in Paris; long after her death, she remains a profound psychological presence in the artist's work, in which the spider is a metaphor for maternal virtues: nurture, patience, protection and industriousness. 'The spider is an ode to my mother,' said Bourgeois of her early drawings of surreal, long-legged, dream-like arachnids.[21] The drawings later became gigantic sculptures cast in bronze and steel,

exhibited at galleries from Ottawa to Leningrad. They are immensely popular, and *Maman* is now on permanent guard outside the Tate Modern, with a view of the dome of St Paul's visible through her tottering legs.

As if to make them less leggy and intimidating, some art images of spiders drop two of their legs, which has the effect of making the spider more insect-like, if not less frightening. An example is the Wren and Spider Roundel, a circular piece of stained glass in the Zouche Chapel of York Minster. Painted in the sixteenth century, it shows a wren, identifiable from its erect tail feathers, investigating a six-legged orb spider in its web. Its significance is unknown – perhaps it illustrates a forgotten proverb – but it is one of the favourite images of the Minster. Nearby is a second, anatomically correct, spider sitting on St James's hat. A spider and a fly also appear on a stained-glass window in the parish church at Merton, Norfolk. As the legend '*Loquimur fugit hora*' ('while we speak, time flies') makes clear, it is a pun. The sense is that we talk too much.

A second giant spider, created by another French artist, François Delarozière, was drafted in to inaugurate Liverpool's year as the cultural capital of Europe in September 2008. This 15-metre, 37-tonne

A six-legged spider and a wren in medieval stained glass from the Zouche Chapel, York Minster.

arachnid made from reclaimed steel and poplar wood, was hailed as the largest piece of free theatre ever staged in the UK. The show began with the spider being hoisted onto a redundant office block close to the city's central railway station to greet the morning's commuters as they emerged into the street. Later, having been 'woken' by fireworks and smoke, it danced on the spot in a convincingly tarantula-like way, before trundling off down the street at a dignified three kilometres per hour; one team of technicians perched on the top, close to the monster's unspider-like water cannon, and another sat under its belly pulling the levers that operated the joints in its hydraulic limbs. Despite the pouring rain, the spectacle was considered excellent entertainment – inspiring, according to the *Daily Mail*, highly pleasurable 'terror and awe' wherever it went. Entomologists felt less comfortable with the press statement describing the great beast as 'an insect'.[22]

Not all spiders are monstrous and terrifying. Spiders don't come nicer than Charlotte in E. B. White's classic children's story *Charlotte's Web* (1952). The wise, grey 'barn spider' learns that a lonely pig called Wilbur has a date with a human family, the Zuckermans, on 25 December – it is to be their Christmas dinner. She saves the pig by weaving complimentary words about Wilbur – 'SOME PIG', etc. – in her webs. These have the desired effect: Wilbur is spared and goes on to win prizes at the county fair. Charlotte, though, having only a spider's short life, duly expires, but not before the pig has adopted her batch of eggs. Though the animals of *Charlotte's Web* have human intelligence, they still behave as animals. Charlotte traps flies and sucks out their body fluids, and there is nothing Wilbur likes more than to wallow in lukewarm filth. The story was made into a cartoon feature in 1973 and, using more convincing digital animation, into a film in 2006.

The beneficial side of spiders has also been enlisted by advertisers. The Lenor range of fabric-softeners showed a friendly spider dangling by a thread next to an unafraid mother and child with the tag line: 'Along came a spider/ Who was quick to provide her/ Lenor for delicate skin.' What can be finer than spider silk?

In films, spiders tend to be portrayed more negatively. In *Arachnophobia* (1990), venomous spiders invade a small American town. The trouble is caused by a 'queen' who lurks inside the coffin of the person she bit during a trip to the Amazon.

Escaping, she mates with local spiders to create a deadly hybrid race, which run amok and bite people left, right and centre. Finally, the queen is traced to a basement where the film's hero, overcoming his terror of spiders, manages to kill her. The film was an exercise in a new genre of horror-comedy, 'scared but laughing'. The sounds of spiders being stepped on and squashed were reproduced by scrunching potato crisps or, for the larger, squishier ones, by jumping on tubes of mustard. The arachnid stars of *Arachnophobia* were played by professional Avondale hunting spiders from New Zealand, chosen for their large size and social habits. They are, as it happens, completely harmless. The same species also put in an appearance at the start of the 2002 film *Spiderman*.

Spider surveys

Spiders attract a small but dedicated band, never more than a few hundred strong, who spend their spare time studying and recording them. Most are members of the British Arachnological Society, which formed in 1968 as the successor body of the Flatford Mill Spider Group. Today, it has about 500 members, half of them in Britain and half living overseas. In 2002, the society published a provisional distribution atlas of 648 species of British spiders. Spider specialists are blessed by an erudite and unusually readable literature, with masterpieces by Theodore Savory, William Bristowe and Paul Hillyard.[23] The standard identification guide, Michael J. Roberts's three-volume *Spiders of Great Britain and Ireland*, is a work of art; so is Stephen Dalton's collection of spider images, *Spiders: The ultimate predators* (2008).

Many spiders are elusive, and surveying them demands patience and equipment more elaborate than the entomologist's traditional bag-net and jam-jar. Peter Smithers of Plymouth University hunts them with a suction sampler, 'a modified, petrol-driven Hoover' that sucks invertebrates out of the vegetation and into a fine mesh bag. It resembles a rocket launcher, sounds like a chain-saw and gets steadily heavier as the spider-hunter's day wears on.

Orb web spiders *Araneidae*

An orb web spun by the Garden spider or one of its relations is among the most ephemeral of animal creations, yet also among the most beautiful – delicate, mysterious and enchanting. The webs are most prominent in early autumn when the spider is fully grown. One spider regularly builds a web over my front-door frame. It is regularly broken by the milkman or the postman (being soft-hearted, I use the back door), but by the next day, with inexhaustible patience and determination, the spider is sitting, head-down as usual, in the middle of a fresh one, and continues to renew her web whenever it is broken until the time comes when she wanders into the hedge to lay her eggs. Some say (wrongly) that a spider eats its web every night, along with anything trapped in it, and spins a fresh one every morning. An old kid's trick to get a Garden spider to show itself is to tickle a strand of the web with a grass blade so the spider thinks it has caught something. It works best with a fresh-made web; if a web looks dilapidated, the spider is probably old and past caring, or dead.

The Garden spider is the best known of all spiders and the one with the most wholesome reputation. It is also called the Diadem, or Cross, Spider from the pattern of dots on its back (they are technically swollen cells filled with guanine, a protein byproduct). In times past, this marked them as a holy talisman, which had the reputation – in parts of Europe, at least – of being a good-luck charm. Even today one can buy necklaces with a little golden orb spider in place of a cross. We perhaps value it more today as a gardener's friend, since it traps harmful insects.

Much of what we think we know about spiders, including the difficulties faced by male spiders, comes from the behaviour of just this one species. The male is much smaller than its mate, and its courtship of the plump matron in the centre of the web is fraught with risk. William Bristowe likened the male spider's tentative swings on a special mating thread to 'a trapeze artist at a circus who decides at the last moment not to entrust himself to a partner who is waiting to grasp him.'[24]

Several other plump orb spiders are common in gardens. The Four-spotted Orb-weaver has a square-shaped arrangement of spots, while the Walnut Orb-weaver has a dark, flattened, crenellated body. The jaws of fully grown female orb spiders are technically capable of breaking the human skin,

An Orb spider at the centre of its web on a dewy autumn morning.

A ball of 'spiderlings', or baby Garden spiders. They will eventually disperse with the help of silken parachute threads.

The Wasp spider, with its characteristic zigzag web.

but these spiders are not aggressive and rarely bite. According to the Natural History Museum, a nip from the Walnut Orb-weaver feels 'like a prick from a bramble thorn'. Far worse is the sensation of walking into a large web at head height, one of the things that tend to happen on those days when nothing goes right.

The exotic-looking Wasp spider has vivid yellow and black bands that always attract attention. Recently it appeared so plentifully in gardens in the London area that it created a record number of calls to the spider department of the Natural History Museum. Its webs, slung well down among the grass stalks in warm, sheltered corners, are positioned to catch the spider's favourite prey, grasshoppers. It is sometimes known as the St Andrew's Cross spider, from the way it holds its legs in an X-shape when at rest, or the Writing spider, from the way it seems to form letters in its web (mainly zigzag ones like N and Z). The Wasp spider lives up to its name in other ways. If mishandled, a large female can deliver a bite as sharp as a nettle sting.

House spiders *Agelenidae*

VN: cobweb spider, funnel spider

House spiders make sheet-like dusty cobwebs and frighten us when they run across the carpet. They are built for running and at one time held the world spider record for speed, though large ones can only sustain this for a few seconds before collapsing in exhaustion (the current record is held by a tropical spider relative, a solifugid, or sun spider, that can outrun a human over very short distances).

There are six British species of house spider (their scientific genus name *Tegenaria* comes from the Latin word for mat, a reference to the shape of their webs rather than their readiness to step indoors). Only two or three of the species enter houses; the commonest is *Tegenaria domestica*, but the biggest is *T. gigantea*, the Giant House spider – both leggy creatures that make us pull up our own legs as they scuttle by. It is the slender, speedy male spiders that we see most often. The more reclusive female spins a tubular retreat behind wardrobes and fittings, in wall and floor spaces or rooms that are seldom used. The well-meaning action of arachnophiles in catching these spiders and releasing them outdoors is misplaced. They belong indoors and will either come straight back in again or perish from cold. Over the centuries, house spiders have become virtually cosmopolitan. They have been carried from country to country in the cargoes of ships and railways, and from house to house on furniture and building materials.

The other species of house spider are more at home outdoors, though they sometimes enter a garage or outhouse. They frequent garden log piles or lurk under bark or wood chips or holes in banks. The biggest of them all is the Cardinal spider, whose hairy legs may, at full stretch, span a saucer (it is one of the world's bigger spiders). But the Cardinal spider is mostly leg with a small body. It is named after Cardinal Wolsey, who is said to have been terrified by them as they raced across the tapestries, looking twice as large by flickering candlelight. In Leicester, where Wolsey lies buried, they say that every time you step on a house spider, the Cardinal stirs in his grave.

Though house spiders rarely bite, a large female can deliver a sharp nip to a finger, which can be psychologically upsetting. In America, the Yard Spider, *T. agrestis*, known there as the Hobo spider, has changed its normally timid behaviour to become

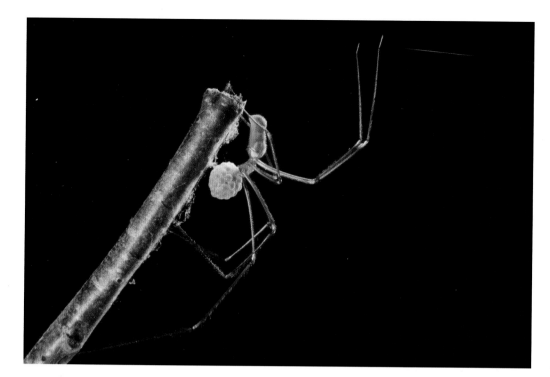

A Pholcus, or Daddy-longlegs spider, carrying eggs.

notorious for biting with little provocation when cornered or threatened. Perhaps the colder winters of North America have forced it indoors. The way to deal with it, they say, is to encourage the slightly bigger Giant House spider, which is not aggressive to humans but will soon evict its rival.

'In our family all big hairy house spiders are called johnny spiders and boris spiders.'[25]

Daddy-longlegs spider

AN: cellar spider, daddy long-legger, Pholcus, vibrating spider

Many homes are now the abode of a smaller spider, which hangs motionless from a scaffolding of fine, barely visible threads among roof beams and undusted corners. This is Pholcus, or the Daddy-longlegs spider, formerly known as the 'cellar spider', a slow-moving beast with a slim, curved body and slim front legs, which it uses like fingers to probe its surroundings (its scientific name, *Pholcus phalangioides,* means 'squint-eyed and finger-like'). It is also known as the 'vibrating spider', from its entertaining habit when threatened of swaying rapidly from side to side to create a visual blur, making it more difficult for a predator to know where to snap or stab. Where Pholcus roams the ceiling, you are less likely to suffer from house spiders. As it fingers its way slowly across the wall,

it is able to rob webs of their prey and even take fellow spiders unawares. I try as far as possible to leave Pholcus in peace. You scarcely notice its webs, and they come in useful when gnats and other annoying insects invade your personal space.

Until recently, Pholcus lived mainly in cellars, but in the past few decades, it has moved upstairs, probably in response to a warming climate or perhaps central heating. Its increase was logged by the young Bristowe, who, as soon as he could afford a motorbike, 'zigzagged across England ostensibly seeking rooms in hotels or lodgings whose ceilings I viewed with nonchalant interest . . . their unwitting cooperation enabled me to draw a map which showed that *Pholcus* inhabited houses coinciding with the narrow southern strip where the average temperature throughout the year exceeds 50 degrees F. North of this strip she is normally confined to cellars.'[26] Since then, the Pholcus strip has moved steadily north towards the Scottish border.

A persistent urban legend insists that Pholcus has more potent venom than other spiders and that we risk inadvertently swallowing one at night. Tests have shown that, while an exceptionally large Pholcus could theoretically pierce human skin, its venom is, in fact, below par by everyday spider norms.[27] Another legend asserts it is not a true spider at all. It is, but Pholcus is often confused with craneflies or harvestmen, which share its common name.

Money spiders *Linyphidiidae*

AN: dwarf spiders, money-spinners (Kent), sheet weavers

In 1939, William Bristowe took a close look at a grass field near Bexhill in Sussex. It had not been heavily grazed or disturbed by ploughing for several years, and Bristowe expected there to be a lot of tiny spiders hidden among the tussocks and surface litter. But even he, the foremost expert on British spiders, was taken aback by just how many. By taking samples from different parts of the field and averaging them out, he calculated a density of between 400,000 and 800,000 spiders per acre that spring. By the following autumn, their numbers had increased to around a million per acre, and in some places, half as many again. Being a methodical man – Bristowe was an industrial chemist and knew all about statistics – he repeated the exercise after two years and found that, in a good year, there might be as many as *two* million spiders to the acre, and

A money spider 'ballooning'.

every one of them a hungry carnivore. He assigned a cautious hundred 'victims' per year per spider and calculated that the weight of food consumed by British spiders each year would be well in excess of the combined weight of the British human population.[28] He was, in fact, ultra-conservative in his figures: garden spiders catch up to 500 small insects *per day*.

The little spiders hang, wrote Bristowe (1958), beneath 'dew-covered hammock webs of exquisite delicacy that glisten in every hedge and even amongst the close-cut grass of a garden lawn . . . fine days stir their multitude into restless activity, leaving a matted sheet of intercrossing drag-lines to cloak the fields with a mantle which shimmers in the evening sunlight like a silver sea.' Only at such times do we gain a true sense of the swarms beneath our feet. Weight for weight, spiders are the greatest consumers of insects on the planet, leaving birds far behind. The RSPB has championed the conservation of insects on the grounds that they feed birds. How much more true that is of spiders.

The vast majority of these spiders are money spiders, ant-sized dwarf spiders averaging only 2 millimetres long. They are members of the Linyphiidae, the largest family of British spiders, with around 250 species and more discovered almost annually. Small though they are, they spin hanky-sized sheet, or hammock, webs in the grass, which are much more prominent when spangled with dew in the morning – some fields can look like one great web. Each individual web is a slightly raised dome anchored to grass with scaffolding threads, strands of silk described by Robert Burton as 'bright ephemeral lines – all length and no thickness'.[29]

Money spiders are light enough to take to the air on parachute strands of silk that are blown far and wide, sometimes far into the upper atmosphere. This is why they can suddenly appear on your arm, seemingly from nowhere, and why they are called money spiders. When one lands on your clothes, or if you spot one in mid-air descending on its thread, it is a sign of good luck and prosperity. Some say you should pick up the money spider and throw it over our shoulder for luck, others that you should take its tiny thread between finger and thumb and whirl it round your head three times, which may be impossible. Alternatively, it is acceptable to put the spider in your pocket. If it dies, you must carry its tiny corpse in your shoe.[30] If the trick works, the spider will bring you money. But if harm comes to the spider, you can forget it.

Gossamer and cobwebs

VN: slammachs (Scot.), sunbeam (Cornwall), Virgin's webs

Gossamer is produced when the fine, filmy, air-light silk produced by money spiders loses its moorings and is blown into the air. From late September until the first hard frosts of winter, the web fragments take flight as the morning sun warms the ground. With exceptionally strong updrafts, practically every web in the field will break from its mooring lines and carry into the air like tiny clouds. They fall to the ground again in the cool of evening, where they catch the dew and glisten like a vast net. The rainbow effect made as the slanting early light is refracted by the myriad drops is known as a dew-bow, an earthly equivalent of a rainbow.

Only a lucky few of us, generally early risers, see what Francis Kilvert saw in early September 1875, after a long and memorably hot summer:

'The morning suddenly became glorious and we saw what had happened in the night. All night long millions of gossamer spiders had been spinning and the whole country was covered . . . The gossamer webs gleamed and twinkled into crimson and gold and green, like the most exquisite shot-silk dress in the finest texture of gauzy silver wire. I never saw anything like it or anything so exquisite as "the Virgin's webs" glowed with changing opal lights and glanced with all the colours of the rainbow.'[31]

Once aloft on a warm thermal, gossamer loses its earthly association with spiders and becomes a kind of gift of the gods. The name is old, but until the scientific age no one knew what it was. Gossamer was among the mysteries discussed over frothy tankards in Chaucer's *The Canterbury Tales*:

Sore wondren some on cause of thunder, (some wonder anxiously).
On ebb and floud, on gossamer, and on mist.[32]

Some held that it represented bits of the Virgin Mary's winding sheet that fell to earth during her assumption to heaven. Chaucer himself made a connection between gossamer, dew and clouds. The fine strands, he reasoned, were 'scorched dew' or 'filmy threads of dew evaporate', rising from the warm earth to join the clouds. This was based on certain observable facts. Gossamer did indeed form on cold, dewy nights and could be seen rising as the sun warmed the ground. As rational a scientist as the seventeenth-century polymath Robert Hooke

believed that gossamer and clouds were made of the same light, filmy substance.

Since showers of gossamer sometimes occurred at the time of autumn goose fairs, some held that it must be down from an exceptionally finely feathered bird. One folk-name for gossamer was 'feathers', and gossamer itself is probably a combination of 'goose' plus 'summer'.

Rising early one fine autumn day in 1741, the young Gilbert White watched in awe as a 'shower of cobwebs' fell on the village from a clear sky. The fields of stubble and clover were smothered in a thick mat of webs like 'setting-nets drawn one over the other'. As the day grew warmer, flakes and rags of web drifted into the still air like thistledown, twinkling in the sunshine as they twisted and turned. Later on, 'the flakes hung in the trees and hedges so thick that a diligent person sent out might have gathered baskets full'.[33] Yet, though White knew that gossamer was produced by spiders, he saw it primarily as a weather phenomenon – that is, due to the action of evaporation on dew. The inference was that the spiders helped to create fine weather, which added to the reasons country people had for not harming them. But White failed to guess that spiders might actually benefit from flying to new locations.

The discovery that gossamer was in fact spider silk failed to end the myth-making. The earliest authority on spiders, Martin Lister (1638–1712), supposed that the animals placidly carried on spinning in mid-air and so were able to control their descent, like a hot-air balloonist, by altering the dimensions of their threads. Some claimed to have watched the tiny spiders swimming through the air with vigorous motions of their eight legs or even shooting along by jet propulsion. As recently as 1940 (in a notably warm and settled early autumn), gossamer seen drifting above the downs of southern England was suspected to be a device of the enemy. When a golfer claimed that his wrists had been blistered by the stuff, a rumour reached the government that a new and mysterious form of chemical warfare was being tested. In Hampshire, the Home Guard was called out to inspect the sinister-looking clouds of white mist gathered over the fields. Fortunately, one of them had read the *Natural History of Selborne* and knew that it was not a cloud of deadly gas but Gilbert White's 'thick coat of cobweb'.

The ancient Greeks knew that cobwebs were good for cuts. Cobwebs absorb blood and so helped to staunch wounds. Such knowledge was passed down in country lore. 'I shall desire you of more acquaintance, good master Cobweb,' said the ass-headed Bottom to a fairy in *A Midsummer Night's Dream*. 'If I should cut my finger, I shall make good use of you.'[34] Webs could even be turned into plasters for cuts and sprains. In the eighteenth century, Eleazar Albin's patent remedy, for example, was to beat up cobwebs with frog spawn and allow the mess to dry on a pewter plate. With this concoction, he claimed to have cured a particularly difficult nose bleed. As late as the 1950s, country people were still gathering webs for the medicine chest.[35]

For our time, the word gossamer has become ineradicably associated with the condoms manufactured by Durex. The word was presumably chosen because it captured the quality of tensile strength combined with near-total weightlessness. Other lendings include a web-programmer called Gossamer Threads and a book with the same title about the making of fine lace shawls.

The Ladybird spider, now confined to a solitary acre of heath in Dorset, where it is carefully protected.

Ladybird spiders *Eresidae*

The Ladybird spider is arguably the most beautiful British spider and one regularly compared with jewels and gemstones. Chris Packham called it 'a glamorous little gem'.[36] The young Gerald Durrell saw it as 'an animated ruby, or a moving drop of blood . . . It was the most spectacular spider that I had ever seen'.[37] Only the male is brightly coloured, with a red, four-spotted body the size of a ladybird and hairy banded legs; the larger, rarely seen female is a velvety black.

The Ladybird spider was hailed by the *Guinness Book of Animal Facts and Feats* as Britain's most elusive spider. It lives in a silk-lined tube, from which it emerges at night to pounce on beetles, woodlice and other prey. Long believed to be extinct, it was refound in 1980 by Peter Merrett on a small patch of heath near Wareham, Dorset. With a body count of only five spiders, its survival seemed to be in doubt, especially as rhododendron was over-running its habitat. Fortunately, careful micro-management, followed by captive breeding and release came to its aid, and the most recent survey, in 2007, recorded 825 webs.[38] This spider is also being introduced to other suitable heathland sites in the area.

The Ladybird spider was one of the first British invertebrates to receive full legal protection. The charity Buglife has adopted it as a pin-badge, an icon of endangered 'bugs' everywhere.

Wolf spiders *Lycosidae*

Wolf spiders, or Lycosids (from *lycos*, the Greek word for wolf), are dapper-looking greyish or brownish spiders that hunt their prey with the help of long racing legs and six forward-facing eyes, like a row of headlights (plus two on the side). They were once believed to hunt in packs like wolves but are, in fact, solitary animals, like almost all spiders. Lacking a nursery web, the female carries her egg sac in her palps and sometimes also hoists her baby spiderlings on her back. The lone male attracts his mate by what passes in spider-land for singing – a low purr or drone made by rubbing his palps. In mid serenade, the spider's heartbeat races to about 70 per minute, apparently carried away by the emotional power of music.

Water spiders *Argyronetidae*

VN: wall-wesher (Scot.), water-baillie (Scot.)

Few apart from pond dippers ever catch sight of a Water spider, and yet its unique life history has played a small part in stimulating the human

A victim's-eye view of the Wolf spider Arctosa cinerea.

The Water spider, with its silvery diving bell.

imagination. A swimming spider is a living contradiction, and the animal, which measures only 10–16 millimetres across its outstretched legs, has long been the object of wonder, a 'little creature of exceeding nimbleness', as Muffet referred to it.[39] Its hind-legs are furnished with long fine hairs to act as paddles, and the shorter hairs on its body trap a bubble of air so that, under water, the spider shines like a ball of mercury (hence the spider's generic name *Argyroneta*, or 'silver net'). Though an air-breathing animal, like all spiders, it is able to live under water by supplying air to its dome-shaped web, or 'diving bell', where most of its activities – mating, egg-laying, consuming prey – take place. A recently coined name for it is 'scuba spider', a diver that swims with the aid of its own 'tank' of air. The spider can even monitor the carbon dioxide level in the bell, topping it up with fresh air once it reaches a dangerous level. Water Spiders are preyed on by fish, and anglers occasionally use a rubber spider, or 'rubber bug', as a lure. They can live in garden ponds, but they will take fish fry and newt larvae. If mishandled, large ones can bite.

Raft spiders *Pisauridae*

AN: fishing spider

No one who is lucky enough to have seen a full-sized raft spider is likely to forget it. Large and hairy, with handsome yellow stripes running down their sides, they live by small pools or ditches, often sitting on a natural raft of moss or a leaf, but sometimes outspread on the water's surface. They are not common, and it was unkind of one of the 1950s *I-Spy* books to include one, albeit for a maximum number of points.

The larger and rarer of our two species, the Fen Raft Spider, made the headlines in the 1990s when

A Raft spider – one of the largest British spiders – dining on stickleback.

its isolated habitat at Redgrave and Lopham Fen in Suffolk was threatened by a nearby borehole. To ensure enough standing water for the spider to continue to hunt, the Suffolk Wildlife Trust rather desperately deepened its pools or excavated new ones, and when even these showed signs of drying out, tried hosing in water from outside. At the last gasp, the borehole was sealed and relocated. The spider survived, just, and in the process helped to highlight the plight of our easily overlooked, smaller animal life.

Lace-web spiders *Amaurobiidae*

AN: weaver spider

These small spiders, also known as weaver spiders, spin delicate, tube-shaped webs in wall cracks, window frames, cellars and outhouses, from which they can be encouraged to emerge at night, ready for the fray, by vibrating a tuning fork (they will sometimes fiercely grab hold of the fork, hence the

old species name of *ferox,* or warlike). When freshly spun, their silk has a bluish tinge. Two common garden species are the Lace Weaver Spider and the Black Lace Weaver Spider, both dark and slim, with faint markings on their velvet-covered bodies. They will seize prey as large as a wasp, and can even bite humans, though the effect is said to be no worse than pins-and-needles.

Jumping spiders *Salticidae*

These small, stocky spiders are delightful to watch for the jerky way they scuttle about on walls and fences, catching some small fly or aphid with a sudden leap (after taking the precaution of first spinning a safety harness). The best-known species is the attractive black-and-white-striped Zebra Spider, which is said to have the best eyesight of any spider – or any invertebrate, for that matter. It does sometimes seem to be as curious about us as we are about it, raising its many-eyed head as if to get a better look. Its scientific name, *Salticus scenicus*, means 'leaping actor' or acrobat.

A related species known as the Distinguished Jumping Spider attracted attention in 2007 when its locality at West Thurrock Marshes beside the Thames estuary was threatened by development. Its name helped; so did a wonderful image of its huge eyes and teddy-bear-like appearance.

Uloborid spiders *Uloboridae*

Uloborids are stumpy-looking spiders that spin large, fragile-looking orb webs but subdue their prey not with a bite but with prodigious quantities of sticky silk. Their victims find themselves on the receiving end of snowballs of fuzzy silk that press against their tiny bodies like burrs. At last, tied up, immovable inside yards of sticky rope, the victim's legs crack, its eyes burst from their sockets, its body caves in and it expires. Only then does the spider move in and start to feed. 'It is a slow eater', mused William Bristowe, who watched the process from start to finish with appalled fascination. It may take 24 hours to finish off a moth or large fly. One species, probably introduced, has been dubbed the Garden Centre Spider for the frequency in which its webs are found suspended between tubs, especially indoors. It is also common in the tropical 'biome' at the Eden Centre in Cornwall.

The Woodlouse spider, with its powerful, shell-piercing fangs.

Woodlouse spider *Dysderidae*

AN: dysdera, sow-bug killer (N. America)

To feed on woodlice, you need strong jaws as well as a strong stomach. The Woodlouse spider has the most impressive jaws of any British spider and is quite capable of penetrating human skin as well as puncturing woodlice. Despite its bulldog jaws, the brightly coloured nocturnal spider is soft-bodied and easily damaged. Not wishing to harm them, our contributor Tony Harwood coaxes them away from his patio with blades of grass that the spiders are easily persuaded to bite. He also creates spider refuges 'in custom-made des-res wood-piles stuffed with dry leaves and old rabbit-bedding.'[40]

Tube-web spider *Segestriidae*

AN: six-eyed spider

The Tube-web spider is perhaps the most intimidating British spider. A fully grown female is at least as large as a house spider, and the species has the reputation, whipped up by the press, of being 'the most dangerous spider in Britain' (which is not saying much). It lurks inside a silk-lined tunnel in a crevice in a wall, using trap lines of silk to alert it to passing prey. When it feels a quiver on the line (or the vibration of a tuning fork), the spider leaps out, grabs the prey and retreats back in again, all in an eye-blink. The best way to get a good look at it is to block its hole quickly with a pencil or twig, but playing with a Tube-web spider is not advisable, for it has a sharp, painful bite. Its normal prey are bees and wasps, which the spider subdues with a swift bite to the head before they can twirl round and use their stings. The Tube-web spider was probably

The outstretched arms of the Crab spider Misumena vatia, *alert and ready on its bluebell perch.*

introduced to British ports in the cargo of ships, and, though it seems to be increasing, the spider is nocturnal and retiring and not likely to terrify us often.

Purse-web spider *Atapidae*

The Purse-web spider, or Atypus, is Britain's only tarantula, a stocky black spider that lives inside a silken tube shaped more like a sock than a purse. At the approach of a bumblebee or beetle, it jumps out, bites the victim and drags it into the sock, all in a flash. The repeated, erroneous mention in older books that this is a trapdoor spider with a telltale hinged plug above its burrow must have sent many spider-watchers on a false trail. In fact the spider can be traced by a finger-like projection of silk protruding from its lair, but finding it takes sharp eyes. The Purse-web spider is, for many, the Holy Grail among British spiders, the most charismatic spider of them all.

Crab spiders *Thomisidae*

AN: ambush spiders

Crab spiders do look a bit like tiny crabs. Their bodies are as wide as they are long, with outstretched legs like a crab's front claws; they even move with a scuttling, sideways gait. Instead of spinning webs, they are ambush predators that conceal themselves in a flower to await an unsuspecting butterfly, moth or bee. Crab spiders habitually take prey much larger than themselves and have even been observed in mid-air, hanging on grimly to a bumblebee or butterfly. They seem to prefer yellow or white flowers. The best-known species, the Flower Crab Spider, has the chameleon-like ability to turn pink, white or yellow according to its chosen blossom. One contributor to *Bugs Britannica* referred to them as 'white-death spiders'.[41]

Those who named crab spiders were no more immune to anthropocentrism than the rest of us. The scientific name of a common, pale-coloured species, *Misumena vatia*, means 'hate-filled and bowlegged' (it is also known, more mildly, as the goldenrod spider). That of an attractive pink species, *Thomisus onustus*, means 'loaded sting'.

Comb-footed spiders and false widows
Theridiidae

VN: cobweb spider, scaffold-web spider

Comb-footed spiders spin their snares and untidy, tent-like webs in nettle beds, bramble patches or the crowns of trees. They entrap their prey with a maze of sticky threads, catching the insect like a hooked fish, which is then wound in by the spider. Our 48 species of native comb-footed spiders are harmless, but an introduced species, the glossy black, wicked-looking False Widow is in a different category. It arrived in shipments from the Canary Isles and is now well established in outhouses and walls in London and the southern counties. Stuart Hine, the spider expert at the Natural History Museum, provoked a short-lived media panic when he predicted that, in a few years, the scruffy cobwebs of False Widows will be found in every garden in southern England.[42]

Though not as dangerous as the better-known Black Widow Spider, False Widows do have a numbing bite similar to a bee sting. They are not aggressive, and the greatest danger comes from spiders that have taken up residence in an old pair of gardening gloves or a scruffy sweater hanging up in the shed. Victims logging on the Natural History Museum website mention a 'sudden onset of intense pain, radiating across thigh . . .'; 'tingling in all fingers', an aching itchy arm and, in the worst case, 'a burning sensation . . . increased in intensity, like being scalded, stabbing pains spread first to armpit, then down right arm' along with flu-like 'sweats and fatigue'. A market trader from Dorchester spent three days in the county hospital with symptoms of heart seizure after an unknown spider, believed to be this species, bit him in the chest.[43]

Two more 'false widows' seem to have established colonies here and there. *Steatoda grossa* is sometimes called the Cellar Spider, though it also lurks in garages or among piles of rubbish. *Steatoda paykulliana* looks the part of a poisonous spider with tomato-red markings on its glossy black body. It has been mistaken for the Black Widow, but the crescent-shaped red or orange marking at the top of its abdomen is diagnostic.

According to urban legend, if you are bitten once by a widow spider you will recover, but a second time means you will die. It is not true.

Harvestmen *Opiliones*

VN: daddy-longlegs, harvest spider, kirsty-kringlick (Orkney)

The harvestmen Leiobunum rotundum, *a common species found near garden walls, nettle patches and shaded tree trunks. The numbers of these button-bodied spider relatives peak around harvest time.*

Harvestmen are those button-bodied spider-like insects with eight thread-like legs that are common in late summer around harvest time. Though distantly related to spiders, they are a distinct and ancient group, whose body parts are fused into a single, round form. Lacking the spider's spinnerets, harvestmen do not make webs but wander about on their long legs, scavenging dead plant or animal material (bird droppings are a favourite). In captivity, they are happy to accept bread and butter. They also prey on live, soft-bodied bugs such as aphids or mites and so are considered to be one of the traditional gardener's friends. Harvestmen have their devotees. Since 1973, the distribution of our 23 native species has been mapped, with the help of a newsletter called *Ocularium*, named from a distinctive raised mound at the front end of the creature bearing a pair of simple eyes.

Harvestmen are commonly known as harvest spiders or, especially in North America, as daddy-longlegs. A legend has grown up, stoked by the internet, that they are venomous and that it is especially dangerous to swallow them. They have been confused both with the Daddy-longlegs spider and with the Daddy-longlegs itself, around which a similar groundless folk reputation has grown. In fact harvestmen lack poison glands or venom. In former times they were considered to be good-luck charms, and harvest workers were careful not to harm them.

In Orkney, where harvestmen were called 'kirsty' or 'kirsty-kringlick', children would enjoy letting them crawl ticklishly over their hands, while reciting a special rhyme:

> Kirsty, kirsty kringlick
> Gae me nave a tinglick.
> Whit shall ye for supper hae?
> Deer, sheer, brett and smeer
> Minchmeat sma or nane ava?
> Kirsty kringlick run awa.[44]

(It translates as 'Kirsty, little ball, tickle my hand. What would you like for supper? Meat, sour milk, bread and butter, mincemeat small or none at all? Kirsty, little ball, run away.')

Scorpions *Scorpiones*

Everyone knows the scorpion. The ancients recognised its shape in the stars and placed it in the zodiac (it is one of the few star shapes that is instantly recognisable, though too low in the sky to be seen well from Britain). The constellation of the Scorpion sits on the opposite side of the sky to Orion the Hunter. The story goes that the Goddess Diana sent a scorpion to sting Orion on the foot after he had made indecent and presumptuous advances towards her. The hero toppled over dead, and the grateful Diana immortalised the scorpion among the stars but as far away from Orion as possible. The ancients believed that scorpion venom is most potent during November, the corresponding month of the zodiac.

The reputation of scorpion venom is highly exaggerated. The sting of all but a few species is no worse than a bee sting. Some scorpions hardly bother with stings at all except to defend themselves. Like tarantulas, they look dangerous while being

A scorpion found-object sculpture by Harriet Mead, made from pliers, screws and other suggestively shaped pieces of metal.

relatively harmless, which lends them a certain cachet as exotic pets. The most popular one is the African Emperor Scorpion, which is big and black with impressive lobster-like claws yet is said to have a calm and docile nature. Its favourite treat is baby mice.

Britain has a little-known wild scorpion, confined to dockyard districts in London and North Kent; it even lacks an accepted English name (its scientific name is *Euscorpius flavicaudis*, meaning 'good-scorpion with yellow legs'). Small and black, with pale legs and a thin tail, it lurks in cracks and holes in old walls where the mortar pointing has crumbled, emerging by night to hunt woodlice, spiders and smaller fellow scorpions. A native of south-west Europe, it was probably brought to London in ships' cargoes in the eighteenth century, and though it has been living here quietly and unobtrusively ever since, it has never strayed far from its port of entry. The English scorpion is most easily found by torchlight, since the animal glows a bright and eerie blue-green in UV light. It can sting, and careful handling is advised.

Pseudoscorpions
Pseudoscorpiones

AN: book scorpion, false scorpion

Though small and unlikely to come to the attention unless looked for, these tiny scorpion-like animals have long intrigued naturalists. Under a lens or, better still, a low-power stereoscopic microscope, they are delightful little beasts, with impressive outstretched claws but blunt bodies lacking the true scorpion's tail-sting. They live in places where there are plenty of mites and small larvae to hunt, such as under bark and in leaf litter and, above all, in bird's nests. One species can even live indoors in stables, grain stores and dusty bookcases, where it hunts booklice and dust mites across the pages of old manuscripts. It may have been the 'book scorpion' spotted by Aristotle among the scrolls in the Athenian library. It was also the 'land crab' discovered by Robert Hooke on the pages of his own *Micrographica*. Hooke characteristically made a fine

A false scorpion (Chthomius ischnocheles) *prowling its miniature tree-bark world.*

119

engraving of it to match his famous giant flea. The next reference came around 1770, when a naturalist noted that a 'lobster-insect' had been discovered by 'some labouring men who were drinking their porter, and borne away by an ingenious gentleman who brought it to my lodging'.[45]

The 30 or so British species (from a world total of 3300) have their own newsletter, *Galea*, named after the animal's spinning organ, and also a small study group, led heroically by Dr Gerald Legg at the Booth Museum of Natural History in Brighton. Subscribers to *Galea* are clearly in the mould of the naturalists of old. Among many other unusual activities, they are urged to dig up moles' nests to find a certain rare species and to sift carefully through the mole's bedding. The group published a provisional atlas in 1980. Pseudoscorpions are regarded as householder-friendly, since they hunt unwanted bugs such bedbugs and clothes moths. Beekeepers are interested in them, since hungry pseudoscorpions could be allies for getting rid of the varroa mites currently infesting hives.

A pair of Sheep Ticks (keds). Tick numbers seem to have increased, perhaps helped by Britain's burgeoning populations of wild deer.

Ticks *Acarina*

VN: fags, kebs (Orkney), keds, sheep lice, sheep pest, sheep-taids, taids

You always know when a tick has got hold of you. The bite itself is hardly felt, but the intolerable itching that follows, often in the middle of the night, has an intensity all its own. In their *An Introduction to Entomology* (1815–26), W. Kirby and W. Spence gave a good account of why most of us would agree with Aristotle that ticks are 'disgusting parasitic animals': they plunge 'their serrated rostrum into the bare places of the body, beginning to suck your blood, going deeper and deeper till they are half-buried in the flesh . . . it is now extremely difficult to extract them, the animal rather suffering itself to be pulled to pieces than let go its hold; so that the rostrum and head, being often left in the wound, produce an inflammation and suppuration which render it deep and dangerous.'[46]

Our flesh responds to the tick's anticoagulant saliva by swelling, sometimes raising up the tick, as though it were diving into its own handiwork. Removing the tick takes special care. It can be forced to loosen its grip with Vaseline or spirit, after which it can be twisted out with pointed forceps (for some reason, an anticlockwise twist seems to work best). Some recommend using a cotton thread, though it needs nimble fingers. There is also a tick-removing tool on the market. The majority of bites are caused by the tick's pinhead-sized nymph, which can take up to three years to develop into the short-lived adult.

Ticks are small, blood-sucking mites that feed exclusively on birds, mammals and tortoises. Britain has 22 species, ranging from the abundant Sheep Tick to rarely recorded species confined in one case to water voles and in another to tortoises in pet shops. Though only one or two of them will bite humans, ticks have been unwelcome familiars since ancient times; Pliny regarded them as one of 'the foulest and nastiest creatures', not least because he thought they gorged on blood until they 'burst with over-repletion and die from actual nourishment'.[47] The word 'tick' dates back to the Middle Ages, but its origin is unknown, though it could be a corruption of 'tike'. Amateur naturalists have tended to leave ticks (and mites) well alone, and the hero of tick studies is a pathologist, D. R. Arthur, who published the standard work in 1963. Coincidentally, Arthur is also the name of the hero of *The Tick* cartoon series, a spoof of American superheroes such as Spiderman. He wears a moth suit with antennae but is often mistaken for a bunny.[48]

The tick cannot jump or fly, nor does it spin webs. Instead many live in nests, while Sheep Ticks wait patiently on the tips of leaves or blades of grass for suitable mammals to brush past. A Sheep Tick detects us from our vibrations, our heat and the small, invisible cloud of carbon dioxide we emit with every breath. It uses its hook-like little limbs to grasp fur or feathers or, in our case, clothing and then wanders about looking for a suitable place to feed. This may take a time, for ticks tend to bite in the night, usually in one of the softer, more humid parts of the body. It will feed for hours, its little body swelling like a plastic bag until it appears ready to burst.

Even ticks were not without their medicinal virtues. 'Many English men have learned by experience', wrote Muffet, 'that one dram and a half of Sheep's Lice given in drink will soon and certainly cure the Jaundies.'[49] How you go about collecting a cup-full of ticks, he does not say.

Ticks are said to avoid people with red hair. One of our contributors can confirm this: 'One of the first environmental conservation tasks I did was helping to control bracken on Bardsey Island, off the coast of North Wales. Someone told us to beware of the ticks, but added that I'd be all right as they don't find redheads palatable. Sure enough, in the 20 years since then, I have only suffered one tick bite, in spite of them crawling on me after walking in tick-infested land.'[50]

Sheep Ticks are on the increase. In the past, there were two peak times, or 'tick rises', one in late spring and the other in the autumn. But mild winters and wet summers have extended the period so that no part of the summer is now free of them. Moreover, there are more deer in the countryside to transmit them. I once made the mistake of sitting in trampled grass where a roe deer had been resting up, and one arm was very soon crawling with ticks.

Ticks, often known as 'keds' or 'taigs', used to be infrequent in eastern Scotland. Colin McLeod, who lives in Fife, says his short-haired dogs used to attract the odd tick when taken for walks across the moors but neither he nor his father or grandfather, both great walkers, were ever bothered by them until about 20 years ago. 'I noticed many more ticks in 1986, when I worked in Strathglass in the Central Highlands. Around the same time, the dogs began to pick them up at Tentsmuir in Fife. Since then there has been a population explosion. Ticks are everywhere, often in great numbers, not just in woods and on moors, but anywhere in the countryside, and even in the grounds of my office, near Perth. The tick season is also longer, lasting from March to November, at least in mild areas. They have become a significant health and safety issue when organising public activities, especially with children.'[51]

Ticks used to be a bit of a joke. Now that they are known to carry Lyme disease, the joke has gone sour. The disease is named after the Connecticut town of Lyme, where an outbreak of tick-related arthritis in children was investigated in 1975. It is now known to be caused by a spirochete bacterium carried in the bodily fluids of the tick. The first warning sign is a bull's-eye shaped rash spreading from the bite. If left untreated, this can develop into flu-like symptoms and aching joints and can go on to cause nerve damage, resulting in extreme fatigue and other symptoms. Prompt removal of the ticks greatly reduces the chances of infection. Fortunately, incipient Lyme disease can be sorted out speedily with a course of antibiotics. There is a rooted view in the medical profession that the disease is more prevalent in the New Forest than anywhere else or that, at any rate, some areas are more at risk than others. In truth, Lyme disease can be caught wherever there are Sheep Ticks, including London parks, though the ticks are certainly more numerous in some places such as Hampshire, west Wales and the Western Highlands than others (with the Midlands being apparently the least tick-ridden part of Britain).[52] Bracken is probably the worst tick dispenser, followed by bilberry, coarse grass and thick leaf litter. Only a minority of ticks will carry the disease, but of course there is no telling which one. The best remedy is prevention by, for example, tucking your trousers into socks and examining yourself in the shower after a trip to tick country.

Sheep Ticks also transmit a livestock disease known as 'louping ill', or 'sheep-trembling ill' (its medical name is ovine encephalomyelitis). It is caused by a virus and can lead, via various distressing symptoms, to an animal's complete prostration. In the case of grouse chicks, it is 80 per cent fatal. The Game Conservancy reports some success with acaricides (pesticides) and vaccination of sheep, both of which reduce ticks to a level where sheep and grouse can co-exist. The danger presented by

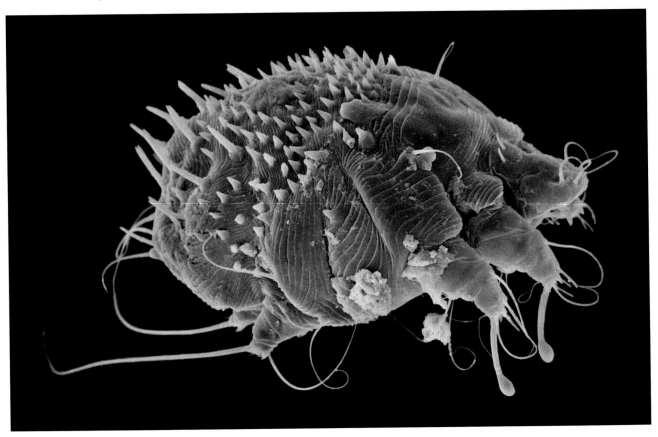

An unseen house guest, a dust mite (x250), scavenger of our daily fall-out of skin flakes. In prime habitats, such as carpets and bedding, there may be about 200 of them for every gram of dust.

the tick has, reportedly, resulted in massacres of mountain hares on shooting estates, since they, too, are known to carry the tick.

It was perhaps the spread of tick-borne illnesses in Europe and America that made possible a film such as *Ticks* (1993). Described as 'vampires of the insect world', these monster-film ticks grow huge and savage after a farmer sprays an illicit crop of marijuana with herbal steroids. The hormonally enhanced bugs take to burrowing inside their victim before bursting out again, *Alien* fashion, in pints of gore.

Mites *Acarina*

VN: midgan (Cornwall), mints or minty

Mites are very small, proverbially so (the name comes from an Old English word for very small), so small, reported Thomas Muffet, 'that Epicurus said it was not made of Atoms but was an Atom itself.' Their somewhat unimaginative collective name is also a mite: a mite of mites – the point being, perhaps, that even a lot of mites is not very much. They are related to spiders and grouped together with ticks in the Acarina, from the Greek word for mite. Most mites are smaller than a pinhead and more or less round. They live by scavenging or sucking the juices of plants and certain invertebrates (diving beetles and dung beetles are peculiarly luckless in this respect). But, unlike ticks, true mites do not suck the blood of mammals or birds.

Using his primitive microscope, Robert Hooke was the first to observe the minute eggs of mites,

The Velvet Mite, a harmless and attractive mite often seen on garden paths but easily mistaken for the more destructive Red Spider Mite.

barely visible to the human eye. At the time, creatures such as these were thought to regenerate spontaneously and be fully grown from filth, and if they laid eggs, it was only for form's sake, for the eggs did not hatch. Hooke readily disproved this theory when he pointed out a host of newly hatched baby mites, 'small moveable specks' but nonetheless 'very prettily shap'd Insects, each of them furnish'd with eight well shap'd and proportion'd legs'.[53]

The extraordinary diversity of mites is indicated by their names. There are soil mites and water mites, spider mites, gall mites, dust mites, harvest mites, flour mites, even sugar mites.

There are some 2100 species of mites in Britain, 130 of them discovered since 1973 (and, of those, 65 were new to science). This, it is thought, is a gross underestimate, but identifying mites is a difficult and specialised field; practically the only well-documented species are agricultural or horticultural pests (our 200-odd water mites are a partial exception, as they were studied when microscopes were popular). Yet mites are among the most abundant animals in the soil and are fundamental to life, as decomposers and recyclers, as well as food for larger invertebrates. Even the least fertile soil, such as dry peat hummocks, is full of mites; one sample contained 18,000 mites per square metre.

Certain mites feed on stored food in kitchens and warehouses. In Scotland, oatmeal once had to be packed extra tight to prevent the free movement of flour mites. The ubiquitous dust mites are probably found in every home, especially in our bedding, where they feed on the flakes of skin we constantly shed (a fair amount of household dust originates from our skins). Fortunately, they are too tiny to be seen, but their dust-like droppings can cause allergies. It is said that feather pillows slowly fill up with damp and mildewed mite droppings if they are not changed.

A cheese infected with mites sometimes acquires a sweet, aromatic smell of mint, hence the term 'minty cheese' and the nickname 'mints' for the mites themselves. The tiny mites burrow into the rind, leaving a dusting of grey droppings, which can cause a mild form of dermatitis known as baker's or grocer's itch. Cheese mites were the subject of the first-ever scientific film documentary, shown at the Alhambra Music Hall in London's Leicester Square in 1903. The audience were treated to a few minutes of magnified mites 'crawling and creeping … like great uncanny crabs.' The film is said to have boosted the sales of cheap microscopes, and for a while, a little bag of mites became a popular microscopic accessory.[54]

The Scabies, or Itch, Mite under high magnification. Allergic reactions to its bites are also known as the seven-year itch. The phrase has long become a metaphor for all that is annoying, as well as the stirrings of infidelity after seven years of marriage.

'Parable', a short, satirical poem by Arthur Conan Doyle, published in 1916, imagined a warm debate among cheese mites about the origin of their live-giving truckle of Cheddar. 'The Orthodox said that it came from the air/ And the Heretics said from the platter.' Not one of them thought of a cow.

Another, once frequent, indoor pest is the Scabies, or Itch, Mite, which tunnels under the skin in S-shaped or zigzag patterns. It produces the condition known as scabies (from the Latin, *scabere*, to itch) or, simply, the itch. As itches go, scabies is said to be one of the worst, especially as the mite prefers places such as the genitals, the top of the thighs or, perhaps the most maddening of all, the webbing between our fingers. It is also one of the species that causes mange in dogs. The Scabies Mite can be picked up when sleeping rough (there was a bad outbreak of it during the Second World War) and is also endemic in places where people crowd together, such as schools and day centres. A

traditional schoolboy remedy was to smear the itch with ink. In most homes the vacuum cleaner has put an end to its activities.

Some particularly troublesome mites are recent arrivals to Britain. The Varroa Mite was first detected here in 1992 and quickly spread throughout the country. It lives by attaching itself to the body of a honeybee or its grub and sucking its bodily fluids. Several mites busily sucking together can weaken a bee and leave it prone to infection. They feed preferentially on the dispensable drones, but in badly mite-ridden hives, drone-rearing ceases and then the mites switch to the grubs of worker bees. This can result in a population crash and, effectively, the end of the hive. Worse still, Varroa Mites transmit viral diseases that can wipe out the colony. They are implicated in the phenomenon known as Colony Collapse Disorder, which is devastating hives throughout North America (*see* Honeybee).

The Varroa Mite can be controlled by commercial 'miticides' (with due care to avoid contaminating the honey) and to some extent by natural oils such as mint or lemon. Many beekeepers use a screen to catch the mites as they drop off the bees on to a sticky bottom board, which ensures they do not reoffend. Unfortunately, the mites quickly develop resistance to routine chemical treatments. DEFRA now advises beekeepers to alternate the treatment to avoid the build-up of resistance, to practise rigorous nest hygiene and to monitor the mite levels so that appropriate action can be taken when needed.

Harvest Mite

VN: August fly, berry bug (Scotland), bloodsucker, chigger, harvest bug, red bug, scrub-itch mite

The Harvest Mite is the cause of a maddening itch, notorious in fruit-picking areas, and seemingly commonest on the hottest days of the year. In the 'raspberry belt' of eastern Scotland, it is known as the 'berry bug', since the peak infestation coincides with the picking season. The orange-red mites are tiny – you could fit a dozen on a pin-head – but they cause itching and skin rashes. The adults are rarely seen; they live on plants and keep out of our way. It is their virtually microscopic, six-legged larvae that cause the problem. They chew the surface of the skin, and it is the enzymes in their saliva that cause itching and sometimes rashes. The irritation tends to appear after the mite has finished its meal and has already departed (it sometimes leaves behind a red dot of blood, which is often mistaken for the mite itself).

In America, where the mites are known as 'chiggers', there is a widespread but unwarranted belief that the mites tunnel under the skin. Another myth is that a good splash of alcohol kills the chiggers and sooths the itching; a burning pain is more likely. Dabs of clear nail polish or vinegar are said to be effective, but the best treatment is a hot shower using plenty of soap. The mites are also deterred by repellents containing DEET. In Britain, harvest mites do not transmit diseases, though in East Asia and the Pacific islands, they carry scrub typhus from rodents to humans and back again. Even so, severe infestations can cause illness, especially in children. The symptoms are said to include a hallucinatory out-of-body experience and a sense of floating.

Pickers of soft fruit such as raspberries (and, in America, blueberries) are especially prone to mite attacks. Gilbert White mentioned this troublesome 'harvest bug' and its habit of getting under people's skin, 'especially those of women and children, and raising tumours which itch intolerably'.[55] Sufferers might spare a thought for the rabbit, which has to live with these mites when they infest its burrow. People who used to spread nets up on the downs to catch rabbits for the pot sometimes paid for it with hours of itching and scratching. In hot years, said Gilbert White, the swarms of mites in the burrows gave a reddish cast to the nets.

'As boys we used to squash those little red mites with our fingers to look like blood.'[56]

Red Spider Mite

AN: two-spotted spider mite
VN: bloodsucker

The Red Spider Mite is an all-too-common pest of glasshouses, where it pierces the leaf cells of a variety of plants, especially tomatoes, cucumbers, carnations and chrysanthemums, resulting in discoloured leaves and sickly-looking growth. In a recent poll of the worst garden pests, it came in as number eight, just ahead of deer and ants (though in a poll restricted to glasshouses the mite would probably weigh in at number one). The spider mite is resistant to chemical insecticides. Outbreaks can be controlled by introducing a predatory mite, available from garden centres, housed in plastic tubes.

Often mistaken for it is the harmless Velvet Mite, which is also red but slightly larger and with a furrowed back. It seems to be most commonly observed around the tables in pub gardens.

SMALL INSECT ORDERS

Insects *Insecta*

At last we arrive at what many will regard as the real bugs: the insects. Insects are the earth's teeming hordes. Though no species grows larger than a mouse, vast numbers of them swarm over land and water, some with wings, others with legs made for running, leaping or hopping, some living in nests, others in balls of foam or protective cases made from gravel or bits of vegetation. They are nature's most versatile animals, the same basic design having evolved into forms as different as a grasshopper, a ladybird, a moth and a housefly. Whether alone or in company, they nibble the leaves, recycle the waste, pollinate the flowers and feed most of vertebrate life. They share our lives and, by turns, fascinate us, help us and exasperate us.

The word insect comes from the Latin *secare*, meaning 'to cut'. It refers to the notched outline of the insect body, in which the head, thorax and abdomen are cleanly separated. The Greek equivalent, *entomos*, gives us entomology, the science of insects. We have given them nicknames such as creepy-crawlies or bugs. Judith Jones knew hard-backed insects as 'crunsters' and flying ones as 'zizzies'. In Yorkshire, the word for a crawly bug was 'wick'; the same word was also used to describe bug-nibbled leaves or moth-eaten garments.

At one time, any small creature could be described as an insect. Science has limited the word to mean invertebrates with six legs. Even so, there are well over a million different insects, around 22,000 species in Britain alone. We begin our tour of this vast group with the most primitive, that is, the ones that probably evolved first, before describing the more familiar groups: dragonflies, mayflies, grasshoppers, butterflies and moths, beetles, flies and bees.

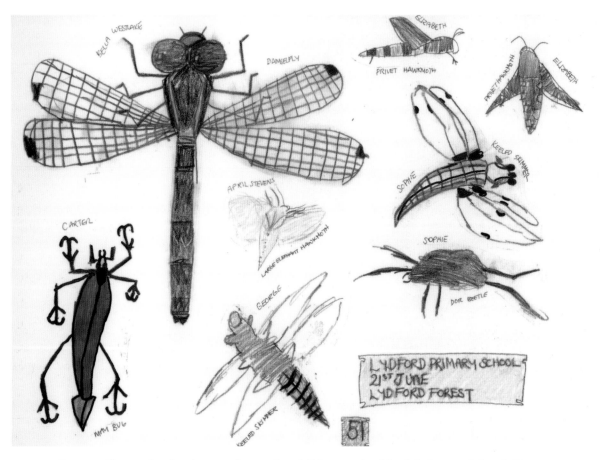

Dragonflies and other insects drawn by children at Lydford Primary School, Devon.

Bristletails *Thysanura*

Bristletails are the most primitive of insects, wingless, with a carrot-shaped body and long bristles (cerci) on their tails, matching the similarly bristle-like antennae on their heads. The bristletails proper, which include the well-known silverfish, generally carry three bristles and are placed in the order Thysanura (fringe-tail). The smaller insects of the order Diplura (two-tails) have only two tails. A third order, the Protura ('simple-tail') consists of minute, sausage-like, soil-living creatures that were completely overlooked until 1907. Most species of bristletails, two-tails and simple-tails, live quietly and out of sight to all but a few enthusiasts and soil scientists. Just two have become better known because they are relatively large and live in houses, often in the fireplace or the kitchen. These are the Silverfish and the Firebrat.

Silverfish are smooth, silvery little creatures, often spotted at night in the kitchen or bathroom scuttling into the nearest crevice. 'They scud away very nimbly to seek some other Hiding-Place', wrote Robert Hooke in the seventeenth century. Their shape is vaguely fish-like, and if you try to pick one up, it is likely to slip between your fingers, leaving a coating of silver scales. For a long time, naturalists were confused about what they were, and many believed them to be the larvae of the clothes moth.

Silverfish eat starchy foods, especially spilled flour, but they can feed on almost anything containing starch or cellulose, including organic glue and paste, scraps of paper or textiles and flakes of human skin (dandruff is caviar to a silverfish). They have been known to tackle shampoo, shaving foam and even leather, not to mention the moulted skins of their own kind. They are also apt to chew the lining of books kept in neglected, damp conditions, such as paperbacks stored in a garage, leaving a characteristically lace-like nibbled edge. Hooke, who called them bookworms, noted that silverfish seem allergic to print and leave the words on the page alone. Where there is nothing at all to eat, they can fast for up to a year. No doubt their hardiness accounts for the success of silverfish worldwide – 'living fossils' in the kitchen cupboard.

Firebrats are less familiar today, but they were once common in the crevices of large stone or brick-lined fireplaces. They have longer antennae than

A Silverfish samples some home-made jam.

silverfish and are brownish in colour. They thrive in the warmth of open fires but not in centrally heated homes and today are commonest in bakeries and around boilers and furnaces. Like silverfish, they feed on tiny scraps of carbohydrate.

> 'As children, we called silverfish "poochies" – possibly from an Indian dialect word for an insect.'

Mayflies *Ephemeroptera*

VN: dayflies, dippers, fish-flies, mays, scurs (Scot.), shadfly, upwing or upwing fly

Anglers' names: brown, drake, dun, olive, spinner, upright, watery

The one thing everyone knows about mayflies is that they live for only a day: 'each ephemeral insect then/ Is gather'd into death without a dawn'.[1] By the evening, after a few hours partying by the water, the mayfly is what angler's call a 'spent gnat', its tiny corpse floating on the water. No wonder mayfly is a byword for brevity. The very name of the mayfly's order, Ephemeroptera (day-wing), hints at the wistful transience of insect life. But that is only the way we see it. As the naturalist Dominic Couzens observes, 'An insect's life is targeted and purposeful: time is immaterial.'[2]

Mayfly adults do not feed and most do indeed die within a day or so, though some mated females might live a little longer. However their aquatic larvae or

A sub-adult mayfly newly emerged from the water. Mayflies are unique in changing their skin at the adult stage from a drab 'dun' to a brightly coloured 'shiner'.

The name mayfly is a misnomer. Different species appear throughout the spring and early summer, and in some cases, there is a second brood later on. But May and June is the peak season, at least on the chalk streams of southern England, the period when the swarms are at their height and even tyros can expect to land a fish or two – known by fishermen as duffer's fortnight. Mayflies are also sometimes known as 'dayflies' or as 'upwing flies', from the way their delicate wings are held at right angles to the body, like dragonflies' wings. In most European languages they are 'one-day flies'.

Uniquely among insects, the mayfly has two winged states, the first being a sober-coloured sub-imago, or 'dun', and the second a brighter, sexually mature stage with shining wings and long graceful 'tails' that fishermen call a 'spinner'. Fishermen use the terms in their colourful names for fishing flies. Unlike science, which assigns strictly one name per species, fishermen may have several names for a variable species such as *Ephemera danica*, which can be a 'greendrake', a 'grey drake' or a 'black drake', depending on its colour and stage of growth. By the same token, another name may rope in a group of similar-looking species, such as the mayfly called the March Brown. Mayfly names have something of the riverside in them, and you can imagine fly-fishermen dreaming them up as they cast upon the rippling waters – names such as Golden Olive Bumble, Pale Watery and Evening Dun. Others, such as 'zonkers', 'buzzers' and 'straddlebugs', have a more contemporary ring.

No one pays more attention to mayflies than anglers. 'Doubt not that Angling is an Art', wrote Izaak Walton, author of *The Compleat Angler*. 'Is it not an Art to deceive a Trout with an artificial Flie? a Trout! He that hopes to be a good Angler must not only bring an inquiring, searching, observing wit but he must bring patience and love and prosperity to the Art itself.'[3] When mayflies hatch, the trout rise to take the flies laying on the water or dancing just above it. Real mayflies are far too fragile to fasten to the end of a hook, and so anglers do the next best thing and imitate them with a more or less realistic artificial fly. The practice dates back far beyond Izaak Walton to classical times, when second-century Macedonian fishermen improved their catch-rate by tying red wool to their hooks.

Fly-fishing was revived in Britain in the late Middle Ages, when Dame Juliana Berners contributed a 'Treatyse of Fysshynge with an Angle' to *The Boke of St Albans* in 1496, including

nymphs live for several weeks or even months on the beds of streams and rivers, while those that survive the winter as eggs may take a year or more to complete their lifecycles. Mayfly nymphs graze algae or scavenge among the stones, and breathe with the aid of feathery tail-end gills. Once fully developed, they abandon their hideouts and swim or float to the surface, where they emerge as adult mayflies, leaving the cast skins or 'shuck', behind. Often mayflies emerge en masse in what fishermen call hatches, swarms of winged flies shimmering as the morning sun strikes the water. Experienced watermen can sense a big hatch coming from signs in the weather and take advantage of the consequent feeding frenzy of trout and other river fish.

descriptions of several fly dressings. Walton himself included two whole chapters on fly-fishing, written by his friend Charles Cotton from his experiences on the Derbyshire Wye. Because of their importance to angling, mayflies were the subject of a serious study by the Dutch entomologist Swammerdam in 1675, well in advance of similar scientific treatises on butterflies, moths or spiders.[4] Perhaps it says something about the state of our water quality today that the species Swammerdam chose to focus on is now extinct in Western Europe.

Early fishing flies were relatively crude and based on only the broader characteristics of waterside insects, most notably their size and colour. The modern era of fly-fishing began with the advent of fishing clubs and popular manuals such as *The Fly-fisher's Entomology* (1836), by Alfred Ronalds. From then on, every fly-fisherman was expected to tie his own flies; as J. W. Dunne rather sternly told the readers in 1924, 'The fisherman who knows nothing of his flies is as great an anachronism as the painter who knows nothing of his paints. More, he is a bad man of business.'[5]

The construction of ever more elaborate flies became something of a fetish, with the flowering of intricate designs based on fur, wool and feathers (hackles) and attached by coloured wires and silk to produce a convincing simulacrum of the real thing. Rarely can such a developed and intricate art have been based on something as humble as a mayfly. The need for such exactness, when few of us, apart from a fisherman, can tell one mayfly from another, is because the right fly has to be matched to the time and place. Trout are fickle fish whose food preference varies from time to time and river to river. For example, the highly successful Pheasant's Tail Nymph is designed to mimic a particular mayfly nymph as it ascends to the surface to emerge. Greenwell's Glory, a famous fly used since the mid-nineteenth century, reproduces the immature mayfly as it settles on the water's surface drying its wings. Lunn's Particular is a 'red spinner', a fly that mimics the motions of a dying mayfly trapped in the surface film. Many such flies were invented by river keepers who also happened to be keen and observant entomologists.

Traditional flies were based on natural materials, and the enthusiast kept a collection of fur and feathers for the purpose. Modern flies, which are more usually bought ready-made, tend to be brighter and less subtle, being made of synthetic fibres. Whether the traditional exactness of these lures is

A hatch of mayflies, a plate from a nineteenth-century work of entomology.

strictly necessary is debatable; modern research suggests that, if they are in the right mood, trout will snatch at any colourful object that catches their eye. The tiny mayfly *Caenis* is sometimes known as the Angler's Curse, because trout dining out on *Caenis* are uninterested in artificial flies.

Izaak Walton subtitled his famous book, 'The Contemplative Man's Recreation'. He founded a long tradition of thoughtful fish contests with Pickwickian traditions of fellowship and good living. One of the oldest and most exclusive fishing clubs (full membership is limited to 25) is the Houghton Fishing Club, whose headquarters are in Stockbridge, Hampshire. Along with the stuffed prize fish in their glass cases, it has famous dry flies mounted in frames, including the club's own Houghton Ruby. Among the milestones of its year on the River Test are the first rise of the grannom fly in April and the mayfly the following month. At an annual mayfly banquet held inside a

The inn sign of The Mayfly, by the River Test near Stockbridge, Hampshire.

tent, also known as the Mayfly, the members raise their glasses to the 'rising generation'. The club journal, meanwhile, is a running commentary on our relationship with aquatic insects, sometimes in elaborate prose, such as the note that runs, 'It is a marked characteristic of certain creatures … to pullulate in abnormal numbers at irregular intervals on the stimulus of some favourable concatenation of physical conditions whereof the nature has hitherto evaded recognition.'[6]

A large number of mayflies have angling names. These are some of the most widely used:

Scientific name	Angling name
Ephemera	Greendrake, Grey Drake, Dark Mayfly, Spent Gnat
Rhithrogena	March Brown, Yellow Upright, Olive Upright
Ephemerella	Blue-winged Olive, Sherry Spinner, Yellow Evening Dun
Leptophlebia	Claret and Sepia Duns
Paraleptophlebia	Turkey Brown, Purple Dun
Siphlonurus	Large Summer Dun, Summer Mayfly
Baetis	Various Olives, Iron Blue, Pale Watery, Jenny Spinner, Lunn's Particular
Cloeon	Pond and Lake Olives
Procloeon	Pale Evening Dun
Centroptilum	Pale Watery Dun, Little Sky-blue, Little Amber, Spurwing
Ecdyonurus	Great Red Spinner, Late March Brown, Green Dun, Large Green, August Dun, Brook Dun
Heptagenia	Yellow Dun, Dusky Yellowstreak, Dark Dun
Ceanis	White Midge, Angler's Curse
Habrophlebia	Ditch Dun
Ameletus	Upland Dun

Products and businesses named after mayflies include a light caravan, a riverside pub in Hampshire, a 1970s rock festival in Oxford, a disposable racing shoe and a brand-name consultancy ('we draw our inspiration from the common mayfly, a beautiful creature that crams its whole life experience into a single day').[7]

Dragonflies *Odonata*

VN: adder, adder bolt, adder-fly, adder's spear (or spik), ather-bell (or bill), ather-cap, balance-fly, blue needle, boult or bolt, bull adder, bull fly (Yorks), bullstang or bulltang or bullting (N Eng.), cow killer, damoselfly or damselfly, darting-fly (Kent), demoiselle, devil's coach-horse, devil's darning-needle, devil's needle, devil's riding-horse, Dicken's (or Dickinson's) riding-horse, Dickinson's mare, ear-cutter, edther, ether's mon or adder's man, ether's nild or adder's needle, fire-flee, fleeing aither, fleeing ask, fleeing snake, flying adder, flying asp, granny's needle, heather-bill or edder-bell (Scot.), heather-bolt (Lancs), heatherflee, hobby-horse, horse-adder (Cornwall), horse-long-cripple, horse-stang, hoss adder (Dorset), hoss-fly (Yorks), hoss stinger (Yorks), jacky breeze, kingfisher, King George, kite-flee, lady fly, leatherwing, locust, may-maid, merry-maid, moutchet (Channel Islands), mule killer, peacock, penny-adder, silver-pin, snake-arrow, spinner, spineroo, spinning jenny, stingin'-ether (Scot.), tenging ether, i.e., stinging adder (NE

Eng.), tom breeze or tom breezer (Norfolk), water-butterfly, water-dipper, waterfly, woodwig

A dragonfly is the most dazzling of insects. An aerial acrobat with long gauzy wings and brilliant spots and stripes of colour on its broomstick body, the dragonfly restlessly patrols the margins of ponds and lakes with a characteristic buzz like a crackle of electricity. It hunts small flying insects by day, using its enormous bulging eyes, which, like ours, see in colour. By moving its wings in a rapid figure-of-eight motion, a dragonfly can turn and loop with great agility, and fly sideways or even backwards. They can be grouped according to their particular habits: dragonflies are broadly divided between hawkers, which patrol up and down or in zigzag fashion, chasers and darters, which make sudden dashes, and skimmers, which brush close to the water's surface. A dragonfly larva, or nymph, is aquatic, and the adults are normally found close to water bodies, though they can wander far. Like butterflies, they are insects of summer and warm sunshine. Cultural references to dragonflies tend to invoke lazy, carefree days by the water.

We also take pleasure in those smaller insects, the damselflies, similar in shape but much smaller and daintier, with needle-like bodies in bright shades of red, blue and green. The two largest have coloured wings and a flopping flight that lent them the apt folk name of 'water butterflies'. Damselflies, too, are hunters of small insects, but they are also food for larger dragonflies. Because dragonflies and damselflies are easy to watch with binoculars, they have become birdwatchers' insects – almost honorary birds – and today are second to butterflies in popularity. In Far Eastern countries, especially Japan, they have long been admired and have inspired a rich and affectionate folklore.

In Western countries, on the other hand, dragonflies were feared by the more superstitious as a kind of devil's insect. Though they are completely harmless, country lore insisted that at least the larger dragonflies could bite or sting. This might have been inferred by their apparently aggressive behaviour. After alighting on your arm, a dragonfly may curl round its long thin body as if about to sting. Dragonflies can also make a chewing motion with their lower jaw as if about to bite. There are stories of dragonflies trying, quite harmlessly, to lay eggs on dogs, training shoes or even bare legs (the species most prone to this is the Southern Hawker; apparently it creates a ticklish sensation). They are also sometimes seen flying around horses and other farm animals in a vaguely intimidating way, probably hawking at flies. All this must have helped to forge a reputation for dragonflies as sinister, evil-natured insects. But there was another reason for fearing them. Medieval fabulists believed on the basis of certain signs that dragonflies were in league with the devil. Some saw them as poisonous winged snakes, others as animated bolts or arrows, or even as devilish darning needles.

The earliest reference to dragonflies is by William Caxton in a printed book of 1483, in which he mentions 'a grete flye called in some places an adder bolte' (a bolt is a short arrow fired from a crossbow).[8] A flying bolt spotted and banded like an adder presumably stung like one too.

Dragonfly itself is probably a folk-name. Like many mythical creatures, dragons were believed to inhabit remote parts of the world, hence that famous phrase of old maps: 'here be dragons'. As everyone knew (for the maps included illustrations), dragons had long thin bodies and broad outstretched wings. Not all dragons were large and terrifying. One that was supposed to inhabit the Welsh hills was a modest, even shy animal that lurked in cowsheds, frightened babies and crept out early in the morning to curdle the milk. At some point, dragon-like insects became known as 'dragon-flies'. The word is introduced in a familiar way, as though everyone knew what they were, by Francis Bacon in a rambling work of natural history in 1626. 'The delicate coloured Dragon Flies may have some corrosive quality', mused Bacon, in the context of the Biblical Plagues of Egypt.[9] They were said to be among the swarms of noxious flies sent by God to teach the Pharaoh a lesson.

For her book on the folklore of dragonflies, *Spinning Jenny and Devil's Darning Needle* (2002), Jill Lucas collected around 80 folk-names, from England, Scotland and Wales. A few, such as 'horse-stinger' are still occasionally used today, but most of them are forgotten. Yet they speak volumes about the sinister image of dragonflies in times past. One set of names, such as 'adder fly' or 'ather-cap', compares them with snakes. In Norway, they had a saying, 'the dragonfly is the brother of the viper' (the grass snake does indeed sometimes share their watery habitat, while adders and dragonflies can be

The face of the Azure Damselfly, one of our commonest small dragonflies

seen sharing the same boggy depression on moors). Some claimed that the dragonfly could actually turn into a snake and that they were, in fact, one and the same creepy, shape-shifting beast.

Another set of names links dragonflies with the devil and his agents. The devil tempted Adam and Eve in the form of a snake. While dragonflies resemble snakes, their long stiff bodies also suggested broomsticks. The devil himself, familiarly known as Old Dick, chose to ride on a winged dragonfly, hence their folk-names of Dicken's or Dickinson's horse. Even the more neutral-sounding name of Balance Fly has sinister undertones. With its hammer-like head and sometimes bulbous 'tail', the dragonfly resembled an old-fashioned set of scales. This was obviously not accidental, and some believed that the devil used the dragonfly to weigh the souls of the dead.

People also noted the dragonfly's habit of swinging or darting to and fro, as though stitching

An Azure Damselfly in flight. The delicacy and grace of damselflies made them a favourite marginal decoration in medieval books of devotion.

Dragonfly dance performed by Plymouth Young People's Dance Company.

an invisible piece of cloth. This produced the folk-name of 'darning needle' or 'devil's darning needle', which survives today in the American name 'darner' for the large hawker dragonflies (though it is the damselflies that most closely resemble flying needles). It was said that, if you fell asleep by a stream on a hot summer's day, the dragonfly might use its long, thin body to sew your eyes shut. Dragonfly-darners were conscripted into the nursery as a warning to children not to tell lies or swear, lest the devil's darner should sow up their mouths. Dragonflies were said particularly to dislike 'screaming children, gossiping, quarrelling or scolding women, and cursing and blaspheming men'.[10] It would seem that the insect, though no doubt the devil's agent, could also provide a useful social service.

Some people, especially in the south of England, warned that dragonflies were insect vampires that could suck your blood, perhaps with fatal consequences. Evidently there was another parenting dimension here for (so it was said) they only stung bad boys; bad girls are not mentioned. To good boys, the insects showed their benign side by pointing out where the fish were settling, always a useful thing to know. Perhaps the story of bloodsucking dragonflies was invented to frighten naughty children.

The point was underscored with a dialect rhyme, based on the dragonfly's local name 'snakestinger':

> Snakestanger, snakestanger, Vlee about the
>   brooks;
> Sting aal the bad bwoys that vor the vish look,
> But let the good bwoys ketch aal the vish they
>   can,
> And car'm away whooam to vry 'em in a pan;
> Bread and butter they shall yeat at supper wi'
>   their vish
> While aal the littull bad bwoys shall only lick
>   the dish.[11]

In Cambridgeshire, by contrast, dragonflies brought good luck. If you spotted one buzzing about above the water, you should cross your fingers and make a wish. If you caught it, you would soon be married. For some reason, this only worked in England. In France, the approach of the dragonfly was akin to the pirate's flag making its way towards you, and the prudent reaction was to get out of its way.

The devilish reputation of dragonflies attached itself most strongly to the large ones (the name bull, as in 'bullstang', means big). The smaller ones,

known as 'damsel-flies', enjoyed a gentler image, for in Muffet's words, they did 'let forth Nature's elegancy beyond the expression of art'.[12] Most damselflies are blue, and alternate names include 'virgo fly', a benign reference to the blue colours worn by the Virgin Mary, and 'kingfisher', a reference to the shimmer and flash of blue as the insect flutters downstream. The old name virgo fly later attached itself to the scientific name of the butterfly-like Beautiful Demoiselle, *Calopteryx virgo*.

Other dragonflies with broader bodies, such as the 'chasers' in the genus *Libellula*, look more like spindles than needles and so might be said to spin rather than darn. Perhaps that is why they used to be called 'spinners', 'spineroos' or, most attractively, 'spinning jennies'. *Libellula* itself means 'little book' and is probably a reference to the way some species hold their wings, at one moment open and outstretched and at the next folded shut like the pages of a pamphlet.

An ironic image of dragonflies emerges in the old name of 'King George' (which they shared with certain butterflies), though the king in question was in fact St George, slayer of dragons, the probably mythical Christian martyr who later became the patron saint of England. According to the story, the saint enjoyed a prestigious afterlife as a warrior-angel mounted on a particularly splendid winged steed. One day, St George failed to control his mount, which suddenly and for no apparent reason started galloping backwards, knocking over all the other angels behind him. This looked suspicious. God ordered an investigation into the incident, and sure enough, it was found that St George's horse had been bewitched by the devil. George was told to dismount, and the moment he did so, the angelic horse turned into a decidedly devilish dragonfly: the saint confounded by his dragon nemesis.

In Mary Webb's fifth and last completed novel, *Precious Bane* (1924), set by the lonely, lapping, tree-ringed waters of Sarn Pool (based on the real-life Bomere Pool in Shropshire), we hear through the voice of Prudence Sarn a glimpse of how dragonflies were seen by Shropshire country folk a century ago (I have picked out the folk-names in italics):

'Dragon-fly, I say, because I doubt some wouldna know what our name for them meant. We called the

Left: *A damselfly victim of the sticky embrace of sundew, an insect-eating plant common in boggy places.*

dragon-fly the *ether's mon* or *ether's nild* at Sarn, for it was supposed that where the adder, or ether, lay hid in the grass, there above hovered the ether's mon as a warning. One kind, all blue, we called *kingfishers*; and another one, with a very thin body, *the darning needle*. Mother used to tell Gideon that if he took dog's leave or did some other mischief the devil would take the needle to him and use the dragon-fly to sew up his ears, so he couldna hear the comfortable word of God and would come to damnation. But I could never believe that the devil could have power over such a fair thing as a dragon-fly.'[13]

Another folk-name is touched on by Frances Brown in her 1990 novel A *Harefoot Legacy*: '"Hope them snake-arrows is down at the pond like we saw this morning. Masses of them weren't there, Johnny, great big bluey-green ones." "Do you mean dragonflies?" asked Liddy. "Yes. But snake-arrows is what the village chavvies call 'em."'[14]

There are also folk-names in Gaelic or Welsh that run through broadly the same range of serpent and needle analogies as their English counterparts. Yet the devil hardly appears in the Gaelic view of dragonflies, and names such as 'blazing fly' and 'needle of the wings' suggest a poetic feeling lacking in the more earthy English names. Most of these names seem more appropriate to hawker dragonflies, but *cuileag-nan-cruinneag* (fly of the damsel) sounds more like a damselfly. Other names include:

Welsh: *gwaell neidr* (adder's knitting-needle), *gyas y neidr* (adder's servant), *gwas y neidr* (snake's servant).

Gaelic: *damhan nathran* (ox viper), *snathad mor na sciathain* (big winged needle), *tarbh nathrach* (bull-snake).

Irish: *cleardhar caoch* (blind wasp), *spear adoir* (mower), *spiogan mor* (big spike: possibly a reference to the sharp ovipositor of the female Golden-ringed Dragonfly).

If this book was Bugs Japannica instead of *Bugs Britannica*, the folk-lore of dragonflies would be far more positive. Dragonflies are revered there above all other insects as cultural symbols, embodying the spirit of the rice plant and so as a harbinger of good harvests. The very name for Japan is *Akitsushmi*, or 'dragonfly island'. The cultural status of dragonflies in China and other Far Eastern countries is almost equally exalted.

A medieval hawker dragonfly from the fourteenth-century Luttrell Psalter.

The devilish reputation of dragonflies is belied by their appearance in religious missals as decorative and seemingly benign insects, their coloured pencil bodies contrasting with the pearly shimmer of their wings. Perhaps the earliest appears as an illumination in the *Luttrell Psalter*, produced in Lincolnshire around 1330. It is recognisably a male Common Hawker. A man is sticking his tongue out at it, below a line in Latin which translates, rather mysteriously, as 'and your teaching has corrected me'. Taught him what, one might wonder – to defy the devil?

The Hastings Hours of around 1480 include a nicely rendered Banded Demoiselle, perched on a blue iris. Possibly it is purely there as decoration, but more likely it has a message. Perhaps it is reminding Lord Hastings that life can be brief – appropriately enough, in his case, for he is the same Lord Hastings who lost his life in the *coup d'état* that put Richard III on the throne. Alternatively, it might be a good-luck symbol, for blue was a colour associated with the Virgin Mary.

Another ancient depiction of dragonflies is on a fresco by Lorenzetti in Sienna's city hall. Painted around 1340 and called the *Allegory of Good Government*, it shows a group of dancing ladies, one of whom wears a garment embroidered with dragonflies. Live dragonflies are buzzing about or resting on outstretched arms and ankles. What does it all mean? One explanation is that the dancing women are the Muses, and the one with the dragonfly dress is Polyhymnia, the muse of rhetoric and geometry. Like Leonardo's famous image of a man describing

The Banded Demoiselle, also known as the 'kingfisher' or 'water butterfly'.

a circle with his outstretched arms, the dragonfly, with wings and body of roughly equal length, could be regarded as a natural image of proportion and balance. In other words, it symbolised an aspect of good governance.[15]

In his moral fable *The Water Babies* (1863), Charles Kingsley makes full use of the dramatic contrast between the 'very ugly, dirty' larva (a description more suited to some species than others) and the angelic adult insect. The transformation of the larva to a shimmering adult dragonfly reflects the water baby Tom's own experience of turning from 'an ugly little black' chimneysweep into a clean water sprite. 'I am the king of all the flies,' says the newborn dragonfly. 'I shall dance in the sunshine, and hawk over the river, and catch gnats, and have a beautiful wife like myself.'[16]

Kingsley was a good naturalist, and his descriptions of water life in *The Water Babies* are both lyrical and realistic. However, he allots to the dragonfly the unlikely role of Tom's friend and mentor. From it, Tom learns not to taunt other water creatures and generally become better behaved. It is a positive spin on the dragonfly, since a real one would have snapped up young Tom as it might a tadpole. Perhaps Kingsley knew of the oriental tales in which dragonflies appear as benign spirits helpful to mankind.

Mary Webb (1924), in the person of Prudence Sarn, describes the beauty of a variety of dragonflies in the Shropshire dialect:

We had a power of dragon-flies at Sarn of many kinds and colours, little and big. But every one was bound in due season to climb out of its watery grave and come out of its body with great labour and pain like the rending of the tomb … There were plenty of dragon-flies about, both big and little. There were the big blue ones that are so strong they will fly over the top of the tallest tree if you fritten them, and there were tiny thin ones that seem almost too small to be called dragon-flies at all. There were rich blue kingfisher flies and those we call damsels, coloured and polished in the manner of luster ware. There were a good few with clear wings of no colour or of faint green, and a tuthree with a powdery look like you see on the leaves of rickluses. Some were tawny, like a fitchet cat, some were rusty or coloured like

Dragonfly *by Harriet Mead, a found-object sculpture created from scrap metal.*

137

The Dragonfly, *a sculpture inspired by helicopters at Boscombe Down, Wiltshire. Created by Charlotte Moreton.*

the copper fruit kettle. Jewels, they made you think of, precious gems such as be listed in the Bible. And the sound of their wings was loud in the air, sharp and whirring, when they had come to themselves after their agony. Whiles, in some mossy bit of clear ground between the trees, they'd sit about like so many cats round the hearth, very contented in themselves, so you could almost think they were washing their faces and purring.[17]

A considerable body of folk or rock music has been inspired by dragonflies, generally helping to provide a hazy, summer's day feeling. For example, in Fleetwood Mac's 'Dragonfly' (1971), this 'king of flies' wears a 'gorgeous opal crown', not a bad description of a hawker dragonfly's bulging, multi-coloured eyes.[18] The languid 'Dragonfly Dreams', by former Genesis instrumentalist Anthony Phillips, makes perfect listening after a stressful day at the office. Odin Dragonfly is a contemporary duo of multi-instrumented female folk-singers with a similar acoustic, back-to-nature sound.

The same image of a dream-like insect somehow embodying the lazy pleasures of a summer afternoon is caught by Eva Ibbotson in her children's novel *The Dragonfly Pool* (2008). The pool, lost in the woods, is a place of refuge and liberation from the stuffy

rigours of adult life. It is the sort of timeless idyll many of us must have dreamed of during lessons.

It is the possibilities of dragonflies as heavenly intercessors or agents of the paranormal that inspired the 2002 film *Dragonfly*, starring Kevin Costner and Susanna Thompson. The tagline is: 'When someone you love dies . . . are they gone forever?' An exercise in that novel genre, an unscary ghost story, it is about a recently widowed doctor who develops a psychic ability to hear ghostly messages from the hereafter. His dead wife's favourite creatures were dragonflies, and their pestering attentions convince the doctor that they are intermediaries from beyond.[19]

In more pragmatic vein, the aerodynamics of the dragonfly's wings are said to have inspired the design of flight blades for the first helicopters. Certainly, the Royal Navy's first operational helicopter was named the Dragonfly (there was also a civilian version known as a Wasp Junior). In homage to this inspirational link, a dragonfly sculpture by Charlotte Moreton, created from an old Gazelle helicopter, now stands by the A303 at Boscombe Down.

Finally, dragonflies are associated with water and, hence, by a small leap of thirst, to drink. The Dragonfly is a fairly popular pub name. There is a pub in Peterborough, a couple of cocktail bars in Edinburgh and a pub in Northampton whose swinging signs feature an Emperor Dragonfly. A bottled beer brewed by Youngs of London called Damselfly is flavoured with wild elderflowers. It is 'light and slightly hoppy with sherbet notes'.

Despite their beauty, dragonflies were never as popular among collectors as butterflies or beetles. Their bright colours fade after death, and museum specimens are disappointing (and made ludicrously poor images when used for identification guides). Live ones are also difficult to rear and keep in captivity. Perhaps for these reasons, until recently only a few species, such as the Emperor or Hairy Dragonflies, had accepted English names. The first attempt to give popular names to all species was made by Cynthia Longfield in 1937,[20] though they are somewhat half-hearted, since she was eager to retain the generic names as far as possible for her 'Common Aeshnas' and 'Common Sympetrums'. In his popular 1970s book, Cyril Hammond introduced full English names for the first time, replacing the aeshnas and sympetrums with names based on dragonfly behaviour, such as hawkers, skimmers and darters.[21]

In 1991, the British Dragonfly Society recommended Hammond's inventions (with a few variants) as standard names, though subsequent authors have attempted to improve on them. There was, perhaps, a political aspect to the introduction of American names in *The Natural History of Ireland's Dragonflies* (2004), for example, by replacing 'demoiselle' with 'jewelwing' and 'emerald' with 'spreadwing'. Philip Corbet and Stephen Brooks were unhappy about the artificial division between dragonflies and damselflies, preferring to call the former 'warriorflies' while preserving 'dragonflies' for the whole group.[22] Others wish us to call them odonates, from the name of their order, Odonata.

The British Dragonfly Society formed in 1983 from a small band of enthusiasts and now has around 1300 members, though these are only the hardcore of a much larger number of dragonfly spotters and recorders. More than 2000 people contributed to its dragonfly mapping scheme, culminating in the *Atlas of the Dragonflies of Britain and Ireland* (1996). Good fieldguides and the development of close-up binoculars have helped to make dragonflies more accessible, and with only 40 species to remember, dragonflies are among the most manageable of insects.

In 1991, a dragonfly sanctuary was set up at the pond of a disused mill-house at Ashton in Northamptonshire. At the initiative of Ruary Mackenzie-Dodds, the mill-house was reconstructed as the National Dragonfly BioMuseum, from which, after viewing the exhibits, the real thing could be spotted by the river and close-ups of larvae viewed by video link to microscopes. Over seven years, it received some 22,000 visitors. The museum has since been renamed the Dragonfly Project and re-sited to Wicken Fen in Cambridgeshire, where dragonfly safaris are also run. A second dragonfly sanctuary opened in 1994 by the Lea Valley Park Authority at Cornhill Meadows near Waltham Abbey in Essex, with an interpretive centre providing multimedia displays on dragonfly ecology. It provides guided walks over the nearby water meadows and riverbank, where up to 21 species can be seen.

Dragonflies were among the world's first flying insects. We have missed Britain's biggest one by 300 million years. About the size of a seagull, it buzzed over the swampy forests of what is now Bolsover, Derbyshire. The first specimen, found in 1978 as a wing impression on the roof of a coal seam, was nicknamed the Bolsover Beast (not to be confused with Bolsover's famously acerbic MP, Dennis Skinner, who is the Beast of Bolsover). It was named *Erasipteron bolsoveri* ('gracefully winged of Bolsover') by Dr Paul Whalley at the Natural History Museum. Shortly afterwards, an even larger one was found in another seam, which was believed to be another species and named *Tupus diliculum* ('giant dragonfly of the dawn'). Yet, despite its impressive size, *Tupus* never achieved the same fame as the Bolsover Beast. Both species belong to an extinct family of huge, 'primitive' dragonflies that differ from living ones mainly in the detail of their wings. They probably hawked over the steaming swamps, with a rustle and clatter. The atmosphere was much richer in oxygen then, and perhaps this high-octane air sustained a much faster metabolic rate, allowing giant dragonflies to speed along at the same rate as modern-day emperors. Fittingly, the dragonfly has become an icon for Bolsover and was used as the logo for the partnership that reclaimed and landscaped the area after Bolsover colliery closed in the 1980s. In what is now Carr Vale Nature Reserve, distant descendents of the Bolsover Beast flit over purpose-built dragonfly pools.

Stoneflies *Plecoptera*

VN: adults: mayflies (N Eng.)
    nymphs: creepers

Stoneflies look a little like flying earwigs (but without the pincers). The larger ones have a hesitant, blundering flight, and instead of alighting gracefully onto a perch like a mayfly, they tend to crash-land like an aircraft out of fuel. Their heavily veined wings are unconnected and beat out of synch, adding to the overall air of bad design. It is easy to imagine the first flying insects as being something like a stonefly, a kind of hopeful amateur that got airborne after a certain amount of muscular effort and wind assistance but which is frankly happier on terra firma.

Stoneflies are distantly related to dragonflies and mayflies but have their own order, the Plecoptera, or 'twisted wing'. They are named not after the adult fly but from its larva, or nymph. Like mayflies and dragonflies, stoneflies have fully aquatic larvae that live on the beds of streams and rivers (and, less generally, in large ponds and lakes). The nymphs are flattened and well adapted for a life clinging to stones in a rapid current; pick up the stone, and the nymph will either cling tight or scuttle off like a crab. Mayfly larvae are found in the same places but they generally have three 'tails', while a stonefly has two.

Stoneflies are typical insects of trout streams and, though seldom as common as mayflies, are particularly attractive to trout, since their clumsy fluttering and dipping creates a commotion on the water's surface, which instantly alerts the fish. For centuries, anglers have fashioned ingenious artificial flies based on stoneflies or their nymphs. The first fishing-fly ever described, in 1496, was based on a stonefly. Stonefly lures are particularly popular on lakes and rivers in the north and west, where these insects are abundant (and where, confusingly, stoneflies are often called mayflies). Stoneflies are intolerant of pollution, and their presence in good numbers is a sign of high-quality water.

Fishermen have a variety of names for stoneflies. Their flattened, bristly-legged nymphs are known as 'creepers'. The adult flies have angling names, such as the 'yellow Sally' – a large stonefly of chalk streams with a flattish, stocky body and pale yellow wings. Certain small, slim stoneflies are known as

'needle-flies', and slightly larger ones as 'willow-flies'. Two that are out early in the year and so are useful at that time are known as the 'early brown' and the 'February red'. Medium-sized dark ones are the 'brown stoneflies', and a bigger species common on chalk streams is, aptly if unimaginatively, known as the 'large stonefly'.

The largest species of stonefly is *Dinocras*, meaning 'terribly big'. A big *Dinocras* crash-landing with a tangible bump on your shirt as you walk along the river bank is a memorable (and, for those of us who like insects, pleasing) experience.

Barklice *Psocoptera*

AN: barkfly, booklouse, death-tick, deathwatch, dust-louse, psocid

These small, ever-nibbling little insects are often known as booklice, though only two or three species out of our 90-odd native and naturalised kinds ever go near a book. A more accurate name, and one preferred by entomologists, is barklouse. They most resemble aphids but have broader heads, with biting jaws and a pair of long antennae; the name of their order, Psocoptera, means 'gnawed wing'. Most species of barklouse scrape a living from pollen grains or the algal film growing on bark or mildewed leaves. Some perform a useful clean-up job in bird nests and squirrel drays. Our contributor Tony Harwood once found his car windows crawling with 'tiny, unobtrusive bark-lice with wings painted with a mottled tracery' while bringing home a load of hazel twigs on the back seat of his car. A great many barklice must end their brief lives in flames in bonfires and wood-burners.

The species known as the Common Booklouse is like a minute, flightless termite and thrives in damp paper stores and libraries. It has long intrigued observers as a devourer of documents, a kind of consumer of history, destroying the very words on the page and so grinding knowledge and wisdom into dust. In fact, booklice prefer binding paste to paper, causing books to fall apart rather than disappear, though they do graze the barely visible mildew that forms on damp paper. Other favourite haunts are damp wallpaper and plaster, mattress fillings and dirty kitchen cupboards, especially if they find a leaking packet of flour, milk powder or semolina. What no booklouse can tolerate is dry conditions (their soft bodies frizzle up when the humidity falls below 60 per cent), and so modern, centrally heated homes are not an attractive habitat. A simple answer to a domestic booklouse problem is a session with the fan heater.

A related species, *Lepinotus*, has a taste for museum specimens, especially fellow insects, and sometimes turns drawers of preserved evidence into a collection of pins, labels and a powdery mess of cast skins and droppings. Museum curators and collectors counter-attack with chemicals such as naphthalene or, increasingly, by placing the drawers in the freezer for 48 hours.

One barklouse (*Trogium pulsatorium*) makes a faint ticking noise similar to that of the Deathwatch Beetle, as it strikes its body against paper and similar materials. It has been nicknamed the 'death tick' or 'deathwatch', since the sound was once believed to presage a death. It shares the same folklore as the better-known Deathwatch Beetle: a knocking summons to the far side.

Thrips *Thysanoptera*

VN: corn flea (NE Eng.), corn lice, harvest bugs, little old men of Wroot (Yorks), midges or midgets, picture-frame insects, storm-flies, thunder-bugs, thunder-flies

Thrips are noted for getting stuck behind picture frames, in our eyes and hair or up our noses on hot humid days. They are adept at squeezing through the tiniest cracks, and when they try nibbling our sweaty skin, they can be maddeningly itchy, especially if we encounter a cloud of them when cycling up a steep hill. We call them thrips, from an ancient Greek word for woodlouse. By the rules of ancient Greek grammar, an individual insect can be called a thrip or a thrips with equal correctness.

Their family, the Thysanoptera, means 'tassel-wing'. Their feathery wings are useless for powered flight but make effective sails, allowing the thrip to be carried aloft like a hang-glider. Swarms of them

Thunder-flies: thrips on a bindweed flower.

suddenly appear in the still, humid conditions that prefigure a thunderstorm, and so they are popularly known as 'thunder-flies' or 'thunder-bugs'. Thrips are particularly attracted to brightly coloured clothing, especially orange or yellow, perhaps in the presumption that we are flowers. They may even attempt to suck our sap, and though their mouthparts cannot penetrate our skin, thrips can cause an allergic rash in a few people.

Thrips normally feed on juice or nectar from flowers and leaves, and since a few of the 185 British species feed on commercial crop plants, they are regarded as pests. Most species, in fact, feed harmlessly on wild plants, while a few attack mites and other pests, as well as fungal spores, and so could be counted as allies. Thrips form a significant part of the diet of house martins and swallows – aerial plankton scooped up as the birds dive low over the cereal fields on humid summer afternoons.

Those that make a nuisance of themselves in glasshouses and on houseplants are not native 'wild' thrips but cosmopolitan species that can only survive indoors. They scrape away at the plant's surface to get at the sap, thereby ruining a plant's fine appearance by dulling or discolouring the leaves. On top of that, they transmit plant viruses. Onions, peas and greenhouse tomatoes are the most vulnerable, while the Cereal Thrip is sometimes a problem on summer-sown wheat. Thrips have a particular liking for celery, and in the celery fields of the Isle of Axholme in Lincolnshire they have long been known as 'the little old men' or 'the little black men of Wroot'.

> 'They were called "thunder bugs" when I grew up in Oxfordshire, but when I moved to the Fens, I found they were called thrips and "midges", the latter often pronounced "midgets". This led to comments about closing the windows when the combines arrive so we don't get "midgets" flying into the house.'[23]

Stylopids *Strepsiptera*

The logo of the Royal Entomological Society is a strange little insect with a squat body and a pair of twisted, fan-shaped wings. This is a stylopid, one of a small group of parasitic insects in the order Strepsiptera, or 'twisted wings'. Only the males possess wings; the strange grub-like females live half inside their host insect, with their bodies partly protruding. These bizarre insects were the special study of the Rev. William Kirby (1759–1850), one of the founders of the society and a senior figure in the early development of British entomology. The society wished to honour him and chose a humble little stylopid discovered by him, *Stylops kirbii*, to do so.

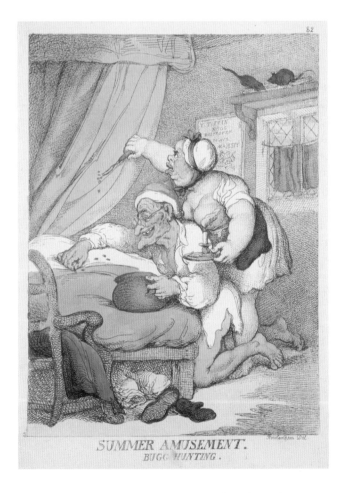

Summer Amusement, Bugg Hunting *(1801), a satire by Thomas Rowlandson.*

Lice *Anoplura* and *Mallophaga*

vn: biddies (Durham), bobo (Orkney), bogs (Lancs.), boo (Scot.), cattle (Scot.), cuties, dickies (NE Eng.), gray horse, ieawse (Lancs.), Jerusalem traveller, mums (Isle of Wight), nits, pert-lice (N Eng.), poulie, scrallybobs (Cheshire), traveller

The collective name for a large number of lice is curiously mild. It is a flock. The expression 'a flock of lice' turns up in one of the first printed books in English, *The Hors, the Shepe and the Ghoos* (1476), when a flock was a company term for any large group of animals; someone even referred to a flock of lions. But perhaps the plump, whitish lice nestling beneath the close gaze of the author of *Hors, Shepe and Ghoos* reminded him of sheep sheltering from wild weather in a fold.

Their few folk-names are equally mild. Louse itself is an ancient word of uncertain origin or meaning but not necessarily the term of abuse it is today. In Orkney, lice were referred to in almost cuddly terms as 'bobos' or 'poolies', both words meaning 'little ball'. A head crawling with lice was 'skrullyan alive wi' lice' or 'skrithan wi' lice'.[24] In America, head lice are called, with due irony, 'cuties'; in northern England, the equivalent term is 'dickies' or 'biddies'. The single word that sums up our real feelings towards lice is lousy. Originally meaning 'covered in lice', it is now a broad term for anything bad, inferior or contemptible.

There are sucking lice (Anoplura), which suck blood, and biting lice (Mallophaga), which scratch away at the skin with their jaws. Both are contained within the order Phthiraptera, meaning 'wingless louse'. We have about 25 species of sucking lice (there are undoubtedly many more out there, but the group is understandably not one that has attracted many naturalists). Human discourse is chiefly concerned with just three: the body louse, the head louse and the crab louse. All are small, wingless and with clinging, claw-like legs. Soldiers living rough in the trenches were well acquainted with the body louse, particularly during the First World War. They returned from the front itching with bites and with the stale whiff of massed lice, and louse eggs, or 'nits', in every crevice and seam of their uniform and underclothes. Soldiers had their own rough-and-ready ways of dealing with them; one was to pass a candle over the seam, as George

De-lousing: a woodcut from a 1491 printed book, Hortus Sanitatis *(The Garden of Health).*

Coppard, who served in the trenches during the Battle of the Somme, remembered:

> The things lay in the seams of trousers, in the deep furrows of long, thick, woolly pants, and seemed impregnable in their deep entrenchments. A lighted candle applied where they were thickest made them pop like Chinese crackers. After a session of this, my face would be covered in the small blood spots from extra big fellows which had popped too vigorously.[25]

Humans and lice have lived together since prehistory, though in modern times they are associated above all with war. Lice contributed their bit to the First World War by transmitting trench fever, an illness that laid low a fifth to a third of the British army between 1915 and 1918 (it was only when the war was nearly over that lice were identified as the cause). When the unbearably itchy bites are scratched, bacteria in the stomach-lining of the louse pass out in their droppings and enter the human body. Among those who endured the painful five-day (quintan) fever was J. R. R. Tolkien, author of *The Lord of the Rings*.

The body louse and the head louse are forms of the same species, otherwise known as the Human Louse. Today, head lice (subspecies *capitus*) are a recurring problem at schools, where close confinement allows them to be passed from one child to the next. One theory for their increase blames enzyme-based ('biological') soap powders. Clothes are no longer boiled in the washer, and therefore some lice may survive the wash. Though lice are associated with dirt, they are not confined to unwashed heads and are commoner on girls than boys, perhaps because girls have longer hair. Up to 5 per cent of the community has head lice at any one time. A survey commissioned by Lyclear, the makers of a medical treatment, found that one in five hairdressing salons see at least one case of 'cuties' every month, and that all hairdressers had met at least one customer with lice. Some forms of head lice have become resistant to the usual insecticides such as permethrin.

Britain was particularly troubled by head lice during the 1940s, when the visiting nurses in charge of inspecting the heads of schoolchildren became known as 'nitty Noras' or 'nitty Nora the flea explorer'. Children with nits were supposed to slop the prescribed liquid over their heads each morning and then comb out the dead bugs with special combs. Infected households were advised to wash all the bed linen and hairbrushes in hot water. Needless to say, children found ways of incorporating the lice into their games. Tony Harwood remembers that 'a favoured hobby at my primary school was preserving particularly impressive headlice, pressed flower-like, between the pages of a book'.[26]

Like fleas, lice are a traditional insult. 'Thou Flea, thou Nit, thou winter cricket, thou', roared Petruchio at a hapless tailor in Shakespeare's comedy *The Taming of the Shrew*.[27] 'Nit' comes from the ancient Greek word for dust. The word nitwit entered the language as a foolish or contemptible person or, in the case of nitpicking, someone who fusses over trifles, the irritating twit who misses the message by seeing only the small print.

The first person to look closely at a louse (as well as a flea) was Robert Hooke, who made a large and nightmarish drawing, which he had engraved in

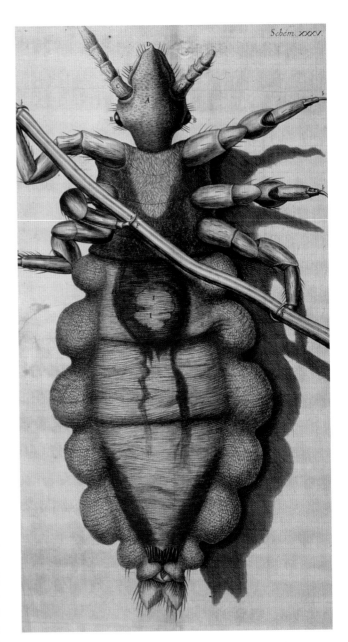

A louse on human hair, an engraving from Robert Hooke's Micrographia *of 1665.*

copper for his great work *Micrographia*. In Hooke's day, lice were thought to spring spontaneously and fully formed from 'humours' on the skin or from corrupt, putrefied blood. Hooke's louse, however, was shown with sex organs, strongly suggesting that it had other ways of multiplying. Hooke was also impressed by the appetite of a louse that he had deliberately starved before allowing it to sink its jaws into his arm. The man of science watched in fascination as the insect, though 'so greedy it could not contain more, yet continued sucking as fast as ever, and, as fast, emptying itself behind'.[28] A louse, he found, did have one weakness: it would die instantly if smeared with the blood of another creature.

Like fleas, the perceived worthlessness of lice lends itself to comedy. Robert Burns' great poem 'To a Louse', written in 1785, is best remembered for the line in its last verse:

> O wad some Pow'r the giftie gie us
> To see coursels as others see us!

Less often remembered is the poem's sub-title: 'On Seeing One on a Lady's Bonnet at Church'. The poem is essentially a comic sermon on the text of 'She who exalts herself shall be humbled'. Burns is sitting behind Jenny, a local girl he fancies but has no hope of winning. Jenny thinks the poet's rapt attention is because of her bonnie looks and the fine, fashionable balloon-like bonnet she is wearing. But she cannot see what Burns sees, a louse 'as plump an' gray as onie grozet' climbing up her expensive headwear. Yet, Burns reflects, ruefully, the bug is one up on him, for it has set its foul feet where he dare not, on Jenny's body. It has bitten her once already and will surely do so again.

> Ha! Whare ye gaun, ye crowlan ferlie!
> Ye ugly, creepan, blastet wonner,
> Detested, shunn'd, by saunt an' sinner,
> How daur ye set your fit upon her,
> Sae fine a Lady!
> Gae somewhere else and seek your dinner,
> On some poor body.[29]

Part of the comic effect comes from the louse's unconscious pretensions. There are plenty of humble folk in the congregation whose bonnets would be a fitter place for the louse – the homely woollen cap of an 'auld wifie', for instance, or the grubby flannel vest of 'some bit duddy boy'. But this mock-heroic louse has chosen 'the vera tapmost, towrin' height O' Miss's bonnet'. The prideful, puffed-up Jenny has been laughably brought down by the lowest creature on earth.

What came first, the louse or the egg? This problem bothered William Kirby, the founding father of modern entomology. Kirby was a deeply religious man who believed in the literal truth of the Bible. In Genesis he read that all creeping things were already created, fully formed, before God created Adam and Eve. But, if so, where did that leave insects such as head lice and fleas that, as parasites, depended on mankind? After long soul-searching, he found a solution. God had indeed created these creatures, but they remained in dormant form, as

eggs, until there were humans to parasitise. Hence, Kirby thought, he had solved the age-old question of which comes first, the chicken or the egg? In the case of lice, it was the egg.

The Crab Louse is a different species, known in Scotland as a 'cart' or 'kartie'. Almost as broad as long and roughly crab-shaped, it has powerful claws for clinging to thick pubic hair and is rarely found far from the human crotch (it is also occasionally found attached to eye-lashes). Unlike the body louse, it does not transmit disease but, of course, extracts a social penalty, as 'crabs' suggest the victim has been rather unfussy in his or her sexual activities. The ritual treatment was to creep off to the clinic, head hanging, to collect a jar of 'blue unction' ointment with which to plaster one's shaven genitals (today, crab lice are more easily banished with medical shampoo). Crab lice are said to have a preference for teenagers and young adults.

Bird lice *Mallophaga*

AN: biting lice, chewing lice, feather lice

Unlike sucking lice, bird lice have functioning jaws, which they use to scrape bits off hair, skin or feathers (their scientific group name Mallophaga means 'wool-eating'), though a few species can also suck blood. There are around 500 species in Britain, but because most are parasites of birds and usually leave humankind alone, they do not excite so much attention. Up to the 1950s, only one book had ever been written about British bird lice, and that was 160 years out of date. Yet even the author of the *Monographia Anoplurorum Britanniae* failed to warm to his subjects: 'Can we believe that man in his pristine state of glory, and beauty, and dignity, could be the receptacle of these unclean and disgusting creatures?' wrote Henry Denny, rhetorically, of course, in 1842.[30]

Some birds suffer more from lice than others. Those which festoon the sleek feathers of swallows, swifts and martins must technically count as migrants since, unlike fleas, some of them are carried away with the bird, returning again in the spring, still busy nibbling skin and feathers and apparently none the worse for the experience. Pigeons, too, carry more than their share, and where large numbers of them roost nearby, the lice can be carried into homes. As a boy, I was nibbled by bird lice escaping from swift's nests in the attic. Some itchy skin blotches were the result, but it must be far worse being a bird.

Fleas *Siphonaptera*

VN: biddies (Cumb.), fleea (Lancs.), flech or fleck (Scot.), lop (NE Eng.), vlea (Isle of Wight), vlee (Yorks.)

Fleas, wrote Thomas Muffet, are 'a vexation to all men'.[31] He might have added 'and women', since housemaids were frequent victims, as were 'wearied and sick persons'. Fleas attack by night, 'seeking for the most tender places', and depart in the morning, 'leaving a red spot as a Trophie of their force'. Like other small, nuisance insects, they were supposed to spring to life by spontaneous generation, newborn from dust and filth. Some claimed that the nascent fleas stirred when dust was moistened by sweat or drops of urine. Physicians such as Muffet were well aware that fleas laid eggs, but it seems they regarded them as an alternative way of developing, as an insurance policy, perhaps – but only a secondary method of procreation. Fleas could be kept away by strewing the bedroom with pungent herbs, especially fleabane and fleawort. Other everyday weeds that sometimes did the trick were pennyroyal, rue, mint, coriander and mustard, or the leaves of bay and walnut trees. Those not wholly convinced of the powers of such natural insecticides could turn to more dangerous concoctions: white arsenic, quicklime laced with hellebore juice or, presumably if all else failed, 'the dregs of mares-pisse'.

Yet Muffet could not hide a certain admiration for this 'Wonder of Nature', this 'bunch backed' little creature 'almost like a Hog', whose 'hinder legs are bent backwards towards their bellies, and their forelegs towards their breasts', and were capable of such prodigious leaps. The name of the flea family, Siphonaptera, means 'wingless pipe'. All fleas are wingless, and apart from their famous jumps into space, are taken from place to place in the fur or feathers of their hosts, transferring themselves from one animal to the next as they nestle together. Some 60 species occur in Britain, all of which are external parasites of mammals and birds. Today, the few that find their way into homes are brought there mainly by cats and dogs. The straightforward solution is to give the pet a bath with plenty of soapy water. For infestations, one answer is a fine powder or spray known as 'diatomaceous earth', made from the spiky, microscopic skeletons of algae. When the fleas swallow it, the tiny 'spicules' puncture their

guts and kill them. Cat and dog fleas occasionally bite us; the more famous Human Flea is now rare in Britain, with remarkably few recent records in the *Atlas of the Fleas*.[32]

Some animals are plagued by fleas more than others. The hedgehog is a notoriously flea-ridden beast; one sick animal at a rescue centre yielded 7100 specimens. Sand martins and house martins have whole tribes of fleas peculiar to themselves; evidently they drop off before the birds depart south but are ready and waiting at their nests when they return in the spring. Moles, voles, badgers and red squirrels are also regular flea hosts. The species that have impinged most on human lives are the Rat Flea and the Rabbit Flea. The Rat Flea is believed to be the vector of the bubonic plague bacillus, which killed up to half the British population during the Black Death, and was also the cause of a mass mortality in India in the late nineteenth century. It bites only the black rat, an animal almost extinct in Britain, and there are no recent records of its flea. The brown rat, though unwelcome in other ways, does not carry the flea.

The Rabbit Flea carries the *myxoma* virus, which was deliberately introduced to Australia to control rabbits and illicitly released into the French countryside in 1952. It found its way to Britain a year later. Dying listless rabbits infected with myxomatosis, or 'myxi', with their horribly swollen eyes, are all too familiar. In ironic counterpoint to the flea-related Black Death, the rabbits in Richard Adams' novel *Watership Down* referred to it as the 'white death'. In its early years, the disease wiped out 95 percent of British rabbits. Though they have developed resistance to the disease and their numbers have partially recovered, rabbits have never again been as abundant as they were before 1953. Their flea is more likely to be seen nowadays festooning the ears of a cat as it returns from a hunting expedition. The Rabbit Flea is native to Britain and normally does no lasting harm to its host. It is our own manipulation of nature using micro-organisms that wiped out the rabbits.

Muffet picked up a tall hunting story of how foxes got rid of their fleas. Living in earthen dens, foxes attracted more than their share of them. Huntsmen, who of all people could appreciate the intelligence of the fox, swore that they had witnessed the animal pulling sheep's wool from the thorns and briars and then, holding the ball of wool in its mouth, running down to the river. By slowly immersing itself in the cold water, the fox ensured that his fleas would migrate to the last bit of dry animal, its jaws, where they would find the warm and inviting ball of wool. When the last flea had crept into the wool, the fox would bark and spit the flea-ridden wool into the water, and 'so very froliquely being delivered from their molestations', would swim back to land, wagging its big bushy tail.[33]

It is not in a flea's best interests to harm its host. Sometimes fleas weaken fledgling birds by drinking too much of their blood, but it is the micro-organisms sometimes carried by them that cause illness rather than the fleas themselves. Pet stores stock an impressive armoury of products to deal with fleas on dogs and cats, from shampoos, sprays, dips and lotions to growth regulators that circulate in the animal's blood and render the flea effectively sterile. But perhaps the best weapon of all is the household vacuum cleaner.

Charles Rothschild was head of Rothschild's bank and a gifted amateur naturalist who took a self-confessedly 'child-like pleasure' in nature. Though originally a lepidopterist, he took up fleas because of their greater scientific challenge. During a collecting trip to the Sudan in 1901, he was the first to describe scientifically the plague-carrying Rat Flea; he named it *Xenopsylla cheopsis* in honour of Cheops, the pharaoh who built the Great Pyramid. After his untimely death in 1923, Rothschild's pioneering descriptive work was continued by his daughter Miriam, who for the purpose kept quantities of live fleas in linen bags and cardboard boxes scattered about her bedroom or under the bed. Her published work on the Rothschild collection spilled into six fat volumes, work requiring untold hours of, as she put it, 'staring at the backside of fleas'. She noticed, in the process, that no two fleas were exactly alike; also that the Rabbit Flea could time its fertility to coincide with that of its host so accurately that 'the baby fleas were able to drop straight on to new-born rabbits'.[34]

The catalyst for the study of such unpopular invertebrates is often a single hyperactive individual. In the case of fleas, the successor to the Rothschilds is Bob George, a former RAF pilot and schoolteacher, who has studied them for 60 years and, in 1964, instituted a national record scheme for fleas. In 1974, the first flea atlas was published, but perhaps not surprisingly, it tended to show where flea experts, rather than fleas, lived. Thirty-eight years later, in 2008, a second atlas was published with far more credible 'dot maps', attesting to a vast amount of quiet activity by Bob George and

A cat flea leaping from its comfort blanket of fur.

his fellows (though Shropshire, the home county of one of them, is revealed by dense clusters of dots).

Sayings involving fleas generally stress their worthlessness. The flea was the smallest of insects that could be seen with the naked eye and therefore ranked least in creation's great scheme, the lowest of the low in life's pecking order. Once, when asked to compare the merits of two very dim poets, Derrick and Smart, Dr Johnson quipped that 'Sir, there is no settling the point of precedency between a louse and a flea'. Both were so despicable that deciding which of them was worse was a waste of time. Similarly, a 'flea bite' is a small thing of no consequence, a mere nothing, a mean, measly contribution barely worth having.

Everyone knows Jonathan Swift's adage that 'Great fleas have lesser fleas'. It is true that some parasites have lesser parasites known as hyper-parasites (though not ad infinitum), but the great satirist was using the lowly flea to highlight the human condition: no matter what our station in life, he was saying, we all suffer from hangers-on. The original version comes from Swift's *On Poetry: A Rhapsody*:

> Hobbes clearly proves, that every creature
> Lives in a state of war by nature . . .
> So naturalists observe, a flea
> Has smaller fleas that on him prey;
> And these have smaller still to bite 'em,
> And so proceed *ad infinitum*.
> Thus ever poet, in his kind,
> Is bit by him that comes behind.[35]

To send someone away 'with a flea in his ear' dates back to the Middle Ages, where it appears among *Scogan's Jests*. It means to deliver a reproof sufficiently devastating to send the miscreant staggering off in shock. The analogy is with a dog driven mad by an appalling itching in a place it cannot reach and so running away in frustration and fear. In earlier times, the phrase could also suggest that someone had heard some bad news and had gone away shaking his or her head. This, apparently, is the normal human reaction to a flea in one's ear.

'As fit as a flea' recalls the flea's prodigious jumping powers. In the north of England, they were called 'lops', from the old word for leaps. Were a flea the size of a man, it could jump over St Paul's or Canary Wharf, while a particularly strong flea could probably go into orbit. The energy produced by a jumping flea is such that, if a flea could continue to jump for 90 seconds together, it would actually boil.

The entomologist and professional Yorkshireman Obadiah Westwood used to say, 'if I could 'op as 'igh as a flea I could 'op to the top of 'Eadington 'ill in an 'op and a 'arf'.[36] Another Yorkshire saying was: 'How sweet, how varry sweet is life. As t'flea said when 'e wur stick it treacle.'

'If you lie down with dogs, you'll get up with fleas.' Human failings, such as dishonesty, are contagious. Get involved in bad company, and you will suffer the consequences. This is an old expression, surfacing long ago as: 'He that goeth to bedde wyth dogges aryseth with fleas.'

At least one flea saying was invented by the Bard himself, in *Henry V*. The French nobles are quarrelling on the eve of Agincourt. One admits that the English are valiant, to which another scoffs: 'That's a valiant flea that dare eat his breakfast on the lip of a lion.'[37] It is all very well being brave, but when you face (as he thinks) certain destruction, the better part of valour is discretion.

My Spanish mother-in-law has a phrase, 'Stranger than a green flea'.[38]

In the Hebrides, when someone is outstaying their welcome, they say: '*Rinn e luath is deargannan ann*' – that is, 'He made ashes and fleas there.'[39]

Fleas were among the most popular objects for early microscopes, so much so that the instruments were nicknamed 'flea glasses'. Robert Hooke's *Micrographia*, published in the 1660s, contains a huge and detailed drawing of a human flea 43 cm across. 'Though this little Creature is almost universally known to be a small brown skipping animal,' commented Hooke, 'very few are acquainted with its real Shape and Figure, with the Structure, Strength, Beauty of its Limbs and Parts, or with the Manner of its Generation and Increase.'[40] The drawing is not in Hooke's usual style; it may possibly be the work of his one-time colleague, the famous architect Christopher Wren. At any rate, the drawing coincided gruesomely with the Great Plague of London in 1665, in which up to 100,000 people died from a disease transmitted by fleas (and

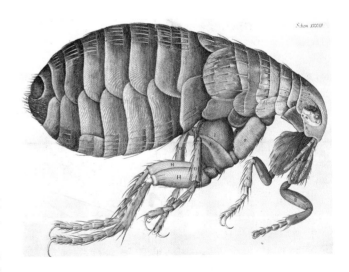

A flea from Robert Hooke's Micrographia: some Physiological descriptions of minute bodies made by magnifying glasses *(1665), published in the same year as the Great Plague of London.*

The Ghost of a Flea (1819–20), by William Blake, an image based on the tradition that fleas are inhabited by the souls of violent, bloodthirsty men.

Man Perceived as a Flea (1985), by Stephen Campbell, a surrealist painting inverting the human-centred view of life.

probably lice). At the time, no one had made any connection between the plague and the flea.

Hooke's flea is shown as he observed it, under his simple 'flea glass', but William Blake's painting *The Ghost of a Flea* shows the world as he thought a flea might see it. A high-shouldered, naked bogeyman – half man, half flea – strides across the boards at night, with stars and a falling meteor adding to the unworldly effect. The creature holds a curved knife. A tongue flickers in its small head as it leers, with what G. K. Chesterton calls 'a moony glitter', at the contents of a large bowl held in its other hand. Like fairy-tale giants and ogres who live in dark, gloomy castles, he is about to take a swig of human blood. Barely visible beneath his 'curiously polish'd suit of sable Armour' sits a tiny flea. Why should so small a thing as a flea have so mighty a 'ghost'? Blake's friend John Varley thought the poet had seen and been influenced by Hooke's huge engraving of a flea and that the Ghost's cup was in fact the aperture of Hooke's microscope.

But Blake was also aware of a folk tradition that saw fleas as husks inhabited by the souls of violent and bloodthirsty men. These brutes and tyrants were providentially confined inside the bodies of the smallest of insects to reduce their rage to a manageable level. Blake is showing us the monster within. In his short biography of the visionary artist, G. K. Chesterton points out that Blake was less interested in the anatomical details of a flea as in its 'idea or principle'. Just as the tiger, for Blake, stands for elegance, and a tree for silent strength, so the flea is about bloodthirstiness: 'the feeding on the life of another, the fury of the parasite'. In Blake's inward eye, the soul of a flea is ten thousand times larger than a flea and so, in a sense, is more solid and real than the insect itself. 'The flea himself is hazy and fantastic', says Chesterton, 'compared to the hard and massive actuality of his ghost. When we have understood this, we have understood one of the great ideas in Blake – the idea of ideas.'[41]

The Scottish surrealist painter, the late Steven Campbell, produced a very different image of the world as seen through the eyes of a flea. His dream-like painting *A Man Perceived by a Flea* has the insect more or less accurately drawn, whereas the man's body and head have dissolved into a mass of bubbles, leaving only his foreshortened legs and feet. This, perhaps, alludes to the distorted vision of an insect's multi-faceted eyes. That something else is going on as well is suggested by the bubble-man's falling hat, his shoeless foot and the second head that has mysteriously sprouted near his waist. Like Blake's vision, these are images of the inward mind, of mental space rather than physical space. The effect is to unbalance our perceptions of reality.

Poetic fleas have a different, sometimes erotic, life inspired by the necessarily intimate contact between person and flea. 'The Flea', by John Donne, draws a surprising mixture of comedy and sensuousness from an encounter with a flea. The protagonist is in bed with his newly wedded wife, who is still a virgin. The man is as keen as mustard, but his partner is a little shy and reluctant. Sharing their bed is a hungry flea, and the poet asks the lady to observe how 'It suck'd me first, and now bites thee' and thus mingled their blood within its tiny body:

> And in this flea our two bloods be.
> Thou know'st that this cannot be said
> A sin, nor shame, nor loss of maidenhead;
> Yet this enjoys before it woo,
> And pamper'd swells with one blood made of
>   two;
> And this, alas! Is more than we would do.[42]

If she will 'yield' to him, she will lose only as much of her honour as she has already lost to the flea. The erotic charge of this poem comes from the contemporary idea of the sexual act as 'a mingling of the blood', in which each partner takes a little of the life from the other. This saucy flea had casually done what the poet still aspires to.

Mankind has exploited the flea, turned the tables, as it were, by seemingly training them to perform circus tricks. Of course, circus-training a flea or any other insect is in reality impossible: insect behaviour is programmed by DNA, not learned. Flea circuses use the scaled-down leg-power of fleas to deceive the viewer into believing what they see. The grandfather of all flea circuses was Bertolotto's, known as the 'Extraordinary Exhibition of the Industrious Fleas' and based in rooms on Regent Street in the early 1800s. With the help of fresnel magnifying lenses, viewers queued up to watch as the fleas were harnessed to little wagons with barely visible wisps of thread or performed acrobatics from a high wire with, as a grand finale, a rendition of the Battle of Waterloo starring a flea Napoleon. Bertolotto, who claimed to treat his flea performers

Dressed fleas, collected by Charles Rothschild while travelling in Mexico in 1905, now in Tring Museum.

with great kindness, later wrote a well-regarded book about them.[43] The trickery lies in harnessing the insects without harming them, after which the flea simply does what comes naturally and kicks out with its hind legs. Today's performing fleas have the benefit of video cameras to project the activities onto a big screen. The Bertolotto of our time is Steve Legg, whose Incredible Flea Circus pulls in the crowds with its Ben-Hur style chariot races and death-defying finale starring Barry and Brenda, the incredible fleas. Presumably Barry and Brenda are replaced regularly, since even the best-fed flea seldom lives more than a season.

Unlike flea circuses, flea-dressing is a lost art. A tiny flea is decked out in wisps of brightly coloured clothes visible only under a magnifying glass. There is an exhibit in the Tring Museum, once owned by Lord Rothschild, of a flea wedding party, including bride and groom and a band, all dressed up in their best, the work of some forgotten genius in nineteenth-century Mexico.

Fleas also inspired music. 'Spanish Flea' is an instrumental tune by Herb Alpert & the Tijuana Brass, which was hard to escape from around Christmas 1965. It was based on a song about a music-minded flea from Madrid, which packed its tiny Spanish guitar and hitched a ride 'inside a dog'. Arriving in London humming its signature tune, the Latino flea was taken up by a music producer and lived happily ever after. Today it may best be remembered by *Simpsons'* fans from the episode in which Homer warbles the mindless words while, unnoticed by him, a riot is taking place just outside.

Fleapits were places where crowds gathered for entertainment and fleas gathered for a blood banquet. The modern-day equivalent of the Elizabethan theatres and cockpits is a run-down town cinema. Flea markets, on the other hand, are noted for cheap, shoddy goods rather than real live fleas. Just as fleas were seen as worthless, so too are the bargains on display. Surprisingly, perhaps, there are even pubs named after fleas. The Fleapit in Bethnal Green specializes in beers made by micro-breweries. There was also a Dumb Flea at Meldreth in Cumberland.

Lacewings and their relatives
Neuroptera

Lacewings *Chrysopidae*

VN: golden-eyes, stink-flies, trash-bugs

The commonest kind of lacewing, which is often found sitting on windowpanes or even on walls indoors, is a delicate-looking insect, with a long green body, beady little eyes and oval wings as intricately veined as muslin. They are considered to be among the principal gardener's friends, since their larvae prey on aphids. Less flatteringly, they are known as 'stink-flies', from their habit of excreting when handled. By some evolutionary quirk, lacewing larvae lack a functioning anus, and so they store up their body waste until the moment when, after changing their skin one last time, they void it all in one go. Apparently, some lacewings can be identified by the shape of this single enormous dropping.

Lacewings are the best-known insects in the order Neuroptera, or 'nerve-wings', so named from the intricate, net-like pattern of veins on their transparent wings. Their appetite for aphids is prodigious. Each adult lays about 300 eggs, and a single larva consumes 1000–10,000 aphids during its development. Hence just one pair of lacewings has the potential to rid our gardens of up to 3 million aphids. One species with a bluish body, *Chrysopa perla*, can now be purchased as a bio-control agent for use in greenhouses. One can also buy custom-made 'lacewing chambers' to hang in a suitably sheltered position as a hibernation rest-lodge for overwintering adults, a gesture of reward for all their help.

Lacewings are delicate and easily damaged by careless handling. Our contributor Tony Harwood offers this tip for rescuers: 'Lacewings usually drop like a stone if you try to catch them. So try placing a receptacle, or your palm, directly beneath one, and wave the other hand close to the insect. It should drop down and remain docile for a few seconds, long enough for you to release it out of the window.'

The largest of our 43 species of lacewing, *Osymlus fulvicephalus*, is a giant, the size of a small dragonfly, with big, floppy, dot-marked wings. It occasionally inhabits damp, neglected corners of the garden, especially near a stream where willowherb or

Left: *The flight of a lacewing. Slowed down, it has a balletic grace and beauty.*

nettles have been allowed to grow. Such conditions seem to breed giant insects: the lacewing shares the mangrove-like shade with a giant daddy-longlegs, the aptly named *Tipula maxima*, which, at six centimetres across, has the largest wingspan of any British fly.

Spongeflies (Sisyridae) are a specialist family of brown-winged lacewings whose larvae live inside freshwater sponges, feeding on their body fluids.

Lacewings have seldom entered our cultural lives except among swarms of other insects, but they do appear quite often as ingredients for magic potions in the Harry Potter stories. Perhaps it's the name.

A sagging interest in lacewings and their relatives was revived in 1988 by a national recording scheme. Participants receive a newsletter, the *Neuro News*.

Alderflies *Sialidae*

Alderflies look like heavily built lacewings or small caddisflies but have distinctive black-veined wings. Though they are common along the banks of streams and rivers in early summer, they have no particular association with alders. The adults are attracted to pale colours and readily settle on our clothes and sleeves. There are six very similar-looking British species. Though alderflies have fierce-looking aquatic larvae that live on the bottom, feeding on smaller worms and insect larvae, the adults are placid

The Alderfly, with its heavily veined wings.

insects that often fall into the water, where they are eagerly snapped up by trout. On days when large numbers of alderflies are about, some anglers use a wet-fly modelled on them, known simply as an 'alder'. A specially made box to hold fishing flies has been marketed as an 'alderfly box'.

Antlions *Myrmeleonidae*

vn: doodlebug, sand dragon

If you see an adult antlion, you might wonder how it acquired its fierce name. Superficially, it resembles a dragonfly, but it has patterned wings and clubbed antennae like a butterfly. Its flight is more like a butterfly's, slow and fluttering, with frequent pauses for rest, draping its long wings over its back. The antlion gets its name not from the rather sedate adult insect but from the pudgy grub, with its outsized pair of pincer-like jaws. The antlion larva excavates a conical pit in the sand and conceals itself in a burrow at the bottom, leaving only its spring-trap jaws poking up. Unwary crawling insects tumble into the pit, where they are dispatched with a bite, pulled into the hidden burrow and consumed. Ants certainly feature among the prey, but almost any wandering creature small enough to fit the antlion's jaws can be on the menu, including other, slightly smaller, antlions. If the victim spots what is going on and tries to scramble out of the pit, the antlion has another trick. It hurls sand grains upwards until a lucky strike sends the victim tumbling downhill for its date with the jaws. In America, where they are common, antlions are called 'doodlebugs' from their habit of making spiral trails in the sand as they look for a suitable place to dig. They are popular insect pets: all they need is a live ant or two every day. They perform for their food with a snap of their jaws.

Until the 1990s, it was debatable whether antlions bred in Britain. The evidence was slender, and if they did occasionally establish a colony, they were certainly rare. A short account, back in 1781, gives the impression, without citing evidence, that in the eighteenth century, it was considered British. An adult was seen clinging to a paling at Garleston, Suffolk, in 1931, and another was attracted to a window light at Corton in 1988. Then in 1994, two adults were spotted by a path near the RSPB's Minsmere reserve on the Suffolk coast, and a third was found 'squashed on the floor of the toilet

A particularly impressive South African species of antlion, sometimes kept as a pet. Antlions are named after their ferocious larvae, which hide at the bottom of conical depressions in the sand, with only their open jaws protruding.

block'.[44] Two years later, hundreds of antlion pits were found, along with 12 newly emerged adults drying their wings. The species was identified as *Euroleon nostras*, a widespread continental species now known in Britain as the Suffolk Antlion. It has become a minor insect celebrity and now appears in brochures promoting walks in the Sandlings area. Recently, another colony has turned up at Wells-next-the-Sea in Norfolk.

Snakeflies *Raphidiidae*

Snakeflies are a small and ancient group of flying insects, distantly related to lacewings but usually placed in an order of their own, the Raphidioptera. You can recognise one instantly by its elongated thorax and head, like the front end of a tiny snake. The fly uses this extra length to lunge at its prey from an ambush-point on a leaf. The female snakefly has what looks like an impressive sting but is, in fact, an ovipositor for laying eggs in the crevices of tree bark. They are not uncommon in open woodland but are generally only seen when they use a passing human as a rest stop or perhaps as a convenient walking tree. There are four British species.

Scorpionflies *Mecoptera*

Scorpionflies look alarming but, like snakeflies, are completely harmless. The name comes from the female fly's curled-over, scorpion-like tail, but the head end looks almost equally intimidating, ending in a sharp, vicious-looking beak. They are ancient insects of hedgerows and wood-edges, with no living relatives, and so are usually placed in an order of their own, the Mecoptera, meaning 'long-wing'. Scorpionflies are noted for their risky dining habits, which include stealing small insects from spider webs, as well as supping on windfall apples shoulder to shoulder with hungry social wasps. We have only four species, including the charming Snow Flea, a dumpy, wingless insect that hops among the moss on moors and heaths in the dead of winter.

The Snow Flea, a strange flightless relation of scorpionflies – a springtail – and one of the few insects that lives on snow.

A scorpionfly (Panorpa communis) *leaves terra firma.*

Caddisflies *Trichoptera*

VN: (adult): rails (Ireland), sedge-flies
 (larva): caddisworm, caseworm, codworm,
 cor bait, stickworm, straw-worm

Caddisflies are best known to fishermen as 'sedges' or 'caddisworms', and they fashion special flies that imitate either the adult fly or its larva. If you live near a pond or river, you may find caddisflies coming to lighted windows; they fly around lamps with an odd clicking sound. It is easy to recognise a caddisfly but much more difficult to distinguish one species from another, since most of our 198 species look disconcertingly similar. Far more distinctive are their larvae, all but one of which live in water, many inside ingenious little cases strengthened with grit or bits of leaves or twigs.

The original name for these insects seems to have been 'caddisworm' or 'codworm'. Thomas Muffet referred to the 'cados worm', while the angler Izaak Walton claimed that the 'Mayflie . . . is bred of the cod-worm or Caddis.'[45] The word caddis meant a strip of cloth. In Shakespeare's *The Winter's Tale*, the wandering cloth-seller and pickpocket Autolycus has 'ribbons of all colours i' the rainbow, points . . . inkles [and] caddysses' to sell.[46] Cloth-sellers like him commonly wore strips of brightly coloured yarn to advertise their trade, and these worms of the streambed similarly wore bits of material for their own purposes. Perhaps the name also has links with 'caddy' as a box or bag, as in tea caddy, or the bag of golf clubs that caddies carry around for their clients.

Adult caddisflies look moth-like but can be distinguished easily by their long, forward-pointing antennae and the characteristic way they hold their wings like a steep-pitched roof over their slim, leggy bodies. Caddisflies lack the coiled proboscis of butterflies and moths, and their wings are covered in short hair instead of scales, hence the name of their order, Trichoptera, or 'hairy wings'.

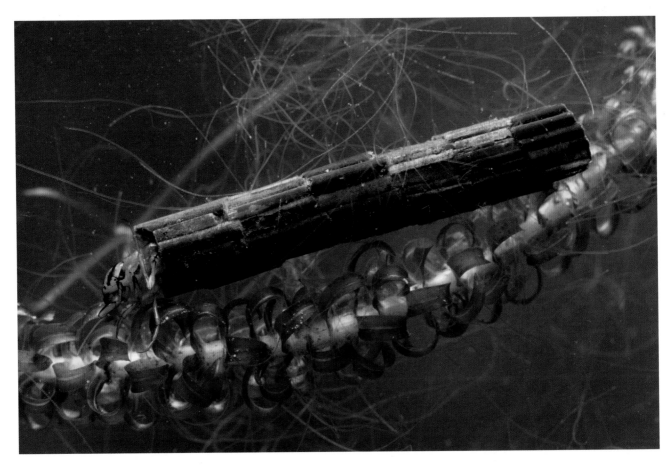

A caddisfly larva. It makes its case from fragments of leaves, chewed to fit and arranged with a bricklayer's care.

Caddisflies are commonest in cold, well-oxygenated water and so are good indicators of water quality. Both the caddisworms and adult flies are important in the diet of fish, especially trout, and hence anglers have a whole terminology for flies based on different kinds of caddis. The commonest ones are 'sedges', named after common wetland plants, but others include 'dancers', 'buttons', 'flags' and 'silverhorns', as well as the 'caperer', 'grannom' and 'speckled Peter'. Each fishing fly has its season, when the corresponding insect is about on the water; the 'grannom', for example, is a handy trout-fly for chalk streams in April.

The following are angler's names for species of caddisfly.

Scientific name	Angling name
Myastacides	silverhorn, dancer
Sericostoma	Halford's Welsh button, caperer
Leptocerus	silverhorn
Phryganea	great red sedge, murragh, speckled Peter
Limnephilus	cinnamon sedge
Stenophylax stellatus	large cinnamon sedge
Rhyacophila	brown sedge
Brachycentrus subnubilis	grannom
Halesus radiatus	caperer
Hydropsyche	grey flag, grey sedge
Goera pilosa	medium sedge
Lepidostoma	silver sedge

There is a single exception to the rule that caddisfly larvae live in water: the elusive Land Caddis, which lives among damp leaves and moss in woodland. It is confined to the part of Worcestershire centred on the Wyre Forest, and though not spectacular (David Harding describes it as 'resembling animated All-Bran'),[47] it has become a minor insect celebrity, both for its rarity and its exceptional habits. The first Land Caddis seen for many decades was on the walls of the tent of the naturalist Norman Hickin, while he was camping in the forest, though to his lasting chagrin, it was spotted not by him but by his young daughter.[48]

Caddisflies have a small but active recording group, currently run by Dr Ian Wallace at the World Museum Liverpool. They are also studied through the Angler's Monitoring Initiative, run by the Riverfly Partnership, which uses the caddisflies' sensitive ecology to assess the environmental health of rivers.

In 2007, four rare caddisflies were added to the list of threatened insects in the UK Biodiversity Action Plan: Small Grey Sedge, Window-winged Sedge, Scarce Grey Flag and Scarce Brown Sedge. The English names were manufactured especially for the occasion. Unless it has a pronounceable name, it may be difficult to persuade politicians that something is worth saving.

GRASSHOPPERS AND CRICKETS
Orthoptera

Grasshoppers *Acrididae*

VN: cricket (Scotland), griglan (Cornwall), ground locust, skipjacks

Nothing in the insect world, except perhaps butterflies, recalls the pleasure of lying among the long grass and staring at the sky as much as do grasshoppers. Poets down the ages have alluded to that merry chirp as an eternal image of high summer, with its dalliances and bucolic pleasures. John Clare, who had the enviable knack of always finding exactly the right phrase, referred

to the grasshopper's 'fretting song' (as opposed to the cricket's 'chickering') or 'treble pipe'.[1] A grasshopper makes its characteristic sound by rubbing its wing-cases against its legs (crickets do it by rubbing their wings together), a process known as stridulation. Unlike Clare, entomologists have struggled to find words for the stridulations of individual grasshoppers. Perhaps the most familiar is the Field Grasshopper's 'short, brisk chirp, repeated at short intervals', but more exotic sounds are the 'bubbles popping' of the Large Marsh Grasshopper or the 'weird metallic scouring' of the Stripe-winged Grasshopper, while the Heath Grasshopper produces a burst of energetic scraping

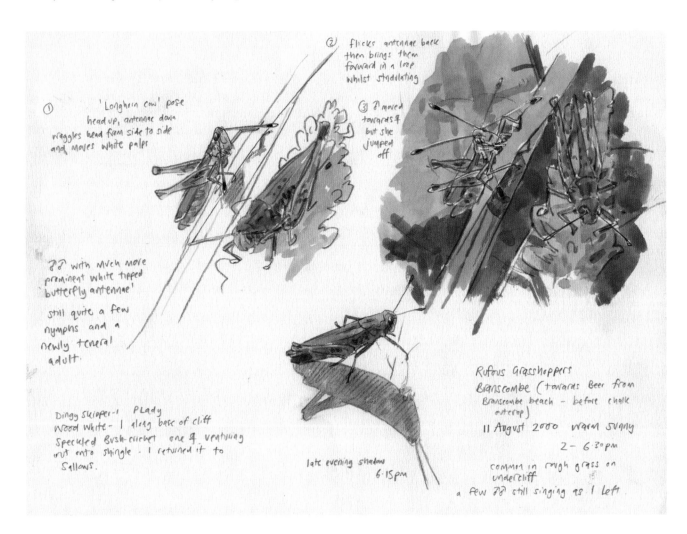

Sketches from Life of the Rufous Grasshopper, *by John Walters.*

The Grasshopper and the Ant, *a linocut by Edward Bawden, from* Aesop's Fables.

that recalls nothing so much as the quacking of an excited duck.

As the naturalist Michael Chinery put it, 'they share with radio announcers the distinction of being better known by their voice than their looks.' Each species of grasshopper or cricket has a diagnostic set of buzzes, scrapes or chirps with which it advertises its presence to a mate. And like birds, its call can be recognised long before you find the small green insect that made it. Even when in full chirp, their wing-cases scratching busily away nearby, they can be elusive, and they tend to stop singing when you get too close. Compared with central and southern Europe, Britain is a poor place for grasshopper diversity. We have only 30 or so species, and many of these are confined to warm places in the south, such as heaths, south-facing downs and coastal cliffs. On the other hand, a few are very common: the majority of everyday grasshopper songs come from the trio of Common Green, Field and Meadow Grasshoppers.

True grasshoppers have powerful back legs for jumping and short 'horns', their wings carefully folded like a fan beneath brittle, parchment-like wing-cases. They range in size from tiny ground-hoppers no larger than a grain of seed to the rare Migratory Locust, with a body the size of a little finger. One thinks of grasshoppers as mainly green, but some forms are brownish, others surprisingly colourful in shades of red, purple and yellow. The Woodland Grasshopper has been described as 'as showy as a spotted woodpecker', while some forms of the Mottled Grasshopper are 'reminiscent of the

dazzle-paint camouflage patterns used on shipping during war'.[2]

There are surprisingly few folk-names for grasshoppers, perhaps because their name is so delightfully folksy already. In rural parts of Cornwall, they have been called 'griggans,' probably from the Cornish word for rough ground, *griglan*. Welsh-speakers know them as *celiog y rhedhyn* or 'cock of the bracken', *jac-y-jwmper* (Jack the jumper), *sboncyn gwair* (sprites of the grass) or, on Anglesey, *Robin shonc* (sprightly robins).

The grasshoppers of folklore, which derive from the Bible, are what we now call locusts. The Greek word *locusta* means any bug with thick, shell-like skin, and so included crabs, lobsters and cicadas as well as locusts (lobster and locust are in fact variants on the same word, as is langoustine, or 'little sea locust'). What they had in common was that these 'locusts' could be all collected as food. John the Baptist survived in the desert on a diet of locusts and wild honey. Hence, in some devotional paintings, he is accompanied by a grasshopper, as if it were a companion or good angel as well as lunch.

The collective term 'a cloud of grasshoppers' refers to the result of a sudden population explosion of Desert, or Migratory, Locusts, once a common and dreaded phenomenon of nature in Africa and the Middle East. From a safe distance, a swarm of locusts looks like a dust cloud, and in ancient literature they were described as numberless as grains of sand on a beach or as the stars in the heavens. A swarm contains something like 250 million finger-sized grasshoppers per square kilometre and a big swarm may cover half the size of an English county. Locusts strip the landscape bare. Hence, they became a potent symbol of an all-devouring destruction, and the image lives on in expressions such as 'the locust years', the term famously used by Winston Churchill to describe the politically wasted years of the 1930s, or in the Biblical original, 'the years that the locust hath eaten' (Joel, 2:25).

Despite their image as scourges of the earth, the swarming tendencies of locusts were also seen as a kind of wisdom. One of the Biblical Proverbs reminds us that 'locusts have no king, yet they go forth all of them by bands'. (Proverbs, 30:27) They are one of the four 'little things' that were considered 'exceedingly wise', along with ants, spiders and 'rabbits'. Proverbs seems to be pointing out a useful lesson in democracy and co-operation. But early Christian commentators saw the lesson in evangelical terms: plagues of locusts brought on a mood of repentance. Others saw in the suffering of the Israelites a reminder that the gentile nations often did uncommonly well in war, despite not being among the elect. Combining the two ideas, the locust came to symbolise the conversion of gentiles to Christianity, which is why, in some devotional images, the Christ-child, like St John, is shown clutching a little green grasshopper.

Grasshoppers also symbolise old age. The allusion is, once again, from the Bible: '. . . the almond tree shall flourish, and the grasshopper shall be a burden, and desire shall fail: because man goeth to his long home, and the mourners go about the streets' (Ecclesiastes, 12:5). An old man nearing the end of his pilgrimage resembles a grasshopper with his stooping walk, his dry and shrivelled skin, his thin legs, his head bent to the ground and his bony elbows projecting backwards. The allusion may have come from Greek mythology. In the legend of Tithonus, the boy's immortal mother asks Zeus to make her son immortal, too, but forgets to ask the god for perpetual youth as well. Tithonus certainly showed signs of going on forever, but unfortunately only in a shrivelled and emaciated state. So his mother changed her mind about immortality and got Zeus to turn him into a grasshopper. The moral is that nothing is wholly fortunate.

A more terrifying form of grasshopper appears in the Book of Revelation when, on the fifth blast of the angelic trumpet, grasshoppers are set to rise from the smoke of Hell, in power, 'as the scorpions of the earth have power' (Revelation, 9: 3–11). These hellish, armour-plated locusts bear crowned human faces and horrible stings with which they torment the ungodly for five months. You can imagine them swooping down like Apache helicopters, stings projecting forward. Their leader, adds Revelation, will be called Abad'don, which means destruction, and in Greek is spelt *Apollyon*. He is one of the nastiest devils in Hell, if not the Devil himself.

In the same spirit, 'grasshopper' has various underground meanings. In the sense of a greenhorn, or novice, the term was born in a seventies television Kung Fu series, in which the blind master could sense what the ignorant novice could not: a grasshopper sitting at his feet. From then on, the student was known as Grasshopper: 'Watch and learn, Grasshopper.' It is used as a street word for someone organising a party or someone who smokes someone else's dope or who 'hops' dope around from place to place.[3] It is also Cockney rhyming slang for a copper, that is, a policeman.

A swarm of migratory locusts from a nineteenth century work of entomology.

In its original sense of something light that moves effortlessly about on grass, grasshopper is a popular brand name for lawn mowers, golf buggies and sports teams and clubs, especially in lawn tennis and bowling. It is the name of a marketing agency with the tagline, 'one jump ahead', a duo of folk singers from Herefordshire, a green cocktail based on crème de menthe and a historic pub in the Kentish Weald. The latter markets a home brew, Grasshopper Inn Ale, described as a light session bitter, but no doubt with a kick in it.

Grasshoppers are proverbially small and live around the level of our feet (hence the phrase, 'when I was knee-high to a grasshopper', meaning when I was very small). In the *Book of Numbers*, they were invoked as a metaphor for the insignificance of humankind when giants walked the earth. Since grasshoppers jump out of the way as humans approach, they were also a common metaphor for timidity. 'Can you make a horse leap like frightened grasshopper?' demands the Lord of his hapless servant Job (Job, 39:20). In his long poem 'Upon Appleton House' (1681), Andrew Marvell overturns the Biblical image of the tiny, timorous grasshopper by imagining what it would be like if we were insect-sized and they giants:

> And now to that abyss I pass
> Of that unfathomable grass,
> Where men like grasshoppers appear,
> But grasshoppers are giants there:
> They, in their squeaking laugh, contemn
> Us as we walk more low than them:
> And, from the precipices tall
> Of the green spires, to us do call.

It may not be squeezing the poem too hard to suggest that Marvell anticipates the idea of ecology and habitats. Early on in the poem, he notes that:

> No creature loves an empty space;
> Their bodies measure out their place.[4]

Just as Marvell's Appleton House seems to ease itself into its setting like a well-worn glove, so insects like grasshoppers fit their surroundings. They measure out a space but they also inhabit a special place.

A grasshopper mind is one that is always jumping about from one thing to the next without settling anywhere. A similar idea lies at the heart of Aesop's famous fable about the grasshopper and the ant. The grasshopper is a wastrel who spends the summer singing, jumping with joy and generally loafing about without a care in the world. The ant, by contrast, does nothing but work, gathering and storing up food for the winter. When cold weather returns, the grasshopper finds itself starving and begs the ant for food. But instead of offering charity, the ant rebukes the grasshopper for its worthless life and sends it on its way.

In the 1934 Walt Disney version of the tale, the queen of the ants eventually took pity on the wretched grasshopper and allowed it board and lodging in return for playing its fiddle. Rather appropriately, the grasshopper's hit tune, 'The World Owes Me a Living', was later given to Goofy. A happier ending, in our view, was the *Muppet Show*'s take on the fable, in which the smug, self-righteous ant is stepped on accidentally by a distracted Miss Piggy, while the grasshopper drives off to Florida in his new sports car.

Aesop's fable is constantly being reinvented.

In a cartoon shown in America during the 1940s, the grasshopper was not unduly worried about food, since he had widely invested in war-bonds. A version currently doing the rounds has the grasshopper calling a press conference at the start of winter to complain about socio-economic inequity. He is given the ant's house.

A poem, 'The Grasshopper', written by the cavalier poet Richard Lovelace towards the end of the English Civil War, inverts the fable into a satire on the state of England. Before he joined the losing side, Lovelace seemed to have everything – talent, money, good looks, pleasant manners, high connections. The one thing he lacked was luck, and everything came tumbling down when, as an obdurate Royalist, he lost in quick succession his land and property, his liberty and his health. By the time he was released from prison, Lovelace appeared, according to John Aubrey (who sketched a vivid portrait of the poet among his *Brief Lives*), a man 'in ragged cloaths . . . and mostly lodged in obscure and dirty places, more befitting the worst of beggars and poorest of servants'.[5]

One might have expected Lovelace to portray the fable in the conventional way as an object lesson in riches to rags, yet instead he is impenitent and defiant. His grasshopper is the embodiment of *joie de vivre*. It swings on an ear of wheat and sucks in 'the joys of Earth and Ayre'. 'Drunk every night with a delicious tear', it lives for pleasure: 'Up with the day, the sun thou welcom'st then/ Sport'st in the gilt plats of his beams.' Soon enough, its time will be cut short by the harvest sickle and the cold of 'dripping December'. But cavalier grasshoppers have another source of warmth: the bond of shared adversity among comrades. The dogged loyalty of defeated cavaliers represents the eternal summer of the soul, which keeps us warm and free even when living inside stone walls with iron bars on the windows.[6]

As well as a symbol of joy, the grasshopper has become an unlikely symbol of wealth and commerce. Its image is found on the mastheads of certain banks in the City of London, and a particularly large golden one crowns the dome of London's Royal Exchange. This grasshopper originated on the arms of the wealthy Gresham family of Norfolk and hence is known as the Gresham Grasshopper. The story goes that an ancestor of the Greshams was left abandoned in a field as a baby, to be rescued in the nick of time when an old lady, drawn by the loud chirping of a nearby grasshopper, spotted the

The Gresham Bank golden grasshopper, inherited by Martins Bank, which was later swallowed by the Barclay's Bank eagle.

Right: *The Corpus Clock, designed by John Taylor. The time-devouring grasshopper alludes to Biblical notions of ravening locusts.*

infant. More probably, the Gresham grasshopper incorporates a pun on the family name; the Old English form of grass was '*gres*', hence Gresham and 'gresh-hopper'. The richest of the Greshams was Sir Thomas, who founded the Royal Exchange in the sixteenth century. The original building seems to have had stone grasshoppers everywhere, plus a golden one on the roof to signify Sir Thomas's vast fortune (gained by evicting his hapless tenants in the north of England and replacing them with sheep).

The multiple grasshoppers on the original Gresham building perished in the Great Fire of London in 1666. The new exchange contented itself with a single golden hopper, but that, too, was lost in another fire in 1838. Fortunately it had been copied for erecting as a weathervane over Faneuil Hall in Boston, Massachusetts, as a way of linking the commerce of the New World with the Old. During

the American War of Independence, strangers to Boston were asked: 'What sits atop Fanueil Hall?', and if they did not know, they faced arrest. The present Royal Exchange opened for business in 1845, and carries a copper-gilt copy of the American copy high up on the weathervane, seemingly skewered by the mast like a museum specimen, though it is now difficult to see unless you happen to be standing in the right spot with the wind in the right direction.

More city grasshoppers lurk at 68 Lombard Street, where Sir Thomas owned a goldsmith's shop and where he founded Martins Bank in 1563. Another was found on the barrel of a cast-iron cannon dredged from the Thames, a reminder of the family's funding of arms manufacture at the time of the Spanish Armada. A golden one in the form of a bush-cricket fittingly straddles the sign of the Norfolk village of Gresham. Gresham School at Holt in Norfolk honoured its founder by co-opting the grasshopper on its own coat of arms; its magazine is called *The Grasshopper*.

In 2008, an unorthodox clock without hands, made by horologist and inventor John Taylor, was unveiled at Corpus Christi College, Cambridge. It is a homage to the eighteenth-century clock-maker John Harrison (of *Longitude* fame), who invented a mechanism that releases the clock's gears at each swing of its pendulum, a device he called the grasshopper escapement. Taylor's clock features a real grasshopper, a 'chronophage' which devours the time second by second as the escape wheel clicks under its straggled legs. 'I wanted to depict time as a destroyer,' said Taylor. 'That's why my grasshopper is not a Disney character. He is a ferocious beast that over the seconds has his tongue lolling out, his jaws opening, then on the 59th second he gulps down time.' On the hour, you hear the sound of a chain dropping into a wooden coffin to remind you of mortality. The Latin inscription below the clock translates as 'The world and its desires pass away.'[7]

It would be an exaggeration to suggest that grasshoppers have inspired much human music, for insect scratching defies easy translation. But Benjamin Britten composed *Two Insect Pieces* for piano and oboe, in which the players portray the bounding gait of the grasshopper, contrasted with the angry buzzing of the wasp. The sound of crickets also inspired the Hungarian-born composer Peter Eötvös to create a chamber-piece of 'organized nature' consisting of nothing but the 'chirring of crickets, cut and combed like Japanese gardens, a five-voiced madrigal-comedy performed by the tiniest musicians in the world'.

Better known is the anonymous children's leapfrog song, sung to the tune of 'The Battle Hymn of the Republic': 'The first grasshopper jumped right over/ the second grasshopper's back.' The song was memorably parodied in *Oh, What A Lovely War*, sung by a pile of slouching Aussie troops as 'One staff officer jumped right over/ the second staff officer's back.'

Despite their attractiveness, grasshoppers have been described (by the presenter and naturalist Chris Packham) as 'the overlooked Orthoptera'. One reason is that collectors tended to give them a wide berth; nor do we, unlike the Japanese, keep them as insect cage-birds. As museum specimens, they are disappointing: the bright colours soon fade and their legs are apt to drop off. But a live

grasshopper has its own kind of angular beauty. The authority on British grasshoppers, Chris Haes, refers appreciatively to the 'prominent veining of the wings; the herring-bone muscles on the hind-legs; the sharply chiselled faces ... and glossy compound eyes ... the intricate colours full of minute but clean detail.'[8]

In the past 20 years, 'orthoptery' has taken a great leap forward, thanks to the availability of good field guides, CD players – the songs of all the British Orthoptera are faithfully recorded on CD discs – and close-up binoculars. With good identification guides, grasshoppers are relatively easy to name, and catching one for inspection is surprisingly easy: hold a glass tube above it and it will hop straight in. Along with dragonflies, they have become popular 'birders' insects'. Some 1500 people took part in the *Atlas of British Orthoptera*, published in 1997.[9]

Bush-crickets *Tettigoniidae*

Like grasshoppers and crickets, bush-crickets are usually heard before they are seen. Fortunately, their various songs are as distinctive – and in some cases almost as loud – as bird calls. W. H. Hudson described the unmistakable trill of the Great Green Bush-cricket (which he also knew as the leaf-cricket) as 'a sustained sound, a current of brightest, finest, bell-like strokes or beats' or as the sound of 'crystal beads dropped in a stream down a crystal stair'. Today's less poetic observers have compared the sound to free-spinning bicycle wheels and fishing reels. It is probably the loudest insect song in Britain. To Hudson, listening to rival male bush-crickets induced a curious effect: 'certain nerves throb with the sound until it seems that it is in the brain, and is like that disagreeable condition called "ringing in the ears" made pleasant.'[10]

The sounds of several other bush-crickets are just as arresting, if less ear-piercing. A Rousel's Bush-cricket in full song sounds uncannily like the crackling sound of overhead electricity pylons. The Long-winged Conehead is a good test for elderly ears: not many people over the age of 50 can still make out its quiet, sewing-machine purr. The flightless Speckled Bush-cricket seems completely silent until a bat-detector catches its high-pitched chatter. The short chirps of the Dark Bush-cricket

The Wart-biter *(centre), one of a set of British insect stamps issued by the Post Office on 12 May 1985.*

is the most familiar bush-cricket song, in some areas as much a sound of autumn as a solo robin (it is probably John Keats' 'hedge cricket'). Attracted to window lights, the Dark Bush-cricket often strays indoors; for the same reason it is a habitué of strip-lit campsite lavatories, where it is regularly mistaken for a spider. A voice in the dark saying 'psst, psst' may well be a Dark Bush-cricket trying to find the exit.

Bush-crickets sing by day as well as at dusk, and only one species is fully nocturnal. This is the Oak Bush-cricket, a small, emerald-green species, which often turns up on windows or under the porch light. It has been called the 'bathroom bush-cricket', because that is where many people encounter it. It also turns up, usually the worse for wear, in moth-traps (and also visits the moth-hunter's treacle). Unfortunately, its moth-like weakness for bright lights means that many Oak Bush-crickets become road victims: 407 out of 468 records from Surrey were squashed specimens on roads.[11]

The male Oak Bush-cricket has an unusual way of attracting a mate: he uses his long hindlegs to drum or tap-dance on a leaf, producing a pattering sound like soft rain. When they tap on the stretched canvas walls of a tent, the resonating sound can be disconcerting, especially for non-entomologists. 'From experience, I can report that, to the occupants

of its chosen tent, the sound is like a distant drum-roll – a little worrying at two o' clock in the morning.'[12]

The rarest but perhaps the most famous of our bush-crickets is the Wart-biter. Its unlikely name is a translation of its Latin name *verrucivorus* or 'wart-eater'. This name was bestowed on it by the father of modern taxonomy, Carl Linnaeus, in whose native Sweden it was said to have been induced to remove warts with a snap of its powerful jaws. The name is enough to make handling wart-biters a nervous business, though in Britain the cricket has always been much too rare to be used in this way. Today it is best known as a species we are struggling to conserve at its few remaining sites by tailoring the management to its supposed needs. For its part, the Post Office put a Wart-biter Bush-cricket on a 29p postage stamp in 1985, one of a set of five Europe-themed British insects.

The word bush-cricket is fairly recent. In older books, the insects are usually called 'long-horned grasshoppers'.[13] They are, in fact, more closely related to grasshoppers than to crickets, and not all of them live in bushes, either. In other English-speaking countries, they call them 'katydids', after the song of certain North American bush-crickets that sounds like: 'Katy did, Katy didn't.'

A Great Green Bush-cricket drying its wings after a last skin-cast in late summer. Its song has been compared with 'crystal beads falling down a stair'.

Camel crickets
Rhaphidophoridae

One of Britain's more bizarre indoor insects is the Greenhouse Camel Cricket, a leggy creature like a cross between a cricket and a cockroach, with bristly front legs, long antennae and a characteristic hump (hence the camel). Being wingless, it cannot sing, but by rubbing one body part against another, it manages a faint scratching sound. In China, camel crickets are cave-dwelling insects. Britain's climate is far too cold for the Greenhouse Camel Cricket to survive outdoors, but small feral colonies have become established in warm corners of zoo buildings and plant nurseries, by boilers and hot-water pipes and in heated greenhouses, especially among ferns and orchids. Camel-crickets have spread around the world as eggs hidden in potted plants, and there may well now be more surviving in artificial surroundings than there are in the wild. Being nocturnal they are easily missed, unless one is in a hothouse at night and sees or hears them scurrying and scratching behind the pipes

The colonies tend not to last very long. Though Greenhouse Camel Crickets are mainly carnivorous, and quite possibly do a useful job by eating insect pests, they are also suspected of nibbling tender young plants. Their usual fate is a dose of insecticide. Fortunately they are tolerated by the kindly owners of a garden centre in Clowne, Derbyshire, where they have been living happily and, it would seem, harmlessly among the plant pots since the early 1990s.

Crickets *Gryllidae*

The chirp of crickets was once so familiar that Charles Dickens could wrap an entire novel around their friendly presence. It was one of the sounds of home, especially in the evening, when the family gathered around the fire; to some a cricket was as good as a canary, to others it was a kind of presiding benign spirit, even a guardian angel, especially, perhaps, because crickets were more often heard than seen. Unfortunately the chirp of the cricket is no longer heard in most homes, and the House Cricket now lives mainly in boiler rooms and on refuse tips, where they are kept warm by decaying matter. Some of our other crickets have fared even worse. The Field Cricket hovers on the brink of extinction, and it seems that the Mole Cricket may have already gone.

Crickets have nothing to do with cricket. The word comes from the Old French *criquer*, an onomatopoeic word meaning 'to crackle or creak' (the game, by contrast, seems to derive from the Old English *cric*, a staff or stick).

Place names containing the word cricket, such as Cricket St Thomas in Somerset, probably have nothing to do with either kind of cricket. The name comes from the Old English word *cruc*, meaning a hill, while the '-et' is a diminutive suffix, hence 'little hill'.

The Cherokees believed that drinking tea brewed from crickets would improve their singing – a divine gift passed on through the insect 'tea leaves'. Perhaps this native lore influenced Buddy Holly, whose 1950s rock-and-roll band was, of course, the Crickets. But the more usual story is that, during the playback of 'I'm Gonna Love You Too', a cricket was accidentally recorded during the final moments of the song. A cricket is certainly a good analogy for Buddy's high-pitched, hiccupping style.

House Cricket, *Acheta domesticus*

VN: chirker (Scot.), crickad (Isle of Man), kricket

The chirrup of House Crickets was once as familiar as the chirp of sparrows. As late as the 1890s, W. H. Hudson, going on his summer evening rounds in the heights above Selborne, Hampshire, could

Hearth crickets: the real thing and brass copies.

hear them shrilling from every cottage. With its association with warm coals and toasted muffins, and the kettle whistling from the hob, the cricket was emblematic of hearth and home.

This cosy domesticity lay at the heart of Charles Dickens' 1845 Christmas book, *The Cricket on the Hearth*, subtitled 'A Fairy Tale of Home'. To him, the cricket was a 'little household god' that watched over the family and its foolish quarrels and ensured that all would be well in the end. The chapters are called 'chirps'. His tale unwinds very slowly (Dickens takes three whole pages to describe the boiling of the kettle). They tell of 'slow, lumbering, honest' but jealous John Peerybingle and his pretty young wife Dot. We are not far into the story when the cricket begins to sing:

Chirrup, chirrup, chirrup! Chirp, chirp, chirp!
Good Heaven, how it chirped! Its shrill,
piercing voice resounded through the house,
and seemed to tinkle in the outer darkness like
a star. There was an indescribable little trill and
tremble in it, at its loudest, which suggested its
being carried off its legs, and made to leap again,
by its own intense enthusiasm.[14]

Dot believes that to have a Cricket on the hearth 'is the luckiest thing in all the world!' In the end, the insect turns into a fairy to tell John Peerybingle that his wife is not having an affair and that he is an idiot. It all ends happily, the actors leave the stage, and the narrator is left alone in his chair: 'A cricket sings upon the hearth; a broken child's toy lies upon the ground, and nothing else remains.'

Though Dickens sugars the story till the bones ache, the role of the cricket as a benign domestic familiar is an old one. Even his title might have been borrowed from John Milton's 'Il Penseroso' (1645),

a poem about a contemplative man who delights in the quieter pleasures of life, such as listening to crickets:

Where glowing embers through the room
Teach light to counterfeit a gloom,
Far from all resort of mirth,
Save the cricket on the hearth,[15]

Another, even chirpier household god is Jiminy Cricket in Walt Disney's film *Pinocchio*. The irrepressible, eternally optimistic Jiminy is there to offer a helping hand and moral guidance – 'always let your conscience be your guide' – and personifies the expression, 'as merry as a cricket'. According to New England folklore (which had a faint echo in old England), killing crickets in the home brings bad luck; compatriots of the departed cricket will wreak revenge by creeping in at night and biting holes in your clothes. Perhaps this hints at a darker side to Jiminy Cricket. His name comes from the acceptable form of yelling 'Jesus Christ!' when you accidentally drop the steam iron on your toe after scalding yourself with the kettle.

Apart from bringing good fortune, crickets are as good as a thermometer. You simply count the number of chirps a cricket makes in 14 seconds. For a Centigrade chirp you add 25, divide by three and then add four. For example, if a cricket chirps 112 times in a minute it will be about 20°C outside. Ideally one would count at least ten different crickets and average them out. 'Cricket thermometers' work best in warm weather, since in cooler conditions, the insects tend to stop chirping altogether. Temperature also affects their pitch, which gave the late Roger Deakin the fantasy idea of an electronic organ that worked by harnessing the variable music of their stridulations. The crickets, encased inside glass tubes, would be warmed and cooled by keyboard control.

> I first met crickets in Ireland in 1949 in the cottage where we stayed. They would creep out onto the hearth by the peat fire. The locals were careful to warn us not to harm them for fear it would bring bad luck to the household. Years later, in the 1980s, I heard a familiar sound in the roofing of our leisure centre in Bury, Lancs, and was amazed to be told it was a colony of crickets. They were proving difficult to eradicate.[16]

Pet shops sell small, black crickets as food for lizards and snakes (their species is rarely specified but most are probably the non-British Southern Field Cricket). Occasionally they escape, and if they find somewhere warm, form feral colonies. 'A feature of Maidstone's town centre is the evocative sound of crickets singing on warm summer nights. These are exotic Black Crickets that have escaped from a pet shop where they were on the menu for much of the livestock. The escapees have established a large colony in the street buildings and outhouses, where they manage to survive our winters, thanks to the residual urban warmth.'[17]

Field Cricket, *Gryllus campestris*

The first detailed account of this enchanting insect was also the first long nature note by Gilbert White, the great naturalist of Selborne. White adored crickets above all other insects (he hardly mentions butterflies). By astonishing good fortune, eighteenth-century Selborne was home to all the British species of cricket (today, nowhere is). The Field Cricket's melodious, penetrating chirp, which can be heard up to a hundred yards away, was, to White, a kind of insect nightingale, 'a train of summer ideas, rural, verdurous and joyous'. The crickets could be heard every year just beyond the village churchyard from the hillside known as the Short Lythe. But though everyone must have heard them, few, it seems, had ever set eyes on the living creatures. One day, Gilbert and his brother Theo decided to track down the source of that mysterious 'cheerful shrill cry'. After a bit of searching among the short grass, they located the songster at the entrance to its earthen burrow, and White was moved to write the following precise and closely observed description of it in his *Garden Kalendar*:

It was 'of the Cricket-kind, with wings & ornamented Cases over them, like the House kind. But tho' they have long legs behind with large brawny thighs, like Grasshoppers, for leaping; it is remarkable that when they were dug-out of their holes they shewed no manner of activity, but crawled along in a very shiftless manner, so as easily to be taken. We found it difficult not to squeeze them to death in breaking the Ground: & out of one so bruised I took a multitude of eggs . . . It was easy to discover the male from the female; the former of which is of a black shining Colour, with a golden stripe across it's shoulders something like that of the Humble Bee: the latter was more dusky, & distinguished by a long terebra at its tail, which probably may be the instrument with which it may deposit it's eggs in Crannies, & safe receptacles. It is very likely that the males only make that shrilling noise; which they may do out of rivalry, & emulation during their breeding time; as is the case with many animals. They are solitary Insects living singly in Holes by themselves; & will fight fiercely when they meet, as I found by some which I put into an hole in a dry wall where I should be glad to have them encrease on account of their pleasing summer sound. For tho' they had express'd distress by being taken out of their knowledge; yet the first that had got possession of the chink seized an other with a vast pair of serrated fangs so as to make it cry-out . . . I could but wonder, that when taken in hand, they never offer'd to bite, tho' furnish'd with such formidable weapons. They are remarkably shy, & cautious, never stirring but a few inches from the mouth of their holes, & retiring backward nimbly into them, & stopping short in their song by that time you come within several yards of their caverns.'[18]

This 'sudden discourse', written on 20 May 1761, is a milestone in the development of natural history; one might almost say it represents the very *beginning* of modern natural history, with its vivid attentiveness. White had a strong sense of wonder and restless inquiry, together with a sharp eye, but there is something else there as well: a deep sympathy for nature in general and a manifest feeling of affection for the Field Cricket in particular. It was a fellow creature, worth studying for its own sake.

Not that White was the first to discover Field

The Field Cricket outside its burrow, exactly as Gilbert White found it at Selborne in 1761.

Crickets. Two centuries before, Thomas Muffet described how children would entice crickets from their burrows with a wriggling ant 'tied about their middle with a hair' or with a straw or small twig.[19] Gilbert White tried this by 'gently insinuating' a grass stalk. The result was startling: the cricket held on by its jaws, bulldog fashion, allowing White to draw it forth from its lair like a cork from a bottle: 'Thus the humane enquirer may gratify his curiosity without injuring the object of it.' Once extracted, the cricket proved surprisingly docile: 'They show no activity, but crawl along in a shiftless manner, so as easily to be taken; and again, though provided with a curious apparatus of wings, yet they never exert them when there seems to be the greatest occasion.' Nor, when picked up, did they ever attempt to bite, though White thought he noticed 'a vast row of serrated fangs'.

Among the few occasions when his cricket made use of its wings was when White attempted to transplant a colony to his garden by boring ready-made holes in the terrace. The crickets hung around for a few days inspecting White's clumsy efforts, but then 'wandered away by degrees, and were heard at a farther distance each morning, so that it appears that on this emergency they made use of their wings in attempting to return to the spot from which they were taken.' White kept another cricket in a paper cage, with plants moistened with water ('If the plants be not wetted it will die'), only to find that the song was a bit too much. It 'became so merry and loud as to be irksome in the same room where a person is sitting'.[20]

John Clare liked to say that he found his poems ready-made in the fields and simply wrote them down. His insect poetry has this quality, a sharp eye added to a heightened sensibility of the lot of a small creature in the hedgerow or hayfield. To him, the Field Cricket was the 'Sweet little minstrel of the sunny summer', 'A chittering sound of healthy happiness/ That bids the passer-bye be happy too'.

> I've seen thy dwelling by the scythe laid bare
> And thee in russet garb from bent to bent
> Moping without a song in silence there,
> Till grass should bring anew thy home-content,
> And leave thee to thyself to sing and wear
> The summer through without another care.[21]

Alas, the more recent history of the Field Cricket in Britain has been far less cheerful. Its numbers have been falling for a long time. The largest and best-known colony, at Fawley in Hampshire, celebrated in the writings of W. H. Hudson, was destroyed when the chirping banks were turned into a construction site for an oil refinery. By 1990, only three small colonies with perhaps 25 breeding females in total were known, and the cricket faced imminent extinction in Britain. Fortunately London Zoo had been rearing a related species and offered to help. In 1992, English Nature took the risk of removing 12 young crickets from the wild to start a breeding colony at the zoo. With the help of a high-protein diet of tropical-fish food, the dozen duly produced 700 offspring. These were released into the wild in two places, and more releases followed, involving catching and rearing up young adults and subsequently liberating them (unfortunately the zoo cannot keep a breeding population alive through the winter). Today there are four populations of Field Cricket extant, all in Hampshire or West Sussex. One of them, suitably enough, is on the boundary of the cricket pitch at Arundel.[22]

The Field Cricket was one of ten stamps released by the Post Office on 15 April 2008 on the theme of 'Insects – UK Species in Recovery'. In the case of the cricket, the title seems, alas, optimistic.

Mole Cricket, *Gryllotalpa gryllotalpa*

VN: bog-moles (Hants), Cambridge nightingale, churr-worm, eve-churr, fern-cricket, jar-worm, locust

Welsh: *Rhing y les*

The song of the Mole Cricket is another of the vanished sounds of the countryside. It was once well known, at least in southern England, as a soft purr drifting in from damp meadows and marshes on warm spring evenings. Gilbert White described it as 'a low, dull, jarring note, continued for a long time without interruption, & not unlike the chattering of the fern-owl [the nightjar], but more inward'. Thanks to its remarkable appearance, with powerful forelegs and a fat, finger-sized body, the Mole Cricket was a famous insect, with country names such as 'fen-cricket', 'eve-churr' and 'churr-worms', 'all very apposite names', according to

White (Mole Cricket itself is an old name; Linnaeus simply translated it into Latin: *Gryllotalpa*). In damp fields around Cambridge, the sound of their churring carried across the college greens and parks, earning them the name of 'Cambridge nightingales'. On still nights, you could hear them up to a mile away from the river.

Like the Field Cricket, the disembodied song of the Mole Cricket was more familiar than its physical presence. By day, the Mole Cricket hides in its underground burrow in loose, moist soil. It emerges on warm, still evenings at the close of day, when Gilbert White would watch its clumsy, buzzing flight 'rising and falling in curves', as though borne down by its own weight (Muffet referred to these aerial bounds as 'leaps'). Muffet thought them 'ugly to the sight and monstrous'. White once found a burrow laid open after a gardener had peeled off some turf with his scythe. Following its course, he found it ended in a brood-chamber 'about the size of a moderate snuff-box' and containing a hundred tough-skinned, yellowish eggs.[23] The Mole Cricket looks capable of delivering a nasty bite, but it rarely, if ever, does. Like the Field Cricket, it is remarkably docile.

White's local farmers welcomed the Mole

The Mole Cricket showing its powerful front digging feet.

Cricket's evening purrs, and for a practical reason. It sang most strongly when the soil was moist and the sun was strong; what was good for the cricket was also good for the harvest. Gardeners were less welcoming. Its burrows leave a raised ridge of soil on lawns (though it does not throw up 'mole-cricket hills'). Since it either pushes plant roots aside or bites them off, the cricket was considered a pest, and so it is still in the Channel Islands. In fact, Mole Crickets are mainly carnivorous. Any damage they do is sustained incidentally during their underground searches for worms and grubs. Some claimed they crept up on sleeping cattle and bit them (though even Muffet thought that was unlikely). Others believed that Mole Crickets possessed an ant-like prudence and gathered grains of wheat, barley and oats to store inside their burrows as winter supplies. They were also said to feed on horse dung. Mole Crickets live a long time for an insect – perhaps two to three years – but they survive the winter by hibernating, not by feeding on stored grain.

Where have all the Mole Crickets gone? They are in all the books and fieldguides but not, it seems, any longer in gardens or the countryside. They were always rather local and restricted to warm valleys and fens. Land drainage, especially during and after the Second World War, seems to have caused their demise, and by the late 1970s, the only surviving colony was on boggy ground near allotments in the suburbs of Southampton, where they were known as 'bog-moles' or 'locusts'. Even there they had gone by 1980. Since then, there were only four confirmed reports, all of single crickets that might have strayed from imported plants or, conceivably, flown across the sea on a warm wind.[24]

Then, in 2005, a breeding colony turned up, not in a nature reserve but in a compost heap in an Oxfordshire garden. It was filmed by the TV presenter Chris Packham, and careful investigation revealed a total of seven adults, though only one of them was a female (she was carrying a packet of sperm, a gift from one of the six males). How they came to be there is uncertain, but it was probably no coincidence that the gardener happened to farm worms. Perhaps they were carried there in a batch of wormy soil from overseas.[25] But gardens, especially vegetable gardens, are as good a habitat as any for Mole Crickets, and also the place where gardeners lifting root crops are most likely to spot them. Anyone lucky enough to turn up a live one is asked to contact the Natural History Museum.

A flying Mole Cricket appeared on the 43p stamp of a set of Endangered Species released in 1998 (though, by then, it was more than endangered).

Wood Cricket, *Nemobius sylvestris*

The Wood Cricket looks like a miniature House Cricket and is more or less confined to woods in the area around the Solent, above all in the New Forest (it turns up in parts of rural Devon, and there is an isolated colony in the botanic garden at Wisley). Its quiet, purring song, a gentle trilling from among the fallen leaves, is one of the distinctive sounds of the Forest in early autumn. The crickets are insect ventriloquists: chirps which seem some distance away may be from crickets at your feet. Sit still for a few minutes, and they may show themselves – tiny insects (the male measures just under a centimetre) with black heads, clambering over the crisp leaves.

Scaly Cricket, *Pseudomogoplistes squamiger*

Our last-discovered wild cricket, the Scaly Cricket, is a mysterious insect, first found close to a car park on Chesil Beach in 1949. The reason it was overlooked for so long is that, as well as being wingless, it is also noiseless. Since the Scaly Cricket is a Mediterranean species, experts jumped to the conclusion that it must have arrived there by artificial means, perhaps in shipments of sand used for the sandbags at Portland Naval Base during the war. That being the most probable explanation, no one took much interest in the silent cricket.

Then, in the 1980s, large numbers of Scaly Crickets were found swarming among stones being laid for a new footpath. Ninety were counted in a discarded margarine tub – all dead, unfortunately – which suggested that there were more of them on Chesil Beach than anyone had realised. Pitfall traps laid in suitable patches of shingle along the pebble beach from Portland to Abbotsbury caught no fewer than 699 of them, alive this time. More Scaly Crickets have turned up on the Channel Island of Sark and on beaches in Pembrokeshire and at Branscombe in Devon, as well as on the opposite side of the Channel in Brittany. Putting all this new information together, the consensus is that the Scaly Cricket is not, after all, a chance introduction but an overlooked native species. As Peter Sutton puts it, it has 'completed its journey to citizenship'.[26]

Stick insects *Phasmida*

Stick insects make excellent insect pets and are easy to keep. They are excitingly large, free of smells and allergies and don't bite or sting, and nearly all of them will accept humble bramble leaves. As long as they are warm and provided with sufficient fresh food, stick insects need little care or attention. Children and teenagers love to let them crawl up their arms in their deliberate, leggy way. The only problem, apart from their propensity to shed limbs when overcrowded or upset, is what to do with the large numbers of offspring. Releasing baby stick insects into the garden, though illegal, is probably the reason why there are scattered colonies of stick insects in south-west England, especially around Torbay, Falmouth and the Isles of Scilly. Elsewhere, they soon die of cold.

All but one of Britain's little-known wild stick insects are natives of New Zealand and better adapted to a cooler climate than most of the world's species. On the island of Tresco in the Isles of Scilly, they probably arrived as eggs in the soil inside plant tubs destined for the abbey gardens. Others probably came in consignments of New Zealand *Pittosporum* planted around the Scilly bulb fields as shelterbelts. Elsewhere they have been released into gardens, such as at St Mawes, near Falmouth, from where they have spread in all directions. A colony at Paignton in Devon was less lucky, for a large Japanese cedar that they had made their headquarters had to be removed for safety reasons. Insecticides bagged another unplanned colony in the Palm House at Torquay.[27] Strangely enough, our naturalised stick insects are difficult to rear in captivity, and their success, half a world away from home, is against the odds.

The largest British stick insect is the oddly named Unarmed Stick Insect, a smooth-bodied species that just seems to grow and grow. A 12.5-centimetre-long specimen found at Port Isaac in 1992 is the longest insect ever seen out of doors in Britain. The species is found in a range of delightful shades, from apple-green to mahogany-brown, while one form is spotted with purple. The brown ones are pale by day but turn redder by night, a chameleon-like trick that the species apparently performs only in Britain. The insect has been present at Treseder's Nursery in Truro since the 1920s and possibly earlier, perhaps introduced in a batch of exotic plants from the Isle of Rossdohan in County Kerry, which had, in turn, obtained them from New Zealand.

The Indian Stick Insect, often kept as a pet or in the school science lab. It sometimes escapes outdoors, feeding on a privet hedge or bramble patch.

Some Unarmed Stick Insects found on a Chinese rose bush in a Falmouth garden in 1981 were collected and given to an entomologist to breed on. The resulting nymphs were distributed to schools throughout Cornwall, where, in the fullness of time, they will no doubt escape or be thrown away, and more colonies will spring up nearby.

The stick insect usually kept in school biology labs is the Indian, or Laboratory, Stick Insect, a rather dull species, which is kept for the ease with which it can be housed and bred. It often 'escapes' but it is sensitive to cold and so rarely survives for long. Its ideal habitat is said to be front-garden privet hedges.

The oddest thing about British stick insects is that they are all females. Males are known in their native New Zealand but not here. From the stick insect's point of view, this is no great loss, since they breed by parthenogenesis – that is, the eggs form without fertilisation by male sperm. Stick insects grow to maturity within a few weeks, and since each one lays hundreds of tiny, seed-like eggs, they have the capacity to multiply very rapidly. Requiring nothing but warmth and a few bramble leaves to chew, they probably face a sunny future in a globally warmed Britain.

Cockroaches *Blattodea*

vn: black beetle, blackclock (NE Eng.), black-worm (Cornwall), Bombay canary, Crotan bug (US), jaspers (Isle of Man), May beetle, shiner, steambug, steamfly, Yankee settler (US)

Cockroaches are not popular. They damage fabrics by their incessant chewing and often leave behind a musky, unpleasant smell, composed partly of their mildewed droppings and partly the pheromones they release to attract a mate. By feeding on decomposing food, they are seen as a health risk. And to most of us, the larger ones appear rather alarming, with their long twitching antennae and flat, greasy-looking bodies and wings. Modern British homes are less cockroach-friendly than in the past, since food tends to be sealed away inside the fridge or freezer or in Tupperware, or instantly disposed of inside plastic wheelie bins. But they are still a problem in bakeries and restaurant kitchens, where, like the dirty child in comics, they are repelled by soap and water.

Cockroach study has been driven by a single motive: getting rid of them. Nearly all research into cockroach lives has been funded by pest-control agencies. The discovery of this quintessential 'bug' in a home is generally followed by a visit from a professional bug exterminator, who spreads on the floor a poison gel, which the cockroaches obediently lap up. The trick is to leave the corpses where they are. Cockroaches are cannibals and, they say, will be attracted by the pungent scent of their poisoned brothers.

Britain's three native species of cockroach are small and unobtrusive (and rather cute) insects of wild places, especially along the shore. The cockroaches that share our homes and kitchens are foreigners that are said to have first reached England from the New World in the hold of a galleon captured by Francis Drake. Cockroach comes from a Spanish word *cucaracha*, made up of *cuca*, meaning caterpillar or maggot, and *racha*, literally a gust of wind. The sense, perhaps, is 'speeding maggot'. Early settlers

Oriental Cockroaches, *by Amy Bartlett Wright, an American-based illustrator of large-scale murals and small-scale insect life. This is the ubiquitous 'black beetle' or 'black jack' of warehouses, laundries, hotels and hospitals worldwide.*

in America saw plenty of them, and by the 1650s, the word had been anglicised to 'cockroche' and, hence, cockroach.

The collective noun is an intrusion of cockroaches. We dislike their smell, the way they slither and scuttle, their association with refuse – like insect rats – and that alien twitch of their too-long whiskers. Above all, we fear their numbers. A moving raft of large, hungry, twitching insects is the stuff of horror films. 'If you want to say something nasty about someone,' said Richard Schweid in his book *The Cockroach Papers* (1999), 'call him a cockroach: that lowest of the low, vilest of the vile, most easily eliminated without a pang of remorse, the cheapest of all lives, an animal only a Jain [a believer in non-violence] . . . would ever think twice about killing.'[28]

In that spirit, during the genocide in Rwanda in 1994, the Hutu Interahamwe referred to their hated rival Tutsis as cockroaches. So, on occasion, do Israeli politicians when discussing militant Palestinians (and vice versa, no doubt). The very names of the commonest cockroach, *Blatella germanica*, are ethnic slurs. In Britain and the United States, it is known as the German Cockroach, in Germany as the Russian, or French, Cockroach, and in Russia as the Prussian Cockroach; it seems to be named after whoever we are or were at war with. Ironically, *B. germanica* originated from none of these places but from Africa, from whence it travelled to the New World in the holds of slave ships. The same is true of the Oriental Cockroach, the Australian Cockroach and the American, or Ship, Cockroach, all of them now cosmopolitan insects that live in association with humans on every continent. Even the generic name *Blatta* is prejudicial: it means 'one who shuns light'.

Cockroaches were long known as 'black beetles', though only the Oriental Cockroach is, in fact, black. The alternative name 'shiner' is more appropriate to *B. germanica*, which has a characteristic sheen like polished wax on its thorax and wings. Folk-names such as 'steamfly' or 'steambug' allude to the cockroach's liking for warm, humid places. In New York, they became known as 'Croton Bugs' after swarms of cockroaches appeared in the Croton Aqueduct, which once supplied the city with water.

> In the Isle of Man we knew cockroaches as 'Jaspers', and in the Merchant Navy these things were 'Bombay Canaries'.[29]

Today, cockroaches are perhaps associated with unfortunate holidays abroad, and it is hard to recapture the fear and loathing that lies behind writings such as John Crompton's *The Hunting Wasp* (1955). Crompton was normally a champion of maligned animals, such as snakes and spiders, but he made an exception for 'the flat obscene cockroach, with its nauseating smell, that squeezes horribly into narrow crevices'. He traced his phobia to an experience on board a merchant steamer, when 'they come out at night in unspeakable slithering masses and eat the refuse and get into bunks and nibble toenails and hair. Cockroaches and rats: can you imagine a fouler combination?' He fell foul of them once again while serving as a mounted policeman in what was then Rhodesia. The body of a suspected murder victim had been left in a hot, windowless hut, and the cockroaches had got to it first. Crompton entered to find the corpse 'shimmering' amid a sea of roaches 'covering first the floor and then the walls, squirming wildly into cracks and crevices and hanging in obscene knotted struggling ropes . . . The entire skin [of the body] was pitted and gnawed and corrugated like wave-marked sand, and this included the scalp from which all the hair had been eaten.'[30] Cooler forensic heads might have seen cockroaches as a useful aid to determining the time of death of the victim, but it only deepened Crompton's conviction of their ineradicable vileness.

Yet cockroaches are not without their defenders. Unlike the rest of his family, Gerald Durrell rather admired the scuttling creatures that overran the family kitchen in Corfu, though his fascination stopped well short of sentimentality:

> I was fascinated by their beauty, for to me they looked as though they were carved out of tortoiseshell, and their egg cases were so elegant, like the most beautiful little ladies' evening handbags. I used to collect these capsules and hatch them out in my room (unbeknownst to my mother); half I would let go and the other half I would feed to my mantis . . . I felt this was fair.[31]

Many share Durrell's liking for them and, today, large cockroaches are among the most popular insect pets, being easy to keep and with fascinating habits. The world's largest cockroach is the Queensland Giant Burrowing Cockroach, which measures up to 8 centimetres long and weighs up to 35 grams, but it is expensive and rather demanding as a pet. Much cheaper and in every way ideal is the remarkable Hissing Cockroach of Madagascar, which whooshes like a steam kettle when aroused. Perhaps significantly, it is wingless, which has the odd effect of making it seem less insect-like and more like a large, friendly woodlouse.

Cockroach fans may be few but they are dedicated. Adrian Durkin, exhibitions officer at Dudley Museum and Art Gallery, was first attracted to breeding them by the 'different forms and the subtle variation in the group', having already specialised in a related group, the stick insects. Meeting others who felt the same way, Durkin decided to form 'an appreciation society', and so in 1986, he founded a missionary group 'to promote the study and culture of cockroaches on a world wide basis'. He called it the 'Blattodea Culture Group' (Blattodea being the scientific suborder of cockroach-kind). 'No one feels threatened by "blattids",' he noted, 'whereas they start getting paranoid if you keep "cockroaches".' Today, the group has a core of dedicated members, a respected journal, *Cockroach Studies*, and a members-only website.[32]

Others, too, have found a positive side to the cockroach. It has inspired poetry, mainly in America, in the surprising guise of ecofeminism, a view that finds connections between the degradation of nature and oppressed womanhood. In her children's story, *Spider Kane and the Mystery Under the May-Apple* (1999), Mary Pope Osborne quotes lines by Christina Rossetti that express the right to life of even the lowliest insects (as we see them):

The last and least of things
That soar on quivering wings,
Or crawl among the grass blades out of sight
Have just as clear a right
To their appointed portion of delight
As queens or kings.[33]

Another boost for the self-respect of cockroaches is Janell Cannon's children's book, *Crickwing* (2000), where the attractive golden cockroach stands as a champion for under-appreciated insects generally. Crickwing lives in the rainforest (a reminder that most of the world's cockroaches live in the wild, often in threatened habitats). The underlying message is that our image of cockroaches is skewed by the few who have made themselves unwelcome in our lives. It is we who threaten the world's cockroaches, not they that threaten us.[34]

An insect that has survived little-changed for 300 million years clearly has a powerful and potentially useful biochemistry. The ancients used cockroaches for cures. According to Pliny, crushed cockroach took the sting out of bites, scabs and ulcers. Ground up in lard and mixed with oil of roses, they soothed aching ears. Cockroaches are still used in traditional medicine around the world; dried or powdered roach has been used to treat asthma in Brazil and dropsy in rural Russia, while cockroach tea, with or without a chaser of boiled cockroach, appears in African-American folk medicine as a cure for stingray burns.[35] According to the American TV show *Ripley's Believe It or Not*, a Scot plagued with digestive problems claimed that a diet of raw, live Madagascan Hissing Cockroaches had put everything to rights, and that he no longer experienced the slightest discomfort.

Most people would find the idea of swallowing a cockroach peculiarly revolting, and it is, of course, exactly this fear and disgust that lies behind a competition held each year in a New York amusement park. Whoever swallows the most live cockroaches inside a minute is declared the winner. The world record is held by a Derbyshire man who managed to down 36 of them. Organiser James Taylor commented: 'it's supposed to be scary, it's icky, it's gross, it's Halloween fun and it's just one small part of the haunted houses and thrilling rides going on.'[36] Medically speaking, raw cockroach is not advisable. Even when raised on a clean diet, cockroaches retain a mild neurotoxin that numbs the mouth and makes them awkward to swallow.

A milder form of cockroach abuse is cockroach racing, an aspect of Australian culture that has not yet caught on in Britain. The world championships are held each year on Australia Day at a hotel in Brisbane. Punters generally bring their own racers, cockroaches with form and names such as Roachback Mountain or Cockzilla, but in the democratic spirit of the sport, anyone without an entrant can buy a roach from a tank at the hotel. The race starts after the umpire unceremoniously empties a bucket of roaches onto a circular track; the first through the finishing hoop wins. In the steeplechase, the racers are encouraged to jump over a length of hosepipe 'to enhance the spectacle and test the roach talent'. Admittedly, without racing colours it is hard to tell one roach from another, but the event takes place amid such beery, patriotic bonhomie that no one seems to mind. Dave Freeman included cockroach racing among his *100 Things To Do Before You Die*.[37]

This is obviously a comedy sport – the glamour of racing contrasted with the least glamorous of creatures. But Australians seem to have a grudging sympathy for an insect underdog that's a born survivor. When the Australian cricket captain Steve Waugh called our Mike Atherton 'the Cockroach', he meant it as a back-handed compliment. Like the cockroach, Atherton was 'extremely difficult to stamp out'.

In the same spirit, *La Cucaracha* is a well-known Latin American song, a kind of Mexican *Yankee Doodle*, whose chorus line includes a punning reference to marijuana, or 'roach'. Its spirit is impossible to translate, but a non-drug rendition of the chorus might be:

Cockroach, oh cockroach
Can't walk any more
Because it don't have, 'cause it lacks
A front leg.[38]

Perhaps because cockroaches are mainly insects of warm, humid climates, they are more significant in American folklore than in British. In William S. Burrough's hallucinatory novel *The Naked Lunch*, the lead character's 'case worker' is a Kafkaesque cockroach, which later hybridises with his typewriter.

Hollywood has capitalised on the cockroach as the quintessential bug, the nightmare insect that always threatens to turn the tables on human-kind and wipe *us* out. *Bug* (1975) used industrial quantities of real-life hissing cockroaches to play imaginary incendiary creatures that emerge from the bowels of the earth after an earthquake. These arsonist cockroaches rub their back legs together in Boy Scout fashion to set the world ablaze and, after some ill-advised cross-breeding, become even more ferocious monsters that feed on human flesh and are impervious to all known pesticides. In *Damnation Alley* (1977), similar monstrous insects, played once again by hissing cockroaches, stalk the planet in a post-nuclear apocalypse. The film *Mimic* (1997) is a fable about genetic engineering. In order to wipe out the cockroaches that are spreading a deadly virus in New York, the mad scientist crosses termites with mantids. This turns out to be a bad idea, since the bio-engineered horror-bugs turn on New Yorkers instead. Cockroaches also appear in *Nightmare on Elm Street 4*, when the fate of one victim is to be turned into her least favourite animal and then promptly squashed by Freddie Krueger.

Such fantasies play on the universal loathing for cockroaches in America. The horror-film cockroach is not so much a real insect as a blend of insect and humankind, blown up to giant size and given a malignant intelligence. But the films do at least play grudging respect to a genuine aspect of the cockroach, its sheer survivability. In the 1920s, a thriving colony of cockroaches was found 2160 feet down a coal mine in South Wales, evidently 'finding the déjà vu Carboniferous atmosphere quite as pleasant as the bowels of London or New York'.[39] If we ever manage to blow our world to bits with nuclear weapons, cockroaches will be one of the animals crawling out from the ruins.

Our attitude to cockroaches remains an enigma. Though certain kinds are popular insect pets, the ingrained image remains of a kind of insect rat, one of the least-loved creatures on earth. Marion Copeland finds that 'it is exactly this ambiguity that sets the cockroach up as satire's darling, and allows it to continue to question boundaries and set question marks after certainties'. It is the 'totem animal for all those who are relegated to the undersides of their cultures despite their virtues and gifts'.[40]

The Common Earwig – 'forky-tail' – on a favourite flower, a daisy.

Earwigs *Dermaptera*

VN: arrywiggle (variously spelt), battle-twig, clipshears (Scot.), clocks (N. Ireland), coachbell (Scot.), codgy-bell (NE Eng.), collieglean (Scot.), crutchybell (NE Eng.), eariewig (variously spelt), earwrig (Somerset), ermit (Scot.), erriwiggle (Norfolk), forker (Scot.), forkie (Orkney), forkie-gollach (NE Scot.), forkin-robin (Yorks), fork-tail, forky-tail (NE Eng. and Scot.), galloch or variants: gollach, gavelock gullack, gowlach, gellick, etc. (Scot.), horny-gollach (Scot.), muiro (Orkney), pincher bug, pincher-wig, pishamere barneybee (Norfolk), scodgebell or scotchybell (NE Eng. and Scot.), switchbell (Scot.), switchpool (Scot.), touchbell (Scot.), touch-spale, twinge, twitch-ballock, twitch-bells (NE Eng. and Scot.), witchy-beetle (NE Eng.), yerriwig (Suffolk)

Earwigs have been our familiars for probably as long as mankind has lived in permanent homes. Their narrow forms squeeze into cracks in window frames, lurk in damp, shaded corners under kitchen sinks or in compost bins and seek appetising snacks in an unwashed pet food dish or swing-bin. They eat almost anything, from other insects such as aphids and mites to living and decaying plant matter. Ideal homes for earwigs include piles of damp newspapers, damp baseboards and, perhaps most of all, boxes of stored apples. They have even been found inside DVD cases. The mild, damp climate of Britain is one of the most earwig-friendly on earth, allowing them to reproduce all year round. They take full advantage of the many opportunities we put in their way to settle down and multiply in our homes and gardens.

Earwig is an old word and one we share with most European languages; the French call them *perce-oreille* and the Germans *ohrwurm*. It derives from the Old English *ear wicga*, meaning, literally, 'one that wiggles in your ear'. Just how earwigs became associated with ears is uncertain. Earwigs like dark, moist cavities and seem the right size and shape to seek shelter there, and so perhaps the relationship was assumed. Possibly, if you slept out of doors on the damp ground, there would be some small chance of attracting an earwig looking for shelter. But rumour went further, attributing malice to the innocent insect and warning that it might bite its way into your inner ear or even wander further

inwards and lay its eggs in your brain. Needless to say, this is a myth, but its plausibility ensures it a long life:

> The old story that earwigs could cause deafness if they crawled into your ear, presumably by biting their way through one's ear drum was believed with real conviction by girls in the 1940s, to judge by the upbraiding I got whenever I put one near their ear.[41]

Robert Burton heard a story of an earwig that had crept into a soldier's ear during an air-raid. With rare sympathy, the solder saw it as a fellow mortal that was taking cover, just as he was.

Small moths and beetles are just as likely to enter human ears as earwigs. The experience is unpleasant but can soon be alleviated by flushing out the pest with warm oil. In the past, remedies were based on enticing the insect to leave voluntarily. One treatment claimed that the insect could be drawn forth, like a cork from a bottle, with the help of a ripe strawberry placed against the ear. A roasted apple worked just as well: 'To draw an earwig out of the ear, roast a sweet apple and plaster the pap of it to the ear on a hot linen cloth, and lie [the patient] still on the same side very quietly, and when you feel it come to the apple, pluck it away suddenly, that it return not back again.'[42]

Another method was to pour juice of wormwood into the ear and stop the hole with the foliage. Should an earwig 'or other verminous creature' creep into your mouth, the solution was simpler: the patient was ordered to munch some garlic. Yet, by paradox, some held that earwigs could be used to cure diseases of the ear, including deafness. Among the tried and apparently tested concoctions was one of ground-up dried earwig 'mingled with hare's pisse' or, perhaps in seasons where hares were scarce, with oil of cloves.

It was said that anyone who dreamt that an earwig had crawled into the ear should expect to hear bad news. In the unlikely event of an earwig crawling into the ear while you were gossiping to someone, it was an infallible sign that you had been telling a pack of wicked lies. To 'earwig' still means to eavesdrop on someone else's conversation. It can also mean to fill someone's mind with insinuations or else to attempt to influence someone by persistent argument.

Earwigs have many folk-names to match their reputation, and some, such as fork-tail or twitch-bell, are still used locally. Scotland has a particularly rich assortment: 'galloch' or 'horny-gollach' is an anglicised version of the Gaelic *goblachan*, meaning forked. The galloch was portrayed in country rhymes as a little devil, complete with horns and scales:

> The horny galloch is an awesome beast,
> Supple and scaly.
> He has twa horns an' a hantle o' feet,
> An'a forkie tailie.[43]

The name 'twitch-bell' is particularly earthy. The original name, mentioned by Thomas Muffet in his *Theatre of Insects,* was 'twitch-ballock' (though Muffet preferred to disguise the name in Latin form as *scrotomordium*). In support, he told a story about his contemporary Thomas Penny, who had been tormented by nipping earwigs inside his codpiece.[44] Entomologists seem to be as reluctant to admit that earwigs can nip as they are to believe that earwigs enter ears. But in the last resort, earwigs can deliver a sharp pinch to the skin, as the naturalist Maurice Burton discovered when one became lost inside his trouser leg.

The earwig of folk legend is the Common Earwig, *Forficula auricularia* (which means 'fork-ear'). It is considered to be a nuisance in orchards and gardens, especially in autumn when, as night temperatures fall, the earwigs seek shelter among the petals of chrysanthemums and dahlias, nibbling holes, which spoil a perfect bloom. The traditional way of catching them is to stuff straw or dried grass into a plastic cup mounted on a short cane in an area where earwigs congregate. The earwigs that make use of this hiding place can then be disposed of or, if you are of a kindly and forgiving nature, released somewhere else.

There are three more native British earwigs, plus a few established aliens. The Lesser Earwig is tiny and dull yellow and lives in dung-heaps. It was more familiar when the streets were caked in horse manure, but nowadays, unless it can find a good stable yard, it has to settle for second-best, a compost heap or a rubbish tip. You may, though, see one flying, buzzing around a lamp before settling on the ceiling. Earwig wings are normally held, elaborately folded, under skin-like flaps; the name of their order, the Dermaptera, means 'skin-wing'. Common Earwigs can fly but rarely do.

The introduced Bone-house Earwig was first found inside a packet of peanuts, but it soon discovered a better home in places where bones were stored before turning into glue. Today, glue is made from inedible chemicals, and the earwig has paid the price of living in a dangerously specialised habitat: it is extinct, more or less.

The Hop-garden Earwig is a reddish-brown species with short wings, worn like a waistcoat several sizes too small for it. In the days between the wars when hop-picking in Kent was a kind of worker's holiday, it was a familiar insect on hop flowers, but insecticides now make hop-gardens dangerous places for earwigs. Instead, it lingers on in thickets and hedges.

Our rarest and most exciting earwig is the Giant, or Tawny, Earwig, a monster up to three centimetres long, with matching pincers like a pair of pliers. It is one of our mystery insects. It is a cosmopolitan species, found on shores throughout the world, including oceanic islands, perhaps moving from one place to the next by clinging to driftwood and floating refuse. In Britain, its misfortune was to choose beaches that are now overrun by holidaymakers. The last time anyone saw one was in the 1980s, somewhere between Sidmouth and Beer in Devon. At least, someone reported spotting a very large earwig and, lacking a camera or cell-phone, made a sketch of it. Unfortunately he then lost the sketch.[45]

Are earwigs, with their long slithery shape and pincers at the wrong end, seen as vaguely phantasmagoric creatures? Earwigs was the name of an early eighties rock band inspired by the psychedelic sounds of the sixties. Or is it just that they have a funny-sounding name? The hero of David Nobbs' *The Fall and Rise of Reginald Perrin* often used the word earwig in surprising contexts as a means of relieving boredom, for example, 'I am a senior sales earwig', 'I didn't get where I am today by saying "earwig" instead of "thank you".'[46]

TRUE BUGS
Hemiptera

The Forest Bug, a typical shieldbug – stout, smart and smelly (its scientific name Pentatoma rufipes *means 'five segments, red legs').*

In the broadest sense, a bug can be any creeping 'insect'. By a more exact definition, a true bug is a member of the order Hemiptera, meaning half-winged. Among them are the shieldbugs, pond skaters and water boatmen, as well as the smaller but much commoner aphids and scale insects. What nearly all have in common is a characteristic way of folding their wings flat across the body in such a way as to leave a distinctive triangle, the scutellum, between the wing cases and the thorax. Most bugs are squat and flattish and feed with the help of a pointed 'beak' on plant sap or the body fluids of prey. True

bugs are among the more primitive insects, and like grasshoppers, their young, known as nymphs, are small, wingless versions of their parents.

Some would restrict the true bugs to a suborder Heteroptera, meaning different-winged. These are distinguished by thickened forewings, which, like those of beetles, form a protective sheath for the delicate flight wings. The 533 British species of the Hemiptera-Heteroptera include most of the larger bugs. The late Sir Richard Southwood suggested they were an ideal group for study, wonderfully diverse, often attractive and neither too many (like beetles, moths or flies) nor too few (like butterflies, dragonflies and grasshoppers).[1] Yet they remain one of the more neglected groups of insects, and there is no dedicated bug society or study group.

The other half of the Hemiptera is the suborder Homoptera (same-wing), a ragbag of mostly small and delicately built bugs with membranous wings, all of which feed on plant sap. The 1066 British species include aphids, froghoppers, scale insects and plant-lice, as well as the only British species of cicada. Among them are numerous forestry, agricultural and garden pests but also legions of harmless little hopping insects, including the one that makes cuckoo-spit. Traditionally, the Hemiptera-Homoptera is the province of agricultural entomologists rather than naturalists. As a result, we know more about the pests than the rest.

Bugs, like beetles, contain an arsenal of smelly defensive chemicals (hydroquinones), which apothecaries once used in traditional medicines. Among an apothecary's remedies might be a jar of dried shieldbugs, smelling gently of almonds, ready for grinding into powder form. Powdered bug was recommended for disorders of the urinary tract and also for quieting fevers and soothing the colic. The powder could also be mixed with honey or rosewater and used as a lotion.

Bugs have had surprisingly little lasting cultural impact. To be as 'snug as a bug in a rug' is to feel cosy, warm and comfortable, the way a bedbug is presumed to feel as it tucks in next to you. The expression dates back 300 years. 'Bug off' is short for 'bugger off' and so not entomological; 'bog off' is a slightly more genteel way of saying the same thing. New boys at school were sometimes called 'new bugs'. Another use of the word is for an addictive hobby: 'He has got the racing bug.'

> Biology masters at public schools were often known as 'Bugs'.[2]

Shieldbugs *Pentatomidae and other families*

VN: stinkbug

Shieldbugs are those squat, geometrically shaped insects often found basking on a leaf or madly running about on the ground. Unlike many insects, they usually allow us to get a good look at them to appreciate their finer points: the way they feed on a flower or leaf, or sway from side to side as they walk, or suddenly take flight with a buzz of their hidden wings.

Shieldbugs are relatively large, often colourful and relatively easy to identify. There are 33 British species, all of them compact insects with a hard carapace and a body shaped somewhat like the shield of a medieval knight. Their less flattering name, stinkbug, refers to the foul-smelling fluid that a shieldbug releases from glands between its legs to discourage predators. Compared to some warm-climate species, the scent of British shieldbugs is mild; it has been compared with rancid marzipan or mouldy almonds. In a Channel 5 poll of the world's smelliest animals, shieldbugs were nominated but, pleasingly, came bottom. Their stink is, though, undoubtedly a warning, for in the natural world a scent of almonds spells cyanide.

The stinkbug provided Alexander Pope, himself known as the Wasp of Twickenham, with a ready-made epithet for his enemy, the foppish Sporus, or Lord John Hervey:

> . . . let me flap this Bug with gilded wings,
> This painted Child of Dirt that stinks and stings;
> Whose buzz the witty and the fair annoys,
> Yet wit ne'er tastes, and beauty ne'er enjoys.[3]

The more distinctive shieldbugs have well-established English names. The Woundwort and the Birch Shieldbugs are named after their food-plants (the importance of knowing the right plants and where to find them makes the shieldbugs botanists' insects). That of the dark-coloured Negro Bug comes from the Spanish word for black. The Sloe Bug is misnamed, for though it feeds on a variety of plants, sloe is not one of them. The Turtle Bug and the Tortoise Bug are named after their shape and appearance. The Bishop's Mitre has a long, triangular projection that resembles a bishop's ceremonial headpiece and helps to disguise the bug among

Firebugs mating heedlessly on a sprig of box. They bear the image of a facial mask on their wing cases, hence the alternate name, Clown-faced Bug.

grains of grass. The Parent Bug is an old name for a maternal bug that crouches over her mass of eggs like an armoured chicken, solicitously guarding her growing brood. The Forest Bug likes ripe apples and cherries, though its 'wild' food seems to be tree sap.

Many gardens, especially those with shrubberies, may contain half a dozen species of shieldbug. The commonest, the Green Shieldbug, is often found on blackberries and also enjoys our raspberries and runner beans, though they are rarely numerous enough to be a problem. Similar but somewhat larger and paler is the Southern Green Shieldbug, or Green Vegetable Bug. It was imported into Britain on tomato plants and until recently was confined to greenhouses. But now it has been found outdoors, including in a nature reserve near Kings Cross Station in London, and will probably become established in the near future. Unlike our native shieldbugs, it has the capacity to become a garden pest, attacking a wide range of crops, from soft fruit to potatoes and beans.

The Firebug is a most distinctive red and black bug, with a pattern and shape eerily like that of a tribal mask. In Jersey, it is known as the Clown-faced Bug. Though very common around the Mediterranean, it is at the edge of its range in Britain and until recently was confined to the rocky islet of Ore Stones near Torquay, where it feeds on the seeds of tree mallow. In recent years, it has begun turning up on the mainland, and with the warming climate, may be on the verge of becoming established along the south coast.

A related family, often counted as honorary shieldbugs, is the Coreidae, or 'squashbugs'. In America, several species are common pests of squashes (our marrows), and the name, though unsuitable over here, has stuck. The born survivor among them is the Box Bug, which was formerly confined to box trees in the neighbourhood of Box Hill, Surrey, but has suddenly and unexpectedly expanded its tastes and moved on to hawthorn and wild roses.

Along with water bugs, shieldbugs are the most popular true bugs. The existence of a book called *The Shieldbugs of Surrey* is a testament to their popularity, and it contains useful hints on keeping them in captivity: 'If a fat bug refuses to eat, then it is probably close to a moult. If a thin bug does not eat, then there's something wrong with the food . . . If a bug is running around madly, then it may be in need of a drink . . . Sometimes a bug may be found lying on its back and waving its legs in the air. This is nothing to worry about . . . the creature may just be stuck.'[4]

Bedbugs *Cimicidae*

The Bedbug, *Cimex lectularius*

VN: crimson rambler, mahogany flat, stinkbug

There is a Spanish expression, 'you can't have more bedbugs than a blanket-full', which is as good a way as any to describe overnight accommodation at certain cheap hostels near airports. Waking up itching and scratching and then noticing the red blips or welts on your arms and chest is never a pleasant start to the day. It is not so much the skin reaction or even the outrage done to your sleeping body but the thought of sharing your bed with a nocturnal bloodsucker. When mothers say 'Goodnight, don't let the bedbugs bite,' to their sleepy children, it is perhaps just as well that the children don't understand.

The Bedbug is a true bug about the size of a ladybird. It is wingless and, unless blown-up after a blood meal, flat. Bedbugs used to be as familiar as fleas. People even knew their smell: the sweetish, slightly rancid, pheromone scent of massed 'stink-bugs' ('smelling of bedbugs' is a frequent phrase in field guides on fungi, presumably dating from the time when most people had experienced it). It was practically impossible to get rid of them, since even the cleanest homes were full of Bedbug refuges, such as straw mattresses or the horsehair insulation in walls. In 1939, half the homes in London were reported to have Bedbugs. Just a few years later, we began to win this particular war, at considerable cost to the environment, with DDT. The Bedbug seemed to be a thing of the past, at least in clean homes in Western Europe. But, like head lice, they are returning, not everywhere – but reported infestations in the London area have risen tenfold since 1996.[5]

One reason for the bug's return is, ironically, our concern for the environment. Modern pest-control tends to avoid poisons that kill the bugs outright in place of less environmentally damaging materials that act on the bug's hormone regulation. Hence there is more room for the bugs to escape. The other reason is the ease and cheapness of foreign travel. Backpackers and green tourists routinely stay in places that may be infected with bugs. The Bedbugs come out at night, bite their victims and leave their tiny eggs in clothes lying in convenient

A Bedbug takes a midnight snack.

heaps; the clothes are then crammed into the rucksack and returned to Britain unwashed. You can pick up Bedbugs on buses and trains, in airport lounges or from other people's dry-cleaning. They hide in sleeping bags, in tatty paperback books, in wall sockets and alarm clocks and in the attractive carving you picked up in a street market. Any modern home is full of potential bug refuges. The only difference is that, in a clean and tidy home you are likely to spot the danger signs sooner.

The call-signs of Bedbugs are blood spots or brown excrement spots on the sheets, and that sweet buggy smell. They live for up to 18 months, and though they need at least one blood meal every time they change their skin, they can survive without food for months. Like mosquitoes, they inject an anticoagulant into us, which causes itching. For the minority who are allergic to insect bites, these can turn into sores and cause other side-effects such as sleepiness. Fortunately, unlike mosquitoes, they are not known to transmit diseases.

Bedbugs were apparently not known in Britain before 1503. According to a John Southall of Southward, who published a highly creditable *Treatise of Buggs* in 1730, they began to be a nuisance in the pre-building boom after the Great Fire of London of 1666, when quantities of imported timber were undocked. Sixty years on, claimed Southall, nearly every house in London was plagued by this 'nauseous venomous insect'. He had a patent remedy to offer. During a trip to the West Indies, Southall had been taken ill with a fever. A slave, noticing bug bites all over Southall's body, produced a 'strong and oleous' lotion made from certain local plants. Having bribed the slave to reveal its contents, Southall took the formula back to London and went into business, marketing the stuff as Nonpareil.

He also set about studying the life of the bug, rearing Bedbugs and making meticulous drawings of every stage in their lifecycle. He left a charming description of an insect whose legs were jointed like a crab and whose head and neck resembled a toad's, from which bristled 'three picqued horns'. Bedbugs, warned Southall, 'are watchful and cunning, and though timorous of us, yet in fight with one another are very fierce; I having often seen some . . . fight as eagerly as Dogs or Cockes, and sometimes one or both have died on the Spot.'[6] He established, accurately enough, that their eggs are fertile only in warm weather and that, contrary to rumour, Bedbugs are not fussy about whom they bite. Diligent searching and cleanliness were the keys to a bug-free house (with, of course, a nightly dose of Southall's patent Nonpareil).

Bedbug art must be rare, but in Kingsclere, Hampshire, there is a golden Bedbug on the weather vane of the church. According to legend, it was put there on the orders of King John after he had spent an itchy night nearby. The church magazine is called *The Bedbug Recorder*.

Two other bloodsucking bugs occasionally bite people. Both the Martin Bug and the Pigeon Bug live in bird's nests and normally suck the blood of the unfortunate birds, though they have been known to stray on to people sleeping below.

Water bugs

Aquatic bugs are among our best-known and most fascinating bugs, including the pond skaters and water measurers that walk on the water, the Water Scorpion and the Water Stick Insect that are adept ambush predators, disguised as leaves or twigs, and the water boatmen, engaging insects that scull about using their long, feathered back legs as oars.

Water Scorpions *Nepidae*

The Water Scorpion looks vaguely like a scorpion, with its grasping forelegs and apparent sting in the form of a long, thin breathing tube at the end of its flattened, leaf-like body. Its dull, matt brown colours blend in with pond debris, but its underside

A Water Scorpion lurking in shallow water disguised as a leaf. It is not related to true scorpions, and what looks like a sting is its breathing tube.

183

is a startlingly bright red, like a bright waistcoat beneath a dowdy coat. Its purpose is presumably to startle potential predators, but in Britain, at least, the Water Scorpion rarely seems to open its wings and almost never flies. It cannot sting, and though it may be capable of biting, it usually prefers to play dead when handled. In America, there is a larger, more aggressive water scorpion that definitely bites; they call it the 'toe-biter'.

The Water Stick Insect is another charismatic bug, almost unbelievably long and leggy, like an aquatic praying mantis. It spends much of its time motionless, watching and waiting from a head-down position on a scrap of weed. Its long legs give the bug an extraordinary reach with which to snatch at passing fish fry or tadpoles. It is a surprisingly good

The Water Stick Insect, a favourite among pond-dippers. It has similar habits to a praying mantis, lying motionless among waterweed awaiting the moment when a victim strays within grabbing distance.

swimmer and can on occasion take flight, when it 'resembles a red damselfly with the body held parallel to the ground'.[7]

Both have long been familiar insects. The sixteenth-century naturalist Thomas Muffet knew them as 'lake scorpions' or 'forked claws' and he included a recognisable woodcut of the Water Stick Insect in his great book *The Theatre of Insects*.[8] In Devon, the insect has been called 'granfer griggs' (a name it shares with the woodlouse), while in America, it is the 'needle bug'.

The Water Stick Insect is comparatively rare. 'When I was a boy, there were a number of insect "Holy Grails", and one of these was the Water Stick Insect,' recalls Tony Harwood. 'I eventually found one in a weedy ditch. Unfortunately, with me at the time was my pet duck, a mallard called Emma, who showed her appreciation by promptly seizing it. There followed some undignified wrestling with the duck as I tried to make her drop it. On other forays, Emma also managed to snaffle a Water Scorpion, a Saucer Bug and some larvae of a particularly interesting cranefly.' The moral seems to be: never go pond-dipping with a duck.[9]

Water boatmen *Corixidae*

How many of us have heard the song of water boatmen? Some of them make characteristic zips, ticks and rasping calls by rubbing special sound-pegs on their front legs. They say one of them, the tiny *Micronecta poweri*, only two to three millimetres long, is one of the noisiest animals on earth relative to its size. It can be heard from five metres away, which may not sound impressive but, scaled up, is the equivalent of hearing a cow or a horse from five kilometres off. This alien sound-world of the pond is unfamiliar partly because the boatmen are at their most vocal at night, especially just after dusk, but perhaps mainly because there are usually too many competing noises, not least among ourselves, for us to hear them well. Surprisingly, the name *poweri* has nothing to do with decibels. It commemorates a Victorian entomologist known as John 'the Indefatigable' Power, who was noted for the lengths he would go to catch bugs, including keeping his field equipment inside a special tall hat.[10]

One of the best places to watch water boatmen is in a cattle trough, which is usually free of fish and other predators and yet contains enough detritus for them to hoover up with their nozzle-

The Water Boatman, or Common Backswimmer, hanging from the water's surface film on the lookout for live prey, from mites to tadpoles and small fish. Its bite is sharp enough to puncture human skin.

like mouthparts. The bugs live in water throughout their lifecycle, and the steep sides and lack of access to a cattle trough are no handicap. There are 38 species of water boatmen in Britain (not counting the predatory 'backswimmers'), but they are all very similar-looking despite having diverse habits and, in some cases, different 'songs'. They swim the right way up and under water with vigorous beats of their long swimming legs, carrying a film of air under their wing cases. None of them can bite, but when frightened, they release a cheesy pungent fluid, which you can sometimes actually smell in the water. In tropical Asia, there is a giant water boatman that is eaten as a delicacy and tastes of gorgonzola cheese.

Water boatmen fly well, and often turn up in large numbers in moth traps. Their efficiency at colonising new sites means they usually find a suitable garden pond within weeks of its construction.

most writers now prefer the American name, backswimmers. These predatory bugs paddle on their backs while moving on the water's surface, swimming legs outstretched. This strange way of life, gazing simultaneously at the sun and the water, has intrigued pond-watchers from Muffet onwards. Muffet even suggested that 'men learnt the art of swimming upon their backs' by copying the backswimmer.[11]

There are only four species of *Notonecta* in Britain, fairly easily distinguished by the patterns on their wing-cases. In their way, they are rather beautiful, with their hull-like bodies, bulging reddish eyes and feathered swimming legs. They feed on a variety of pond life, from water mites to tadpoles and small fish, immobilising them with a toxic bite. They are well capable of jabbing human skin with a painful bite, perhaps mistaking an outstretched finger for an unusually large worm.

Backswimmers *Notonectidae*

AN: water boatman

Confusingly, the larger *Notonecta* water bugs are also known in Britain as water boatmen, though

Saucer bugs *Naucoridae*

The Saucer Bug is a handsome and common bug of clean, weedy ponds whose streamlined head-end looks a little like that of a villain with a stocking pulled over his face. It has a relative in fast-flowing

The vanishingly thin Water Measurer, built for water-walking.

rivers known, logically enough, as the River Saucer Bug, which is flat and round, resembling a large bedbug. Both have a powerful, instinctive bite that is said to feel like a bee sting.

Water-walkers

VN: water skater, water strider, wherryman

An animal that walks on water compels admiration. Pond skaters (Gerridae) are those elongated bugs that scuttle along on the water's surface, with their long, thread-thin legs dipping into the film. They have also intrigued us by the X-shaped angle of their legs, as if the bug was a living compass. Hence, in some cultures (not ours), the pond skater has become a symbol of direction. Altogether, it is a mysterious insect whose way of life suggests that it is not entirely of this world, just as its fragile form hints that its time with us will be short.

Pond skaters hunt by feeling vibrations with their velvet-covered feet. A sudden disturbance in the water, indicating a drowning insect, sets it racing forwards using its middle pair of legs for propulsion and its back pair for steering (the remaining, smaller pair is used to grab the prey). The bug keeps dry by means of a waxy coat and water-repellent hairs, which act on the same principle as those non-absorbent towels you find in expensive hotels. When not feeding, mating or sleeping, pond skaters

are usually washing. They do this by flipping themselves over to dip their top halves in the water in a move Jonty Denton describes as 'akin to a self-tossing pancake'.[12]

It is useless trying to keep pond skaters in an aquarium. They run around in a panic, jump in vain against the glass walls and eventually manage to stun themselves and drown. Whereupon the remaining pond skaters will stop to feast on the corpse of their fellow captive before resuming their hopeless attempts to escape. In America, pond skaters are called water striders or waterskates. Other names of New World origin include 'water scooter', 'water skater' or 'skeeter', 'waterskipper' and, because they walk on water, 'Jesus bug'.[13] It seems that Americans are more pond-skater-aware than us.

The Water Measurer, also known as a 'water gnat', is one of the thinnest insects on earth. They seem virtually linear, all length and no breadth. Their name echoes the way they habitually move in a slow, measured way as if pacing out the distance, though they are, in fact, in search of gnat larvae or water fleas too small or sick to resist. They can even survive in temporary pools by patiently sheltering under stones and debris until the puddle fills up again.

Water crickets (Veliidae) look like small, stout pond skaters and are found scuttling about on the water's surface at the edge of ponds and the quieter reaches of rivers. Muffet knew them as 'water grasshoppers'. In America they are commonly called small 'water striders' or 'riffle bugs'.

The capsid bug Miris striatus, *one of a large group of vegetarian bugs that feed on flowers and seeds.*

Capsid bugs *Miridae*

AN: grass bug, leaf bug, mirid bug, plant bug

The capsids, which are characterised by relatively soft forewings, are the largest family of bugs. They feed on developing buds and fruit, a habit that has brought a few species into conflict with gardeners. The commonest sign of capsid damage is distorted, crinkly leaves full of holes. When the bug sups at a flower or leaf bud, it injects toxic saliva into the plant tissue that kills the cells around the site of the wound. Then, as the bud unfurls, the dead parts of the leaf rip apart like perforations on a stamp. Vulnerable plants include chrysanthemums, hydrangeas, dahlias, fuchsias and forsythias, and among vegetables, beans and potatoes. The bug responsible is often the Common Green Capsid,

a typically leggy bug with an oval body. Another garden-plant-muncher is the dull brown Tarnished Plant Bug, which might move there from its base in the nettle patch we left for the butterfly caterpillars in favour of flowers and fruit trees. Another fruit-tree specialist, the Apple Capsid, sucks the juice of developing fruit leaving scabs on the apple. The damage is only skin deep and does not affect the taste, but unfortunately it does affect their saleability, especially in supermarkets. Short of spraying, they say the best way to avoid capsids is to pick them off in May.

A few capsids are predators, and an American species, *Deraeocoris nebulosus*, has been used as a bio-control agent against mites and scale insects.

An assassin bug (Himacerus apterus), a formidable predator with grasping front legs and a long retractable 'dagger'.

Assassin bugs *Reduviidae*

VN: ambush bugs, kissing bugs

Assassin bugs are predators. They are named after their habit of waiting under cover to ambush their prey, which they dispatch with a sharp proboscis like a poisoned stiletto. Once the victim has stopped struggling and its innards have been turned into soup, the proboscis becomes a straw through which the bug drinks its victim's flesh. Some species have bristly, sticky legs to hold the prey down while they feed. Since their prey includes garden pests, assassin bugs are regarded as a good thing.

Most assassin bugs hunt by night and so are not often seen unless looked for. The most familiar British species is the Fly Bug, since it is large and attracted to light and so occasionally found in moth traps or on a window. The Fly Bug stridulates like a grasshopper when handled, but handling is not recommended as it has a painful bite. Related but daintier bugs in the family Nedidae are known as damsel bugs.

Assassin bugs are better known in the New World and tropical Africa, where certain species are spectacularly large and brightly coloured. These are sometimes kept as slightly scary pets in America though not, it seems, in Britain. The favourite is a five-centimetre monster, the Wheel Bug, so named because its thorax has a spiny crest shaped like a cogwheel.

New World assassin bugs have at least one footnote in British history. While collecting and sleeping rough out on the pampas during the voyage of HMS *Beagle*, Charles Darwin had been bitten repeatedly on the face by 'a great black bug'. It was probably a kissing bug, so called because of its genial habit of biting our softer parts, including the lips, while we sleep. Kissing bugs can transmit disease, including a wasting illness known as Chagas disease. In later life Darwin was always feeling unwell; his trouble has been dismissed as hypochondria, but it may have been the drawn-out sequel to a forgotten bug bite in his adventurous youth.[14]

Other families of bugs include the unimaginatively named ground bugs (Lygaeidae), which are often found scuttling at speed over bare spaces. Most ground bugs feed on plant seeds, hence their alternate name, seed bugs. Cone bugs (*Gastrodes* species) are seed bugs adapted for life high up among the pines and spruces.

Hoppers, aphids and scales *Homoptera*

The New Forest Cicada. Its high-pitched song is a test for sensitive ears.

Cicadas *Cicadidae*

Many of us associate the noisy buzzing of cicadas with languid evenings in the Mediterranean. Yet Britain has its own wild cicada, *Cicadetta montana*, a little-known bug confined to the New Forest. We might celebrate it more were it not for the fact that the British cicada is, to our ears, almost silent. Few adults can detect it, though W. H. Hudson claimed to have heard it once, or what he assumed to be it: 'a sustained sound . . . the beats or drops of sound which compose the grasshopper's song, and run in a stream, were more distinct and separate, giving it a trilling rather than a reeling character'.[15] He preferred it to the 'brain-piercing, everlasting whirr' of its Mediterranean relatives.

The New Forest Cicada sings only on hot days, two hours either side of noon, and stops at the slightest breeze or disturbance. The males have been found perched on twigs, where they quickly slip to the other side out of view like a squirrel if they sense our presence. A colony of them was studied and monitored for 40 years, first by Jim Grant, and then, after his untimely death in 1991, by his wife, Lena Ward. In 1962, when the project began, there were a hundred singing males, but numbers have fallen steadily over the years, and today, it seems, there are none left. Cicada colonies routinely move from place to place in search of suitable open scrub in sunny places, but their open, bushy habitat, usually in small, sun-warmed forest glades, is often under threat from grazing ponies as well as invading bracken. Though global warming should, in theory, help our cicada, it will be of no avail if it also means wetter and windier summers. And if winter rainfall increases, so does the danger of the cicada nymphs drowning in their burrows.[16]

189

Froghoppers *Aphrophoridae*

*The larva of a froghopper (*Philaenus spumarius*) inside its protective covering of 'cuckoo spit'.*

VN: cuckoo-spit insects, cuckoo's spittens (Scot.), gowk's spittle (Scot.), puddock (Scot.), spittlebugs, toad-spit, wood-seer (Northants)

Anyone who has wandered through the grass in early summer, especially early in the morning, will know cuckoo spit, the mysterious froth that coats the grass stems. Since it had no obvious source, it was once assumed to be the spittle of birds passing overhead. Those who examined the froth more closely found a tiny green grub inside, but that seemed only to deepen the mystery. From ancient times onwards it was believed (unlikely as it seems) that this tiny being was a baby cuckoo. The reasoning went like this: cuckoos had no known nest; Aristotle had taught that certain animals were not born sexually but generated spontaneously in carrion, dung, pond-slime or, in this case, spit; so instead of laying an egg like other birds, the cuckoo spat its young into the world.

Eventually it became apparent that the tiny creature smeared in spit was not a bird but an insect. In his 'inquiry' into vulgar errors and perceived truths, the seventeenth-century writer Sir Thomas Browne firmly dismissed the cuckoo theory, concluding that the grub was a young cicada, 'bred out of cuccow spittle or Wood-sear; that is, that spumous, frothy dew or exudation.'[17] Yet the name cuckoo spit lived on, perhaps because it appears at around the time when the cuckoo is calling. It could be seen as a talisman of the spring in the same way that certain early flowers are known as 'cuckoo flowers'.

The bug inside the spit is in fact a perfect miniature of the adult insect, known as a froghopper. In America they are known as 'spittlebugs' or 'spitbugs'. The insect does look vaguely like a tiny frog, with its plump shape, powerful back legs and bulging eyes, and the adult also leaps in a frog-like way. The spit has been called 'frog-spit' or 'frog-foam', and in America 'toad-spit' or 'snake-spit' (the latter names suggest that the 'spit' is poisonous, though it isn't). In Scotland, cuckoo spit is 'gowk's spittle' or 'gowk's spittens', from the Scots dialect word for a cuckoo. Latinised spit appears in the scientific name of the commonest species, *Philaenus spumarius*.

The nineteenth-century poet John Clare knew the grubs as 'woodseers' or 'wood prophets', noting how they 'lye in little notts of spittle on the backs of leaves & flowers' and appeared in plenty in wet weather. They were, said Clare, 'one of the shepherd's weather glasses. When the head of the insect is seen upward it is said to token fine weather, when downward on the contrary wet may be expected.'[18]

There is no longer any mystery about how the spit is produced. The grub sucks plant sap, much of which passes through its little body and out again, under pressure. The grub blows a little air into the sticky sap and, hey presto, it bubbles up like bath foam. In other words, Clare's 'notts of spittle' are a heroic example of insect flatulence. The idea of an animal building itself a shelter by farting into its food never fails to entertain budding young naturalists.

In *The Very Quiet Cricket*, the children's-story writer Eric Carle takes us on a journey through the grass blades, meeting all kinds of insects buzzing, humming and stridulating. But none sounds weirder than the spittlebug 'slurping in a sea of froth'.[19]

In Scotland, we called the green nymph a 'Puddock'. I've never heard it called that anywhere else. Puddock is the Scots name for a frog.[20]

Aphids
Aphididae and other families

VN: blackfly, blight, greenflies, plant-lice, smother-flies

One hot day at the beginning of August in 1774, the Hampshire village of Selborne was surprised by what Gilbert White described as 'a shower of *aphides* or smother-flies'. They settled on every hedge and garden, 'blackening all the vegetables where they alighted.' White's annuals 'were discoloured with them, and the stalks of a bed of onions were quite coated for six days after'. He believed this invading 'army' had come from the hop-gardens of Kent and Sussex, since 'great clouds' of aphids had been spotted coming from that direction 'all along the vale from Farnham to Alton'.[21]

Aphids are still, of course, troublesome insects in gardens, not only because their endless sucking blocks the flow of the sap and so weakens the plant but also because they can be vectors of plant viruses such as 'sugar beet yellow' and 'potato mosaic'. Greenfly and blackfly appear in swarms, clustered on the growing parts of the plant, and seem to multiply before our eyes. For most of their lives, aphids reproduce without sex, so that each newborn nymph is a genetic carbon-copy of its lone parent. Moreover, aphids are built like Russian dolls: inside each mature female, or 'stem mother', there is a developing nymph, which in turn contains the embryo of a grandchild aphid. This enables aphids to multiply with disconcerting speed, so that a single female can produce a whole herd of offspring within days.

Such fecundity excites the statistician: if an aphid and all its progeny lived to reproduce at the same rate, the planet would, by the end of the year, have become an aphid mountain of around a quadrillion individuals. In short order, they would suck every plant dry, use up the oxygen and wipe out virtually all life, including themselves. Aphids obviously never achieve more than a tiny fraction of their full reproductive potential, but in the right conditions, they can locally become more abundant than any other insect on earth. A large field of alfalfa, a particularly aphid-susceptible crop, may contain up to four tonnes of aphids. Hollywood, obsessed with giant mutant insects, has overlooked this bug's staggering reproductive potential.

A leaf-hopping bug and beetle on a Victorian wooden carving at Studely Royal, Yorkshire.

One of the most familiar garden aphids is the blackfly, or Black Bean Aphid. It clusters as 'blight' on the undersides of leaves and the tender shoot tips of plants, especially beans and peas. Apart from spoiling the crop, these aphids encourage a black mould that grows eagerly on their sticky-sweet droppings. As every rose-grower knows, aphids have an infuriating way of clustering on the tender, sappy shoots and flower buds, ruining any chance of producing prize-winning blooms. These are Rose Aphids or greenflies, which can be pink as well as green, with characteristic black 'knees'. The traditional way of dealing with them is soapy water, followed by a dusting of derris, but greenfly are very persistent, and prevention is better than cure. They are sensitive to nicotine, and a time-honoured method for deterring them indoors was to blow cigarette smoke on to infected plants. Later in the year, they lose interest in roses and migrate to other flowers such as scabious and teasels.

Other garden pests include the Woolly Aphid, or American Blight, a purplish aphid that feeds and multiplies under protective tufts of waxy threads. A New World native, it was first noticed in an English garden by Sir Joseph Banks more than 200 years ago. By the 1800s, it had become a periodic nuisance in orchards, and in one particularly bad summer, stopped cider production throughout Gloucestershire. It is still a common pest on apple trees. The pale green Peach-potato Aphid is the vector of more than a hundred plant viruses, and because of its phenomenal rate of reproduction, quickly develops a resistance to insecticides. The big, grey Lupin Aphid is a relative newcomer from

Mother greenfly and her babies – a Mother's Day card from an entomologist.

America and seems to have no natural enemies in Britain; aphid predators such as hoverflies and ladybirds seem to leave it alone. Short of hand-picking, the only way to deal with these aphids is a spray containing rape-oil. The Green Spruce Aphid is a serious defoliating pest of Sitka Spruce plantations.

In his song 'Greenfly and Rose', Robert Calvert, poet, performer and lead singer with Hawkwind in the 1970s, compared aphid-afflicted roses with a love affair: they blossom briefly and then they droop. Aphids, he suggests, dream of roses for breakfast, lunch and tea. They live to eat; eating is what they are good at. They would consume the whole world with their little sucking mouths if they could, even the sun and the stars.[22]

Schoolchildren played a game with greenfly known as 'flea-darts'. The darts were the ears of wall-barley grass, whose points, when thrown with skill, stuck in clothes and hair. The 'fleas' were the aphids that lived between the ears of the seed-heads, which added a scary dimension to the game, as if the aphids would promptly turn into head lice. The victim was expected to cry, 'flea darts injected!'

Does anyone remember the greenfly plague in the early 1980s? I was sitting outside a pub in Staffordshire next to a group of bikers, and the air was thick with greenflies. I watched with amazement while one biker used a beer-mat to scrape together a thick line of greenfly, and then snort up the lot through a rolled up banknote, much to the loud approval of his mates.[23]

Aphids are preyed on by a large number of insects, most notably lacewing and hoverfly larvae and both adult and larval ladybirds. Yet they are not entirely defenceless. In spring 2007, scientists at Imperial College London discovered that certain aphids are able to resist their predators by, in effect, turning themselves into suicide bombers. The topical resonance with our own world ensured that the discovery, which would otherwise have remained buried deep in a scientific journal, made the headlines. Cabbage Aphids are tiny greenish insects, some with wings, some without, which feed on brassicas in the spring and early summer. They are preyed upon by large numbers of insects, including ladybird and hoverfly larvae, and give the appearance of being completely helpless, unable either to run away or to resist. But brassicas contain blistering agents in the form of mustard oils, and the aphids store them in their body fluids as potentially explosive chemicals called glucosinolates. In the event of an attack, a chemical sequence comes into play in which the stored explosives are ignited by enzymes produced in an aphid's muscles. The aphid is blown apart, in the process flinging stinging mustard oil into the face of the predator. The research team from Britain and Norway confirmed their findings by offering different plants to the aphids. Those which fed on plants rich in glucosinolates had the highest success rate in fending off predators.[24]

Honeydew

Most of us will have experienced mysterious stickiness on the car roof, often after unwisely parking beneath a lime or sycamore tree on a hot day. This is honeydew, dropping like sugary rain from the bottoms of vast numbers of tiny aphids and scale insects feeding in the foliage. The aphids use their mouthparts to puncture leaf tissue until they locate the phloem (the duct which transports sugar-rich sap from the leaves to the trunk and roots). Having done so, the aphid hardly needs to do anything more, for the sugar-rich liquid gushes out under pressure straight into their gut. Aphids process at least their own weight of phloem sap every day. Why do they need so much? Because though plant sap is rich in simple sugars, it is poor in the protein the aphid needs to grow and reproduce. Hence, to process enough for its needs, an aphid must spend most of its life (20–40 days) feeding. Of course, this means it consumes vastly more sugar than it requires and so excretes most of it in concentrated form as bubbles of honeydew. At peak times, a medium-sized sycamore can contain around 2 million aphids, equivalent in weight to a large rabbit – a highly incontinent rabbit. As the aphids move around in their slow, deliberate way, the honeydew coats the leaves, brambles and other vegetation below and is eventually washed into the soil by rain or, in autumn, after leaf-fall.

This perpetual fall-out of sugar is a bonanza to a whole ecosystem of micro-organisms, fungi and insects. Honeydew is an important food source for many invertebrates, from butterflies and moths to wasps and flies; it is probably the main reason why butterflies such as hairstreaks can live in the treetops (you can watch them imbibing honeydew on bramble leaves, completely ignoring the flowers). In warm, damp weather, honeydew develops a sour smell as natural yeasts develop on the film of dew and begin to ferment. At such times, wasps in particular show signs of disorientation, which is probably the insect equivalent of intoxication. Without aphids in the trees, forests would be much less rich in insect life.

Ants famously obtain honeydew directly from the aphid by collecting it as droplets in their jaws. This is often referred to in decorous terms as 'milking', with the aphids acting as surrogate cows, but this is a polite euphemism for what really happens. When Woody Allen, playing a fussy ant called 'Z' in his film *Antz*, was offered a drink of aphid beer, he replied: 'Call me crazy, but I have a thing about drinking from the anus of another creature.'[25] But, at whatever risk to their dignity, the aphids benefit from the relationship, since the ants drive away their many enemies, including those fierce aphid-eaters, ladybirds and lacewing larvae.

Less positively, honeydew provides a nutritious substrate for sooty moulds, which ruin the appearance of ornamental plants and eventually weaken them by preventing photosynthesis. The mould grows anywhere, including windowsills and car panels, and can need vigorous scrubbing to remove. Occasionally, the honeydew itself can be bothersome, coating every leaf with viscous goo. Gilbert White experienced this during the exceptionally hot summer of 1783, when 'honey-dews were so frequent as to deface and destroy the beauties of my garden'. He noticed that the substance was often 'loaded' with aphids but assumed that they were eating it rather than excreting it. He reasoned that the honeydew was formed by the 'effluvia of flowers' being drawn into the air by a 'brisk evaporation' which fell as dew by night as the air cooled.[26] The name honeydew was coined in the belief that it formed from the saturated air like dew or as manna from the heavens.

Honeydew honey, made from bees that collect the 'dew' instead of nectar and pollen, is a rich substance described as 'the Marmite of honeys', for it is not only dark but also strong to the point of becoming savoury. Often sold as forest honey or pine, fir or beech honey, depending on which tree is involved, it has a higher proportion of antioxidants and complex sugars such as maltose than lighter floral honeys. It may also contain natural yeasts and so be slightly alcoholic. Honeydew honey is said to be good for maintaining or developing beneficial bacteria in our gut (often known as the 'gut flora'). Little of it is made in Britain but it has long been a speciality of the Black Forest in Germany, where the hives are placed among pines and other trees leaking with the dew from armies of aphids and scale insects (because honeydew lacks the nitrogen-rich element of pollen, the bees need to be fed protein supplements). In the 1970s, the technique was passed on to New Zealand, where beekeepers have successfully made a southern hemisphere version from honeydew leaking from *Nothofagus*, or southern beech trees.

Whiteflies *Aleyrodidae*

Whiteflies are aphid relatives with wax-coated wings and a resemblance to tiny, pale moths. The Greenhouse Whitefly is a non-native insect that arrives here on imported plants and thrives in glasshouses; it is also beginning to survive the British winter. A parasitic wasp specialising in targeting this whitefly has appeared from nowhere and can now be bought from garden centres. The Cabbage Whitefly lays its oval, pale yellow eggs in neat curves and circles on the underside of cabbages and other leafy brassicas. They do little damage in themselves, but their droppings encourage sooty mildew to develop and spoil the crop.

Whitefly on a cabbage leaf.

Jumping plant lice *Psyllidae*

VN: suckers

Psyllids are tiny relatives of cicadas, which, despite their plump, awkward-looking little bodies, can jump as nimbly as grasshoppers. Like aphids and whiteflies, they suck the sap of tender plants, and their sticky droppings encourage mildew. Several species also cause plant galls. They generally come to our attention only when they are damaging garden fruit trees and other crops, and this distorts our perception of them. The best-known psyllid is the Bay Sucker, which occasionally swarms on potted bay trees at the front of smart hotels or as the centerpiece of a herb garden. The Apple Sucker is responsible for sticky leaves on apple trees.

Against our perception of them as horticultural pests, an orange-winged psyllid from Japan, *Aphalara itadori,* has been put forward as a potential bio-control for one of Britain's most invasive plants, Japanese knotweed. Hitherto, the plant has been almost impossible to control, since it can regenerate from root fragments and can force its way through tarmac and even concrete. Using chemicals to eradicate it root and branch would cost about £1.5 billion.[27] But, as some pundits pointed out, the world is full of the catastrophic consequences of introducing alien species into the wild. Introducing the bug may seem tempting, but it is a risky course to take.

Scale insects *Coccidae*

VN: mealybugs

It is hard to see scale insects as relations of aphids and whiteflies; indeed, they hardly look alive. Scale insects are round and flattened, seemingly legless and generally motionless and resembling warts or fish scales. The more active ones, like tiny woodlice, are known as mealybugs (Pseudococcidae) from their scurfy bodies. But those in the super-family Coccoidea are more or less immobile. They cluster on the same patch of stem or bark, sucking the sap throughout much of their brief lives and excreting sticky honeydew over the leaves. Some shelter under a coating of pearly wax or fluffy threads. Most scale insects we find are female; the tiny winged males live only a few hours.

Scale insects have made their mark on history in various ways. Accumulations of honeydew produced by a desert species of scale insect is the most likely explanation for the mysterious manna on which Moses and the Israelites are supposed to have been miraculously fed. Another species is the source of the red dye cochineal, once used to colour the British army's red coats. The best cochineal came from North America, but there was a cheaper European equivalent known as Polish cochineal; both were eventually superseded by natural plant dyes. An Asian species of scale insect, the Lac Bug, was responsible for a sticky natural resin called shellac, which has been put to a large variety of uses, including a high-gloss varnish, a colourant, a natural

Waxy scale insects on a lime leaf.

A 'fancy portrait' cartoon from Punch, *1890, highlighting the Phylloxera bug's uncanny ability to attach itself to the best vineyards and most valuable vines.*

wax and a candy coating for certain sweets. Before cheaper, chemical derivatives became available from the 1930s onwards, the average household was full of brittle, shellac-derived materials.

Today scale insects are better known as pests of trees and gardens. A Royal Horticultural Society poll in 2003 rated the Cushion Scale and the Soft Scale as among the top-10 garden pests, especially in glasshouses.[28] They are resistant to insecticides, and the recommended way of dealing with them is bio-control in the form of a parasitic wasp.

Perhaps the most conspicuous scale insect is the misnamed Horse Chestnut Scale (though it does occur on horse chestnuts it prefers limes and sycamore). White puffballs spun by the scale are often spotted on street trees in London; beneath them are batches of eggs laid by the females before dying. Though unsightly, the puffballs seem to do no harm to the tree, and the scale insect is a good food source for ladybirds.

Phylloxerans *Phylloxeridae*

A *Punch* cartoon of 1890 shows a plant bug known as Phylloxera in full evening dress, smoking a cigar and sampling a range of fine vintage wines. 'A true

gourmet, he finds the best vineyards and attaches itself to the best wines', runs the caption. Phylloxera (the names means 'dry leaf') is a tiny, pale yellow, sap-sucking insect related to aphids, which devastated the French vineyards in the late nineteenth century and went on to destroy more than two-thirds of the grape vines of Europe. It feeds on the roots and leaves of grape vines, causing deformities that result in secondary fungal infection, which eventually kills the plants.

French wine growers resorted to desperate measures. One was to bury a live toad beneath the vine in the hope of drawing 'poison' from the plant. When toads failed, the vineyards were replanted using stock grafted on to the roots of New World vines. Since Phylloxera is native to North America, the indigenous vines have developed resistance which can be passed on through grafting without effecting the natural vitality of European vines or the distinctive taste of Old World grapes. New vineyards have also been planted on sandy soil, which the bug cannot colonise. Certain European islands, including Britain, escaped the Phylloxera 'epidemic'. Though the bug has been found in Britain, it may be that our climate is too cold for it.

BUTTERFLIES
Lepidoptera

The original butterfly? The male Brimstone is butter-yellow though named after evil-smelling sulphur.

Their bright colours make our butterflies by far and away the most widely loved group of insects, interesting to watch, easy to identify (and so to become our familiars), challenging to paint and photograph and, in a different era, satisfying to collect. Biologically, butterflies are a relatively small branch of the Lepidoptera (scale-wings) a distinct group of insects with patterned hindwings and clubbed antennae. Culturally, we tend to see them as joyful spirits, happy, frivolous and carefree – in other words, their actions and their beauty create such feelings in ourselves. We love them, pursue them and long to know them better.

Large moths are mainly nocturnal and so less familiar. We see them only briefly, buzzing at a lamp or passing through the beam of a headlight or kitchen window. They are mysterious beings of the

dark, with a matching ghostly reputation, and when we find them by day, they seem to be asleep or in a trance. Many moths are better known by their big, horned or hairy, day-feeding caterpillars.

But what, technically, is the difference between a moth and a butterfly? Surprisingly little. The average moth is somberly coloured to blend in with its surroundings when at rest during the day. It often has a plump, hairy body over which it wraps its wings like the folds of an old coat. Butterflies all fly by day, are more or less brightly coloured and rest with their wings over their backs, pressed closely together. Butterflies have clubbed antennae, while those of moths are shaped like feathers or wire. But there are exceptions: the day-flying burnet-moths also have clubbed antennae, albeit of a heavier type. Butterflies tend to flutter, while moths, whose wings are linked up by a coupling device, tend to buzz; but certain moths, notably the geometers, also have floppy, fluttery flights (though they rarely seem to fly very far).

Butterflies and moths share a similar life history. An adult lays eggs that hatch into caterpillars. The latter feed on vegetation over several weeks and change their skin several times as they grow. When fully grown, a caterpillar sheds its skin for the last time and changes into a pupa or chrysalis – a resting stage before the emergence of the adult insect. The butterfly or moth duly emerges from the shell of the pupa, expands and dries its wings and flies off. After mating, the female then lays her eggs, and the cycle is repeated.

Male and female butterflies sometimes have strikingly different colours, with the male generally being the brighter. Only the male Orange-tip has orange tips, for example, and most of our blue butterflies have dull brown females. The reason lies in their behaviour. Male butterflies must be conspicuous to attract a mate; females need to be better camouflaged for the serious business of egg-laying. Most adult butterflies and moths live only a few weeks or, in the case of the smaller ones, perhaps less than a week. The full lifecycle will take two to three months or, for those species with just one generation per annum, a full year. The adult insects feed on nectar from flowers and other sources of liquid sugar, such as sap or honeydew. Some moths hardly seem to feed at all, living instead on the food reserves stored as fat inside their plump bodies.

Virginia Woolf loftily considered that day-flying moths are not worthy of the name of moth: 'They do not excite that pleasant sense of dark autumn nights and ivy-blossom which the commonest yellow-underwing asleep in the shadow of the curtain never fails to rouse in us. They are hybrid creatures, neither gay like butterflies nor sombre like their own species.' Others might equally consider that certain butterflies hardly live up to their image. The skippers in particular share the buzzing flight and piggy little bodies of moths, so much so that they were once known as flying 'hogs'.

There are only 70 or so British butterflies (depending on how many strays from the continent you choose to include), but the far more numerous 2000-odd species of moths vary from minute 'micros' to hand-sized silk moths and hawkmoths, and they include moths with no wings or with 'feathers' or 'plumes' instead of wings, and others that look

more like wasps or bees. Butterflies are few enough in Britain to make it easy to name them all. Indeed, our relatively tiny band of admirals, tortoiseshells, blues, browns and whites must be among the best-known and best-studied group of insects on earth.

Butterflies

VN: aurelian, butterie (Scot.), butterloggy (NE Eng.), butterlowie (Durham), flinder (Kent), flutter-by, loggerhead or loggerheed, lowy (NE Eng.), scotchie (Durham)

How does one measure pleasure? Of all insects, butterflies mean the most to us, not because they are useful like honeybees but because they brighten the day with their beautiful colours and patterned wings. They have been called 'sky-flakes' or, in the words of John Keats, 'little bright-eyed things/ that float about the air on azured wings'. Miriam Rothschild wrote how 'They flutter erratically through our lives, like stray but familiar thoughts.'[1] Yet the universal appeal of butterflies, which is shared throughout the world, is hard to define in words. Advertisers and companies seize on the butterfly (often portraying it in phantasmagoric colours) to sell their products or enhance their own image, but what quality are they trying to convey? Is it simply beauty, a sense of freedom or an inner spiritual vision brought to a bottle of shampoo or a packet of soap? Butterfly advertising is all the more persuasive because it is non-prescriptive: the meaning of the bright-winged insect is in the eye of the beholder, or customer, and all the more effective for it.

The value of butterflies has to be seen in terms of senses and feelings because, in earthly terms, they seem worthless. In former times, people spoke of something being 'not worth a butterfly'.[2] With the exception of a few garden pests (or rare and valuable specimens), they lack economic significance. They are not even important pollinators. Yet their magic finds us in the first moment when we, as children, reached out to a butterfly settled on a flower. As adults we see in them our own fantasies of childhood – innocent, wandering and joyful. In the mind's eye, butterflies both adorn and define wild nature, whether it is Marbled Whites and blues fluttering over a chalk bank or White Admirals and fritillaries swooping over a woodland glade, or tortoiseshells and Brimstones crowding on a garden buddleia.

Part of the appeal of butterflies lies in their seeming fragility. Their wings are like coloured tissuepaper and their bodies frail and spindly. They scarcely seem able to survive summer droughts, gales and thunderstorms, and it was once believed that they live for only a day or two. Yet, like all insects, butterflies are accomplished survivors. If they can avoid being eaten by birds or spiders, most British species live for at least two or three weeks. A few survive the winter frosts by hibernating, and others endure long energy-draining migrations from the Mediterranean or even North Africa – the English Channel is no barrier. One butterfly, the Monarch, has occasionally crossed the Atlantic.

The early entomologists were fascinated by the miracle of the transformation from an earthbound caterpillar to a bright-winged insect. As Eric Carle recognised in his *The Very Hungry Caterpillar* (1969), we tend to see caterpillars as ugly and greedy, stripping one leaf after another down to the midrib, leaving a scattering of droppings. Adult butterflies, on the other hand, are the closest things in nature to our idea of a spirit, bright, fleeting and evanescent. It was natural for the religiously inclined to see such transformations as a reflection of the journey of the soul after death, from a corpse to an angel.

Yet we call them butterflies. Why we do is unclear, but the word is extremely old. It first surfaces in the Old English form of *butterfleoge* in an Anglo-Saxon manuscript from the eighth century. Yet the only obvious connection between butter and butterflies is that some butterflies are yellow. Michael Chinery suggested that 'butter' is a corruption of 'beauty',[3] but the Oxford English Dictionary has no doubt that the Old English *butter* meant butter. Many books suggest, without much supporting evidence, that the all-yellow male Brimstone was the original 'butter-fly'. Another theory links butterflies to the 'butter season', that is, the growing season of grass, when butterflies (like most insects) are on the wing. Yet another, which borders on being a joke, is that butterfly is a metathesis, a rearrangement of the word 'flutterby': butterflies, after all, do flutter by. This would be plausible only if butterfly was a modern word.

Yet it is unmistakably ancient, being shared by all the German-speaking languages of northern Europe, suggesting it has a common root far back in prehistory. In Old Dutch it is *botervlieg*, in Old German, *butterfliege*. A clue to its possible original meaning lies in the alternative German word for butterfly – *schmetterling* – from a dialect word meaning cream or sour milk. Another mid-European folk-name for butterfly was *milchdieb* (milk-thief). In Teutonic myth, witches stole the milk from other people's cows; they were known as the *milch-diebin,* or milk-stealers. Were butterflies once seen not as bringers of pleasure but as malign spirits in league with witches? Do, in fact, butterflies 'steal' milk and butter? Apparently. Though there are few recorded instances of the phenomenon in Britain, women churning butter out of doors in old-fashioned wooden tubs in parts of Eastern Europe were sometimes seen 'surrounded by a cloud of butterflies of all kinds'.[4] Perhaps the insects are drawn to a chemical pheromone in buttermilk. Perhaps butterflies fluttering around dairies and butteries were once a common but now a forgotten sight in pre-industrial England.

Or is this all too far-fetched? The word scholar Wilhelm Oehl believes it is more likely that butterfly is based on some forgotten primal word like 'boto' or 'buto', and if so, since we do not know what 'boto' meant, the name is meaningless. It is just a word.[5]

The Latin word for butterflies is *papilio*, which in time became the French *papillon*. In the past, British lepidopterists often called butterflies 'papilios', perhaps because it sounded more educated. *Papilio* and pavilion share the same Latin root, meaning a tent. Butterflies have broad, coloured wings like a stretch of spotted or striped canvas. In French slang, a *papillon* is also a name for a parking ticket. They are attached to the car's windscreen using the wiper blade, which resembles the long, thin body of a butterfly as the ticket flaps in the wind. Coincidently, French parking tickets are yellow, the colour of butter …

The bow-tie shaped strips of Italian pasta are *farfalles,* or butterflies. The Spanish associate butterflies, like ladybirds, with the Virgin Mary: their word is *mariposa*, which is difficult to translate but means, roughly, 'Mary alights'. The Russian name *babochka* seems to touch on both meanings. Pronounced in one way it means bow-ties but in another it could mean little woman or, in the diminutive, *baba,* or witch. They have a second butterfly word, *dushichka*, meaning little soul.

The collective names for butterflies are a flight, a rabble, a rainbow or a kaleidoscope, perhaps depending on whether they are seen as attractive or a threat to your cabbage patch. The butterfly

The Fairy Queen's Carriage *towed by 12 fine 'thoroughbreds' (1870), by the prolific Victorian illustrator Richard Doyle, captures the ethereal, dreamy quality of butterflies.*

traditionally symbolises sportiveness or the irresponsible, carefree life (something they share in the folk consciousness with grasshoppers). A social butterfly is a light, flippant, objectless person, perpetually fluttering from one pleasure to the next. The phrase has also been used in the cab trade for taxi drivers that operate only during peak times in summer, when the living is easy.

Miriam Rothschild combed the anthologies to find the following words used to describe butterflies:

Simple	Dizzy
Gilded	Chaste
Angelic	Languid
Joyous	Silly
Careless	Peerless
Idle	Elegant
Inquisitive[6]	

There are many ways in which butterflies have been used as metaphors for human experiences. 'Butterflies in the stomach' refers to the invisible fluttering one feels in one's bowels before some important event such as an interview, getting married or going over the top to brave the enemy machine guns. A 'butterfly kiss' is a rather fey embrace in which one flutters a person's cheek with one's eyelashes. 'To float like a butterfly and sting like a bee' was Mohammed Ali's way of describing his particular boxing technique.

The phrase 'to break a butterfly on the wheel' was coined by Alexander Pope for using a disproportionate effort to accomplish a small thing.

It was famously cited by William Rees-Mogg, then editor of *The Times*, to pour scorn on the attempts by the unenlightened state to imprison Mick Jagger and Keith Richards of the Rolling Stones for possession of small amounts of soft drugs after a police raid on Richards' home in 1967.

In his brief poetic career, before he was killed on the Western Front, Edward Thomas captured the small details of nature in a way that still tugs at the heartstrings. 'The Brook' is a still, quiet poem about a nameless butterfly on a sun-baked stone which basks with open wings for a moment, 'as if I were the last of men/ And he the first of insects to have earth/ And sun together and to know their worth.'[7] When asked why he had enlisted in a front-line regiment in the army at the age of 37, Thomas picked up a handful of English earth and replied, 'literally for this'. One is reminded of this, somehow, in the last scene of the film *All Quiet on the Western Front*, when the soldier in the muddy trench reaches his hand out to a butterfly, and is shot.

The literature of butterflies is primarily scientific, though they are often drafted into stories to evoke the pleasures of summer or the pursuit of a precious rarity. Rudyard Kipling's *Just So* story, 'The Butterfly that Stamped', is a morality tale about husbands and wives and how the women manage to come out on top even when their husband is an all-powerful sultan. The butterfly seems to be the weakest of creatures, yet Kipling's talking butterfly is vain and boastful, claiming it has only to stamp its little foot and the palace and its gardens would disappear in a clap of thunder. The sultan uses the lying butterfly to play a trick on his women, but unknown to him, his cleverest wife has stage-managed the whole thing. A set of stamps issued by the Post Office in January 2002 to honour Kipling included 'The Butterfly that Stamped', featuring a Swallowtail.

British artists have long produced exquisite paintings of butterflies, mainly for entomological publications. From the very beginning, in works such as Eleazar Albin's *A Natural History of English Insects* (1720) or Benjamin Wilkes's *The English Moths and Butterflies* (1749), the illustrations were far more gorgeously rendered than strict scientific purposes would warrant. Eighteenth-century butterfly artists commonly showed butterflies floating and settling over elaborate still-life representations of flowers, natural vegetation and even entomological forceps and bottles. Wilkes even experimented with the kaleidoscope-like patterns and forms made by butterflies arranged in various ways. In the nineteenth and most of the twentieth centuries, by contrast, butterflies tended to be shown pinned and set, like specimens in a museum drawer, often exquisitely painted but essentially lifeless. Recent times have seen a welcome revival of paintings and illustrations showing them in their natural setting, with close attention to accurate ecological detail.

Perhaps Britain's largest butterfly image was the 2008 Udder Farm Maize Maze in Congleton, Cheshire, an area the size of six football pitches cut in the shape of a butterfly (modelled on the angular-winged Small Tortoiseshell). Inside it was a butterfly quiz trail and two butterfly-garden rest-stops for those trying to find their way out.

Perhaps the best-known butterfly images in contemporary art are by Damien Hirst, who used the disembodied wings of tropical butterflies to create geometric designs that resemble kaleidoscope patterns or stained glass. To Hirst, butterflies are a metaphor for mortality. He once filled a room with hundreds of live butterflies, some of them emerging from chrysalises attached to blank canvases on the walls of the gallery. In his 2007 collection 'Superstition', he expands on the theme of butterflies as iconic motifs of beauty and fragility. The sense of chill and foreboding they bring to the perceptions of the viewer are in tune, perhaps, with our new sense of butterflies as talismans for climate change and vanishing wild habitats.

The most famous musical butterfly is Cio-Cio-San in Puccini's opera *Madame Butterfly*. In the novel on which the opera was based, the heroine's name is Madam Chrysanthemum. The American short-story writer John Luther Long made the character more appealing by stressing her boundless loyalty, changing her name in the process. The tiny, youthful and doomed Madame Butterfly embodies the innocence and fragility of her namesake, and provided a suitable theme for what Puccini called 'great griefs in small souls'.

Butterflies have also been drafted into popular music, often as images of freedom. Charlie Gracie's 1957 UK hit 'Butterfly' compares an object of desire to a free-ranging butterfly whose wings he longs to clip and make his own. In the songs of the psychedelic sixties, they also helped to evoke a warm, dreamy atmosphere. The Hollies 1967 flower-pop album *Butterfly*, for example, evoked love among the butterflies amid lemonade lakes and candyfloss mountains. Two decades later, the singer-songwriter Paul Weller found that walking among butterflies helped to etch in his memory the summer holidays that 'went on forever' and to suggest a sense of being at one with nature, at once blessed and in bliss.[8]

In totally different mood, 'Butterflies and Hurricanes' by the progressive-rock band Muse is perhaps the only hit song about chaos theory. To show how humble individuals can unwittingly make a big difference, it advances the theoretical ability of a butterfly to redirect a hurricane by flapping its wings. There are apparently several versions of the song, one with thought-provoking strings and a Rachmaninov-like interlude on the piano.

The 1970s BBC sitcom *Butterflies*, by Carla Lane, used the insects as a vague metaphor for wish-fulfilment and the romantic dreams of the hen-pecked, flakey housewife Ria, played by Wendy Craig: should Ria spread her wings and fly? Her husband, played by Geoffrey Palmer, is a gruff, butterfly-collecting dentist. Disappointingly, real butterflies hardly appeared at all, apart from the pinned ones in the opening and Dolly Parton's song reminding us that 'Love is like a butterfly, that rare and gentle thing.'[9]

Collecting butterflies was one of the stock British hobbies, with its own rich fund of lore and history. Typical of them is the canon-in-residence Dr Vesey Stanhope in Trollope's *Barchester Towers*. The joke is that the canon is almost never in residence and is generally to be found, net in hand, around the shores of Lake Como (to the bishop's intimidating wife Mrs Proudie, it is bad enough for a canon to collect butterflies but even worse when they are *Italian* butterflies). There have been many anthologies of prose and poems inspired by butterflies that capture the fun of the chase and the pleasure that even the most obsessive collector took in the beauty of the live insect. Many entomologists began their careers by collecting butterflies as a child; collecting celebrities include the novelist Vladimir Nabokov, Prime Minister Neville Chamberlain, zoological plutocrat Walter Rothschild and a clown, Grimaldi. Alfred Russel Wallace, Darwin's co-discoverer of natural selection, was a professional collector (Darwin himself collected beetles), as was Henry Walter Bates, who wrote the first scientific accounts of animal mimicry. Nineteenth-century novels reflect the popularity of the hobby in their regular depiction of clergymen, doctors and sporting gents with their nets and cases of butterflies.

Collecting British butterflies has gone out of fashion, but many still enjoy the challenge of photography (which digital technology has made easier), while others rear butterflies for eventual release. The first person to rear all the British species was probably F. W. Frohawk, whose folio-sized *The Natural History of British Butterflies* (1924) illustrates every stage of the lifecycle of each species in unsurpassed detail; at four species per year, it took him half a lifetime. Perhaps the most popular butterfly hobby today is recording, whether as part of a national or county-based survey or along planned walks or transects, which enable the actual numbers of butterflies to be compared from one year to the next. Many English counties now have their own butterfly atlas with maps recording the distribution of every species and their fluctuations in numbers from one year to the next. Many conservation groups have also become experts at managing habitats to benefit rare butterflies. An increasing number of us devote weekends to clearing scrub on hillsides for the blues or coppicing woods to maintain colonies of glade-loving fritillaries.

The umbrella body for such activities is Butterfly Conservation, the largest invertebrate conservation charity in Britain, with more than 10,000 members. It organised the Millennium Atlas project, which drew attention to the parlous state of nearly half our resident butterflies and also to the remarkable changes in their distribution we are seeing as a result of climate change. The charity, which also takes our moths under its wing, campaigns for 'a world where butterflies and moths can thrive for future generations to enjoy'.[10]

Caterpillars

vn: brottlick (Orkney), canker (Norfolk), canker-worm, eruca, hoss-steng, looper, oubit, palmer-worm, pilgrim, pilgrim-worm, shitshooter, teller (Cheshire)

The destiny of a caterpillar is to nibble at a leaf until the time comes when, with a last skin change, it turns into a pupa, or chrysalis (the shell of silk that some moth caterpillars build before pupating is known as a cocoon). Caterpillars are simply the early stage of a moth or butterfly and so are analogous to fly maggots or the grubs of bees. Many are attractively coloured, to disguise themselves as they nibble, while a few are brightly coloured to warn predators that they taste nasty. Some have horns that look dangerous (a bluff), others are hairy and a few have hairs that sting. Most caterpillars feed on leaves

Red Admiral and Peacock caterpillars and chrysalids. A beautifully observed drawing from Larvae and Pupae of British Lepidoptera *(1878), by Theo Johnson.*

A 'woolly bear', the caterpillar of the Garden Tiger Moth.

or other parts of plants such as flowers, roots or seeds. A few can digest animal products such as hair, feathers or wax and are prepared to tackle even such things as bird pellets, animal hide – or other caterpillars.

Garden and crop pests aside, caterpillars have a mostly wholesome reputation, and many children enjoy rearing them in jam-jars or (for the more serious enthusiasts) muslin cages. Yet their cultural image, formed in Biblical times, is quite different. The hungry caterpillar became a metaphor for wastefulness and for wearing away of human resources and aspirations. Being worthless themselves, they devoured things of real worth, notably crops but also valuable fabrics and our very clothes. In the Bible, God regularly punishes transgressors with 'armies' of 'cankerworms' that nibble roots and so cause the crops to wither and blight, or 'palmerworms' that feed above ground, leaving behind stripped and withered fields. A third kind of caterpillar, generally simply called 'moth', eats our bedding and garments and turns our cherished possessions into dust, like an animal

form of rust. The Biblical caterpillar lives only to consume and destroy.

The word caterpillar combines an old word meaning 'ravaging' with what seems to be a word for 'cat' (from the Old French word *chatepelose*). If so, it combines two different associations, the Biblical ravager of the nations and a more amiable hairy caterpillar such as the woolly bear, the wonderfully bumbling caterpillar of the Garden Tiger Moth. Somehow, caterpillar, with its allusions of cat and pillar seems just the right word for a thin, looping, slightly lumbering creature. The alternative, larva, seems over-clinical for marvellous creatures such as the woolly bear or the caterpillar seated on a mushroom and smoking a hookah in *Alice in Wonderland*.

Yet the word larva is another word with hidden meanings and complexities. The novelist John Moore pointed out that larva originally meant the walking spirit of a dead person and carries the implication that it is the dead in pursuit of the living. Such a spirit is faceless, and so larva carries the additional sense of a disguise:

Alice meets the caterpillar, an illustration by John Tenniel for Lewis Carroll's Alice in Wonderland *(the creature's first two pairs of forelegs have become its nose and chin).*

By a most daring fancy, our old naturalists adopted it as the scientific name for a caterpillar; because such a creature wears a disguise, the future insect is not recognisable in the present grub, its form is 'a mask' which will one day be cast off. The name dates, of course, from the days before science and the humanities set themselves at odds; a good natural historian was generally a fair classical scholar, and he used the classics to make his communications concerning science more vivid, imaginative, logical and accurate. So science and poetry coexisted – the use of 'larva' for a caterpillar . . . is a truly poetic employment of words.[11]

In the past, caterpillars were often called 'palmers' or 'palmerworms'. The name is obscure today, but at one time, a palmer was a familiar wandering figure, a pilgrim on foot bearing a palm as the sign of a pilgrimage. The analogy is probably with the habit of caterpillars basking or wandering on beaten tracks, in reality either warming up in the sun or looking for somewhere safe to pupate. Izaak Walton refers to the restless movement of the 'Palmer Worm', 'not unlike the waves of the sea [which] will not content himself with any certain place of abode . . . but will boldly and disorderly wander up and down and not endure to be kept to a diet or fixt to one particular place.'[12]

In the north of England, large, hairy caterpillars were often called 'woubits' or 'oobits' (also spelt as oubuts, wobats or oobity-worms). The name, which means 'a bit of wool', has since attached itself to humans, too: a woubit is a derogatory name for a small, shabby and, presumably, hairy person. In Charles Kingsley's cod-Scots poem, it seems that oubits were of interest as potential fishing bait:

> This feckless hairy oubit cam' hirpli' by the linn,
> A swirl o' win' cam' down the glen an' blew that oubit in:
> O when he took the water, the saumon fly they rose
> An' tigged him a' to pieces sma', by head an' tail an' toes.[13]

Another name for a hairy caterpillar, which dates back to the Middle Ages (it is mentioned by Chaucer), is 'walbode', the Middle English version of 'woolly bear'. The word might have been used for any suitably hairy caterpillar, but it was attached most of all to the larva of the Garden Tiger Moth, which is still known in Scotland as 'hairy worm' or 'hairy grannie' (and, in bygone Cheshire, as 'the devil's coach-horse'). Anglers know it as 'the woolly bugger'. Hawkmoth caterpillars, which have a spike on their tail, were, like dragonflies, known as 'horse stingers' or 'hoss-stengs'. They do not, of course, sting, but their tail-spikes certainly make them look as though they could.

On the Isle of Wight, they invented an imaginary and very large caterpillar known as the Gooseberry Wife as a bogey to deter children from picking the gooseberries: 'If ye goos out in the garden, the Gooseberry Wife'll be sure to ketch ye.' Red, injurious caterpillars that swarmed on the island's cabbages were called 'mallishags'. Those that made nests of webbing in the bushes were known in Sussex as 'puckets'.

The more scholarly used the Latin word for a caterpillar, *eruca* (the word survives as 'eruciform', meaning caterpillar-shaped). For example, the

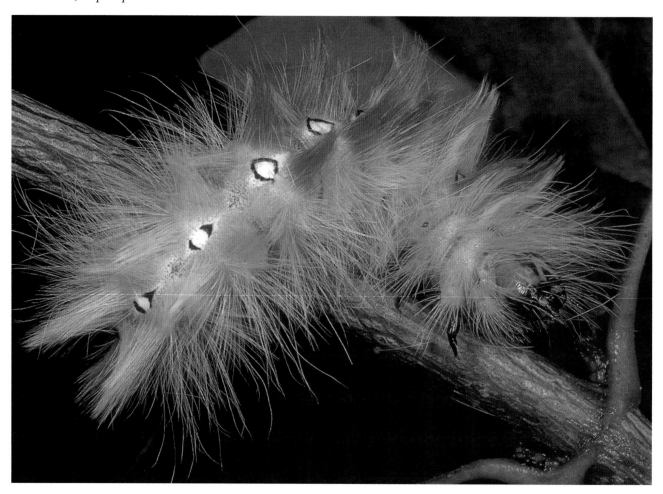

The flamboyant caterpillar of the Sycamore Moth mimicking a feather (the adult moth, by contrast, is dull grey).

seventeenth-century English naturalist John Ray called the zigzag larva of the pebble moth the Terrible Eruca. The less scholarly called them reptiles, presumably because caterpillars looked like small serpents.

Children have their own names. Ian Wallace remembers calling caterpillars 'shitshooters'.[14] Andrew Bissitt, who grew up in Salford in the 1960s, had nicknames for a whole range of species he found in the local park: 'That of the Grey Dagger moth we called a "streamliner", while the Poplar Grey caterpillar we called "Hairy Mary". The "German Racer" was another hairy one, while "Yellowbelly", which was bright yellow with black spots, might have been a sawfly larva. We would go to any lengths to obtain them, climbing the tree, or lobbing a sod of earth at branches out of reach. They were lovingly cared for in a pickle jar until we went on holiday in August, when the survivors were released.'[15]

The Very Hungry Caterpillar by Eric Carle is a colourful classic story for young children, first published in 1969 (the original idea had been to call it *A Week with Willi Worm*, but Carle was persuaded that caterpillars are more likeable than worms). The genius of the story lies in the way the ravenous little beast, eating its way through different vegetables and fruits, gnaws holes in the book. In the process, toddlers painlessly learn how to count up to five and the seven days of the week. Rather hopefully, the publishers add that the story will also tell them a little about nutrition. Ex-President Bush listed this among his favourite boyhood books, which caused surprise at the time, since he was 23 when *The Very Hungry Caterpillar* was first published.[16]

The slightly surreal nature of caterpillars continues in pop lyrics. In 'Caterpillar Girl', a hit song by alternative band The Cure, the lyrics are sunk in a dreamy, psychedelic haze. Caterpillar girls are sweet, languorous and colourful, but eventually they fly away, having turned into butterflies. To Ray Campi, caterpillars were more lively, dancing creatures, 'fat like a cat, skinny like a pillar', rocking and rolling on a 40-inch log.[17]

Very young children learn about caterpillars and the way they walk from the rhyme 'Arabella Miller', sung to the tune of 'Twinkle-Twinkle Little Star' and accompanied by some creepy finger-walking up the arm:

> Little Arabella Miller
> Found a hairy caterpillar.
> First it crawled upon her mother,
> Then upon her baby brother.
> All said: Arabella Miller,
> Take away that caterpillar.[18]

The name Arabella Miller was borrowed by a company that produces organic cotton T-shirts for babies and toddlers bearing 'mini-beast' designs. Its logo is a bobbly caterpillar sporting a non-entomological pair of antennae.

Caterpillars and entomology have only the most tangential association with the Caterpillar Club, formed by a parachute company during the Second World War. Its members are all survivors from enemy action who escaped from their burning planes by parachute. At that time, parachutes were made of silk by the Irvin Air Chute Company. Silk is, of course, a natural product made from the spinnings of a caterpillar, the silkworm, and just as an airman bails out from his burning plane and floats earthwards on his parachute, so the adult moths clamber out of their silken cocoons before flying away. By 1945, some 34,000 airmen had been admitted into the club, though time has diminished its membership. Caterpillar Club members proudly wear a pin in the form of a wriggly golden caterpillar with ruby-red eyes.

Pupa: the sleeping stage

The destiny of every surviving caterpillar is to turn into a pupa or chrysalis, the immobile stage of apparent near-death before the emergence of the adult insect. This interlude between grub and winged insect has long entranced naturalists, who saw in it an echo of the mystical transcendence from death to life. To Vladimir Nabokov, it provided the 'immemorial link' between the gravity-bound pupa in its earthen tomb to the airborne moth that emerges from the ground, climbs up into the air and flies off into the night.[19]

The same word that has given us puppy, for a baby dog, and poppet, an outmoded term of endearment, has provided us with pupa, the resting stage of an insect. It comes from the Latin for a young girl or, by association, a doll. John Moore saw this word-play as another stroke of linguistic genius: 'as you will realise if you look at the underside of a moth's pupa and see the shape of its face, eyes and embryonic wings like little arms sedately crossed in front of its body, wrapped as if in swaddling-clothes which emphasise its likeness to a doll.'[20] Another analogy would be with an Egyptian mummy. Meanwhile, the silken shroud that many caterpillars spin around their pupal chamber is known as a cocoon, from an old word meaning shell.

By tradition, the pupae of butterflies alone are known as chrysalises or chrysalids. Chrysalis comes from a Greek word meaning golden and refers to the metallic flashes on the pupal skins of some butterflies (they probably assist with camouflaging). In the eighteenth century, a group of entomologists meeting in London called themselves the Aurelians, from the Latin equivalent. By coincidence or not, they included a disproportionate number of silversmiths and goldsmiths; the greatest of the early collectors, Dru Drury, was a goldsmith. In Scots dialect, butterfly chrysalises were known as 'Tammie-nid-nods'.

Pupa: the resting stage of the Privet Hawkmoth. The projection on the right houses the developing moth's enormous tongue.

Butterfly species

The Adoration of the Magi, *attended by symbolic butterflies* (bottom left), *by Albrecht Dürer (1504).*

Skippers *Hesperiidae*

Chequered Skipper, *Carterocephalus palaemon*

AN: Scarce Skipper (1819), Spotted Skipper (1853)

Modern butterfly books begin with the skippers as the most 'primitive' British butterflies (in older books, they were placed at the end for the same reason). With their short wings and tubby little bodies, they seem half butterfly, half moth. The Chequered Skipper is the prettiest and also the rarest of the skippers. It was discovered on 8 May 1798 near Bedford by Charles Abbot, one of the first in a long line of butterfly-collecting prelates. The new butterfly was 'copiose', he wrote in wonder, and if you missed it with the first swipe, it would oblige you by quickly settling again, being 'far from timid'.[21]

Abbot proposed to call it the Duke of York Fritillary, but he was ignored. The butterfly was later found in many woods between Bedford and Lincoln, with a few outlying colonies elsewhere, but it was always regarded as rare. Its presence was one of the reasons why Charles Rothschild chose to buy a country estate at Ashton Wold, near Oundle in Northamptonshire. He built a pub for his estate workers originally called The Three Horseshoes but later renamed The Chequered Skipper. A handsome sign was made with a lifelike image of the butterfly picked out in hobnails. After a fire in 1996, the pub was rebuilt and restored. A replacement iron butterfly now welcomes the World Conker Championship which meets every year on the green outside.

Long thought to be an exclusively English butterfly, the Chequered Skipper baffled butterfly-watchers by turning up in, of all places, western Inverness-shire in 1942. Lt Colonel Cyril Mackworth-Praed, stationed with his regiment at Inverlochy Castle, reported how 'I could not believe my eyes when the first one settled in front of me.'[22] Surprisingly, the discovery did not spark a hunt for more Scottish Chequered Skippers, and it was not until the 1970s that a methodical search was conducted by the Scottish Wildlife Trust. It revealed, again to complete surprise, that the butterfly was widespread over a limited part of the western Highlands; it even flew on road verges. Recommended places to see it between mid-May and the end of June are Butterfly Conservation's nature reserve at Allt Mhuic, by Loch Arkaig, and the National Nature Reserve of Glasdrum Wood, by Loch Creran.

In England, the Chequered Skipper has fared less well. A long, slow and, it seems, hardly noticed decline set in during the twentieth century, probably linked to changes in the way woods were managed. The densely stocked timber forests and pheasant coverts of post-war England were much less butterfly-friendly than the former, more open, coppice woods with their glades and broad rides full of flowers. Despite the protection of some of its best colonies as nature reserves, the Chequered Skipper was extinct in England by the mid-seventies. A plan to reintroduce it in the nineties came to nothing. It seems there is too little suitable habitat left for reintroductions to have any reasonable chance of success. At least we now know why it died out.

The Chequered Skipper has a walk-on part in Arthur Conan Doyle's best-known Sherlock Holmes story, *The Hound of the Baskervilles*. The

The last Chequered Skipper in England, picked out in iron nails on a pub sign at Ashton, Northamptonshire, close to the woods where it once flew.

villain, Stapleton, alias Baskerville, is a keen butterfly collector with 'the most complete collection in the South-west of England'. He was having a word with Dr Watson about the treacherous terrain of Dartmoor when 'a small fly or moth fluttered across our path'. '"Oh, excuse me an instant",' cries the polite villain, '"it is surely *Cyclopides*. He is very rare, and seldom found in the late autumn" . . . In an instant Stapleton was rushing with extraordinary energy and speed in pursuit . . . bounding from tuft to tuft behind it, his green net waving in the air.'[23] *Cyclopides* is the old generic name of the Chequered Skipper, though autumn is not its season nor Dartmoor its habitat.

A Chequered Skipper flying towards its favourite bugle flower appeared on the high-value (25p) stamp, one of a set of four butterfly stamps issued by the Post Office on 13 May 1981. They were designed by Gordon Beningfield (1936–98), an artist who discarded the then convention by showing butterflies not as museum specimens but as living insects going about their business. He painted as we see them, from a distance, often as tiny bobs of colour amongst tangled vegetation. His butterfly paintings, published as *Beningfield's Butterflies* in 1978, were revolutionary in their day; his technique of sketching and painting butterflies and moths from life has been continued with the same fidelity and panache by Richard Tratt.

Large Chequered Skipper, *Heteropterus morpheus*

AN: *le Miroir*

The Large Chequered Skipper is only borderline British. It is, or was, confined to the island of Jersey, where it is known by its French name, *le Miroir*, a reference to the pale circular markings on its hindwing, like tiny hand-mirrors or beads of water on a glass. It is believed to have been introduced to the island in hay imported from France during the wartime German occupation. But 'the Mirror' struggled to survive, and none has been seen since 1996.

Small Skipper, *Thymelicus sylvestris*

AN: Streaked Golden Hog (male), Spotless Golden Hog (female) (1704)

Welsh: *Y Gwibiwr Bach*

The Small Skipper is a little fox-brown butterfly of long grass and field corners. It is named, like all skippers, from its skittish flight. Moses Harris described how the butterflies fly 'with a kind of skipping motion, which is affected by reason of their closing their wings so often in their passage'. Similarly, the Small Skipper's scientific name *Thymelicus* also refers to skipping. In ancient Greek drama, the original Thymelicus was a dancer, who would trip about the stage, pausing now and again to make stiff gestures with his arms. The butterflies were once also called 'hogs' from their dumpy, pig-like bodies (evidently the word was pronounced 'og'). The Small Skipper was the 'Golden, or Spotless, Hog'. By comparison, Small Skipper is a poor name; it is in fact one of the bigger skippers, only two out of our eight British skippers being consistently larger.

The Golden Hog is expanding northwards. In 2007 it crossed the Scottish border for the first time.

Essex Skipper, *Thymelicus lineola*

AN: Scarce Small Skipper (1896), Lineola Skipper (1897), New Small Skipper (1959)

The Essex Skipper looks almost exactly like the Small Skipper. It takes a close view of their antennae to separate them: the Essex has black tips, and the Small pale brown ones. Their similarity explains why the Essex Skipper was the last resident British butterfly to be discovered (in 1890), despite being quite common. It was first found in Essex, and though it is now known to be much more widespread, the name seems indestructible, having early shaken off such feeble alternatives as Lineola Skipper or Scarce Small Skipper. This skipper has proven an equally adept coloniser in North America, where they call it the European or New English Skipper.

There is an Essex Skipper Inn in Harlow New Town, Essex. Unfortunately, its sign shows not a butterfly but a seasoned East Anglian mariner.

Lulworth Skipper, *Thymelicus acteon*

The dark brown Lulworth Skipper has kept the same name since its discovery, near Lulworth in Dorset, in 1832 (the actual place was Durdle Door, a few miles to the west, but perhaps it was felt that 'Durdle Skipper' lacked dignity). Its discoverer, J. C. Dale, collected butterflies from horseback, and one can imagine him wielding his baggy net like a polo mallet. He routinely rode for 40 miles to the coast and back home again to Glanvilles Wootton with a box full of bugs in his saddle-bag.

Collecting the Lulworth Skipper became something of a ritual. Throughout the Victorian age, men in their Sunday best headed towards a spot known as the Burning Cliff, where the butterflies flew in abundance among the long grass. Many stayed at the Square and Compasses Inn at Worth Matravers, which now houses a small museum. The butterfly is probably commoner today than in the nineteenth century. Its food-plant – the coarse, tussocky tor-grass, so tough that nothing but a starving sheep will touch it, has spread along the south coast, and the butterfly has followed it.

Silver-spotted Skipper, *Hesperia comma*

AN: Pearl Skipper (1766), August Skipper (1795)

The Silver-spotted Skipper is a tough little butterfly that flies fast and close to the ground with a bee-like blur of its fawn wings. They say it is a waste of time looking for it unless numerous chalk pebbles peep through the grass. Even then it is quite hard to spot unless you happen to see one basking with open

Grizzled skippers and a Small Blue congregating on a patch of moisture on a hot day.

wings on a patch of bare, sun-baked soil or feeding from a thistle head.

Not long ago, the Silver-spotted Skipper was billed as the British butterfly least likely to succeed. A nationwide survey in 1982 revealed that its numbers had fallen precariously low. Only 49 scattered colonies remained, and half of those were unlikely to survive long. Yet, against the odds, its fortunes have turned around; a repeat survey in 2000 found 257 colonies, a threefold increase, and the warm summer of 2003 proved its best year for a long time. Conservation bodies can take part of the credit, but the skipper has undoubtedly benefited from the long hot summers of the 1990s and early 2000s.

Large Skipper, *Ochlodes venata*

AN: Chequer-like Hog (male), Chequered Hog (female) (1704), Cloudy Hog (1717), Wood Skipper (1819)

Welsh: *Y Gwibiwr Mawr*

The Large Skipper is an attractive butterfly of woodland borders and bramble thickets, whose wings seem deceptively orange in the sunshine.

It patrols a regular 'beat', darting aggressively at what it perceives as rivals and chasing them off with what one author characterises as 'unnecessary force'.[24] With such behaviour in mind, its scientific name *Ochlodes* can be translated as 'turbulent' or 'unruly'.

Dingy Skipper, *Erynnis tages*

AN: Handley's Brown Hog Butterfly (1706), Handley's Small Brown Butterfly (1717)

Welsh: *Y Gwibiwr Llywyd*
Irish: *Donnan*

The Dingy Skipper is our most moth-like butterfly. It folds its short, flecked-grey wings over its stumpy body like a moth, and if one did not know otherwise, it would be easy to mistake it for one (it flits from flower to flower on downs and banks, often in the company of a similarly-sized moth, the Burnet Companion). Its unflattering name is at least an advance on an earlier effort, 'Handley's Small Brown Butterfly' (named after a totally forgotten Mr Handley). Like the Large Skipper, the Dingy has an unexpectedly bloodcurdling scientific name: *Erynnis*, named after the Erynnes, or Furies, of ancient Greek myth, which harried wrongdoers and hounded them from place to place. The name invokes the butterfly's restless flight, rarely settling for long and always on the move 'as if perpetually chased by the avenging goddesses'.[25]

Grizzled Skipper, *Pyrgus malvae*

AN: Our Marsh Fritillary (1699), Brown Marsh Fritillary (1717), Grizzled Butterfly (1749), the Grizzle (or Grizzel) (1769), Spotted Skipper (1795), the Mallow (1813), Mallow Skipper (1819)

Welsh: *Y Gwibiwr Brith*

For many years this, the smallest British butterfly, was known as the Grizzle (or the Gristle), not because it looked miserable but because its flecked grey and white wing pattern suggested the greying hairs of a senior citizen. In France, a similar name, *grisette*, is used for the Dingy Skipper. For a while, a genetic variety called 'ab. *taras*' was thought to be a separate species, named the Scarce Grizzle. Another early name was Marsh Fritillary, but that was later and more suitably bestowed on one of our fritillary butterflies. England is one of the few places where the Grizzled Skipper can be recognised easily; in most other European countries there are numerous look-alikes that differ only in tiny details.

In flight, the Grizzled Skipper buzzes like a small grey moth, and, like the Dingy Skipper, is easily mistaken for one. It has a liking for quarries and abandoned industrial sites with plenty of flowers during its brief flight-time in late spring. The rate at which such brownfield sites have been filled in, built over or 'redeveloped' with lawn grass and street lights has propelled both the Grizzled Skipper and the similarly inclined Dingy Skipper on to the growing list of butterflies to be concerned about.

The Swallowtail butterfly in its Broadland setting.

Swallowtails *Papilionidae*

Swallowtail, *Papilio machaon*

vn: Royal William (1704), Queen Butterfly

Swallowtails are among the world's most elegant butterflies – combining large size, contrasting, often yellow and black, colours and prominent hindwing 'tails'. There are many kinds of swallowtails, but in Britain, our lone species is *the* Swallowtail. Though it is a common butterfly over much of Europe, here it is confined to the Broads in East Anglia, where its powerful, gliding flight over reedbeds and ditches is one of the iconic images of the Broads, along with windmills, wherries and bitterns.

Given its rarity in Britain, it seems surprising that the Swallowtail has always been one of our best-known butterflies. A passably accurate woodcut of it and its distinctively banded caterpillar was reproduced for Thomas Muffet's *Theatre of Insects* in the 1590s. Yet, though rather taken with its 'flame-coloured eyes',[26] Muffet had no name for it; nor did John Ray, writing a century later. In the early eighteenth century, what must have seemed like an appropriately grand name was found for it: the Royal William, in honour of the late king William III (better known as William of Orange). It was doubly suitable as the butterfly had lately appeared in the royal gardens at St James, then the London residence of the king. Once 'King Billy' had become a fading memory, it was widely assumed that Royal William must be the William, Duke of Cumberland, the Butcher of Culloden and Handel's Conquering Hero.

By the 1760s, the name Swallowtail had superseded earlier names. Possibly it was borrowed from the French, who call it the *Grand Porte-Queue*. The British Swallowtail is regarded as a distinctive subspecies, or race, *britannicus*, which is paler and more heavily marked than its congener on the continent and is confined to marshland. Its gaily striped caterpillars feed on milk parsley, which grows only in reedy dykes and wet meadows. Despite the loss of much of its former habitat to farmland or scrub, the Swallowtail is still quite common in the Broads, though heavily reliant on conservation work. But it mysteriously died out at its other stronghold at Wicken Fen, and attempts to reintroduce it there in the 1990s were fruitless.

The Fall of the Rebel Angels *(1562), by Pieter Bruegel the Elder. The lead devil (in the middle) has turned into a swallowtail, his minions into moths.*

Jack Dempster, of the then Institute of Terrestrial Ecology, found out why. The milk parsley plants are smaller there and do not project much above the surrounding marsh. In consequence, too many of the young caterpillars were killed by spiders.

When Vladimir Nabokov, the great Russian-American novelist, first spotted a swallowtail, his eyes nearly popped out of his head:

> . . . a splendid, pale yellow creature with black blotches, blue crenels, and a cinnabar eyespot above each chrome-rimmed black tail. As it probed the inclined flower from which it hung, its powdery body slightly bent, it kept restlessly jerking its great wings, and my desire for it was one of the most intense I have ever experienced.[27]

A fellow novelist, Frederic Prokosch, remembered Nabokov imagining out loud what it must be like to be a butterfly:

> . . . to feel the air skimming under my outstretched wings, to feel the leaves caressing my scales, to hear the petals under my proboscis, to feel the autumn in the depth of my thorax and the scent and far off storm in the beads of my antennae. And also to feel the delight of the larvae as it gnaws at the nettles and the delicious growth of wings in the depth of a cocoon. That's what it means to be a butterfly: an entire labyrinth of ecstasies.[28]

Any lepidopterist could tell him that a butterfly makes a chrysalis and a moth a cocoon. Still, the words ring true, and Nabokov was a very imaginative man.

Swallowtails also appear in western art, usually as no more than a decoration but occasionally with deeper significance. One such image is in Pieter Bruegel's picture *The Fall of the Rebel Angels*, painted in 1562. The butterfly is accurately painted,

*The Swallowtail sign of the entomological suppliers
Watkins and Doncaster, which hung above a
barber's shop in the Strand during the early 1950s.*

but its wings are attached to a demonic little creature
about to be struck down by the avenging sword of
St Michael. More butterfly or moth wings are visible
among the crowd of warring angels, and they all
belong to the rebels. Bruegel's demonic butterfly
wings are probably a reference to the *Book of
Revelation*, which relates how, as the rebel angels
were evicted from heaven, they lost their glorious
swan's wings and took on a form emblematic of their
wickedness. Most artists gave them parody wings
belonging to bats or insects. By providing what
appears to be Satan himself with the beautiful shining
wings of a Swallowtail, Bruegel may be reminding us
of the beauty Satan once had. They will doubtless
fall off as he plunges to Hell and be replaced by the
hideous black wings of a vampire bat.

The logo of Watkins and Doncaster, the suppliers
of entomological and scientific equipment, is a
Swallowtail. In the 1950s, their sign, hanging above
a barber's shop in the Strand, was one of London's
minor landmarks.

Scarce Swallowtail, *Iphiclides podalarius*

The Scarce Swallowtail is a splendid butterfly but
only doubtfully British. There seems to have been
an unspoken desire to claim it for our own, for it

was often included in books or series of cigarette
cards as though it was a British insect, but the
evidence for its existence is very thin. The story goes
that, one summer in 1822, the Reverend Frederick
William Hope, founder of the Hope Entomology
Department at Oxford, spotted one in his garden
at Netley Hall in Shropshire. He rubbed his eyes,
dashed inside for his net and managed to catch it.
Later, he spent half the day chasing another one.
The finding of its caterpillar two years later seemed
to prove that Netley had a small breeding colony.
But yet another Scarce Swallowtail spotted in 1828
feeding on a ripe peach, proved to be the last. Later
it turned out that a neighbour, a Mrs Plimley of
Longnor, liked to paint butterflies and had probably
reared then from continental pupae and released
them in her garden.

In the Liverpool Museum collection is a battered
specimen of the Scarce Swallowtail with several
holes punched through its wings and the following
label: 'Jeancourt, June 1917, blown up by a German
3-inch shell and picked up half-dead.'[29]

Apollo, *Parnassius apollo*

AN: Mr Ray's Alpine Butterfly (1704), Crimson-
ringed Butterfly (1832)

The Apollo resembles the costume of a snow-queen
in a pantomime, its wings translucent as muslin,
dabbed with white and black, and with great cherry-
red circles (which give it a definite resemblance to
nougat). It was named after the sun god Phoebus-
Apollo, for the butterfly flies only in sunshine, high
among the mountain peaks – the traditional home
of the gods. These attributes are underscored by
the butterfly's generic name *Parnassius*, after the
sacred mountain Parnassus near Delphi in Greece,
associated with Apollo.

It is not a British butterfly, though like the
Scarce Swallowtail, it has often accompanied our
native butterflies in books. All the early authors,
from Thomas Muffet onwards, include it, though
without supporting evidence. James Petiver called
it Mr Ray's Alpine Butterfly, though the specimen
Ray supplied to him had come from Switzerland.
Occasional records, like the Scarce Swallowtail
caught in a sunbather's hat at Dover in 1955 or the
one spotted from a sailing boat off the Isle of Wight
in 1865, may be wind-blown strays from Norway
or France.

Whites *Pieridae*

Wood White, *Leptidea sinapis*

AN: Small White Butterfly (1699), Small White (1710), White Small-tipped Butterfly (1717), Wood Lady (1799)

Irish: *Banog choille*

The small, chocolate-tipped Wood White has a remarkably feeble, floppy flight: it is the one British butterfly you can reach out and touch as it flaps past. It is believed to be a primitive butterfly – that is, one that evolved longest ago and has changed least. Its long, narrow wings and slender body give it a faintly otherworldly air.

The Wood White has always been regarded as rather rare. In *Brendon Chase*, a story about some runaway boys going feral in the woods in the 1920s, a butterfly-collecting vicar, the Reverend Whiting, spots one and heads off in pursuit, allowing the boys to make a discreet exit.[30] Today, the Wood White's biggest colonies are in the rides of large woods maintained by the Forestry Commission or along the coastal undercliff in Devon and Dorset. Older books often repeat the canard that its caterpillar feeds only on 'tuberous pea' (if so, a suicidal strategy, for the true tuberous pea is even rarer than the Wood White in Britain). In fact, the butterfly feeds on a wide range of common vetches and trefoils.

Réal's Wood White, *Leptidea reali*

AN: Long-willied Wood White

A chance discovery made in Ireland in 2001 solved a minor butterfly mystery: why Irish Wood Whites fly in the open countryside but English ones stick to woods and shade. They are, in fact, different species. The Irish one was officially named Réal's Wood White after its French discoverer but has also been unofficially dubbed the 'Long-willied Wood White', in recognition of the new species' more generous proportions.[31] It is widespread in Ireland but seemingly absent from Britain. The 'long willie' can supposedly be inspected by a little gentle squeezing without harming the butterfly, but it sounds rather unkind.

Clouded Yellow, *Colias croceus*

AN: The Saffron Butterfly (male), Spotted Saffron (female) (1703), Clouded Saffron, Clouded Orange (1795), Redhorn (c19)

Welsh: *Iar Fach Felen*
Irish: *Buiog chroch*

In flight, a fresh Clouded Yellow looks like a golden guinea glinting in the sun. It flies fast and straight, and many a collector of the past has recalled with an obvious visceral rush those mad steeplechases across a down or sea cliff with a butterfly net trailing in the wind. Perhaps this was the 'gilded butterfly' that would have brought some consolation to the old *King Lear* as he imagined life in prison with his Cordelia:

> . . . so we'll live,
> And pray, and sing, and tell old tales, and laugh
> At gilded butterflies[32]

Shakespeare mentions them again in *Coriolanus*, in the scene in which we hear about the hero's horrible little boy:

> I saw him run after a gilded butterfly, and when
> he caught it, he let it go again, and after it again,
> and over and over he comes and up again,
> catched it again; or whether his fall enraged him,
> or how 'twas, he did so set his teeth and tear it.
> O, I warrant, how he mammocked it![33]

Praising a boy for ripping the wings off a butterfly offers us a glimpse into the sort of upbringing Coriolanus himself might have had. Stern military men of his sort have no time for natural beauty; it simply enrages them.

The Clouded Yellow appears accurately figured in various religious images of the fifteenth and sixteenth centuries, most suggestively in Albrecht Dürer's *Adoration of the Magi*, painted in 1504. Two butterflies are quietly sucking nectar from the blossoms of a small weed, oblivious to the drama of the nativity. One is a Painted Lady, the other a Clouded Yellow (and, as it happens, a male). They are too prominent to be mere decoration, and Dürer was no doubt aware that in the ancient world the word for soul and butterfly was one and the same: *psyche*. For those who could read the picture, the butterflies symbolised the brevity of earthly life and the immortality of the soul: one butterfly to represent the Virgin Mary, the other perhaps the male 'gilded butterfly', the Christ-child.[34]

213

Still earlier, Clouded Yellows appear on medieval illuminated manuscripts, such as a *Book of Hours*, belonging to Anne of Brittany, a duchess of English descent, dating around 1500. On one panel, the decorated border contains not only the butterfly but also a recognisable portrait of its full-grown caterpillar. Earlier still is the manuscript of medieval legends known collectively as the *Romance of Alexander*, kept in the Bodleian Library in Oxford and dating from around 1340. It is full of little marginal scenes of everyday life – jousting, hunting, cockfighting, playing the pipes – and among them are pictures of men and women catching butterflies, apparently by swiping at them with the sleeves of their jackets. Some of these butterflies are clearly Clouded Yellows.

The first name of the Clouded Yellow was the Saffron Butterfly. It took an artist, Moses Harris (1731–85), to invent the lovely name by which we know it today. The Clouded Yellow is a migrant from North Africa and southern Europe that arrives in varying numbers each year, most commonly in late summer. Occasionally and unpredictably, it appears in vast numbers, and such episodes were known by collectors as 'edusa years', after the butterfly's former scientific name, *Colias edusa*. One such year was 1868, when an 11-year-old boy sat on the cliffs near Marazion in Cornwall and saw, in the distance, 'a yellow patch out at sea, which as it came nearer showed itself to be composed of thousands of Clouded Yellows, which approached flying close over the water, and rising and falling over every wave till they reached the cliffs, when I was surrounded by clouds of *C. edusa* which settled on every flower.'[35]

The warm summers of the 1940s saw a record number of edusa years – no fewer than six between 1941 and 1950. A former soldier, reminiscing on the local television news in 2007, recalled seeing what he thought was a cloud of yellow chlorine gas approaching the Sussex coast at about the time of the Battle of Britain and duly reported it to the coastguards. The greatest number of Clouded Yellows ever seen was from the decks of a steamer off Start Point in Devon in October 1947, when a vast cloud of yellow wings was seen moving steadily south-south-west across the sea like a weather front. Whether they ever made landfall or were blown off course and perished out at sea no one

knows. After 1947 there were no more edusa years until 1983. Two more modest invasions followed in 1996 and 2000. On warm pockets along the south coast such as Bournemouth, the caterpillars are now overwintering successfully and so producing butterflies much earlier in the year than they are normally seen.

The Clouded Yellow was the name of a 1951 film starring Trevor Howard as an ex-secret-service agent, who lands what he hopes will be a quieter job cataloguing a collection of butterflies. Described as 'a taut and convincing thriller', the plot unfolds with some murderous goings-on at a stately home, culminating in a lengthy, suspenseful chase across England. Jean Simmons plays the trapped butterfly.

Pale Clouded Yellow, *Colias hyale*

AN: Clouded Sulphur

Welsh: *Y Felen Welw*
Irish: *Buiog liath*

One of the classic horror stories of collecting is about the man who caught 800 Pale Clouded Yellows. That really is a lot of Pale Clouded Yellows. To put this dubious feat into context, it exceeds by a large margin the entire number of Pale Clouded Yellow reported since 1950. The story emerged in

The jacket design by Tom Adams of John Fowles' novel The Collector, *linking a pinned specimen of a Pale Clouded Yellow with a lock of a girl's hair – both the butterfly and the girl have been captured and locked away.*

Left: *The Clouded Yellow – the 'gilded butterfly'.*

an exchange of letters in *The Entomologist* in 1875, when a correspondent claimed that someone had 'boasted roundly of the exploit' and another admitted that it was him.[36] His name was H. Ramsay Cox. He had, he explained, been staying on the Isle of Wight with two fellow collectors, and it took them three weeks to catch that many. If so, and assuming that it took a minimum of ten minutes to pin, set and label each butterfly, and that they worked an eight-hour day, the preparation time involved would have been 14 weeks. Most of the 800 would be given away or swapped. H. Ramsay Cox recommended the exercise as 'thorough and innocent enjoyment' and as 'science in its original and pure manner'.

The Pale Clouded Yellow has ceased to be a regular migrant to Britain and is now usually relegated to the back of guidebooks. It is possibly being passed over for pale-coloured forms of the Clouded Yellow. In northern Europe, Pale Clouded Yellows used to settle and lay in fields of clover and lucerne cut for fodder; most such fields now grow oil-seed rape or autumn-sown barley and wheat.

Berger's Clouded Yellow, *Colias alfacariensis*

AN: New Clouded Yellow, Scarce Clouded Yellow

This was the last butterfly to be added to the canonical list of 69 British butterflies. Being almost indistinguishable from the Pale Clouded Yellow, it was unknown to science until 1945, when a Belgian lepidopterist, Lucien Berger, realised that this butterfly was not a single species but two very similar ones. The key difference lay in their respective caterpillars; the 'New Clouded Yellow' is more spotted and striped and has a different food-plant, horseshoe vetch. Berger's discovery paper was published in 1947, and immediately British lepidopterists started looking more closely at their rows of Pale Clouded Yellows. Many turned out to be the new species. By fortunate chance, 1947 was a vintage year: one man hunting the cliffs near Folkestone caught five New Clouded Yellows in one day. Since then, sightings have been few, though a small breeding colony was discovered at Portland in 1991 and a female was seen laying eggs elsewhere in Dorset in 1996. The official name was changed from New Clouded Yellow to Berger's Clouded Yellow in 1982.

Brimstone, *Gonepteryx rhamni*

AN: Pale Brimstone (female) (1695), Straw Butterfly (1717), Sulphur Butterfly

Welsh: *Melyn y Rhafnwydd*
Irish: *Buiog ruibheach*

The bright yellow male Brimstone cheers us up early in the year, long before the first swallow, as a harbinger of spring. It is the insect equivalent of celandine, an icon of the season's turning. The Brimstone is one of our most individual butterflies, its angular, strongly veined wings mimicking leaves when the insect is at rest, with its wings tightly closed over its back (this is one of the few butterflies that never basks with its wings open). Strange to say, it is not universally popular. Some say that a Brimstone in the garden is a sign of bad weather to come.

A hoax butterfly made by carefully painting patches on to a set specimen of a Brimstone. Preserved in the Linnaean Society collections, it fooled people long enough to be given the scientific name Papilio ecclipsis.

'Brimstone' is one of the oldest butterfly names. It appears on the first page of the first volume of Petiver's catalogue of butterflies and moths (1695), as though it were already an established name. Brimstone is another word for sulphur. The volcanic products that rained down on Sodom and Gomorrah in Genesis were 'fire and brimstone', while 'brimstone and treacle' was the disgusting substance ladled down the gullets of the unfortunate boys in *Nicholas Nickleby*. Sulphur is a good match for the bright yellow of the male butterfly (the paler female was Petiver's 'straw butterfly'). In France

Translucent Black-veined White butterflies, like animated seed-cases.

and Germany, the match is lemons (*le Citron, Zitronenfalter*). Some claim that the Brimstone, being the colour of butter, is the original 'butter-fly'. There is also a Brimstone moth, which is similarly bright yellow but much smaller.

The Brimstone has a range that coincides almost exactly with its food-plants, buckthorn and alder buckthorn. Its recent increase in range to North Wales and Cheshire is attributed to the planting of buckthorns in amenity schemes.

Black-veined White, *Aporia crataegi*

AN: White Butterfly with Black Veins (1717), Blackvein White (late c18), Hawthorn White

Is there anyone still alive who has seen a native, British-born Black-veined White? The last of them disappeared around 1925. There have been a very few recorded since that date, but these are probably strays from continental Europe or illicit attempts to reintroduce it (until the 1940s, this always local

and now extinct butterfly was categorised officially as a pest). The wings of the Black-veined White are wonderfully minimalist: pure white with translucent panels and the veins picked out in black. It has a diaphanous beauty all its own, with its floating flight and wings that seem to carry their own light. In Britain, the Black-veined White used to form localised colonies that fluctuated in size from year to year. By the first decade of the twentieth century, it was more or less confined to the hedgerows and orchards around Canterbury. No one knows why it died out. One theory proposes long-term climate change with the *coup de grâce* being a series of wet Septembers. It could equally be an increase in hungry birds. This butterfly seems to be vulnerable at the chrysalis stage in early autumn, since, unusually, it is brightly coloured and easy to spot.

A famous attempt was made to reintroduce the Black-veined White at Chartwell, Winston Churchill's home overlooking the Kentish Weald near Westerham. Churchill had become quite interested in butterflies while a prisoner of war in South Africa. He had visited the nearby Butterfly

Farm at Bexley, run by L. W. Newman and his son Hugh, and asked them to come up with a plan to increase the number of butterflies in his garden. Then war intervened. With more spare time on his hands after being voted out of office in 1945, the great man returned to his garden projects and summoned Hugh Newman to Chartwell to discuss it further. Releasing the Black-veined White was Newman's own idea. Churchill initially demurred, fearing damage to his fruit trees, but on being assured that the butterfly preferred laying its eggs on hawthorn to anything else, Churchill gave the green light. Acquiring eggs from a continental supplier, Newman positioned nests of young larvae on the Chartwell hawthorns and surrounded them with protective muslin 'sleeves'. Unfortunately, when the time came for the sleeves to be removed, Churchill's gardener misunderstood his instructions and simply cut off the twigs – sleeves, larvae and all. Newman tried again, but though the caterpillars grew and pupated in a satisfactory way, not a single butterfly emerged the following year. He suspected that the local tits had gobbled up all the pupae during the winter.[37]

Large White, *Pieris brassicae*

VN: cabbage butterfly, Cabbage White, Frenchmen (Lincs), hairy mollies (Ireland), kailworm (Scot.), papishes, pelmers, summer snowflakes

AN: Greater White Cabbage-Butterfly (1703), Great White Butterfly (1720), Large White Garden Butterfly (1749), Large Garden White (c18)

Welsh: *Iar Wen Fawr*
Irish: *Banog mhor*

The caterpillars of the Large White (the Cabbage White), roam in a pack, stripping the fleshy leaves of cabbages down to their ribs and leaving them enveloped in an acrid cloud of mustard-oil gas. Large Whites are most frequent in late summer, when their numbers are enforced by immigration, and in a bad year, it will be a very well-defended cabbage patch that they do not manage to penetrate.

Gardeners who would never dream of harming a Red Admiral or tortoiseshell, and even leave a few nettles for them, think nothing of squashing cabbage caterpillars or the clusters of their yellow, bottle-shaped eggs. At some point in the distant past, the Large White must have laid on wild mustards and

cresses, but its main food-plant has long been planted brassicas in gardens and allotments, including cauliflower, broccoli, swede, turnip, radish, Brussels sprouts and, of course, cabbage.

Miriam Rothschild actually liked Cabbage Whites and welcomed them to her greenhouse. 'As a white butterfly flaps past, it rouses in us a sudden sense of recognition, of pleasure and empathy', she explained. 'Somehow they flutter erratically through our lives like stray but familiar thoughts.' The 'cabbage butterfly' has almost certainly been a familiar of mankind for as long as we have grown cabbages. In *The Canterbury Tales*, a 'boterflye' makes a brief appearance among the kale, implying that for Chaucer and his contemporaries, the Large White was the archetypal butterfly. [38]

The bristly green, black and yellow caterpillar of the Cabbage White is notorious not only in Europe but also in both North America and Australia, where it was accidentally introduced and now thrives. In the United States, it was 'the imported cabbage worm', in Japan 'the European cabbage butterfly'. Nearer to home, it was known in Ireland as 'hairy mollie', and in Scotland as the 'kailworm' or 'green kailworm'. The custom of naming noxious insects after a recognised enemy meant that, in strongly Protestant communities in Ireland, they were 'papishes' and gathered up for burning on Oak Apple Day (29 May). In Lincolnshire, perhaps around the time of the Napoleonic Wars, they were called 'Frenchmen'.[39] In the New Forest and perhaps other parts, they were known as 'pelmers' or 'palmers', a name for wandering 'hairy worms', derived from the poor, palm-carrying pilgrims of medieval England. Paul Waring recalls his grandfather using this name during a population explosion of Cabbage White caterpillars in the New Forest, when vast numbers wandered away from a field of brassicas looking for somewhere to pupate. Some found such a place in the folds of the curtains of nearby houses, but many more were 'squashed into slurry' on the roads.

By imbibing mustard oil from their food, the Large White's caterpillars are distasteful to birds and so feed openly and in full view. This at least makes them easy to spot and remove. Some say that you can avoid trouble ahead by catching and killing the first cabbage white to appear in the garden. Gardeners since Pliny (who recommended strewing the cabbage patch with 'nitre or salt earth' or the ashes of a bonfire) have devised different ways of deterring them. In recent times, netting and

Damage to Brussels sprouts caused by Large White caterpillars.

Planting 'egg-crows' among the cabbage patch to deter Cabbage White butterflies.

a sprinkling of derris dust were the main deterrents, but a coating of washing-up detergent is said to be equally effective. The caterpillars can also be deterred with a selective bacterial agent such as Thuricide. Some gardeners swear by interplanting with marigolds (said to have insecticidal properties) or nasturtiums (as alternative butterfly food) – a tip dating back to the sixteenth century and Thomas Muffet, who also found that his cabbages remained caterpillar-free if he interplanted them with vetches. One website recommends posting eggshells on sticks as 'egg-crows'. Apparently, the butterfly mistakes the shells for a rival butterfly and so beats a hasty retreat.

Despite their interest in our cabbages, white butterflies in the spring have been seen as good-luck charms. If the first butterfly of the year is white, then a prosperous season might follow. An early brown butterfly, on the other hand, warns us to tighten our belts: a difficult year lies ahead. The analogy was bread. White butterflies stood for white bread, once a luxury food, while brown bread

was cheaper and more likely to appear on poorer tables. Needless to say, this piece of lore has dated badly, and the comparison of Large Whites with cheap ready-sliced bread has a different resonance today.

Large Whites have a powerful flight and no difficulty crossing the English Channel. Just occasionally they arrive in enormous numbers. At Sutton Broad in Norfolk in 1912, a large patch of sundews caught an estimated 6 million of them, part of a vast swarm that had recently arrived from across the sea and settled on what had looked to them like nectar. Back in 1508, the skies over Calais temporarily darkened as 'an innumerable swarm of white butterflies as thick as flakes of snow' flew over the town. At one point they were so dense that onlookers in the fields outside the town could barely see its walls. Another witness to one of these summer snowstorms described the butterflies coming in from the sea like 'animated snowflakes for the wind to try'. There are occasional plagues of the caterpillars, too, though the British have never experienced them in such numbers as an observer in Kiev, who watched a moving carpet of them swarm over the railway lines to be 'crushed like pâté by the locomotive'.[40]

The scientific name of our white butterflies, *Pieris,* commemorates the classical Muses who lived at Pieria at the bottom of Mount Olympus, home of the gods. The Muses bestowed divine gifts on deserving human beings, such as the ability to write outstanding songs or poems. *Pieris brassicae* could be translated as 'muse of the cabbage patch', though why a pest should be thought deserving of such a name is a mystery. It was also a scientific mistake. The name of a genus is supposed to be unique to a particular group of animals or plants, but the cabbage white's name is shared between the butterflies and a group of shrubs of the heather family, of which the best known is the lily-of-the-valley bush, *Pieris japonica.*

Large Whites feature prominently in several films. The opening sequences of *The Innocents* (1961), based on *The Turn of the Screw* by Henry James, introduce white butterflies to suggest the ghostly nature of the story. The butterflies were bred specially by the entomologist and broadcaster Hugh Newman, though he was not invited to the actual filming: 'I heard later that a great many butterflies were wasted and, in my opinion, they were not shown to their best advantage,' he grumbled.[41] Other entomological references used in the film include a spider crawling across the face of a statue and butterfly-eating bugs, suggesting corruption and obscenity lurking in the shadows.

Large White butterflies also had a role to play in the Rolling Stones concert in Hyde Park in July 1969. A few days earlier, their guitarist Brian Jones had been found dead in his swimming pool. Mick Jagger, dressed in white, read out some lines from Shelley's *Adonais*: 'Peace, peace! He is not dead, he doth not sleep . . . ' after which several hundred cabbage whites were shaken free from their cardboard boxes. Some had expired in the heat, but enough survived to form an impressive cloud of aerial confetti.[42] The butterflies symbolised the passing of Jones' soul from earth to sky, in keeping with the ancient belief that white butterflies embodied the escaping human psyche after death.

This touching ritual did not amuse Thomas Frankland, chairman of the newly formed charity British Butterfly Conservation Society (now Butterfly Conservation). Writing to *The Times,* he deplored 'the wanton releasing of butterflies in a park without food-plants in the centre of a large city' and challenged 'Mr Jagger' to buy as many again and 'entrust them to my Society so that they can be released throughout Britain to give pleasure to many who are saddened by the disappearance of butterflies.'[43] Later, the caterpillars of Mick Jagger's butterflies were said to have 'devastated' gardens and allotments for miles around.

Small White, *Pieris rapae*

VN: Common White, Cabbage White, Small Cabbage Butterfly

AN: Lesser White Cabbage Butterfly (1703), Smaller Common White Butterfly (1710), Small White Garden Butterfly (1749), Small Garden White (c18), Small Cabbage Butterfly (1819), Small White Cabbage (1856), summer snowflakes

Welsh: *Iar Wen Fach*
Irish: *Banog bheag*

The Small White shares its larger relative's taste for brassicas (its scientific name is borrowed from the cultivated turnip, *Brassica rapa*) and, like it, is commoner in gardens and allotments than in the open countryside. The Small White is less of a pest as it lays its eggs singly and so rarely attacks cabbages in large numbers. On the other hand, its velvety-green caterpillars are harder to find and remove, for they tend to hide on the underside of the leaf and also to bore into the heart of a cabbage, spoiling it with their droppings. There are two broods, but for every member of the pure-white spring generation, there are likely to be a score or more of the duskier-coloured summer butterflies. Research by Jack Dempster in the 1970s found that there is a cost-free way of keeping the garden relatively free of Small Whites: go easy on the weeding. The more weeds there are, the greater the number of predators, particularly harvestmen and beetles. Indiscriminate insecticides risk killing off friends as well as enemies, and then the enemy comes back without the natural predators that keep its numbers in check.

Small Whites have a liking for white or blue flowers. I remember one hot year when every lavender flower seemed to have at least one butterfly attached to it, like another set of petals. They attack cabbages, but they are butterflies, too.

Green-veined White, *Pieris napi*

AN: Common white-veined Butterfly (1699), Green-veined Butterfly (1720), White Butterfly with Green Veins (1749)

Welsh: *Iar Wen Wythiennog*
Irish: *Banog uaine*

This is our rural white, which is commonest in sheltered marshy places and road banks where its favoured food-plant, garlic mustard, grows. Unlike the cabbage white, it has never departed from its ancestral wild food and leaves our vegetables alone (it is much maligned by its scientific name, *napi*, meaning swede). As the 'green-veined butterfly', its common name has been in use since 1720. In North America, it is the 'mustard white'.

This is one of our indestructible butterflies. There is hardly a time of year (except winter) when it is not on the wing, and in warm years, a third brood will fly far into the autumn. It also occurs practically everywhere in Britain, from the Channel Islands to Orkney (which it colonised in the 1930s). Its only weakness is hot summer droughts, but it soon recovers. Perhaps it is surprising that so common and widespread a butterfly has attracted so little 'lore'.

Bath White, *Pontia daplidice*

AN: Mr Vernon's Half-mourner (1699), Greenish Half-mourner, Green Chequered White (1803), Chequered White (1853)

The chequered Bath White, so common in the Mediterranean, is a rare migrant to Britain. According to William Lewin, who published a book of butterfly paintings in 1795, it took its name from 'a piece of

A mating pair of Orange-tips, perfectly camouflaged against the foamy foliage of cow parsley.

needlework executed at Bath by a young lady from a specimen of this insect said to have been taken near that place'. But it was the anonymous lady who lived in Bath, not the butterfly. The last time this butterfly visited Britain in numbers was 1945 when, for a few days in July, it was quite common on parts of the south coast. Bernard Kettlewell (who thought he must be dreaming) caught 37 of them while on holiday in Cornwall. Since then, the Bath White has resumed its usual rate of immigration at one or two records per year, invariably along the south coast.

The Bath White had an older, more cryptic name: the 'Half-mourner' or 'Vernon's Half-mourner' (a name it shared for a while with the unrelated Marbled White). What was a half-mourner? In times gone by, mourning for a dead husband or other close relative was carefully regulated. In Victorian times, the newly widowed woman would drape herself in widow's weeds, that is, black crepe and bombazine, symbolic of spiritual darkness. After a discreet interval, she was allowed to wear lighter colours, while retaining the symbolic black in the form of a shawl or a veil, and it was this black-and-white stage that was known as half-mourning. The pattern of the Bath White, with black worn mainly around the edges of its wings, is reminiscent of this lacy combination.

Surprisingly, this rare butterfly was known from early times and seems to have established itself as a temporary resident near Cambridge. E. B. Ford illustrates a rather battered specimen from the Hope Collection at Oxford dated 1702 in the belief that it was 'one of the oldest butterflies extant'.[44] Yet even this was not the first Bath White. An even earlier one was caught in Hampstead and given to James Petiver, who figured it in his first specimen catalogue of 1695.

Orange Tip, *Anthocharis cardamines*

AN: White marbled Butterfly (1699), Wood Lady (1748), Prince of Orange (1748), Dutfield's Wood Lady (1766), Lady of the Woods (1775)

Welsh: *Boneddiges y Wig*
Irish: *Banog rinnbhui*

Few insects are more emblematic of the seasons than the bright little Orange Tip as it flutters along lanes and hedge-banks in May. Its appearance often coincides with the first spell of really warm weather, with the hawthorn coming into blossom and the fluffy

avenues of Queen Anne's lace appearing along the roadsides. The Orange Tip is a feel-good butterfly; it cheers us up with its dainty, pretty wings, especially that piercing circle of orange on the forewing of the male. In France, it is known as *Aurora*, representing the glowing orange sun at daybreak. Happily, Orange Tips are doing well in Britain and expanding northwards at the rate of several miles a year.

Orange Tip eggs are easy to find on their main food-plants, lady's smock and garlic mustard, since they, too, are bright orange. For children who think it is impossible to find so small a thing as a butterfly's egg, 'nesting' for Orange Tips can be great fun. They are also easy to rear so long as you confine them to one caterpillar per plant (otherwise they tend to eat one another).

Hairstreaks, Coppers and Blues *Lycaenidae*

Green Hairstreak, *Callophrys rubi*

AN: Holly Butterfly (1717), Green Butterfly (1749), Green Fly or Bramble Fly (1766), Green Underside (1819)

Welsh: *Brithribin Werdd*
Irish: *Stiallach uaine*

The Green Hairstreak is unique in having all-green underwings that contrast with the all-brown topside and make it difficult to spot when at rest on a leaf. It is one of those butterflies you tend to spot when you are not really looking, as it flies skittishly close to the ground on a flowery down, around gorse bushes or along the sunny border of a wood. It is rarely seen in numbers and forms scattered colonies of as few as 20 to 40 individuals. Its original name was the Green Fly, or Holly Butterfly, from a supposed but mistaken association with holly. Its scientific name means 'pretty eyebrow of the bramble'.

Brown Hairstreak, *Thecla betulae*

AN: Brown Double Streak (male), Golden Brown Double Streak (female) (1703), Golden Hairstreak (1710), Hairstreak Butterfly (1720)

Welsh: *Brithribin Frown*
Irish: *Stiallach donn*

The Brown Hairstreak is one of the most elusive British butterflies, partly because it is uncommon but also because the adult spends most of its life out of sight among the treetops. In places it can be watched only with binoculars, but in others the butterflies descend to feed on late summer flowers such as fleabane and thistles and can then be approached and photographed. The great enemy of the Brown Hairstreak is the flail. The butterfly lays its eggs on blackthorn, either in hedges or the thickets that often surround woods on sticky clay soil. Unluckily, its eggs overwinter on the kind of projecting twigs that are routinely smashed into splinters by whirling, tractor-drawn chains.

The early entomologist James Petiver (1663–1718) was convinced that the Brown Hairstreak was two species. One, the male, he called 'the Brown Double-streak', and the other, the female, with big orange patches on its wings, 'the Golden Brown Double-streak'. The surprise is that he knew it at all. Another surprise is that Petiver's original specimens still survive, preserved between transparent slivers of mica, and almost as fresh as the day they were caught, more than 300 years ago.

The White-letter Hairstreak – the original 'hair streak', with its W-letter.

Purple Hairstreak, *Quercusia quercus*

AN: Mr Ray's Purple Streak (1702), Mr Ray's Blew Hairstreak, Our Blue Hairstreak (1717)

Welsh: *Brithribin Borffor*
Irish: *Stiallach corcra*

The Purple Hairstreak is a small, dark butterfly with a jinking flight and is usually spotted by training binoculars on a high oak branch. Close up, it shares the same iridescent colours as the Purple Emperor as well as the emperor's woodland habitat, and in many woods the butterflies dance together in the treetops. John Masefield's description of the Purple Emperor, 'that dark prince, the oakwood haunting thing/ Dyed with blue burnish like the mallard's wing' is equally apt for the male Purple Hairstreak. [45]

Unusually, this butterfly seems to be most active in the afternoon and evening and has even turned up in moth traps. It was first discovered by none other than the great British naturalist John Ray, who spotted a couple 'paired on nettles' near his home in Braintree, Essex, in 1692. Later he also found its caterpillar, which he described, aptly enough, as 'somewhat like a woodlouse'. Ray evidently bred it through, as his *History of Insects* contains a short description of caterpillar, chrysalis and both sexes of the butterfly. In recognition, his friend Petiver named it 'Mr Ray's blew (sic) Hairstreak', or 'Mr Ray's purple Streak'.

White-letter Hairstreak, *Satyrium w-album*

AN: Hairstreak (1703), Dark Hairstreak (1775), Black Hairstreak (1808), White-w Hairstreak (1853)

Welsh: *Brithribin Wen*

The White-letter Hairstreak feeds only on elm, and the death of most of our elm trees from Dutch elm disease in the 1970s seemed to threaten its future. Yet the butterfly hung on and even increased its range by laying on the low, scrubby elms still surviving in the hedgerows. More recently its numbers seemed to have fallen again (though, for such an elusive insect, it is hard to be sure). You now stand a better chance of seeing it, typically as a distant, dark butterfly flickering above the leaves, in northern England and the Midlands than in its former strongholds in the south.

This was the original hairstreak, so named from the white line that runs along the hindwings, ending in a wiggle shaped like a 'W'. It was illustrated by Petiver in 1703 as 'the Hairstreak', and later it was listed as the 'Dark' or 'Black' Hairstreak, confusingly so, since the latter name was later transferred to a different species. It was creditable that Petiver knew it at all, since the White-letter Hairstreak is another elusive butterfly that only occasionally descends from the treetops to sip at privet or bramble blossom.

The novelist Vladimir Nabokov relived the moment when he first spotted a White-letter Hairstreak, then known as *Thecla*:

> I remember one day when I warily brought my net closer and closer to a little *Thecla* that had daintily settled on a sprig. I could clearly see the white *W* on its chocolate-brown underside. Its wings were closed and the inferior ones were rubbing against each other in a curious circular motion – possibly producing some small blithe crepitation pitched too high for a human ear to catch. I had long wanted that particular species, and, when near enough, I struck. You have heard champion tennis players moan after muffling an easy shot. You have seen stunned golfers smile horrible, helpless smiles. But that day nobody saw me shake out a piece of twig from an otherwise empty net and stare at a hole in the tarlatan. [46]

The butterfly's modern genus name, *Satyrium*, denotes a satyr, one of the rustic deities, a woodland creature half-man, half-goat, and bearing a pair of lusty little horns (the butterfly wears these on its hindwings). The satyr name turns up again in the Satyrinae, the subfamily of the butterflies known as the 'browns'. Maitland Emmet, the twentieth-century scholar of butterfly names, suggested that the jerky flight of hairstreak butterflies put someone in mind of the bouncy goatish dance of satyrs as they cavorted with nymphs in classical paintings. He also suspected a pun on a plant known as 'saturion', once a notorious aphrodisiac. It seems there was sometimes a satirical purpose behind the naming of names.

Black Hairstreak, *Satyrium pruni*

AN: Dark Hairstreak (1854)

This elusive, dark little butterfly was unknown in Britain until 1828. The circumstances of its discovery were rather odd. A collector had bought some specimens from an Ipswich-based dealer called Seaman under the impression that they were White-letter Hairstreaks but which later turned out to be a new and unknown species. Seaman, realising he was on to a good thing, claimed to have caught them in Yorkshire. The actual locality, which he tried to keep secret, was Monks Wood, near Huntingdon. In due course, Seaman was rumbled, and Monks Wood immediately became a magnet for collectors. It was partly this residual fame that resulted in Monks Wood becoming one of the first National Nature Reserves in 1953 (despite having been clear-felled during the First World War) and, later, the site of Monks Wood Experimental Station, a powerhouse of ecological study from the 1960s until its regrettable closure in 2008.

The name Black Hairstreak was stolen from the butterfly now known as the White-letter Hairstreak, and so any reference to a Black Hairstreak in older literature could mean either species. It is not a very good name in any case, because apart from some spots on the underside, there is no trace of black on it.

Small Copper, *Lycaena phlaeas*

AN: Small Golden Black-spotted Meadow Butterfly (1699), Small Tortoiseshell (1717), Copper or Copper Butterfly (1766), Common Copper (1803)

Welsh: *Copor Bach*
Irish: *Coprog bheag*

The Small Copper is a bright and active little butterfly, often seen perched on a flower, from which it makes threatening lunges at any passing insect or merciless pursuits of a female. Its metallic, coppery wings had lent it the name 'copper butterfly' by the 1760s; later on it was renamed the Small Copper after a second, larger one was discovered. Rather mysteriously, it was unknown to the first generation of collectors. There is a particularly pretty form with a row of blue spots on the hindwing, like a coronet of sapphires.

Large Copper, *Lycaena dispar*

AN: Orange Argus of Elloe (1749), Great Copper (1798)

When I was about six, my father bought me *The Observer's Book of Butterflies*. I remember turning to the Large Copper page and thinking what a fine-looking butterfly it was, the best of the lot in my opinion. Reading on, I was disappointed to learn that it was too late to see one, for the very last British Large Copper had been 'taken in 1851, in Bottisham Fen, by Mr Wagstaff'.[47] It sounded as though this Wagstaff had single-handedly wiped it out. Was there a statue of him in Bottisham, one wondered, his butterfly net raised over the last Large Copper of them all?

In its heyday in the first half of the nineteenth century, the Large Copper occurred widely across the flat-lying Fens and Broads of eastern England, and perhaps elsewhere. Its flame-red wings fluttered over wet meadows and fen ditches, where the butterfly laid its eggs on water dock. The ensuing plump green caterpillars were so well adapted to life near the water that they could survive floods, staying for a while in a trance-like state completely submerged. Today we can only dream of these brilliantly coloured butterflies flashing like flames in the sunshine, for the places where they flew have all been drained or have become overgrown.

The British Large Copper was bigger and brighter than those on the continent. The species was first described scientifically from British specimens and so was given the proud name of *Lycaena dispar britannica* (*dispar* means different and refers to the contrasting patterns of males and females). It seems that local people knew all about the butterfly long before the scientific community became aware of it. Browsing through the minutes of the Spalding Gentleman's Society in 1982, a local historian, E. J. Redshaw came across an entry dated 28 September 1749 with coloured drawings of a pretty butterfly that was unmistakably a Large Copper. It had been caught by the then secretary of the society, a John Green, who had 'scetch'd into the Book these very exact pictures'. He named it *Argus Aurantius Elloensis*, or 'the Orange Argus of Elloe' (Elloe was a fenny district in South Lincolnshire, since drained).[48]

Why did the Large Copper become extinct? P. B. M. Allan claimed that it was 'putting a price on its head that exterminated *dispar*'.[49] Collecting the larvae or pupae and selling them at sixpence

Collector's items: specimens of the extinct British race of Large Coppers (left) *and the introduced Dutch race* (right).

or a shilling to collectors became a profitable side-business for agricultural labourers in the Fens. Dealers, too, made their profit, charging a shilling or two for a set specimen. Yet collecting seems to have been a sustainable activity for as long as the butterfly's marshy habitat remained intact. Its disappearance coincided with the drainage of Whittlesey Mere in 1851, which destroyed its best-known breeding grounds, conveniently close to Holme and Yaxley railway stations on the main line from London. The butterfly lingered on for a decade or two in the Norfolk Broads (so Mr Wagstaff was not the great exterminator after all) but was apparently extinct in Britain by the 1870s.

In the 1920s, attempts were made to introduce foreign races of the butterfly to suitably fenny parts of Ireland and to Wood Walton Fen, the one small part of the old fens that remained suitably wet and open. The Dutch race of the Large Copper flew at Wood Walton in varying numbers until the late 1960s, helped by periodic top-ups from captive stock. Unfortunately, the whole stock perished in a flood in 1969, and more recent attempts to re-establish it there came to nothing. The view today is that a much larger area of pristine habitat would be necessary to sustain a breeding population.

The Norfolk Broads offers the best scope for an experimental reintroduction, but for the moment the project is on hold.

Once the last butterfly had gone, its price rose steeply. In 1871, dealers still had a large stock of them, and British Coppers could be bought for under a pound each. Towards the end of the century, however, they were in short supply, and collectors were willing to part with five guineas or even more for fine specimens of the rarer female butterfly. By the 1920s, specimens were fetching around £15 at auction. Today, there are probably around a thousand set specimens of British Large Coppers still in existence, most of them in museums.

Scarce Copper, *Lycaena virgaurea*

AN: Middle Copper (1803)

The Scarce, or Middle, Copper is one of our minor butterfly mysteries. There are travellers' tales, especially from the South-west, of mysterious butterflies with fiery wings that some say must be Scarce Coppers, but they remain no more than rumour and conjecture. There is some slight evidence that the butterfly did once occur in Britain, and in his book *Butterflies* (1945), E. B. Ford revived interest in the subject by presenting an actual specimen, a very ragged one taken some time around 1800.

Long-tailed Blue, *Lampides boeticus*

AN: Tailed Blue (1860), Pea-pod Argus (1870), Large-tailed Blue (1896), pea blue

A lavender-blue butterfly with fine 'tails' on each hindwing, this is a Mediterranean species that occasionally strays as far north as southern Britain. It has bred on more than one occasion, usually in the London area and most recently in 2003, but it does not seem able to establish itself for long. It is also carried here as a larva in foodstuffs, such as a batch of Kenyan mange-tout peas, from which a butterfly emerged in 1998; another Long-tailed Blue was found in the same year on the window of a greengrocer in Essex. The best year ever was 1945, when 38 Long-tailed Blues were recorded during a vintage year for migrant butterflies.

The only part of Britain where the Long-tailed Blue appears regularly is the Channel Islands. Frank Lowe, who had a large vicarage garden in Jersey, wrote to *The Standard* in 1902 to boast that he had managed to bag 11 one day and 22 the next, and a total of 80 in all. A less-than-impressed reader accused him of a 'lust of destruction'.[50] Perhaps this touched his conscience for when, a few years later, Lowe reported another invasion of Long-tailed Blues, he added that he had captured only two for examination purposes and then let them go.

Small Blue, *Cupido minimus*

AN: Bedford Blue (1819), Little Blue (1853)

Welsh: *Glesyn Bach*
Irish: *Gorman bheag*

The Small Blue is well named: it is, indeed, the smallest British butterfly. It is possibly also our most sedentary one, with most adults never straying more than a short distance from their food-plant, kidney vetch (though a few may wander for miles). The Small Blue was briefly known as the Bedford Blue after collectors found a large and convenient colony near that town.

The scientific name *Cupido* commemorates

Cupid, the god of love, usually represented as a cherubic and flutter-winged toddler holding a tiny little bow and arrow. There is no obvious connection with the butterfly except that it is obviously little, a fact underlined by its species name *minimus*.

Short-tailed Blue, *Everes argiades*

AN: Bloxworth Blue, Small-tailed Blue (1896)

The Short-tailed Blue is a vagrant insect that is occasionally blown across the Channel from its natural home in the hay meadows and scrubby wood-edges of France. The first pair was caught by the gloriously named Octavius Picard-Cambridge at Bloxworth Heath in Dorset in 1885; many prefer his name, the Bloxworth Blue, to the blandly descriptive Short-tailed Blue.

Silver-studded Blue, *Plebejus argus*

AN: Small Lead Argus (1717), Lead Argus

Welsh: *Glesyn Serennog*

The Silver-studded Blue is the blue butterfly of heaths and bogs, as well as certain limestone headlands and cliffs. Despite the destruction of many lowland heaths, it has fared better than its habitat and is still a signature species of the Purbeck heaths

The Silver-studded Blue and its heathland habitat. Watercolour by Tim Bernhard.

of Dorset and the open spaces of the New Forest. Its secret may be resilience. In summer 2006, Thursley Common in Surrey was burned from end to end by accidental fires, and yet only two years later, the blue was back, fluttering over the embers and ashes of its habitat. It has also been successfully released in places where it had died out such as Ockham Common in Surrey and Kelling Heath in Norfolk.

Its scientific name, *Plebejus,* commemorates the common people of ancient Rome, the plebeians or 'plebs'. This became a whimsical name for some of the smaller butterflies, such as the blues and skippers, but is now confined to just this one. The Silver-studded Blue defies its derisory name by sporting distinctive and shining silver 'studs' on the edges of its hindwings. Its species name, *argus*, was the legendary character with eyes all over his head (see Peacock); the 'eyes' are the black dots underneath its hindwing, each of which is circled with white.

Brown Argus, *Aricia agestis*

AN: The Edg'd Brown Argus (1704), Argus Blue (1775), Brown Blue (1795), Black-spot Brown (1819)

Welsh: *Y Gwrymn Glas*

The Brown Argus is a brown among blues, a modest butterfly of downs, dunes and, increasingly, brownfield sites in towns and urban wastes. It is sometimes found resting on grass stems in dull weather or roosting after sunset with its orange 'argus-eyed' underwings to the fore. This is not a butterfly to attract much attention but it is an interesting example of a species that has widened its range through a change in behaviour. Older books say its caterpillar feeds on rockrose, but in urban locations and on set-aside fields, it now prefers annual weeds in the form of cranesbill plants.

Northern Brown Argus, *Aricia artaxerxes*

AN: Brown Whitespot (1795) or Whitespot Brown (1819), Scotch Argus or Scotch Brown Argus (1803), Scotch Brown Blue, The Artaxerxes (1813), Castle Eden Argus (1828), Durham Argus (1832), Dark Argus (1856), Scotch White Spot (1906)

The Northern Brown Argus was once thought to be Britain's only endemic butterfly, but, disappointingly,

DNA studies show that it is the same species as a similar butterfly that lives in Scandinavia. It was first discovered in 1793 at Arthur's Seat in Edinburgh and christened 'the Whitespot' from a prominent spot in the forewings. As a new discovery, they were heavily collected. Local boys made pocket-money by chasing after the butterflies 'with orange-coloured nets, and bottle them up wholesale, five or six together, alive, in the same receptacle, generally a matchbox'. In 1857, someone placed an ad in *The Entomologist's Weekly Intelligencer* offering to purchase 'about Twenty Gross in good condition, either alive or set'.[51] Another famous locality was Castle Eden Dene in County Durham, where it was naturally known as the Castle Eden Argus.

Common Blue, *Polyommatus icarus*

AN: Little Blew Argus (1699), Blue Argus (male), Mix'd Argus (female) (1704), Ultramarine Argus (1742), Caerulean Blue (1832)

Welsh: *Glesyn Cyffredyn*
Irish: *Gorman coiteann*

Though it no longer justifies the name common, this blue is still widespread in Britain and occurs in many habitats, from coastal dunes to the uplands, though it is not a regular visitor to gardens. Its species name, *icarus*, derives from Icarus, the unfortunate boy in Greek myth who flew too close to the sun on his home-made wings and fell from the sky into the sea. Perhaps it was considered a suitable if slightly ironic name for a sun-loving butterfly or possibly it was because its blue wings match the colour of both the sea and the sky. Island races of the Common Blue are sometimes significantly different from mainland forms, for example, often brighter or slightly larger. To find out why, they were studied by the ecological geneticist E. B. Ford (1901–88) and colleagues over many years and are part of the evidence of how the rate of evolution increases on isolated island communities.

> Occasionally people describe a 'beautiful, bright blue' butterfly to me, and ask its name. Almost without fail their excitement dies when I tell them it is a Common Blue. I now tend to use the name which I first heard a few years ago, the Icarus Blue (after its scientific name, *P. icarus*). Now that keeps the smile on their faces.[52]

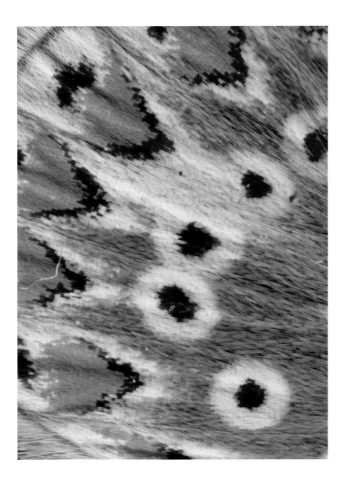

Butterfly-wing patterns are made up of tiny scales. This is the underside hindwing of a Common Blue.

Common Blues awakening at sunrise.

Chalkhill (or Chalk Hill) Blue, *Lysandra coridon*

AN: Pale blue Argus (1704)

This pretty butterfly, whose colour matches the washed-out blue of a hazy summer sky, was named after Coridon, an Arcadian shepherd in Virgil's *Eclogues*. The link is with the Chalkhill Blue's habitat: lonely, windswept downs, the province of shepherds and their flocks. Of all British butterflies, the Chalkhill Blue displays the greatest genetic variety. Scores of different forms or aberrations have been named, and in the past they were collected like rare stamps. An extreme variety, such as a butterfly with streaks instead of spots, or a hermaphrodite half blue and half brown, was the entomological equivalent to collectors of a stamp printed upside down or in the wrong colour.

Certain places were noted for their Chalkhill Blue 'aberrations', and during the butterfly's flight time (which coincided with the summer holidays), collectors would descend in large numbers, like prospectors in a gold rush, each keen on establishing his or her own beat on the short-cropped turf. One such place was Shoreham Bank on the Sussex Downs, where local naturalist Andy Horton's family still remembers 'the butterfly men' with their baggy nets and satchels trailing past their home on the way to the downs.[53] The butterflies have declined since then, not from collecting but due to the spread of scrub over the formerly bare downs following the wiping out of rabbits after an outbreak of myxomatosis in the 1950s.

Royston Heath, in Hertfordshire, was perhaps the most famous hunting ground of all. It could be reached by the London train, and in its heyday in the early twentieth century, every hotel and boarding house in the area would be booked by collectors during the peak week at the end of July. In a good year, the butterflies would be present in their tens of thousands, recalling the 'sky-flakes down in flurry on flurry' in Robert Frost's poem 'Blue Butterfly Days'.[54] On dull days, you could find them at rest in sheltered dells, up to four or five butterflies on a single grass stem. Most of the butterflies were perfectly safe. The collectors sought only the rare genetic 'aberrations', and if they caught as many as a dozen in a day, they could consider themselves very lucky. Outstanding varieties would be shown and passed around in the pub afterwards, for despite the inevitable rivalries, collecting was essentially a companionable hobby. Why certain downs were rich in varieties and others not is still a mystery. It may be just that they were the largest populations of Chalkhill Blue, and so the most subject to genetic variation.

Adonis Blue, *Lysandra bellargus*

AN: Clifden Blue (1775), Dartford Blue (1853), Celestial Blue (c18)

The Adonis Blue is the brightest and prettiest of the blues. The male has wings of an intense, iridescent blue that flash in the sun as the butterfly patrols the downland turf in search of a mate. John Keats must have remembered it when he wrote of 'little bright-eyed things/ That float the air on azure wings'. Its modern name commemorates Adonis, the classical model of male beauty, beloved of Aphrodite. The name was originally bestowed as a scientific one in 1775 and became the accepted English name only after Richard South used it in what became the standard textbook, *Butterflies of the British Isles*, in 1906. In the nineteenth century it was generally known as the Clifden Blue, named after the chalk hills near Clifden (now Cliveden), Buckinghamshire, where it was then common.

Miriam Rothschild, one of the few modern scientists to retain an awareness of poetry in nature, was fascinated by how physics and chemistry combined in this butterfly's wing membranes to create a radiant blue that both absorbed and reflected light. 'Do they focus light rays from without or reflect them from within?' she wondered. 'We do not know.'[55] The iridescent scales brush off easily, producing the fine 'fairy dust' beloved of poets such as Heinrich Heine, whose butterflies 'teasingly scatter their coloured diamond dust in the flowers' eye'.[56]

The Adonis Blue is a choosy insect. In Britain it requires short turf in full sun with plenty of horseshoe vetch and a generous supply of the right sort of ant to protect its slug-like caterpillars, rewarded by a sugary solution from a special gland.

By the 1980s, its numbers had fallen to the point when extinction seemed a real possibility; 'What ails Adonis?' asked a paper in the first issue of the conservation journal *Ecos*. Fortunately, thanks in part to conservation activities but still more to a succession of hot summers in the 1990s, the butterfly has picked its way back from the brink. At a monitored 'butterfly transect' at Fontmell Down in Dorset in August 2003, there were 'more Adonis Blues … than the entire total for any other year since monitoring began there in 1980'.[57]

Like the Chalkhill Blue, the Adonis Blue is a variable butterfly with many remarkably beautiful 'aberrations'. Hence it was assiduously collected. One unlikely specialist was the famous clown Grimaldi, who called it the Dartford Blue after his favourite collecting ground. His collection was lost after burglars broke into his London apartment. Finding no jewels but row after row of exquisite butterflies, they smashed them all to bits with what Charles Dickens described as 'the most heartless cruelty and absence of all taste for scientific pursuits'. The broken-hearted Grimaldi sold his collecting gear and took up pigeon rearing.[58]

The name Adonis Blue has been borrowed for a variety of buddleia with deep-blue flowers, as the title of a set of nature poems by Donald Ward (1909–2003) and for a collection of studios and flats on the site of Wimbledon Football Club.

Mazarine Blue, *Cyaniris semiargus*

AN: Dark Blue (1795)

The seventeenth-century French statesman, Cardinal Mazarin, is credited with the discovery of the 'brilliant cut' treatment of precious stones. Such gems were once known as 'mazarines', and it was the image of a lustrous, shimmering jewel that lies behind this butterfly's puzzling name. Though its shade is relatively dull compared with the Adonis Blue, the scales flash in the sunshine like light on the cut surface of a sapphire. Unfortunately, the Mazarine Blue is another of our extinct butterflies. Never very common, it seems to have been an immigrant that established temporary colonies on clover fields and downs. It had more or less gone by 1880, though it persisted in north Lincolnshire until 1904. There has never been any serious attempt to reintroduce it.

Holly Blue, *Celastrina argiolus*

AN: Blue Speckt Butterfly (1717), Azure Blue (1775), Wood Blue (1795)

Welsh: *Glesyn yr Eiddew*
Irish: *Gorman cuillin*

It is easy to recognise a Holly Blue. While other blues fly close to the ground, this one flutters along at about head height, patrolling an ivy-covered wall or inspecting a line of holly trees. It is a garden butterfly. Fittingly, Holly Blues seem tame and, when settled, are almost oblivious of human observers. There are two generations: the one in the spring is a beautiful fresh sky-blue, accentuated by flashes of its white underside; the summer one is a duller shade of lavender blue, and the female is suffused with dark grey, like an approaching thundercloud. Only the spring butterflies lay on holly; the summer one prefers ivy. The old name of the Holly Blue is Azure Blue.

Large Blue, *Maculinea arion*

AN: Mazarine Blue (1797)

Between the extinction of the British Large Copper around 1860 and its own extinction 120 years later, the Large Blue enjoyed (if that is the right word) the reputation of Britain's rarest butterfly. It could be found at a scatter of places across south-west England, though seldom commonly and with a disconcerting tendency to die out without apparent cause. Accordingly, it was collected as purposefully as antique porcelain or rare stamps. The record Large Blue obsessive seems to have been Baron J. Bouck, whose collection, auctioned after his death in 1939, contained more than 900 British Large Blues. One raid on a newly discovered Cornish colony in 1896 reportedly stripped it of 2660 specimens, with some collectors bagging 500–600 each.[59]

Yet it was not collecting (or not only collecting) that drove the butterfly to national extinction by 1979. Of all butterflies, the Large Blue is the most sensitive to environmental change, though the reason why was not thoroughly understood until it was too late. Collectors had seen the butterfly laying eggs on wild thyme and had tried to rear it, though never with success. Its secret was revealed in 1916 when T. A. Chapman found a full-grown caterpillar inside an ant's nest and, after accidentally killing it, had the presence of mind to dissect its stomach contents. To his surprise, he found it full of the remains of ant grubs. A few years later, the butterfly was successfully reared for the first time by F. W. Frohawk and Captain J. B. Purefoy, with the help of captive ants. Such was the butterfly's dependence on ants that its caterpillar would die without its final feast of ant grubs. Nor could they be any old ant. As Jeremy Thomas discovered in the 1970s, it had to be a particular species of black ant, *Mymica sabuleti*. On top of that, the butterfly needs well-cropped, sunbaked ground on south-facing slopes, which in turn depend on grazing by rabbits or sheep, plus periodic burning of invading gorse to keep the ground open and sufficiently warm. It seems to have been myxomatosis in the 1950s and the subsequent lack of close-grazing that sealed the butterfly's fate, while two wet summers in a row were enough to wipe out the very last colony.

Since the late 1980s, the butterfly has been painstakingly reintroduced from Swedish stock believed to be almost identical to the lost British race. The Swedes were delighted to help, but British law was more obstructive. Jeremy Thomas and his team had to obtain three sets of licences: to import the caterpillars, to release them into the wild and, subsequently, to monitor their progress. The first experimental reintroduction was made in 1983 in an old site in a steep valley on the edge of Dartmoor. After signs that it was doing well, the butterfly was introduced at nine more sites in the Cotswolds, in the Polden Hills of Somerset and in north Cornwall. One now large and flourishing colony at the National Trust's Collard Hill in Somerset is open to the public, and more showcase sites are likely to follow. The Large Blue is back, and looks set to stay.

New discoveries have deepened the wonder of the Large Blue's lifecycle. The caterpillar is now known to mimic the chemical signals of ant grubs. This fools any worker ant encountering it into carrying the caterpillar into the underground ant nest and 'repatriating' it among the real ant grubs, which it will then feed on. Using new microtechnology, the caterpillar's barely imaginable life was filmed in detail for the first time for David Attenborough's 2005 BBC series *Life in the Undergrowth*. The team discovered that the caterpillar not only smells right to the ants but also effectively serenades them by rubbing its segments together, producing a sound 'not unlike the contented murmurs of a brooding hen'.[60] Meanwhile, a parasitic wasp has turned

The Large Blue, one of a set of British Butterfly stamps designed by Gordon Beningfield and issued by the Post Office in May 1981.

the tables on the caterpillar by secreting its own chemicals that panic the ant defenders, so leaving the way clear for it to attack the Large Blue caterpillar. It poses a nice ethical question: having reintroduced the Large Blue, should we also reintroduce its natural parasite?

The Large Blue appeared feeding on the flowers of wild thyme on the 18p stamp of the Butterflies set issued in 1981.

Metalmarks *Riodinidae*

Duke of Burgundy, *Hamearis lucina*

AN: Mr Vernon's Small Fritillary (1710), Cambridge Small Fritillary, The Burgundy (1766), Duke of Burgundy Fritillaria or Fritillary (1766)

Welsh: *Y Goeg Fritheg*

The Duke of Burgundy (formerly the Duke of Burgundy Fritillary) is the only European member of a large Neotropical family known in America as the 'metalmarks' after the silvery spots on some of them. It is a strange little butterfly, seldom seen in more than ones and twos and found mainly on sheltered pockets on the downs, where its food-plant, the cowslip, covers the ground. Formerly it was more widespread in open woods, where its nocturnal caterpillar fed on primrose leaves. The male Duke of Burgundy is an aggressive little butterfly, always alert for intruders into its territory, whether bees, other butterflies or even birds, and seeing them off in a quick darting flight before returning to its perch on a leaf or flower. Its idea of

courtship is a sudden dash followed by what looks like butterfly rape.

The name is a complete mystery. The Duke of Burgundy was a title borne by semi-independent rulers in France until 1477, after which it was sequestrated by members of the French royal family. The first person to use this name for the butterfly in print was Moses Harris in 1766, but he was evidently drawing on accepted tradition, for he adds that it was 'commonly called the Burgundy'. Maitland Emmet suggested that the butterfly was named after a plate in a book.[61] In the eighteenth century, artists would dedicate a copper-engraved plate to a nobleman or distinguished colleague in exchange for their patronage. Perhaps the Duke of Burgundy, who at that time was also the Dauphin of France, had commissioned a plate of this butterfly in some forgotten entomological tome. Or perhaps it was just pure artistic licence. An attempt to change the name to the Speckled Darter was, fortunately, ignored.

The species name, *lucina*, is named after the goddess of light, and seems to be based, like the German name *Perlbinde* (pearl-bind), on the pale spots on the butterfly's underside. Because it shared the same chequered colours of the unrelated fritillaries, the butterfly was long known by the cumbersome name of Duke of Burgundy Fritillary.

Nymphs *Nymphalidae*

White Admiral, *Ladoga camilla*

AN: White Leghorn Admiral (1703), White Admirable (1749)

Welsh: *Y Fantell Wen*

The White Admiral is a beautiful black and white butterfly with an elegant, effortless gliding flight all of its own. It is usually seen flying in the dappled light of overshading trees but sometimes in full sun feeding on bramble flowers. It was named the White Admiral to distinguish it from the Red Admiral (which was known up to that time simply as 'the Admiral'; for an explanation of the admiral name, *see* Red Admiral). The White Admiral was noted for its striking *nigrina* form, in which most of the white is replaced by black; though it is rare in the wild, you can 'manufacture' it by chilling the chrysalis in the fridge.

Harlow, in Essex, has a large number of pubs and bars named after butterflies and moths, sometimes in a punning context. Among them is the White Admiral. But, though the butterfly does inhabit the woods nearby, and perhaps even visits the pub garden, the sign shows a human white admiral – none other than Nelson who, at the time of the Battle of Trafalgar, was Admiral of the White.

Purple Emperor, *Apatura iris*

AN: Emperor of Morocco, Mr Dale's Purple Eye (1704), Purple Highflyer or Emperor of the Woods (1749), Purple Shades (1795)

Welsh: *Boneddiges Borffor*

The Purple Emperor is the most majestic of all British butterflies. It soars, glides and wheels above the upper branches of the forest, occasionally offering us a distant view of iridescent purple on its velvety, dappled wings. 'Above the sovereign oak, a sovereign skims', wrote George Crabbe of Suffolk, 'the purple emp'ror, strong in wing and limb'.[62] Yet obvious beauty and effortless flight are only part of its aura: what lends this butterfly its peculiar allure is its mysterious life, spent mostly out of sight, among the treetops. It is not attracted to flowers and seems to obtain most of its energy needs from

A female White Admiral basks on a maple leaf.

Left: *A male Purple Emperor breakfasting on a dropping.*

sap and honeydew. It does, however, have an unsavoury appetite for carrion or fresh droppings, and collectors have used a variety of bizarre and smelly baits to lure the butterflies from the canopy.

All this gives the Emperor a character; it is conventionally seen as a butterfly monarch with depraved tastes. Perhaps everyone remembers the first time they spotted the Emperor, the patient wait as the sun climbs above the trees, the glimpse of something dark, the flash of purple, and then the butterfly itself, outspread majestically on a pile of dog poo. I remember vividly the one that appeared from nowhere one sultry day to circle my car and was away again before I could fetch my binoculars; the one I somehow spotted among the midsummer shadowlands from the paired antennae projecting from a rhododendron leaf; the one I managed to catch and brought triumphantly home to photograph, only to lose it immediately when it shot up and out of a vent in the conservatory. At such a moment one relives the anguish of the old naturalist Joseph Dandridge (1665–1745) who, in the course of chasing after the butterfly, had been apprehended as an obvious lunatic, and, as he was wrestled to the ground, could only wail: 'The Purple Emperor's gone, the Purple Emperor's gone!'[63]

Linnaeus gave it the name of *iris,* the goddess who appeared to mortals in the guise of the rainbow. Being classically trained, he was perhaps thinking of the moment in Virgil's *Aeneid* when 'dewy-winged Iris flew down through the golden sky, drawing countless wavering colours from the sun's rays' – a good poetic description of the Emperor's flickering iridescence. He might also have known Alexander Pope's 'Rape of the Lock':

> Dipt in the richest tincture of the skies,
> Where light disports in ever mingling dyes,
> While every beam new transient colour flings,
> Colours that change whene'er they wave their
>   wings.

The genus name *Apatura,* on the other hand, seems to be a deliberately obscure word pun. Fabricius, the eighteenth-century entomologist responsible, delighted in verbal trickery and might have missed his vocation as a crossword compiler. He may have been thinking of the Ionian festival of the *Apaturia,* in which revellers imbibed quantities of alcohol beneath the forest trees. But it is also close to the Greek word *apatao,* meaning 'to deceive', and so perhaps Fabricius' idea of a joke.

The literature is full of hyperbole (but surprisingly few facts) about 'this noble Fly', this 'Royal Game'. One author devoted two pages of purple prose to his first capture of this 'Allied Sovereign' with a 50-foot net, toasting it over dinner with '*vive l'Empereur*' (a touch ironic, given that his Emperor was in fact dead and impaled on a pin).[64] Alone among butterflies, the Purple Emperor had the aura of big game, and collecting it appealed to the sort of person who shot large animals and lined the panels of his hall with their heads. 'You can't think how I put my whole soul into egg and butterfly collecting', wrote Frederick Courtney Selous after rain had put an end to a promising Purple Emperor hunt, 'and how I boil over with impotent rage at not being able to attain the object of my desires.' Another Victorian entomologist had better luck, but having caught his Emperor, 'felt a pang of sorrow' that he hadn't caught *two.*

Perhaps the person who best personified this curious duality – greed attended by reverence – was a former African big-game hunter, I. R. P. Heslop. A one-time District Commissioner in Nigeria, where in the 1930s he discovered a subspecies of pigmy hippo and shot a lot of elephants, Heslop spent much of his retirement chasing and studying Purple Emperors. He left a permanent record in a self-funded book, *Notes and Views on the Purple Emperor* (the original title was to have been *How To Collect the Purple Emperor*) – a compendium which Matthew Oates has called 'a masterpiece in obsession, a meditation on an all-pervading passion'.[65] Heslop had probably seen more Purple Emperors than anyone alive, and had acquired a large collection of them with the help of an extraordinary 'high-net', a series of ferrule-linked bamboo poles that lofted a baggy net high above the rooftops. Yet, like most collectors, Heslop was too intent on catching butterflies to spend time watching how they attracted a mate, defended a territory and laid their eggs. 'As an ecologist, he was incapacitated by his desire to net just about every specimen he saw,' says Oates. Near the end of his life, Heslop did some totting up and worked out that 'by coincidence I have caught exactly as many Purple Emperors as I have shot elephants'.

Did all this collecting have any impact on Purple Emperor numbers? F. W. Frohawk thought so, recounting in his *Complete Book of British Butterflies* (1934) a tale about a dealer and his chum who stalked the butterfly day after day in what was once a noted stronghold at Chattenden Woods in Kent. Attracted by bait, 'no fewer than ninety-seven of these beautiful butterflies were captured in a few days . . . It is not surprising that the Purple Emperor rapidly became scarcer in that particular spot owing to this destruction carried on by these two men year after year. The butterfly finally disappeared altogether from that famous locality.' The consensus today is that changes in forestry practice have had more far-reaching consequences that collecting ever had. The Purple Emperor has, in fact, survived the poisoning of oaks and the clear-felling of ancient forests better than most woodland butterflies.

The mystery of how the Emperor spends his days has been partially cracked by Matthew Oates, who is perhaps the first naturalist to have watched the butterfly *from above*, from the ladder of a hired cherry-picker. 'Until one has spent an afternoon looking down upon the Emperor's machinations', he wrote in 2006, 'one has not experienced the Emperor at all . . . Seen from above, the iridescent colours of the fresh male Purple Emperor continuously and miraculously flash through a spectrum ranging from electric blue through various shades of violet, through royal blue, into jet black, and into and out of the rich purple of the Roman Emperors. Simultaneously the small ferruginous-pink [eyespot] in the hindwing flickers on and off . . . the overall effect is awesome.'[66]

Oates has also experimented with baits designed to attract Emperors for wing-tagging purposes. Successful baits used in the past varied from a fortuitous load of pig manure dumped in a corner of Bentley Wood to rancid cheese. Oates remembers the legendary collector Baron Charles de Worms rubbing Danish Blue into a forest gatepost while 'clad only in a string vest, Boy Scout shorts and hob-nail boots'. Every seasoned Emperor hunter seems to have had his own special bait, which could be deer skins, dead animals, treacle, rotting bananas or 'some combination of beer, sugar and strawberries'. Oates himself has hopefully tied a large, decaying salmon to a high oak branch, but the most effective bait of all came to him after a visit by a world authority on Purple Emperors, Yasutaka Murata. He had brought with him a Malaysian delicacy called *belachan*, a mess of spiced, curried shrimps that had been allowed to fester and rot. This noisome stuff did indeed prove a magnet for the local Emperors, but something else ate it during the night, and two days later Oates found the corpse of a recently dead fox nearby. One butterfly's meat is indeed someone else's poison.

Albin's Hampstead Eye, *Junonia villida*

AN: Meadow Argus (Australia)

This 'butterfly that never was' is one of the classic mystery stories of entomology. According to legend, Eleazar Albin was walking on Hampstead Heath one day early in the eighteenth century when he spotted and captured an unusual butterfly. He gave it to James Petiver, who depicted it as 'Albin's Hampstead Eye' in a volume of British butterflies, which he published in 1717, adding that it was 'the only one I have yet seen'. In those days, when little was known about the distribution of British butterflies, it seemed natural to regard it as an overlooked native species. In due course, it was even given a scientific name *Papilio hampsteadiensis*. Petiver's slope-winged Hampstead Eye passed its way from book to book, but no one ever saw another. Eventually the mystery was solved: it was not and never had been a British insect. The butterfly is a native of Australia and known in those parts as the Meadow Argus. How it came to be flying on Hampstead Heath is still a puzzle, but the most likely explanation is that it never did, and that Albin or Petiver had somehow muddled their labels. The most likely explanation is that it arrived in Britain long dead in a consignment of foreign insects, perhaps from Amsterdam Island in the Indian Ocean, which was visited by trading vessels at that time.[67] Albin's specimen still survives in the collections of the Natural History Museum.

Red Admiral, *Vanessa atalanta*

VN: The Alderman, Frenchie, King Georgies

AN: The Admiral (1699), The Admirable (1749), Red Admirable, Scarlet Admiral (1795)

Welsh: *Y Fantell*
Irish: *Aimireal dearg*

Its brilliantly coloured red, white and black wings make the Red Admiral at once one of the most unmistakable and most attractive British butterflies. We used to associate it with fallen apples and Michaelmas daisies, and sultry late-summer afternoons in the deckchair. As a migrant that, until recently, never survived a British winter, it was commoner in some years than others, but there was rarely a year without at least a few on the late garden flowers. In the past ten years the Red Admiral has begun to survive our milder winters and so become a resident. There are now few months when it does not appear, and Red Admirals can often be seen fluttering around houses on sunny days in the dead of winter. Its spiky caterpillar feeds, like peacocks and tortoiseshells, on stinging nettle.

There has been much debate about this butterfly's name, which is widely held to be a corruption of admirable: hence, the 'Red Admirable'. That view was shown to be wrong by Maitland Emmet, who found literary references to 'Admiral' that long preceded the use of 'Admirable' and proposed a convincing explanation of what Admiral actually meant.[68] In one of his early eighteenth-century insect 'catalogues', James Petiver defined admirals as 'such butterflies as generally have a white, yellow or other field in the midst of their upper wings; and the rest of other colours' (by 'field' he meant a patch). The obvious analogy is with a naval flag. When an admiral was on board his flagship, an ensign was hoisted consisting of a plain field with colours in the corner. The colours of this butterfly were reminiscent of the Union Jack, the flag of the United Kingdom, which had come into being around the time Petiver was cataloguing his butterflies. Admiral may, however, be a much older folk-name, for we share it with Germany, Sweden and the Netherlands.

Admirable, by contrast, first surfaces in 1749, when Benjamin Wilkes, a semi-literate artist and engraver, guessed that this might be the butterfly's original name, from its 'great Variety and Beauty of its colours'. Subsequent authors jumped to the conclusion that Admiral was only a corruption of Admirable, but they had the facts in reverse. In the Channel Islands, the butterfly is still known as the Alderman, perhaps another corruption of Admiral, while in Cornwall, Essex and the Black Country, it was sometimes called 'King Georgie' (along with the Peacock and Small Tortoiseshell). Perhaps this is another naval analogy, based on the cross of St George, which adorned naval ensigns before 1707; or the butterfly might have reminded people of the red coats worn by the king's soldiers. In parts of Yorkshire, Red Admirals and Small Tortoiseshells were also known as 'Frenchies'.[69]

The Red Admiral's scientific name *Vanessa* is one of science's little in-jokes. The original Vanessa was the nickname of a teenage girl tutored by Jonathan Swift and was based on her real name of Hester Vanhombrugh, that is, 'Van-ester'. It seems that she and Swift had an affair and that he celebrated her 'bright looks' in his poem 'Cademus and Vanessa'. But

Vanessa is also a learned pun involving a Greek word *phaino*, meaning bright or shining. The eighteenth-century entomologist Johan Christian Fabricius thought it a suitable name for some of our brightest and most familiar butterflies, including the tortoiseshells and the Peacock as well as the Red Admiral, though subsequent work has whittled it down to just this butterfly and its closest relatives abroad.

The species name *atalanta* commemorates an Arcadian heroine of myth, a famous beauty and hunter who, though pledged to perpetual virginity, fell for the charms of a youth named Meleager and then joined Jason and the Argonauts. Several of our most attractive butterflies are named after similarly seduced 'nymphs'. Perhaps the butterfly's fiery red bands reminded Linnaeus of the legend in which Meleager's life was guaranteed by the Fates so long as a particular firebrand was not burned. When, in an act of revenge, the brand was hurled into the flames, Meleager perished. All this is now forgotten, and the name of the Red Admiral is often misspelt 'atlanta' after the better known Atlantis myth.

The colours of the Red Admiral have entranced artists for hundreds of years. It appears on a number of still-life paintings and other works of art, where the butterfly seems to convey a coded meaning. A dramatically early example is the *Luttrell Psalter*, dating from around 1330, when a recognisable Red Admiral is pursued by a bird. The context suggests this is not simply a bird in search of a snack but an image of sexual conquest (as a nearby squirrel, a medieval symbol of female sexuality, implies). Red

Exit Red Admiral pursued by a fantastical bird – a decorative detail from the early-fourteenth-century Luttrell Psalter, *perhaps on the theme of the pursuit of beauty.*

Admirals also adorn the margins of *The Romance of Alexander* (see Clouded Yellow), produced at around the same time, where they are shown being caught by ladies with small nets.

Other paintings may draw on a lost folklore of butterflies that seems to have been shared by many European countries. In one early example, a Red Admiral flutters past a portrait of Margharita Gonzaga painted around 1440 by Antonio Pisanello, against a background of pinks and columbines. The butterfly appears again, painted with great fidelity, in a watercolour by Jacques le Moyne de Morgues of around 1568. It might simply be that the artists liked its bold, bright colours and worked them into the design, but more likely, just as particular flowers bore special messages, these 'winged flowers' had a particular significance. It is probable that the Red Admiral represents sin or temptation.[70] The flickering band of scarlet on the butterfly's forewings, vivid against a dark, smoky background, suggest the flames of a smithy – hence its French name, *le Vulcain*, after Vulcan, the blacksmith of the gods. But, to Christians, it also suggested the flames of Hell. This allusion is more explicit in certain seventeenth-century Dutch paintings such as *The Madonna and Child with Two Butterflies* by the Jesuit artist Daniel Seghers. The Virgin's gaze is directed towards a white butterfly, and the Christ Child's hand is raised as if to reach out to catch it. Yet, unexpectedly, his eyes are fixed on the Red Admiral that hovers out of reach in the corner of the picture. The white butterfly evidently stands for the unblemished Christian soul, while the red one is an embodiment of evil and temptation. The picture is telling its audience that the Christian must strive for goodness but be aware of sin.

Another, still more explicit picture is a still-life called *Lobsters and Fruit*, painted by Jan Davidszoon de Heem around 1670. Its theme is gluttony, and the table is piled high with mouthwatering food. An upturned goblet suggests someone has already eaten and drunk so much that he has fallen off his chair. Like the frontispiece to a celebrity cookbook, the picture is dominated by a huge red lobster. It is reminiscent of the Devil with his traditional horns and suit of red. The message is rubbed in further by a beautifully painted Red Admiral fluttering over a bowl of fruit. The lesson is that greed leads to ungodliness. This surprisingly hellish image of the Red Admiral was gradually forgotten during the Enlightenment, when artists started to draw butterflies for their own sake. But perhaps the story of a 'red butterfly' said to have been hunted in the north of England and the Borders as a witch is an echo of a previous, more sinister characterisation.[71]

Butterfly place names are rare to non-existent, but there is a Red Admiral pub at Broughton Astley in Leicestershire, and this time the pub sign shows a butterfly, not a naval captain.

Painted Lady, *Cynthia cardui*

VN: Bella Donna, Good King Henry

AN: The Thistle (1766), Thistle Butterfly

Welsh: *Iar Fach Dramor*
Irish: *Aileann*

The summer of the Painted Lady was 1996. Suddenly, this elegant, flesh-pink butterfly was everywhere, on thistle heads and in gardens, crowding the buddleia flowers. Those lucky enough to be walking on

The Painted Lady and 'The Marmoress', or Marbled White, from The Aurelian *by Moses Harris (1766),[72] generally agreed to be the most beautiful and accurate of all the eighteenth-century insect books.*

the south coast at the time might have witnessed hundreds of paint-fresh butterflies coming in from the sea, flying fast and straight but pausing to refuel on the cliff-top flowers. That July, every thistle in my village fields had been stripped by its spiky caterpillars, which then vanished, leaving behind only webs, cast skins and mounds of droppings. There was a more modest immigration in August 2006 on the East Anglian coast and a larger one in 2009, when thousands of butterflies were seen throughout England during a hot spell at the end of May; unusually heavy rain followed by a mass flowering in their breeding grounds in the Atlas Mountains had produced a population explosion of butterflies.

The Painted Lady is a migrant that visits Britain every year but is unable to survive our winters (though the season is getting longer: in 2004, a butterfly was spotted as early as February). Where the butterflies come from is still a mystery. There is evidently a vast breeding ground somewhere in north-west Africa, perhaps on the edge of the Sahara desert, but no one has yet found it. But we now know that at least a few Painted Ladies make a return journey from Britain to the Mediterranean and North Africa at the end of summer. In 2009 there were many reports of butterflies heading out to sea from the south coast of England, and a few marked individuals were seen hundreds of miles to the south.

The name Painted Lady is at least 300 years old, and is probably derived from the heavily made-up ladies of fashion (but not necessarily vice-girls) of late-seventeenth-century London. When freshly emerged, the butterfly's wings are a warm-brown flesh tone and the wing-tips are marked with black and white to suggest deep eye-shadow. An alternate, perhaps even older, name was 'bella donna'. It means 'pretty lady', but belladonna, the juice of the deadly nightshade, was used to give the eyes attractively large pupils, rather like the black and white eye-markings in the butterfly's forewings. The Painted Lady's genus name, *Cynthia*, was a popular name with lyric poets and was sometimes used as a coded reference to the Virgin Queen, Elizabeth. In the eighteenth century, the butterfly was also known, briefly and prosaically, as the 'Thistle Butterfly'.

A close relative of the 'bella donna' is the American Painted Lady, also known as Hunter's Painted Lady, a rare vagrant that occasionally visits Britain from its native North America or, more likely, from Spain, where it is now established. Judging from the few British records, the best hope of finding it would be to inspect the buddleias and hanging baskets on railway stations. In 1998 a few arrived in Britain on the tail of Hurricane Earl.

Small Tortoiseshell, *Aglais urticae*

VN: Frenchie, King's Drummer (pre-1939), King Georgies, Witch (Scot.)

AN: Tortoiseshell, Lesser or Common Tortoiseshell (1699), Nettle Tortoiseshell (1795), Nettle Butterfly

Welsh: *Iar Fach Amryliw*
Irish: *Ruan beag*

The Small Tortoiseshell is one of our most familiar butterflies. It visits gardens to feast on buddleia and ice-plants and is also the butterfly most likely to hibernate inside the house. The butterflies enter houses on hot days, too, especially in late summer, as if prospecting for their winter quarters. As long ago as the 1590s, Thomas Muffet noted 'how commonly they found in houses sleeping all the Winter like Serpents and Bears, in windowes, in chinks and corners. Where, if the Spider do not chance to light on them, they live till the Spring.'[73]

Tortoiseshell is another of our old butterfly names. John Ray listed a lesser and a greater tortoiseshell in his *History of Insects*, published posthumously in 1710, and James Petiver illustrated a common, or lesser, tortoiseshell at around the same time. The first to use the name Small Tortoiseshell in its present form was Benjamin Wilkes, in 1741. It would certainly be hard to find a better name for this orange, white and black butterfly, so like the thin slivers of turtle-shell (tortoiseshell) used as veneer for tea caddies and furniture. It would be tempting to assume it is a folk-name, but tortoiseshell was little known in Europe before the late seventeenth century (it was one of the products that Britain began to import in quantity from China in trade ships). The fashion for tortoiseshell coincided with the growing curiosity for the natural world, including butterflies. But for imported tortoiseshell, we might have named this one the 'little fox', as in Germany, or the 'little stinging nettle' (*Ortiguera*) as in Spain.

Around Blackburn, Lancashire, they had a special name for the Small Tortoiseshell: the 'King's Drummer'. 'My godfather says that's how the local boys knew them in the days before the Second World War, from the red uniform with

The Small Tortoiseshell – garden delight.

black epaulets. I do not know how widely known this name was but I'm aware there were other local names for various butterflies and moths that never made their way into books and so are now lost. I wish I could remember half of what my grandfather told me about them.'[74] Another forgotten country name was 'King Georgie', which it shared with the Red Admiral.

'My mother used to call them Red Admirals.'[75] So did mine (meaning tortoiseshells).

As a garden butterfly, the Small Tortoiseshell is the very emblem of sunny days in the garden. It sums up in its colourful form all our associations with butterflies in general. Yet, as with the Red Admiral, artists could turn its beauty into images of temptation and sin. For example, the butterfly makes a surprise appearance in *The Garden of Delights* by Hieronymus Bosch, painted in Holland around 1500. Bosch specialised in scenes of hell and damnation, but the central 'garden' in which the butterfly appears looks more like Disneyland. It is crammed with naked souls having the time of their lives, dancing, riding on fairground creatures, eating strawberries and indulging in sexual antics in the shrubbery. But Bosch would not be Bosch if all this fun did not have a sinister side. What lies in wait for these souls is displayed on the panel on

the right, where earthly pleasures have turned into eternal, hellish torment. This Disneyland is in fact a false paradise, a garden of sin. Because gluttony and lust are enjoyable, Bosch has filled his garden with multicoloured beasts, including a kingfisher, jay, goldfinch and green woodpecker. His Small Tortoiseshell is a strange little creature with forewings only, and those back to front, and its meaning is complicated by the fact that it is shown feeding on a thistle (which is, indeed, a favourite nectar source of this butterfly). In the Victorian 'language of flowers', the spiny thistle stands for the pains of death, while in contemporary religious paintings, the butterfly stood for the salvation of the soul. Might Bosch have intended the combined image to represent a teetering balance between salvation and damnation, between Heaven and Hell?[76] It certainly seems to be a picture within a picture, whose message echoes that of the whole painting, the soul's journey from birth to death. Not that Bosch (being Bosch) was optimistic about our chances of redemption – *see* the Meadow Brown.

Until very recently, the Small Tortoiseshell was one of the commonest and most familiar butterflies. Gardeners would often set aside a patch of nettles for it (though recent evidence suggests that it seldom breeds in town gardens).[77] But since 2005, its numbers have fallen alarmingly, especially in southern England (though by 2009, it was appearing in larger numbers). The problem seems to be a parasite, a tiny fly called *Sturmia bella*, which lays its eggs on nettle leaves where the butterfly's caterpillars are feeding. The caterpillars unknowingly ingest the eggs with their food, whereupon the eggs hatch inside them. After feeding on the juices of the caterpillar and then pupating, the flies eventually burst out through the butterfly's dead chrysalis. The parasite was unknown to Britain before 1999, and it is tempting to link its sudden, casual colonisation with climate change. The Small Tortoiseshell is unlikely to die out, but it may become more reliant on immigration, especially in late summer.

There is also evidence that the butterfly is hibernating inside houses less often. In the past, Small Tortoiseshells (and sometimes also the Peacock) often spent the winter on the ceiling of a spare, unheated bedroom or other parts of the home where the temperature is cool and fairly constant (in my house they found such a place high above the stairwell). Today's centrally heated homes are probably too warm for it.

A Small Tortoiseshell perched on some out-of-scale dandelion clocks was the first-class stamp in the set of four butterfly designs by Gordon Beningfield in 1981.

Large Tortoiseshell, *Nymphalis polychloros*

AN: Great (or Greater) Tortoiseshell (1699), Elm Tortoiseshell (1795), Elm Butterfly, Wood Tortoiseshell

Welsh: *Iar Fawr Amryliw*

Collectors in the eighteenth and nineteenth centuries knew this butterfly much better than we do. It is in all the early illustrated books, some of them also showing the egg, the gilded chrysalis, and the spiky caterpillar chewing on an elm leaf. The Large Tortoiseshell was a peculiarly elusive butterfly, emerging in late summer only to go more or less immediately into hibernation. In favourable localities such as the New Forest, it could appear in relative abundance in one year and seemingly vanish in the next. The evidence suggests it was an immigrant that established colonies here and there but never became fully established. The last time the Large Tortoiseshell was seen in reasonable numbers was during the long hot summer of 1947, when it fed on garden flowers or flew along leafy lanes bordered by elms in East Anglia. Recent sightings might originate either from stray butterflies or from releases, but the species seems to be effectively extinct as a breeding resident. In the *Millennium Atlas of Butterflies*, it was relegated to the back of the book as a mere vagrant.

Camberwell Beauty, *Nymphalis antiopa*

VN: Mourning Cloak

AN: Willow Butterfly (1749), Grand Surprize (1766), White Border or White Bordered (1803), White Petticoat

How was one of our rarest and most exotic butterflies named after an inner London suburb? Because it was there, when Camberwell was still a pleasant rural village, that it was first discovered in Britain. 'This is one of the scarcest Flies of any known in England', noted Moses Harris, 'nor do we know of above three or four that were ever found here, the first two were taken about the middle of August 1748, in Cool Arbour Lane near Camberwell . . .'[78] Cool Arbour Lane was described 'a pleasant thoroughfare lined with willows'.[79] It still exists, now Coldharbour Lane and part of the A2217, but it is no longer leafy nor particularly pleasant, and crime has lent it a new nickname, Crackharbour Lane. Yet its association with the butterfly is not completely forgotten. The Camberwell Beauty flies again on tiles on the side of the old swimming baths and above the entrance to the local park.

Before Harris renamed it, this butterfly was known as the 'Grand Surprize' (spelt in eighteenth-century fashion with a zed). It was also called, more prosaically, the 'Willow Butterfly' or the 'White Border' (the latter reflected an erroneous belief that English Camberwell Beauties had white-bordered rather than yellow-bordered wings). We turned our backs on the butterfly's European name of 'Mourning Cloak' (which is also its name in North America). Catching a Camberwell Beauty in England was a thrilling, once-in-a-lifetime event; it was no occasion for mourning.

One of those lucky enough to catch one was the poet Siegfried Sassoon. One day he was disturbed from his reading by a butterfly imprisoned between the skylight and a piece of gauze tacked over it to soften the glare:

By standing on a chair – which I placed on a table – I could just get my hand between the gauze and the glass. The butterfly was ungratefully elusive, and more than once the chair almost toppled over. Successful at last, I climbed down, and was about to put the butterfly out of the window when I observed between my fingers that it wasn't the Small Tortoiseshell or Cabbage White that I had assumed it to be. Its dark wings had yellowish borders with blue spots on them. It was more than seven years since I had entomologically squeezed the thorax of a 'specimen'. Doing so now, I discovered that one of the loftiest ambitions of my childhood had been belatedly realised. I had caught a Camberwell Beauty.[80]

Camberwell is not far from the London Docks, which lent credence to a theory that the butterflies were carried to Britain as stowaways on timber ships from Scandinavia. But in fact the butterfly reaches us under its own power, since its best years, known as 'antiopa years' after its scientific name, have always coincided with stable high pressure systems across the North Sea. Antiopa years occur

Hugh Newman and his wife Moira releasing bred Camberwell Beauties in Greenwich Park, 1956.

about once a decade, but the occasions when hundreds of the butterflies suddenly appear on the coast are far fewer. So far there have been only four such years: 1846, 1872, 1947 and 1976. We saw more of them in 1995 and 2002, but the numbers were more modest. East Anglians have the best chance of seeing a Camberwell Beauty, and there are more records from buddleia bushes in gardens and town centres than from the open countryside.

Though the butterfly is quite easy to rear in captivity and is probably sometimes illicitly released, the British climate prevents it from breeding successfully (its discovery year, 1748, when caterpillars were reportedly found in plenty, seems to have been a rare exception). This did not prevent the late L. Hugh Newman from releasing large numbers of bred Beauties at Lullingstone Park and elsewhere, perhaps in the hope of overwhelming climatic imperatives by sheer numbers. None survived and there are no plans to repeat the experiment.

The name *antiopa* is a Latinised version of a mythological princess, Antiope, who was seduced by Zeus in the form of a satyr. The scene has been painted by Titian, Correggio and other Old

Masters. Perhaps the sombre colours of the hairy, goat-footed Zeus seemed an appropriate analogy for this dark-coloured butterfly. Antiopa is also one of the fair women seduced by Duke Theseus, with Titania's help, according to the fairy king Oberon in *A Midsummer Night's Dream*.

The Camberwell Beauty was used as a trademark by Samuel Jones & Co who manufactured gummed paper at a factory in Camberwell. The butterfly was picked out in coloured tiles on the factory wall until its demolition in 1982. Eventually, as already noted, it was rescued and transferred to the side of the former swimming baths. Its name was also borrowed by Jenny Eclair as the title of her debut novel in 2000 about 'life, love and shagging the plumber'.

Peacock, *Inachis io*

AN: Peacock's Eye (1699), Peacock-eye, Harvest Butterfly

Welsh: *Y Peunog*
Irish: *Peacog*

The Peacock butterfly is another familiar, much-loved and quite unmistakable garden butterfly. Thomas Muffet was the first to pen a printed appreciation (though he had no name for it) as 'the Queen or chief of all', comparing its wings with 'four Adamants glistering in a beazil of Hyacinth' which 'show wonderful rich, yea almost dazzle the Hyacinth and Adamant themselves; for they shine curiously like stars, and do cast about them sparks of the colour of the Rain-bow.'[81] The Peacock's original name was the 'Peacock's Tail', which referred, of course, to its similarity to the iridescent eyes in the peacock's tail feathers. At some point the name was shortened to Peacock (a rare variety where the eyes are suffused is known as the 'blind peacock').

The Peacock butterfly appears towards the end of July and flies until early autumn before entering hibernation quarters, often in outbuildings (wartime concrete pillboxes were a favourite place). A few emerge battered and chipped in the first warm days of the spring, when they are often seen basking on paths. The Peacock has one of the most familiar butterfly caterpillars, black and spiky, and sometimes found feeding in great numbers on patches of nettles in a sunny location or singly wandering over the garden path. Muffet perpetuated a country belief that it could sting: 'at first a pleasant itching . . . but

Originally named the Peacock's Tail butterfly, today we know it, simply, as the Peacock.

after that a pain hard to be endured'. It was known as the Nettle Caterpillar, which might have contained a double meaning: that it ate the nettle and stung like a nettle. It is, in fact, completely harmless and the spikes are a bluff.

The Peacock is increasing its range and in recent years has colonised the far north of Scotland. In 2004, a Peacock was found hibernating in a peat stack on Lewis, the first time the butterfly has been recorded from the Outer Hebrides. On the other hand, its numbers were fewer than usual in 2007 and 2008. It might have been the bad weather, but there are fears that the parasitic fly which decimated the Small Tortoiseshell may also be targeting the Peacock.

The Peacock's scientific name, *Inachis io*, alludes to another ancient myth, which explains the origin of the peacock's tail. Io was another seduced nymph, the daughter of King Inachus. In order to disguise Io from his wife's prying eyes, Jupiter turned her into a heifer. Io, still helplessly lovely and desirable even in the form of a cow, was given to the care of Argus, a heavenly herdsman whose hundred eyes made escape impossible. At length, her father discovered Io grazing in a field. The winged god Mercury helped her to escape by telling Argus a long and immensely boring story that resulted in every one of his eyes closing in sleep. Then, rather unsportingly, Mercury got out his sword and cut his head off. This displeased Jupiter's wife, but she managed to collect all of Argus's eyes and attached them to her favourite bird, the peacock, 'covering its tail with jewelled stars'.

The Peacock is one of the few butterflies that can make a dry, rustling sound with its wings. 'Growing up in Birmingham in the 1940s and 50s, I recall my mother's description of overwintering butterflies, usually concealed on curtains in the house, as "bobowlers", or possibly "Bob Howlers" . . . It seems only to apply to butterflies such as the Peacock, not to moths.'[82]

A Peacock flying towards a thistle head completed the quartet of butterfly stamps printed by the Post Office in 1981.

Comma, *Polygonia c-album*

AN: Silver, Pale, Jagged-wing and Small Comma (1717)

Welsh: *Adain Garpiog*

Around 1695, Charles duBois, a silk trader and businessman who was interested in butterflies, drew a little picture of the Comma butterfly in his notebook. Its wings, he noted, were ragged and a 'sad brown', but bore a distinctive 'very white mark' like a C on the underside. The only name he had for it was '*papilio alis lacinatis*', 'the butterfly with ragged wings', but the 'C-mark' soon became a 'comma', a name by which it has been known ever since. In France, they ignore the mark altogether and call the butterfly *Robert le Diable* after its devilish, jagged wings.

Though the Comma is common today in gardens and hedge-banks, in the nineteenth century it was regarded as scarce and rather special, a strange butterfly that preferred hop-yards to open countryside. The decline of the hop industry and the use of chemical insecticides should logically have spelled its doom, but instead the Comma seems to have changed its behaviour, laying on stinging nettles and elm trees instead of hops and now gradually expanding its range all over England and lowland Wales. It is currently the most rapidly spreading British butterfly, moving north at the rate of 10 kilometres per year.

Map Butterfly, or European Map, *Araschnia levana*

The Map is a 'nearly British' butterfly, named after a supposed similarity of its wing patterns with countries on a globe. It occurs in France and the Netherlands but has not yet managed to hop across the Channel to lay its eggs on Kentish nettles. There have been several attempts to introduce it, most famously in 1912, when continental Maps were released in the Wye Valley. They seemed to be doing well until a local collector, disapproving of foreign butterflies, took it upon himself to exterminate every one. Either he succeeded or else the butterfly was unable to adapt to life on the Welsh Marches.

Fritillaries *Argynninae*

Fritillary butterflies are named after the Latin word *fritillus*, meaning a dice box. According to the poet Horace, Roman gamblers kept their dice in a special cylindrical container, which was fretted on the inside to make an impressive rattling noise. Though no genuine Roman *fritillus* has survived, the best ones seem to have been inlaid with a black and white chequer pattern. By the sixteenth century, the same word, anglicised as 'fritillary', was in use for a type of lily with a box-like flower and a contrasting, dark and light pattern. A century later, certainly by the time John Ray was compiling his *History of Insects* in the 1690s, butterflies with similarly chequered wings were also being known as fritillaries because, noted Ray, 'the black spots are arranged like a chessboard (*tabula schaccaria*)'.[83] There may have been some punning word-play involved, as a similar French word, *fretiller*, means to flutter.

There are eight resident British fritillaries and one scarce migrant. Nearly all of them have declined in recent years, some at a speed that has baffled conservationists. Freshly emerged, they are a wonder to watch, their wings flashing orange and gold in the sun, and their effortless gliding flight is made even more beautiful by their natural surroundings. Fritillaries are butterflies of scented woodland glades and flowery banks, downs and dunes. Today, alas, many species are increasingly confined to protected sites and nature reserves.

Small Pearl-bordered Fritillary, *Boloria selene*

AN: Small Pearl Border Fritillary (1742), May Fritillary (1795), Pearly Border Likeness (1819)

Welsh: *Britheg Berlog Fach*

The Small Pearl-bordered and Pearl-bordered Fritillaries both have distinctive rows of silver spots on the underside of their hindwings. They look very similar on the wing but can be distinguished by their underwing pattern, the Small Pearl-bordered being more contrasted and with a few extra spots. Their similarity was acknowledged in an older name for the Small Pearl-bordered, Pearly Border Likeness. Small Pearl-bordered Fritillary is a poor name by comparison; not only is it too long but it is not

Small Pearl-bordered Fritillaries, formerly known more elegantly as May Fritillaries or the Pearly Border Likeness.

even accurate: the two pearl-bordered fritillaries are about the same size.

The Small Pearl-bordered Fritillary flies on boggy moors, coastal cliffs and open woods. Being less reliant on woodland management, it has declined less than its Pearl-bordered namesake and is commoner in the western half of Britain.

Pearl-bordered Fritillary, *Boloria euphrosyne*

AN: April Fritillary (1699), Pearl Border Fritillaria (1766)

Welsh: *Britheg Berlog*
Irish: *Fritilean pearlach*

Fritillaries are graceful butterflies, and generations of classically educated entomologists saw in them parallels with the nymphs and graces of Greek mythology. The Pearl-bordered Fritillary takes its Latin name *euphrosyne* from one of the Three Graces, the one that personified elegance, beauty and joy. The butterfly's appearance in the spring was especially joyful because it coincided with the greening of the woods with their floods of primrose and bluebell and the birds in full song. Before the Gregorian calendar was put back by 11 days, the butterfly was on the wing early enough to be called the April Fritillary (after the calendar changed, it became the May Fritillary).

Sadly, autumn has come to the 'April Fritillary'. Half a century ago few would have believed that such a common butterfly could be reduced to just 170 colonies in the whole of Britain, with fewer and fewer every year despite the best efforts of Butterfly Conservation and other wildlife charities. Since 1997, it has been lost from Dorset, Somerset and Kent, and it hangs on by a whisker in several other counties. Its weakness seems to be the caterpillar's need for warmth after emerging from hibernation in early spring, when it spends much time basking in the sunshine. Our woods are shadier than in the past, and all too many fritillary-friendly glades, with their patches of violets and warm, dry basking spots have been replaced by a tangle of coarse grass and brambles. The outlook is grim.

Weaver's Fritillary, *Boloria dia*

This small, continental fritillary was named after Richard Weaver, a well-travelled nineteenth-century entomologist who made many new insect discoveries and set up a well-regarded natural history museum in his native Birmingham. Alas for him, he is mainly remembered now for *Boloria dia*, which he thought he remembered catching somewhere near Birmingham around 1820. He probably muddled his labels, for no one else has ever found this butterfly in Britain. Ironically, it is now known as Weaver's Fritillary throughout Europe.

Queen of Spain Fritillary, *Argynnis lathonia*

AN: Lesser Silver-spotted or Riga Fritillary (1710), Scallop-winged Fritillary (1795)

First known as the Riga Fritillary or the Lesser Silver-spotted Fritillary, this beautiful butterfly is spangled with silver on its characteristically angular hindwings. It was given its present name by Moses Harris, but unfortunately he omitted to tell us why.[84] Perhaps its silver spots suggested to him the shimmering satins and jewels worn by the Hapsburg royalty in Spain.

The Queen of Spain Fritillary was once thought to be a rare resident (it kept turning up in a particular Cambridgeshire wood), but today it is rarely more than an occasional migrant. The early 1940s saw a slight increase in records from single to double figures, and there was another short-lived increase in the 1990s, when evidence of a small breeding colony was found on the Suffolk coast near the RSPB's Minsmere reserve. This seems to have died out, but the butterfly again bred on wild pansies on field borders near Eastbourne in 2009, and may be on the verge of settling here.

Niobe Fritillary, *Argynnis niobe*

AN: Abbot's Fritillary (1829)

There was money to be made from rare butterflies in the nineteenth century, when more than one crafty trader took to releasing continental butterflies in likely places and presenting them to clients as overlooked British species. One of these was the Niobe Fritillary. According to George Parry, a commercial dealer in Canterbury in the 1880s, it flew in a deep chalk valley near Wye in Kent, 'a convulsion of Nature, with almost perpendicular sides . . . where an alpenstock would not be despised by any but an entomologist.' Parry seems to have kept the chasm well supplied with butterflies, for the Niobe Fritillary continued to appear there year after year and was presented in books of the time as a genuine native species.[85] Eventually Parry's activities were exposed, and the butterfly suddenly disappeared. The classical Niobe was another much-abused nymph who was turned into a weeping rock.

High Brown Fritillary, *Argynnis adippe*

AN: Greater Silver-spotted Fritillary (1699), Violet Silver-spotted Fritillary (1795)

Welsh: *Britheg Frown*

This beautiful butterfly, once fairly common in open woods in England and Wales, has become increasingly scarce over the past half-century and is now confined to just a handful of scattered localities. Since 1982, three quarters of its sites have been lost. Its last, best hope lies in the perpetuation of the open woods around the head of Morecambe Bay and on the southern fringes of Dartmoor, the geographical extremes of its former range. Research suggests that the butterfly needs large areas of bracken where its caterpillars can bask in the spring, coupled with plenty of violets. This combination depends on the right level of grazing, but the system of open-range agriculture that maintained it is in terminal decline.[86]

The name 'High Brown' has been misunderstood. Many of our butterflies were named by artists and pattern designers. The word 'high', when applied to a colour, simply meant 'rich'. Hence 'high brown' meant rich brown wings, not high-flying habits.

A 'butterfly landscape' – Silver-washed Fritillaries in a woodland glade – by Richard Tratt. Unusually for an insect painter, Tratt uses oil on canvas. He normally sketches the landscape on the spot but finishes the detail of the butterflies in the studio.

Dark Green Fritillary, *Argynnis aglaia*

AN: Darkned (sic) Green Fritillary (1742), Silver-spotted Fritillary (1795), Queen of England Fritillary (late c18)

Welsh: *Britheg Werdd*
Irish: *Fritilean dughlas*

The Dark Green Fritillary is a butterfly of blustery places, mainly on chalk hills or coastal dunes and cliff-tops. To cope with the wind, it has a powerful elegant flight and glides from flower to flower with only an occasional whirr of its golden-brown wings. Butterfly photographers wait for it to settle on a favourite purple flower, especially a tall thistle. Of all our fritillaries, this one has declined the least. Perhaps the secret of its success is versatility. It occurs in a variety of habitats and so avoids the isolation of other species trapped inside their shrinking woodland or marshland habitats.

The Dark Green Fritillary's odd-sounding name refers to the undersides of its wings, which are patterned in green, though not in a dark but a fresh apple-green shade. Dark and green are unrelated words: the butterfly is not dark green, but dark *and* green. The female butterfly is suffused with dark scales, which serves to distinguish it from the

slightly smaller, brighter High Brown Fritillary. As for the species name, *aglaia* was another of the Three Graces, personifying charm, grace and beauty; an apt enough name for this beautiful butterfly.

Silver-washed Fritillary, *Argynnis paphia*

AN: Greater Silver-streaked (or -stroaked) Fritillary (1699), Great Fritillary (1769), Silver Streak Fritillary (1795), Silver Stripe Fritillary (1798)

Welsh: *Britheg Arian*
Irish: *Fritilean geal*

The beautifully named Silver-washed Fritillary is the largest of our fritillaries and is a majestic sight as it glides and soars through the dappled woods of high summer, supping on the nectar of bramble blossom and other flowers. More than most butterflies, Silver-washed Fritillaries are a kind of birder's insect with elaborate courtship behaviour in which the male follows its mate on a trail of scent, repeatedly swooping under and over her. 'It glides', writes Jeremy Thomas, 'to investigate any golden object, but is especially attracted to movement.' This habit was well known to collectors, who would make orange paper models and wave them on the

A Marsh Fritillary at rest, with the light shining through its translucent wings.

end of fishing lines, netting the rival butterflies as they approached.[87]

This butterfly was so common in the New Forest in the 1890s that the artist F. W. Frohawk could count 40 or more on a single bramble bush. The hot summer of 1976 was probably the last time when such sights were witnessed, but it still flies in reduced numbers in open woods over much of southern England. Silver-washed Fritillary was a name apparently coined by Moses Harris, a watercolour artist, from the wash of silver across the pale green undersides of its hind wings. A dramatic dusky form of the female butterfly with a greenish sheen is known as *valezina*. Unlike the normal form, it prefers shade and can even fly in cloudy weather. Frohawk so admired it that he named his daughter Valezina in its honour. So did Frohawk's butterfly-collecting friend, John Bagwell Purefoy, whose day job was manufacturing corkscrews. A type of double-action screw-thread corkscrew is still known in the trade as the Valezina Corkscrew, in honour of Valezina Purefoy, by way of a glamorous butterfly.

Marsh Fritillary, *Euphydryas aurinia*

AN: Dandridge's Midling (sic) Fritillary, Small Black Fritillary (1717), Small Fritillary Butterfly (1749), Dishclout or Greasy Fritillary (1766)

Welsh: *Britheg y Gors*
Irish: *Fritilean reisc*

This bright little butterfly came within a whisker of being known for all time as the 'Greasy' or 'Dishclout Fritillary'. Moses Harris, who gave us such otherwise inspired names, was in this case chiefly struck by 'the under Side of the upper Wing [which] always appears greasy'. 'Greasy Fritillary' remained the name of choice of many authors well into the last century. Fortunately the name Marsh Fritillary, after its habitat, won out in the end.

This is, or was, a butterfly of wet marshes and fens, though it is just as likely to be seen nowadays on chalk downs, where its food-plant, devil's-bit scabious, grows in damp hollows. Like other fritillaries, it has greatly declined. The Marsh Fritillary was famous for the way its numbers

247

varied from one year to the next. There would be occasional years when its population exploded and vast numbers of its stumpy, black-spiked caterpillars appeared on the move. In Church Stretton the roads and fields were 'blackened' by countless caterpillars one year in the 1880s.[88]

In nineteenth-century Ireland, these mysterious caterpillar plagues could be even more extreme. In County Clare, they spoke of a 'shower of worms', while the Rev. S. L. Brakey found them 'so multitudinous that a black layer of insects seemed to roll in corrugations as the migrating hosts swarmed over one another in search of food'.[89] After an outbreak in County Fermanagh, which was reported in Parliament, people were barricading their doors with peat bricks and burning shovelfuls of spiky caterpillars on bonfires.

Many nature-reserve managers would welcome even one shovelful of Marsh Fritillaries today, having worked hard to retain tiny populations of the beleaguered butterfly.

Glanville Fritillary, *Melitaea cinxia*

AN: Lincolnshire Fritillary (1703), Dullidge (i.e. Dulwich) Fritillary (1717), Plantain Fritillary (1749), Glanvil Fritillaria (1766)

The rare Glanville Fritillary helps to define the part of the Isle of Wight known as the Undercliff – an elegant golden-brown butterfly gliding from flower to flower under a bright blue sky and with the sea behind its wings. It flies for only a few weeks in early summer, but later on, its stubby black caterpillars can be found feeding on plantains in warm, sunny hollows on the broken ground that tumbles down to the beach. Being easy to rear, the butterfly has been released in various warm, sheltered places on the mainland, where it has sometimes become established for a few years.

The Glanville Fritillary is the only resident British butterfly named after a person (such names are more generously bestowed on moths). Moses Harris summed up what was remembered about Lady Glanville:

She was 'the ingenious Lady Glanvil [sic] whose Memory had like to have suffered for her Curiosity. Some Relations that was disappointed by her Will attempted to let it aside by Acts of Lunacy, for they suggested that none but those who were deprived of their Senses, would go in Pursuit of Butterflies.' At

the hearing, the greatest naturalists of the day, John Ray and Sir Hans Sloane, founder of the British Museum, were supposed to have supported her, and their testimony 'satisfied the Judge and Jury of the Lady's laudable Inquiry into the wonderful Works of the Creation'.[90]

It reads almost like a morality tale. The deceased Lady Glanville, traduced by her relatives, becomes a martyr to entomology, a pursuit regarded as so self-evidently worthless that anyone who indulged in it must be considered out of their wits. But all is set right in the end when the two worthies convince the judge of the fundamental importance of scientific inquiry.

Unfortunately the story had been distorted with the telling and is, to put it bluntly, not true. It took exhaustive enquiries by W. S. Bristowe, the expert on spiders, to establish that the lady's name was not Elizabeth but Eleanor and that she was not a titled Lady. Born Eleanor Goodricke in Yorkshire, around 1654, she inherited property in the fullness of time, including Tickenham Court, near Clevedon in Somerset, which she made her home. She first married Edmund Ashfield, an artist from Lincolnshire, by whom she had three children, and then, after his untimely death, Richard Glanville, by whom she had four more. Richard was abusive and violent and on at least one occasion threatened to shoot her with a loaded pistol. By 1698, the marriage had failed, and Richard, anxious to lay his hands on her money, began to circulate stories of Eleanor's disreputable pursuits, notably her interest in insects. He either persuaded or forced her children to sign affidavits against her. Shrewdly, Eleanor turned over her properties to trustees and bequeathed her estate to her second cousin, Sir Henry Goodricke, leaving nothing but some small legacies for her four surviving children and nothing at all to Richard Glanville.[91]

That is the background to the celebrated court case at Wells that followed Eleanor Glanville's death in 1709, aged about 55. The will was challenged by her eldest son, Forest, but not solely on the grounds of her interest in butterflies. Witnesses testified that she had, on occasions, dressed like a gypsy and had even been observed wandering about 'without all necessary cloths'. Forest himself claimed that Eleanor had disinherited her children on the grounds that she thought they had all turned into fairies.

Butterflies certainly came into it. Witnesses were found to recall how she used to lay a sheet beneath some spreading oak and beat the branches with a

This coloured copperplate engraving by James Dutfield in 1749, part of a never-published work on British butterflies and moths, matches the rare Glanville Fritillary and its early stages with their correct food-plant, ribwort plantain. The other butterfly is the Orange-tip, then known as the 'Wood Lady'.

pole to 'catch a parcel of worms'. Worse, she was known to pay as much as a shilling for such plainly worthless things. Evidence like this seems to have convinced the Wells magistrates that the late Eleanor Glanville had indeed been of unsound mind, and

in 1712, the wretched Forest won his case, and the will was set aside. Hence there was no resolution in favour of science, no happy ending, no Ray or Sloane to ride to the rescue (for, by then, John Ray had been dead seven years).

Among the carefully packed butterflies Eleanor Glanville sent via the mail to Petiver in London was an unknown fritillary she had captured near Lincoln. He named it the Lincolnshire Fritillary, though it was subsequently renamed the 'Dullidge' Fritillary after being found near Dulwich. But its association with the ill-fated lady was remembered, and the gallant Moses Harris made amends by substituting the name by which we know it today.

Heath Fritillary, *Mellicta athalia*

AN: May Fritillary (1699), Straw May and White May Fritillary (1717), Pearl Border Likeness (1766), Wood Fritillary

A woodland glade carpeted in flowers with these attractive chequered butterflies circling and settling is a rare delight that lingers in the memory. The Heath Fritillary was noted for 'following the woodman', for it laid its eggs in the sunny clearings left after the wood had been cut. Strangely enough, the Heath Fritillary was not known to live on heaths until the 1980s, when several large colonies were found in the open on Exmoor. Despite that, Heath Fritillary is an old name. It was also once called May Fritillary or Pearl Border Likeness, both of which names were confusingly shared with the Small Pearl-bordered Fritillary.

In the 1970s, the Heath Fritillary seemed threatened with extinction in Britain. Fortunately, Martin Warren, now head of Butterfly Conservation, dedicated five years to finding out what had gone wrong, and, after some timely management on nature reserves in Kent, Essex and Cornwall, its numbers have built up again. It is still rare, but Britain is only an outpost for this species: the Heath Fritillary is in fact one of the most widely distributed butterflies in the world, with names in more than 30 languages.

Browns *Satyrinae*

Speckled Wood, *Pararge aegeria*

AN: Enfield Eye (1704), Wood Argus (1749)

Welsh: *Brych y Coed*
Irish: *Breacfheileacan coille*

Few of us would bother to note the time and place where common, everyday butterflies come and go, and so the late Roger Deakin's characteristically precise note on a small brown butterfly may be unusual: 'A speckled wood butterfly on the windowpane to the north of the study. Always on the north windows. Always speckled wood. Three spots on the hind wing, one spot on the higher. It sits on the windowpane trembling, like living stained glass. Pale beige windows in its brown wings. The serrated outline of a leaf on its wing edges/borders. Target-shaped spots. The dark brown penumbra shows up the spots.'[92]

The Speckled Wood is the butterfly par excellence of dappled light on shaded lanes and rides and is often seen perched on a leaf in a pool of sunshine. It is noted for gladiatorial fights, the rivals whirling round and round one another and spiralling upwards in a column of light, their wings and bodies continually clashing and colliding. The winner, nearly always the incumbent, returns to the same perch on the sunlit leaf. The territory it defends so energetically is tiny – often no more than a few square metres.

This common woodland butterfly was originally known as the Enfield Eye, for it occurred on Enfield Chase, near London, or the Wood Argus. The name of Speckled Wood was invented, or at least perpetuated, by Moses Harris. It is one of the few butterflies to have benefited from our shadier woods, and it has been slowly but steadily expanding its range over the past half-century. Increasingly it is being seen in gardens. Recently it appeared for the first time in one of the few patches of woodland on the island of Lewis. The Speckled Wood has one of the longest seasons of any British butterfly, emerging in the spring as early as March or even February, with late broods that can persist well into the autumn.

Wall Brown, *Lasiommata megera*

AN: The Wall, London Eye (1717), Great Argus (1749), Orange Argus (1795), Gatekeeper (1819)

Welsh: *Iar Fach y Fagwyr*
Irish: *Donnog an bhalla*

Until recently, the Wall Brown, the brightest of the browns, was a common and familiar butterfly; it visited gardens, where it would settle on bare soil and paths, basking on the warm surface. As if to prove the truth of its name, it liked the sunny side of walls, and indeed has wing markings that are reminiscent of bricks. Unfortunately, it has suffered a severe population crash, leaving many parts of the countryside Wall-free. The authors of *The Millennium Atlas* blame the abandonment of traditional grazing on natural grassland and perhaps also the decline of close grazing by rabbits.[93] Fortunately, it has held its own on parts of the coast and in the north of England, where it thrives on some industrial brownfield sites.

The Wall Brown was always a well-known butterfly. A beautifully painted one appears as early as 1614 perched on a rose in a still-life painting by the Dutch artist Ambrosius Bosschaert. Its earliest recorded name was the clumsy 'Golden Marbled Butterfly with black eyes' of John Ray, after which others named it the 'Great Argus' or the 'London Eye', after the eyespots in its forewing. By 1765, however, there was a new name, as Moses Harris explained:

> This Fly is very common in Fields and by Road-sides. It delights to fly along very low in dry Ditches, seldom straying from the Bank, or Field, where it was bred; but, when it comes to the End of the Bank, will return back again, frequently settling against the Bank, or perhaps against the Side of a Wall; and for this Reason, called WALL FLIE.[94]

Mountain Ringlet, *Erebia epiphron*

AN: Small Mountain Ringlet, Small Ringlet (1841)

The Mountain Ringlet (older books call it the Small Mountain Ringlet, though there are no large kinds) is our only alpine butterfly, confined to boggy slopes on the higher peaks of the Lake District and the central Highlands of Scotland. Since it flies only in bright sunshine and only for a short period in midsummer, it is also among our least-known butterflies. The warming climate seems to be slowly driving it further uphill – which, in the Lake District at least, means there will soon be nowhere to go. Butterfly Conservation predicts its extinction in England by the 2050s. Hence this modest brown butterfly has at last achieved a kind of melancholy fame as a victim of climate change and an icon of the fragility of life in a rapidly changing world. Perhaps its future was always implicit in its doleful Latin name: *Erebia* is the dark chasm between earth and the pagan underworld; *epiphron* means thoughtful.

Scotch Argus, *Erebia aethiops*

AN: Scotch Ringlet (1832)

The name of this dusky northern butterfly has understandably never been popular in Scotland, where 'Scottish' or 'Scots Argus' would seem more polite. But the name comes from a distant time when 'Scotch' was the normal word (as in butterscotch or scotch whisky), with no insult intended. A dark brown butterfly with attractive orange patches on its wings, it is one of only three butterflies that are commoner in Scotland than England (the others are the Northern Brown Argus and the Mountain Ringlet). Not wishing to travel that far, English collectors tended to congregate at its most southerly location at Grassington in the Yorkshire Dales, which, by all accounts, sustained a massive annual assault until the butterfly died out there around 1935.

Arran Brown, *Erebia ligea*

AN: Arran Argus (1853), Scarce Scotch Argus (1856)

This continental 'ringlet' is another of our butterfly mysteries. Did it really occur on the Isle of Arran, where Sir Patrick Walker is supposed to have caught a couple while grouse shooting in 1803? Or was it another result of museum entomologists muddling their labels? In support of its existence are specimens labelled from different parts of Scotland: the Isles of Bute and Mull, Rannoch Moor and Galashiels in the Borders. On the other hand, the Arran Brown is a reasonably distinctive butterfly and could not, surely, have escaped detection for so long. But it is hard to prove a negative, and many prefer to keep an open mind about it. Whether or not it ever occurred there, the butterfly's name is firmly established, both in Britain and abroad, as the Arran Brown.

Marbled White, *Melanargia galathea*

AN: Our Half-Mourner (1695), Half-Mourner (1710), Common Half-Mourner (1717), Marble Butterfly (1749), Marbled Argus (1795), Marbled Butterfly (1819), Marbled White Half-mourner (1841), Marmoress (1844)

Welsh: *Iar Fach Gleisiog*

The Marbled White is a familiar black and white butterfly of chalk downs and, increasingly, other grassy places in the south and Midlands (plus scattered records further north, which are believed to have been releases). It has a slow, lazy flight, frequently settling on scabious, knapweed and other late-summer flowers, where the butterflies are very easy to approach. It was formerly known by the arguably more attractive names of 'Marbled Argus', the 'Half-Mourner' (*see also* Bath White) or the 'Marmoress', the latter name meaning 'marmoreal' or marble-like. Surprisingly, no one thought of the name by which it is known in Germany: *Schachbrett*, the chessboard.

The Marbled White is a common butterfly but one prone to extreme variation. Two of the most valuable butterfly specimens ever auctioned were an all-white and an all-black Marbled White, which, after passing from one collection to the next, together fetched £110 in 1946.

Shortly before her death in 2005 and while in her nineties, Miriam Rothschild discovered that Marbled Whites are poisonous. Since her childhood she had assumed that such an eye-catching butterfly must be distasteful to birds, but only late in life, with advanced chemical analysis available, was she able to prove it. It seems that some caterpillars of this species feed on grass that has been infected by ergot fungus (the same fungus that, in infected rye-bread, caused convulsions and even gangrene). The caterpillars store the toxins so that at least a proportion of them are dangerous enough for birds to leave them alone. Ergot is also a powerful aphrodisiac, which led Miriam to quip that the Marbled White's life may be short but is no doubt merry.

Grayling, *Hipparchia semele*

AN: Black-eyed Marble Butterfly (1699), Tunbridge Grayling (1717), Rock Underwing (1742), 'Grailing' (1766), Great Argus (1795), Rock-eyed Underwing (1853)

Welsh: *Iar Fach y Graig*
Irish: *Donnog aille*

The Grayling is a large brown butterfly of hot dusty places on heaths and seashores. It has a characteristic habit of flying up from the path from almost beneath your feet, gliding for a short distance and then settling again. When at rest, the butterfly angles its wings to preclude any shadow, with the result, thanks also to its mottled grey hindwings, that its outline is almost invisible. Grayling is still spelt in the eighteenth-century way and means 'the little grey one'. The first recorded specimen was given to John Ray in 1697 'by Dr David Kreig of Annaburg in Saxony, found on the Gogmagog Hills in Cambridgeshire.'[95] Later authors played around with the name, spelling it 'Grailing' or 'Grayline', while others renamed it 'Rock Underwing' or 'Great Argus' (after the conspicuous 'eyes' on the forewing).

The Grayling's Latin name, *semele*, will be well-known to music-lovers from Handel's opera of that name. The lovely Semele became the lover of Zeus, mightiest of the gods, but perished in smoke and flames after she had rashly persuaded the god to appear to her in all his Olympian glory. Fortunately, Zeus managed to rescue her unborn male child, who eventually became a god himself and then rescued his unfortunate mum from Hades. The theme appealed to Handel, who gave the opera some of his best tunes, such as 'Where'er you walk'. Coincidentally, this is a reminder of the path-dwelling habits of the Grayling. And some forms of the butterfly do have a smoky look.

Gatekeeper, *Pyronia tithonus*

AN: Originally spelt 'Gate Keeper'. Lesser Double-eyed Butterfly (1699), Hedge Eye with Double Specks (1717), Orange Field Butterfly (1749), Large Gatekeeper (1775), Clouded Argus (1795), Large Heath (1803), Small Meadow Brown (1819), Hedge Brown

Welsh: *Y Porthor*
Irish: *Geatoir*

'Gatekeeper' perfectly describes this familiar orangey-brown butterfly's habit of settling and flying by hedgerows, often on patches of ragwort and bramble blossom by the entrances to fields. Some authors have preferred Hedge Brown, but the older name is now once again in vogue. The Gatekeeper is one of the signature insects of late summer, one of the last of the year's butterflies to emerge, and all the more welcome for that. Common and apparently indestructible, it is, like many other butterflies, slowly expanding its range northwards. The Gatekeeper's scientific name *tithonus* commemorates, without relevance, a mythical youth who asked for immortality but forgot to make it clear that he meant perpetual youth. So he became permanently old and doddery, until Zeus took pity and turned him into a grasshopper (*see* Grasshopper).

Life with the Meadow Browns. While a pair mate on a bracken frond, a rival male prepares to attack.

Meadow Brown, *Maniola jurtina*

AN: Brown Meadow Ey'd Butterfly (male), Golden Meadow Ey'd Butterfly (female) (1699), Brown Meadow-Eye and Golden Meadow-Eye (1717), Large Meadow Brown (1853), Meadow Brown Argus

Welsh: *Gwryn y Ddol*
Irish: *Donnog fheir*

Figures from butterfly recording schemes suggest that the Meadow Brown is our commonest butterfly. In good summers, at least, it flutters over wild banks and corners of tall grass by the hundreds if not the thousands. Yet, thanks to its dark and subdued colours, and perhaps also because it is one of the few butterflies to remain on the wing in dull, cloudy weather, the Meadow Brown has long been associated with mournfulness. Its scientific name *Maniola* is the diminutive form of *Manes*, the soul or spirit of the departed. It was coined in 1802 by Franz Paula von Schrank, a one-time professor of theology, who applied it to a wide range of dull, dark butterflies appropriate to 'the denizens of the nether regions'. It seems that, wearing his classical hat, Schrank saw the browns as 'the children of dusky Proserpina', the wife of Pluto, lord of the underworld. Wearing his theological one, he might also have seen them as lost souls in Hell.[96]

That he was responding to an age-old tradition is suggested by *The Garden of Delights,* by Hieronymus Bosch, in which a demon wearing the Meadow Brown's wings is having an unpleasant word with a petrified sinner. It is probably no accident that the image lies on the same horizontal plane as the Small Tortoiseshell in the bright and cheerful 'garden' in the central panel (*see* Small Tortoiseshell). Perhaps Bosch is showing us a metamorphosis: assuming the Small Tortoiseshell stands for innocence and the possibility of salvation, then the Meadow Brown is definitely one of the damned.

Ringlet, *Aphantopus hyperantus*

AN: Brown-eyed Butterfly with Yellow Circles (1699), Brown and Eyes or Brown Seven Eyes (1717), Wood Ringlet (1853)

Welsh: *Iar Fach y Glaw*
Irish: *Fainneog*

The Ringlet was named at a time when women wore their hair in fashionable Jane Austen curls. The name refers to the neat white circles on the butterfly's underwings, its sole claim to distinction, for the upper wings are a dark, sombre brown. In France it is *le Tristan*, the sorrowful one, while the Germans call it *Waldvogel*, the wood-bird. The mournful reputation of the Ringlet is underlined by its ability to fly in damp, overcast weather. In north-east Scotland, the rings are often replaced by mere dots, while a rare and beautiful variety has large, almond-shaped rings.

The Small Heath, perhaps our most understated and overlooked butterfly. Its familiar name was first used in print by John Ray, more than 300 years ago.

Small Heath, *Coenonympha pamphilus*

AN: Golden or Selvedg'd Heath Eye (1717), Little or Small Gatekeeper (1766), Small Argus (1795), Least Meadow Brown (1853)

Welsh: *Gweundir Bach*
Irish: *Fraochan bheag*

Perhaps surprisingly, Small Heath is one of the oldest butterfly names. Ray used it without comment in his *History of Insects* (1710), and most subsequent writers have followed suit, despite later attempts to rename it Golden Eye, Heath Eye, Small Argus or Little Gatekeeper. In Ray's time, the word 'heath' meant land that was rough and uncultivated but not necessarily heather-covered. It describes this butterfly's habitat perfectly. The Small Heath flutters, always close to the ground, on sheepwalks, commons and waysides, where it was, at least until recently, one of the commonest butterflies of spring and summer. It is still one of the most widely distributed, ranging from the Channel Islands to the Outer Hebrides (but not Orkney and Shetland).

Like other once-ubiquitous animals (sparrows, cockchafers, Small Tortoiseshells), we took the Small Heath for granted. No ecologist showed much interest in it, since it is the rare butterflies that attract research funds and conservation money. Yet the Small Heath is no longer as common as it was. The first warning signs came in Butterfly Conservation's Millennium Atlas survey, which revealed numerous local extinctions and an apparent decline right across its range. Perhaps, since it is dependent on fine-leaved grasses, it may be suffering from an overall coarsening of wild vegetation, possibly as a result of nitrogen pollution. All of a sudden, the humble Small Heath is now 'high priority', at least for research purposes, in the Biodiversity Action Plan.

Large Heath, *Coenonympha tullia*

AN: Manchester Argus (1795), Scarce Meadow Brown (1798), Small Ringlet, Marsh Ringlet and Scarce Heath (in the belief that it was three species) (1803), Silver-bordered Ringlet (1832), July Ringlet, Heath Butterfly (1853)

Welsh: *Gweundir Mawr*
Irish: *Fraochan mor*

Since most entomologists lived in the south, this northern brown was long regarded as a rare butterfly. It was known for a while as the Manchester Argus since it was from the bogs near the manufacturing city that collectors went to look for their specimens. Later on, when the butterfly was found to be much more widespread, it was believed that there was not one Large Heath but three, distinguished by the size of the 'eyes' on their wings and known respectively as Small Ringlet, Marsh Ringlet and Scarce Heath. They are now known to be local forms of the same thing.

Cicero, or 'Tully', the great Roman man of letters, might have been disappointed to find the sole mention of his name in the insect world attached to this dull brown butterfly of northern bogs, and in a feminine form moreover. The Large Heath's scientific name can be translated as 'Tully's common nymph'.

This is another butterfly facing a bleak future. Though it is currently doing well enough, computer predictions suggest that climatic conditions will no longer be suitable for it over most of Britain by the end of the present century.

Monarchs *Danaidae*

Monarch, *Danaus plexippus*

AN: Archippus (1897), Black-veined Brown (1924), Milkweed (1906)

Welsh: *Iar Fawr America*
Irish: *Bleacht fheileacan*

Whole books have been written about the spectacular long-distance migrations of the Monarch butterfly and the extraordinary 'butterfly trees' where they spend the winter. There they cluster thickly on branches like dead leaves, which explode with colour as the butterflies disperse in the warming sun. The flight of the Monarch is fast and sustained. It once had the reputation of a super-butterfly, which could flash past at racing-car speeds, though when timed, it turned out that the cruising speed of a Monarch is closer to that of a cyclist, around 18 kilometres an hour, with short bursts of up to 48kph. Even so, with a favouring wind behind it, the butterfly is theoretically capable of crossing the Atlantic in two to four days without refuelling.

The Monarch is a New World butterfly that has become established in other parts of the world, but in Britain it used to be almost as rare as an American robin. The first was caught at Neath in South Wales in 1876, and over the next 64 years only 148 more were reported, and some of those were seen from the decks of ships. Then in 1968, 63 were seen, followed in 1981 by about 135. More recently, 1995 and 1999 were notable 'plexippus years', with around 150 to 200 sightings apiece, mainly along the south coast in September and October. A timely butterfly hotline has helped hundreds of butterfly-watchers to see a genuine British Monarch. They are commonly found feasting on buddleia with other butterflies, but several records have been road casualties. The best places to go Monarch-watching are promontories on the south-west coast, such as Prawle Point in Devon. At the Lizard in Cornwall and the Isles of Scilly, some guesthouses even find it worth advertising the possibility of seeing Monarchs.

E. B. Ford left a memorable account of the day he bagged a Monarch at Kynance Cove in Cornwall in August 1941. 'Glancing to the left, [I] saw a Monarch Butterfly about twenty feet away flying inland perhaps fifteen feet from the ground. It was

A newly emerged Monarch drying its wings. The butterfly never breeds in the wild in Britain, since we lack its only food-plant, milkweed.

slowly flapping and gliding and looked immense, and the honey-coloured underside of the hindwings showed clearly. It quickly reached a small rocky hill and disappeared over the top.' Ford gave chase and eventually 'beheld with joy the Monarch about fifty yards away. It was hovering over a path, no more than a foot above the ground, and then slowly rose . . . I caught it with a single stroke of the net.' For Ford, the collecting urge came second to his scientific curiosity, and his first impulse, knowing that the butterfly stored toxins from its poisonous food-plant, was to wonder what a Monarch tasted like: 'A faint musky odour hung about it, and I was greatly tempted to bite into it to determine if it were unpalatable.' Alas, 'having regard to the interest of the specimen in other ways, I thought it well to restrain my curiosity in this respect.'[97]

Until recently, British Monarchs were usually called Milkweeds, after the name of their food-plant (which does not occur wild in Britain). In his landmark *A Natural History of British Butterflies*, F. W. Frohawk preferred 'Black-veined Brown'.

MOTHS
Lepidoptera

Moths, butterflies and other insects with a sprig of periwinkle, *by Jan van Kessel the Elder (1628–79), an early master of insect life, who painted with oils on copperplate.*

VN: bats, bob-owler or bob-howler (W Eng.), bustard or buzzard, hully-butterflies (Cumbria), loggerhead (Northumb.), meggyhowler or maggie-owler (Cornwall), miller, morth (Norfolk), mote (Glos), night buggerts (Lancs), owl or owlet, pisgies, soul, wick, witch

The late Roger Deakin noticed something that many of us must have felt when we saw a moth close up for the first time, that 'moths are somehow more cuddly, more like mammals, than butterflies'.[1] The larger moths are hairy, like tiny winged mice, with furry teddy-bear-like forelegs (the 'fur' consists of long, modified scales rather than hair, but its

purpose is the same: to keep the moth warm). They are often content to sit on our hand and to explore our skin, feeling their way with their antennae and clinging with surprising tenacity with their clawed feet. The soft, subtle hues and patterns of moths are as appealing as the bright colours of butterflies. Though they disguise the moth when at rest on bark or a leaf, they seem to go beyond the necessities of nature and to produce beauty for its own sake.

An evening with a moth lamp is one of the most exciting ways of visiting the world of insects. On a warm summer night, moths large and small appear out of the darkness into the pool of white light from a mercury-vapour lamp suspended over a white sheet. As they arrive, there is growing expectation and intense concentration from the circle of enthusiasts, their faces cast into light and shadow as if from a fire. There is, as Deakin discovered, 'the unmistakable air of theatre'.[2] The moths settle on the sheet, where they are identified on the spot or boxed for a closer look later on. The expert present intones their wonderful names: 'Clouded Silver, Dark Spinach, Heart-and-Club, Setaceous Hebrew Character . . .' Then, after their brief contact with the moth recorders, the moths are released back into the night to continue their mysterious lives.

Moth, like butterfly, is a word that runs counter to our sense of them as attractive insects. The Old English *motha* (pronounced with a hard 'th') was a maggot. The word was, and to some extent still is, synonymous with the ever-nibbling larvae of the clothes moth and other small, damaging grubs. Nor did the pre-scientific age confine the word to the Lepidoptera. The original 'moths' included completely unrelated insects such as silverfish and cockroaches (or 'moths called Blattae', as Muffet called the latter).

When the word moth appears in an ancient text, it is almost invariably in the context of a destroyer of fine textiles. Psalm 39 speaks of beauty 'consumed away like a moth fretting a garment'. Proverbs 25:20 compares 'a moth in clothing or a maggot in wood' to the gnawing of sorrow at the human heart. According to Matthew 6:19, Jesus himself urged us not to 'lay up for yourselves treasures on earth where moth and rust doth corrupt'. The metaphor is of a slow, remorseless gnawing away.

Adult moths were seen as sinister creatures of the dark, the realm of ghosts and disembodied souls. 'Soul' was, in fact, one of the moth's folk-names. Large, pale-winged moths were held by some to be the souls of the recently departed. A large moth seen in the room of someone dead or dying was the visible embodiment of a soul quitting the body. In Welsh folklore, these moth-souls were allowed to take their farewell of the earth before flying off into the darkness. They should not be harmed and should be assisted by the opening of a window.

Such Gothic fantasies were alive and well in nineteenth-century Cornwall when Arthur Quiller Couch penned a dark little poem, 'The White Moth' (1895). Here is the opening and the conclusion:

The light above the poet's head
Streamed on the pane and on the cloth,
And twice and thrice there buffeted

On the black pane a white-winged moth:
'Twas Annie's soul that beat outside
And 'Open! Open! Open!' cried.

And as she blundered in the blaze
Towards him, on ecstatic wings,
He raised a hand and smote her dead;
Then wrote, *'That I had died instead.'*[3]

Moths were also known as witches, embodying more sinister forces of the dark (an American moth, one of the largest moths in the world, is known as the Black Witch, though its appearances are said to be a sign of good luck). Welsh folklore held that, when witches die, their souls pass from their bodies in the form of a large, perhaps dark, moth. If a black moth lands on you by day, it signifies death, not necessarily yours, but certainly someone's. To this day, a few people are unaccountably frightened by moths, especially black ones. Moths (and other insects, especially dark creepy-crawlies) are still called 'wicks' or 'wick things' in northern England, a name inherited from the Old English *wicca*, meaning wizard or witch.

Another folk name was 'miller', a name most appropriate for pale moths with powdery scales; the Victorian poet John Byrne Warren referred to 'owl-white moths with mealy wings'.[4] Large moths that enter houses through the window and buzz loudly around the lamp were known as 'buzzards' or, in Lancashire, 'night buggerts'. In Birmingham and the counties bordering Wales, they have long been called 'Maggie-owlers' or 'bob-owlers', presumably because, like owls, they are brownish and nocturnal.[5] Yet another old name of obscure meaning, used in parts of northern England, was 'loggerheads'.

Some said moths, like spiders, can predict the arrival of a message. A moth flying persistently near you was a sign that you were about to receive a letter; the size of the moth indicated the length of the correspondence, so a big moth might mean a parcel or perhaps an important message. Careful observation of the moth's habits brought further clues: if it flew once round a lamp post, you could expect a postcard, but three times round definitely meant a parcel. In some cultures, a moth that landed on you was a sign that good fortune was on the way (in Britain this was usually transferred to money spiders).

Moths and psyche

Writers down the ages have been haunted by the resonance between the human soul and the lifecycle of a moth. Before passing from an earthbound grub to a winged insect, the moth seems to pass through death. The pupa not only appears dead; it also resembles a graven effigy on a tomb or sarcophagus. The miraculous emergence of the winged insect from its mummy-like tomb echoed the rebirth of the soul after death, which lay at the heart of many religions, some Christian, some pagan. Just as a moth flies off into the dark of night, so with the human soul after death. In his *Ecclesiastical History of the English People*, the Venerable Bede (673–735) compared this soul-journey with the flight of a sparrow through a warm hall on a winter's night. The bird enters from unknowable darkness and exits into unknowable darkness. Its brief crossing of the hall is its life as we are aware of it. A moth might have served better as a metaphor, with its eerie transcendences and mysterious life in the dark.

Like the Egyptians, the classical Greeks believed in an afterlife. Their word for the human soul and for a butterfly or moth was one and the same: *psyche*. It was Socrates who first conceived the idea of a non-physical soul, an airy spirit-life beyond human imagination. For Aristotle, it represented the ultimate perfection towards which life is directed. There were parallels in the functions of a growing moth, each metamorphosis leading towards the perfect winged 'imago'. In classical art, the soul is often symbolised by a white moth or a dove, and in certain ancient texts, the souls of the dead assume the form of moths and butterflies as they travel either heavenward or down to the underworld.

In Plato's version, a chariot of heaven-bound souls was driven by Eros, the god of love, thus establishing a connection developed in subsequent tales of Psyche, the female personification of the soul, and her heavenly lover Eros. With Eros reduced to a fleshier Cupid, the story of Psyche became a major theme in classical art and poetry. Psyche is represented in female form as an allegory of resurrection. Representations on Roman tombs show her with moth-like wings that prefigure the angels of Christian tradition. Psyche's insect wings make a return in eighteenth-century neoclassical art, most famously in Canova's marble of Cupid and Psyche, whose round, moth-like wings contrast with the excited feathers of Cupid's outstretched wings. Elsewhere, as

The Soul of a Witch *by Nancy Farmer.*

in a much-reproduced painting of Cupid and Psyche by François Gérard, the latter is shown wingless and, as usual, bare-breasted, but with a symbolic white moth (Gerard draws it as a butterfly) hovering over her head as Cupid plants a kiss. The soul-moth is preparing to settle on Psyche at the exact moment of the kiss, reminding the classically educated viewer that the maiden is about to obtain immortality.

In the last lines of his swoony poem 'Ode to Psyche', John Keats explicitly identifies Psyche with a moth, a winged soul fluttering towards the candlelight:

> And there shall be for thee all soft delight
> That shadowy thought can win,
> A bright torch, and a casement ope at night,
> To let the warm love in![6]

The writer and poet Robert Gittings was a biographer of John Keats and probably had his 'Ode to Psyche' in mind when he wrote one of his best-known poems, 'The Great Moth'. Short and gentle, it describes the restoration to life of a moribund moth on a rain-lashed window by the 'slightest goodwill gesture' of a bowl of honeysuckle. Gittings' moth does not simply recover and fly away but arises 'from the dead triumphant', while those watching it felt 'the catch of hope and courage of heart/ As if with plumes of grace to hover/ A spirit took our part.'[7] The analogy we are expected to draw is with the risen Christ, but the poem also taps into the pagan tradition of moths and souls that inspired artists including Keats and Canova. In strict entomological terms, the great moth is probably a Convolvulus Hawkmoth, a 'visitant to our dumbly human home' with its 'rose-barred body and vibrant wings' (and it does indeed feed on honeysuckle flowers).

The Death of the Moth and Other Essays was the title of a volume by Virginia Woolf published the year after her death by drowning in 1941. The moth in question had 'hay-coloured wings fringed with a tassel of the same colour' and fluttered at a windowpane while Virginia was reading: 'One could not help watching him. One was, indeed, conscious of a queer feeling of pity for him. The possibilities of pleasure seemed that morning so enormous and so various that to have only a moth's part in life . . . appeared a hard fate, and his zest at enjoying his meagre opportunities to the full, pathetic.' The moth seemed to put its heart and soul into its fluttering as though filled with a spark of divine energy: 'He was little or nothing but life . . . as if someone had taken a tiny bead of pure life and decking it as lightly as possible with down and feathers, has set it dancing and zig-zagging to show us the true nature of life.'

When the author looked up again from her book, something had changed, and the moth's 'dancing' had become stiff and awkward. 'After perhaps a seventh attempt he slipped from the wooden ledge and fell, fluttering his wings, on to the back of the window sill . . . he could no longer raise himself; his legs struggled vainly . . . the moth having righted himself now lay most decently and uncomplainingly composed. O yes, he seemed to say, death is stronger than I am.'[8]

Virginia Woolf saw this small, insignificant death in terms of the vast forces of energy that animate the natural world. At the moment the moth was dancing at the window, the ploughed fields outside were alive with rooks, 'soaring until it looked as if a vast net with thousands of black knots in it had been cast up into the air; which, after a few moments sank slowly down upon the trees until every twig seemed to have a knot at the end of it.' Then, as rooks do, they dispersed, and all became quiet again. It was at that moment that the moth expired, as though the energy force had suddenly been withdrawn and all there was left for the little creature to do was to surrender its life. That same force, as she might have sensed it, had her in its grip, trapped behind the windowpane. Perhaps only a few weeks, or even days, later, Virginia Woolf walked into the River Ouse and drowned herself.

The belief in moths as transcendent agents is still found in some parts, perhaps especially in rural Ireland. Frances Cooke was in Ireland sorting out her late father's effects when a moth (a Cinnabar) suddenly appeared on the window. After her return to England, leaving a family friend to complete the house clearance, she received the following note: 'The minute I opened the door, this lovely butterfly soared all around me; it followed me everywhere into the garage and back into the house. I really knew who it was. As I left, I wished it all the very best in Heaven . . . that little butterfly looked really pleased.'[9]

This story had a sequel: 'Shortly afterwards, I visited Brownsea Island in Poole Harbour to see the red squirrels. I was sitting on the beach under an oak tree when a moth landed on me. It was what I had always called an "angel-shades". When I checked in the field guide, I was disappointed to learn its name is not angel-shades but *angle-shades*. So I must accept that I had no private angel looking after me – though one cannot be certain of course.'

Moths and light

To fly 'like a moth to a flame' is to be helplessly attracted to someone or something. The moth seems to be playing with fire, a dangerous game for a slight, combustible insect. John Gay used the phrase in *The Beggar's Opera*: 'How, like a moth, the simple maid/ Still plays around the flame!'[10] Shakespeare made a similar analogy in *The Merchant of Venice*: 'Thus hath the candle singed the moth', crows Portia as another suitor bites the dust.[11]

Singed moth is one of those once-familiar household smells we lost when candles were replaced by the electric light. Moths do bang into electric bulbs or rattle around in the protective cage below old-fashioned streetlights, but they soon reach a state of quiet stupefaction and then dry out rather than burn. With candlelight, their date with the flames was more of an elaborate death-dance; the moth flew around the room casting flickering shadows on the wall, circling closer and closer until its wings touched the naked flame, then fell like a burning spitfire or, becoming stuck in the hot candle-wax, was burnt to a cinder. The moth's helpless draw to the flame was as proverbial as its appetite for woollen cloths. In his novel *Green Mansions*, W. H. Hudson recalled the 'faint indistinct sound like a dream in the night' as a moth perished by candlelight.[12]

Emptying the moth trap at Kingcombe Field Centre, Dorset.

In his persona as Archy the cockroach (who was too small to hit the letters and shift key on his typewriter simultaneously), Don Marquis, the New York journalist, was transfixed by the mad behaviour of moths as they flew to their death in the lamplight:

> He was trying to break into
> an electric light bulb
> and fry himself in the wires . . .
>   . . . i wish
> there was something i wanted
> as badly as he wanted to fry himself.[13]

Shelley had the moth fly towards the stars in a metaphysical flight from reality:

> The desire of the moth for the star,
> Of the night for the morrow,
> The devotion to something afar
> From the sphere of our sorrow.[14]

Real moths prefer warm, overcast nights without moon or stars. They live in a world of pheromone (hormone scent) trails and barely imaginable sonic vibrations. The most likely explanation of why moths revolve around the lamp, as Nabokov puts it, 'like the moons around Jupiter',[15] is to do with the

workings of their compound eyes. What the moth sees is a dazzlingly bright spot surrounded by a dark halo. It seems that the moth is not attracted to the light so much as trying to escape its painful glare by seeking the darkness it detects around it. The result is that the moth flies not directly towards the lamp of a moth trap but past it, in repeated flights, until it accidentally collides with a pane of the trap and falls in. Ordinary tungsten lights appear relatively dim to moths, but the brilliant ultraviolet beams of mercury-vapour lamps pull them in from far and wide. Modern sodium street lamps, by contrast, seem to put them into a torpor; instead of fluttering towards the light, the moths seem to sit quietly in the shadows as though it were daylight. This must be one reason why there seem to be fewer moths in built-up areas.

Moth names

By long tradition, the British divide their moths into the large and the small. The former, which includes nearly all the more familiar moths, are known as macro-lepidoptera, or 'macros', the latter as the micro-lepidoptera, or 'micros'. All the macros have English names, but most of the micros do not. In part, it is a matter of familiarity. Nearly all the well-known moths are macros, and so are most of the moths recorded by moth-trappers and catered for by fieldguides. There have been attempts to provide English names for some of the micros, but they are usually ignored. The latest effort, made for legal and conservation reasons, includes such gems as the Large Gold Case-bearer, the Liquorice Piercer, the Greenweed Flat-body and the Scarce Four-dot Pin-palp.

Another part of the reason for a lack of common names is that macro and micro-moth enthusiasts are distinct breeds. The macro-expert runs a light trap and might also smear rum-flavoured treacle on to tree trunks or suspend a clothesline dipped in Beaujolais, known as a wine-rope, from branches to attract thirsty moths. The much smaller, elite band of micro-experts tend also to be botanists, skilled in searching for the telltale leaf blister or mine that hides a caterpillar. They breed their charges in small boxes, and though they might resort to a beekeeper's smoker to disturb small moths lurking in the grass, they rarely use a butterfly net. If they are collectors (and micro-experts have to be to some extent, if only to keep voucher specimens for their records),

The new Darwin Centre at the Natural History Museum, its design inspired by an insect cocoon. Though 'never fully revealed to the public' the structure 'invites visitors to explore it from many angles'. Suitably, the eight-storey-high cocoon now houses the museum's insect collections.

they need the ability to set moths as small as a whisker and as delicate as a snowflake with absolute precision. As people with superior skills, they are inclined to look down on big-moth folk. The latter, for their part, have been known to dismiss searching for small moths, rather mysteriously, as pig hunting. Both groups look down on those who only chase butterflies.

Our big-moth names are long established, surprisingly so considering how few people are conversant with their finer points. Moth names are often wonderfully harmonious and, with their slightly unworldly air, also intriguing. They include very un-moth-like names that are either obscure or nonsensical, such as 'nycteoline', 'eggar' and 'ingrailed'. They include 'footmen' and 'lackeys', 'festoons' and 'tussocks', 'rustics' and 'quakers'. To those who love moths, such names are as familiar and comfortable as an old pair of slippers. Yet they are undoubtedly strange and seem to have very little to do with the modern world.[16]

Many of our moths have carried such names for

two or even three centuries. You can sometimes trace the moment when a name came into being by perusing the gorgeously illustrated insect books of the time. For example, in 1720, the illustrator Eleazar Albin engraved a pretty gilded moth, whose 'light parts', he wrote, '[are] like burnished Brass'. When that moth next appears in the literature, it had become the Burnished Brass, a name it retains to this day. Similarly, when Albin made a portrait of a hitherto nameless moth that emerged 'at the latter End of December', it was not long before (hey presto) everyone was calling it the December Moth.[17]

When people first started taking an interest in moths, few species had any kind of name. The first attempt to supply names was made by James Petiver around 1700, though his 'Dandridge's small greenish moth', 'Tilman Bobart's straw moth' or 'Glanville's copper spotted moth' have failed to stand the test of time (some might regret the passing of his 'leopards' and 'furbelows' – named after the pleated border of a skirt).[18] Sheer inventiveness reached a climax in the works of the watercolourist Moses Harris, who coined such poetic names as the Seraphim, the Phoenix and the Argent-and-Sable. His True Lover's Knot has, he explained, a little double-bow hidden in its forewings exactly like the one that ties the extended forefingers of a lovelorn swain to his intended bride.[19]

Every moth name tells a story. Here is a sample.

Lady Portland's moth

The Duchess of Portland, Margaret Cavendish-Bentinck (1715–1785) was one of the original 'bluestockings': aristocratic and intellectual women who met to discuss such matters as the mysteries of the natural world, the economics of free trade and the shortcomings of men. Among the extremely rich duchess's curio collections, libraries, aviaries and hot-houses of her country seat at Bulstrode, Buckinghamshire, was one of the finest collections of moths and butterflies in England. Her intention, according to her admirer, Hugh Walpole, was to have 'every species in the three kingdoms of nature described and published to the world'. The duchess spent part of each year at a property near Weymouth, where she employed a collector, one Professor Yeates, to look out for specimens. Among his bag for 1750 was a new and pretty greenish moth, which became known as the Portland Moth. The name no

The Mother Shipton moth hides a silhouette of the famous Yorkshire sorceress in its forewings.

doubt had a double meaning: the moth came from Portland, but it also honoured the famous duchess. And though it has not been seen anywhere near Portland for at least a century, it retains the name to this day. The duchess is also remembered as the owner of the famous Portland Vase, which she probably used to hold plants for her caterpillars.

The witch of Knaresborough

Everyone loves a creature with a hidden message in its wings. The moth called the Mother Shipton contains in its wing markings the face of an old woman – a crone with beady eyes, a hooked nose and a pointed chin. The original, famously ugly Mother Shipton is said to have lived in a cave by the River Nidd near Knaresborough, Yorkshire, where she had the reputation as a prophetess (and, some said, a witch). Still called Mother Shipton's Cave, it became one of England's first tourist attractions, where hats and other articles left in the water would slowly seem to turn to stone. This kept the fame of Mother Shipton alive and, in due course, her name was borrowed for the moth. Moses Harris, who evidently had scruples about using the names of real persons, preferred 'the Mask', while Linnaeus saw instead of a face a letter M and so named it 'mi'. But

children always enjoy seeing the funny face in the wing, especially when no one else can see it.

Haworth, Blair and others

A dim little moth called Haworth's Minor honours a once-famous entomologist, Adrian Haworth (1767–1833), a man who died of cholera shortly after watering his garden plants. The name came with a little encomium, like a medal, thanking Howarth for his 'splendid cabinet, so liberally opened to his friends [entitling] him to the thanks of every one engaged in the study of this beautiful Order.'[20]

Blomer's Rivulet was discovered, appropriately enough, by a Captain Blomer, a soldier in Wellington's Peninsular Army and a founder-member of the Royal Entomological Society. He caught the orange-tipped moth in Castle Eden Dene, a renowned Victorian beauty spot in County Durham and, as was then the custom, sent a specimen to the artist John Curtis to draw its portrait. Curtis obliged with a colour plate showing the moth fluttering over the Dene's other great attraction, the rare and exotic Lady's Slipper Orchid.

Dr Kenneth Gloyne Blair, formerly assistant curator at the Natural History Museum, was fortunate enough to have no fewer than three moths named after him: Blair's Wainscot, Blair's Mocha and Blair's Shoulder-knot. He discovered them in retirement, on the Isle of Wight, always a good place to intercept rare migrant moths. He was doubly lucky in that one of them, Blair's Shoulder-knot, is now common. Its caterpillar feeds on leylandii hedges and has spread over much of Britain during the past 50 years. Its northward march took it to Kirkcaldy in 2007, the constituency of the Prime Minister Gordon Brown, where, by chance, it was spotted by an enthusiast called Prescott. Everyone concerned had a jolly good laugh about that, according to *Butterfly*, the magazine of Butterfly Conservation.

Moths that sign their name

Several moths with metallic marks on their wings are grouped together in the genus *Autographa*, which means 'written with my own hand', as though the moths themselves had made the marks. One of these is the Silver Y, a name that is often mistaken for a typo; many are the times when an entomologist has written 'Silver Y', only to have it corrected to 'silvery'. A related moth has the letters N and I in its wings, hence the name Ni Moth.

The rare Heart Moth is patterned with a pair of 'o's, hence its scientific name, *Dicycla oo* (though it is easy to assume that the 'oo' is made by an excited collector). The scientific name of the Poplar Lutestring incorporates the same idea: *Tethea or*, the moth with 'OR' in its wings. Its relative *Tethea ocularis* (meaning eyes) is known in English as the Figure of Eighty moth, which is really 'OR' in reverse.

The Hebrew Character moth contains a black marking that Hebrew scholars could no doubt identify. The non-related Setaceous Hebrew Character combines this marking with a hairline and so became the nom de plume of the eccentric collector Baron de Worms, who was both Jewish and follically challenged. The more subdued mark on the Chinese Character moth resembles the indented maker's mark on an oriental pot. But that is only how we see it; the moth itself is doing its best to camouflage itself by looking like a bird dropping.

Some cryptic names

Moses Harris had a weakness for heraldry. His Argent and Sable moth is a pretty day-flier whose wings are chequered black and white like the flag that ends a motor race. Its strong pattern made the moth the perfect logo for Butterfly Conservation's moth-recording scheme and annual Moth Night.

Merveille du jour was an expression that meant, roughly, 'the best thing I've seen all day' (as opposed to *mauvais de semaine* – 'the worst thing I've seen all week'). The pretty Merveille du Jour moth has dappled green wings, but it is wildly misnamed, being strictly nocturnal and almost never seen by day. Its Latin name *aprilina* is also nonsensical, for the moth appears in October. More than one Irish moth recorder calls it 'the green fella'.

The Spectacle, appearing to wear a pair of round glasses or airman's goggles.

The Merveille du Jour, marvellously camouflaged on lichen.

Names of doubt and confusion

Every moth enthusiast rejoices in a quartet of moths called the Uncertain, the Confused, the Suspected and the Anomalous. Uncertainty and confusion among experts is always reassuring, and they are certainly honest reactions to the mind-numbing plainness of these particular moths. Perhaps future discoveries of equal drabness will merit similar names, perhaps the Ambiguous, the Doubtful, the Dreary or the Hopeless. The saddest name so far was given to a dull little moth that the normally generous Moses Harris dubbed the Dismal. Later on someone must have taken pity, for it is now known as the Dingy Shears.

A pair of Lime Hawkmoths, or 'Olive Shades', the female at the top.

Hawkmoths *Sphingidae*

VN: match-owlet, sphinx; caterpillars: cannoch-worms, hornworms, horse-stingers, hoss-stengs, nanny-vipers

Nearly 300 years ago, Eleazar Albin noted that certain large moths were 'very swift of flight, for which reason they have the name of Hawk Moths'.[21] In those days, hawk could be loosely applied to any small bird of prey, including falcons and harriers. The one that inspired the name of these noble and powerful moths is almost certainly the kestrel, for certain hawkmoths share its well-known ability to hover in mid-air, wings whirring. Like kestrels, the moths' long, narrow forewings enable them to fly fast and straight. The archetypal hawkmoth is probably the Hummingbird Hawkmoth, which not only feeds at the hover but flies by day and so always draws attention.

An alternative name, which is still widely used in America, is sphinx. A French naturalist had been impressed by the cigar-sized caterpillar of the Privet Hawk and especially by its habit of sitting up in an apparently thoughtful pose. In this posture it resembled images of the Sphinx of myth, a sinister character with a woman's head and breasts and a lion's body. Naturalists, exercising their imagination to the limit, saw such features in the reared-up front end of the caterpillar, perhaps in much the same way that sailors fantasised manatees into mermaids. The name survives today in *Sphinx*, the genus name of the Privet Hawkmoth, and in Sphingidae, the family name of all hawkmoths (it is also the species name of the Sprawler Moth, which rears up, legs sprawling, when alarmed).

There are 12 native and regularly visiting British hawkmoths and several more scarce migrants. The following species are those which come to notice most often and which have at least the makings of a cultural profile.

Lime Hawkmoth, *Mimas tiliae*

Given their size and general magnificence, most of our hawkmoths have surprisingly boring names. Many, like this one, are simply named after their larval food-plant (in this case, the lime tree). The Lime Hawkmoth did at least have an alternative name, the Olive Shades, though this has fallen into disuse. It is perhaps our most familiar hawkmoth, being common in towns and cities in the southern half of England, where its distinctive blue-horned caterpillars feed on street limes, pattering the pavement with their droppings. It is almost a signature moth of suburban London. Once a Wimbledon semifinal was interrupted for a short while by a moth that had chosen the Centre Court for its siesta; it was gently removed on the end of a racket by one of the players. I hope he won.

Poplar Hawkmoth, *Laothoe populi*

This is our commonest hawkmoth, at least in the country, and probably our commonest large moth. It turns up in most garden moth traps sooner or later. Children love to let the great grey moths perch on their fingers or noses or crawl up their arms, and are always surprised by how tenaciously the moth can grip, like a koala bear, using its tiny, clawed legs.

Eyed Hawkmoth, *Smerinthus ocellata*

A moth sometimes holds a surprise in its hindwings. At rest, the Eyed Hawk looks like just another hawkmoth, in various shades of brown, but when annoyed, it flicks open its forewings to reveal a pair of glaring blue eyes set in a crimson background. These eyes are, of course, a wing-pattern, but they very effectively transform the insect from a moth into an angry face. To add to the surprise, the moth also shakes menacingly. As the would-be predator hesitates, the Eyed Hawk makes its escape.

This big, attractive hawkmoth, often bred by children in jam-jars, is found in gardens and unsprayed apple orchards, though its big, warty caterpillar is more easily found on small bushes of willow and sallow around the edges of marshes and damp woods.

Privet Hawkmoth, *Sphinx ligustri*

The Privet Hawkmoth is the largest moth regularly to visit a light-trap. It arrives with a loud buzz under the considerable power of its long, hawk-like wings, and its great form easily dominates the night's catch. Its equally enormous green caterpillar lives on suburban privet bushes and is surprisingly

hard to detect until you spot the droppings, each the size of a peppercorn.

This was one of the few moths that country people distinguished from the common herd. Thomas Muffet described and illustrated it accurately, though, as usual, he had no name for it. His near-contemporary, the angler Izaak Walton, noted that the caterpillar was the size of a 'peascod'. He once put one in a box with a sprig of privet and watched in awe as it fed 'as sharply as a dog gnaws on a bone'.[22]

Death's-head Hawkmoth, *Acherontia atropos*

VN: bee robber (Ireland), bee tiger, death-bird, ghost, jessamine or jasmine hawkmoth, potato hawk, locust, tatur-dog

The Death's-head Hawkmoth is a harmless moth that nonetheless inhabits the darker side of our imaginations. Impressively sized, with wings the size of a small bat and a body the size and weight

The Death's-head moth, or 'Bee tiger', a plate from The Aurelian *(1766) by Moses Harris.*

The Hireling
Shepherd *(1851), by*
William Holman
Hunt (1827–1910).
Nature is shown at
her most luminous
beneath the midday
sun, but the shepherd's
unconventional gift
is a Death's-head
Hawkmoth.

of a shrew, it bears on its thorax the unmistakable image of a skull. Its occasional appearances at lighted windows or to lantern light were seen as an omen of death within the family. The moth was also considered to be a kind of insect Hell's Angel, a tyrant moth that slew its smaller kindred. 'As great tyrants prey upon and exhaust the nobles of lesser races,' noted Muffet, 'so these night-fliers beat with their wings and slay the day-flying butterflies sheltering under the foliage.'[23]

The biological purpose of the death's-head marking is still uncertain. One theory is that it resembles a bee as seen through an insect's eyes and so fools it into deciding that the moth is one of them. This ruse is necessary, since the Death's-head has a habit of entering beehives to steal the honey and uses bee-like pheromones (scents), to avoid being stung. In times past, it was known as the 'bee tiger' or the 'bee robber'. The moth has a short, stout proboscis, which is badly adapted for reaching nectar at the back of flowers but ideal for lapping up the sap oozing from trees or honey in the comb.

Other names for this most charismatic of moths were borrowed from its larval food-plant, or supposed food-plant. The eighteenth-century artist and naturalist Benjamin Wilkes knew it as the 'jasmine hawkmoth', noting that it had been 'bred by Mr Dandridge from a Caterpillar that was found on the Jessamine . . . the moth came forth the end of October following.'[24] Another name, belying the

moth's tigerish reputation, was the 'potato hawk'. Its monstrous yellow caterpillars were sometimes found by workers during the potato harvest, quietly grazing on the leaves. Country people called them 'tatur-dogs' or 'locusts', from the ravenous way they chewed through one plant after another.

The moth, always more familiar in central Europe than in Britain, was feared by the superstitious, who knew it as the 'death-bird' or the 'ghost'. Some said it could blind a man with the deadly dust from its wings. In Brittany, they believed it spread plague and disease, being clearly an agent of the devil. The moth's scientific name borrows from its hellish reputation. It combines the Acheron, the dark river that flows through Hell, with the *Atropi*, or the Fates, a trio of witch-like figures that hold the thread of life (the moth has also lent its name *atropos* to the leading independent journal on British moths and dragonflies).

The Death's-head was too rare in Britain for such tales to take serious hold, but stories were told about its sinister visitations. Two specimens preserved in the University Museum in Cambridge are said to have disturbed King George III in his bedchamber and, it was conjectured, might have contributed to his bouts of madness. Another, apparently true, tale concerns the youngster who was given a specimen as a present. He displayed it in pride of place in a case on his bedroom wall. Some time later he fell ill, and an old woman was brought in to officiate as a nurse. She spotted the moth at once and cried: 'No wonder your son is ill! He'll never be well so long as *that* thing is in the house.' The boy's mother was persuaded to throw the unlucky object away, but that was not enough. To avert the evil emanating from the dead moth, it had to be burnt. Thereupon the patient quickly recovered.[25]

In certain ways, the Death's-head Hawkmoth lives up to its reputation. Almost alone among British moths, it can make a shrill squeak like a mouse by squeezing air through its proboscis. The sound, like its skull marking, is said to have the effect of quieting bees during a raid on the hive. Some have also noticed its faint musky scent like jasmine flowers. This may be a sexual attractant, since the moth can turn it on or off at will, or perhaps it is yet another weapon in its arsenal of defences.

Another attribute, which collectors have noticed, is that the moth is remarkably hard to kill. In 1881, someone called Annie Dows wanted one for her collection. 'Upon my first taking it,' she noted, 'it emitted a shrill cry, which continued without ceasing until I put it in my killing box.' Even then the chloroform failed to do more than knock it out, and the next morning she found the pinned, eviscerated, cotton-wool-stuffed moth very much alive, 'and had the pin through the thorax not been a very strong one [it] would have liberated itself.' She was able to put the poor moth out of its misery only by soaking it in benzoline.[26]

The most sinister aspect of the moth, however, was as a visitant, a harbinger of evil to come. In Hardy's *The Return of the Native*, a nocturnal dice game played on the heath between Diggory Venn and Damon Wildeve is interrupted by the moth, prefiguring trouble ahead:

'Nearly twenty minutes passed thus. The light of the candle had by this time attracted heath-flies, moths and other winged creatures of the night, which floated around the lantern, flew into the flame, or beat about the faces of the two players . . . Ten minutes passed away. Then a large death's head moth advanced from the obscure outer air, wheeled twice round the lantern, flew straight at the candle, and extinguished it by the force of the blow.'[27]

Similarly, the moth provides the clue to Holman Hunt's apparently happy painting *The Hireling Shepherd*, first exhibited in 1851. At a glance, this is a sun-sparkled scene of young love and pastoral bliss: the virile young man snuggles up to his comely lass with a cute little lamb in her lap. He is presenting to her a moth he has found, but it is a Death's-head moth. We then notice that the shepherd's neglected

A close-up of the real Death's-head, a mimic queen bee.

flock has wandered into the corn; several sheep have fallen over and seem unable to get up. The girl's lamb is gorging on green apples, which will give it the colic. Even the girl seems to have a dawning awareness that something is not right.

The Death's-head Hawkmoth was famously at the centre of *The Silence of the Lambs*, a novel by Thomas Harris, made into a celebrated horror film starring Jodie Foster and Anthony Hopkins. A serial killer on the loose has the strange habit of leaving the pupa of the Death's-head Hawkmoth inside the mouths of his victims (technically speaking, the film uses the pupa of another species because it looks more dramatic). It is the key to the killer's twisted ambition to metamorphose himself. Agent Clarice Starling, played by Foster, knows she has found the monster's lair when she spots a Death's-head moth fluttering in a darkened house. A computer-enhanced version of the moth appears prominently

jodie foster / anthony hopkins / scott glenn

the silence of the lambs

from the terrifying best seller

A computer-manipulated Death's-head moth, the sinister trademark of the serial killer in The Silence of the Lambs.

on the film posters, sitting spread-winged on the lips of the wide-eyed Jodie Foster. Close inspection reveals that this death's head is not that of the real moth but a representation of three naked women in the form of a skull, taken from a painting by Salvador Dalí called *In Voluptas Mors*. The idea is based on a line from *The Worshipper of the Image*, by Richard le Galliennes: 'The eyes of Silencieux were wide open, and from her lips hung a dark moth with the face of death between its wings.' It is a modern echo of the ancient belief that the souls of the dead escape from the earthly body as moths.

Convolvulus Hawkmoth, *Agrius convolvuli*

The original name for this large grey moth was the Unicorn Hawk, referring to the long projection at the head end of its pupa that houses the moth's exceptionally long proboscis. The Convolvulus Hawk is an immigrant that arrives in irregular numbers in late summer and often visits gardens, especially where night-scented flowers, such as tobacco plants, are grown. Late evening is the best time for watching it feeding at the hover on wings larger than those of some hummingbirds. The moth has become much more common in recent years, and people operating moth-lamps on the south coast in early autumn can now expect to see one sooner or later. One lucky trapper met with dozens, swooping around his head, possibly a rather unsettling experience. Coastal bird observatories regularly report their large mottled and spotted caterpillars feeding on bindweed in the garden.

They say you can sometimes make out a monkey's face on the moth's thorax if you stare hard enough.

Elephant Hawkmoth, *Deilephila elpenor*

The Elephant Hawkmoth is one of our most beautiful moths, as bright as a butterfly in shades of olive-green and salmon-pink. Its strange name is supplied by the remarkable caterpillar, which has an extensible snout that, in combination with a pair of eyespots, gives it the appearance of a legless pig. Indeed, the Elizabethan physician and proto-entomologist Thomas Muffet, who first described it, called it *porcellus*, the little pig. When fully extended, the snout becomes more like a trunk, and so other early entomologists, perhaps better acquainted with elephants than Muffet, renamed it the Elephant Hawk, keeping 'little pig' for its diminutive cousin, the Small Elephant Hawk. It could equally well be called the snake hawk, for, when alarmed, the caterpillar contracts its trunk and swells up impressively with bulging false eyes, giving it the look of an angry serpent. The caterpillar feeds on willowherb in marshy places, including gardens, and is one of the few which can actually swim (when it might resemble a small grass snake). The moth itself is sometimes affectionately known as the Pink Elephant.

'When I was 12, the fields behind my parent's house in Dewsbury, Yorkshire, teemed with insect life. In July and August I would collect Elephant Hawkmoth caterpillars from the rosebay willowherb which grew in profusion on waste ground. I would often come back with twenty or so dark brown "elephants" which I would feed, allow to pupate and wait for them to hatch the following

A Hummingbird Hawkmoth hovers at a cigar flower (cuphea). *It will return day after day to a favourite border or buddleia bush.*

June. Although this was a magical experience for me, my mother was less impressed as I frequently came back not loaded with "catties" but also with my black school duffel-coat totally covered in difficult-to-remove willowherb seeds. I looked like a very odd Christmas snowman.'[28]

Hummingbird Hawkmoth, *Macroglossum stellatarum*

At St Ives, where the young Virginia Woolf spent her summer holidays, the Hummingbird Hawkmoth was a frequent and familiar visitor, known as 'merrylee-dance-a-pole', from its zigzag, hovering flight, as though tethered to an invisible stake. Elsewhere she describes its 'tremulous ecstasy' when feeding at a flower.[29]

In his *The Book of a Naturalist* (1919), W. H. Hudson quoted from a letter sent to him by 'a lady some years ago' about another encounter with merrylee-dance-a-pole, commenting that its warmth of tone and generosity of sentiment made a sad contrast with run-of-the-mill nature writing:

Only on the hottest and longest of summer days did the radiant being delight our eyes; to have seen it conferred high honour and distinction on the fortunate beholder. We regarded it with mingled awe and joy, and followed its erratic and rapid flight with ecstasy. It was soft and warm and brown, fluffy and golden, too, and created in our infantile minds an indescribable impression of glory, brilliance, aloofness, elusiveness. We thought it a being from some other world ... and I longed to be a Merrylee-dance-a-pole myself to fly to unheard-of, unthought-of, undreamed-of beautiful flowery lands.

The warm summer of 2006 was a vintage year for Hummingbird Hawks. In many places in the Midlands and south, these exotic moths, whose wings are lost in a fawn blur, like a large spotted bee, would be seen hovering at buddleia or clover or buzzing along hot, dusty tracks. There was a similar influx in summer 2000, when they were reported from parks and gardens the length of Britain. They can be attracted to gardens by planting nectar-rich flowers such as petunia and honeysuckle, though they are said to prefer red valerian above all flowers, especially when grown on walls in the full sun.

> Almost every year I have spotted them in our garden and observed that, despite the wide range of flowers, they only seem to feed on the same pink phloxes, or occasionally on pink hydrangea.[30]

Hummingbird Hawks occasionally fool urban journalists into filing sensational reports about escaped hummingbirds (global warming, indeed). But the moth has become more familiar of late, and there are reports of it successfully hibernating in greenhouses and sheltered places. The moths are known to 'trap-line' flower beds – that is, to return to the same patch at the same time each day. This has prompted animal behaviourists to test the moth's visual memory and find that it does indeed have the ability to learn and memorise particular colours and hence return to a favourite object.

Hummingbird Hawkmoths are sometimes known simply as 'hummingbird moths' or, more confusingly, as 'bee-hawks'. We have a pair of genuine bee mimics, the Broad-bordered and the Narrow-bordered Bee Hawkmoths. Both make very convincing mock-bumblebees, with their plump, fuzzy bodies and transparent wings. They fly by day with a bee-like buzz and hover at flowers like bees; they can be distinguished from real bees by their longer antennae and quieter hum.

Pine Hawkmoth, *Hyloicus pinastri*

With so many of our moths in decline, it is comforting to find at least one that has increased. A century ago, the Pine Hawk was regarded as a rarity, but the planting of pine and other conifers on commons and heaths has aided its natural spread across southern and eastern England. By the 1990s, it had become established as far north as Yorkshire.

It is a common visitor to garden moth traps, where its handsome, arrow-like shape and white-dusted grey wings make it a favourite.

Spurge Hawkmoth, *Hyles euphorbiae*

The original name for this beautiful migrant moth was the Spotted Elephant, a reference to its polka-dotted caterpillar but also, metaphorically, to its fabulous rarity. The first one was caught near the home of the butterfly-collecting Duchess of Portland in 1776 and duly took its place in her cabinet. Around a quarter century later, a sensational find in north Devon suggested that the Spurge Hawk was an overlooked breeding species. A William Raddon of Barnstaple claimed he was hunting butterflies over the nearby dunes of Braunton Burrows when he discovered the moth's spotted caterpillars 'aplenty' on plants of sea spurge growing near the shore. Gathering an armful of the plant to feed them, he found that they, too, were crawling with baby caterpillars. It is a nice story, and ensured that the moth took its due place in every book as an overlooked resident. Unfortunately, it is probably untrue. Raddon was apparently a part-time dealer in natural curios and had an obvious motive in broadcasting such tales.[31] In fact, with an average of just one moth every four years, the Spurge Hawk is hardly British at all.

A similar tall tale is told of the 'luck' of the Victorian collector A. B. Farn. Having inspected and rejected a pair of 'reputed British' Spurge Hawks for sale, he supposedly returned home to find a freshly emerged Spurge Hawk clinging to his front doorknob.[32] Possibly someone was playing a practical joke, or perhaps this is an apocryphal tale that grew even taller with the telling.

Prominents and kittens
Notodontidae

The prominents are a group of good-looking moths with fluffy forelegs, chunky, furry bodies and wing-patterns designed to mirror as closely as possible the textures and tones of bark. Their 'prominent' part is a triangular projection on each forewing shaped like the fin of a shark. Its function is probably to help break up its outline when the moth is at rest (it obviously works, for the moths are very hard to find by day). But in the days before light-traps, the caterpillars were better known than the moths, and the scientific names are often taken from their characteristics, such as the Pebble Prominent, whose species name *ziczac* recalls the zigzag shape of its larva, or *dromedarius*, the Iron Prominent, which has a camel-like hump.

The English names, by contrast, refer to a character of the adult moth. The Pebble Prominent, formerly known as just the Pebble, takes its name from a round, pebble-like wing mark. The Coxcomb Prominent has a tall, pointed thoracic crest like a jester's cap. The Iron Prominent has rust-like markings on a steely grey background. The male Plumed Prominent has large, feathery antennae. The name of the Swallow Prominent, however, is not so clear. Though it bears the usual 'prominent' tufts, nothing about the moth or its caterpillar is obviously swallow-like. Most likely, the name is a corruption of sallow, its larval food-plant (there is also a Lesser Swallow Prominent moth, whose food-plant is birch).

To P. B. M. Allan, the twentieth-century moth expert, whose literary soubriquet was the Old Moth Hunter, the Swallow Prominent was 'aesthetically the perfect insect . . . He is, to me, the *summa perfectionis* of outline, of tints, of design; the perfect *tout ensemble*.' Yet its caterpillar is, by contrast, among the ugliest: 'What plan had Dame Nature in mind', complained Allan, 'when she ordained that so fair an insect should spring from so foul a grub? His skin shines as though it were slimy. It wrinkles in the wrong places. He takes up ungainly attitudes. He obtrudes his dirty yellow belly to your gaze whenever he can. He is a most obnoxious beast. I could readily believe that he smells.' What really annoyed him was that it was almost impossible to rear: '"Thank you; but I prefer to die" is the attitude of about fifty per cent of him.'[33]

Lobster moth, *Stauropus fagi*

The Lobster Moth is a big, furry, browny-grey moth that looks nothing like a lobster. The name celebrates its caterpillar, one of the most extraordinary in the natural world, whose forelegs resemble outstretched claws and whose body swells and cantilevers back on itself like a lobster's tail (the

A full-grown Lobster Moth caterpillar, once believed to be a poisonous beetle.

lobster stage is preceded by one in which the young caterpillar looks like an ant, with six long, spindly legs). Until people managed to rear it and watched what one entomologist called 'the crustaceous fish' miraculously turn into an ordinary looking moth, the caterpillar was considered to be a kind of beetle, related to the Devil's Coach-horse. Thomas Muffet warned that it could sting or even poison horses.

Lobster Moth (1999), by the Aberdeen-born writer Niall Duthie, is an ingenious tragicomic tale of two men living in different times but with connected lives. The theme is about the nature of interpretation, and the moth, the embodiment of a collector's desire for a rare moth, is also a symbol of metamorphosis, from caterpillar to moth or from one person to another.

More straightforward is *Lobster Moths*, Diane Massie's children's story of a professor and his cat. Both are avid moth collectors, the Prof for his collection, the cat for its dinner. They get their comeuppance when the 'lobster moth fairy' turns them into moths, promising them 'big troubles' to come.[34]

Puss moths and kittens

VN: millard, miller

Before entomology became a science, people noticed moths and caterpillars only when they were exceptionally distinctive or common or when they caused damage to our fabrics, crops and gardens. No caterpillar is more distinctive than the Puss Moth, with its plump, swollen body, mask-like 'face' and pair of twitching 'tails'. As long ago as the sixteenth century, it was known as 'vinula', after the creature's wine-coloured 'saddle'; *'Elegans mehercules eruca!'* wrote Thomas Muffet in admiration. 'By Jove, what a handsome caterpillar!'[35] Izaak Walton was equally impressed by its 'eyes black as jet; his forehead purple; his feet and hinder parts green; his tails two-forked and black'. Towards winter, the caterpillar spun its cocoon, 'a strange shell or crust, called an aurelia,' in which it passed the winter as 'a kind of dead life'.[36] Whether or not a moth emerged from this aurelia in the spring, he does not say.

It was Moses Harris who discovered what the waving tails did: 'When provoked, he [the caterpillar] thrusts out two red arrows of a tender elastic substance . . . and upon a repeated insult, ejects from thence a thin liquor, which they have often squirted

Lifecycle of the Puss Moth *by Richard Lewington.*

in the face of them which attempt to injure them.'[37] The 'liquor' is formic acid, and the caterpillar has an accurate range of about 60 centimetres. It does not blister the skin, but a squirt in the eye can sting.

The name Puss Moth was current by the early eighteenth century, but does it refer to the caterpillar or the moth? Both have feline attributes. The caterpillar has a pair of false eyes that look like cat's eyes, and it flicks its tail when irritated. But equally, the moth has a Persian-cat fluffiness, with woolly legs. Its smaller relatives are known as kitten moths. In America, the puss caterpillar is an unrelated species with stinging hairs, also known as an asp.

'Some years after the First World War,' wrote L. Hugh Newman, 'I was lunching with a young aircraft designer who mentioned that they were having difficulty in finding suitable names for various types of planes then being evolved. "Why not use moth names?" I suggested. "Puss Moth, for instance." "Not a bad idea," he said, "I must remember that."'[38] By coincidence or not, the Puss Moth biplane appeared a few years later, followed in due course by the Gipsy Moth and Tiger Moth.

Tussock moths *Lymantriidae*

The nine British species of tussock moths (plus two more which have died out) are all furry, medium-sized moths, some of them with gleaming white, ghost-like wings. Their caterpillars are similarly hairy, and some bear tufts or 'tussocks'. The species that gave its name to the whole family is the Pale Tussock, whose tessellated caterpillar bears a row of beautiful white tufts along its back. It is often seen basking on warm woodland paths in the early autumn and used to be common in hop-yards – hence its country names of 'hop-dog' or 'hop-cat'.

The small, rich-brown moth known as the Vapourer is often seen flying by day, jinking along walls and windows in search of the flightless female. At one time, it was also known as the Lime-tree Tussock, from the moth's habit of flying around street trees in London. The name Vapourer probably refers to the caterpillar, which has spouts of long, dark hair that look like a conventional drawing of vapour escaping from a nozzle. But it might allude to the invisible pheromone 'vapour' of the female moth that draws in the winged males from far and wide. Collectors took advantage of the male Vapourer's sense of chemical detection by hanging a boxed female from a branch and waiting for the males to assemble. The practice was called assembling or 'sembling'.

The Yellow-tail and Brown-tail moths have stinging caterpillars that are best not handled. The Brown-tail has loose hairs that can cause a skin rash or inflammation if they get into the eyes. The moths themselves are an innocent pure white, contrasting with a dab of bright yellow or brown at the ends of their bodies. The female camouflages her eggs with hair from her swollen, coloured 'tail', which may also keep them warm. The fur covers the moth's genital area, which probably explains the scientific name of the Pale Tussock, *pudibunda*, meaning 'blushing', or maidenly modest.

The caterpillars of the Brown-tail live colonially in nests on trees and shrubs. Sometimes their numbers build up to the extent that they defoliate the whole plant, leaving bare twigs and messy tents of silk. Among the worst affected trees are apples, plums, pears and cherries. Though the caterpillars rarely cause permanent damage to a tree, they are at their peak of growth in the spring when the trees are in blossom. Hence a bad attack can rob orchards and gardens of most of their fruit. Perhaps fortunately,

A colour plate by William Curtis, from A Short History of the Brown-tail Moth, *published in 1782.*

the moth is confined mainly to south-east England, especially the coast and the Thames estuary. A century ago it was regarded as rare, so much so that collectors were asked not to take too many.

The worst outbreak of recent times was in 1947–8, when the caterpillars defoliated hedgerows and trees on Canvey Island and other parts of the Essex coast. There was a similar explosion of Brown-tails in London in 1782. Prayers were offered to avert the evil, and practical steps were taken in the form of a pamphlet that has been hailed as the first scientific investigation of a horticultural pest. Written by William Curtis, editor of the *Botanical Magazine*, it delved into the life-history of the moth, whose 'caterpillars are at present uncommonly numerous and destructive in the Vicinity of the Metropolis', leaving ragged webs on 'almost every hedge, tree and shrub in London.' There were then no horticultural advisors or government scientists to allay the imaginary terrors of the public, still liable to see such things in apocalyptic terms, and so Curtis stepped in with a reasoned investigation aimed at giving 'a true idea of the nature of these Insects'. He rightly concluded that Brown-tail numbers are controlled primarily by their parasites, the 'grandest' of which was an ichneumon wasp. He was also right to link the outbreak with exceptionally hot weather and correctly predicted that the caterpillars would disappear of their own accord inside a year or two.[39]

Curtis's advice for dealing with the Brown-tail was remarkably similar to what local authorities are offering today. Since the caterpillars spend most of their time snug inside their nests, spraying the nests with rat poison or chimney soot or, in our own time, with permitted insecticides, is useless. The practical solution is to prune the bushes and burn the webs and the larvae inside them on a bonfire. In 1782, parishes employed the urban poor to cut off and collect the webs at a shilling per bushel, casting them into the flames under the eye of the local church warden. In a single day, four-score bushels of caterpillars were collected in the parish of Clapham alone. In the 1990s, a more merciful bio-control method was introduced at Portsmouth: pheromone lures, which divert the female moths and so prevent breeding.

Lutestring moths *Thyatiridae*

Our nine species of lutestring moths include two of our prettiest, the Buff Arches and the Peach Blossom – the moth-world's answer to Laura Ashley wallpaper. Some of these moths, notably the Satin Lutestring, have curiously glossy wings. The name lutestring comes not from lutes but from an appropriately shiny fabric known as lustrine, once used to make dresses and ribbons.

Laura Ashley colours: the Peach Blossom Moth.

Eggars *Lasiocampidae*

The eggars are another small family of ten resident species, which includes some of our largest and best-known moths, notably the Fox Moth, the Drinker, the Oak Eggar, the Lappet and the Lackey. They are all thick-set, hairy moths in warm brown or yellowish colours and with similarly plump, hairy caterpillars. Some of the caterpillars have irritant hairs that allow them to feed and bask by day, and has made them and, in some cases, their silken cocoons as familiar as the adult moths. They are eaten with gusto by cuckoos.

Eggar is an obsolete word that refers to the oval, egg-shaped cocoons of the Oak Eggar moth. They are easy to spot on commons and moors and were once considered by country folk to be silk-wrapped eggs. Some people believed the eggs to be laid by moths, but others, having perhaps observed hairy larvae in the vicinity, claimed that it was the *caterpillars* that had done the laying. Either way, they were 'eggars', a folk-name that has made its way into entomology.

P. B. M. Allan must have had his tongue firmly in his cheek when he suggested in *A Moth-Hunter's Gossip* (1937) that the female Oak Eggar moth, with its soft, broad, yellow wings, was probably named after an omelette. But the whole name is nonsensical: the Oak Eggar does not live or feed on oak trees, nor does its relative the Grass Eggar depend on grass. Like the names of several other moths, the early entomologists got their facts wrong, but the names have stuck because no one ever saw any need to change them. Nonsense names are part of the charm of moths.

The male Oak Eggar has a madcap, zigzag flight that makes it very difficult to catch. Allan recalled an encounter with the moth one hot afternoon after, it appears, a liquid lunch:

> Oak Eggars drive me nearly mad . . . He flies like no other insect inhabiting these islands. He flies like a mad airman in a cranky aeroplane in a nightmare. He zooms and sideslips and corkscrews, and all the time he has his eye on me and comes nearer and nearer. It is utterly impossible to disregard him . . . His mad dance fascinates me. He is as a stoat performing acrobatics before a rabbit, as indeed I am in his presence, ever wheeling nearer and nearer,

A female Oak Eggar Moth: teddy-bear fluffiness.

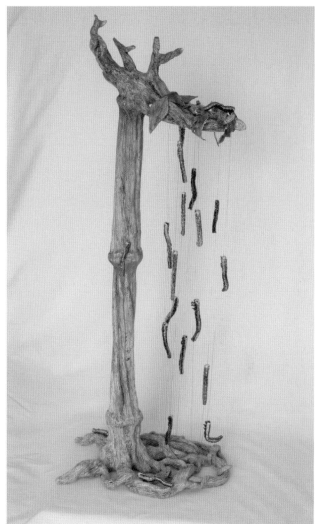

Abseil – Lackey Moth Caterpillars, *a sculpture by Jill Moger in stone, wire and porcelain.*

until he is within striking distance . . . As he approaches, I grip my net tightly, and my arm quivers. Suddenly he comes straight at me. I make a terrific swish – my hat flies off – he buzzes round my head – I leap at him, into the middle of a bramble bush – swish, swish – I step into a rabbit hole – he zooms up fifty feet and disappears through a chink in the oak-trees. I quiver with rage and curse him loud and long, and get my fingers full of thorns in disentangling my net from the brambles.[40]

Other eggars are named after their caterpillars. The Drinker Moth's hairy larva is often found on grass stems, apparently drinking the dew. This habit was noted long ago by a Dutch naturalist Jan Goedart, who in 1662 spotted one 'dipping its head in the water and then lifting it up as hens do, which it repeats over and over again.'[41] He named it the Drinker, a name Linnaeus borrowed for its scientific name, *potatoria* (in fact many other caterpillars also 'drink' in this way). As for the adult Drinker moth, Roger Deakin (2007) suggested you imagine something 'soft, pale bear-brown, furry, chubby, sturdy,' 'a teddy bear with a handlebar moustache, its antennae branched into delicate combs, like the cow-catcher on an old American steam locomotive.'[42]

The equally hairy caterpillar of the Fox Moth has distinctive pale rings and is often found sunbathing on paths in the spring. When disturbed, it curls up tight into a ball, and this, together with its stinging hairs, gave the caterpillar its old country name of 'the devil's gold ring'. The name Fox Moth dates from 1720 and is most appropriate to the russet-coloured male moth, whose jerky flight in the afternoon sunshine makes it one of the more familiar large moths. Moreover, it frequents commons and sandy places used by foxes. The Fox Moth and its relatives are the best match for the 'hully butterflies', a name used in the Furness district of Cumbria for large, heavy moths.

The Lackey Moth is a common, though much declined, moth whose caterpillars spin tents on low shrubs especially, it seems, in supermarket car parks and new housing estates. The eighteenth-century naturalist Moses Harris tells us why it was so named: the caterpillar had 'strips of different colours' – blue, red and white – which reminded people of the livery lace then worn by household servants, or lackeys.[43]

When fully grown, the Lappet Moth has one

Birds, Butterflies and a Frog (*1688*) *by the Dutch still-life artist Melchior d'Hondecoeter. Most of the 'butterflies' are, in fact, Emperor Moths, attracted to the scent of a captive female moth, a collecting method known as 'assembling'.*

of the largest caterpillars of any British moth, fat, brown, magnificently hairy and the size of a cigar. It is less familiar than one might expect because it is active only by night, when it feeds on low hawthorn, blackthorn or sallow bushes. The name lappet is applicable both to the moth and its larva. The former has scalloped edges to the wings similar to the leather lappets on medieval tunics, while the caterpillar has a similarly shaped row of fleshy false feet running down the length of its body. Their effect is to 'fuse' the caterpillar to the twig so that, despite its great size, it is hard to spot.

A moth that has caused controversy in Scotland is the Pine-tree Lappet, recently found in mixed woodland near Inverness. The Forestry Commission, noting that the moth is a listed pest species of pine plantations in Europe, was all for wiping it out before it could spread any further. On the other hand, as the entomologist Mark Tunmore pointed out, it is not impossible that the Pine-tree Lappet is an overlooked native species, in which case it should be protected. Besides, he added, it is hardly possible to target one kind of moth without hurting others.

Emperor moths *Saturniidae*

The Emperor Moth is our only native silk moth, a modest-sized relative of the Atlas Moth; it is also related to the commercial silkworm. It is instantly recognisable by its peacock-like eyespots (hence its scientific name, *Saturnia pavonia*). The male moth can be seen flying by day on commons, moors and open woods in an erratic, zigzag way as it picks up the scent trail of a female moth. The peacock eyes probably deflect a predator's attention from the moth's plump, banded body to the more expendable parts of its wings. They also help to make the moth appear threatening and impressive, like a baleful mask, which it accentuates with menacing quivers of its wings. None of this seems to impress small birds of prey such as the merlin, whose regular plucking posts are often surrounded by snapped-off Emperor Moth wings in the spring (the plucking posts are, in fact, a useful way of recording merlins as well as big moths).

Silk is produced not by adult moths but by their caterpillars. The silk of the Emperor has no commercial value, but the ingenious construction of its cocoons was commented on in 1766 by Moses Harris:

The Web or Case wherein they change to the Chrysalis is greatly to be admired, being so wonderfully formed for the security of the enclosed Insect; the entrance or part designed by Nature, for the coming forth of the Moth is so contrived, that it is almost impossible for any Insect to enter; and should they attain the Mouth of the Case, which they cannot do, without being very much embarrassed with the Web, they will meet with a second and more impassable defence, which is set with a sort of Spikes, which all meet in a point or centre, something like the contrivance which is common to be seen in some sort of Mouse-traps, which easily admits the Animal one way, but wholly forbids and opposes its return.[44]

Commercial silk is produced from the cocoons of a flightless silkmoth, *Bombyx mori*, whose larvae are known as silkworms. Silk-weaving originated in China, but the skill was imported to Europe during the Middle Ages. From the late eighteenth century onwards, Britain began manufacturing silk, with a trade centre at Spitalfields in London and, later, in factories in a number of industrial towns. Several of the leading silk-pattern designers, such as Joseph Dandridge and James Leman, were keen naturalists, who reared, studied and collected insects and were probably responsible for the large number of fabric-based names among our moths. British silk fabrics used imported raw silk, but in the 1930s, Lady Hart-Dyke developed a small-scale, home-grown silk farm at Lullingstone Castle in Hertfordshire, where 21 acres of mulberry bushes fed enough caterpillars to produce 20 pounds of silk per week. For reasons of prestige, British silk produced the wedding dresses of both the Queen and, after the farm moved to Dorset in 1975, of Princess Diana.

The beautiful Kentish Glory moth is a distant relative of the silk moths and is placed in a family of its own, the Endromidae. It has a fluffy body, to keep out the cold, and warm brown, delicately blotched and striped wings. This is another moth with a nonsensical name, and for the saddest of reasons. It was indeed once found in Kent, having been caught there for the first time in mid-April 1741, 'flying in a wood in the day-time, near Cookham, by Westram [i.e., Westerham] in Kent.'[45] But it died out there in the nineteenth century and is now extinct in England. The moth's remaining stronghold lies at the opposite end of the country, among scrub birch on the moors of north-east and central Scotland.

Tiger moths *Arctiidae*

VN: coach-and-horses, hairy Hubert (NE Eng.), loggerhead, oobit, oolly-worm, Tommy Tailor, woolly bear, woubit

John Keats wrote of the 'tiger-moth's deep-damask'd wings'.[46] Damask is woven silk, producing characteristically smooth, velvety and richly coloured patterns, and is a perfect analogy with the wings of the Garden Tiger and its relatives. The moths look as though they have flown on silken wings out of a tapestry or Pre-Raphaelite painting.

Yet their name is a misnomer. Most tiger moths are spotted, not striped, and they should strictly speaking be leopard moths (only one British species, the Jersey Tiger, has tiger-stripes). Leopard was indeed the name James Petiver, the father of butterfly names, used for them, but the later naturalists preferred tigers. Meanwhile, their family, the Arctiidae, is named after bears (from *arctia*, Greek for 'bear'), a reference to their 'woolly bear' caterpillars. The smaller moths are 'ermines', after their pale, black-flecked wings, similar to the ermine furs worn by royalty. There is also a whole subfamily of 'footmen' moths, which share the stiff, narrow outlines of eighteenth-century household servants.

The Garden Tiger is one of the best-known British moths. Its hairy, fast-trundling caterpillar was known in the Middle Ages as the 'walbode' or 'wall bear', and in more recent times as 'Tommy

Tailor', 'coach-and-horses' or, most often, as the 'woolly bear'. In nineteenth-century Shropshire it was considered lucky to have a Tommy Tailor creep up on you. The adult moth has been called 'loggerhead' in northern England. It has bright red or orange hindwings as a sign that it is distasteful; like other moths in this family, it stores toxic alkaloids to deter predators. The woolly bear, too, has a defence in the form of stinging hairs, though only people with sensitive skin are at risk.

The Garden Tiger has, unfortunately, become much less common in recent years, especially in eastern England. It may have been evicted from some public spaces by spraying and tidying up, but there is strong circumstantial evidence that the main reason is climate change. The species hibernates as a half-grown caterpillar and needs reasonably cold winters to avoid waking up. Damp, mild Januaries are its downfall.

Certain other tiger moths, by contrast, are commoner than they were. The Scarlet Tiger flies by day in marshy places, with vivid flashes of red, black and white, and seems to have benefited from the spread of its food-plant comfrey on riverbanks, as well as the moth's ability to disperse widely to take advantage of changing circumstances. The genetics of the Scarlet Tiger were studied intensively at Oxford University by E. B. Ford and his colleagues to elucidate how evolution by natural selection worked in the field. Some of the footman moths have also increased since the lichens on which they depend have benefited from the cleaner air, especially in towns and cities.

The Cinnabar is another common and familiar day-flying moth, so-named because its wings are the colour of the mineral cinnabar, once used as an artist's reddish-pink pigment. It, too, has a familiar caterpillar, sometimes known as a 'football jersey' from its orange and black stripes. Cinnabar caterpillars are a natural control for ragwort. On a warm, sunny day, a single one can strip a ragwort plant in minutes. Hence the moth has been used as a would-be bio-control of the ragwort 'yellow peril' in America and Australasia. Expectations were eventually disappointed, though to begin with the moth did make inroads into the ocean of ragwort on the overgrazed plains of Australia.

In Britain, too, farmers and landowners have experimented with Cinnabars, with some success. But it is unlikely that their numbers can keep pace with the spread of ragwort because, as the ecologist Jack Dempster demonstrated 20 years ago, vast

A Garden Tiger Moth on a stained glass window dated 1939 at St Mary's Church, East Brent, Somerset.

Cinnabar caterpillars, or 'football jerseys', on ragwort.

numbers of their pupae are eaten every winter by moles. When, in a panic reaction to reports of horses dying from consuming ragwort, the Ragwort Control Act was passed in 2003, the accent was on prevention rather than control. In places where the ragwort had taken over, DEFRA's advice was to mow or to spray. No one suggested using Cinnabar Moths.

Tiger moths lent their name to a famous biplane designed by de Havilland in 1931 and which served the Royal Air Force as a trainer and glider tug until the 1950s. Based on the design of the earlier Gipsy Moth, the Tiger Moth also saw civilian use as a crop-sprayer and is still used by flying clubs throughout the world. The aircraft's name is quite meaningless: De Havilland was in the habit of naming its biplanes after moths (*see* Puss Moth), and this particular name just sounded good.

Noctuids *Noctuidae*

Most of the grayish or brownish moths that appear on the windowpane after dark will be Noctuids. They are the largest family of larger moths, with just over 400 British species. By custom, all have English names, even those such as Lorimer's Rustic or Spalding's Dart, which are recent discoveries or long-distance vagrants known only by a record or two. The family includes migrants, such as the Silver Y moth, which often arrives in vast numbers from Spain in late summer. Most species have bald, worm-like caterpillars and only one generation per year. Britain's smallest 'macro' moth is a noctuid. So is one of our largest, the rare and beautiful Blue Underwing.

The names of noctuid moths have exercised the imaginations of past entomologists to the limit. They found poetry and expression in the drabbest of moths and fashioned names from the merest hint in their wing markings, among them being darts, brocades, shears, daggers, ears, shoulder-knots, arches and coronets. Brownish or grey moths lacking such marks were often called clays, drabs or quakers. Others, such as sallows, sword-grasses or the sweet-gale moth, were named after their real or supposed food-plants. Snout moths have long noses (actually, palps); fan-feet have curious tufts of hair on their legs. Sharks have grey, tapering bodies. Certain names are simply descriptive: golden twin-spot, double-line, rosy marbled, dot moth. Others seem to have been composed in a dream-like state of consciousness: heart and dart, green-brindled crescent, silver cloud, the alchymist. Just a few are named after their caterpillars. That of the sprawler has an odd way of rearing back and sprawling its fore-legs in what it intends to be a threatening manner.

A few noctuids, notably the Turnip Moth and the Cabbage Moth (which Moses Harris sympathetically called the Old Gentlewoman), whose caterpillars are known as cutworms, can be a minor nuisance in gardens and allotments but are rarely present in large numbers. Species in the genus *Spodoptera* are notorious crop pests in warmer countries, where they are known as leafworms or armyworms. In Britain, however, where they are only occasional immigrants, we know them as 'willows'. The injurious moth known to the world as the bollworm is, in Britain, called the Scarce Bordered Straw, a rare and cherished migrant (though, with help from global warming, it certainly has pest potential in the near future).

Perhaps the most headlined noctuid of recent times is the pretty, reddish Pine Beauty, which normally lives at low density on natural and planted Scots pines, doing no harm. In the late 1970s, however, it suddenly became a serious pest of pines planted on peat in the far north of Scotland where, in the absence of its natural predators and parasites, the moth quickly multiplied. Forestry companies went to great lengths to try to control it, including spraying insecticides from aircraft and using pheromone lures designed to prevent mating. By chance, the Pine Beauty was targeting conifers planted as a tax dodge on what until then had been pristine peat bogs. Many conservationists, I suspect, saw the moth as an avatar of vengeance for the environmental damage caused by tax-avoidance planting in the 1980s.

Among the largest and most attractive noctuids are the underwing moths, some of which form a distinct subfamily, the Catocalinae. The forewings of the Red Underwing are grey and mottled for a life spent resting quietly by day on willow stumps. But

A Dark Crimson Underwing Moth painted by Richard Lewington, wings partly open to reveal what Linnaeus saw as the moth's gaudy undergarment.

when disturbed, it flies off rapidly with a sudden red flash. Its surprise hindwings are bright red with a black band, intended to give a would-be predator an unsettling moment and so allowing the moth time to get away. The effect is even more dazzling by torchlight, when the banded underwings seem to flicker and flash as the moth passes overhead.

This flashing habit seems to have caught the imagination of the great Swedish naturalist Carl Linnaeus (1707–78) when he came to name these moths. In each case he found a Latin name allusive to marriage: the Red Underwing became *nupta*, meaning a bride; the Common Yellow Underwing became *pronuba*, that is, a bridesmaid; while the Dark and Light Crimson Underwings were named *sponsa* – meaning 'sponsored in marriage' – and *promissa*, or 'pledged in marriage' (hence both names mean fiancée). What was going on in his mind? Linnaeus did not elaborate, but in his book on moth names, Maitland Emmet suggests it was all about underwear. 'Did eighteenth-century brides in Sweden wear gaudy underwear to stimulate the groom, or did Linnaeus think they ought to do so?'[47] Linnaeus, it seems, was in the habit of naming pretty moths after women, as in the Scarlet Tiger, *dominula* (lady of the house), and the Cream-spot Tiger, *villica* (lady of the villa). It was the flash of bridal knickers, whether red, yellow or crimson, that struck the mind of the great man as he ogled the great moths flickering by the light of his lantern.

The largest and most magnificent of the underwings is the Blue Underwing, also known as the Clifden Nonpareil or Clifden Beauty. Moses Harris, as usual, explained why: 'The first to be taken in England was at Clifden in Buckinghamshire in July. It was taken hanging against the pedestal of a statue, having just come out of a chrysalis, and was drying its wings.' This wonderful moth, he added, was now 'in the possession of Esquire Lockyer of Ealing'.[48]

The much less spectacular Orange Upperwing moth is the rather unlikely object at the heart of Allan Shepherd's modern fable *Curious Incidents in the Garden at Night-time* (2005). The moth, 'a fleck of honey-glazed orange fibre on a highway of bark', was last seen in the author's corner of Wales in 1994 and is now believed to be extinct in Britain. Its return, in the story at least, is a gift from the night.[49]

Looper moths *Geometridae*

VN: geometers, inchworms, measuring bugs, span-worms

The Geometridae is our second largest family of larger moths, with around 300 British species. They are often called geometers ('earth measurers') or loopers after the characteristic gait of their long, thin caterpillars. Their true legs at the front are separated from the false feet near the back, obliging them to move by looping and stretching their bodies (the pay-off is that they look like twigs or leaf stalks when at rest). Some, including the moths known as thorns, have realistic-looking prickles, bumps and scars that resemble leaf-bases. They are, in effect, the stick insects of the Lepidoptera.

Looper caterpillars are also known in America as inchworms, span-worms or measuring bugs. The inchworm's moment of fame came in the 1952 film *Hans Christian Andersen*, when, with a chorus of children chanting the times-table in the background, Danny Kaye croons to a caterpillar on a rather unrealistic herbaceous border.[50]

The seventeenth-century naturalist John Ray named several looper caterpillars after his three daughters, who brought him insects when he was too ill to hunt for them himself. Among them were Katherine's Eruca, Katherine's Oak-Geometer, Katherine's Ash-Geometer and Jane's Chickweed Caterpillar. One with a big head he simply called Grout-head.[51]

The adult moths generally rest with their wings flattened against the surface or, in the case of the attractive Orange Underwing, folded around a twig. Others park their wings over their bodies like a pitched roof, while a few press theirs together over their backs like a butterfly. The smaller geometers have a weak, fluttering flight, and some fly at dusk rather than at night. Collectors would hunt them in the twilight with butterfly nets in an activity they called 'dusking'. Many species are more easily found as larvae by searching or collecting quantities of their food-plants.

The entomologists of old loved the subtle shades and tints of these moths, bestowing on them such

Inchworm, the stick-like caterpillar of the Swallow-tailed Moth.

names as emeralds, carpets and beauties. The name Carpet Moth is apt to be misunderstood; it came about not because these moths nibble holes in rugs (they don't) but because of a fancied resemblance to eighteenth-century textile designs. A subset of small moths that settle with outspread wings is known as the pugs. They acquired the name at a time when pug dogs were popular lady's pets (Lady Bertram had one as a lap dog in Jane Austen's *Mansfield Park*). Any connection between a moth and a glum-looking dog may be hard to spot, but fortunately, the entomologist Adrian Haworth was there to inform us that 'the hindwing is shorter than the forewing, just as the lower lip of a pug-dog is shorter than its upper lip'. Their scientific genus name *Eupithecia* means 'pretty dwarf'.

The early appearance of certain geometers was the cue for a set of appropriately seasonal names: the Early Moth, the March Moth and the Spring Usher, followed in the fall by the Autumnal Moth, the November Moth and the Winter Moth. There are even a couple of high-summer names: the July Belle and the July Highflier (which has a relative, perhaps coined by a frustrated collector, called the Ruddy Highflyer), not to mention the August and the September Thorns.

A few loopers come to our attention because they occasionally defoliate trees. The main culprits are the caterpillars of the Winter Moth and the Mottled Umber (whose scientific name is *defoliaria*). The adult moths lay their eggs in midwinter so that their caterpillars can emerge just in time for the tenderest (and most nutritious) leaf growth in the spring. Gardeners would paint a band of creosote around their fruit trees to trap the wingless female Winter Moths as they crawl up the trunks to lay their eggs. Because they occur in enormous numbers, Winter Moth caterpillars are a key food source for breeding birds, notably Blue Tits and Great Tits. The latter times its clutches to coincide with the peak season for caterpillars.

Another well-known looper, the Magpie Moth, used to swarm over currant bushes in gardens. Both moth and caterpillar are brightly coloured and easy to spot, but birds avoid them as they store toxic biochemicals. Magpie Moths are much less common today, possibly because currant bushes are less often grown in gardens, possibly because, when they are, they are sprayed. Virtually every moth that depends on currant bushes has similarly declined, including the misnamed Spinach Moth and the V-Moth, so-called because of the V-shaped markings in its forewings.

In terms of its contribution to fundamental science, one of the most significant of all insects is a looper, the Peppered Moth. The normal form of the moth is pale and speckled (hence, 'pepper'), but in a famous example of evolution in action, a black form of the moth appeared in grimy industrial cities in the nineteenth century, which seemed to be a perfect working demonstration of Darwin's theory of natural selection. Since the black moths were less visible than the normal form on soot-blackened trees, more black ones survived to reproduce, and so the darker form gradually took over from the pale form. Scientific proof for this phenomenon became the life's work of a retired doctor, Bernard Kettlewell. His results were called into question by

intelligent-design advocates in the United States, but they were re-evaluated by the late Professor Michael Majerus at Cambridge and found to be correct. Industrial melanism is not confined to the Peppered Moth, for there are dark forms of many species, some of them now commoner than the typical form.

The Peppered Moth was the title of a 2001 novel by Margaret Drabble, which explored the fortunes of four generations of a family in a Yorkshire mining town. The moth symbolises Drabble's focus on heredity and how genes, DNA and the environment change or challenge individuals and influence their lives and behaviour.

Burnet moths *Zygaenidae*

VN: bloodsuckers, saund-sleeper, seven-sleeper (Cornwall)

Burnet-moths are day-flying insects that behave in a similar way to butterflies, visiting (and pollinating) flowers in the warm sunshine. Both the moths and their stumpy yellow-and-black caterpillars are conspicuous; they have no need for camouflage as they store toxic chemicals from their food-plants, vetches and trefoils. Even the papery cocoons are easy to spot on tall grass stems, often with the extruding remains of the dark pupa.

Numerous burnet moths buzzing around are as much a sign of environmental health as a singing skylark. Wherever there are downs, dunes, meadows and marshes with plenty of wild flowers, the moths seem to thrive, but they soon disappear when the habitat is drained or re-sown. There are seven species, ranging from the widespread and often common Six- and Five-spot Burnets to the endangered New Forest Burnet, long extinct in the New Forest but surviving precariously at the opposite end of Britain, on the west coast of Scotland. Equally rare is the Scotch, or Mountain, Burnet which is confined to a few hilltops in the Cairngorms and so vulnerable to climate change.

The early entomologists were not sure what to make of burnet moths. They seemed to represent a half-way stage between butterflies and moths, behaving much like butterflies but resting like moths with their wings angled like a pitched roof. Burnet seems to be an old folk-name similar to brunette, meaning dark-coloured. It has been suggested that the name also comes from their habit of sitting on salad burnet flowers. The moths are sometimes known as bloodsuckers, from their red hindwings and red-spotted forewings rather than any imagined sanguinary habits.[52]

Everyday insects such as burnet moths have an important, if unsung, role in getting some of us hooked for life on insects: 'My earliest memory of

Moth Balls II, by Claire Moynihan, a collection of hand-embroidered alpaca-wool felt balls inspired by museum collections of moths: 'I aim to celebrate the underrated moth, whilst commenting on the irony of our description of certain moths as "pests".'

insects is of collecting "red flies" in a jam-jar during the mid-1940s on the dunes at Ainsdale, Lancashire, when I was about three. These were actually burnet moths, which were abundant on the waste ground adjacent to the sand-dunes. I was already fascinated by insects when I went on to graduate in zoology, then a PhD on defoliating caterpillars, followed by a 25-year-career lecturing in ecology. So my early interest in creepy-crawlies paid off.'[53]

Forester moths are lesser-known cousins of the burnets and share their day-flying habits but have shiny green wings. There are three species, none of which occur in forests (except, maybe, in very large forest glades) but live on flowery hillsides and meadows. The name probably derives from the moth's colour: medieval foresters (as well as Robin Hood) are said to have worn 'Lincoln Green' tunics.

Clearwings *Sessiidae*

The novelist Vladimir Nabokov was fascinated by clearwings. These are moths that not only look like wasps but also behave like them, with very unmoth-like twitches of their long antennae. They seemed to him to have 'carried to a point of mimetic subtlety far in excess of the predator's power of appreciation'. Hence, 'I discovered in nature the non-utilitarian delights that I sought in art.'[54]

One clearwing is such an effective hornet-mimic that, at a glance, it is hard to tell them apart, and the smaller species mimic solitary wasps. The best known of our 16 species is the Currant Clearwing, whose caterpillars used to mine the twigs of currant

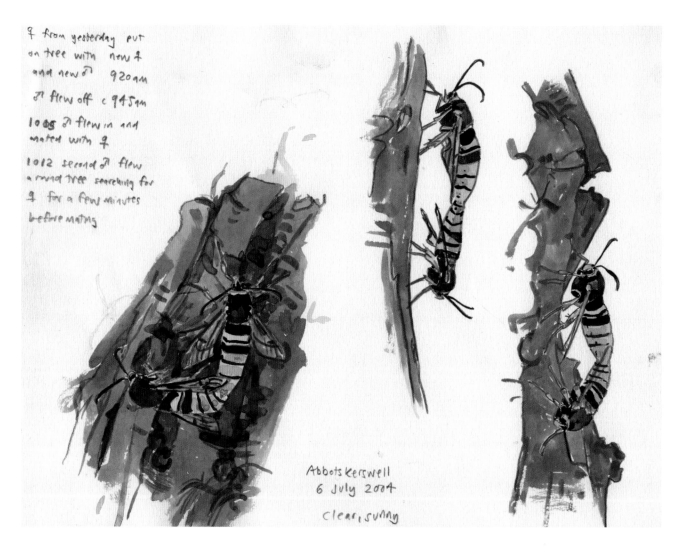

Lunar Hornet Moths, watercolour sketches by John Walters. 'Working in the field presents many challenges, such as the weather and the speed at which these small creatures move, but I enjoy the challenge and feel that the work captures some of the life and vitality of the subjects.'

bushes in gardens and allotments but has greatly declined since the 1960s. 'In North Lincolnshire we knew clearwing moths – especially the Currant Clearwing, which was quite common in gardens – as "stingers".'[55] A new one, dubbed the Raspberry Clearwing, was discovered in 2007, mining the stems of raspberry bushes on fruit farms in Cambridgeshire.

Adult clearwings are difficult to spot, and collectors used to look instead for the frass (droppings) and exit holes of their caterpillars. Now that pheromone lures are available, the moths have become much easier to detect and are proving commoner than was realised. They will come to the right lure in many gardens, and on a good day the males may buzz around the scent like wasps at a picnic.

The Goat Moth, named after the rank smell of its caterpillar, one of the few able to digest wood cellulose.

Goat moth *Cossidae*

VN: augur worms, carpenter moth, willow borer

The Goat Moth is named after the rank smell of its large, wood-boring caterpillar. Carl Linnaeus, who named the moth *cossus*, after a grub that the Romans enjoyed eating as a delicacy, was under the impression that the Goat Moth, too, was edible. Relatives of the Goat Moth known as witchety grubs are certainly eaten as bush-tucker in Australia – they are regularly served up raw to contestants on *I'm a Celebrity, Get Me Out of Here!* – but I have still to find anyone who has actually eaten the British species.

Goat Moth caterpillars are among the few insects that can digest wood cellulose. They live in burrows in the trunks of old willows and apple trees and give away their presence not only by their large, round exit holes (often oozing sap) but also by a pervasive smell of ripe billy goat. The adult moth is fat-bodied with short, broad wings etched with blackish veins quite unlike those of any other British moth. But it is rarely seen and is not attracted to light. It has been known to circle, slowly and ponderously, around trees painted with entomological sugar, but all to no purpose, since it has no functioning mouthparts and cannot feed.

The best way to find a Goat Moth is to look for a Goat Moth tree. The moth is known to return to the same tree for generation after generation until the tree is so perforated by the caterpillars that it dies. Supposedly, you can extract the caterpillar without harm by wiggling a piece of grass bent into a loop inside the hole. The caterpillar sinks its jaws into the grass, allowing you to draw it out. Goat Moths can be reared on a diet of beetroot inside a metal box; the usual wooden cages are no use, since the caterpillars soon gnaw their way out.

In 1760, the Dutch naturalist and engraver Pieter Lyonnet published a remarkable monograph on the Goat Moth caterpillar. Over a series of exquisitely detailed copperplate engravings, he displayed its innards, from its outsized salivary glands to more than 4000 individually labelled muscles, half of them in the caterpillar's powerful intestines. Lyonnet's laborious dissections are still among the most detailed ever performed on any insect – and definitely the best-illustrated.[56] Not content with that, he went on to tackle the pupa and the moth in a second volume but died before it could be brought to press.

The Goat Moth is the sort of insect that gives rise to macabre stories. One of them is about a moth-collecting canon who thought the vaults of his cathedral, with their constant cool temperature, would be just the place to leave his cage of caterpillars over the winter. The result was a series of large holes in the coffins laid there and a macabre exhumation resulting, to everyone's consternation except the canon's, in the release of several large, dark moths. The other story involves a wooden box containing a full-grown Goat Moth caterpillar carelessly left on a grand piano in the drawing-room. By early morning the box was empty and a hole had appeared in the piano lid. Early the morning after, they heard the strains of Mendelssohn's 'Spring Song'. Said the entomologist to his wife, 'There's that damned Goat Moth.' He was wrong, as it happened. It was his daughter who had got up early to practise.[57]

Bird cherry draped by the webs of ermine caterpillars.

Tent-dwellers and leaf-miners

Micro-moths, even common ones, rarely come to our attention. We are more likely to notice their caterpillars. Some live communally, spinning silken tents or webs. Others 'mine' leaves in a distinctive way, leaving wavy patterns or blotches. Others still live inside cases, like caddisflies. Among the most visible are the little ermine moths (Yponomeutidae), so called because the adults have pure white wings dotted with black. In a good ermine year (which might be once a decade), you can spot the spindle bushes in hedges a mile off by the massed webs of the Spindle Ermine, while in northern parts, it may be hard to find a bird cherry that has not been draped and defoliated by the Bird Cherry Ermine.

Occasionally ermine moths make headlines. 'Tree in web of horror', was the banner headline in the *Diss Mercury* one day in June 2007, above an image of someone gazing open-mouthed at a favourite cherry tree completely swathed in webbing like the stockinged face of a bank robber. It took just a week for the caterpillars to strip the nine-metre tree of every leaf. 'It looks like something from a horror film,' exclaimed an onlooker.[58] Yet, even after such a spectacular demonstration of web-spinning, the tree usually bounces back in full health the next year.

Leaf-mining moths, by contrast, have caterpillars small enough to tunnel under the surface of a leaf, leaving a silvery trail or blister peppered with droppings where the leaf cells have been nibbled out. Among the miners are the smallest moths of all, the barely visible Nepticulidae, known in the trade as 'neps'. Connoisseurs of micro-moths can usually identify the species from the food-plant and the geometry of the mine without needing to find the adult moth.

Native leaf-mining moths are fairly harmless. Among those that frequent gardens are species that mine the leaves of roses, apples, azaleas, leeks and laburnums, but they rarely cause serious damage to the plant. The most notorious species, the Horse Chestnut Leaf Miner (whose scientific name is appropriately pronounced 'orrid-ella'), is a recent invader, first found in Eastern Europe, from where it suddenly irrupted westwards, as if determined to reach the bountiful horse chestnuts of Britain as quickly as possible. After the discovery of the first specimen on Wimbledon Common in 2002, it spread over much of England, leaving mature horse

The Many-plumed Moth, with its bizarre feathered wings.

Horse chestnut leaves riddled with leaf-mining caterpillars. Badly infected trees go brown prematurely.

chestnuts scored and blotched with moth mines until, by the end of July, they often appear coppery brown at a distance. The moth presumably lacks the normal checks and balances to its numbers and has proved impossible to control.

This tiny and rarely noticed moth has achieved rapid and spectacular spread without being a good flier. It is believed to have been assisted by wind and, probably, road vehicles. You can imagine a big horse chestnut leaf in which a dozen moth pupae are embedded getting lodged in the radiator of a lorry and blowing free at a service station a hundred miles up the motorway. The Victorians' habit of planting horse chestnuts in groves and avenues has also helped the moth; isolated trees often seem to escape it. There is no hard evidence that the infestation will cause permanent damage to our chestnuts, but repeated defoliations will certainly weaken the trees and lay them open to fungal infection. Local authorities are understandably becoming reluctant to plant horse chestnuts. And without horse chestnuts, there will be no conkers.

Plume moths *Pterophoridae*

Plume moths are extraordinary little moths whose wings appear to be replaced by feathers. Added to this eccentricity, is a unique resting posture, with the moths' outstretched wings and body forming a letter T superimposed on to the X of their spindly legs. The commonest species, the pure-white Large White Plume is found in gardens. Its species name *pentadactyla* means 'five fingers' (from above, there appear to be only four, but a fifth is tucked underneath). The Many-plumed Moth looks like a tiny feather fan when at rest with its wings outstretched.

There are 42 British species of plume moths, a few of which have taken the suicidal-seeming course of depending on one rare and declining food-plant such as marsh gentian or mossy saxifrage. The plume, so to speak, goes to *Buckleria paludum*, which has the nerve to feed on an insect-eating plant, the sundew. None of the British plume moths are of economic importance, unlike in North America, where several are garden pests and several more used as bio-control agents for invasive plants. There is, however, current interest in the Ragwort Plume as a potential, though not very promising, bio-control for ragwort. Though it takes only two of its tiny caterpillars to strip a plant completely, in Britain, they seem to prefer the harmless and non-invasive marsh ragwort.

Grass moths, china-marks and wax moths
Pyralidae

The Pyralidae is a large family of small, often day-flying moths, the Pyrales. Our 208 species include familiar moths with long-established English names, such as the Small Magpie and the Garden Pebble. Today, helped by the fact that some Pyrales turn up in moth traps, they are often treated as honorary macros, and an increasing number of people are recording them. In an attempt to popularise them further, English names have recently been invented for most species.

Among the Pyrales is a small group of moths whose caterpillars are aquatic. They have long been called china-marks because of a fancied resemblance to the potter's mark on antique porcelain. The largest species, the Brown China-mark moth, is also called 'sandwich man' or 'taco man' in America, because its caterpillars live between two flat pieces of leaf. It is often responsible for the neat holes mysteriously cut from the floating leaves in garden lily ponds.

Our four native china-marks have been joined by several more, arriving in imported waterweeds, turning up most often in garden centres and aquatic nurseries. Fortunately they do not seem to compete with the native moths. A related species, the Water Veneer, emerges in July in swarms, flying so low over the water that they seem to be skating. It visits lighted windows or the moth trap, often in enormous numbers, and with its narrow, semi-transparent wings, it is easily mistaken for a caddis-fly.

The Pyrales include attractive, small day-flying moths such as the Mint Moth and the Mother of Pearl Moth, which as a nettle feeder must be grateful for those patches of nettles well-meaning gardeners leave for the butterflies. They also include the grass moths, or Crambids, which fly up in numbers when we walk through long grass in the summer.

The Pyrales also include a number of minor garden or warehouse pests. Some of the latter are cosmopolitan 'indoor moths', whose caterpillars feed on stored products. Some are named after their preferred food, so that we have the Raisin Moth, the Dried Fruit Moth, the Dried Currant Moth, the Cocoa Moth and the Mediterranean Flour Moth. The family has its equivalent of the Brown House Moth in the Large Tabby, which is not as sweet as it sounds. Linnaeus named it *pinguinalis* (meaning grease) and believed it fed on 'fats, usually butter, etc., in houses and kitchens, *occasionally in the human belly*, the most loathsome of worms.' The latter assertion is an old urban legend – there are no Tabbies in bellies – but its caterpillar certainly thrives on refuse and filth, including undigested straw in horse dung. But while you might not welcome it in the boudoir, it is completely harmless (and now rather scarce).

The Wax Moth, also known as the Honeycomb Moth, is another once-troublesome Pyrale. It is a small brown moth with broad, distinctively notched forewings that lives in abandoned beehives or where the bees have been reduced to a dejected state by disease or starvation. Good beekeeping hygiene leaves little space for the Wax Moth, but a bad infestation can reduce much of the honeycomb to dust and droppings, and can cause asthma or conjunctivitis to those exposed to it. The caterpillars, known as waxworms, are reared commercially as 'lizard chocolate', a treat for reptile pets; the larvae have an unusually high fat content, thanks to a life spent gorging on beeswax. They are said to be palatable to humans, too, at least for those with a taste for exotica. Amanda Callaghan likes the 'wonderful soft feeling' of the grubs (though, being full of bacteria, they should not be eaten raw) and makes a 'waxworm brittle' with blanched and dry-roasted waxworms in place of the usual peanuts.[59]

Beekeepers are still occasionally troubled by the Lesser Wax Moth – which, if allowed to multiply, can induce the bees to desert the hive. When they cannot get wax, the caterpillars will stolidly munch their way through dried fruit or even dead insects. There is also the Bee Moth, a nondescript brown moth that lives inside wasp nests as well as beehives. Its caterpillar first helps itself to debris before, gaining courage as well as size, progressing to the comb and finally to the brood itself.

Tortrix moths *Tortricidae*

It is easy to identify a tortrix moth from its broad, oblong wings, but recognising the species is less so, for this is a large family and includes moths that are highly variable. Many tortrix moths have attractively patterned wings, and they are sufficiently good fliers to turn up in small numbers in moth traps. Their caterpillars normally live inside a curl of leaf, secured with a thread of silk, hence their alternative name of leaf-rollers.

Inevitably it is the ones that feed on plants of economic importance that come to our attention. This family has more than its share of crop and

Codlin Moth
Life Cycle,
*by Jonathan
Latimer.*

garden pests (no fewer than 189 Eurasian species, not all of them British, are so listed). The plants most at risk are fruit trees, strawberries, carnations and cyclamens. Gardeners concerned about tortrix moths can buy a tent-like trap with a sticky floor to hang over a favourite bloom.

One of our most familiar small moths is the Green Oak Tortrix. In some years it is so abundant that you can hear the rain-like patter of the caterpillars' droppings as they hit the dry leaves below the oak canopy in which they are feeding. Since oak leaves quickly fill up with tannins and so become inedible, the moths have to time their hatches to coincide exactly with the moment the tender leaves unfurl from the buds. Though Oak Tortrix occasionally defoliate whole trees, their appetites rarely bring permanent damage, especially since oaks have evolved a back-up strategy with a spurt of new leaves (the so-called lammas leaves) in late summer.

The most notorious tortrix is the Codlin (or Codling) Moth, also known as the appleworm. A codlin is a traditional variety of cooking apple, though the moth will attack any kind of apple, as well as pears and walnuts. Its grub, feeding near the core of the apple, is much less common today. It

has been assailed with some of the world's harshest pesticides, including the arsenate of lead with which orchard-growers would paint their trees in the days before DDT. A milder way of deterring them is to band each trunk with corrugated cardboard, which catches the grubs as they leave the tree to pupate. The scent, codlemone, which the moths use to attract a mate, has now been synthesised and is used to detect imminent Codlin Moth attacks, after which action can be taken. It is likely that the moth is losing the war.

A tiny, rare tortrix known only by its cumbersome scientific name *Choristoneura lafauryana*, made a brief outing in the headlines in the early 1990s when its only known locality was thought to be threatened by the Dersingham bypass in Norfolk. With amused irony the local press dubbed it the 'mighty moth'. It turned out that no one had seen the little moth there for years (the last record was 1962), and the bypass went ahead.

Swifts *Hepialidae*

The world's first moths might have looked like swift moths. They have long, narrow, primitive wings like a dragonfly or a lacewing that, unlike those of other moths, are not linked by a hook-and-catch device. This means that swift moths flap their wings like butterflies in a way described by the old entomologists as 'feverish' – hence their family name, Hepialidae, from the Greek *hepialos*, meaning 'to shiver'. The name swift might have been borrowed from the narrow-winged bird, though Moses Harris claimed it was because the moths 'fly low and very swift'. They are 'swifts' in most other European languages, though in France they prefer *la Louvette* – 'the she-wolf' (the reason for that becomes clear when you look closely from the side at the long-snouted head of a swift moth).

There are five British species. The caterpillar of the Common, or Garden, Swift feeds underground on the roots and lower stems of grasses and also garden crops including lettuce, strawberry and potato. By damaging the roots and thus drying out and ultimately killing the plant, it is ranked as a pest of lawns, though it is seldom common enough to become a serious one. It is also an occasional nuisance in fields of cereals, especially maize.

The best-known species of swift is the largest, the Ghost Moth, or Ghost Swift, so-named from the remarkable ghostly dances performed by the male moth at twilight. The males have pure white wings and are attracted around dusk by the pheromones of the dowdier females hidden in the long grass. Once they are close to the source, the males compete in ghostly dances just above the level of the grass stalks, their white wings hovering like balls of mist and sometimes swinging from side to side like the pendulum of a clock. A dozen or more male moths may join these bewitching dances, for which Bernard Kettlewell coined the name 'pendeculating'. The female moth, having chosen the most promising male, darts towards him and head-butts him into the grass. The subsequent night of love passes out of sight somewhere among the vegetation.

The entomologist Kenneth Gloyne Blair was convinced that the Ghost Moth was behind the phosphorescent will-o-the-wisp: ghostly, flickering lights occasionally seen over marshy ground. He was 'almost certain' that at least some instances of the pale hovering light is moonlight reflected on the male Ghost Moth's shining wings. 'Many of you lepidopterists,' he told a gathering of entomologists in London in 1922, 'have no doubt seen the appearance of a shining luminous object hovering in one spot for a time, and then moving off to repeat the motions a few yards away, and then off again, and then disappearing altogether, only to appear again a few moments later.'[60] Few have seen the wisp in recent times, and the Ghost Moth is reported to be less common than it was.

Clothes moths *Tineidae*

vn: letter fly (Orkney), mouch (Orkney), mouds (Scot.), silver-moths

The 'moths' of the Bible and other early texts were the grubs of clothes moths. They have lived with humans for thousands of years, nibbling away at animal skins and woollen fabrics. Perhaps even today the first image to come to mind when people hear the word moth is a tiny, dismal insect that chews holes in jumpers. The moths themselves do not nibble – that is done by their caterpillars.

Clothes moths are a small group of species within the family Tineidae (from the Latin *tinea*, meaning a gnawing worm). They are dowdy little moths that tend to run rather than fly when disturbed. What makes them a byword among insect pests is their ability to digest keratin, the tough substance at the heart of feathers, hair and skin, as well as toenails and dandruff. The commonest clothes moth today is the Case-bearing Clothes Moth, so named because its caterpillar lives inside a caddis-like tube (the so-called Common Clothes Moth, known in America as the Webbing Clothes Moth, is no longer common). Clothes moth caterpillars feed on garments made from natural fibres, but having a finely tuned sense of smell, are more likely to be attracted to fabrics soiled by sweat, blood or urine than clean clothes smelling of fresh air and soap. Some species have been known to sample such unlikely foods as hot spices, tobacco and hemp. Clothes moths have a remarkable resistance to drought; they are one of the few insects that can survive in that indoor Sahara the airing cupboard. Their ancestral habitat was probably bird nests and animal dens. Despite their habit of leaving behind a mess of droppings and

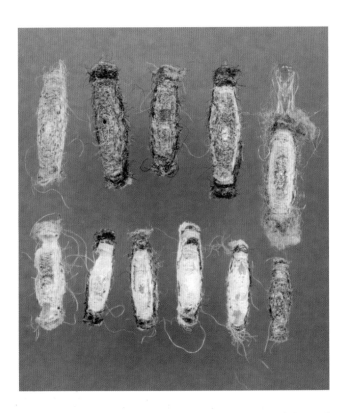

Sporting colours. Case-bearing Clothes Moth larval cases, the result of an infestation of a sock drawer.

cast skins, clothes moths are among nature's useful scavengers – humble insects feeding on the crumbs left over by bigger, more important animals.

Some members of the Tineidae have more adventurous tastes than the Case-bearing Clothes Moth. Of the little beige moth known only as *Tenaga nigripunctella*, the Victorian writer, C. G. Barrett noted that 'its larva may be suspected of tastes and habits which can hardly be described as decent, much less fastidious.'[61] He meant that they lived in outdoor lavatories, mainly, it seems, outdoor lavatories in Wales. Several Tineids like to chew the corks of wine bottles, though their natural pabulum is bracket fungi. *Haplotinea insectella* inhabits hencoops, while *Tinea fictrix* is happy among rat droppings in the holds of ships, though it has also been reared on an imaginative cocktail of maize, copra dust, bat guano and pigeon nests.

Certain nuisance moths in other families are named after their particular diet. The Tapestry Moth was once notorious for chewing woven wall hangings, but since it cannot survive long in centrally heated rooms, it is now confined to old, draughty halls. The Skin Moth feeds in the wild on bird dung and owl pellets but is also said to have a distressing taste for corpses. It acquired its name from a penchant for stored animal products such as skins and untreated leather and is, or was, a pest in museums. The Corn Moth lives on stored grain, and dried fruit and mushrooms, a diet that translates well from the wild to the kitchen cupboard.

The Brown House-moth is among the commonest small indoor moths today. Though its caterpillar may chew fabrics, it is more of a generalist, consuming any kind of homely refuse, from dead bats to ancient crud decomposing quietly beneath the fridge. A Brown House-moth on the wall is nature's way of telling you to get the hoover out. Its generic name is one of entomology's occasional in-jokes: *Hofmannophila*, or 'I like Hoffman', seems to be a dig at a forgotten German entomologist with a presumed personal hygiene problem.[62]

Clothes moths were traditionally deterred with mothballs, compacted balls of naphthalene or other industrial chemicals, the strong scent of which is injurious to the moths and their larvae; for the same reason it was also used to safeguard insect collections. In most modern homes, clothes moths are no longer a serious pest and, as a group, have declined severely. One reason is the widespread use of pesticides. Another is the universal availability of efficient vacuum cleaners and central heating, both deadly enemies of indoor insects. The *coup de grâce* was the appearance of man-made fibres such as polyester and nylon, which even a clothes moth cannot digest. In consequence, some species, such as the Tapestry Moth, are reverting to their ancestral habitats, in this case, owl nests. We are, however, experiencing a modest revival in clothes moths now that global warming is allowing them to breed faster and more often. One of the country's most important costume collections at Killerton House near Exeter was under attack recently.

FLIES

Two-winged flies *Diptera*

Who loves a fly? In Christian iconography, flies represent many unflattering things, which put together made them seem like the embodiment of sin and vice. To begin with, they are seen as impudent. Though the least of God's creatures (in Biblical terms), flies will settle on prince and commoner alike without distinction. Lacking any kind of scruple, they will even perch insouciantly on the bosom of a queen. In some medieval images of the Virgin and Child, a buzzing fly is there to remind us of the corruption from which we are being redeemed.

Flies were considered to be the antithesis of the industrious and useful honeybee. While bees make honey, flies 'take their pleasure promiscuously, restlessly, unswervably, unashamedly.'[1] They trample on their food and are so attracted to sweet, alcoholic liquors that their tiny corpses can be found floating in the glass. This carefree lifestyle naturally turned flies into subjects for moral allegories about the consequences of pleasure-driven lives: drowned in wine or singed by candle flames. Compared with prudent, sagacious insects such as bees and ants, flies were seen as totally irresponsible.

Everyone knows that flies fly with sublime indifference from dead rat to picnic basket, from nappy bucket to patisserie, bearing scraps of their previous meal on their dirty little legs. As Steven Connor puts it, 'Flies are vehicles, vectors that set at naught our safe demarcation of spaces. Perhaps they are a kind of anti-angel, which spreads malaise and unease rather than good news.'[2] Yet, despite their obvious love of filth, it was only towards the end of the nineteenth century that certain flies became associated with disease (*see* Housefly).

Flies were also considered unusually lustful. Aristotle was the first but by no means the last to remark on the difficulty of pulling apart a pair of copulating flies. 'The gilded fly does lecher in my sight', shouted the mad King Lear, 'let copulation

thrive!'[3] To Aristotle and Shakespeare, flies embodied carnal sin, the weaknesses of the flesh. Bees and ants, it was noted, hardly ever copulate. Unlike the disgusting fly, they work hard, collecting and storing food and feeding their young. They co-operate, while flies merely swarm.

Flies also served as a symbol of brevity, of the tragic shortness of mortal existence. Being the least of insects (they were sometimes referred to as 'atomies'), created spontaneously, it was believed, from mud and filth, their short, buzzing, pointless life was over in little more than a day. They reminded Christians of the frailty of mortal life; that 'time flies'. They were firmly earth-bound insects, associated with death and corruption, unlike butterflies and moths, which represented the eternal soul.

But for all the aspersions cast upon the fly by Christian moralists, the very qualities that invited derision also instilled a grudging respect. The fly, after all, was his own master: 'Each fly is king of his own country', wrote Edward Halford Ross in 1913. 'He knows no laws or conventions, he can go where he likes and feed where he likes.' To John Ruskin, there was even a touch of the political radical about a fly: 'He has no work to do – no tyrannical instinct to obey . . . free in the air, free in the chamber . . . he rises with angry republican buzz. What freedom is like this?'[4]

Here and there, a fly can be found in the stained glass of church windows. Their main purpose was as moral reminder for the congregation, though some said that they were also there to discourage living flies. The adage was: *similia similibus curantur*, that is, 'like is cured by like' – a kind of spiritual fly-spray. Such may be the idea behind the fly on a diamond of glass in the cloisters of Chester Cathedral shown in earnest conversation with a monk. Such flies were a quiet, talismanic nod to the sleeping devilry of Beelzebub and his buzzing army.

Flies, strangely enough, were considered good-luck charms. If a fly fell into your drink, it was a sign of good fortune (if only because the alcohol would probably kill any bacteria carried by the fly). It was also lucky to see a fly in the home at Christmas. Why? Because, it was reasoned, flies are killed off by cold weather, and so any that are still alive in midwinter must be exceptionally lucky ones. The

Left: *A housefly cruising over a continental shelf of bread.*

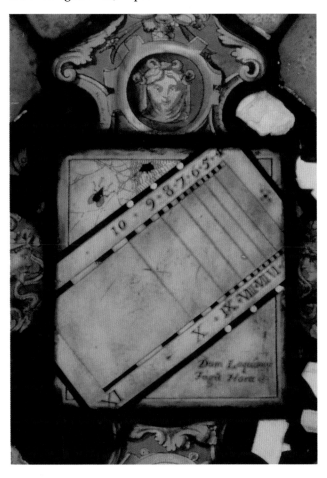

A visual pun on the saying 'time flies', part of a seventeenth-century glass window at St Peter's Church, Merton in Norfolk .

houseflies. One tenth of all species known to science are flies.

The collective noun for flies is a business or swarm. Perhaps 'business' is a pun on 'buzziness'.

The divine purpose of flies

'God in his wisdom invented the fly', remarked Ogden Nash, 'and then forgot to tell us why.'[5] St Augustine thought he knew why: God sent the fly to punish human arrogance. Thomas Muffet also had an answer or rather three answers. First, they helped mankind to forecast the weather. Biting flies such as gnats descend from the upper regions of the air just before rain, when, being hungry, they 'more diligently' seek after our blood. So swarms of midges, reasoned Muffet, are an infallible sign that rain is on the way. Second, flies provide medicines for us when we are sick and are also food for 'divers other creatures'. Finally flies 'show and set forth the Omnipotency of God and execute his justice; they improve the diligence and providential wisdom of men.'[6] So, in a sense, and however annoying they might be, flies are necessary.

It is not clear what medicines were provided by flies, since Muffet cites no instances. But, by the doctrine of signatures, the thorax of a fly, with its sparse hairs, resembles the head of a balding man. This hinted strongly that they could be enlisted in cures for hair loss. Surprisingly, there is a measure of truth to this piece of folklore. A scientist at Harvard tested the saliva of sandflies on the shaved rumps of mice and found, to his surprise, that 'the hair grew back so quickly it was annoying'.[7] It seems that the protein that prevents blood from clotting also helps to stimulate the flow of blood and so renews falling hair. Unfortunately the results obtained from bald human volunteers were inconclusive.

hope was that some of this fly luck would rub off. Another explanation in keeping with the short-lived benevolence we feel towards our fellow men on the birth day of Our Saviour is that the 'Christmas fly' is a divine visitor and so should not be killed.

These folk beliefs embrace not all biological flies but just a few familiar ones, notably the ubiquitous housefly and other chunky, buzzing insects such as the bluebottle or the fleshfly. All 'true flies' belong to the order Diptera (two-wings), insects with only one pair of functional wings, the second pair having been modified to form little club-like projections called halteres (named after the counterweights that long-jumpers once used to assist their leaping). These help the fly to balance and navigate. The Diptera is the second largest order of insects in Britain, with around 6670 species and new ones being discovered every year. It includes no fewer than 41 families, among them the craneflies, mosquitoes, blackflies, horseflies, robberflies, hoverflies and

The worthlessness of flies

Flies, being small, without virtue and generally present in vast swarms, rivalled fleas and lice in being the most worthless of the earth's creatures. Nothing, it seemed, was paltrier than a fly. In one of Aesop's fables, a wretched little fly sits on the wheel of a chariot and crows, 'See what dust I make.' The dust, of course, is nothing to do with him. Aesop's fly is the exemplar of all those who puff themselves up as important but are, in fact, insignificant.

Another fable contains a similar moral at the fly's expense. The fly spots a camel carrying a heavy load. 'I will rest on its back,' thinks the fly, and buzzes down to settle on the camel's ear. This is a long way off the ground and the fly, having its due of cheek but very little brain, thinks, 'I'm even taller than the great camel.' After a long journey, the camel rests and the fly drops to the ground. 'I hope I have not been too heavy a burden,' it squeaks, with the insolence of its kind. The camel replies disdainfully, 'I did not know you were there, and so I won't feel any different now that you are gone.' The moral? He that is nothing but thinks he is something is still nothing. Doctor Johnson had his own version of the fable: 'A fly, Sir, may sting a stately horse and make him wince; but one is but an insect, and the other is a horse still.'

A cautionary tale by the Brothers Grimm is called, with due irony, 'The Brave Little Taylor'. The hero, having killed seven flies with one blow of his needle, thinks that qualifies him to set off and put the world to rights. Even the child reader can see that the tailor is absurd: like the flies he has swatted, his feat is worthless.

The many verbal expressions involving flies tend to continue the same theme. Here are a selection.

A fly in the ointment is a small but irritating flaw that spoils everything. The phrase is Biblical (Ecclesiastes, 10:1): 'Dead flies cause the ointment of the apothecary to send forth a stinking savour; so doth a little folly him that is in reputation for wisdom and honour.' In ancient times, ointment was valuable and expensive, and used on solemn and ceremonial occasions, as well as medicinally.

There are no flies on him indicates that a person is shrewd and won't be caught napping. This may be a reference to Solomon's Temple where, according to legend, no flies were ever seen, despite the ever-present temptation offered by blood from the corpses of animals prepared for sacrifice.

An eagle does not hawk at flies. Little worthless things are beneath the contempt of a great man or woman.

Fly-blown means fouled and spoiled by flies. It was once considered that baby maggots were blown on to the meat by flies, hence 'blowflies'.

You catch more flies with honey than vinegar. You get further with charm than with sharpness or aggression. Just as flies are supposed to prefer sweet things to bitter ones, so people respond better to kindness and consideration. This expression gives a more positive slant on flies, though in reality houseflies prefer filth to honey.

A fly on the wall. Originating in America, this means to be in a position to be able to observe freely without being noticed. Of late, the expression is used most often about voyeuristic television documentaries, notably *Big Brother*.

Dropping or *dying like flies* refers to the fabled transience of a fly's life but also evokes the horror of an epidemic or a battle, when death loses its individual sting and becomes a statistic. Flies, someone said, bring us disconcertingly close to ourselves.

Literary flies

The buzzing of flies was often used by poets as a metaphor for dreams. Distracted wits or intemperate desires were attributed to notional flies or their maggots buzzing and biting inside the brain. To be 'governed by a maggot' was to be in the uncontrollable grip of an obsession or delusion. To do something 'when the maggot bites' was to give way to a mad impulse, while to be 'maggot-pated' was to be full of fantastical whims and notions. Paradoxically, while such behaviour would normally disadvantage the sufferer, it was the very stuff of romantic poetry. P. B. Shelley speaks of 'busy dreams, as thick as summer flies'. John Keats evokes the bewildering thoughts that are 'born of atomies/ That buzz about our slumbers, like brain-flies,/ Leaving us fancy-sick'.[8]

Samuel Wesley, father of the famous Methodist preacher, chose the title *Maggots* for his first book of poetry in 1685, opening with the lines: 'The Maggot Bites, I must begin:/ Muse! Pray be civil! Enter in!/ Ransack my addled pate with Care/ And muster all the Maggots there!'[9] When the poetical maggot awoke hungry, it was time to reach for the quill pen.

The phrase 'Lord of the Flies' is inherited from ancient temple religions when flies buzzed over the pools of blood and scraps of meat left after the sacrifice of a bull or sheep. In what one might think was a counterproductive gesture, the Greeks even sacrificed animals to Zeus in his guise as Apomyios, the *averter* of flies. In Christian demonology, the Lord of the Flies is Beelzebub, Satan's right-hand man. Beelzebub has come down in the world. He once had great stature as *Boal-zebub*, but his cult was decisively trashed by Elijah and he was relegated to Hell and put in charge of flies which buzz and sting. In the English Mummers' Plays, he is more humble still, 'a jolly old man' reduced to scrounging pennies from the crowd in his copper pan after the show.

William Golding chose *The Lord of the Flies* as the title of his first novel to underline the savagery that lies just beneath the surface of our civilised lives. Put a group of boys in a jungle without any adult authority figure to keep their worst instincts in check, and murder and mayhem will follow, believed Golding, unimpressed with the veracity of Victorian boys' stories such as *The Coral Island*. The 'Lord' remains off-stage throughout the novel, but the boys fear its counterpart, the Beast, and stick a flyblown pig's head on a stake as an offering to the presiding god. Only the saintly Simon recognises, in a transcendent moment, that the Beast does not live on top of the mountain, or at the far end of the island but much closer to home. 'You knew, didn't you?' the fly-encrusted skull seems to tell him. 'I'm part of you.'[10] Peter Brooke's 1963 film of *The Lord of the Flies* made compelling use of the constant buzzing of flies drawn to human sweat.

Irvine Welsh's dark comedy *The Granton Star Cause* is a twist on Kafka's *Metamorphosis,* in which a man is turned into a bug. God appears to a hopeless amateur footballer, Boab Coyley, in the form of a foul-mouthed down-and-out who, as punishment for wasting his life and opportunities, turns Boab into a housefly. Boab takes advantage of the fly's talent for spreading disease to exact a deadly revenge on those he blames for ruining his life, before, ironically, being swatted by his own mother.[11]

W. B. Yeats' poem 'Long-legged Fly' is about the mind in quiet contemplation. Caesar in his tent looks far away, absorbed in thought, 'his eye fixed upon nothing':

> Like a long-legged fly upon the stream
> His mind moves upon silence.[12]

It is a very quiet poem. Inward contemplation is both intense and delicate, like a gnat that floats on the air above a stream or a pond-skater moving on the water's surface, an atom of thought contemplating eternity.

Flies also appear in films, usually horror films. *The Fly* (1986) was film-director David Cronenberg's characteristically gruesome remake of a 1958 low-budget film, itself based on a short story by George Langelaan. The tale involves an invented 'teleport' that transfers a person from place to place, but inevitably, things go horribly wrong when, unnoticed, a fly buzzes into the machine. In the first film, the inventor simply exchanges some of his body parts with the fly, but in Cronenberg's version, the human and the fly exchange genetic codes, producing a rubble-skinned, 185-pound man-fly with a craving for chocolate bars. He can walk on the ceiling. Some believed that the film was an allegory of the AIDS epidemic, but Cronenberg denied that was his intention. It is remembered for its catch-phrase, 'Be afraid. Be very afraid.'

In Henri-Georges Clouzot's classic 1953 film *The Wages of Fear (Le Salaire de la Peur),* a fly makes a telling contribution to an erotic scene when it crawls languidly across a woman's bare breast.

Flies in art

Painted images of flies commonly appear in art, especially still-life paintings, as emblems of sin and corruption. Contemporary art has provided a new twist on the traditional image by incorporating actual live flies and their maggots into artwork. The most famous exponent of this kind of insect art is Damien Hirst, who while still a student produced the first of the 'animal' installations for which he became famous. Entitled *A Thousand Years*, it was a tank of flies and maggots feeding on a rotting cow's head. A proportion of the emerging flies were continually zapped by an 'Insect-o-cuter'. Tender stomachs were said to have turned over when *A Thousand Years* was first exhibited at the Royal Academy, though it was admired by Francis Bacon and quickly bought by Charles Saatchi. Hirst has since produced two canvases of squashed flies titled *Devil Worshipper* and *Who is Afraid of the Dark?*

Much more sympathetic to flies and their kind is Julia Lohmann's 'curation' of 'maggot-art' featuring 'performances and artwork by maggots.' She calls her creations *Maggotypes* or *Maggoteers*. 'Our aim,'

Maggot art by Julia Lohmann: 'We "curated" a number of exhibitions featuring performances and artwork by maggots under the titles Maggotypes *and* Magnificent Maggoteers . . . *Our aim was to transform people's perceptions of maggots, creatures that are normally perceived as a disgusting, squirming mass of nonentities. We documented the artwork created by maggots and their subsequent transformation into flies in a book.'*

says Lohmann, is 'to transform people's perceptions of maggots, creatures that are mostly perceived as a disgusting, squirming mass of nonentities. We designed special questionnaires, asking the maggots about their gender, names and dreams for the future, politics, eating habits etc. Once the maggots had answered they suddenly became individuals with a name and personality. Our hitherto rather squeamish audience asked us: "So, what's going to happen to Bob, now? You aren't going to kill him, are you?" – Mission accomplished.'[13]

Fly swats

According to Suetonius, the Roman Emperor Domitian had an unusual hobby. He would spend hours alone catching flies and then stabbing their tiny bodies with a needle-sharp pen. Once, when asked whether anyone was with the emperor, his secretary answered wittily, 'No, not even a fly.' Others claimed Domitian enjoyed setting up miniature gladiatorial combats between flies and spiders.

As anyone who has ever tried knows, swatting flies is surprisingly difficult. The fly is magnificently nimble and able to detect the slightest movement. In an instant (the response time has been measured at 200 milliseconds), they seem able to calculate the

Live and let live: 'The Fly', from William Blake's Songs of Innocence and of Experience *(1794).*

incoming blow and take evasive action. Summer 2008 saw an outbreak of fly-swatting tips and anecdotes in national newspapers. One correspondent to the *Daily Telegraph* claimed to be a crackshot with a peashooter, another an adept with an elastic band ('One elastic band. One steady aim. One wall cleaner.'). Mike Marsh of Sheffield swore by his 'spring-loaded fly-gun that fires a soft plastic pad retrieved by a 4ft string. It is good practice for the partridge season.' Catching flies in flight with one bare hand is also said to be excellent practice for fielding at cricket. Surprisingly, none of the correspondents mentioned the most effective fly-swat of them all: a rolled-up copy of the *Daily Telegraph*.

The ultimate in fly-swats is the Bug Zapper, a battery-powered weapon, shaped like a small tennis racket, that delivers a crackle of electricity through the metal strings which not only swats the fly but dispatches it with a sizzle. A fine example of twenty-first century overkill, some might think, it lacks the decent sense of fair play shown by the customised German fly-swat which has a hole in the centre and the motto *Gib der Fliege eine Chance*: 'Give the fly a chance'.

Not everyone reacts to buzzing flies with rage. Uncle Toby in Laurence Stern's *Tristram Shandy* is presented as obsessed with military matters but strangely benevolent towards flies. After suffering a fly buzzing around his head all dinner time, he succeeds in catching it only to release it gently outside. 'This world surely is wide enough to hold both thee and me,' says wise old Uncle Toby.[14]

William Blake, too, shows a Buddhist-like feeling for a fly in his *Songs of Innocence and Experience*. For Blake, the least of life is still life; his fly is not a contemptible speck or a devil in disguise but a fellow creature. He brushes the buzzing insect away, presumably kills it, and then reflects on what he has done: 'Am not I/ A fly like thee?' Yes, indeed, 'For I dance/ And drink, and sing,/ Till some blind hand/ Shall brush my wing.' Then, concludes Blake, 'Then am I/ A happy fly,/ If I live,/ Or if I die.'[15] In other words, if we are no better or worse than a fly then, surely, we are equal to the fly.

Perhaps the tenderest moment in Shakespeare's shock-horror play *Titus Andronicus* is when the protagonist's brother Marcus strikes a fly that has settled on his dinner plate. Titus, who has just seen the executed heads of two of his sons, a daughter raped and mutilated, and been tricked into chopping off his own hand, appears shocked at this casual slaughter of an insignificant insect:

> How if that fly had a father and mother?
> How would he hang his slender gilded wings
> And buzz lamenting doings in the air.
> Poor harmless fly,
> That with his pretty buzzing melody
> Came here to make us merry, and thou hast
>   killed him.[16]

Charles Tennyson Turner (1818–79), the elder brother of Alfred Tennyson, showed a like sympathy in his humorous sonnet 'Calvus to a Fly'. As evening closes in, a fly is drawn to the bald head of the poet, which gleams in the lamplight as he reads a book of verse. Despite its 'shrill sound and constant touch', the poet wishes it no harm but reflects that a moment's irritation – a bad poem, say, would cause his 'hasty hand' to make a scapegoat of the fly and crush out its life with a careless splat:

A mated pair of craneflies, generally known as daddy-longlegs.

'And thou mayst perish in that moment's spite/ And die a martyr to thy love of light.'

Tennyson Turner's sensitive heartstrings were plucked once again in his more despondent poem 'On Finding a Small Fly Crushed in a Book'. This time there was little left of the squashed insect but its gauzy wings, which to the poet were of angelic beauty, utterly transcending a life devoted to dung and filth:

Oh! That the memories which survive us here
Were half so lovely as these wings of thine!
Pure relics of a blameless life that shone
Now thou art gone.[17]

Craneflies or daddy-longlegs
Tipulidae

VN: arry-long-legs or harry-long-legs (Cheshire), grandfer longligs (Isle of Wight), granfer griggles (Devon), granny nobble-knee (Kent), jenny-lang-legs (Scot.), jinnyspinner (Cumb.), kirsie-kringlo (Orkney), meggie-nettles, meggie-speeder or meggie-spinner (Scot.), speeder jenny, speederlegs, spinnin jennie (Scot.), spinnin Maggie (Scot.), tom-taylor (Cornwall)

Why do daddy-longlegs have long legs? They neither wade in water like herons nor use the extra height to feed like a giraffe. For a flying insect, six dangling and readily detachable legs could be considered a drawback. The most likely reason is that, in flight, their legs act like a cat's whiskers, helping them avoid bumping into things. They also act as balancers for the fly's long, thin body, like the

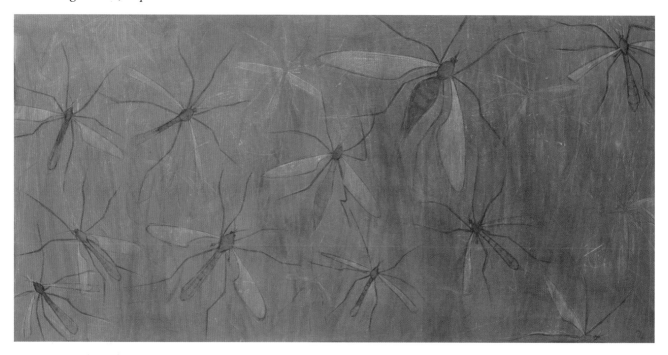

Dance of the Daddy Longlegs *(mixed media on board), by Annabel Harris, whose work, influenced by Japanese art, brings out the shimmer and sense of movement of live insects.*

pole of a high-wire artist. Perhaps they also divert the attention of predators from the less disposable parts of the fly or enable the flies to escape from spider webs, minus a leg or two. For the female fly (the mummy-longlegs?), its long limbs help to stabilise the body during egg-laying, like a high tripod. It seems to work: the craneflies, to which the daddy-longlegs belong, are among the world's oldest and most diverse families of flies; today one fly in ten is a cranefly.

Daddy-longlegs is the age-old name given to the large craneflies that visit gardens and lighted windows in late summer. As if to correct any assertion that the 'daddies' are male, a one-time alternative name was 'granny nobble-knee'. Their long legs make you think of spiders, so among their other country names are 'meggie-spinner', 'spinnin jennie' and 'speederlegs'. The folk-name 'meggie-nettles' reflected a belief that, looking like spiders, they could also 'sting' like them. A similar mistaken notion of cranefly behaviour lies behind the American names – 'mosquito hawks' or 'skeeter eaters' (as well as 'gallinippers', 'golliwhoppers' and 'Texas mosquitoes' – that is, giant mosquitoes).

Daddy-longlegs trouble some people with their wobbly, skittish flight. Indoors they seem careless of life; they frazzle in lampshades, drown in washbasins or toilets and shed their legs at every collision. Their fragile build excites childish cruelty. Children would once rip off the cranefly's legs, one by one, like petals from a daisy, while reciting a customised version of 'Goosey, goosey, gander':

> Old Harry Long-legs
> Cannot say his prayers
> Catch him by the left leg
> And throw him down the stairs[18]

Yet some people, especially in rural North America, would never dream of harming a daddy-longlegs. The insect was linked in some mysterious way with cows. If a farmer ran over one with his plough, the milk would go dry. If he could not find his cattle, the daddy-longlegs could help him: by picking one up by a trailing leg, its other legs would point in the right direction (this also applied to the harvestman, which is also called daddy-longlegs in North America). Others say that if you kill a daddy-longlegs you will be stung by a wasp. Probably at the root of this lore is the vague resemblance of a daddy-longlegs to that better-known good-luck talisman, a spider.

Seldom has the daddy-longlegs appeared in such numbers as September 2006, when every step in the grass seemed to kick up clouds of them. Such abundance revived the urban myth that the daddy-longlegs is poisonous, some say the most toxic

Cranefly Ale, brewed by Castle Rock, Nottingham, in association with the Nottingham Wildlife Trust.

insect of all. Children, perhaps adults, too, feared the remote possibility of a daddy-longlegs dropping from the ceiling into their mouths while they were asleep or, worse, of the appalling possibility of one mistaking your mouth for its natural habitat – a moist, mossy ditch. Yet another modern myth insists it has poisonous fangs. In fact, the flies are non-toxic and non-biting (they barely feed as adults) and cannot harm us in any way.

Perhaps our uneasy relationship with the daddy-longlegs is compounded by a sense of pity for their apparently dysfunctional design, as Craig Brown suggested at the height of the 2006 cranefly explosion:

> It is, I suppose, this sense of their utter uselessness that makes us pity them, and perhaps even, in our more downhearted moments, identify with them. Their life is all such an effort – and to what purpose? . . . Swarms of male daddy longlegs dance around like drunken morons, on the lookout for lady friends. Copulation sounds a grim affair for both parties. 'The male genitalia include a pair of claspers which grip the female genital valves,' says one encyclopaedia, 'but in order to do so the male's abdomen has to be twisted through 180 degrees'. Their only other pleasure in life seems to be cleaning their legs, which they do obsessively after each meal, pulling them one at a time through their jaws. After all this, they bluster into a light-bulb, have a pot-shot taken at them, nose-dive into a basin, lose half their legs, crawl around for a bit, lose the other half, and then die. It's not a life to be envied, I think, as I reach for the dustpan and brush.[19]

In 2007, the Nottinghamshire Wildlife Trust teamed up with Nottingham's Castle Rock Brewery to improve the daddy-longlegs' public image with an ale called Cranefly. Launching the product, the trust explained that though craneflies 'can be a bit annoying' it urged people to give them a break. 'They are a generally positive part of our natural heritage. The larvae are a major food source for birds such as rooks and the adults are eaten by everything from spiders to bats.'[20] The brewery's previous outings on behalf of maligned insects include Hoverfly and Flying Ant beers.

Daddy-longlegs is a composite name for three common and similar-looking species. The daddy of them all, *Tipula maxima*, is a rather grand insect and by far the biggest British fly in terms of wingspan. It has mottled, veined wings reminiscent of clear church windowpanes. It is an insect of damp woods and large, wet nettle-beds by streams, and so the least likely of the three to enter the house.

Their larva, known as a 'leatherjacket' (and also, in some areas, as 'leatherback' or 'leatherback slug'), is a tough-skinned grub that feeds on grass roots and sometimes emerges at night to chew the blades. This can create bare patches of soil – as at Lord's cricket ground in 1935, when thousands were collected up and burned – and the first sign of leatherjackets is often starlings or rooks scratching at the surface. The customary way of dealing with them was to tip a bowl of washing-up water over the soil to force the grubs to the surface and summary execution. Most of the chemicals that were used against leatherjackets are now banned, but gardeners have a new weapon in the form of nematode bio-controls.

Certain other large craneflies redeem the plain looks of the daddy-longlegs. The rare Hornet Cranefly is a brightly striped wasp mimic with gorgeously plumed antennae and was once considered a prize among collectors (and hence worth money). Another large cranefly, the White-footed Ghost, has acquired cult status among fly specialists largely because of its memorable name, though its habitat also has a romantic air: its ghostly feet dance over the chilly waters of moss-draped springs and ghylls.

Some six families and 329 species of flies are very loosely aggregated under the common name of craneflies. All have elongated bodies and long spindly legs, and when at rest with outstretched wings, some of them do recall a flying, long-legged bird. The family Tipulidae – some 89 species – includes the daddy-longlegs and its closest relatives. Other families include the winter gnats, which bob harmlessly at lighted windows during the dark months of the year.

> In my family craneflies have always been known as 'eergie things'. They are the only animals I dislike, especially the way they fly straight at your head and try to dangle their horrible spindly legs all over your face, maliciously, and with intent to wound. That's what it seems like, anyway![21]

> I'm not that squeamish, in fact I love spiders, but I can't be doing with daddy-long-legs. One went up mum's skirt when she was little. I always say to people that I don't like them because they are clackety; when you hold them in your hands they rattle, and they have way too many legs somehow.[22]

Mosquitoes *Culicidae*

VN: buer or buver (NE Eng.), gnat, midge, mingins (Norfolk), mozzies, nudge (Cheshire), widgeon

A mosquito can sense your breath in pitch darkness from more than 30 metres away. It homes in on a guiding beam of carbon dioxide expelled from your lungs and takes a morsel of your blood without you noticing. While doing so, it can also unwittingly transmit some of the world's most dreaded diseases, among them yellow fever and malaria. Though mosquitoes are too similar-looking to have individual common names, some of their scientific ones are provocative enough: *Aedes irritans*, *Culex perfidiosus*, *Aedes excrucians*, *Psorophora horridus*.

People used to speak of a mosquito's sting, but the more correct term is bite. Some object to that,

Mosquito larvae anchored by their breathing tubes to the surface film. Breaking the film with oil will cause them to drown.

too, pointing out that the mosquito lacks jaws and teeth. Instead, it has a pair of lancets folded around a feeding tube, or proboscis, that can pierce the flesh like the most subtle of hypodermic needles. The nearest parallel, therefore, is to a blood test. Having taken what it requires, and to get airborne as quickly as possible, the mosquito expels its waste on to the bite. It is these body fluids, and not the bite itself, that causes the itchy bump we call a mosquito bite, and this is also the route by which mosquitoes transmit disease. Only the females need a blood meal now and then, the males supping as harmlessly as butterflies on nectar and sap.

Technically speaking, true mosquitoes are confined to a single family of flies, the Culicidae. The word mosquito is of Spanish-American origin and means, simply, little fly. Until at least the nineteenth century, Americans called them 'muskets', while for a long time, the English stuck to their own word, 'gnat'. In some parts, mosquitoes are also referred to indiscriminately as 'midges'. Mosquito comes from the Latin word for fly, *musca*, which in turn is based on the Greek word *muia*, which supposedly emulates the sound it makes. The Romans had another stab at reproducing that whining buzz in *zinzala*, which is what they called a gnat. The Jews had perhaps the most authentic mosquito sound of all, pronounced *zvuv*.

The collective name for non-biting gnats is a cloud, horde or clout, yet for midges it is a bite and for mosquitoes a scourge. Some 33 species of mosquito are recorded in Britain, a modest number compared to the 1600 known species worldwide. There are two groups, the Culicines, which rest with the body roughly parallel to the surface, and the Anophelines, which rest with the body sharply inclined. Both bite but, in Britain, only the Anophelines are known to transmit disease.

The worst biter among British mosquitoes is probably *Culiseta annulata* (it lacks an accepted English name), which is large with spotted wings and banded legs and can breed happily in water tanks, wells, troughs and even buckets. It also hibernates indoors. Its bite can causes skin blisters and swelling, and after a bite on the back of his hand, our contributor Steve Palin's fingers 'were like pork sausages, and it was very sore'. He phoned the local hospital, where a tunnel-vision consultant dermatologist tried to reassure him that 'you needn't worry, sir, we don't get mosquitoes in this country'.[23]

One mosquito is unique to the London Underground. Known formally as *Culex pipiens* form *molestus*, and informally as the London Underground Mosquito, it first came into prominence during the Blitz, when Londoners using the Underground platforms as bomb shelters found themselves mysteriously covered in bites. In 1998, Kate Byne and Richard Nichols discovered that this subterranean mosquito is genetically distinct from its relatives above ground and, indeed, that the two no longer interbreed. Hence, though the Underground was dug only a century ago, its resident mosquito is already well on the way to becoming a new species, a process that, according to Darwinian theory, should take thousands of years. Moreover, different genetic strains have evolved in different tube lines, so that eventually we might speak of the Bakerloo Mosquito or the Circle Line Mosquito.

What seems to have happened is that, when the mosquitoes began to breed in the dark, in the stagnant puddles below the streets of London, they found themselves in a radically different habitat. The winters were milder and frost-free, allowing them to breed all year round. On the other hand, their usual hosts, birds, were absent. Instead, the mosquitoes found an ample substitute host in rats and mice, and also the herds of two-legged animals that periodically milled around under the bright lights.

Mosquitoes are said to be more attracted to women than men. One of our contributors says he is hardly ever bitten, yet 'my poor wife is absolutely massacred every time she goes out'.[24] Tony Harwood recalls summer walks through damp woodland with the 'handsome Banded Mosquito thronging in clouds around the unfortunate women and children while completely ignoring the men.[25]

Until the 1890s, malaria, one of the greatest scourges of mankind, was believed to be caused by damp and 'infected' air hanging over marshy ground; the name comes from the Italian for 'bad air'. It took a long time to link the disease with mosquitoes. The missing link was a protozoan parasite, a trypanosome, which the French scientist Alphonse Laveran isolated from mosquito blood in the 1880s. But it was not until 1897 that Britain's Ronald Ross proved that the trypanosomes were carried from host to host in the guts of a mosquito. The ancients were not wrong to associate malaria with bad drainage, but they mistook the character of the disease.

As well as spreading malaria, mosquitoes are

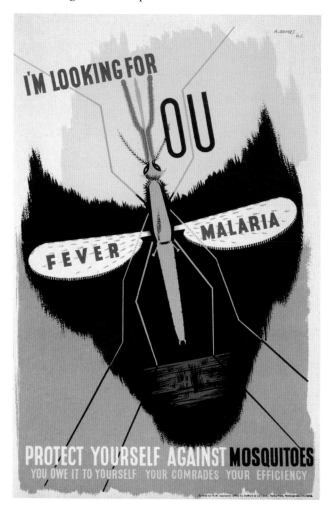

Malaria poster (1941), by Abram Games, with the wings representing eye-sockets in a skull. Proof that mosquitoes were the vectors of malaria and other diseases provided a strong incentive to study insects.

also the carriers of yellow fever, dengue fever, West Nile fever and many other infectious diseases. Fortunately, in Britain, they are less of a danger. A mild form of malaria known as the ague used to be common, especially in marshy areas. All six British species of *Anopheles* mosquitoes can transmit it, but the most effective vector is *Anopheles atroparvus*, a species that breeds in saline pools by the coast. By the late nineteenth century, ague and other forms of malaria in Britain had been all but eliminated by the drainage of marshlands and the availability of the anti-malarial drug quinine (which could be taken in the painless form of a gin-and-tonic). But there were outbreaks of malaria during and after both World Wars, when troops invalided home were sent to convalesce in what it was hoped would be the mild and pleasant climate of the Kentish and Essex

seafronts. Perhaps the memory of these places as hotbeds of ague was already fading.

Mosquitoes are, of course, a nuisance, even when they are not passing on malignant viruses and parasites. They are commonest in coastal districts as well as around large sewage works in cities. In some areas, their persistent biting forces the residents to use mosquito nets on their beds. In other places, that whining mosquito in the bedroom probably bred in the water butt or a blocked drain just outside. The problem can be minimised simply by covering all rainwater receptacles with a gnat-proof lid. Mosquitoes tend to be commonest in wet years; the sodden summer of 2007 saw a large increase in callers to the NHS seeking advice on bites.

Mosquito control was pioneered in Britain by an amateur entomologist and unsung hero, John Marshall, in the 1920s. Believing in fighting from the front, he chose Hayling Island near Portsmouth, a notorious mosquito breeding ground, as the location for what became the British Mosquito Institute. By experiment, Marshall discovered that mosquitoes need stagnant water to breed and that, by clearing and maintaining the local ditches, he could prevent them from gaining a hold. Where that was impractical, he poured oil on the surface, thus breaking the film and effectively drowning the mosquito's eggs and larvae. His work influenced mosquito control worldwide; in 1938, Marshall published his magnum opus, *The British Mosquitoes*, still the standard text on the subject. His methods are still used to control mosquitoes on Hayling Island today, where the Institute's old buildings are now part of the Seacourt Tennis Club (though local legend insists that the island's famously bloodthirsty mosquitoes are escapees from Marshall's laboratory).

Mosquitoes in fable and rhyme

Mosquitoes represent the power of the small over the mighty. In Aesop's subversive fable about the lion and the mosquito, the insect stings the king of beasts on the nose, causing him to thrash about in vain at his invisible enemy and end up wounding only himself. Thus, moralised the Renaissance scholar Aldrovandi, 'the lion surpasses all animals in strength, spirit and body . . . yet the tiniest midge in Mesopotamia subdues it.'

Mosquitoes may successfully torment the king of the beasts, but many people must have wondered

'Then in a wailful choir the small gnats mourn . . . borne aloft or sinking as the light wind lives or dies' –
John Keats, 'To Autumn' (1819).

why they were 'necessary' and fashioned myths to explain their origin. One such tale leans on the ancient myth of Pandora's Box to explain how mosquitoes were accidentally spilled on to the world when they escaped from confinement; it was, in that sense, no one's fault. Another story blames a malignant, blood-drinking giant. He caused havoc until Jack the giant-slayer found a way of destroying the giant's immortality by burning his body to ashes. The giant got his revenge when each particle of ash turned into a blood-drinking mosquito and were then scattered by the wind to the four corners of the earth.

It is easy to portray mosquitoes as agents of a motiveless malignancy, but compared to human bloodsuckers, they have a kind of innocence: they do what they do out of biological necessity. In his satirical poem 'The Mosquito Knows', D. H. Lawrence implies that humans are far worse than biting insects, for we know no such restraint. Lawrence was living near the well-named Mosquito

Coast of America at the time and no doubt had insects on the mind. His mosquito is a non-biological 'he':

> The mosquito knows full well, small as he is
> he's a beast of prey.
> But after all
> he only takes his bellyful.
> he doesn't put my blood in the bank.

'I like to write when I feel spiteful', wrote Lawrence. 'It is like having a good sneeze.' A second, longer poem, 'The Mosquito', appeared in his collection, *Birds, Beasts and Flowers* (1923), which includes some of his writing on the otherness of the non-human world. It addresses the insect (non-gender this time) directly, half playfully, half wonderingly, as it stalks the poet in a 'sly game of bluff' with its 'small, high, hateful bugle in my ear'. The poem seems to progress in real time; the author and his insect tormentor apparently read each other's thoughts before the mosquito obtains what it came for and the poet his revenge:

Blood, red blood
Super-magical
Forbidden liquor
I behold you stand
For a second enspasmed in oblivion,
Obscenely ecstasied
Sucking live blood,
My blood.

The poet wonders at the strange, airy grace of the insect. Why does it have such high legs? 'Is it so that you shall lift your centre of gravity upwards/ And weigh no more than air as you alight upon me?' With its 'thin wings' and 'streaming legs' it sails 'like a heron, or a dull clot of air/ A nothingness.' Its very lack of substance – 'a winged phantom' – enables it to 'waft away on the very draught my anger makes in snatching.' The poem ends in a splat:

Queer, what a big stain my sucked blood makes
Beside the infinitesimal faint smear of you!
Queer, what a dim dark smudge you have
   disappeared into![26]

The De Havilland aircraft company liked to name their planes, civil and military, after insects, presumably to emphasise their light and airy qualities. The most successful of them all was the twin-engined Mosquito. Like its insect moniker, this classic aircraft of the Second World War was gossamer-light, relatively quiet and packed a sting. Different forms of it were used as light bombers, dayfighters, nightfighters, photo-reconnaissance planes (usually still with a bomb or two in the bay) and anti-shipping strike aircraft. The Mosquito entered service in 1941 and, being built largely of wood but bearing two mighty Rolls Royce Merlin engines, it was very fast – faster than most enemy fighter planes. A later version, called the Hornet, was the fastest-ever wooden plane.

Midges *Ceratopogonidae*

vn: meeo (Orkney), midget, midgies, mudge, no-see-ums (America)

There is a Scottish saying: 'The midge is as big as a mountain.' Gaelic has a different version: '*Chan eil moran eader a blo's a' mheanbh-chuileag,*' meaning 'there's not much between a cow and a midge,'[27] that is, nothing gets in the way of a female midge and its appetite. The so-called Highland Midge is widespread in Britain, but nowhere does it make its presence felt more than in the Highlands and islands. Midges attack in swarms, and a bad set of bites can look like a skin rash. The intense itchiness wears away quickly and leaves no unpleasant after-effects, but as I can attest, a face full of midges makes you briefly want to tear your skin off. In parts of western Scotland, midges make outdoor life difficult if not unbearable on warm, damp, windless days. Up to 20 per cent of working days each summer are lost to forestry workers in midge country. Half the visitors to some of the grandest scenery in Europe said they would be put off visiting the area again because of midges, and Scottish tourism claims to lose £286 million a year because of them.

Midges are tiny but can be present in vast numbers. On their ideal wet peat moor with scattered pools, there can be up to a quarter of a million per square metre – a kind of midge-fog. Traps commonly collect a million in a night. Highland midges bite humans, cattle and deer indiscriminately, and one of the reasons for the movement of Highland red deer to higher ground in summer is to escape them.

Is there anything to be said for the midge? Because of their sheer numbers, midge larvae have ecological significance. By burrowing in the wet soil and acting as mini-earthworms, they are important decomposers. And by rendering parts of the Highlands barely habitable, they have at least helped to keep wild, open landscapes free of human habitation. Scottish tourist sites tend to treat the midge as part of Highland life, as part of experiencing wildest Britain. As if to bear witness to the fact, a midge sculpture by Anthony Bennett was unveiled at Inverness Museum and Art Gallery in 2008 to mark its 'open doors' festivities.

Technology has come to the aid of the walker and camper in the Highlands. Midge forecasts based on a combination of trapping data and standard weather

MegaMidge
or Culicoides
Impunctatus
Giganticus, *by
Anthony Bennett,
now on display at
Inverness Museum
and Art Gallery.*

forecasts are now routine in the western Highlands and are available online (there are also 'midge maps' on Google). Walkers can choose from a wide range of midge repellents. Sprays, wipes or roll-ons containing DEET (diethyl toluamide) are effective, and after a liberal application, you can watch hungry midges doing sudden U-turns as they make contact with the chemical. There are natural alternatives based on citronella and eucalyptus oil, and if all else fails, midge hoods are available everywhere in the Highlands.

Seasoned walkers and campers have had their own midge remedies. Some relied on the preventative properties of brewer's yeast. Others use orange peel or Marmite, or simply trust in light-coloured clothing. It was common practice for campers to tie sprigs of aromatic bog myrtle leaves to the tent post (the plant was also used in the Highlands to deter clothes moths). Fishermen would stick a few sprigs in their hats. In 1995, a commercial repellent based on bog myrtle, gathered from the wild on the Isle of Skye and steam-distilled to produce a volatile oil, was manufactured by Scotia Pharmaceuticals under the name Myrica. Unfortunately the project foundered before the repellent could be put on sale.

Evenings on the terrace overlooking spacious harbours or distant mountains have been made comfortable by another invention, the midge-eater. Midges are drawn to our bodies by our smell and especially by the invisible trail of carbon dioxide we leave. The midge-eater, which looks like a portable stove, releases the gas to draw them into a disposable bag. It can chew up tens of thousands of midges with calm efficiency, and the sight of the bulging bag full of what look like greyish soap flakes is an impressive indication of what the evening might have been like without this clever invention.

Despite DEET and midge-eaters, midges seem to be broadening their range, both spatially and temporally. In the past, midge days were more or less confined to the summer months, especially July and August, but today there are plenty of midges around in the spring. Eastern Scotland was, until recently, not much troubled by midges, but they are now a nuisance, at least in wet summers, in Edinburgh and the Lothians (though the hot weather in 2006 killed them off).

With the arrival of blue-tongue disease in Britain in 2007, biting midges became a potentially serious problem for cattle and sheep farmers. Blue-tongue is a non-contagious animal disease caused by a virus that is spread by midges. Until 1998, it was confined to southern Europe and North Africa, but it has been spreading north, perhaps through global warming, perhaps also because the virus is now

307

carried by midges that occur in northern Europe, including the Garden Midge. By 2006, it had reached Germany and the Netherlands, and by the following September, the first case in Britain was diagnosed at a Rare Breeds farm near Ipswich (there were no new cases reported in 2008). The symptoms are those of a bad cold, the swollen 'blue' or cyanosed tongue appearing in only a minority of cases. There is no effective treatment available other than vaccination. DEFRA's response was to restrict the movement of cattle within areas designated as Blue-tongue Protection Zones. Its recommendations include the draining of wet patches where the midges may breed. Unfortunately, a lot of other insects, most of them harmless and benign, also breed on wet patches.

Non-biting midges are of interest mainly to fishermen. Forms of the slender larvae of chironomid midges contain an iron-rich substance, similar to the haemoglobin in human blood, that helps them to breathe in the anoxic sludge at the bottom of ponds. Known as bloodworms, they are used as fish food (a source of iron, they are also high in calories and are 60 per cent protein). Trout fishermen have made ingenious wriggly flexiglass flies to imitate them. Bloodworms can be bought live or freeze-dried as cubes or pellets. Most if not all of them come from the wild, sieved from the mud at night when the 'worms' are active. Colourless forms are known as glassworms.

Adult gnats are important food for trout and other fish, as well as swallows and martins hawking over the water. Among the fishing flies based on them are summer flies named 'racehorses' or 'buzzers', from the gnat's habit of flying close to the water's surface. Other famous gnat flies include the Golden Dun Midge, the Blagdon Buzzer, the Ruby Gnat and the Blae and Blacks.

Scientifically speaking, the word midge embraces several families of small, gnat-like flies, few of which actually bite. They include phantom midges (Chaoboridae), owl midges (Psychodidae), gall midges (Cecidomyiidae) and meniscus midges (Dixidae). The most abundant of all are midges with feathered antennae (Chironomidae) that form large mating swarms near water and often occur in swarms in the dead of winter. All except the gall midges have aquatic larvae, and none can bite us. The bad reputation of midges is based on a single family, the Ceratopogonidae, or biting midges, and above all, on just one species, the Highland Midge.

Blackflies *Simulidae*

VN: Blandford Bomber, Blandford Fly, buffalo gnats, reed smuts

The most notorious blackfly in Britain is the Blandford Fly or 'Blanny Bomber', the worst of all the small, dark biting flies that haunt the riverbanks and marshes. It is widespread but is associated above all with the town of Blandford Forum in Dorset, where it breeds in the shallows of the River Stour. It first came to public notice in the 1960s, when people began to visit their GPs with bubbly skin lesions, especially on their shins. Once the culprit had been identified, legends sprang up to explain the apparently sudden arrival of such un-British flies. Some said they came in with a consignment of butterflies from South America. Others believed that they were unwittingly introduced as eggs in the mud-caked boots of soldiers at nearby Blandford Camp. The most persistent story blamed sinister experiments in the biology lab of Blandford's Bryanston School (by way of evidence, it was pointed out that the fly is particularly common around boarding schools near the river).

Things reached a head in 1972 when 600 people needed treatment within a four-week period. The Blandford Fly had another vintage season in 1988, when 1400 people suffered bites and lesions, and questions were asked about it in Parliament. Being English, we turned it all into a bit of a joke. One resident suggested adding the words 'Home to the Blandford Fly' to all road signs. With its growing fame, the fly made an appearance as a cunning eco-terrorist weapon in *Creeping Jenny*, a 1993 mystery novel in which wicked plotters plan to release swarms of the flies during the Queen's visit to the Chelsea Flower Show. The fly itself appeared on a locally brewed bottled ale called Blandford Fly (though more recently, the undistinguished-looking fly was replaced by a fly fisherman). The ale contains zingibain, a natural enzyme found in ginger and said to be good for bites. Could it be that large quantities of this elixir are the best way of preventing blackfly bites!

Blackflies are small, squat little flies barely five millimetres long, with blackish bodies and dark-veined wings. There are about 40 species, all of which live in wet places, especially on the banks of fast-flowing rivers and streams. Like mosquitoes

Blandford Fly, a locally brewed bottle ale celebrating the River Stour's notorious biting fly.

moreover, have extended their time of emergence. People living within a kilometre of the river are now advised neither to lie naked on sunbeds on blackfly days nor to expose their legs by the river on warm, windless evenings. Insect repellent is a partial solution. Some prefer to use nature's own repellent and rub themselves with tansy. It smells like tomcats but is said to deter the flies.

Blackflies, both as larvae and adults, are eaten greedily by trout and other fish. Anglers cash in by tying small black imitation flies called reed smuts. They work best during a mass emergence of the insects, when the artificial fly is sunk just beneath the surface and wriggled about as realistically as possible.

and horseflies, the female blackfly needs occasional blood meals to accumulate body protein for her eggs. Fortunately, only the Blandford Fly seems to specialise in humans. Other blackflies prefer mammals or birds. In North America and Africa, where they are known as buffalo gnats, blackflies have been known to drive horses and cattle into a frenzy.

The early stages of blackflies are aquatic, but unlike the agile larva of a mosquito or gnat, the blackfly larva is a passive beast which attaches itself to a rock and simply filter-feeds on suspended matter in the water. When fully fed, it pupates inside a brown cocoon the shape of an ice-cream cornet, and the fly duly emerges in the late spring. The young adult floats elegantly to the surface inside a silvery bubble of air – a brief, incongruous moment of beauty and wonder.

Early attempts to control the Blandford Fly by cutting or dragging out river-weed were ineffective as well as environmentally damaging. Fortunately, an alternative weapon was found in the form of a naturally occurring bacterium called *Bacillus thuringiensis israelensis,* or 'Bti', which carries a toxin fatal to blackflies. From 1991, the riverbanks were routinely sprayed with the agent at emergence time, and reported cases of blackfly bites fell by 80 to 90 percent. The bacillus is said to be host-specific so that other species, even other blackfly species, are not harmed. It is, it seems, a shining example of a biological pesticide that really works.

The fly, though, is not going quietly. In an impressive evolutionary fight-back, some have already acquired immunity to the bacillus and,

March flies *Bibionidae*

vn: black gnat, hawthorn fly, love bug, St Mark's fly

'The air was heavy with St Mark's flies', said Roger Deakin. 'They are top-heavy insects, with a thorax like an old Dragon Rapide biplane and a body that tapers to nothing. Their flight is jerky and uncertain. They kept taking off like Bleriot on a maiden flight, dropping out of the sky quite suddenly, only to catch themselves, as if on an invisible safety net, and set some new and equally aimless course. Their larvae live on the roots of wet grasses, and they must all have emerged at the same moment without any clear idea about the direction their lives should take. Truly a fly for our times.'[28]

While walking over wet meadows on a warm day in April, it is hard to avoid these harmless black flies. They emerge towards the end of March, and by midday, many will be doubled up in midair copulation – amorous tendencies that resulted in another country name, 'love bug'. The flies visit flowers and are believed to be useful pollinators. The St Mark's fly is so called because it appears around St Mark's Day (21 April). It is wolfed down in quantities by trout, and on the days when it is swarming some anglers swear by an imitation fly called 'Bibio'. Our non-biting March flies should not be confused with the fierce March flies of Australia and other countries, which are relatives of what we call horseflies.

The other common March fly is the Fever Fly,

St Mark's fly, the blackest of blackflies, noted for its aimless, chaotic flights over marshy ground.

which has a smaller head and more transparent wings. It swarms on flowers in the spring and is sometimes called the Blossom Fly. The name Fever Fly is a mystery, since the fly does not transmit disease, nor was it used by apothecaries in fever cures. Perhaps, it refers to the fly's chaotic, feverish flight.

Soldierflies *Stratiomyidae*

Why *soldier* flies? Flies, after all, do not move around in battle groups, nor do they conduct wars. These particular flies are, though, decked out in bright and gleaming colours and, with one wing crossed smartly over the other and with their margins as parallel as a sentry's rifle, they seem to 'stand on duty'. The English names recently invented for all 47 British soldierflies have a marked military flavour: there are legionnaires, centurions and plain soldiers, in addition to a hierarchy of ranks: majors, colonels, brigadiers and generals.[29] All British soldierflies are considered to belong to the officer class, though there is a junior-sounding Common Orange Legionnaire and a Pygmy Soldier, while the Delicate Soldier sounds as though it was excused boots on parade.

What distinguish a soldierfly are its colours, especially metallic greens and vivid yellows, like dabs of poster paint on a plastic model. They look like hoverflies but are less proficient fliers and have more flattened bodies, with distinctive antennae that

project forward like little black daggers. They are active in warm weather and are most often seen on flowers, especially umbellifers such as hogweed and water dropwort. Their main claim to fame today is as habitat indicators. Soldierflies are pernickety insects that require precise habitat conditions. Their larvae need seepages and trickles of lime-rich water (some of the lime ends up in their cuticle) or wet moss, and the flies are often early victims of drainage. At one time, these soldiers seemed to be losing the battle.

Fortunately, they are more resilient than was once thought. Many are not so much rare as hard to find. Alan Stubbs found a perfect lure for both the adults and their larvae in fruit skins: for some reason, soldierflies find a partially rotted hemisphere of grapefruit irresistible. Today's soldierfly specialists tend to eat grapefruit for breakfast and pack their knapsack with the peel. Another breakthrough in understanding was the discovery that the adult flies do not hang around their breeding sites but congregate in bushes. Soldierfly hunters no longer squelch fruitlessly through the mud but wander around the edge, peering at leaves. The erstwhile, ominously empty, distribution maps have started to fill with dots.

The soldierfly called the Barred Green Colonel has been described as the nation's rarest fly (though there are many other contenders for that title). The Forestry Commission has come to its aid in Dalby Forest, Yorkshire, by introducing longhorn cattle. The idea is to create water-filled hoof holes, which represent luxury living for the fly. The herd will also graze on invasive vegetation such as rushes and birch saplings, which threaten to overrun the site. It seems that what rare insects such as the Barred Green Colonel need is not a protective fence but the right kind of low-intensity farming.

Not all soldierflies are so dainty. The Black Soldierfly does not occur naturally in Britain, but its larvae are mass-reared indoors as food for lizards. As a soldierfly, its behaviour is out of order, swarming around chicken coops and dung heaps. The advantage to herpetologists is that its larvae are rich in calcium, containing 20 times as much of this bone-building element than other maggots. In America, they are known as 'phoenix worms', while over here they are marketed as 'calci-worms'.

Left: *The Banded General Soldierfly, its yellow markings gleaming like fresh paint.*

Snipeflies *Rhagionidae*

VN: down-looker fly

Bulging-eyed and spindly-legged, snipeflies are found in the sort of marshy places where you might expect to see snipe. However, the name is more likely taken from the way the fly's body tapers sharply to an attenuated point like a bird's beak. The alternative name of 'down-looker flies' comes from the fly's habit of invariably settling face down.

A related family, Therevidae, with similarly pointed bodies, is known as stiletto-flies. The small family Xylophagidae, or awl-flies, has distinctive awl-headed maggots.

Horseflies *Tabanidae*

VN: borrill (Yorks), breeze (or breeze-fly), brim, brimp, bumbore (NE Eng.), burrel-fly, clag (Ireland), cleg (or clegg), clinger, crawgon (Isle of Man), deerfly, doctor, dun-fly, gad-fly, gled (or gleg) (N Eng., Scotland), goad-bee, goad-fly, horsestinger (Glos.), nimble dick (Kent), old maid (Glos.), stout or stowt (Hants), swap (Cornwall), thunder-fly (Herts), waps (Cornwall), whame-fly

Gaelic: *croaghan*

It sounds strange and contradictory, wrote Alan Stubbs, that an insect with such ugly habits should be so beautiful.[30] Horseflies, or clegs, are the largest of the blood-sucking flies, and when they bite they hurt. Not for them the painless whisper of the mosquito's quiet stiletto. There is a Scottish expression: 'Whaur the midgies mazy dance, Clegs dart oot the fiery lance.'[31] A fly that can puncture the hide of a cow or horse experiences no trouble at all with human skin. As Thomas Muffet wrote more than 400 years ago, the horsefly 'carries before him a very hard, stiff, and well compacted sting, with which he strikes through the Oxe his hide; he is in fashion like a great Fly, and forces the beasts for fear of him only to stand up to the belly in water, or else to betake themselves to wood sides, cool shades, and places where the wind blowes through.'[32]

The unexpected beauty of horseflies resides

mainly in their bulging eyes. Those in the genus *Chrysops* are green or bronze with reflected spots surrounded by a rainbow-coloured halo. Those of *Tabanus* have shimmering bands of iridescent colour. Even the dullest and commonest horsefly, the notorious cleg, has intriguing zigzag golden bands that flicker across its eyes as the fly contemplates its next victim. The colours vanish after death, so that museum specimens contain no hint of the psychedelic aura of the living fly.

The Roman Pliny the Younger named large biting flies *Tabanus*, which survives as the generic name of our largest horseflies. Countrymen did not usually distinguish the different kinds of large biting flies, and so the name 'gad-fly' is a mishmash of horseflies, warble-flies or any other biting fly (or supposedly biting fly) that torments livestock. A 'gad' is a spike. The name was in use in Shakespeare's day and is proverbial: a human gadfly is someone who stings and annoys, a satirical journalist, for example.

The large *Tabanus* horseflies are particularly common in the New Forest, where they were known as 'stouts' or 'stowts', from their thick-set bodies. On the Gower, and perhaps elsewhere, they were 'brims', while on the Isle of Man they were 'crawgons'.[33] The *Chrysops* horseflies are often known as deerflies, perhaps because they are common on moors where deer roam. They are also known as thunder-flies.

The commonest word for horseflies, cleg (sometimes spelt with two 'g's), comes from an Old Norse word and so may have been introduced here by Vikings. In other places settled by Vikings, such as Iceland, they are 'kleggi', while in Scotland they are sometimes 'glegs', and in Ireland 'clags'. Some confine 'cleg' to a particular species, the dark-bodied, dusky-winged Common Cleg, *Haematopota* (which means 'blood-drinker') – by far the commonest horsefly and the one that bites us most often. Another name that alludes to its subdued colour is dun-fly. We are lucky that British clegs tend to attack us in ones and twos and not, as in some countries, in swarms. Who, for example, would want to live in Horsefly, a town in British Columbia?

Horseflies are summer insects and are most active on hot, windless days. They commonly emerge from their pupae in the morning but take time to warm up and so tend to be most active around midday and into the afternoon. Horseflies lay their eggs in moist soil and so are commonest in wet places such as damp meadows, stream banks and marshes. Like their mothers, the larvae are agile predators. One large species is known to eat 'earthworms and fly larvae, including their own kind, and are prepared to bite anything else offered, such as fingers and frogs.'[34]

Despite their size and ferocity, horseflies are by no means top predators, even among insects. They have parasites galore and regularly fall prey to robberflies, spiders and swallows. Their larvae, too, are gobbled up in their thousands by wading birds. The best places to see horseflies, at least in terms of diversity, are the New Forest and the Purbeck heaths of Dorset. This might be a disincentive to most people, but greater biodiversity does not necessarily increase one's chances of being bitten. Most horseflies prefer the blood of deer, feral ponies and free-range cattle to that of humans. We are not a normal part of their diet.

Those people who wish to find horseflies look for them in puddles where the flies congregate in hot weather – or make a trap to catch them, such as a malaise trap, a kind of muslin tent with a collecting bottle at one end. The simplest way is to leave your car in the full sun in a likely spot with the window down until the interior is like an oven. Dark coloured cars seem to be the most attractive. One hot day in 1995, the Scottish town of Inverary was shocked to find quantities of huge flies basking on cars throughout the town and by the dozen on the front window of a car showroom. It was a mass emergence of the seldom-seen Dark Giant Horsefly, one of the world's largest horseflies.

Only the female horsefly bites, for like other blood-sucking insects, she needs a blood meal as a fast-fix to accumulate enough body protein to develop her eggs. It takes six days for a fly to digest a full blood meal and get hungry again. Most horseflies that come our way are females. When it bites, the fly injects a drop of saliva containing an anticoagulant to prevent the blood from clotting. During feeding, colourless fluid may pass out of the fly's anus. It is the response of our skin to substances left behind by the fly, not to the bite itself, which causes a nasty swelling reaction in some people. Fortunately, British horseflies do not transmit diseases, though there is a small risk of secondary infection if the bite is scratched (in Africa, deerflies are the vectors of a tiny worm that bores into the eye). Curiously enough, it is perfectly safe to handle horseflies; they don't bite in defence but only when their body processes compel them to.

Horseflies drink correspondingly more blood

Head on: the vast coloured eyes and biting gear of a Tabanus *horsefly.*

than midges and mosquitoes. The smaller ones will take about 20 to 30 milligrams if given the chance, the larger, bee-sized ones up to a disconcerting 200 mg. Of course, humans seldom allow them to take that much, but a large swarm of horseflies could be distressing for a tethered animal. Muffet (who also knew them as 'side-flies') preserved a story, perhaps a Tudor legend, of a horse that was bitten to death by these furious insects. Unable to run away, it was, 'by reason of the multitude of them, killed in less than six hours; they had drawn out so much blood that the spirits failing he fell down dead.'[35]

Different kinds of horseflies tend to bite different parts of the body. The cleg has a preference for wrists or bare legs and, being silent on the wing, rarely gives any warning of its approach. When a big *Tabanus* approaches, it is likely to circle round your head before disdainfully buzzing off, in Alan Stubbs' words, 'looking for something bigger and better.'[36] When it does bite, it usually zooms in close to the ground and alights on the legs or ankles or behind the knees, making a deep, loud buzz as it does so. *Chrysops* flies higher and tends to settle out

of sight on the back of the neck with a trademark high-pitched buzz. *Hybomitra* (distinguished by its hairy eyes) has a taste for the tender flesh near the top of the thighs – if you happen to be in its marshy haunts on a hot day wearing shorts. Horsefly experts claim to distinguish the various species by the pitch of their hum.

Some people are more attractive to horseflies than others. Women are bitten more often than men (though clegs are less fussy). 'Your chances of becoming a good lure,' says Stubbs, are increased by wearing dark cloths (black, brown or red) … It is probable that running about to make yourself hot and sweaty will make you even more irresistible – to horseflies, that is.' 'The susceptibility of women to horsefly bites is well-known,' notes Tony Harwood. 'An entomologist friend sometimes uses his wife as unwitting bait. He will invite her out for a nice country walk and, once horsefly habitat has been reached, will lurk behind a short distance, net in hand.'[37]

Flat-flies *Hippoboscidae*

AN: louse-flies

Miriam Rothschild once imagined that, if 'we could talk to birds as we talk to one another we would probably find that flies ... provide one of the major topics of conversation.' By day, flies form part of the diet of birds, but by night the tables are turned with a vengeance. Among the biting flies that assail sleeping birds are housefly-sized objects known as flat-flies or louse-flies. For a small bird such as a robin, the discomfort of a pair of these clambering about must be like 'a man with a couple of large shore crabs scuttling about in his underclothes.'[38]

Flat-flies are beautifully camouflaged to resemble the feather colour of their host (a lovely iridescent green on the wood pigeon, for example). They are perhaps best known to ringers or grouse-moor keepers, for they have a disconcerting habit of slipping off their avian victim and on to your sleeve or into your hair (Muffet noted, accurately enough, that 'they never fly forward but sidelong, as it were, hopping and skipping as they go'). The bite of a flat-fly is neither dangerous nor painful, but because the fly is a parasite, it has an element of add-on horror.

The flat-fly family also includes the wingless Sheep Ked and the Forest Fly, which ignore humans but bite cattle, horses and deer. These bizarre flies do not lay eggs but, like us, produce just one baby at a time, nourishing it internally until giving birth to a fat and fully developed maggot, which pupates almost immediately. A related family of wingless flies, the Nycteribiidae, lives among the fur of bats.

Bee-flies *Bombyliidae*

One of the small pleasures of spring is watching bee-flies. They are most commonly seen hovering over sunny banks visiting early flowers such as primroses, ground-ivy or, in gardens, aubrietia. They hover-steer from one flower to the next, probing the blossoms like tiny hummingbirds. There is something comforting, as well as slightly comic, about a bee-fly – a tiny, furry ball of an insect, with a long, stiff tongue sticking out in front like a drawn sword. But the fly's pleasant looks and habits are misleading. As a grub, it is a carnivore, growing fat on the combs and larvae of bees.

Nearly all the bee-flies you will see are likely to be the Common, or Dark-edged, Bee-fly, distinguished by a chocolate-brown band along the border of its wings. The other eight native species are all seldom-seen habitat specialists, confined to dunes, southern heaths and coastal cliffs. One all-black continental bee-fly, only doubtfully recorded from Britain, has the terrifying name of *Anthrax anthrax*. But, in Greek, *anthrax* means nothing worse than a lump of coal. (The disease anthrax was so named because the infected animal seemed to burn from within, like coal).

The Western Bee-fly, a fuzzy winged ball with a proboscis like a blade.

Right: *A conopid, or Thick-headed Fly* (Physocephala nigra), *a parasite of bumblebees.*

Hunchbacked flies
Acroceridae

A fly that feeds on spiders is an amusing twist on traditional folklore. To look at them, these flies are not obvious predators. They are dumpy and humpbacked, with tiny round heads tucked under, hence their name of hunchbacked flies or, less memorably, small-headed flies. The adults cannot feed; indeed they can barely fly; 'Their design,' remarks Alan Stubbs, 'does not strike one as airworthy,'[39] and they spend their short lives basking or walking over foliage or sometimes borne along on the wind passively, like tiny balloons.

Their unexpected taste for spiders comes at the larval stage. To survive, a newly hatched grub has to grab hold of a passing spider. In pursuance of this seemingly impossible objective, the tiny maggot jerks itself along like a self-propelled tiddlywink, using its tail bristles as propulsion. Its next task is to hang grimly on to one of the host's eight legs and then chew its way inside. Over the ensuing days, the grub sets off on a journey through the innards of the spider, being careful to avoid the vital parts until the last minute. It is probable that only exceptionally lucky maggots succeed in becoming a hunchbacked fly.

Many of these winged, parasitical Quasimodos themselves fall victim to parasites, notably a wasp, *Ectomnius rubicola* – which, to continue the unlikely tale, packs its nest exclusively with the drugged but still-living bodies of hunchbacked flies.

Robberflies *Asilidae*

AN: assassin-fly

The name robberfly suggests an ambush predator that lies in wait for its victim. In this case, it is not the victim's goods that are robbed but its life. A robberfly has piercing mouthparts and toxic saliva that immobilises its victim, allowing the fly's long, bristly legs to grip and carry it away. Its alternative name is assassin-fly.

Britain is too cold and wet for all but a few robberflies; we have 28 species compared with France's 150. Even so, we do have one of the most spectacular species, the Hornet Robberfly – a hornet mimic and Britain's largest fly. Robberflies are very active and have prodigious appetites: a large one may consume a thousand prey items over its two-month life on the wing. It has an appearance of 'intense awareness, pivoting its body towards potential targets, ready to pounce.'[40] Its large eyes are mounted on a smallish, swivelling head so that the fly can see behind as well as forwards. It can also, it seems, use binocular vision to calculate the distance of a prey animal with precision. Yet though they might look capable of biting, robberflies do not bite people, and if you catch one in your hands, it seems at a loss to know what to do.

The Hornet Robberfly never fails to elicit a gasp from the crowd, but unfortunately it has declined greatly due in part to the veterinary drug ivermectin, which renders the dung of cattle and sheep effectively sterile. The fly lays its eggs in dung and depends on an ample supply of dung insects and maggots as food. Having robbed the robberfly of its means of survival, we are now trying to make amends with an action plan for its survival. As a large and colourful fly, it has become an icon for the fragility of insect life, as well as a lead for the conservation of that neglected and threatened ecosystem, natural dung.

Robberflies would undoubtedly be better known if there was a good fieldguide. Unfortunately for us, the standard work is in Swedish, and it was published 80 years ago.

A prey's eye view of the Hornet Robberfly, displaying its long grasping legs.

Hoverflies *Syrphidae*

VN: flower flies, sweat-flies, Syrphids

Hoverflies are among the friendliest and least disconcerting of flies, hovering so effortlessly at flowers, a thin whine coming from their blurred wings. Like ladybirds, the larvae of some hoverflies have a vast appetite for aphids and so are considered gardeners' friends. They are attractive as well as friendly, with their yellow and black stripes or furry, bee-like bodies. Obligingly, they lose all their wariness when feasting on flowers or basking in the sun and allow us to admire them at close quarters.

Hoverflies are defined by a structure in the middle of their wing, called a *vena spuria*, or false vein. It is this that enables their wings to flex and hence hover, with a simple up-and-down wing-beat (as opposed to the exhausting figure-of-eight acrobatics that a hummingbird must undergo to stay airborne). A hoverfly may beat its wings several hundred times per second to stay stationary in the air, and it is also this simple beat that gives the fly its characteristic steady, straight flight, more like a bee than a fly. Some hoverflies actually look like bees or (less convincingly) like wasps. Though no hoverfly can sting or bite us, when attracted by our personal pheromones (scents) or the smell of sweat, they may deliver a defensive pretend-sting – perhaps the origin of the myth that large hoverflies have stings. They can easily be distinguished from wasps and bees by their lack of long antennae and single pair of wings (bees and wasps have two pairs).

There are 276 species of hoverfly in Britain, varying from the size of a bumblebee to small slender flies hardly bigger than a gnat. In abundance, they vary from the orange and black 'marmalade hoverfly', which can be found on every hogweed flower or ivy blossom, to the impossibly rare *Callicera spinolae*, which was once thought to be confined to pair of 'water-filled rot-holes in two beech trees at a site in Cambridgeshire'[41] – not quite so hopelessly rare today but still confined to a handful of sites.

Hoverflies are the most popular group of flies.

The hoverfly Volucella bombylans, *a bumblebee-mimic.*

Many gardeners go out of their way to attract them. They have even been called 'the butterflies of the flies' (in America they are known by the more attractive name of flower-flies). There is a first-rate handbook available,[42] and identification courses are regularly held at field-centres. A British Hoverfly Recording Scheme was set up in 1976, and a distribution atlas was published in 2000, with more than 375,000 individual records. Recorders are served by a newsletter. There is also an online system for 'predicting hoverfly assemblages across Europe,' called Syrph the Net, a play on their family name, Syrphidae (from the Greek word *syrphos*, meaning a gnat).

The main barrier to their popularity, apart from the similarity of many species, is their lack of English names. Some have established nicknames, such as the 'marmalade hoverfly', whose orange stripes resemble peel, or the 'tiger hoverfly', whose thorax is striped with yellow and black. A pair of long-tongued hoverflies have been dubbed the 'Heineken flies' because they reach the flowers that other hoverflies can't reach.

Hoverflies are important pollinators. They are useful yardsticks of biodiversity and, like butterflies, are believed to be sensitive indicators of environmental change. Many species live in specialised habitats such as decaying wood or rot-holes in old trees, where the larvae feed mainly on bacteria and other micro-organisms, or the sugar-rich sap running from fissures in the bark. The larvae of the *Microdon* hoverflies live inside ants nests and are armoured for protection from bites. Several feed on yeasts or fungi. Some of the biggest species breed inside the nests of bumblebees and social wasps. Many hoverflies visit gardens, but the less common ones tend to be confined to wild sites such as open woods with plenty of old trees and dead wood (the ancient pine forests of Scotland have their own exclusive suite of them), or warm, open heaths and uncultivated downs.

It is easy to attract hoverflies to the garden. The adults depend on the nectar and pollen of flowers (they are among the few insects that can digest pollen, crunching it up into its component grains and then swallowing them). Among the most attractive plants to hoverflies are Michaelmas daisies, ice-plant, *Phacelia* and candytuft, as well as flowering shrubs such as apple. Some gardeners use 'companion planting' to enlist them in aphid control. Among insect-friendly plants commonly interplanted among vulnerable flowers and vegetables are alyssums, buckwheat, chamomile and yarrow. The technique also has potential in fields of wheat, where the cereal aphid is a problem.

Hoverflies appreciate a sunny border of wild flowers. Hogweed, with its flat, floral larders of smelly pollen, probably heads the list, but other favourites include dandelions and hawkbits, bindweed and thistles. In wilder places, enthusiasts have experimented with artificial rot-holes carved out of pine stumps or made from plastic bottles filled with wet sawdust and slung from trees. 'If we can provide nest boxes for birds, dormice and bats, why not breeding bottles for hoverflies?' asks Alan Stubbs.[43]

Droneflies

Droneflies are large, bee-mimicking hoverflies, so named for their resemblance to a dark male bee, or drone. They visit garden flowers with a distinctly bee-like buzz, and newspaper reports of unusually late swarms of honeybees on the Michaelmas daisies often turn out to be droneflies. The females hibernate in crevices in walls or in outhouses or sheds, where they can be seen droning around on mild, sunny days in late winter. Hence this is one of the few insects that can be seen at any time of year.

Adult droneflies behave like conventional hoverflies. But their larvae are the amazing rat-tailed maggots, which can live happily in a bucket of water on a diet of liquid manure or rich compost. The aerial-like 'rat tails' that dimple the water's surface are breathing tubes of adjustable length. They allow the soft-skinned maggots to survive in grossly polluted, virtually oxygen-free water, growing fast and fat on the organic gunk seeping from manure or silage. When it is fully grown, the maggot simply floats to the surface, where it pupates. To look at the clean, handsome, bee-like adult fly, you would never suspect it of such a prenatal existence.

Needless to say, children love rat-tailed maggots. 'My four-year-old daughter Amelia is keen on creating liquid concoctions which are dotted around the garden in every available receptacle. These foul brews contain generous portions of washing-up liquid, compost, and worse, and are very attractive to droneflies. They are soon populated with rat-tailed maggots. They thrive, much to Amelia's delight, until the rain dilutes the brew, after which other beasties, such as mosquito and midge larvae, move in.'[44]

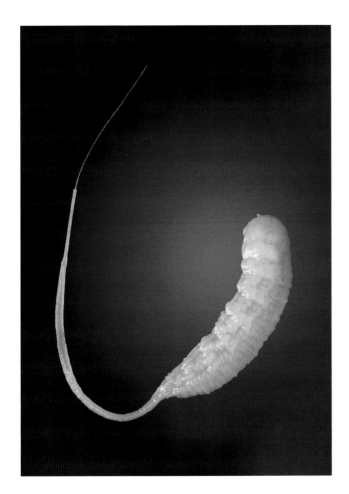

A rat-tailed maggot, the strange larva of the dronefly. The 'rat's tail' is an elongated breathing tube.

In his 1997 poem 'The Rat-tailed Maggot', the punk poet Attila the Stockbroker found comic literary possibilities in the beast's noisome life, 'feasting on Decomposing Vegetation/ And breathing through a Membranous Extension/ Which penetrates the water's surface tension . . . Our dear protagonist pupates/ (Along with many thousands of his mates)/ In dried-up hollows made from Cattle Piss.'[45]

A stained-glass dronefly sits on a sundial in a window in Bucklebury Church, Berkshire. The picture, which dates from the mid-seventeenth century, is a visual pun on the expression 'how time flies'. The fly is drawn with care, and the entomologist Malcolm Storey, who lives nearby, believes it was done from life. In summer 2007, the church was flooded with slurry from a pig farm, creating a dream habitat for rat-tailed maggots.

Bulb Flies

AN: Amaryllid fly, large bulb fly, large narcissus fly

While most hoverflies feed harmlessly on nectar, sap and aphids, three species are characterised as pests because they feed on bulbs: the Greater Bulb-fly and two smaller ones that share the same name of lesser bulb-fly. Their larvae mine into bulbs and feed from within, gradually hollowing out the interior. They are more of a nuisance in horticulture than small gardens, where there are rarely enough of them to do much damage. Yet, 'why worry at the inconspicuous loss of an occasional bulb?' asks Alan Stubbs, when the adult perpetrators are so attractive and pleasing to see. If you spot the telltale hole when collecting bulbs for storing over winter, you need only squeeze the bulb, and the maggot will pop out like a cork.

Bulb-flies prefer some bulbs to others. They are attracted to daffodils, but tulips are usually free of them. The Greater Bulb-fly has a taste for amaryllis lilies in conservatories and greenhouses. The lesser ones sometimes invade the vegetable patch in search of onions and other alliums, as well as parsnip or potato tubers and rhizomes. In the countryside, they are believed to be sustained on a diet of bluebells. The adults, meanwhile, feed innocently on dandelion flowers.

Fruitflies *Tephritidae*

VN: picture-winged flies, vinegar flies

Fruitflies are the small flies with patterned wings that you may find floating in a glass of wine or whisky the moment you take your eyes off it. They are also called vinegar flies, from the belief that their tiny bodies generated spontaneously in sour wine. In fact, fruitfly larvae feed exclusively on soft, decaying fruit, in flowerheads or, in certain cases, inside galls. Apart from their suicidal craving for alcohol, fruitflies would be barely known outside entomological circles were it not for one species that has become the most studied animal on earth.

Drosophila melanogaster is generally known as *the* fruitfly (*Drosophila* means 'dew-lover') and is the standard experimental animal of the genetics

319

lab. The genetic variation of flies was first noticed more than 2000 years ago by Aristotle, who noted that their offspring were 'never identical in shape with the parents, but something imperfect.' His observation was confirmed in the twentieth century when Thomas Hunt Morgan of Columbia University, New York, found numerous anatomical variations among the progeny of his stock of fruitflies, some with deformed wings, others with white eyes instead of the usual red.

Morgan saw the potential of flies for investigations into the biology of inheritance. Not only did the fruitfly mutate into myriads of easily recognisable forms but it also has a short lifecycle and is easy to breed. A thousand years of human genetics can, for fruitflies, be compressed into a single year. The fly also has unusually large chromosomes that can be extracted and counted relatively easily. During the 1930s, Morgan bred industrial quantities of them and, by studying their patterns of inheritance, built up detailed genetic maps. For the first time, the genes responsible for a particular characteristic could be located on the chromosome. Morgan's one-time co-worker Hermann Muller also found that bombarding the flies with X-rays would increase the rate of genetic mutation. Apart from its applications to fundamental and applied research, Muller's discovery casually spawned a genre of horror films in which insects and spiders accidentally exposed to radiation became monstrous as well as, somehow, more intelligent.

Since the 1970s, there has been a new focus of fruitfly research in embryology. The ease by which the fly can mutate makes it the ideal subject for investigations into developmental processes. In other words, biologists want to know how a fruitfly is built. St Augustine once said that only God could make a fly. While we can't make a fly, we have at least unravelled God's blueprint. By 2000, the entire genetic code of the fruitfly had been worked out. Altogether, by dint of the massive research effort devoted to it, this lowly fly has become a kind of genetic ambassador, a representative of all living forms.

Houseflies *Muscidae*

VN: adult fly: flee;
     maggot: mawk, maygut (Lancs.), wick (Cumbria), worms

Thomas Muffet summed up the charms of houseflies in words that are hard to beat: 'All of them are begotten of filth and nastiness, to which they most willingly cleave, and resort especially to such places which are so uncleanly and filthy; unquiet they are, importunate, hateful, troublesome, tumultuous, bold, saucy.'[46]

Houseflies are our constant familiars. They accompany us wherever we settle and wherever we go, feeding where we feed, sharing our domestic space. They breed among the warm, smelly products of decomposition in dustbins and uncollected rubbish. They are what the French poet Andre Bay called 'the constant, immemorial witnesses to the human comedy'.[47]

It was possible to like houseflies, or at least to show sympathy with them as co-tenants. John Clare likened them to chubby fairies as 'things of the mind'. After 'dancing in the window all day from sunrise to sun-set they would sip of the tea, drink of the beer, and eat of the sugar'. The owners of many clean cottages and genteel houses allowed them 'every liberty to creep, fly, or do as they like', or so he claimed. 'They are the small or dwarfish portion of our own family, and so many fairy familiars that we know and treat as one of ourselves.'[48]

Certain ancient writers also wrote about houseflies with, if not the same degree of obvious affection as Clare, at least with a certain respect. Plutarch was struck by the contrast between the fly's proximity and its untamable nature. Of all the creatures that share our dwellings, only the fly and the swallow, he thought, cannot be domesticated. Flies were 'indocile and unteachable creatures, who, though they use the company of men daily, are by no means tamed, neither do they show the least courtesy, or the least show of a grateful mind . . . Both of them are by nature very suspicious, always fearful of treachery, afraid to be caught.'

Perhaps this aloofness could be put down to an apparent absence of feeling on the fly's part. The Italian humanist Leone Battista Alberti marvelled how a fly could endure such changes of fortune without showing so much as a flicker of emotion on

The face of a housefly (coloured artificially).

its 'frozen face'. 'I am ready to declare', he wrote, 'that the fly is the only creature blessed with such equanimity that it has never anywhere been seen to laugh, or weep, or furrow its brow, or clear its forehead in face of any adversity or good fortune. The set of its features is always the same.'[49]

Despite their attraction to dirt and filth, houseflies were ironically once regarded as being on the right side of public hygiene. They were God's binmen or 'winged sponges', helping to clean up and removing putrefying matter from our midst. In addition, their buzzing was considered wholesome and helped to keep the air pure and well-ventilated. Those who studied them closely realised that flies were fastidious insects, constantly cleaning and grooming themselves with a rub-down from their bristly legs, paying special attention to the eyes, mouthparts and other parts on whose smooth functioning the insect depends.

It was only towards the end of the nineteenth century that the image of houseflies – along with mosquitoes, lice and fleas – took a nosedive when it became clear that they were vectors of disease. Not only did they excrete on our food but, in doing so, spread the germs of sometimes fatal diseases such as typhoid and diphtheria. In the brief Spanish–American War of 1898, more soldiers died of typhoid than of wounds. The subsequent enquiry found conclusive evidence that the infection had been spread from one patient to the next by clouds of flies. It led to a campaign to change the innocuous name housefly to 'typhoid fly' and its dubbing in the press as 'the most dangerous animal on earth'. Later, more diseases were added to the charge-sheet: diarrhoea and dysentery, cholera, tuberculosis, polio – eventually 60 in all.

In Britain, the housefly was accused of spreading summer diarrhoea, a serious, sometimes fatal illness, after feeding on street manure from horses. The timely replacement of horse-drawn buggies with motor vehicles removed that particular problem, but from then on, the housefly was constantly held up as a kind of flying parcel of germs. Influential in America was *The House Fly: A Slayer of Men*, published in 1911, followed two years later in the UK by the more moderately titled *The Reduction of Domestic Flies* (1913), by Edward Halford Ross. Though less hysterically militant in tone than his transatlantic counterpart, Ross laid the deaths of 1800 children in a London enteritis epidemic squarely at the door of the housefly. That human progress should have been incommoded by so wretched a creature almost won Ross's reluctant admiration:

> [It] is a wonderful thing to consider that houseflies should have been the means for the prolongation of war, the expenditure of many lives and much money; and the cause – a tiny creature like the domestic fly. The idea would be almost ludicrous were it not so pitiful and humiliating.

The hue and cry against the fly was championed by public-health programmes and kept on the boil by posters and, at least between the wars, by songs. One of these, devised around 1930, was 'The Song of the Fly':

> Straight from the rubbish heap I come
> I never wash my feet.
> And every single chance I get
> I walk on what you eat.[50]

The image of a filthy and malignant creature, a kind of demon for the health age, was combated with a range of ingenious traps and poisons, from sticky paper and petroleum flit-guns to a special tinplate fly-prison, in which you could gloat over the tiny captives 'caged as prisoners of war'.[51] How effective were they? Housefly numbers remained high until the 1950s, but in recent times, they have become much less common, so much so that swarms of the true housefly have become comparatively rare in Britain. Large numbers of flies found indoors are more likely to be Cluster Flies (q.v.) while the fly on the windowpane is more likely to be a Lesser Housefly (one rule of thumb is that the Lesser Housefly usually settles on the window or wall and *the* Housefly, *Musca domestica*, on the ceiling). The buzzing of flies, once as much part of summer as the hum of bees, has quietly departed. The decline of the housefly probably began a century ago with improved sanitation and diminishing amounts of manure and rubbish littering the streets. Since then, successive assaults of petrol, DDT, dustings and sprays, flypaper and Vapona seem to have done their work. Probably the *coup de grâce* for houseflies was the fridge. Today, we probably enjoy the most fly-free lives in the history of civilisation.

Houseflies have one lonely use. Someone found it worth designing a fishing fly based on it, 'dressed with a body made up of mixed fibres from both a rook's and a dark heron's wing feather, a dark grizzled or black hackle and wings of dark starling, or else two grizzled cock hackle points tied back over the hook.'[52]

Housefly horrors (all true)

Some six million bacteria can live on a single fly.

The housefly is suspected of transmitting some 65 diseases, among them cholera, typhoid, dysentery, anthrax and leprosy.

A housefly has no jaws. Instead it vomits on its food, using its acidic body fluids to mash up the food and turn it into a sticky puddle. Even more unfortunately, a housefly's vomit can contain parasitic worms. They also blow bubbles in it.

A well-fed fly defecates every four and a half minutes.

The fly is constantly using its legs for a good rub-down 'like the arms of a Sybarite luxuriating in bath oil.'[53] Unfortunately, like the ring around the bathtub, the accumulated dirt has to go somewhere, and that somewhere is probably inside the house.

If a pair of houseflies laid its full cargo of eggs in April, and all the offspring lived to breed in turn, by August the number of their descendents would be 191 quintillion, that is, 191 followed by eighteen noughts. This is more than there are stars in the known universe or sand grains on a beach. Most people would agree this is too many flies.

Horn Fly

Another of the other nearly lost insect wonders is the Horn Fly. A small, swarming fly with red eyes, it is active only in hot weather, when it rubs a cow's skin with its rough-edged tongue and feeds on the resulting secretions. The Horn Fly was named from its habit of clustering around a cow's horns. Its main claim to immortality is its lightning reaction to the animal's defecation. The Horn Fly is said to be so quick off the mark that an egg can be deposited in the hot stream of dung before it even hits the ground. Immersed in their warm, dungy world, the maggots grow quickly, feeding on bacteria rather than the dung itself, and the fly's whole lifecycle is completed in two weeks flat.

From the farmer's point of view, Horn Flies were a nuisance. Large swarms of them made the animal's life a misery, causing loss of condition and reducing milk yields. Insecticides, particularly ear-tags impregnated with pyrethroids, have greatly reduced their numbers, but the *coup de grâce* was an unintentional consequence of using invermectin to de-worm cattle. It renders cow-dung sterile and so inedible to the likes of the Horn Fly (and to many other, entirely harmless insects that depend on dung).

Sweat flies and dump flies *Hydrotaea*

AN: headfly, sheep's head-fly

The Sweat Fly (*Hydrotaea irritans*) is the small, dark fly that buzzes around our heads on a hot summer's day, especially in woodland, and annoys farm livestock all day long. Though attracted by human sweat, its favourite victims are sheep, especially Swaledale and Scottish Blackface breeds. Like the Horn Fly, it has rough 'teeth' on the end of its tongue that the fly uses to rasp away at the animal's skin and lap up the blood and lymph. In doing so, it can transmit the bacteria responsible for summer mastitis in cattle, and so the fly is a potential pest on dairy farms. Again, the veterinary answer is ear- and tail-tags that slowly release insecticide. Because the fly lays its eggs on dung in wet places such as pond margins, farmers are also advised to keep their animals away from the water; this, of course, has had a knock-on effect on wildlife through the drainage or neglect of farm ponds.

In America, a related species, the Black Dump Fly, also called the Garbage Fly, is used as a bio-control agent, especially on poultry farms. Though its maggots develop in refuse, they are predators on other, more harmful fly maggots. Dyed red, its maggots are also sold to anglers as 'French red devils'. It is probably as escapees from angler's bait tins that the occasional Black Dump Fly has been recorded in Britain, generally from landfill sites.

A greenbottle, watercolour by Carol Mullin.

Blowflies *Calliphoridae*

VN: bee (Orkney), crowan (Isle of Man), fishy bee (Orkney), fish matlo or matlo (Orkney), maak flee (Lancs.), maulie fly (Scot.), mawk-flee (Cumbria), mother-margets or margays (Cornwall), muck fly

Blowflies are familiar large, stoutly built flies, most of which breed in carrion and decaying animal matter. The name is a reminder of the old, entirely fallacious belief that the fly blew its eggs on to rotten meat like a boy with a peashooter. Among the best-known blowflies are the bluebottles, the greenbottles, the cluster flies and the flesh flies. Bluebottle is an old name shared with the Portuguese Man-o'-war and certain blue flowers. The adult fly has a hard, blue gleam on its oval body; it was seen as an animated 'bottle of blue'. It is also known, especially in America, as the 'blue-assed fly', an appropriate colloquialism for a notably robust insect; its equally robust scientific name is *Calliphora vomitora*. Bluebottles announce their appearance with a loud buzz, and are often a sign of a dead mouse or some other animal corpse in the vicinity.

Bluebottles and greenbottle flies are the most likely candidates for the 'gilded flies' of the poets. King Lear mentioned the gilded fly along with the wren as one of nature's most lecherous beasts (they copulate without shame – and in front of a king!). The glister of their bodies showed the fine workmanship of the creator in even the meanest of forms. But it also suggested meretricious display and deceitful flattery, since, beneath the show of beauty, there lurked unpleasing habits. 'These, with a gilded fly we snare,' mused the eighteenth-century satirist Charles Hanbury Williams, but 'ah! fair fools, beneath this shew/ Of gaudy colours lurks a hook'.[54]

Anglers call the maggots of bluebottles 'gentles', an old word that is sometimes abbreviated, with unconscious irony, to 'gents'. Farmed gentles are sold by angling suppliers, generally by the half-pint, and are kept in tins filled with wet bran and sawdust. They are available as white maggots or dyed in various cheerful colours to attract the fish. Some anglers prefer to breed their own gentles from dead pheasants and other road carrion. Angling terminology has special names for different kinds: 'gozzers' are succulent, thin-skinned maggots; 'squatts' are small and oval in shape; 'pinkies' (which are probably greenfly maggots) are small and, well, pink. At one time, every coarse fisherman kept a tin of maggots in his pocket. Today, more and more anglers are turning to artificial pellets, which have the advantage of being neither smelly nor wriggling when you hook them. In Scotland, blowfly maggots are known variously as 'mauks', 'mauches' or 'maiths', while a flyblown corpse is a 'maithie'. In Orcadian dialect, which has absorbed many Old Norse words, the word is 'arboo' (though they also use 'maith').

I once accidentally swallowed a bluebottle and still remember its angry buzzing as it slid down my throat. The naturalist William Buckland deliberately ate one out of curiosity and pronounced it the worst thing he had ever tasted, worse even than cooked mole, and *that*, he said, was pretty bad.

Stripping a corpse

They say that just three blowfly maggots can compete with a lion at the speed in which they can strip a carcass down to the bones. This is not, of course, true, but it does reflect the extraordinary efficiency with which maggots dispose of dead bodies. It is the fate of most corpses left unburied to be consumed by blowfly maggots. 'Food for worms' is the proverbial end to which we must all arrive one day. What Steven Connor calls this 'grim synanthropic ring-a-roses danced out between flies and men' is nicely summed up by the French poet Raymond Queneau: 'When one sees flies, one thinks: *they came from maggots*. When one sees men, one thinks, *to maggots they will come*.'[55] Attracted by the smell of putrefaction, the flies home in and stack their parcels of tall, bottle-shaped eggs by the soft bits and the body's natural orifices. The maggots feed fastest in hot weather, but their squirmy metabolic activity also creates its own heat, raising the temperature inside the hide by as much as 20°C. Finally, they pupate within the corpse and duly emerge as adult flies. A world without bluebottles would soon choke under a mattress of stinking, decomposing flesh. They are our friends, despite themselves.

Bluebottles and other blowflies are used in forensic work to determine a body's time of death. This is possible because putrefaction passes through a series of stages, marked by a procession of organisms. The bacteria get there first. Microbial activity inflates the body with gas and fluids, and at the first hint of a pong, the blowflies arrive, generally during the first 12 hours after death. Within another day, their eggs have hatched and the body is soon seething with maggots. The wriggling mass produces a puddle of digestive secretions, turning the tissues into goo before being slurped into thousands of little mouths. The maggots grow at a rapid rate, casting their skins three times before pupating within the corpse. The emergence of the adult flies within only ten days completes one of the speediest lifecycles in the natural world and gave rise to the belief that flies emerge spontaneously from carrion and filth: 'from filth they come and to filth they return'. If there is any flesh left on the corpse, the emergent bluebottles promptly and thriftily start on a second generation. Hence, dating the corpse using blowfly maggots is straightforward: the oldest maggots are the biggest, and once they have been identified and their growth-rate determined, the forensic scientist will know roughly how long the body has lain outside. For example, a corpse with maggots but no pupae will probably be less than ten days old.

The longer the corpse stays unburied, the richer the ecosystem it supports. A human body is big enough to support three generations of blowflies, and their maggots in turn attract predators and parasites – beetles, mites, and even parasitoids that

Gentles, or Bluebottle maggots.

lay their eggs inside the maggots. Some 10 to 20 days after death, the bloated body collapses, and the accumulated fluids drain from the body and leak into the soil. After a month or so, most of the flesh will have been removed, and so the body is no longer of interest to a blowfly. Its by now cheesy consistency is attractive to certain beetles, and after the corpse has been reduced to bones, hair and dry skin, certain Tineid moths become interested, especially in the matted hair. Finally, when only bones are left, half-buried in the ground, they may be scrunched up or dispersed by a passing fox or stray dog.

As forensic techniques improve, it may soon be possible to detect poison as a murder weapon even after the body has been reduced to bones. Just as DDT used to pass through the foodchain from mosquitoes to birds of prey, so drugs and toxins pass from the corpse to the bugs that eat the corpse. They are retained in their cast skins and empty puparia even after the insects have departed. It is also possible to deduce if a body has been removed by identifying the maggots or insect debris left behind.

Blowfly maggots are not, unfortunately, confined to corpses. As every livestock farmer knows, they will also lay eggs on the dead tissue of live animals, an action known in the trade as flystrike. The predilection of the flies for the soiled backsides of sheep is the reason why lambs' tails are docked soon after birth. The year 2006 was a particularly bad one for flystrike on sheep, with maggots fattening up on necrotic tissue on the most inaccessible parts of the animals, keeping hill farmers and vets busy all summer. What may be happening is that, because the blowflies' usual diet of corpses has been denied them by farming hygiene regulations, they are laying on the next best thing: dead tissue on live animals.

Ever since classical times, maggots have been used to clean infected wounds. In the 2000 film *Gladiator*, Russell Crowe resorts to self-cure by dropping maggots from his revolting dinner into his festering wounds. Not only do maggots remove the putrefying tissue but they also kill bacteria and so stimulate the growth of healthy replacement tissue. Maggot therapy eventually went out of fashion, only to be rediscovered by Napoleon's surgeons during the Revolutionary Wars. During the First World War, maggots bred specially under clinical conditions were used on wounded soldiers, especially in cases of bone infection. Today 'maggot debridement therapy', or MDT, is widely used in hospitals and is now orthodox health care for cleaning out necrotic tissue in a wound; put simply, the maggots seem to be better at it than we are. But after a few unfortunate cases of blowfly maggots getting out of hand and starting to devour the living flesh, only the petite pink maggots of greenbottles (known medically by their generic name *Lucilia*) are now used. Unlike bluebottles and fleshflies, greenbottles do not transmit disease, and they adhere strictly to dead tissue. They arrive clean and sterile inside their tubes and are simply poured into the wound. The *Lucilia* do the rest, chewing away infected tissue and secreting bactericidal substances as they go. You can even get them on the National Health Service.

A different kind of Bluebottle is the squeaky-voiced Boy Scout in the *Goon Show*, the one who holds surreal conversations with his equally stupid friend Eccles and is often 'deaded' by the end. Spike Milligan never explained his choice of the name, but it gave him an opportunity for a terrible gag early on in Bluebottle's showtime career: 'I'm a Bluebottle.' 'What's that you're reading?' 'A flypaper.'[56]

Bluebottles and greenbottles feast on the corpse of a rabbit.

means corpse-eater). In former times, fresh meat came into that category, forcing people to keep the butcher's cuts and joints inside a special meat safe with a perforated zinc door.

Fleshflies do not bite, but they will visit festering wounds and try to lay a few maggots. Perhaps it was this habit that William Cowper had in mind when concluding his diatribe against contemporary novelists in *Progress of Error* (1782): 'Far, far way these fleshflies of the land/ Who fasten without mercy on the fair,/ And suck, and leave a craving maggot there.' In Ben Jonson's satirical play, *Volpone,* Flesh-fly or Mosca is a corrupt and self-serving parasite. 'Well, Flesh-fly,' someone warns, 'it is summer with you now; Your winter will come on.'[57]

Cluster Fly

The Cluster Fly looks like a large housefly with fine, golden 'fur' on its thorax. It lives harmlessly out of doors in summer but enters buildings to hibernate once the weather turns colder. Like starlings or tortoiseshell butterflies, it passes the winter in company, and it is then that you appreciate the truth of its English name. I once stayed in a top-floor room in an Edinburgh tenement where flies had taken over. Something had killed them, but there were perhaps a million dead flies on the floor and more banked up against the window, with a sickly smell in the air that was not entirely fly-spray. They are said to choose the same place, year after year, so perhaps their descendents are still there in that room to greet the next lodger. Fortunately, Cluster Flies are not a health risk. Their eggs are laid in the soil, where the young maggots bore into earthworms.

Fleshfly

The Fleshfly is a large, handsome fly with a striped thorax, red eyes and noticeably large feet. It has intrigued naturalists by its 'advanced' behaviour, marking its territory with khaki-coloured droppings, while the males compete for the best perch by energetic, bird-like bouncing contests. The female gives birth to live maggots, which feed mainly on carrion (its scientific name *Sarcophaga*

Dung flies *Scathophagidae*

VN: midden flee, muck flee (Scot.), shairay flee (Scot.), sharmy matlo (Orkney)

Dung flies are much maligned. Their generic name *Scathophaga* means dung-eater, but most species feed on plants, rotting matter or insects. Even the ubiquitous Yellow Dung Fly, the one that swarms on fresh cow-pats, does not feed on dung itself but on the maggots of other insects within the dung. Some naturalists have, rather generously, dubbed them 'teddybear flies' from a fancied similarity of their bristly yellow hairs to those small, cheap teddies with fuzzy fur. As a predator of potential nuisance insects, it is one of the friendly insects of the garden. The mating behaviour of the dung fly has been studied in detail by ecologists as a template for Darwinian theories about sexual selection and survival.

Like other insects that use dung, the Yellow Dung Fly has become another victim of the veterinary drug ivermectin. Under laboratory conditions, a drop or two can kill half the population of dung flies within 24 hours (and go on to kill the rest a little later). In smaller doses, ivermectin has what is euphemistically known as sublethal effects, producing flies with wing abnormalities unlikely to live long enough to mate.

Cheese Fly *Piophilidae*

VN: bacon flies, bacon skippers, cheese hoppers, cheese skipper, ham skippers

The ant-sized Cheese Fly is seldom seen today, but until perhaps the 1940s, its small, hopping maggots were a familiar problem-insect in the larder, preferring above all else a ripe truckle of Cheddar. When disturbed, the maggot would, by bending itself into a ring, catching the skin of its tail with its jaws, flip into the air like a flea. Some hostesses served the cheese with the 'flies' on, claiming they improved the flavour.

In Sardinia, Cheese Fly maggots are intentionally introduced into *pecorino* cheese to produce *casu marzu* (meaning 'rotten goo'), a semi-liquified, decomposing stink-bomb served with or without the wriggling white maggots. The taste, they say, is strong enough to burn the tongue, but it is the most beautiful gift you can give to a Sardinian shepherd. But swallowing live cheese fly maggots is not advisable. The maggots are not always killed by stomach acids, and they can survive for a while in the gut and begin to nibble the lining.

Cheese Flies will also lay on bacon, ham and other preserved meats, hence their alternative names of 'bacon skipper' and 'ham hopper'. Modern food-hygiene regulations and the fridge have all but wiped them out.

Cheese Fly maggots will take up residence in a corpse three to six months after death and so can help forensic scientists estimate the time of death. A rare relative of the Cheese Fly is known as the Dead Donkey Fly, because the last British specimen was recorded from the corpse of a donkey. Dead Donkey Flies move in at the end-stage of a decaying carcass, when there is little left but skin and bone; possibly the maggots feed on bone marrow. Dead donkeys and horses are no longer left lying about in today's countryside, and so the fly has been robbed of its habitat.

Truffle Fly

The Truffle Fly, a small, fawn-coloured fly with long, dangling legs, is drawn to the scent of truffles – those smelly, underground fungi on which its tiny maggots feed. Their habit of dancing and swarming over the ripe truffles, half buried and more than half hidden among the leaf mould, makes them a useful ally of the truffle hunter.

Warble-flies and botflies
Oestroidea

VN: Bomb-fly, breeze, brimp (Kent), cattle grubs, gadfly, heel-fly, nimble dick (Kent), ox-warble fly, warback (Scot.), whame, wringle-tail

Welsh: *Robin y gwrrwr* (Robin the driver)
Gaelic: *croaghan*

Warble-flies were the cause of the original mad-cow disease. Cattle seemed to know when the large, bee-like flies were about, perhaps recognising their distinctive hissing buzz. They responded by vigorously shaking their heads and flicking their tails or, if all else failed, by taking evasive action, rushing about with their tails held high and their necks outstretched. Such mad behaviour was known as 'gadding'. In extreme cases, maddened cows would lose all sense of direction and crash into gateposts or barbed-wire fences, sustaining cuts and bruises or even broken bones. A French peasant girl learned to imitate the warble-fly's sinister hum and used the trick to induce stark terror in peacefully grazing cattle.

Unlike horseflies, the adult warble-fly does not bite or suck blood and cannot, in fact, feed. Instead, it lays its eggs on the cow's skin. These eggs can be swallowed when the animal grooms itself. They hatch inside the cow's guts, and the little maggots then chew their way out towards the cow's hide and end up inside customised lumps of inflamed, hardened skin – the 'warbles'. A badly warbled cow is a sorry sight – its hide perforated, its body riddled and its milk reduced to a trickle.

There are two warble-fly species, which differ mainly in their behaviour. The commoner one, *Hypoderma bovis* (*Hypoderma* means 'under the skin', as in hypodermic syringe), zooms in fast and lands on the cow to lay its eggs, either on the cow's leg above the hock or on its body. The other, *Hypoderma lineatum*, adopts a different strategy by sneaking towards the cow at ground level in a series of hops and then crawling up the unsuspecting animal's leg, hence its American name of 'heel fly'.

The warble-fly was a serious scourge of cattle farmers and, as late as 1977, it was still bothering more than a third of British herds. Hypodermosis, as warble-related damage is called, caused a loss of around £13 million a year, mainly in damaged hides.

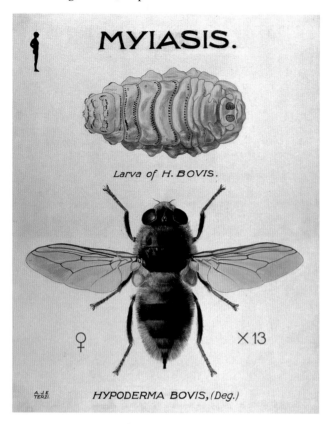

MYIASIS.

Larva of H. BOVIS.

♀ × 13

A.J.E.
TERZI

HYPODERMA BOVIS, (Deg.)

The corrugated maggot and bee-like adult of the feared Ox-warble Fly. Coloured drawing by A. J. E. Terzi.

became available in the form of organophosphorus pour-on pesticides such as Phosmet and Fenthion. These killed the maggots before they could reach the cow's hide, unlike derris dust, which only worked when maggots are actually crawling out of the animal. But the warble-fly responded by developing a resistance to the poison.

The real turning point in the war against the warble-fly came in 1982, when hypodermosis was made a notifiable disease. This gave inspectors the power to restrict the movement of infected herds and require them to be treated. It meant, effectively, that the fly could now be not only controlled but also eradicated. So it proved. A year later 'only localised areas of low incidence remained', and by 1985, the disease had declined from 38 percent of British herds to less than 0.01 per cent. There have been minor setbacks when the disease was reintroduced from imported cattle, but the warble-fly is now effectively extinct as an agricultural pest and quite possibly extinct in fact.

The success may, however, have come at a price. Some believe that pesticides have lowered disease resistance in cattle and so were an indirect cause of BSE in cattle in the 1990s. Today, the drug ivermectin is used in place of the highly poisonous organophosphates of the '60s and '70s.

In times past, there was comparatively little a farmer could do about it. The seventeenth century had a special prayer against the warble-fly, intoned over the infected animal just before sunrise to exorcise the maggot as though it were an evil spirit: 'In the name of God the Father, the Sonne and the Holy Ghost,' the priest would iterate, 'I conjure thee, O worm, by God the Father, the Sonne and the Holy Ghost, that thou neither eate nor drink the flesh, blood or bones of this horse; and that thou hereby maiest be made as patient as Job and as good as St John Baptist when he baptised Christ in Jordan. In the name of the Father, Sonne and Holy Ghost.' He concluded the ceremony by saying three Paternosters and three Aves in the animal's right ear, to the glory of the Holy Trinity. And, perhaps because all the best things came in threes, the prayer was often repeated three days running.[58]

By the early twentieth century, a reasonably effective treatment was available in the form of monthly doses of derris. From the 1930s, British farmers were ordered to treat all infected cattle in this way, but in the mid-1960s, a more effective remedy

Sheep Nostril-fly, *Oestrus ovis*

AN: Sheep Nasal Botfly

This time, the victims are sheep. The Sheep Nostril-fly is a distinctive insect with a big head and a warty, wrinkled, oval body, resembling a tiny flying toad. The fly does not feed and spends much of its brief life at rest on walls. It gives birth to live maggots, which allows the fly to buzz straight into a sheep's nostril and drop its maggots inside the warm, humid nasal cavity. From there the maggots wriggle their way into the sheep's frontal sinus, attach themselves by their mouth-hooks and feed on mucus. On such a diet, they are slow to develop, and it takes about nine months before the maggots are fully grown – plump and a couple of centimetres long. By this stage the sheep is sometimes experiencing breathing difficulties, gasping and sneezing and shaking its head, and possibly even wandering about in a daze in the condition known as 'blind staggers'. Eventually the maggot is ready to pupate. It withdraws its hooks, releases its hold and, when the sheep makes one last culminating sneeze, is shot out of its slimy lair into the countryside.

As with the warble-fly, insecticides have reduced nostril-flies to the point that they are no longer a widespread nuisance. Isolated cases can now be dealt with by a quick squirt of ivermectin in the nostrils. Feral goats are sometimes attacked by the fly, and there have also been instances of sheep farmers accidentally getting nostril-fly maggots caught in their eyes, resulting in a painful but temporary and easily cured irritation. Once, a shepherd boy was found to have a flourishing colony of nostril-flies in his own sinuses, suggesting that the inner cavities of sheep and humans are not dissimilar, at least from the nostril-fly's point of view.

Botfly

VN: burrell-fly, horse-bee, whame, wringle-tail

Bot is an old word for a maggot, probably deriving from the Gaelic *botus*, or belly-worm. Viewed without prejudice, the once-common Horse Botfly is a handsome insect, with its bee-like covering of yellow brown hair and elegant, tapering body, distinguished by a pair of swollen, circular bumps. It neither bites nor feeds but buzzes around in the stableyard for a few days, mates and then dies. Before doing so, the female would lay her eggs on the fetlocks of a horse, and the animal would then lick off and swallow them. Thus, wrote one entomologist, 'unconscious of what it is doing, it unwarily introduces into its own citadel the troops of its enemy.' The maggots find their way into their host's stomach, where they attach themselves to the lining with small, grapnel-like hooks and grow fat, crenellated and barrel-shaped (hence their old name, 'burrell-flies'). When ready to pupate, they release their hold and pass out of the horse in its dung. A related species took a more leisurely passage through the horse's guts, finally anchoring itself to the animal's anus, from which it protruded obscenely for a while before dropping to the ground.

Botflies were familiar enough to have rustic names such as 'wringle-tail' or 'whames'. They terrified horses, wrote Thomas Muffet, which 'at the least touch they endeavour by what means possible with their tails, feet and mouths to drive [them] away.' Though botflies do less damage to their reluctant host than warble-flies, the horse may suffer indigestion and bellyache and some ensuing loss of condition. The greater harm is economic, especially to racehorse owners trying to get their animals into top condition before a race. Ivermectin and similar veterinary drugs have greatly reduced the incidence of botflies in Britain, and they are now quite rare.

In Britain, we are fortunate that botflies ignore humans. In Central America, the fearsome *torsalo* (*Dermatobia hominis*) does not confine itself to livestock. It craftily attaches its tiny egg onto the belly of a passing insect, usually a mosquito. The mosquito takes the young *torsalo* to a human being where the tiny maggot drops off and embeds itself into the skin. There it forms its own 'warble' and feeds on the flesh. Any attempt to pull it out may result in bits of the maggot being left inside to cause infection. The sores are painful, but the psychological scars of carrying a flesh-eating maggot may be worse. Fortunately, only those who spend time living rough in tropical forest are likely to get on intimate terms with the *torsalo*. One who did was Aaron Dallas, who returned from a backpacking holiday in Belize with what he thought were mosquito bites on the top of his head. Peering closely at the inflamed, weeping bumps, the doctor noticed a sudden movement just beneath the skin. 'I'd put my hand back there and feel them moving,' Aaron told a saucer-eyed journalist. 'I thought it was blood coursing through my head. I could hear them. I thought I was going crazy.' The experience made 'my stomach turn over', he added, though 'it's much funnier to everyone else'.[59]

Deer botflies were once believed to be the world's fastest flying insects. An American entomologist, Charles H. Townsend, claimed to have clocked them speeding at up to 400 yards per second, or 800 miles an hour. For many years the botfly's unlikely feat was repeated uncritically in the *Guinness Book of Records*. But when the claim was examined, it fell to bits. To sustain such a speed, the fly would need to consume more than three times its body weight in high-energy food *every second*. Moreover it would be effectively invisible: all the observer's experience of it would be a sonic boom as the burning fly broke through the sound barrier, while anyone standing in the way would be knocked over with the fly embedded deep in his tissues. Using the original report as a basis, the fly's true speed was recalculated at a far more sedate 25 miles per hour.[60]

BEETLES
Coleoptera

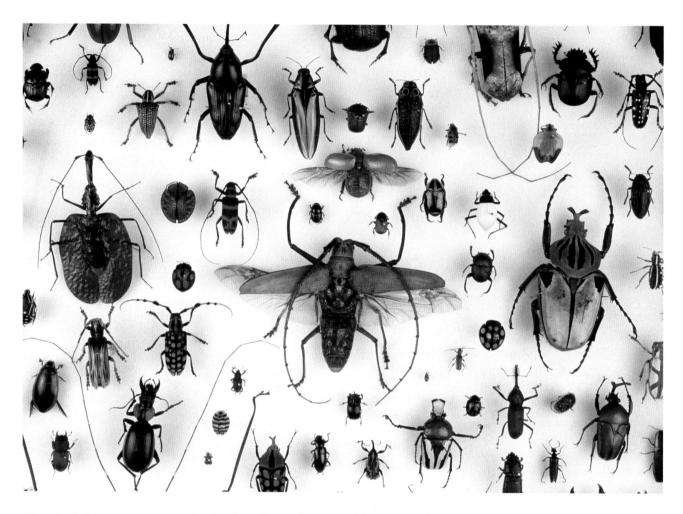

Wonderful diversity - part of a display of mainly tropical beetles in the Natural History Museum. There are 400,000 species of beetles in the world.

VN: bum-clock, buzzard-clock, clock, clock-bee, clocker, crag (Isle of Man), gablo (Orkney), klok, snarly-warly (Devon)

'Whenever I hear of the capture of rare beetles,' wrote Charles Darwin near the end of his life, 'I feel like an old war-horse at the sound of a trumpet.'[1] In his youth, especially while an undergraduate at Cambridge, Darwin had been a keen beetle-collector. To the end of his life, he recalled the exact appearance of a certain rotten post or hollow tree where he had found an especial specimen, and his first outing in print was an illustration in a journal of a beetle captioned 'captured by C. Darwin, esq.'. The extraordinary number and variety of British beetles entranced Darwin. They had clearly got him asking *why*, even before his famous world voyage on the *Beagle*.

If diversity and adaptability are the yardsticks for success, beetles are the most successful animals on the planet. There are 50 times as many species of beetles (400,000) as mammals (8000), and the gap is widening all the time as new species of beetles pile up at the rate of a thousand a year. If every living animal was set out in a row, one in four would be a beetle. In fact, one in ten would be a particular

330

kind of beetle, a weevil. There are more weevils in the world than all the mammals, birds, reptiles and fish put together, an unnecessarily large number one might think. No wonder the evolutionist J. B. Haldane famously exclaimed that 'the Creator, if he exists, must have an inordinate fondness for beetles.'[2]

Moreover, there are almost certainly more unknown beetles than known beetles. Terry Erwin of the Smithsonian Institute in the US made an intensive study of just one species of tree in Panama, which produced a grand total of 1200 species. Of those, 163 species were found only on that kind of tree, and there may be as many as 50,000 kinds of tree in the tropics (and not all of those have been discovered, either). Erwin did the maths and came up with a theoretical total of 8 million species of beetle in the tropics alone.[3] And, since not all beetles live in the tropics or in trees, even that may be an underestimate.

In Britain, we have found only 4034 beetles, and, thanks to Darwin and others like him (three quarters of the British beetles were discovered by Victorian collectors), we can be fairly certain that this is within a short distance of the real figure. In Darwin's day, beetles were the largest order of insects, but they have since been driven into third place by the Hymenoptera (most of which are parasitic wasps) and the true flies, or Diptera. Among the British beetles are some of the best-known and, in certain cases, the best-loved insects: ladybirds, stag beetles, glow-worms, diving beetles and whirligigs. They live in every type of habitat, from the shoreline to the mountaintops, not excluding lakes and rivers; a few have even adapted to an indoor life in factories, warehouses, kitchens and bakeries. They vary from insects no larger than a dot to the great silver diving beetle and the stag beetle – two of our largest and certainly our heaviest insects.

The ecological role of beetles was summed up neatly, if outrageously, by the writer A. A. Gill: 'Beetles do just what they say on the box . . . beetles embody all the talents of the middle classes. They are not aristocratic, vain esoterics, like butterflies and moths, or communists, like ants and bees. They're not filthy, opportunistic carpetbaggers like flies. They are professional, with a skill. They're built for a job, and get down to it without boastfulness or hysterics. And there is nowhere that doesn't, sooner or later, call in a beetle to set up shop and get things done.'[4]

Beetle names and expressions

The word beetle comes from the Old English *bitan*, meaning 'little biter' (their order, the Coleoptera, means sheath-wing, named after the tough cases that protect the delicate, folded wings). Ancient names often refer to a key quality of an animal. Beetles have proper jaws, like pairs of pliers, and some of the bigger ones can nip. Hence, just as spiders are creatures that spin and wasps those that weave, so beetles are the little beasts that bite. The other thing beetles do is to scuttle around on their long legs. Old English has a word for that too: *webila*, a word consonant with weave, in the sense of running back and forth. Later generations transferred the word to a particular group of beetles, the weevils.

The rural name for any big buzzing insect was a clock. Large flying beetles could be 'clockers' while particularly loud ones were known, rather splendidly, as 'bum-clocks' after their humming sound. Orcadians pronounced it with a Scandinavian twist as 'klok', while in the Faroes, such beetles are *klukkas*. The beetle's buzzing flight is known as a drone, as in the well-known line from Thomas Gray's 'Elegy': 'And all the air a solemn stillness holds,/ Save where the beetle wheels his droning flight'.[5] In Scotland, flying beetles were sometimes known simply as bees. Another Orkney name for a beetle is 'gablo'. It is derived from *gobhal*, the Celtic name for fork, and so might have been applied originally to the earwig.[6]

Clocks and buzzing are combined in the folk-name of 'buzzard-clock', which Alfred Tennyson used in his dialect poem, 'Northern Farmer Old Style'.

> An' I hallus coomed to 's choorch afoor moy
> Sally wur dead,
> An' 'eerd 'um a bummin' awaay loike a
> buzzard-clock ower my 'ead . . . [7]

Beetles lend themselves to various expressions, some of which are based on their scurrying gait. For example, to beetle away means to hasten away quickly, probably without dignity. Ground beetles share with cockroaches the danger of being crushed by a human boot, and beetle-crusher was the callous name of crepe-soled shoes worn by Teddy Boys in the 1950s. The same name is used for a stomping clog dance originating from Somerset.

In the game of Beetle, teams sitting at separate tables compete to complete a picture of the

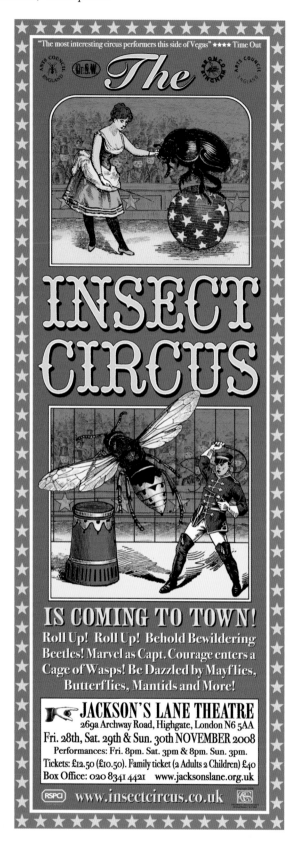

The Insect Circus comes to town – a 'travelling museum' of insect dioramas and ingenious automata starring 'dancing snails, trained butterflies, wasp tamers and balancing bugs'.

eponymous insect. The beetle is drawn in parts, each one decided by a roll of the dice, 6 for the body, 3 for each of the legs, 1 for each of the antennae, and so on. To make it a bit harder, the parts must be drawn in the right order, for example the beetle's head must be in place before the eyes and antennae can be added. The first team to complete their task shouts out 'Beetle!', bringing an end to the play. A sequence of games is called a beetle drive, in mockery of a whist drive.

The expression beetle-browed usually means to have notably shaggy eyebrows. It may have an origin in the curiously tufted antennae of certain beetles, such as cockchafers. It once meant to have a furrowed brow. In the narrative poem 'Piers Plowman', written around 1360, the character called Avarice is appropriately 'bitel-brouwed' with bleary eyes and is clearly absorbed by money matters. A word book of 1611 combined the two meanings: either 'having very great eye brows' or 'frowning or looking sowrely; surlie or proud of countenance'.

Possibly beetle-browed may refer not to an insect but to the kind of wooden mallet known as a betel mallet, which was used for driving in wooden wedges or for putting a glossy finish on cloth by flattening the fibres. Betel, which is pronounced in the same way as beetle, comes from the Old English word *beatan*, to beat. To soften the blows, the head of the betel mallet was covered in leather, which soon frayed along the sides and hung like a fringe.

It was probably coincidence that the Beatles rock band had fringed mop-top haircuts. There are several versions about how the fab four acquired their name. In John Lennon's fantastical explanation to Beatles fans, it came in a vision: a man appeared on a flaming pie and told them that, 'From this day on you are Beatles with an A'. The usual story is that the name was a play on Buddy Holly's band the Crickets but that Lennon, never able to resist a pun, quickly changed 'beetles' to 'beatles'. There seems at least a possibility that one of them remembered the film *The Wild One*, in which the character played by Lee Marvin says to Marlon Brando, 'we all missed you. The beetles missed yuh, *all* the beetles missed yuh.' Apparently 'beetles' was a slang name for a biker's moll in the 1940s, similar to 'chicks'.[8] Perhaps the name of the Liverpool suburb of Bootle also had something to do with it. Appropriately enough, stag beetles appear on the coat of arms of Sir George Martin, the Beatles' musical producer and presiding genius.

Games and pop music aside, the beetle's

contribution to the arts seems fairly modest. *A Beetle called Derek* was an 'environmental magazine programme' for television, written and presented by Andrea Arnold and Roger Deakin, which ran for three series in 1989, 1990 and 1991. The title was taken from a poem by Benjamin Zephaniah, who took part in the show as a kind of court poet. The series was made in the studios at Vinters Park, Maidstone, possibly the only TV studio to be situated inside a nature reserve.

The main character in Paul Shipton's Bug Muldoon books is a beetle of an unspecified type. He is an insect private investigator, writing in the crisp, no-crap style of Raymond Chandler or a 1940s film noir: 'I'm not one of those insects who's drawn to danger like a moth to a flame. A bug's gotta earn a living, is all.'⁹ Bug Muldoon's insect cosmos is an ordinary suburban garden with its small inhabitants: spiders, toads, hedgehogs. In *Bug Muldoon and the Garden of Fear*, he looks into some peculiar goings-on in the regimented society of an ant nest. In the sequel, *Bug Muldoon and the Killer in the Rain*, he daringly enters the house, a fearful place where no insect in its right mind would normally tread, and finds some even more peculiar inhabitants. Written for children, the books pack in a lot of sound natural history within the parameters of an exciting detective story.

Gavin Maxwell's autobiography of childhood, *The House of Elrig* (1965), devotes the chapter 'Aunts and Insects' to his youthful passion for entomology, including an anecdote about his elder brother Eustace, who 'ran howling to my mother about a terrible pain in his ear, that, he blubbered, was due to a large green beetle inside it. This diagnosis was not unnaturally treated as fanciful. However, at the second drop of soothing ear lotion, out walked a large green beetle.'¹⁰ Young Eustace was a keen entomologist who collected almost every kind of insect – but not beetles.

Ground beetles *Carabidae*

VN: black bat (Midlands), black-clocks, black jack (NE Eng.), caregg (Isle of Man), nipping clock (Lancs.), rain clocks, snodderwigs (Cornwall), switch (Cheshire), twitch clog (Cheshire), twitch-clock (Lancs.)

To judge from everyday expressions, the archetypal beetle is fast-moving and black. An old expression said that someone was 'as blind as a beetle', as though being black deprived beetles of eyesight (all of them do have eyes, though, like bats, most black beetles hunt at night). Another saying was 'as deaf as a beetle', as though beetles also have hearing difficulties.

Black beetles are more properly known as ground beetles and resemble the archetypal beetle, being shiny, leggy and neatly divided into head, thorax and abdomen. There are 340 British species, most of them active predators and all built for speed. Some, such as the colourful tiger beetles, are active by day in hot, sunny weather, but most ground beetles hunt by smell at night and ride out the daylight hours under stones or in holes. Most ground beetles are blackish or dark brown, but some, including the largest, the Violet Ground Beetle, have a beautiful purplish sheen. A ground beetle is best not handled; in defence it can void a noxious, irritating fluid from its rear end. Contributor Alex Ramsay was unexpectedly sprayed in the face by a large female ground beetle, 'with a stinging fluid from a distance of 10 centimetres.'¹¹ Some species will make an alarmed squeak, and the biggest can nip with their pincer-like jaws.

In folklore, black is the colour of bad luck. A black ground beetle running around on the floor inside the house is regarded as an unlucky sign and a particularly unlucky one if it runs over your shoe. Nevertheless, in one of those no-win situations so common in country wisdom, it is not a good idea to step on a beetle, either, for this could bring on bad weather or worse. 'We knew the big *Pterostichus* ground beetles as "rain clocks" because it would rain on the next washing day, if we stamped on them.'¹²

The Alexander Beetle of A. A. Milne's Pooh stories was drawn as a ground beetle by his illustrator E. H. Shepherd. In *Winnie the Pooh*, he has a small part in the famous 'Expotition to

A Violet Ground Beetle's business end.

the North Pole', as the last and least of 'Rabbit's friends-and-relations' (presumably he was a friend). A nervous insect and always last in the line, he is so frightened by everyone saying hush, seemingly at him alone, that he buries himself 'head downwards in a crack in the ground, and stayed there for two days until the danger was over, and then went home in a great hurry, and lived quietly with his Aunt ever-afterwards.'[13] Alexander Beetle had made an earlier appearance in Milne's poem 'Forgiven', about a boy (presumably Milne himself) who kept a beetle in a matchbox. Nannie, in search of a match, accidentally lets the beetle out. They search the garden for the holes where beetles hide, making 'the sorts of noises that beetles like to hear'. The beetle, or at any rate *a* beetle, is eventually tracked down and reunited with its box, with 'Alexander' written 'very blackly on the lid'. The poem, always a children's favourite, was set to music by Melanie Safka. Alexander Beetle made a cameo appearance on the *Muppet Show* as a performer in a Bug Band that performed only

Beatles hits. The Muppet Alexander was red and blue, suggesting that Alexander might have been a Bombardier Beetle.

Danger lurks for every ground beetle from an unlikely source – discarded drink containers. 'I never cease to be shocked at the damage to wild-life inflicted by carelessly discarded bottles and tins,' says Tony Harwood. 'Recently I discovered over 50 lesser stag beetles in a single vodka bottle, and I regularly find hundreds of trapped ground beetles. Their vulnerability seems to be linked in part to sex. Often a single female will be found surrounded by scores of males, lured to their death by pheromones from the female in the bottle. The toll on our invertebrates resulting from the current epidemic of littering and fly-tipping can only be imagined.'[14]

Bombardier beetles

VN: doodlebugs

The original bombardier was a non-commissioned officer in the British army who specialised in hurling bombs or grenades. The same name was given to a modest-looking orange and blue ground beetle, which defends itself by firing boiling chemicals from a gland in its rear end. The chemical stored by the Bombardier Beetle is based on hydroquinone and hydrogen peroxide, the same explosives that have been used in liquid bombs manufactured by *jihad* terrorists. When threatened, the beetle releases the chemicals, adds some enzyme to speed up the reaction and blasts its pursuer between the eyes with a boiling, foul-smelling mixture of irritant and explosive. To the human observer, the beetle seems to emit a small puff of smoke accompanied by a soft 'pop', and it is primed up and ready to fire again within minutes.

A relative, the Streaked Bombardier Beetle, has been named Britain's rarest beetle, for it was known only from a pile of builder's rubble overgrown by weeds situated close to the Thames Barrier in East London. Before the bulldozers arrived, volunteers tried to catch as many of the elusive bombardiers as they could in a 'fingertip-search through chunks of concrete, twisted metal and weeds'.[15] Some 61 beetles were eventually rescued and transferred to a customised pile of rubble in a safe place, though the charity Buglife would much have preferred

The Green Tiger Beetle, displaying its toothed biting jaws.

to protect the original pile. 'Previous bug translocations have had poor results and it can be very hard to artificially recreate the exact habitat conditions that a species requires,' said a spokesman.

Tiger beetles *Cicindelidae*

Tiger beetles are active predators that hunt by sight, running down prey on their long spread legs. A tiger beetle in full chase has been clocked at five miles an hour, which scaled up, would make it one of the fastest animals on earth. There are five British species, of which by far the commonest is the Green Tiger Beetle (more commonly known as *the* tiger beetle), often found basking or running along paths in the spring, especially in sandy places. Tiger is in this case a metaphor for speed and fierceness; the beetles are armed with impressive secateur-like jaws that can deliver a sharp nip.

Dor beetles and dung beetles
Geotrupidae and Scarabaeinae

VN: clock beetle, dirt bee (Scot.), dirt flee (Scot.), dor bug, dor fly, dumbledor, dung beetle, lousy watchman

The Dor Beetle is often found lying helplessly on its back, legs wiggling wildly. It is frequently infested with mites, hence its country name the 'lousy watchman' (watchman is a pun on clock, a common name for a large beetle). Dor is an old name for a person of feeble wits: to give someone 'the dor' meant to make a fool of him. Like clock, it was also a name for large, clumsy beetles but eventually settled on just this one, perhaps because it is our commonest large beetle.

A Dor Beetle is a four-square, bulldog-like insect with a metallic sheen and spiky mole-like legs for digging. Like the more widespread dung beetles (Scarabaeinae), it lives on dung. This is not an especially nutritive substance, and both the beetle and its larva need to digest their own weight of it each day. Hence, over a lifetime of about a year, a Dor Beetle will shift and recycle a fair-sized mound,

335

The Beaulieu Dung Beetle (museum specimen). Its brief moment in the sun came in 1996, when the then Environment Minister, John Gummer, approved of its legal protection, noting that 'the beetle is part of God's creation, whose loss would diminish us all'.

an ancient burial chamber beneath a barrow. The male helps by clearing away the excavated soil and bringing in fresh burdens of dung, leaving behind a dollop in each chamber. Once the beetle has laid a single egg in each chamber, its job is done. The larvae chew dung for several weeks before pupating and emerging from the ground in the spring as beetles.

The very last of Aesop's fables, the one he supposedly told as preparations were being made to execute him, was about a dung beetle and an eagle. A hare was being chased by an eagle and ran to the dung beetle begging it to save him. The beetle implored the eagle in the name of Zeus to respect the hare's sanctuary, but the eagle brushed it aside and, tearing the hare to shreds, ate it. In revenge, the beetle followed the eagle to its nest and spitefully smashed all the eggs – twice over. In despair, the eagle flew up to Mount Olympus and laid its latest egg in the lap of Zeus, chief of the gods, beseeching the god for his protection. The beetle's vindictive response was to stuff itself with dung and fly straight into the face of the god. Startled by the filthy creature, Zeus tottered to his feet, forgetting all about the egg, which fell to the ground and broke. When he learned the full story, Zeus scolded the eagle for violating the god's sacred name. But to prevent the vengeful beetle from wiping out the race of eagles, he separated them by placing the beetle underground. Aesop's audience applauded – then seized the great fabulist and threw him off a cliff.

The hero of Aristophanes' play, *Peace*, rides to the gods on the back of a dung beetle – a thrifty choice of mount, since the beetle could feed on the rider's excrement. From a human perspective, dung beetles live unenviable lives. In J. K. Rowling's Harry Potter books, Harry's malignant adopted parents, the Dursleys, live in mortal terror that Harry will turn them into dung beetles. And yet Dumbledore, the wise old wizard, is named after one of the old country names for a Dor Beetle.

The study of dung beetles involves practices that do not always mesh well with domestic priorities. A friend, who had better remain nameless, found that the best way to find them was to return from the field with a sack-full of dry cowpats and unload them into bathwater. The beetles then floated or swam to the surface, after which the bath could be tidied up using the shower hose. Though my friend had carefully hosed away the filth, he neglected to notice that some of the beetles had taken shelter in the overflow. They came out in force, antennae bristling, just as his wife lowered herself into the hot

and it is in part the endless munching of dor beetles that saves the environment from sinking under animal waste. The American Institute of Biological Sciences reckons that were it not for dung beetles, the US cattle industry would have to spend $280 million dollars every year cleaning up.

Like many insects that live on filth, the Dor Beetle is surprisingly clean and fastidious. When not feeding, it is usually grooming, brushing stale titbits of soil or dung from its whiskers as though washing its face. It operates at night in pairs, seeking out a suitable pile of dung, not too fresh but not too stale, under which the female will dig a deep hole with various small chambers off to the sides, not unlike

A Minotaur Beetle inspects a rabbit pellet.

water. Fortunately, not being an expert on beetles, she put it down to the bird nests in the eaves.[16]

The Minotaur Beetle is another stocky black beetle distinguished by a pair of forwardly pointed horns (plus a third smaller one in the middle). To the classically minded, its monstrosity suggested the minotaur of Crete, half-man, half-bull, that lived inside a maze of tunnels. Like the Minotaur, the beetle excavates a burrow with numerous blind-alleys, or brood chambers. Prominent horns on a male are usually a sign of a carefree, idle life devoted mainly to eating and fighting. Impressed by its apparent martial ardour and tunnel-living, Linnaeus named this one *Typhaeus typhoeus*, after Typhoeus, or Typhon, the father of winds (or typhoons), who was imprisoned in a cell at the bottom of Mount Etna, from whence he continues to hurl fire and molten rocks at the sun.

The Minotaur is the only British beetle to push balls of dung (in the ready-made form of rabbit pellets) in the manner of the better-known but only distantly related scarab beetles of southern Europe and the Middle East. The ancient Egyptians perceived the sun as a ball of dung pushed across the sky by an invisible dung beetle and so used the scarab as the earthly representation of their sun god. The myth was compounded by the mysterious appearance of newly emerged beetles from the dung balls, suggesting a magical reincarnation akin to that of the sun god himself. For their part, the ancient Cretans represented their sun god as a bull, suggesting further mythological links between the Minotaur Beetle and the Egyptian scarabs.

Another group of big black beetles are known as rhinoceros beetles from the single curved horn on the heads of the males. Several British beetles bear such a horn, though the name is most often attached to *Sinodendron cylindricum*, a smaller relative of the Stag Beetle. True rhinoceros beetles, which do not occur in Britain, are said to be able to lift up to 850 times their own body weight, which, transferred to a human scale, would equal seven double-decker buses piled on top of one another. Like many animal facts and feats, this is misleading, for a human-sized beetle would not be able to lift so much as a feather duster – its respiratory system condemns it and all other insects to a relatively small size (the crucial insect statistic is not size but numbers). Thanks to their remarkable 'horns', rhinoceros beetles have long been well known to casual observers. They were once considered to live like an insect Phoenix, dying at the end of the year, only to be reborn instantly from the products of their own putrefaction.

Chafers *Melolonthinae* and other families

VN: billywitch or Billy Witch (East Anglia), bracken clock, bummler (NE Eng.), chovy (Norfolk), cob-worms, doodlebug, dorrs, dumbledarey, humbuz (Glos.), June bug, kittywitch, may-bittle (Glos.), maybugs, midsummer dor, mitchamador (East Anglia), oak webs or oak-wibs (S. Wales), rookworms, snartlegog (Devon), spang beetle (East Anglia), tom beedel (Lancs.)

'Chafer' or 'chovy', originally spelt 'ceafor' or 'cefer', is an old word for a beetle; it meant one that chews or gnaws (hence the German word for a beetle, *kaefer*). Charingworth in Gloucestershire and Keverstone in Durham might have been named after swarms of chafers. Those we call by this name are today restricted to a subset of the scarab family, and they include some of our most attractive beetles, such as the brilliant metallic green Rose Chafer and the smaller green and brown Garden Chafer. Less common is the Bee Beetle, whose furry thorax and barred abdomen, added to its habit of immersing itself in thistle heads, give it a passing resemblance to a bumblebee. The largest and best-known species is the Cockchafer. Its curious name could indicate maleness, size or perhaps even familiarity, as in 'cock sparrow'. The Cockchafer is certainly unmistakable, with its grooved, bullet-shaped body and impressive tufted antennae, like a couple of frayed paintbrushes.

Cockchafers are commonest in areas of dry, warm soils. Their local nicknames, mainly from East Anglia, include 'chover', 'kittywitch', 'midsummer dor' and 'mitchamador', and they are still often known as 'billywitches', or 'maybugs' from the time of their peak emergence. Some related, smaller species are called June bugs or July bugs.

> At the time of the V1 flying bombs, in 1944, cockchafers were known in the north-London area as 'doodlebugs'. The beetle often flew through open bedroom windows, making a clattering noise, which abruptly ceased when they came to rest – just like the V1 doodlebugs, whose jet engine would cut shortly before the explosion. (Dr Colin Welch)

Cockchafers normally wake up towards dusk and are attracted to lights and windows, arriving with a characteristic buzz and clatter. You find them on the sill the next morning looking dazed. Many motorcyclists will be familiar with the sharp crack of a maybug hitting a crash helmet. In Italy, they call it and some larger relatives *buffone* – clowns. Cockchafers are a particular nuisance in moth traps: they bash into the panes, fall into the trap half-stunned and spend the night thrashing about on their backs getting covered in the scales of shredded moth.

Unlike their relations the scarabs, chafers are plant-eaters that live on roots, flowers, leaves or decaying wood (one species even lives on refuse inside ant nests). The fat, white grubs of the Cockchafer gnaw on roots, and in years of exceptional plenty – known as 'mass flights' – can be significant pests of lawn grass and root crops, especially potatoes (they are also intermittent pests of cereals). In 1574, they were so numerous in the Severn valley that their drowned bodies blocked the wheels of the watermills. In 1868, they were said to have blackened the skies over Galway.

Before the advent of pesticides, villagers would make rather hopeless efforts to catch as many chafers as they could before the beetles could breed. In a uniquely medieval method of pest control, the court in Avignon, stung beyond endurance by the ravages of the Cockchafer, sentenced the beetle to exile in a cordoned off piece of woodland. In our own time, insecticides almost succeeded in wiping it out, but its numbers have risen slightly since the introduction of EU-wide restrictions on environmentally damaging pesticides. Today, Cockchafers are controlled with bio-agents such as fungi and nematodes. Crows and rooks, meanwhile, dig eagerly for them, hence their country name, 'rookworms'. In parts of Europe, if not in Britain, the beetles and their 'cobworms' were also eaten by humans, roasted or stewed.

The Summer Chafer is a smaller, hairier version of the Cockchafer with less flamboyant antennae. The adults swarm around particular trees or, in open areas, any other vertical objects – including, on occasion, golfers. Its species name, *solstitiale*, commemorates the beetle's appearance around midsummer. Before pesticides reduced their numbers, Summer Chafers could in peak years defoliate trees and even whole woods. In 1770, Gilbert White recorded in his journal that the beech trees around Selborne were 'quite stripped of their leaves by chafers' and 'never recover their beauty again the whole season'. They

Right: *A Cockchafer takes flight.*

provided a feast for the local rooks, which 'pursue & catch the chafers as they flie'.

The Garden Chafer, which has a metallic green thorax and a brownish body, is often found in gardens and orchards and is distinctive and common enough to have acquired alternative names: 'bracken chafer', 'fernshaw chafer' and 'field chafer' among them. In Wales, a well-known trout fly, the *coch-y-bonddu* (literally 'the red one of the black thorax'), tied from the red hackles of a cockerel and the tail feathers of a peacock, takes advantage of the beetle's habit of landing on the surface of mountain lakes.

In *Lucky Jim*, Kingsley Amis used the word cockchafer, presumably in the sense of 'wanker', as one of the inventive insults aimed at Jim's boss, Professor Welch, strictly behind his back, of course. 'Look here, you old cockchafer, what makes you think you can run a history department, even at a place like this, eh, you old cockchafer. I know what you'd be good at, you old cockchafer . . .'

Burying beetles *Silphidae*

AN: carrion beetle, sexton beetle

Burying beetles, often called sexton beetles, are insect undertakers. Five of our six species have black and orange markings and characteristic clubbed antennae, while the sixth, the slightly larger *Nicrophorus humator*, is all black. They come to lighted windows and moth traps and excite our pity because of the masses of tiny mites that often infest them.

With their keen sense of smell and powerful flight, burying beetles are quick to locate and reach any recently dead mouse or small bird, which they bury by excavating a grave beneath the corpse and then dragging it in, a process that takes them around eight hours of steady digging (the idea is to deny the meat to their many rivals, such as bluebottles or

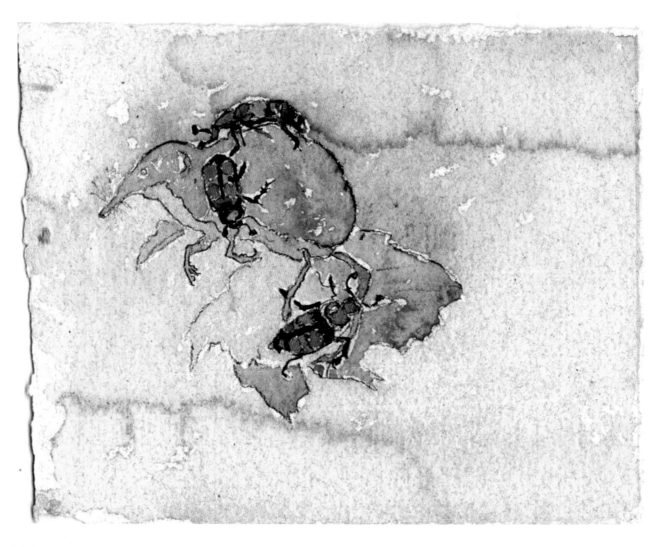

ants). The beetles line the makeshift crypt with the corpse's feathers or hair and inject it with antibiotic chemicals that slow down the process of decay. Eggs are then laid on the body that thereafter supplies all the nutritional needs of the developing grubs. Unusually, burying beetles look after their brood, culling excess grubs to ensure the survival of the rest when there is insufficient to go round. With larger corpses, such as deer, the beetles make no attempt to bury the remains but simply wallow in the warm, liquefying flesh beneath the leathery hide.

Unlike the scarab beetles of southern Europe with their iconic balls of dung, British burying beetles have excited little lore or wisdom. They have at least inspired a novel, *The Burying Beetle* (2005) by Ann Kelly, about a 12-year-old girl with a life-threatening heart condition. At one point the lonely girl becomes fascinated by a burying beetle and its strange behaviour, which 'forces her to confront her own mortality and, like the burying beetle, bury things past and live.'[17]

One of the stock stories of entomology is the apparently true tale of what happened after a noted beetle expert, A. M. Massie, and a companion found a dead tramp in a ditch while bug-hunting in the New Forest. For a moment Massie contemplated the entomological possibilities of the corpse before saying: 'You take the feet and I'll take the head.' Together they shook the body over a sheet spread for the purpose and, sure enough, out fell numerous beetles, including some rarely seen ones. These survive to this day in the collections of the Natural History Museum, labelled 'Dead tramp. New Forest. A. M. Massie'. Another story is less plausible. Finding himself out of pocket, Massie ordered dinner at an expensive hotel and surreptitiously emptied some beetles into the soup. He thereupon complained indignantly, and the hotel manager, anxious to avoid a health inspection, offered him his dinner on the house.[18]

Left: Sexton beetles on a dead shrew, Lydford Forest, Devon *(watercolour), by Jennie Hale.*

Rove beetles *Staphylinidae*

VN: cock-tail, coffin-cutter (Isle of Man), *Dar Daol* or *Deargadaol* (Ireland), devil's coach-horse, devil's coach-man, devil's footman, devil's steed, staphs

About a quarter of all British beetles, nearly a thousand species, are rove beetles, sometimes called 'staphs' after the family name, Staphylinidae. Named after the habit of some larger ones of wandering about along paths, they all share the same long, slim shape with short wingcases that leave most of the body segments exposed (despite that, most staphs fly well). Certain red and black rove beetles contain a toxin stronger than cobra venom called paedurin after the generic name of the rove beetle, *Paedurus*. It has been used in the treatment of chronic ulcers. To gain a sense of the irritant chemicals carried inside these beetles, you need get only a small bit in your eye: it stings.

Most rove beetles are little-noticed scavengers, but a few of the larger ones are fierce predators. The best-known is the Devil's Coach-horse, also called the Common Black Cocktail from its habit of rearing up its tail like a scorpion when threatened. There was a story that the beetle would point its upraised body in the direction of someone it wanted to curse. Its dark and evil look spawned many other tales that vastly enlarged its devilish powers. According to Irish mythology, it can kill merely by a look, like a gorgon or a cockatrice. It was said to imbibe its evil powers by eating the bodies of sinners for, being the Devil's own beetle, it was drawn to sin like a wasp to strawberry jam. It could mysteriously appear in the hand of someone who had had dealings with the Devil.

In Ireland it was known as *Dar Daol*, or *Darragh Daol* – the Devil's beetle. People were urged to exterminate this harmful insect whenever they found it, but great care was required in doing so because of its magic powers. If you simply crushed it, you could expect something unpleasant to happen to your foot. By the same token, retribution might follow if you struck it with a stone or a stick. The only safe way to dispose of a Devil's Coach-horse was to lift it with a shovel and hurl it on to the fire. Some said that you could turn its powers to your advantage. Irish reapers are said to have imprisoned the beetle within the handles of their scythes to improve their skill.

Folk stories sprang up, especially in Catholic Ireland, involving the Devil's beetle in the life and passion of Christ. In one version, the beetle appeared to do its dirty work after Jesus had performed a miracle on a field of corn and produced a host of golden sheaves only hours after the crop was sown. The day came when soldiers were looking for Jesus to arrest him and asked the labourers whether the Lord had passed that way. 'Yes, He had,' they said, truthfully. 'He passed by on the day the corn was sown.' Since that seemed to mean months ago, the soldiers would have turned back had not *Dar Daol* suddenly raised his ugly head and croaked the words, 'Yesterday, yesterday.' With those words, the soldiers realised that Jesus was still in the neighbourhood, with the consequences we all know.

By the time Richard Lewis wrote his horror story, *The Devil's Coach Horse* (1979), subsequently made into a film, the beetle had lost its witch-like powers only to gain new ones through a more earthly transformation. The story begins with a plane full of scientists on the way to a biological convention. They were carrying live insects, including *Dar Daol*. When the plane crashes the beetles survive by eating the dead scientists and so acquire a taste for human flesh. Soon swarms of flesh-eating Devil's Coach-horses are munching their way through the cast. But, as post-Darwinian insects, they serve no power but their own brute biology.

Does anyone still believe in the *Dar Daol*? Today the Devil's Coach-horse, as an insect predator, is hailed as the gardener's friend, supposedly doing a useful job by preying on garden pests. Could this be the start of a contemporary myth? The Devil's Coach-horse is a fascinating animal, but its image as gardener-friendly may be exaggerated. In fact, it preys on friendly and useful earthworms.

Dar Daol: *the Devil's Coach-horse.*

Stag beetles *Lucanidae*

VN: billywitch (East Anglia), Branson bucks, cherry-eater (Kent), devil's beetle, devil's imp, face-catchers, hornbug, horny bug (Surrey), horse-pincher, oak-ox (Acton, London), thunder-beetle

Is the Stag Beetle our most iconic insect? Its image appears everywhere, on pottery, cards and stamps, in advertising and most recently as a symbol of conservation and wildlife in need (it is the insect emblem of the People's Trust for Endangered Species). Yet there must be many people who have never set eyes on a real live one. More commonly seen, and often mistaken for it, is the Lesser Stag Beetle, which is smaller and lacks the impressive 'antlers' of the male Stag Beetle. The real Stag Beetle is rather scarce and confined mainly to south and eastern England. It is said to be commonest in the parks and hospital grounds of south London, and three quarters of all Stag Beetle records are from private gardens.[19]

The male beetle's antlers are modified jaws used for fighting rivals in sumo-style wrestling competitions, each beetle trying to tip the other onto its back. 'When I was a boy in Ipswich,' recalls Colin Hawes, 'young lads used to keep them in matchboxes so that the beetles could be put together to fight.' Despite appearances, the male is harmless; it is the antler-less female that delivers a sharp nip if mishandled. Nevertheless, some people still consider them dangerous and react by stamping on them.[20] The Stag Beetle's plump white grub lives in rotten wood, and so the species is found where there are old trees, stumps and log-piles in parks, commons, open woods and large gardens. It can take three years or more for the grub to develop to full size, and it pupates inside an underground cocoon the size of an orange. The adults start to emerge in May, with a peak around midsummer.

Stag Beetles have long been regarded with a mixture of admiration and fear. They were reputed to have the power to summon thunderstorms, perhaps in an echo of Norse mythology, in which the beetle

Right: *Male Stag Beetles dueling like Sumo wrestlers. The loser is about to be thrown off the branch.*

A 500-year-old Stag Beetle by Dürer.

is a favourite of the thunder god Thor. Moreover, they are sometimes seen drinking the sap exuding from lightning-damaged trees and called thunder-beetles. A captive Stag Beetle kept inside your hat will supposedly protect you from being struck by lightning. The beetles are most often seen in flight in still, humid weather, and in Suffolk, a flying male Stag Beetle is said to indicate fair weather ahead.

Their nicknames include 'billywitch' (a name shared with the cockchafer), 'oak-ox', 'horny bug' and 'horse-pincher'. There were probably many other names now lost. In 1688, when the naturalist John Ray visited the Dorset village of Branson (now Bryanston), he was told they were called Branson Bucks, after the paired horns of the male Roe Deer. Earlier still, in Shakespeare's day, its names included 'hart's horn', 'the bull' and 'the flying stag'. Nicknames for Stag Beetles are still being coined; in Kent, they have been called 'face-catchers' from their habit of flying at head height.

Some said that Stag Beetles, when impelled by a mischievous spirit, would use their outsized jaws to carry glowing coals that they would use to set ablaze hayricks and thatched roofs. In the New Forest, where they were unusually common, the beetles were blamed for crop damage and nicknamed the 'devil's imps'. Their mere appearance was enough for them to be pelted with stones by indignant yokels.

The beetle is also associated with a Greek musician, Cerambos, a master player of the lyre, who was turned into a Stag Beetle after offending a deity. His instrument, minus its strings, was henceforth carried on the head of the beetle. Children would catch the beetle, cruelly chop off its horned head and pretend to play the tiny lyre. The beetle was sometimes hung around the neck as an amulet or good-luck charm. Boiled in wine and 'anointed to the arteries of the arms', it could help cure the agues.

A more benign image of the Stag Beetle appears in certain images of the Madonna and Child, notably those by Albrecht Dürer. Stags were highly prized and much admired beasts that acquired a faint tang of holiness from being pitted against the serpent in one of those good-versus-evil morality dramas beloved of the Middle Ages. Some of this rubbed off on to the Stag Beetle, which became a kind of insect stag. Its presence near the Madonna is as a witness to the Christ-child, the lord of animal creation, whose coming vanquishes evil and guarantees salvation.

Dürer obviously admired Stag Beetles because, in 1505, he went on to paint one simply for its own sake, shorn of religious imagery. The result is one of the first realistic representations of an insect in western art. It is shown in a lively bulldog posture, full of fight, its head raised and mandibles opened wide. Dürer probably made the drawing from nature, with a close eye for the detail of its hard wing cases, massive square head and spiky legs. 'It is indeed true', commented Dürer, 'that art is omniscient in nature, and that the true artist is he who can bring it out.'[21] He illustrated the point with a beautifully rendered portrait of a tuft of grass.

Stag Beetles were all over the media on 27 May 2008 after Bill Oddie improvised a commentary over a pair of mating beetles on the popular television programme *Springwatch*. 'He crash-lands on top of a likely looking lady,' he intoned, adding, in an excruciating pun, 'One thing is for sure, this boy is horny.' The tableau continued with Oddie switching to a squeaky voice to impersonate the female beetle: 'Come on, big boy, come and get it . . . Oh, be gentle with me,' before concluding, in a suave George Sanders voice, 'And rather surprisingly, he is.' The complaints came flooding in.[22] There is, admittedly, something comic about the idea of Stag Beetles in love. Whether seen as lovelorn robots or clattering knights, they appeal to English schoolboy humour.

Stag Beetles are popular pets in Japan, and high prices are paid for them, though trade in the European Stag Beetle is illegal. Greater threats to our beetle come from road traffic (Stag Beetles are often found stunned or dead on pavements and in gutters) and the tidying up of old woodlands.

The Stag Beetle is the only British insect to have appeared on a postage stamp twice. The first was on a set of five insects designed by Gordon Beningfield and released in 1985. It also took the starring role on a set of ten insects released in 2008; the Post Office 'presentation pack' includes a group of conservation volunteers 'building a log pile to encourage the insects to breed'.

Just now and again someone witnesses something like this:

> We held a dinner party in our garden one warm evening near the beginning of June. During the course of it, between twenty and thirty Stag Beetles, both male and female, buzzed across the garden, much to the distress of some of the ladies, and the delight of all of the men. They came from the direction of the river and flew on towards a marshy meadow. We have seen the occasional one since then, but never a repeat of that massed flight.[23]

underground wireworms, but a good hoeing brings them to the surface where birds can be relied on to do the rest. A bio-control in the form of a host-specific nematode worm is now available.

Conversely, there are rare click beetles indicative of ancient forests and parks, which we are trying hard to conserve. One of these is the bright red Cardinal Click Beetle, whose slim body suggests a churchman in his robes (the redness matches its habitat, the red-rotten heartwood of decaying oaks). One of the rarest is the Violet Click Beetle, which is confined to a handful of decaying beech trees in southern England. It appears to scavenge among the droppings and leaf mould within the hollow trunk, though the adult is more usually found on hawthorn flowers. When a gale smashed one of its few known trees, a beech in Windsor Great Park, the trunk was painstakingly reassembled from some of the shattered pieces by the then wildlife ranger Ted Green. From what was known of the beetle's habits, he also created customised click beetle food from a mixture of sawdust and droppings. Another conservation practice is artificially to age a tree by judicious planning to increase its attractiveness for beetles and other insects.

Click beetles *Elateridae*

VN: elater beetle, skipjacks, wireworms

Click beetles are distinguished by their ability to snap themselves into the air with an audible click. They achieve this trick by arching back until a peg on their underside connects with a hinge that releases the tension and sends them spinning into the air. It not only helps them to escape from predators but also comes in useful when the bullet-shaped beetle is on its back trying to right itself. There are 60 British species of click beetle, some of which feed as larvae in the rotten wood of old trees, while others mine plant roots and tubers. Broadly speaking, the former are considered to be priorities for conservation and the latter to be pests.

The larvae of click beetles are stiff, thin and yellowish, and known as wireworms. Several species feed on cereals and root crops, especially potatoes. In the past they could sometimes infest fields of cereal crops to such an extent that the farmer had little alternative but to leave the land fallow for a year. Chemical methods are ineffective against

Soldier beetles *Cantharidae*

VN: bloodsuckers, hogweed bonking beetle, sailor beetle, souk-the-bluid (Scot.)

The best-known soldier beetle, often called *the* soldier beetle, is the ubiquitous *Rhagonycha fulva*, an orange beetle that clusters on the heads of hogweed and other flowers in summer. It is commonly known as 'bloodsucker' from its reddish colour (the beetle feeds harmlessly on pollen) and, more recently, as the 'hogweed bonking beetle', a reference to the beetle's promiscuous sex life. Soldier beetles are often found in copulating pairs that stay hooked together while feeding and even flying.

Roger Key told us the origin of this name: 'It was put in as a joke name in the Invertebrate Site Register during the late 1980s, and it simply stuck. The only official complaint we received was from a vicar in North Yorkshire, who was definitely not amused. The name was eventually edited out, but by then it was too late: the name was already entomological legend.'[24]

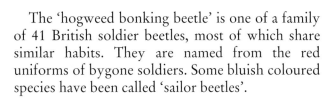

The Red Soldier Beetle, alias the 'bloodsucker' or 'the hogweed bonking beetle', is often found copulating while feeding on flower heads.

A glow-worm at sunset.

The 'hogweed bonking beetle' is one of a family of 41 British soldier beetles, most of which share similar habits. They are named from the red uniforms of bygone soldiers. Some bluish coloured species have been called 'sailor beetles'.

Glow-worms *Lampyridae*

vn: fire-worm, glass-worm, lightning bug, May-worm, shine-worm, shiney bug or shining bug (Kent)

The twinkling goblin light of the glow-worm must be one of the most exciting and mysterious sights of the insect world. When they shine like fallen stars among the grass blades, it feels as though you have strayed into a fairy tale. That cool green radiance – W. H. Hudson called it 'golden-green'[25] – intense and yet without illumination, excites even the most jaded sense of wonder. Yet finding the 'worm' is not always easy, especially when the insect-stars are buried among dense vegetation or grass tussocks. When you do eventually locate it, you find a strange insect, looking a little like a woodlouse, its shining abdomen curled upwards, as if it has somehow dipped its tail in luminous paint. It is, in fact, a wingless beetle. Only the female glow-worm glows in this way, and it is done to attract a mate – another nondescript beetle, this time with wings.

We have been eulogising glow-worms since ancient times. Pliny referred to them as 'glittering flies' and 'earthly stars'. Shakespeare knew their 'pale ineffectual fire' that shone without heat. Webster, in *The Duchess of Malfi*, compared it with deceptive glories that 'far off shine bright,/ But looked to near, have neither heat nor light.'[26] To

Wordsworth, the glow-worm was an 'earth-born star', to Samuel Taylor Coleridge a 'love torch'. A lesser poet, Thomas Lovell Beddoes, saw not fires or torches but the thing itself, 'our still companion of the dew ... with his drop of moonlight.'[27]

In William Blake's poem 'A Dream', the glow-worm becomes an angelic insect lantern-bearer, appearing at the call of a lost 'emmet', a comforting light to a tiny ant, lonely and lost among the dewy grass. 'What wailing wight/ Calls the watchman of the night?' asks the glow-worm.

> I am set to light the ground,
> While the beetle goes his round:
> Follow now the beetle's hum;
> Little wanderer, hie thee home![28]

It is one of Blake's 'perfect, self-sufficient moments', like being tucked up in bed, warm and comforting. In his dream world, insects look after one another.

John Clare, always more realistic in his portrayal of insects, knew and responded to real glow-worms in the hummocky fields near his home in Helpstone, Northamptonshire. 'The Glow-worm', composed around 1820, was among his first published poems:

> Tasteful Illumination of the night
> Bright scatter'd, twinkling star of spangled earth!
> Hail to the nameless colour'd dark-and-light,
> The witching nurse of thy illumin'd birth.
> In thy still hour how dearly I delight
> To rest my weary bones, from labour-free;
> In lone spots, out of hearing, out of sight,
> To sigh day's smothered pains; and pause on thee,
> Bedecking dangling briar and ivied tree,
> Or diamonds tipping on the grassy spear;
> Thy pale-fac'd glimmering light I love to see,
> Gilding and glistening in the dew-drop near:
> O still-hour's mate! my easing heart sobs free,
> While tiny bents low bend with many an added tear.[29]

The Elizabethan authority Thomas Muffet had less time for poetic fancy, describing the insect in matter-of-fact terms as 'a slow-paced creature' that fed on herbs and whose arrival in midsummer was 'a sign of the ripenesse of Barley, and of sowing Millet and Pannick'. They made excellent angling bait, he added, 'being fasten'd to the hook'. A glow-worm set in the middle of the house, he added, 'drives away Flies'.[30]

In plain biochemical terms, the light of the glow-worm is made by a chemical, luciferin (from *lucifer*, or light-bearer), which produces light as a byproduct of oxidation. The poets were right: the reaction is extremely efficient, transferring nearly all the energy into light (the opposite of an old-fashioned phosphorescent light-bulb, where 90 per cent of the energy is wasted on heat). The enzyme responsible, luciferase, has been isolated and synthesised and used to illuminate biological processes. Bio-engineers have managed to implant the genes that produce luciferase into the tissues of various lab animals to provide a built-in micro-light on the processes going on inside the cell.

W. H. Hudson was convinced that their light varies in power according to the degree of excitement felt by the glow-worm, noting that it becomes brightest when the male beetle is standing by. At the climactic moment, the glow-worm begins a sensual swaying motion at the centre of a spotlight 'as if enclosed within an invisible globe'. Yet the winged male, so it seemed to Hudson, fears the light and slinks around the edge of the circle, drawn in eventually by a trail of scent, and not because of the light but in spite of it. Hence the glow-worm's glow, he thought, was 'no more use to it than the precious jewel in the toad's head is to the toad'.[31]

The glow-worm is a member of the small family Lampyridae, which also includes the firefly of southern Europe. The females normally shine just after dark on warm, still midsummer evenings. In his journal, Gilbert White noted that on '14 June the glow-worm appears'.[32] Glow-worms inhabit grassy or scrubby places, especially on banks and waysides, and occasionally, for the very lucky, in gardens. Sheltered banks with lots of empty snail shells (glow-worm larvae feed exclusively on snails) are likely places to look for the glow-worm lights, and some of the best sites are on disused railway embankments. The easily overlooked male glow-worm is sometimes lured off-track by lighted windows and lamplight.

Glow-worms seem to be declining, though no one knows why. They may be victims of light pollution, or perhaps the modern landscape has less room for the kind of warm, sheltered, snail-shell places they like. Since 1990, Robin Scagell has run a UK glow-worm survey in an attempt to find some answers.[33]

Can you read by glow-worm light?

Once, when I found myself lost in an alpine valley after dark without a torch, I enlisted the help of local glow-worms to try to read the map but found them quite useless. Others have had more luck. The naturalist Alfred Leutscher hung up jam-jars full of glowing insects as tent lanterns. Graham Bathe's great uncle remembered people positioning glow-worms around their caps and reading a newspaper by their light.[34]

Thomas Hardy brought in glow-worms to further the plot of *The Return of the Native*. In their celebrated card-game, the 'reddleman' Diggory Venn plays Damon Wildeve at dice amid the heath at night. After their lantern is extinguished by an unlikely blow from a great moth's wing (an ominous portent in the world of Thomas Hardy), their gambling session is able to continue with the help of the light of some neighbouring glow-worms, 'faint greenish points of light among the grass and fern'. 'Shaking the glowworms from the leaf [Venn] ranged them with a trembling hand in a circle on the stone, leaving a space in the middle for the descent of the dice-box, over which thirteen tiny lamps threw a pale phosphoric shine ... It happened to be that season of the year at which glowworms put forth their greatest brilliancy, and the light they yielded was more than ample for the purpose, since it is possible on such nights to read the handwriting of a letter by the light of two or three.'[35]

Winston Churchill once remarked, 'We are all worms. But I believe that I am a glow-worm.'[36]

Fireflies

Fireflies are rare visitors to Britain, too rare to have attracted any homebred folklore. Their name was borrowed by the Fairey aircraft company for the Firefly, perhaps incorporating a pun on 'fire'. A successful carrier-born fighter with folding wings, it entered service in 1944 and was used by what was then the Fleet Air Arm in the fifties.

Ladybirds *Coccinellidae*

VN: bishop barnabee (or bishie-barnabee, bushie-barnabee), bishop-is-burning, bracken clock (Lancs.), burnie-bee, bushy bandy (Suffolk), clock-leddy (Scot.), clock-o'clay, cow lady, cushcow or cushy cow, cushcow lady (Yorks.), dowdy cow (Scot., Yorks.), dundy-cow (Yorks.), farmer's friend (Warwicks), fly-golding (Sussex), God's horse (Lancs.), God's little cow, God's O-mighty cow (Devon), golden beetles (Suffolk), golden knop, goldie bird, golding (Kent), king alison (Scot.), king-coll-awa or king galowa (Scot.), king's doctor Ellison (Scot.), lady beetle, ladybug, lady-cai (Cheshire), lady clock, lady-couch (Scot.), ladycow, ladyfly, Lady-from-London (Isle of Man), Lady-lanners (or landers) (Scot.), lamblady (Lincs.), marygold, May cats, merrigo (Kent), ply-golding (Kent), red-coat (Scot.), reed sodger (Northumb.), sodger (Scot.).

Scottish Gaelic: *daolag dhearg bhreac* (red spotted little beetle)

Welsh: *buwch fach adda* (little cow-bird), *buwch fach goch gwta* (little short red cow), *buwch fach gwta* (little short cow), *pryfyn dom* (dung fly), *Sian ffa* (Jane the bean)

Irish: *boin de* (God's little cow), *boin samraich* (little cow of summer)

Ladybirds enjoy one of the shiniest reputations of any British insect. They are brightly coloured – the ladybird of images and stories always has a red coat with black spots – with a delightfully round, chubby shape that appeals to our inner natures and especially to children. They are small and non-frightening, even touchingly vulnerable, almost like tiny animated toys. Their wholesome image was seized eagerly by the famous series of illustrated children's books and by the almost equally famous designer of children's clothing sold, until recently, at Woolworths. We continue to appreciate ladybirds as adult gardeners, in the confidence that they are helping us in the perennial fight against greenfly and other pests. The apparent contradiction between the ferocious predator of our gardens and the sweet little ladybirds of books, key rings and magnetic toys bothers nobody. We see them as friendly and as our friends. Perhaps, among all the image-making of modern consumerism, there still lingers a touch of the otherworldly about ladybirds in

Britain. When a threat to their continued existence emerged, ironically enough from a fellow ladybird, the Harlequin, public concern has rivalled that of the plight of the honeybee.

Ladybird names

Why a ladybird – that is, why 'lady' and why 'bird'? The name's origin dates back to the Middle Ages and the cult of the Virgin Mary. In religious art, the clothes worn by Our Lady were deeply symbolic. Often her garment is blue, the most expensive colour dye, to represent her divinity, but in other images, including a famous one by Leonardo da Vinci, she wears red, probably to represent the blood of Christ (the same idea, in a more secular context, must lie behind the cocktail known as a Bloody Mary). At the same time, the cult of the Virgin incorporated the mystic number seven: the Seven Joys and Seven Sorrows of Mary. For that reason, the colour and pattern of the common Seven-spot Ladybird conveyed to the medieval mind a divine message – that the beetle was blessed by Heaven as a kind of angelic insect and a bringer of joy and sorrow in equal measure. 'Our Lady's Bird' was the embodiment of goodness in a small, round body. Such an insect could never be a mere bug: it was a bird, a winged messenger of Heaven. By Shakespeare's day, it had become a term of endearment, like sweetheart. 'What, lamb! What, ladybird!' coos the nurse in Romeo and Juliet.[37] The collective name of ladybirds is a loveliness. It is bad luck to kill or harm one.

The ladybird's special status is shared by the whole Christian world and, indeed, beyond. Across Europe from Ireland to Turkey the superstitious saw it as a good-luck charm: a benevolent bug or blessing beetle. In Germany, the ladybird is (among other things) *Marienkafer*, Mary's beetle, or *Marienvoglein*, Mary's Bird. In France, it is the *bêtes de la Vierge*, the Virgin's beast, or *bête a bon Dieu*, the Good Lord's beast. Russia shares with far-off Spain the name of God's little cow, *Bozhia Korovka* or *Vaquilla de Dios*. In Denmark it is *Mariehone*, Mary's hen, and in Sweden, *Maria Nyckelpiga*, Mary's key-maid, the lady who holds the key to Heaven. An Italian country name is *Sarpa de la Madona*, the Virgin's shoe, while in Croatia, the ladybird is, rather mysteriously, 'God's little ship'.[38]

Apart from their Christian names, ladybirds have

Seven-spot Ladybirds feasting on aphids gathered on thistle heads.

acquired a variety of local or folk names that rival those of woodlice in inventiveness. Many seem to come from rhymes that were usually recited to a ladybird perched on your finger, incorporating a wish for the intercessionary ladybird to take to Heaven on its gauzy wings. The Scottish name 'King-coll-awa', for example, echoes the customary parting words: 'Tak up your wings an' flee awa'!' In different parts they were known as 'redcoats' or 'red sodgers', 'clock o' clays', 'cushcows' and 'goldiebirds'. Appropriately enough, most ladybird names (including their scientific names) are feminine.

In Canada and the United States, ladybirds are usually known as ladybugs, though Englishspeaking Australians and South Africans agree with us that they are ladybirds. Certain scientists insist they are lady *beetles*. Their taxonomic rectitude has overtaken their cultural awareness.

To the poet John Clare, the beetle was the 'ladycow' or 'clock o' clay'. 'Here I lie, a clock o' clay/ Waiting for the time of day', was his parody of Shakespeare's 'Where the bee sucks/ There suck I'. Robert Southey knew it as the 'burnie-bee', writing appreciatively of its 'ruby shard/ With many a tiny coal-black freckle deck'd'.[39]

A more mysterious ladybird name, still used in East Anglia, is 'bishop' or 'bishee' barnabee. The alternative name, 'bishop-is-burning' or 'bishop-that-burneth', may be a corruption of 'barnabee', or it might be a lingering folk memory of a holy man with a similar name who was martyred for his faith by being burned at the stake. Unfortunately history has no candidate for the role. Saint Barnabas, a companion of St Paul, has only the most tenuous link with ladybirds in that his feast-day is in midsummer, thus tying in with their German nickname of 'midsummer beetles'. But perhaps the link is not with historical personages so much as the ladybird's cardinal cloak, the colour of fire.

Fly away ladybird. In flight the ladybird loses its sweetness and becomes insect-like.

Ladybird rhymes and games

Ladybirds bring luck, and the very best kind comes when one settles of its own accord on your outstretched finger and leaves it voluntarily or assisted by no more than the gentlest puff of air. At such moments it has long been the custom to ask the ladybird a question. For example, to obtain a ladybird weather forecast, you hold it up on the fingertip of your left hand (others say the right) and recite:

> Ladybird, ladybird, tell to me
> What the weather is going to be;
> If fair, then fly in the air,
> If foul then fall to the ground.[40]

On the third line, some say you should flip the ladybird into the air. If it falls to the ground without attempting to fly, rain will follow. If it flies away, the sun will shine. Given that a ladybird is more likely to unfurl its wings and fly when it is warm and humid, the rhyme is to some extent self-fulfilling.

Ladybirds will also tell you the time. One version of the corresponding rhyme puns on the country name for a beetle, a 'clock':

> Click, Clock, Clay. What time of day?
> One o'clock, two o'clock, three o'clock
> Click, clock, clay.

The exact hour depends on which direction the ladybird flies away; due north means it is twelve o'clock.

The most exciting of the ladybird's auguries is its ability to foretell your marriage partner – though only for girls. The insect cannot, of course, provide the future marriage partner's name, but it can at least indicate the direction he will come from. Once again, you solemnly hold up the ladybird:

> Fly away east or fly away west,
> And show me where lives the one I like best.[41]

Then the girl watches with interest to see whether it flies towards a pretty country village full of rich, handsome, good-natured bachelors or towards a sink-estate with serious youth crime. This rhyme and its little game date back at least to the seventeenth century and perhaps earlier. John Gay (1685–1732), author of *The Beggar's Opera*, knew a more formal version:

> This lady-fly I take from off the grass,
> Whose spotted back might scarlet red surpass,
> Fly, lady-bird, north, south, or east, or west,
> Fly where the man is found that I love best.[42]

In Scotland there was a longer version outlining the various travel options open to the ladybird. It is based on another ladybird name, 'Lady Lanners':

> Lady, Lady Lanners
> Tak up your clowk about your heid
> An flee awa to Flanners.[43]

Ladybird, ladybird, Fly Away Home *(pen and ink and watercolour), a bleak image by Arthur Rackham for* Mother Goose, the Old Nursery Rhymes.

Two and two make four: mating Two-spot Ladybirds.

In Norfolk and Suffolk the invocation is to 'Bishie Barniebee':

> Bishie, bishie, Barnabee
> Tell me when my wedding will be

One of the sillier ladybird games is to find out someone's age by counting the number of spots on a ladybird's back. Since the seven-spot and two-spot ladybirds between them account for 80 per cent of all British ladybird records, the answer will normally be either two or seven. Others insist that the spots tell us the ladybird's own age, in which case it presumably grows another spot as it gets older. Two Liverpool children were overheard discussing a ladybird that had settled on the window: 'How many spots has it?' 'Two.' 'That's how old it is – two!'[44] Other versions have the ladybird telling us how many happy months are due, how many children we will have or how much money will land in our laps. In every case, the 22-spot ladybird would seem a lot luckier than the two-spot ladybird.

The best-known rhyme about ladybirds is surprisingly dark:

> Ladybird, ladybird,
> Fly away home.
> Your house is on fire,
> And your children are gone.
> All except one, and that's Little Anne
> For she has crept under the warming pan.

This nursery rhyme first appeared in *Tommy Thumb's Pretty Song Book*, published in 1744, but is probably older. Like the games of fortune, the custom is to recite the rhyme to the ladybird sitting on your fingertip as if to warn it of approaching catastrophe. Versions of it are chanted by children over half of Europe, which suggests the rhyme has deep cultural and historical roots. But what is it about? One theory claims it originates from the custom of burning refuse in hop-yards after the picking season is over. As George Orwell memorably described in his 1934 novel *A Clergyman's Daughter*, poor families from London's East End used to troop out to the Kentish countryside in late summer for a paid holiday picking hops. Ladybirds, babies and all, clustering among hop blossoms or attempting to hibernate among the straw would perish in the bonfires that signed off the hop season.

For those who believe that our nursery rhymes are rooted in historical circumstance and are not

351

merely nonsense, you can cherry-pick through other possibilities. One parallel is the burning of the Catholic martyrs (that is, those faithful to the cult of Our Lady) under Henry VIII. Or perhaps the rhyme's roots are deeper still and lie in the replacement of pagan, temple-based religions by Christianity in the late Roman Empire, or that the ladybird 'flying away' symbolises the end of the old matriarchal religions of northern Europe and their replacement by the male sky-god Odin.[45] There is even a Scottish version that links the rhyme to the Highland clearances in Scotland when so many widows 'flew away' to America:

> Dowdy-cow, dowdy-cow, ride away hame.
> Thy house is burnt, and thy bairns are taen,
> And if thou means to save thy bairns
> Take thy wings and flee away.

What all the rhymes stress is that ladybirds are special and should not to be harmed, and, in the end, perhaps that is their point. They remind children that ladybirds are benign and useful creatures. 'As children in Conwy in the 1940s,' remembers Bob Powley, 'we loved ladybirds and liked them to crawl over us – until, that is, they produced wings and flew, which terrified us, presumably because of their suddenly altered appearance. When they resettled, they were our friends again.'[46]

Perhaps in courteous acknowledgement of the Virgin's special care of them, folk medicine has tended to leave ladybirds alone. However, ground-up ladybird was sold by apothecaries as *Pulvis dentrificius* and used as tooth powder. It was also said to be helpful to sufferers of the measles (presumably because of the spots) or the colic.

Literary ladybirds

Everyone loves a ladybird. Perhaps the regularity with which they are made into key rings is an echo of the medieval story that they held the keys to heaven. They also sit on every cover of the well-known Ladybird Books (a trademark registered as early as 1915, though not used until the 1940s). The colourful little beetle presides over the books like a little child-friendly house-god (its species oscillates between the two-spot and the seven-spot, though at one point, a non-biological ten-spotted ladybird was used). Appropriately enough, one of the strengths of the Ladybird Books in their heyday was their beautifully illustrated artwork of wildlife and nature.

Literary ladybirds are not always so benign. What makes *The Bad-tempered Ladybird* (1977) by Eric Carle so funny is that it subverts the customary image by presenting a thoroughly disagreeable ladybird, smug, boastful and incompetent. The simple story proceeds through a succession of challenges made by the idiotic ladybird to bigger and bigger beasts, starting with a stag beetle, then a praying mantis, then a lobster and culminating with an ill-advised duel with a whale, which casually flicks the bad-tempered ladybird far over the waves and back to its original perch without even noticing it. There the chastened bug accepts a plate of aphids from its mate with humble thanks.

Some of the modern lore about ladybirds is interestingly downbeat. They did not bring much luck to Nancy Sinatra in 1967; her song 'Lady Bird', performed with Lee Hazlewood, was replete with metaphors of flight and downfall; this lady bird flew too high and burned her wings. The 1994 Ken Loach film *Ladybird Ladybird*, a gritty docudrama about a mother's fight to retain her children, took its cue from the rhyme, 'Ladybird, ladybird, fly away home'. The protagonist had four children with as many fathers (all flown). She finally meets a good man only to attract the attention of care workers after a fire in which her children are harmed. Branded an unfit mother, the future looks bleak for this ladybird.

Far more comforting is the image of the Ladybird range of children's cloths. Legend has it that the ladybird first appeared in a dream to Johannes Pasold, the eighteenth-century founder of a family knitting-and-weaving business in what was then German Bohemia. The ladybird seemed to him the perfect symbol for cloth that was silky and smooth, pleasing to the eye, hard-wearing and fun to wear. After moving to Britain in 1932, Pasold's began to specialise in soft children's cloths, especially for the under-fives, and, in the process, replaced its original Glacier-Mint-style polar bear with a more cheerful ladybird. The ladybirds on the tower of Pasolds' knitware factory in Langley, Berks, would light up at night and became a well-known local landmark until the structure was demolished in 1982.

Predator and prey. A 22-spot ladybird in pursuit of a greenfly.

Types of ladybird

There are 53 British species of ladybirds (Coccinellidae, from *coccum*, meaning red), of which 28 are the familiar brightly coloured, spotted ones. Many of them are named scientifically after their spot number, so that the Seven-spot Ladybird is *Coccinella septempunctata* ('the seven-spotted little red one', normally rendered as *7-punctata* to save space). Besides the Seven- and Two-spot Ladybirds, we also have ladybirds with 4, 5, 11, 13, 14, 16, 18, 19, 22 and 24 spots; there is even a second Seven-spot ladybird, the Scarce Seven-spot. Other species have been named from the shape of their spots, such as the Kidney, Eyed and Hieroglyphic Ladybirds, or the plants they inhabit, such as the Larch, Pine and Bryony Ladybirds. Ladybird scientific names all bow to the tradition that these beetles are feminine; the names of most other beetles tend to be masculine.

With the availability of good fieldguides, more people can identify species of ladybirds, and nicknames have sprung up. The Pine Ladybird, which is often found feeding on scale insects among their protective layers of fleecy down, has been dubbed the 'shepherd's-pie ladybird'.[47] Perhaps the 'lunchbox ladybird' will catch on for the yellow, polka-dotted 16-spot ladybird, which seems to turns up at picnics, 'running frantically up and down grass stems'. The Scarce Seven-spot has been called the 'ants'-nest ladybird' from its habit of preying on aphids close to the nests of wood-ants.

Mankind and ladybirds have always rubbed along well together. Ladybirds are common in gardens, where, in Surrey at least, all but 3 of our 28 spotted species can be found, attracted by the generous supply of aphids. In the right area, ladybirds can be incredibly common; the entomologist Richard Jones reported a million-ladybirds field in Kent, calculated from a discovered mean density of five ladybirds per square metre. Many will remember the swarms of ladybirds, like blood-spots in the grass, during the long, hot summer of 1976. 'My mother told me that the plague of ladybirds made shutting your window a crunchy business, and that my pram needed a mesh cover,' remembers one contributor.[48]

The best ladybird-finders are children. The Bryony Ladybird was discovered for the first time in Britain by five-year-old Alysia Menzies, who spotted it on her garden swing (luckily her grandfather was interested in beetles). Alysia's ladybird was one of several rare beetles to turn up in her corner of Surrey, a mystery known in beetle circles as the Molesey Phenomenon. Happily, ladybirds are quite easy to keep as pets in small plastic boxes so long as you keep them well fed with live aphids, a pastime any rose-growing parent will want to encourage.

Perhaps surprisingly, ladybirds have only once appeared on a British stamp. On the 22p stamp of the Insects set by Gordon Beningfield, released in 1985, a Seven-spot Ladybird sits rather awkwardly on a clover head.

A UK Ladybird Survey with its own website[49] scours the country for ladybirds, with the help of its dedicated finders, young and old. Recently it has helped to track the spread of the Harlequin Ladybird (*see below*) across Britain.

Harlequin Ladybirds clustered characteristically in a corner of a room.

The advance of the Harlequin

The Harlequin Ladybird is a new arrival to Britain that is fast spoiling the reputation of ladybirds as benign and trouble-free insects. As its name implies, the Harlequin comes in a bewildering variety of colours, orange with black spots, black and red or black with orange spots. It was first spotted in a pub garden in Essex in the autumn of 2004, since when it has spread rapidly over much of southern and eastern England. One of the first mass-sightings was on the walls of Maidstone's town hall, which it 'painted a cherry-red'.[50] Clusters of Harlequins are now a common sight on windowsills in autumn, seeking sheltered corners and crannies for hibernation.

The Harlequin is not only a pretty ladybird but also a ladybird killer. The late Michael Majerus, whose recording network monitored its spread, believed it to be the worst threat our native ladybirds have ever faced. The Harlequin seems immune to the usual checks – parasites and diseases – that keep insect numbers in balance, and hence, like all invasive incomers, it holds a considerable competitive edge over native species.

The Harlequin has quickly become the most unpopular ladybird in history; indeed it is changing the image of ladybirds. 'They destroy wallpaper, curtains and carpets if they are not found,' warns Matt Shardlow of Buglife, 'and they poo a sticky black substance everywhere.'[51] They also smear surfaces with 'reflex blood' that seeps from their joints – a foul-smelling substance that stains fabrics yellow and which squirts out if you try to squash them. On top of that, they can deliver a surprisingly painful nip. In a Royal Horticultural Poll held in 2008, the Harlequin Ladybird had rocketed to second place among the least popular invertebrates, just behind garden slugs. The response to this ladybird is, increasingly, 'see it, crush it.' But do they all know which is the Harlequin and which the benign and beloved Seven-spots and Two-spots?

A native of Asia, Harlequins were used in the 1980s in Europe and America as an aphid bio-control. Some of them inevitably escaped into the wild, where they developed their distressing appetite for other ladybirds as well as orchard fruit and vines (where their acrid defensive juices taint the wine). In the New World, colourful swarms of Harlequins became as much a part of the late autumn as garden bonfires and trick-or-treats, hence its nickname 'the Halloween ladybug'.

Scientists are currently working desperately to discover a reliable bio-control agent, one that will not also attack our innocent native ladybirds. Meanwhile they say the best way to fend them off is to wipe the windowsills with vinegar to overcome the scent of the ladybird's pheromones. Others have resorted to vacuuming them up and lugging Hoover bags full of dead ladybirds to the incinerator.

Larder beetles *Dermestidae*

Few insects are more universally hated by bug collectors – a pretty tolerant lot on the whole – than carpet beetles. There are two common ones, the Fur Beetle, which is about the size of a peppercorn, and the slightly smaller Varied Carpet Beetle, both of which are dark and round and pull in their legs when disturbed. Their larvae are the notorious 'woolly bears' that live underneath old woollen carpets or on natural fibres caught up in the skirting. Infestations can sometimes be traced to a forgotten sweater or blanket, a stored carpet or even a bird nest in the loft or chimney. As anyone who owns an insect collection will know, they have a perverse taste for dried insects, often seeming to choose a particularly rare and valuable one to destroy. By consuming specimens from the inside out, they quickly reduce it to a skin, a pin and a pile of droppings. Since mothballs, Vapona and other useful insecticides were withdrawn from sale in 2005, museums have been reduced to passing their collections through a freezer (though some curators claim this is an improvement on the efficacy of most poisons).

Other 'dermestid' beetles are more likely to invade places where food is stored. The once notorious Bacon, or Larder, Beetle has more or less disappeared from domestic kitchens, but it is still an occasional nuisance in meat- or milk-processing plants as well as museums, where it is potentially interested in anything that retains a hide or dried muscle, no matter how old. The scavenging is done by the beetle's larvae, which can create a double dose of grief by chewing into soft wood or insulation before pupating. The slightly smaller Hide, or Leather, Beetle has similar habits and is commoner, though rarely noticed.

The Khapra Beetle, a tiny yellowish brown flightless beetle, specialises in breweries. It is a common pest of malting silos and, with its close relative, the Warehouse Beetle, has become one of

A collection of butterflies destroyed by the Museum, or Carpet, Beetle which consumes dried insects from the inside out. Today's collections are preserved by passing them through a freezer.

Larder Beetle (highly magnified and coloured by computer).

the world's worst pests of stored products. It is hardy and unusually long-lived; the adult beetle can go for months or even years without feeding. It will chew the glue from books and cardboard boxes and nibble the backs of priceless oil paintings and has even been known to find sustenance in a bags of bolts. What until recently was industry's answer to a bad infestation of Khapra Beetles was fairly drastic: the premises were sealed off and highly toxic methyl bromide (also a powerful ozone depleter) was pumped in at up to four kilograms per 30 cubic metres of space. Now that most uses of methyl bromide have been banned in the EU, the pressure is on to find a more environmentally friendly substitute.

Plaster beetles *Lathridiidae*

Plaster beetles are a collection of tiny, black beetles, not much larger than dots, that sometimes appear from nowhere on damp, newly plastered walls and ceilings. They are harmless in the sense that they feed not on the plaster itself but on the invisible mildew that forms on it, and once the plaster has dried out, they normally disappear; if they don't, the underlying problem may not be the beetles but the damp.

Furniture beetles and woodworms *Anobiidae*

The 52 British species of Anobiidae include some of our most dreaded insect pests or, as entomologists prefer, 'insects of economic importance'. Leading the list, at least in historical terms, is the Biscuit Beetle, alias the Bread, or Drugstore, Beetle – the infamous 'weevil' that infested the biscuits of Nelson's navy. As far as sailors were concerned, any small insect was a weevil (larger ones were cockroaches). They were also known as lice. Ship's weevils are a part of the Hollywood image of bygone seafaring, but in reality, they became a problem mainly in hot, damp climates when the thrice-baked hardtack would soften enough to interest the beetle. The trick was to tap the biscuit to knock out the grubs. A captain of Nelson's era knew the maggots as 'bargemen' and recalled that the biscuits were best eaten in the dark.

The small, brownish Biscuit Beetle still makes a nuisance of itself in the food industry. In 2001, 3 million Twix bars worth £800,000 had to be withdrawn from sale after an inspector spotted the telltale black flecks of Biscuit Beetle droppings in the supply of flour. As well as biscuits and chocolate bars, the beetle also enjoys pasta, corn flakes, muesli, nuts, rice, dried beans and dog biscuits, and willingly chews through packaging, including tinfoil, to get at them; the one thing that defeats a Biscuit Beetle is Tupperware. The beetle has also developed an unlikely taste for prescription drugs, hence its alternative name of drugstore beetle. It is a serious nuisance in libraries and museums, where it gnaws into leather-bound books and preserved specimens.

The Tobacco, or Cigarette, Beetle has the ability to curl up into a ball. Like Virginian tobacco, it is a New World native that has spread around the world, living unobserved inside tobacco bales in warehouses and thence makes its way into cigar boxes. At a time when the majority who do not smoke are encouraged to execrate the minority who still do, it is perhaps hard to commune with the grief felt by anyone who has opened a pack of fine Havana cigars to discover that the beetle has got there first. Manufacturers go to great lengths to avoid it by fumigating their warehouses and using vacuum chambers to crush any beetle eggs lying dormant in the tobacco. This beetle has remarkably strong tastes. Apart from tobacco, it can make short work of ginger, cayenne pepper, paprika, chilli or curry powder.

Woodworms

VN: cannie (Scot.), chackie-mill (Scot.), deid-watch (Scot.), elf-mill

The Death-watch Beetle has put fear into the superstitious down the ages with its sinister tapping, like the tick of an old pocket-watch or the pulse of the heart. When the Death-watch knocks, it's said that death is in the air. It might be death for you, it might be for someone else, but for whomever the beetle knocks, the countdown to eternity has begun. The sound, which resembles a pencil rapping against a desktop, is made when the beetle head-butts the roof of its tunnel, enabling the sound to resonate down the chamber. It is in fact the beetle's mating call, made on warm, quiet nights, mainly in the spring. Given the sharpness and clarity of the knock, the beetle that makes it is surprisingly small – about the size of a grain of rice. It is dark and nondescript, and with its head tucked in under its thorax, looks a little like an old lady wearing a bonnet and shawl. To most, the Death-watch Beetle is not a living entity so much as a sinister tap, plus the dust of its droppings as they accumulate beneath the timbers.

The beetle digests wood with the help of fungi in its intestines, though it also feeds on mildew. It is associated above all with broad oak rafters in historic buildings, especially churches and cathedrals (Salisbury Cathedral had a bad attack of them in the 1990s). Chemical fumigation sometimes requires the closing of the church, when, appropriately enough, a warning sign featuring a skull and crossbones appears on the locked doors.

In his satirical rhyme, 'Wood: An Insect', Jonathan Swift compared an unpopular ironmaster, William Wood, who had made a fortune from minting inferior coins known derisively as Wood's Halfpence, with this worst of beetles:

The Third is an Insect we call a *Wood*-Worm,
That lies in old *Wood* like a Hare in her Form;
With Teeth or with Claws it will bite or will
    scratch,
And Chambermaids christen this Worm a Death-
    watch,
Because like a Watch it always cries *Click*:
Then Woe to those in the House who are sick,
For as sure as a Gun they will give up the Ghost[52]

Did the beetle really strike terror into men's hearts? In 1787, the antiquarian Francis Grose included it in a three-page inventory of death-omens. The beetle is among the downy owls and death-moths that afflict the drooping mind in John Keats's 'Ode on Melancholy'. Its knock seems to have preyed most on the minds of the bedridden, sparking morbid thoughts. Oliver Goldsmith reported the anguished drip-drip effect of nocturnal noises on the troubled mind:

> I sat silent for some minutes and soon perceiving the ticking of my watch beginning to grow noisy and troublesome, I quickly placed it out of hearing; and strove to resume my serenity. But the watchman soon gave me a second alarm. I had scarcely recovered from this, when my peace was assaulted by the wind at my window; and when that ceased to blow, I listened for the Death-watch in the wainscot . . . I saw no misery approaching, nor knew any I had to fear, yet still I was miserable.[53]

For the dying, the knocking of the Death-watch Beetle must have felt like the summons of Judgement Day. In his late poem 'Forlorn', Alfred Tennyson summed up:

> You that lie with wasted lungs
> Waiting for the summons . . .
> In the night, O the night!
> O the death watch beating![54]

The narrator of Edgar Allan Poe's short story 'The Tell-tale Heart' (1843) murders an old man and buries his body under the floorboards. That might have been that, except for the sound of the man's heart apparently still beating through the floor, 'a low, dull, quiet sound, such as a watch makes when enveloped in cotton'.[55] It is never entirely clear whether this is in fact the quiet thumping of the 'deathwatches' in the wainscoting or a hallucination, but it induces floods of guilt and remorse and brings the story to an appropriately miserable, Poe-like conclusion. Perhaps he got the idea from Henry Thoreau, who claimed that 'every pulse-beat [of the human heart] is in exact time with the cricket's chant and the tickings of the Death-watch on the wall'.

The beetle continues to be a harbinger of doom. In Alice Hoffman's spooky novel *Practical Magic* (1995), its sudden appearance indicates the immediacy of someone's death; the film version has Sandra Bullock desperately tearing up the floorboards to try to save her husband by killing the tapping beetle. In

Holes and tunnels made in antique furniture by the Death-watch Beetle.

Ray Bradbury's *Something Wicked This Way Comes* (1962), a sinister, tattooed character called Dark has a singular trade: 'To examine, oil, polish and repair Death-watch Beetles.' The beetle has also been a metaphor for a psychological trouble, a woodworm of the mind. When the *Daily Express* offered Ian Fleming a small fortune for the rights to serialise the Bond books as cartoon strips, the author felt 'something of a deathwatch beetle inside', causing 'disgust with the operation to creep in' (though he nonetheless took the money).

Woodworm is a collective term for the nuisance beetles whose grubs bore holes inside building timbers or furniture. Commoner today than the Death-watch Beetle is the Furniture Beetle, the scourge of antique furniture, which is similar in appearance and habits but lacks the trademark knocking. A third common species is the Powderpost Beetle, which prefers fresh timber because of its high starch content. Infestations of the Powderpost Beetle can be identified from the floury frass piled up around the emergence holes.

Insecticides to get rid of woodworm were developed in the 1920s by Harold Maxwell Lefroy, Professor of Entomology at Imperial College. Called in to investigate an outbreak of Death-watch Beetle in Westminster Hall in 1924, his chemical remedy was so successful that he set up a small factory to market it under the brand name of Ento-Kill Fluids. When he came to register a company, he changed the name to Rentokil, now an international pest-control company. Unfortunately Lefroy himself soon became a victim, indeed a martyr, to the deadliness of his own products. While testing a new insecticide in his poorly ventilated laboratory,

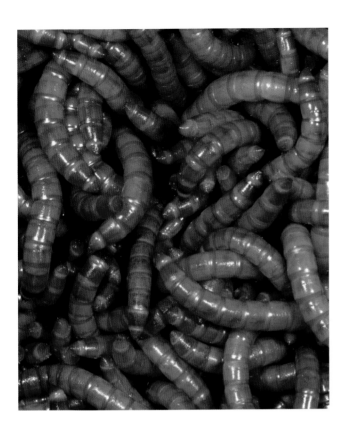

Mealworms, food for birds but also nutritious for humans.

he was overcome by the fumes. His last words are said to have been, 'The little beggars got the best of me that time.'

The woodworm is an unlikely witness of world-changing events in Julian Barnes' subversive novel *A History of the World in 10½ Chapters* (1989). The book relates episodes from the past in different narrative styles that shed light on how we see and relate to the past. Barnes' all-seeing, highly observant woodworm is a stowaway on Noah's Ark, where it spends most of its time thinking about sex; its noisy mating ritual almost leads to its discovery and certain extinction. The woodworm notices that the patriarch and his family seem less interested in saving the animals than in sorting them into 'clean' and 'unclean' kinds, thereafter eating the former and neglecting the latter. By the end of the voyage the most beautiful and magical creatures have all been eaten, and it is a much reduced biodiversity that steps gratefully from the Ark and runs away. 'Man is a very unevolved species compared with animals,' muses the humble stowaway.[56] In Barnes' historical scheme, the woodworm represents an alternate, repressed version of events, the voice of the outcast down the ages.

Mealworms *Tenebrionidae*

Mealworms are the larvae of a small, black beetle. In nature, they live in bird nests and other places where dead animal matter, droppings and other edible leftovers accumulate. In the unnatural world of our homes they lurk in cellars, stores and occasionally cupboards where food debris is not cleaned away regularly. Like most beetles that dare to enter our domain, a dustpan-and-brush and perhaps a good scrub with soapy water is all it takes to get rid of them (they are potentially more of a pest in grain stores).

Mealworms are sold in every pet store and tackle shop, raised on a diet of bran or oatmeal. As the product of a clean diet, they are safe to handle. Commercial growers use a chemical hormone that not only prevents the grubs from pupating and turning into beetles but also forces them to become larger and fatter than their natural counterparts. Mealworms are a standard food for the growing number of pet lizards and are a cheap and useful form of protein for cage-birds and chickens. There are even special mealworm containers available for feeding the birds. With patience and a few wriggling mealworms, you can get robins to feed from your hand.

We can eat mealworms, too; they are rich in fatty acids – useful for repairing nerve and brain tissue – and are sold as novelty candies at Fortnum and Mason and other luxury stores. Some people use crushed dried mealworms to make a protein-rich flour – excellent for nutritious, Mexican-style tortillas – or to add to egg-fried rice, along with chopped onion, soya sauce and a little garlic. At least one entomologist enjoys mealworm bolognese with spaghetti.

Relations of the mealworm include the flour beetles, known as the Rust Red Flour Beetle and the Confused Flour Beetle (named from its similarity in appearance, not because the beetle itself is confused). They are also known as 'bran bugs'. The tiny beetles appear from nowhere as black flecks in open packets of flour, though they will eat a range of milled grain products, including breakfast cereal, cornmeal, crackers and starch. Flour beetles have even nibbled baits laced with arsenic. These are true indoor beetles, found in larders, warehouses and factories throughout the world but never, so far, in the wild. They are apparently able to reproduce from one generation to the next encased inside a packet of flour without further contact with the outside world. Fortunately, they do not transmit disease.

Thomas Muffet described the big, black Churchyard, or Cellar, Beetle as 'a shamefaced creature and most impatient of light, not so much for its ill-favouredness, but the guiltiness of its conscience in regard of the stinke it leaves behind it.'[57] This is a flightless beetle that lives in damp cellars, stables, barns and other dark, humid places and was once familiar to householders from its habit of hiding in outdoor lavatories, or 'base places', as Muffet referred to them. The beetle's smelly reflex fluid contains skin irritants, and its scent suggested to one Victorian coleopterist the odour of decaying coffins.

In Muffet's day, however, few insects were considered entirely useless, and a Churchyard Beetle mashed up with old wine, honey, apple juice, tar, onions, pomegranate rind and *unguentum Syriacum* was said to have a soothing effect on a sore ear.

Relatives of the Churchyard Beetle, known as darkling beetles, are implicated in a semi-mythical but undeniably distressing condition called canthariasis – the invasion of body tissues by beetles. The story goes that the beetle grubs may be swallowed accidentally in foul graveyard water and may survive their journey to the stomach. There they grow fat on half-digested leftovers and are duly returned to the world via the victim's rectum. There are also horror stories, though not from Britain, of beetles invading the rectums of people sleeping rough on the floor and crawling into their gut. The beetles are not parasites, only opportunists, and, it seems, they eventually wander out again.

Oil beetles *Meloidae*

VN: blister beetle, Meloe, oil-clock

The oil beetle is one of Britain's strangest looking insects. About two and a half centimetres long, it is black or blue-black with a round head and a plump, tapering body and a soft, oily lustre suggestive of a half-sucked piece of liquorice. Its short, functionless wingcases sit on the beetle's body like a too-tight waistcoat, or, in Henri Fabre's words, 'yawning over their back like the tails of a fat man's coat.'[58] The beetle's 'oil' – in fact, a defensive and caustic haemolymph – oozes from between the joints of its legs. Early beetle-watchers believed that this orange liquid was beetle-honey (though the tiniest taste would have put them right), whereas it is, in fact, a blistering agent, a necessary defence for a large and possibly tasty beetle that cannot fly or even run very fast.

Oil beetles are most often seen wandering on bare soil in the spring, especially on coastal footpaths or in heathland, open woodland and flowery meadows. The adult beetle feeds on flowers and leaves, with an unexplained preference for buttercups. Its liking for dry places and crumbling banks is due not so much to the adult's needs as those of its bizarre larva. Oil beetles are parasites of small, solitary bees and lay their eggs close to bee holes. An egg hatches not into the usual maggot-like grub but a little leggy creature known as a triungulin, like a cross between a louse and an earwig. The triungulin clambers up a nearby

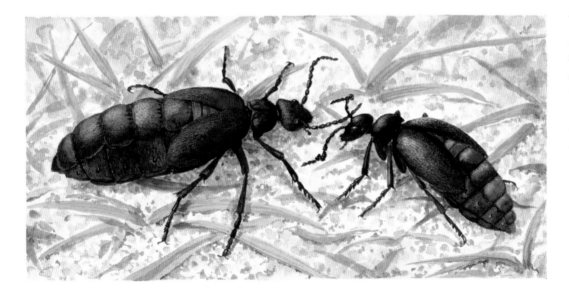

Like a fat man wearing a tail-coat: Oil beetles *(watercolour), by Carol Mullin.*

buttercup and awaits the arrival of a bee. If its luck is in, it grabs hold of the bee's fur with its hook-like front legs and is carried back to the bee's nest. There the larva transforms into a fat, legless grub and helps itself to honey, pollen and bee eggs. After subsisting on this rich diet all summer, the grub duly pupates, and the beetle emerges the following year.

Such a lifestyle is hazardous, not so much from any danger of being stung as from the huge odds against the triungulin coming across the right kind of bee. Such strategies unravel when the host numbers are lower than usual because of bad weather or habitat destruction. Britain has become a very hazardous place for oil beetles. Of the nine recorded species, five seem to be extinct. But they are easily overlooked, and one supposedly extinct species, the Short-necked Oil-beetle, recently turned up on National Trust land in South Devon (it had last been seen in Essex in 1948). Buglife runs a national oil-beetle survey that it hopes will offer clues as to why the beetles are declining.[59]

The caustic haemolymph of oil beetles had its uses in traditional medicine, though in Britain the beetles were perhaps too rare to become regular items in the apothecary's window. In Spain, where the beetle is known as *frailecillo* ('the little monk'), it is still used, immersed in bottles of olive oil, to ease sciatic pains. A stronger concoction of bottled beetle was also used to burn off sores and carbuncles and to treat 'wounds made by a mad dog'.[60] In Germany, powdered beetle was added to beer to make a drink called *kaddentrank*, which put a sick person 'into a sudden and great sweat' and so drew forth the injurious 'humours'.[61]

Blister Beetle

VN: Spanish fly

Spanish fly is a potion that can supposedly turn modest girls into nymphomaniacs. It is made from the ground-up remains of an insect, though a beetle rather than a fly. Stories from ancient times magnified its merits as an aphrodisiac, and the Empress Livia reputedly kept a supply to hand out at orgies. In eighteenth-century France, you could buy Spanish fly in the form of sweets, *pastilles a la Richelieu* or as *bonbons a la Marquis de Sade*.

The substance at work in Spanish fly is not an aphrodisiac in the usual sense but a highly toxic irritant. First isolated pharmaceutically in 1810, it is called cantharidin, from Cantharides, the medicinal name of the beetle. It creates the illusion of sexual arousal by inflaming the urinary tract. In excessive doses, Spanish fly is said to cause priapism – a persistent and embarrassing erection which (say the sufferers) is more painful than erotic; the last thing on the mind of a victim of priapism is sex.

The insect behind the myths is the handsome Blister Beetle, emerald green with black antennae. Only the male can synthesise cantharidin, but it passes some of it on to its partner as part of a courtship ritual. The beetle is a southern European species that only rarely visits Britain, but English apothecaries would buy stocks of it on the international market and store the dried bodies in glass jars ready for grinding up. Their chief medical use was not as a love potion but as a rather drastic blistering agent. Its virtue, noted Muffet, 'consists in burning the body, causing a crust to corrode, cause ulceration, and provoke heat'.[62] The powder was used to burn off nail deformities, corns and other 'cancerous sores'. Even stronger, indeed explosive-sounding, caustic agents could be prepared by mixing cantharides with pepper, quicklime or nitre (the main chemical constituent of gunpowder).

Overzealous users faced burns, nausea, internal bleeding, renal damage and seizures. Cantharidin has, however, retained a role in modern medicine as a test agent for anti-inflammatory drugs and as a growth-inhibiter of cancer cells. It is also said to be an ingredient in certain hair-restorers. Some pharmacies still rely on the beetle as a source of cantharidin, and there are concerns that the resulting exploitation of the wild Blister Beetle is not sustainable.[63]

A solo piece for acoustic guitar called 'Spanish Fly' is a popular choice of ring-tone on mobile phones. But the tune suggests a buzzing fly, not a beetle.

Longhorn beetles
Cerambycidae

VN: capricorns, longicorns

Longhorns are among our most charismatic beetles – medium to large insects with long, solid bodies and even longer, jointed antennae that twitch constantly as they make their way about. A few are sufficiently distinctive to have well-established names such as the Musk Beetle or the Wasp Beetle (though most British longhorns were given English names recently to encourage more people to record them and hence help to conserve them). The largest 'horns' relative to the beetle's size are born by the Timberman, named from its fondness for fresh-cut pine logs, which carries a pair of stiff ones three times the length of its body. The larvae of most longhorns feed under tree bark or tunnel deep into the wood and are considered to be ecologically beneficial as recyclers. With practice, most species can be identified in the field. A *Provisional Atlas of British Longhorn Beetles* was published by the Centre of Ecology and Hydrology in 2008.

The few species that can cause damage by tunnelling into house timbers are non-native imports. By far the commonest is the House Longhorn, or Old House Borer, a cosmopolitan beetle that has spread around the world in the wood of packing cases. It is now found in building timbers the world over, with a preference for softwood beams. By the time the large emergent holes appear, the beetle's fat larvae may already have reduced much of the wood to powder. The beetles sometimes escape into the wild, where they tunnel into the trunks of pine trees, and suburban Surrey and Hampshire have the nucleus of a wild population, based on planted pines on sandy heaths. Local authorities in the area have imposed strict building regulations, requiring all softwood timbers to be treated before construction. This seems to be working; there have been few recent reports of longhorn trouble.

The greatest longhorn of them all is the Capricorn Beetle, a five-centimetre giant whose magnificent antlers would span the width of a saucer. It is known to have inhabited England in the Bronze Age, because its signature timber holes, large enough to insert a finger into, have been found in ancient bog-oaks preserved in the Fens. Supposedly long extinct in Britain, ponderous Capricorn Beetles

The Wasp Beetle. Its movements, as well as colours, mimic those of wasps.

still occasionally emerge from imported timbers, to the awe and astonishment of all concerned. In June 2006, Ben Perrot, a furniture restorer from Llanelli, spotted one sitting on an oak plank 'like a monster from *Dr Who*'[64] and thought at first that it was a plastic toy from a joke shop. Another (possibly a different though equally large species) was found on the floor in a house in Warwickshire, having emerged from some recently installed beams. It was gingerly captured and taken to a butterfly farm in Stratford, where the much-travelled Capricorn was thoughtfully given a pineapple to eat.

> A friend of mine says he can never enjoy a logfire because he cannot help listening for the popping sound of invertebrate larvae as the wood burns. Last year his concerns were justified when a couple from Pershore, Worcestershire, noticed that a striking pair of red beetles was sitting on their hearth next to a basket of oak logs. A local expert identified them as Scarlet Longhorns, vanishingly rare in the UK and seemingly a first record for the county. After much detective work the source of the logs was traced back to the Wyre Forest, but, annoyingly found they had been cut from the Shropshire side.[65]

A Capricorn Beetle, grandest of the longhorns, long extinct in Britain but may be staging a come-back in imported timbers.

Leaf beetles *Chrysomelidae*

The shiny, brilliant green Tansy Beetle, also known as the Jewel of York, is one of our prettiest beetles and was said to have been collected in the nineteenth century as sequins for ladies' dresses. In this century, it has become one of the minor icons of insect conservation, thanks to the efforts of Dr Geoff Oxford and colleagues to conserve it on one of its last sites, the flood-meadows of the Vale of York. The Tansy Beetle takes sedentary living to extremes, seeming to spend its entire life on the same patch of tansy, its slug-like larvae chewing the pungent leaves, and the adults nibbling at pollen on the yellow flowers. But what might sound like the recipe for a perfect self-contained existence has backfired. The Tansy Beetle needs tansy plants growing in moist soil in river valleys where regular flooding keeps the ground suitably damp while also deterring beetle predators such as moles and ants.[66] We are running out of such places; nor does it help that tansy is often mistaken for ragwort and eradicated.

> I remember going to Clifton Ings during the summer term in the 1950s to collect Tansy Beetles. We never had any problems finding them – some plants could have twenty or thirty. We would put them in a shoebox with some leaves and take them home or to school. We held Tansy beetle races along two pieces of taut string although I do not recall any champions or any big bets being wagered.[67]

The Tansy Beetle is just one of about 260 British species of leaf beetles, many of which share its colourful metallic gleam. As the name implies, they are all herbivorous, and their mass assaults leave a plant perforated, wilting and covered in larval droppings. The family includes the tiny flea beetles, which hop out of harm's way as if on springs, and the tortoise beetles, whose wingcases and thorax are fused to form a tough, tortoise-like carapace. The largest British species is the well-known Bloody-nosed Beetle, common on paths in chalk and limestone areas, which sometimes secretes a reddish defensive fluid if picked up. Altogether this is one of the more popular and accessible beetle families, and an *Atlas of the Seed and Leaf Beetles of Britain and Ireland* was published in 2007.

The family includes several attractive, if

The Lily Beetle, now a serious scourge of garden lilies.

unwanted, garden beetles. The Mint Beetle is a brilliant orb of metallic green, whose dark larvae can strip a patch of mint with speed and efficiency. A relative newcomer from America is the Rosemary Leaf Beetle, another breath-stopping beetle, with green and candy-pink stripes. Like the Mint Beetle, it has a counter-intuitive urge to make a beeline for plants famed for their insect-repellent chemicals, including rosemary but also thyme, sage and lavender. Nibbling causes the plants to sicken and eventually die as they succumb to toxins in the beetle's saliva. Experiments are under way to see whether camphor extracted from these herbs could be used to trap the beetle before it can get any further.

The Lundy Flea Beetle, confined to the island of Lundy – 'Britain's little Galapagos' – where it forms part of a unique group of insects dependent on the endemic Lundy Cabbage.

The Colorado Beetle, a notorious pest of potato crops, represented in nineteenth-century British cartoons as an undesirable immigrant or an invading horde.

The most troublesome leaf beetle of all is the pretty, red Lily Beetle (or Red Lily Beetle). Its larvae are found feeding on the leaves of garden lilies or fritillaries and amuse children with their 'coat of dung', a disguise made from their own droppings. A spray with the alarming name of Ultimate Bug Killer Concentrate has been developed to deal with these beetles, but a more bug-friendly alternative is to keep a lookout for the beetle's bright orange egg-batches in the spring. If picked up, the Lily Beetle is said to utter an audible squeak.

The world's best-known and worst-feared leaf beetle is the Colorado Beetle, a gaily striped, yellow and black insect the size of a large ladybird, which wrought havoc on the potato crops of nineteenth-century America and, later, more patchily, in Europe. In the 1870s, when the scare was in full swing, legislation was introduced in Britain to ban imported potatoes from affected areas. The cover of the magazine *Funny Folks* alluded to the scare by featuring a cartoon of an invading army of Colorado Beetles storming up the beach at the White Cliffs of Dover under the banner of the Stars and Stripes. Awaiting them is a pair of stout John Bulls, each armed with a knapsack sprayer. This early insecticide was Paris Green, an arsenic compound based on an artist's pigment. There were also dark rumours that Irish Fenians intended to release the beetle – 'Paddy's pest' – on English potato crops in

revenge for the Irish potato famine. Its potential use as biological warfare led to the beetle's name being used as an insult. Just as certain traditional enemies of the state have been called cockroaches, so the leaders of Irish Home Rule were labelled Colorado Beetles in some High Tory circles.

Fortunately, the beetle never did succeed in invading Britain. But what it did do, suggests J. F. M. Clark, was to colonise a 'small patch of Britain's collective imagination'.[68] The scare led directly to government investment in insecticide production. It was the advent of the age of industrial agriculture and our uneasy reliance on toxic chemicals manufactured in the laboratories of ICI.

Malachite beetles *Cleroidea*

Though fully as attractive as it sounds, the Scarlet Malachite Beetle is very rare and confined to a handful of places, all of them on village greens in the south of England, where the beetle feeds on buttercups. Buglife is championing it by investigating its life-history and promising to reintroduce the beetle to lost sites. The beetle's growing public profile was sealed when the *Independent* ran its photograph across its front page on 24 June 2006. Its commoner but less colourful relative, the Common Malachite Beetle, occurs in gardens, where it feeds on slugs.

Weevils *Curculionidae*

VN: doodlebugs, snout beetles

To entomologists, if not to sailors, weevils are small beetles with characteristic long snouts, or rostrums, that feed on plants or seeds. Weevils form one of the largest beetle families, with around a thousand British species (one beetle in four is a weevil). They are botanists' insects, for many are tied to particular food-plants. Among the stranger weevils is one that tiptoes over duckweed, another that has learned to swim and has an underwater larva, and a whole subgroup that feeds only on the powder-puff flowers and creeping stems of dodder. They should not be confused with the unrelated 'weevil' of ship's biscuits (*see* Furniture Beetles).

Several weevils have clashed with mankind, eating things of value to us, notably stored grain and garden flowers. They came to the granaries of the Bishop of York, reported the twelfth-century gossipy writer Matthew Paris, and destroyed his grain – a meet punishment for one who was notoriously mean to the poor. This species was the Grain Weevil, which is small and hardy enough to burrow into stored grain and complete its entire lifecycle inside a sack. When badly infested with weevil, the grain becomes damp and strung together as if caught in a cobweb. This increases the danger of secondary infection by *E. coli* bacteria, as well as causing the grain to spoil or sprout. Even in Matthew Paris's day, this was not a new pest; the weevil's remains are common in excavated Roman granaries.

The dull-black Vine Weevil would be near the top of the pest list in many British gardens. Its grubs gnaw the roots of a wide range of garden plants, especially primulas and strawberries, causing them to wilt and die. A bio-control in the form of a nematode worm is now available. 'We knew Vine Weevils as "doodlebugs".'[69]

Weevils have themselves been used as a bio-control in aquaculture for the invasive water fern *Azolla*. The species, a North American weevil, *Stenopelmus rufinasus*, otherwise known by its trade name Azollacontrol, is a water-walking weevil that, once released, looks after itself.

The weevil that contributed most to the world's economy, however, is the Cotton, or Boll, Weevil that devastated the American cotton industry in the 1920s. It earned the weevil a place in popular culture via the blues, and in the long run, it proved a blessing in disguise, for the beetle helped to nudge the economy of the South away from a reliance on a monoculture of cotton (which is why, in the town of Enterprise, Alabama, there is a statue of the weevil as a 'herald of prosperity').

The colourful Hazel Weevil. Its larvae feed inside rolled-up hazel leaves.

Bark beetles *Scolytinae*

VN: ambrosia beetle, pinhole borer, shothole borer

The bug that killed the elms was a bark beetle. The tiny Elm Bark Beetle unknowingly carries within its body the spores of the fungus that clog up the channels of the tree and ultimately cause its death. This is Dutch elm disease. A virulent form of it reached southern England in elm logs imported from the European mainland in the late 1960s. In ten years, the disease had destroyed an estimated 25 million elms throughout England and Wales, and with the trees went a cherished form of countryside of fields and lanes lined with tall, billowing trees. The reason so small an insect can have so great an impact on the landscape is that the beetle releases powerful pheromones that attract others when a suitable host tree is found. They reproduce and multiply rapidly in galleries beneath the bark, which, as the tree dies, sloughs off and reveals the beetles' lairs underneath. The loss of most of our elms did not entail the loss of the beetle. It can invade regenerating elms after 20 or so years of growth, leaving another kind of landmark, small skeletal trees with corky, diseased bark within an otherwise healthy hedgerow.

The Elm Bark Beetle is one of approximately 60 species of small, dark, bullet-shaped beetles that tunnel under the bark of trees. You may witness a mass emergence when the heat from a log basket placed near the fireplace disturbs them. Bark beetles spend most of their lives within their galleries, mating, feeding and laying their eggs, and leaving only tiny perforations in the bark once they emerge as adults to take to the air for their brief nuptial flight (hence their nicknames 'pinhole borer' or 'shothole borer'). Most bark beetles feed not on the wood itself but on rotting sawdust or mildew. Those known as ambrosia beetles eat the ambrosia fungi that they cultivate within their tunnels. The word ambrosia was borrowed whimsically from the food of the gods, an elixir that brought immortality to the drinker.

Some bark beetles are attracted to sick or damaged trees, drawn in partly by the scent of ethanol in the sap. Different beetles target different trees, among them oak, ash, larch, spruce and pine, though they seldom become serious pests except to conifers grown in plantations. The Great Spruce Bark Beetle, a non-native species brought here in imported

Elm Bark Beetle galleries. These tiny beetles contributed to the destruction of 25 million elm trees.

timber, can attack apparently healthy trees, and the Forestry Commission has released the predatory beetle *Rhizophagus grandis* in an attempt to control it. Another potential plantation-pest species is the Engraver Beetle, named after its scientific name *Ips typographus*, noted for the deep, sometimes letter-like grooves it leaves under the bark of pine trees.

Water beetles *Hydrophilidae* and other families

VN: water-clocks

The idea of a swimming beetle has always held a special appeal, and water beetles include some of our largest and most attractive beetles. They even have their own society, the Balfour-Browne Club, named after a noted expert on water beetles. It is a small but highly committed group, which runs a mapping scheme, publishes a regular journal, *Latissimus* (named after Europe's largest diving beetle), and acts as an expert international body for their conservation.

What attracts people to water beetles? Jonty Denton suggests 'it is very hard to put into words: the pure streamlined form of a diving beetle does more for me than any Ferrari, and the pursuit of our fauna will entail a tour of much of our great wild country from the Broads and coastal marshes to the tarns and lakes of the Highlands. Perhaps the greatest joy is that the season starts early and is a great cure for the winter blues. Delve around in mild weather in March and you will find things already in full swing . . .'[70]

There are about 280 fully aquatic water beetles and another hundred or so that live on the banks and margins of ponds and streams. Since even water beetles need land to pupate, good beetle ponds have natural, shallow margins and crumbling banks. Some species are happy with puddles or marshy land so long as there is standing water. A well-known method of persuading them to show themselves is to stamp about in welly boots until the beetles rise to the surface. Enthusiasts call this THD, or Temporary Habitat Destruction.

Until recently, most water beetles were known only by their scientific names. A few have group names such as diving beetles, riffle beetles and whirligigs, while one distinctive small species is named the Cherrystone Beetle from its uncanny resemblance to a spat-out cherry pip (for the same reason it is also called the Lentil Beetle). A recent attempt to provide popular names for a much larger number includes half-humorous or cryptic names such as the Shirt, the Prosthetic and the Jockstrap Beetle.

One of the few water beetles distinctive enough to be recognised by the non-expert is the Screech Beetle. When handled, it makes a startling noise – not exactly a screech but more a loud and rapid zip. It is also, perhaps more accurately, known as the Squeak Beetle.

Diving beetles *Dytiscidae*

Our best-known water beetles are powerful, solid-looking insects with hair-fringed hind-legs that enable them to dodge and dive with surprising agility. Diving beetles are fierce carnivores that can devour full-grown tadpoles and small fish. Their five-centimetre larvae are even more impressive, with huge outstretched jaws that snap shut like hinged traps. Since diving beetles can rapidly clear a tank or a small garden pond of fish, they make doubtful neighbours. Hold one, and you can feel its power as it wriggles, but grasp it firmly by its sides or it may draw blood with either a bite or a prick from its spiny legs.

There are six British species of diving beetle, all of which have been given modern English names. The commonest is the Great Diving Beetle. Two others have been dubbed Black Belly and the Wasp from their distinctively black or yellow-striped underbellies, while the Enigma 'should be found on the Somerset Levels and other apparently suitable sites, and isn't'.[71]

Spangled Water Beetle, a rare beetle confined to a pond in Wolmer Forest, Hampshire. The modern name was inspired from this very image, but unfortunately the 'spangling' is largely an artefact of flash photography. In normal light the beetle is a dull, mottled brown.

Common Whirligigs, or 'whizabouts'. Their eyes are split to enable them to see above and below the water simultaneously.

Silver water beetles *Hydrophilidae*

The Great Silver Beetle is a magnificent black beetle the size of a Brazil nut that looks enormous in a pond-net when clambering laboriously out of a mass of weed (its even more monstrous larva is the size of a hawkmoth caterpillar when fully grown). Silver beetles are so named from the film of air they carry on their undersides, which looks like polished metal under water. In Victorian times, the Great Silver Beetle was popular in parlour aquariums and could be bought from aquarists or pet shops at between a shilling and half a crown for a pair.[72] At such prices, commercial collectors took to ransacking the ditches around London, raising fears that the beetle might be endangered. As late as 1959, the author of a popular guide to beetles suggested that the Great Silver Beetle should be protected by law.[73] In fact, though the beetle has declined and is now confined mainly to field drains in low-lying coastal areas, it is not considered to be at risk, though some conservationists would like it to be protected as a flagship species. Like the diving beetles, the Great Silver Beetle needs careful handling: the defensive spines on its hind legs and underside can prick and draw blood.

Whirligigs *Gyrinidae*

VN: apple-smellers, mellow bugs, skeeters (Scot.), water cleaner (Scot.), whilligogs (Cornwall), whizzabouts (Cornwall)

Whirligigs (sometimes spelt whirlygigs) are small, sleek, black beetles that scud over the water's surface, gyrating madly around and leaving circular ripples in the water (their scientific name *Gyrinus* is the same as the word gyrate). They are adapted to life on the water's surface, buoyed up by a silver air bubble carried beneath the wingcases, while their uniquely split eyes allow the beetle to see above and below the water simultaneously. Their middle and hind legs are shaped like switchblades, snapping open on the forward stroke and folding up again to minimise resistance on the recovery. The middle pair does most of the swimming, with the hind legs providing extra power for a getaway. Translated into human size, this arrangement would allow the beetle to flash across the water at 290 kilometres per hour. Whirligigs can also dive, with a rapid spiral trajectory. They live mainly on the dead or dying creatures that fall and float on the water, though the beetle, as well as its larvae, also takes live prey such as small worms and gnat larvae. Though they are common in ponds and other still waters, the best place for whirligigs in Britain is western Scotland.

Whirligigs secrete a defensive chemical with a tangy scent that earns them their folk-names 'apple smellers' or 'mellow bugs'. The scent varies between species, and to our noses is not unpleasant, varying from strong and yeasty to an autumnal whiff of cider. When really alarmed, whirligigs ooze a milky substance; its purpose may be to cloud the water allowing the beetle to make a sharp exit, like a squid squirting ink.

There are 12 species of whirligig in Britain, some of which can be distinguished only by examining their rear ends through a microscope. The Common Whirligig is well named, for it is commoner than all the others put together. Like diving beetles, whirligigs have newly coined names, some of which are appropriately playful. The Highland Whirligig sounds like a Scottish folk-dance, while the Artist is a play on the beetle's scientific name *urinator* (hence piss-artist).[74]

Hilaire Belloc probably had the whirligig in mind in one of his moralistic rhymes for children:

The waterbeetle here shall teach
A sermon far beyond your reach:
He flabbergasts the Human Race
By gliding on the water's face
With ease, celerity and grace;
But if he ever stopped to think
Of how he did it, he would sink.

Moral: Don't ask questions![75]

Nancy Mitford adapted this poem (with some help from Evelyn Waugh) for her 1962 collection of essays *The Water Beetle*. The disarming title suggests that Nancy, too, would sink if she brooded too much on why we act as we do.

The Whirl-Y-Gig is an alternative nightclub billed as London's leading 'Global Community Dance Event', where whole families hop, skip and presumably whirl under rainbow-rippling lights. The experience is described in New Age terms as creating 'a bubble of positivity (sic) in which the potential for ordinary ecstatic experience becomes possible'. Towards the end of the evening, a silk parachute descends and fans the panting dancers before they are released into the dark London night. The point is that this is a very whirly gig.

WASPS, BEES, ANTS
AND THEIR RELATIVES

Hymenoptera

Few insects have had a greater impact on mankind than the Hymenoptera, which includes the ants and the bees. Though the order contains vast numbers of little-known species, it also includes the social insects – those that build elaborate nests and form societies of workers, drones and queens. They bring to a creative peak the ability of animals to organise themselves into societies or, in E. O. Wilson's phrase, to become super-organisms. Certainly, what strikes us most about bees, wasps and ants is their co-operative behaviour, whether it is bees manufacturing honey and wax or ants constructing a nest as complex as a city. Though ants and bees have much about them that seems cold-blooded, alien and instinctive, their sense of order has appealed to thoughtful humans down the ages, from philosophers and politicians to architects and mathematicians.

The Hymenoptera are also the most important pollinators on earth. Bees, with their special leg-baskets, actively collect pollen from flowers, but wasps and sawflies also carry it away stuck to their bodies. Without insect pollinators, most plant life would soon cease to exist, something with which we have become uncomfortably aware with the decline of honeybees and bumblebees.

The Hymenoptera is by far the largest order of insects in Britain. It includes all insects with nipped 'waists' and two pairs of functional wings. As well as the celebrated social insects, the order contains legions of tiny, often parasitic wasps that go largely unnoticed, though every garden will contain hundreds of them. Altogether more than 8000 species occur in Britain (with more being discovered nearly every year). We now know about nearly twice as many hymenopterans as beetles and three times as many as butterflies and moths. The variety of ways of living that can be packed into the same basic body form is, in this case, more than the mind can easily comprehend.

Sawflies *Symphyta*

Sawflies are more familiar as grubs than as adult insects. They are the caterpillar-like larvae, some of which appear in gardens on the leaves of currant bushes or roses. Sawflies are named from the adult female's distinctive rasping sheath, which she uses to open an incision in a twig or leaf stalk into which she deposits her eggs. Adult sawflies can be distinguished from small bees and wasps by the absence of the usual pinched waist. They are rather weak flyers and tend to be spotted only when looked for. Their better-known larvae can be distinguished from butterfly and moth caterpillars by their larger number of fleshy false feet: six or more pairs compared with five or fewer.

All sawfly larvae feed on plants, and most are confined to closely related groups of plants – they are 'botanists' insects'. Their reputation has been distorted by the few that are pests in gardens and crop fields. Some of these are no longer common. The Turnip Sawfly, for example, was once a serious pest of brassica crops. Its larvae have black skins and were known in rural parts as 'blackjacks' or, regrettably, 'niggers'. They feed communally, in the usual sawfly manner, rapidly stripping a leaf to a skeleton and then moving on to the next one. The worst infestations came in hot years, when whole fields could be reduced to leaf skeletons and bare stalks smothered in droppings and cast skins. Farmers had no choice but to pick them off. One enterprising landowner paid children to knock the larvae off with a long pole, and then he sent in a flock of chickens to finish them off. Country children learned to be dexterous blackjack pickers, with a going rate of sixpence per pint of larvae. Another way of tackling the insects was to repeatedly run a long rope over the field or to tie branches of gorse to the wheels of a cart to knock them off.

The Turnip Sawfly was more or less wiped out by the first generation of industrial insecticides, apart

Sawfly larvae react to alarm by curving back their bodies into S-shapes.

from a temporary return in the southern counties during the Second World War. In the warm summer of 2005, however, larvae were found in many fields of oil-seed rape in southern and eastern England, and also in gardens, and with global warming behind it, blackjack seems poised to return.

A more familiar garden pest is the Gooseberry Sawfly. Its black-speckled larvae, about 20 millimetres long when fully grown, are easy to recognise, as is their habit of clinging to the edge of a leaf in a characteristic S-shape. An early sign of their presence is the appearance of perforated holes in the leaves, after which the fast-growing larvae can eventually strip a gooseberry or currant bush. They never attack the fruit, but a defoliated bush will produce a poor crop the following year. They can be controlled by picking the larvae by hand or, better still, searching for the telltale dotted line of eggs running along the leaf veins in April. In more thrifty times, the larvae were traditionally fed to the hens. At least one gardener chucks a few peanuts below each bush and leaves the rest to the birds. Another keeps his bushes sawfly-free by inter-

planting them with garlic. In the mid-1890s, many gardens in Yorkshire experienced Gooseberry Sawfly assaults. A year or two later they were all gone, not because the gardener's efforts had been particularly successful but through the natural ministrations of a parasitic wasp (parasites normally need a year or two to catch up on their prey).

Other garden sawflies include the Rose-slug, or rose slugworm, which gnaws characteristic 'windowpanes' in rose leaves before chewing them off entirely. The yellow-skinned larvae are transparent, and the rose-leaf mulch can be seen inside their guts. Another familiar species is the Solomon's Seal Sawfly, which works its way down the leaf at impressive speed, leaving only a ragged line of veins. The pale grey larvae are active in late summer, after the plant has flowered, and the Solomon's Seal usually bounces back the next year. One gardener swears by hoeing around the base of the plants to expose the larvae to birds. Another uses a jet of water to knock the larvae off the plants. Squirt them hard enough, he says, and they never manage to find their way back.

A Giant Wood-wasp, or horntail, lays its eggs deep into a larch trunk.

An occasional bane of orchard owners is the Apple Sawfly. The seldom-noticed insect lays its eggs on apple blossom in the spring, and its larvae burrow under the skins of the developing apples, leaving ribbon-shaped scars which ruin them for commercial purposes. Sometimes the grub burrows into the green apple, causing it to drop early. Some orchard owners use sticky white boards to detect the adult sawflies and, if necessary, take action. The Apple Sawfly is said to prefer traditional breeds of apple such as James Grieve or Worcester Permain. Its grubs are easily mistaken for those of the Codlin Moth; one key difference is, supposedly, that sawfly droppings smell, while moth droppings are odourless.

The most impressive sawflies are those known as wood-wasps. These lay their eggs inside wood with the help of a long, stiff ovipositor that is easily mistaken for an outsized sting (though these 'wasps' are harmless). The largest is the Giant Wood-wasp, also known as a 'horntail', which mimics a hornet so well that many people would need a lot of convincing that its centimetre-long 'sting' is used only on trees. With it, the horntail bores its way into the tissue of a pine trunk to lay its eggs. It sometimes appears in numbers on new housing estates when the adults emerge from building timbers, and it is also, in my experience, a frequent visitor to tables in pub gardens.

Among the specimens preserved at the World Museum in Liverpool is a female Giant Wood-wasp with its impressive tail spike. According to the label,

it was handed in by a member of the public during the Second World War, believing it to be a secret weapon dropped by a German plane.

A related but slightly smaller species, the Sirex Wood-wasp has been accidentally introduced to North America, probably in wooden packing crates, and is fast colonising the New World pine forests there. Unfortunately, it carries a pathogenic fungus that can kill pine trees. This in turn has ominous implications for American birds dependent on pine, such as the native Kirtland's warbler.

A still smaller species, the Alder Wood-wasp, had its moment of glory in 1960 when Eric Thompson, then a lecturer in forest biology at Oxford, made a ground-breaking film called *The Alder Woodwasp and its Insect Enemies*. Thompson got over the problem of concentrating sufficient light to film the insects without roasting them by devising a Heath Robinsonesque contraption incorporating hair-driers and beakers of boiling water. The film followed the life of the wood-wasp as it courted and then laid its eggs, only to have them fall victim to no fewer than four parasites. The film, Thompson's first, won the 1960 Nature Film Competition and was subsequently shown on BBC Television's *Look* programme and thence around the world. Thompson went on to found Oxford Scientific Films, whose premises were sited in a quarry at the bottom of his garden. His subsequent films included studies of tiger beetles, caterpillars, fish-lice and the Black-widow Spider.

Gall wasps *Cynipoidea*

As the horticulturalist Stefan Buczacki used to advise gardeners, if your plants are going to be attacked by a pest, at least be thankful if the symptoms are attractive. Plant galls come in a variety of often pleasing shapes and colours. There are those resembling ripe fruit called cherry and currant galls, some that look like vegetables, such as the bean or artichoke galls, and a few that recall the sewing box, with names such as silk-button gall and robin's pincushion. Some galls are inconspicuous, while Oak Apples grow to at least the size of a crab apple. A few galls have attracted superstitious lore, and one, the Marble Gall, proved surprisingly useful – it could be nurtured as a source of ink. Britain's Oak Apple Day must be one of the few national festivals in the world to commemorate a gall made by a tiny, nondescript insect.

A gall is a swelling on a plant resulting from invasion by a parasite, a fungus, bacteria or bug. The most attractive are caused by the tiny larvae of insects, generally a midge, scale-insect or gall wasp. The plant reacts by producing layers of protective tissue and sealing off the wound. Sometimes these blemishes are large and characteristically shaped: this becomes the gall. A plant gall lasts months, enabling the tiny grub inside to feed up on plant tissue before pupating and finally emerging through a pore in its, by now, dry and often woody home.

Oak Apple

Oak Apple Day is held on 29 May to commemorate the restoration of the monarchy in 1660 after the ultimate failure of the English Republic. It was the restored King Charles II's birthday and also the day he entered London in triumph. At the procession, the loyal populace was encouraged to wear sprigs of oak in remembrance of the occasion when the king, fleeing from Cromwell's soldiers, hid himself among the upper branches of a great oak near Boscobel House.

Oak Apple Day survived by evolving into a May Day assertion of worker's rights. The chant of the day was: 'Twenty-ninth of May, Twenty-ninth of May/ If you don't give us a holiday, we'll all run away.' Though the day and its ceremonies have since been swallowed up by the May Bank Holiday, Oak Apple Day is still celebrated here and there, notably at Castleton in Derbyshire, where the Garland King rides through the streets swathed in greenery and a fresh branch of oak is affixed to the church tower.

At Great Wishford in Wiltshire, the villagers designate Oak Apple Day for a noisy annual demonstration of their freedom to collect 'dead snapping wood boughs and sticks' from the Lord's land at Grovely Forest. The custom is proclaimed as early in the day as possible with a great communal shout of 'Grovely! Grovely! Grovely! And all Grovely!' To underline the message, they cut green boughs of oak and carry them in procession back to Great Wishford to decorate house doorways and

An oak gall opened to reveal its tiny wasp inmate.

Oak apples. Oak Apple Day, on 29 May, ostensibly celebrates the restoration of monarchy but is also an occasion for noisy assertions of common rights, feasting and partying.

the church tower. Finally, amid more communal shouting, a particularly large leaky bough is carried all the way to Salisbury Cathedral, where dancing and a sit-down lunch are held. The folk memory of the Merry Monarch has long since dimmed, and one suspects that his day was grafted on to something far more ancient – an assertion of customary rights and freedoms with, perhaps, distant echoes of green men and trees inhabited by gods.

Oak Apples are round, crab-apple-like growths that appear on oak twigs in late spring. When fresh they can resemble small, red apples, but later in the year they turn pale brown with a texture like cork. The gall is created by a tiny orange gall wasp, *Biorhiza pallida*, whose grubs live in chambers inside the soft, spongy tissue and duly emerge through a small pore.

There are few uses for Oak Apples. They are inedible and too light and spongy to play with, nor have they found any significant medical applications. But they are strange and unexpected, and it is not surprising that superstitions have grown up around them. Farmers could tell the future weather by inspecting an Oak Apple on Michaelmas Day, 29 September. If it contained a 'worm', the rest of the year would be pleasant and disaster-free. If a 'fly', the weather would be moderate. But an empty Oak Apple meant bad weather and so, perhaps, poor harvests and diseased livestock. The joke was that, by 29 September, most Oak Apples lingering on the tree will be blackening and almost certainly empty.

Marble Gall

AN: bullet gall, chick-chacks or shick-shacks, Devonshire gall, oak nut

Oak Marble Galls are smaller, harder and rounder than Oak Apples. They are tough enough to make worthwhile wooden marbles, and their country name 'chick-chacks' mimics the clattering sound they make when rolled together. In the North Devon village of Dolton, there was even a Chick-chack Day, when members of the local Friendly Society would turn out on parade wearing their finest clothes to celebrate the freedoms of the village.

Marble Galls first appear as small, green spheres on the leaf buds of oak in the spring but later turn brown and woody. Each contains a single grub living like a seed in an apple, and they are often found broken open on the ground where woodpeckers have cracked the gall like a nut to extract the grub inside. The insect responsible is a tiny and rarely noticed wasplet, *Andricus kollari*. A native of the Middle East, it was introduced to Britain in a consignment of Marble Galls imported to Devon in the 1830s as a dye-source for cloth and ink manufacture. A related species, *A. fecundator*, produces distinctive Oak Artichoke Galls, like giant buds, on oak.

The galls are rich in resins and tannic acid, which made them a useful source of black dye. Iron-gall ink was the standard writing ink throughout Europe until the nineteenth century and is still manufactured today by artists interested in reviving traditional craft methods. It could be home-made from local materials: a basket of galls, a few nails and some vinegar, plus a little gum Arabic to seal the ingredients. After their experimental introduction to Devon, Marble Galls spread rapidly in the wild, provoking fears in the press that the acorn crop would be ruined and farmers thereby deprived of valuable autumn 'pannage' for their pigs. The acorns survived, but in terms of ink-making, home-grown galls proved a disappointment. Britain's climate produces only small amounts of the necessary tannins compared with imported galls from the Middle East. Marble Galls did, though, have another, lowly use. Dried, powdered and mixed with hog's lard, they were used as an ointment for piles.

Knopper Gall

Knopper Galls come from the word knop, meaning a small, protuberant object. They are the result of a gall wasp larva developing inside an oak bud early in the spring, which swells into a spiky, green ball-mass attached to, if not smothering, the developing acorn. Some of these knoppers warp into folds like an old dishcloth; others turn into spiky, green maces. The wasp responsible, *Andricus quercuscalicis*, is a recent introduction, first noticed in 1956, but the past 30 years have seen an explosive increase, and by 2007, the gall had spread over Britain as far north as Ayrshire. To complete its lifecycle, the wasp requires the juxtaposition of different oaks, the native Pedunculate Oak and the introduced Turkey Oak. The latter has been grown as an ornamental tree in parks since the eighteenth century and has since spread into the wider countryside as an unwanted weed tree. As the Turkey Oak spreads, so do the inconspicuous wasps and their galls.

Knopper galls on oak.

Cherry galls caused by the wasp Cynips quercusifolia.

Foresters fear that these galls may be reducing the regeneration of native oaks by turning their acorns into sterile galls. Whether or not the oak itself suffers, the lack of ripe acorns has a knock-on effect on birds and animals that depend on them, such as voles and the owls that feed on voles. To control Knopper Gall, the Crown Estates have taken to weeding out Turkey Oak, but on private estates, the Turkey Oak is often a valued landscape tree for, being otherwise virtually insect-free, it bears an unblemished foliage (as though sprayed by an insecticide). They are unlikely to be taken out for the sake of native oak.

Other oak galls

Among the commonest oak galls are the spangles, which form on the underside of leaves and are so-named because they often decorate the surface like a constellation – the star-spangled oak-leaf. They vary in number from one year to the next, probably in response to the parasites that share the gall wasp's abode. One kind, formed by a black gall wasp (whose species name, *quercusbaccarum*, means 'oak-berry'), is shaped like a spotted doughnut or tiny flying saucer; another, created by a related species, is more like a miniature coin or a silk button from a dinner jacket. The tiny grub inside each spangle or button continues to grow after leaf-fall, and those that survive the winter release a minute adult wasp to continue the cycle. These spring-hatched

wasps lay not on the leaf buds but on the trailing strings of oak flowers, producing an alternate and very different kind of gall that closely resembles a redcurrant (a resemblance that does not extend to their taste).

Round, red galls like ripe cherries form on the underside of oak leaves injected by yet another species of gall wasp (whose species name, *quercusfolia*, means oak-flower). Green at first, they turn cherry-red towards the end of summer, and can occur singly or in clusters. The tufts of cotton-wool you sometimes find attached to an oak leaf are yet another kind of gall, produced by a gall wasp whose name *quercusramuli* means 'little oak twigs'.

Robin's Pincushion

AN: bedeguar gall, moss gall, mossy-rose gall

Robin's Pincushions are those familiar, red, feathery tufts on rose stems that are found all year round but are especially obvious in the autumn. They are caused by the Bedeguar Gall Wasp, a characteristically minuscule gall wasp with a black head and an orange body. The name bedeguar derives from the Persian *bad-awar*, meaning 'brought by the wind', while the 'Robin' in Robin's Pincushion is not a bird but the 'shrewd and knavish' sprite Robin Goodfellow, otherwise known as Puck. Robin wears red and is associated with natural objects of that colour. He is said to be quick at needlework and so might

Robin's Pincushion, a gall of wild roses caused by the tiny wasp Diplolepis rosae.

Ichneumons
Ichneumonoidea

Charles Darwin saw the life-history of parasitic wasps as incompatible with a benign creator. 'I own that I cannot see as plainly as others do,' he wrote to an American correspondent, 'and as I should wish to do, evidence of design and beneficence on all sides of us. There seems to me too much misery in the world. I cannot persuade myself that a beneficent and omnipotent God would have designedly created the *Ichneumonidae* with the express intention of their feeding within the living bodies of Caterpillars, or that a cat should play with mice.' To his friend Joseph Hooker, Darwin put it another way: 'what a book a devil's chaplain might write on the clumsy, wasteful, blundering, low, and horribly cruel works of nature!' If one were looking for a message in ichneumons and their like, it would be the lack of any moral sense or benign spirit in nature.[1]

Ichneumon is a Greek word meaning tracker, in the sense of 'one who follows foot-steps'. The ancient Greeks were alluding to the persistent way in which a parasitic wasp follows its intended victim. Another early name was the grave-digger wasp, for these wasps buried their prey as 'the living dead'. In the Middle Ages, the name ichneumon was shared, unlikely as it seems, with the mongoose. It was said that the mongoose deliberately allowed itself to be swallowed whole by the crocodile; once inside the crocodile's guts the mongoose would use its sharp teeth to devour the beast from within. This fable was an object lesson in how small and nimble beasts could outwit huge and mighty ones. Some bestiaries turned Ichneumon the Mongoose into the fabulous Echinemon, which would disguise itself with the mud of the Nile in order to ambush and overcome its enemies.

What looks like the adult ichneumon's sting is, in fact, the wasp's ovipositor, which it uses like a hypodermic needle to inject eggs into its host. Some wasps have enormously long ovipositors with which they can penetrate layers of corky wood to reach a grub inside the tree. By paralysing but not killing its victim, the ichneumon wasp ensures a supply of fresh meat sufficient to sustain the development of its grub. To ensure that the meat stays fresh, the grub instinctively consumes the host's tissues first and its vital organs last. This form of parasitism

have need of a pincushion. On the other hand, he is also a trickster, and so you would expect Robin's Pincushion to be a fake.

Robin's Pincushions were said to have magical properties. Dried and reduced to a powder, they could be a diuretic, a cure for colic or a remedy for toothache. Or they could be burned to ashes, mixed with honey and used as a hair gel to prevent you from going bald. They were rated by some as an astringent and helpful in controlling the levels of bodily fluids. Hidden beneath the pillow, they ensured a good night's sleep. In nineteenth-century Northampton, schoolboys would wear Robin's pincushions in the cuffs of their coats as good-luck charms; they were said to prevent floggings.

This is a compound gall that encloses up to 50 chambers, each containing a single grub. All the wasps that emerge in the spring are infected by a bacterium that turns them into females. For want of any males, they reproduce asexually, producing genetically identical offspring. When treated with antibiotics, the wasps resume normal sexual relations with an equal number of males and females. Their mad pincushion world is a self-contained mini-ecosystem, with parasites, hyperparasites and scavengers that graze on the grub's leftovers or droppings. A medieval theologian might have called it a community of the damned.

*An ichneumon wasp (*Ophion luteus*) injecting its eggs into an unfortunate hawkmoth caterpillar destined to be gradually eaten alive as it supplies fresh meat for the grubs.*

seems nightmarish, but perhaps the limited nervous system of insects limits the host's suffering. Caterpillars seem to carry on feeding normally despite the developing grubs inside them, and only near the end do they suddenly sicken and die. The makers of the film *Alien* capitalised on the horror of being eaten alive and found an extra vein of insect nastiness by giving the beast the sliding jaws of a dragonfly nymph and the intelligence of a man.

Ichneumons are insect parasites and do not attack vertebrate animals. The females of large ones are, however, theoretically capable of piercing the skin with their ovipositors. The large, orange *Ophion luteus*, which is attracted to light and so familiar to moth-trap users, has been known on rare occasions to experiment with human skin, which feels, says one 'moth-er', 'like having a red-hot needle thrust into one's flesh.'[2] The largest of ichneumons, *Rhyssa persuasoria*, is a parasite of Greater Horntail grubs, which it can reach through an inch or more of pinewood with the aid of its long ovipositor. Its scientific name translates as 'the persuasive burglar'.

Parasitic wasp species are extremely diverse, though it is easy to overlook their presence. Jennifer Owen spent 30 years documenting the insects in her modest-sized suburban garden in Leicester.[3] Of the 1602 species of insect she identified, no fewer than 529 were ichneumon wasps (of which 15 were new to Britain and 4 new to science). Later on she added a further 74 species. The Biology of Urban Gardens (BUGS) project in Sheffield agreed that parasitic wasps were the most abundant flying insects in gardens, far more so than bees, moths or even flies.[4] It may be that, for every species of free-living insect, there also is a parasite. Certainly, many parasitic wasps are host-specific. The Holly Blue butterfly, for example, attracts the attentions of a sinisterly handsome wasp, *Listrodomus nycthemerus*, whose onslaughts account for the boom-and-bust cycles of that butterfly – frequent one year and virtually absent the next.

Right: *Cocoons of a small parasitic wasp (*Apanteles *sp.), clustered on a dying caterpillar.*

Solitary wasps

Britain has only eight social wasps but about 230 species of non-social kinds, known as solitary wasps. Being solitary, they are rarely seen in large numbers, and though they are attractive and have diverse and interesting lives, only a few species are sufficiently well-known to have common names.

One of these, the Potter Wasp, is a handsome insect, gleaming in yellow and black stripes. It is also one of the most familiar, thanks to its neat, flask-shaped nests built from wasp saliva and mud. Sometimes several nests are found glued together on sprigs of heather or on a crumbling wall, but they remain separate dwellings containing one grub each and not a true colony.

Similar in appearance and lifestyle are the mason wasps (Eumenidae), which build their nests in sand or crumbling mortar in brick walls (and also plant stems and beetle holes). Several are specialist feeders; the commonest captures and provisions its nest with weevil grubs, which are then eaten alive by its larva.

Another family, the spider-hunting wasps (Pompilidae), are themselves somewhat spider-like, with long legs and a habit of running along the bare ground, and are commonest on sandy heaths and dunes. The female is fascinating to watch as she scuttles about with her antennae twitching expectantly, examining every hole and crevice for spiders and then flying forward close to the ground for a few feet. A spider is brought down usually after an exciting chase and paralysed by a sting, normally with surprisingly little resistance. Then its still-living but helpless body is dragged along and bundled down the wasp's nest burrow as a gruesome feast for its grub, the wasp sometimes thoughtfully severing the spider's legs first. By comparison, the male wasp's life is short and idle, and he is more interested in flowers than spiders.

The digger wasps form the largest family of solitary wasps (Sphecidae), with some 120 British

A Potter Wasp cramming a still-living caterpillar into its home-made larder.

bees, flies, froghopper nymphs and even beetles. One genus of digger wasps, *Argogorytes*, is the sole pollinator of the Fly Orchid. Male *Argogorytes* wasps, which normally emerge a little earlier than the females, are attracted to the orchid by a pheromone that excites them sufficiently to attempt to mate with the flowers. Both orchid and wasp still occur on Downe Bank in Kent, where Charles Darwin conducted his ground-breaking studies of orchid pollination.

Perhaps the best-known diggers are the sand wasps, whose red and black, pear-drop bodies seem attached to the rest of the insect by a mere thread. Despite this, they are robust enough to drag caterpillars many times their weight to their burrows or lift small pebbles in their jaws. Sand wasps are found mainly on dunes or heaths and sandpits inland. In America and other parts of the world, insects referred to as sand wasps belong to a different group of digger wasps, the Bembicinae, which more closely resemble social wasps.

One digger wasp, the Bee-wolf, or Bee-killer, Wasp, has gone from rarity status to local abundance in just a few years, almost certainly as a result of climate change. The wasps' larvae are raised on honeybees, and it is fascinating to watch a wasp return to its lair with the bee strung underneath, like a helicopter carrying a heavy load. In favoured places, such as the south-facing walls of sandy quarries, Bee-wolves are now present in such enormous numbers that they must be adding to the problems of beekeepers, at least locally. Coincidently, Bee-wolf, or Beowulf, is the first great hero figure of

species. They are distinguished by their broad hammer-heads, often huge eyes and exceedingly narrow waists. As their name implies, they excavate nest holes in warm, dry banks, which they provision with live prey, often caterpillars, but also aphids,

A Sand Digger Wasp carrying a paralysed grub to its burrow.

A hunting Bee-wolf Wasp.

English literature, though scholars believe he was probably named after a woodpecker rather than a bee-eating wasp.

The Nobel Prize-winning animal behaviourist Niko Tinbergen chose the Bee-wolf as the subject of his university dissertation. What fascinated Tinbergen were the wasp's uncanny homing instincts and its ability to identify its own burrow among hundreds of identical-looking ones. By experimenting with different arrangements of twigs, pebbles and piles of sand, he was able to show, to the satisfaction of his chiefs, that it is all just a matter of good eyesight. The Bee-wolf recognises its home by local landmarks all but invisible to us, just as we manage to navigate our way home without thinking through the maze of identikit suburban streets. They remind us that wasps may not have large brains by mammalian standards, but that they are very good at being wasps.

Ruby-tailed wasps *Chrysididae*

VN: cuckoo wasps, jewel wasps, ruby-tails

These attractive small wasps gleam in the sun with jewel-like greens, blues and reds. They are often seen running jerkily on walls searching for the nest-holes of mason wasps. Ruby-tailed wasps are nest parasites, or cuckoos, of digger wasps, and lay their eggs in the nests of other solitary wasps and bees – evicting or eating the rightful brood, like a cuckoo. A tough skin saves the adult from the stings and

*A ruby-tailed wasp (*Chrysis viridula*) in its flamboyant livery.*

jaws of larger wasps, added to which the ruby-tail can curl up into a tight ball like a woodlouse. It has a sting, but this is non-functional.

Among the least known British insects are some very small, ant-like parasitic wasps related to ruby-tailed wasps and known as 'debs' (from the initials of their families, Dryinidae, Embolemidae and Bethylidae). There is said to be only one person in Britain who can identify them, not that that is unusual, for it seems there is generally only one DEB specialist around at any given moment. The first of them was active in the 1830s.[5]

Velvet ants *Mutillidae*

Velvet ants are, in fact, wasps. But the female, clad in a livery of soft hair, is wingless, and the effect of a dark-coloured, wingless wasp is curiously ant-like. Like ruby-tailed wasps, velvet ants lay their eggs inside the nests of other wasps or bees, and the resulting larvae go on to kill and devour their hapless hosts. The velvet ants make up for ther lack of mobility with their powerful, curved stings which in America gave them the nickname of 'cow killers' or 'mule killers' and the common name of 'cow ants', as if their sting was bad enough to kill large animals. It cannot, but the sting of a female velvet ant is nonetheless very painful. When mishandled, it makes an angry, high-pitched hum – a broad hint to drop it quick.

Social wasps *Vespinae*

VN: apple-bee, apple-drane (or drone) (SW Eng.), drane, henries, jaspers, sow-waps (queen wasp, Sussex), stingers, vespas, waeps, wamp (Cumbria), waps (wapses), whamp (Northumb.), woppy (Northumb.), wops, yellow jackets

Few of us love wasps. Their stripy forms buzz around menacingly at barbecues and picnics, and when they sting, it hurts. You can half forgive a bee for stinging because you sense that they do so only in defence of their colony. But wasps can sting and sting again, and they seem aggressive in their persistence and desire to share in our outdoor feasting. Hence wasps have long held the reputation

A Common Wasp inspects a fallen apple.

of a devil's insect. Aristotle was doing no more than repeating the popular view when he pointed out that, unlike bees, a wasp has few virtues and no soul. There is a legend that explains how wasps came into the world: the Evil One watched God making bees and naturally grew jealous; so he went away and made some 'bees' of his own.

On the other hand there was a grudging acceptance of their valour. Homer compared Achilles' band of Myrmidons with wasps – dangerous when roused. In classical myth, wasps were associated with conflict or war or, in the case of Aristophanes' play, *The Wasps*, with annoying swarms of jurors. Yet early Christianity surprisingly inverted their evil reputation by comparing a wasp stinging a grasshopper with the triumph of good over evil, a militant winged avatar defeating an idle earthbound hopper. Dead wasps could also be worn as amulets or on a necklace to ward off illness. Like so much animal lore, the basic idea was inherited from ancient Greece and Rome, where dead insects were held to

have mysterious powers of healing. The worse the insect, perhaps, the greater its inherent power.

Wasp is an old word of uncertain meaning. In Old English it was spelt *waesp*, and later as *waps* or *wopses*, which are still alternative names for wasps in deeply rural districts (being 'wapsey' means to be spiteful). Wasp may be linked to the word web, and if so, means 'the weaver' or 'web-maker', a reference to the elaborate tiered nests of social wasps, made from chewed-up wood-pulp spread into combs.

Everywhere in England wasps are still known as 'jaspers'. The name is sufficiently well known for a garden wasp trap to be marketed as a Jasper Grasper. It is an old word that has probably survived because it sounds right, though no one seems to know where it comes from. It may be a corruption of 'vespa', the ancient name (and current scientific name) of a social wasp. Or perhaps it was named from the striped semi-precious stone of that name. Others suggest, perhaps more plausibly, that it derives, like

A Saxon Wasp returns with fresh material for its papier-mâché nest.

wasp itself, from the old Norman-French word, *guêpe,* or *guespe.* Flying insects, such as hoverflies, which look like wasps but do not sting, have been mockingly called 'japsers'. Wasps are also called 'henries' or, in the orchards of Devon, 'apple dranes' or 'apple drones'. 'My grandmother always called wasps Jasper, spiders Horace and flies Clarence.'[6]

There are just eight species of social wasp in Britain, including the large and impressive hornet. The commonest are the Common Wasp and the German Wasp, but the differences between all the species are too slight for these to be anything more than book names (social wasps can be told apart by distinctions in the nose-like markings on their faces).

All social wasps build nests of fantastic complexity and lightness. Unlike bees, wasps have no wax glands to make combs. Instead, their nests are built from well-chewed wood-pulp moistened with saliva to produce a kind of papier-mâché very similar to egg cartons. Tiers of paper cells open downwards, each of which will contain an egg laid by the queen. Most

nests are underground, inside mouse-holes or in hollow trees, but occasionally one is built in a porch, shed or outhouse, either in a corner or hanging from the roof like a Chinese lantern. In warm, sheltered places or snug inside compost heaps, wasp nests are now sometimes active until December.

These intricate and beautiful constructions are as wonderful as anything the insect world can produce, and they can house as many wasps and their developing grubs as the population of a country town. One of the largest ever recorded, as big as a medicine-ball, is on display in the Oxford University Museum. But wild nests are probably never this big: this one was built by captive wasps, pampered on a rich diet of sugar and beer.

One of the larger nests, usually hidden away from prying eyes in thick shrubbery, is that of the Median Wasp, a recent colonist to Britain. This is a little larger and darker than other wasps, and the queen approaches the size of a hornet. Its arrival in the 1990s was accompanied with alarming press reports

German Wasps attending their breeding cells. Wasp nests made of well-chewed wood pulp are intricate and beautiful constructions. A single nest can house as many wasps and grubs as the population of a country town.

of 'French killer wasps' and assertions that the Median Wasp outdoes all others in aggression and stinging power. Once the headlines faded away, so did the wasp's notoriety. If disturbed by a gardener, the wasps defend their home instinctively, like any other wasp. But otherwise the Median Wasp tends to avoid us and, unlike the Common Wasp, rarely causes trouble at the barbecue.

Most of us know the pain of a wasp sting. My worst experience was being very thoroughly stung on the bottom by wasps that had somehow become entangled in the foam-rubber seat of my car, a bright yellow Citroen (which they had perhaps mistaken for a giant buttercup). Wasp venom is chemically complex but contains a protein known as Antigen 5, which produces an allergic reaction in some people. The pain can be eased with various substances. In the past, some swore by the curative properties of calamine lotion, others of home-grown remedies such as vinegar, dock leaves, ice-cubes or even mud. Nowadays, commercial anti-histamine lotions do the job effectively.

If there are other wasps about, the chance of being stung again is greatly increased. A few unfortunate people have a personal pheromone that makes them particularly attractive to wasps and bees and so are more at risk, especially after a wasp's advances have been repulsed. In terms of anaphylactic shock, the worst places to be stung are the neck, face or scalp. A danger for those who wear glasses is being stung on the eyelid by wasps that find themselves trapped, but they say the most painful place of all is the nipple: 'It feels like it's been torn off and the space filled in with vinegar,' remembered one victim on an internet forum. We can at least take consolation in that a sting from a wasp, bee or even a hornet is most unlikely to bring anything other than strictly temporary discomfort. Statistically, we are more likely to perish from swallowing a peanut the wrong way.

'I developed a morbid fear of wasps at an early age. As a young child I remember feeling something hit the top of my head, and reached up to grab it, whatever it was. It was a wasp, and it promptly stung me on the hand. The sting swelled up like a balloon. That was 40 years ago, and now, like the

Business end: a queen Common Wasp's formidable sting.

man who was once bitten by a snake and is now scared of rope, whenever I feel the slightest tickle of a hair, I shake my head furiously, and flail my arms around hysterically.'[7]

There is more than one way of deterring wasps. Some go to great trouble to locate and destroy the nest, while others try to kill queen wasps early in the year to prevent them from building nests in the first place (this may be the factual basis for the belief that killing the first wasp of the year brings good luck). Wasps were a problem in Selborne during the hot summer of 1783. The 'myriads' would have devoured all the produce of my garden, remembered Gilbert White, 'had we not set the boys to take the nests, and caught thousands with hazel-twigs tipped with bird-lime.'[8] To make sure they did not return the following year, White sent these useful boys out into the countryside again the following spring to destroy every queen they could find.

The modern way of evicting wasps is to take advantage of pheromone technology to release a scent that mimics a rival wasp nest. To make it even more effective, the commercial device known

as a Wasp Deterrent even *looks* like a wasp nest. You hang it on your patio and allow its secret scent to drift on the breeze. Any wasp in the vicinity will, it is claimed, turn tail and buzz off in mortal terror. Then you can sit back and relax, with the ugly bag swinging backwards and forwards spilling insecticide all over the barbecue.

'I am often asked what wasps are *for*,' said the broadcaster Chris Packham. In the anthropocentric terms of the question, one possible reply is that social wasps are basically carnivores and that large numbers of caterpillars and other pests are consumed by their growing brood. Wasps generally acquire their sweet tooth only late in the summer. With their nest duties over, there is a sudden glut of idle worker wasps free to indulge their tastes. By buzzing around the picnic, they are seeking what they have denied themselves all year.

Another often-asked question is 'Does Anything Eat Wasps?'[9] The answer is yes, lots of things, from badgers and hawks to various invertebrate parasites, but perhaps the wasp's most deadly enemy is the spider. Our correspondent Tony Harwood regularly finds 'a litter of dead worker wasps on the floor of the shed and, often, the dead body of the queen herself, beneath the beginnings of her nest' – a summer's work undone in a single raid.[10]

Wasp sayings

Wasps are proverbially angry, irritable insects. To say someone is waspish means he or she is feeling tetchy, ill-tempered or vindictive. 'If I be waspish, best beware my sting', warns Kate in *The Taming of the Shrew*. And in *Julius Caesar*, Brutus baits the angry Cassius, promising, '. . . from this day forth/ I'll use you for my mirth, yea, for my laughter,/ When you are waspish.'[11]

'To stir up a wasp's nest', a phrase at least 300 years old, means to make trouble, albeit unwittingly. Wasps are instinctively protective of their elegant paper nests. Damaging a nest in the presence of a buzzing, angry swarm is to invite retribution and grief. The saying is used in various ways but usually with the sense of deliberately provoking a furious response, whether by words or by rocket-launchers. But it is also said in tones of regret: 'When I said that, I had no idea it would stir up a wasp's nest.' 'Wasp's Nest' was one of Agatha Christie's first

Hercule Poirot stories, published in the *Daily Mail* in 1928 and made into a TV film in 1989. But the title is metaphorical; the only wasps in it are human ones.

A wasp-waist is an unnaturally slender waist, like the near-thread that separates a wasp's thorax from its body. The effect, which exaggerates a woman's hips and bust, was at one time considered the reigning standard of female beauty. The effect was achieved using industrial-strength underwear such as tightly-laced corsets and girdles. Among the medical problems experienced by the unfortunate women striving for a waist the size of a flower pot were cracked and deformed ribs, weakened muscles, dislocated internal organs and breathing difficulties. The look also increased the risk of miscarriages and death in childbirth. 'One must suffer to be beautiful,' gasped one Parisian beauty, who had managed to achieve a figure of 36-12-39.[12] The corsets themselves were known as waspies.

Literary wasps

Edward Taylor was a Puritan poet who used insects and other 'fustian animals' to lend colour and expression to his intense religious feelings. His convictions gave him an unusual close, even spiritual empathy with his subjects, including those that buzzed or stung. 'Upon A Wasp Chilled With Cold' is a portrayal of an insect in distress. The wasp behaves as if it possesses rationality and the capacity for gratitude, and is addressed as 'she' (most wasps that come our way are indeed female). She sits half-frozen in a puddle of winter sunshine 'rubbing her … pretty toes, and fingers ends'. The poet imagines the warmth beginning to pulse through 'her velvet capital', thereby setting off some mysterious inner process of self-healing, 'As if her satin jacket hot/ Contained apothecary's shop/ Of nature's receipts'. As the wasp 'hoists sails/ And humming flies in thankful gales', the poet acquires a sense of the mighty divinity that lies within even so insignificant a being as 'this little downy wasp'.[13]

By contrast, 'The Wasp's Nest', by George Macbeth, is a matter of cold, twentieth-century practicality. The previous season's wasps are floating belly up in the gutter, killed by the October cold, but a single wasp is left, 'the bloat queen,/ Sick-orange, with wings draped, and feelers trailing', 'her heavy power to warm the cold future/ Sunk in

unfertilized eggs.' If she survives 'all nest summer … the stepped roof will swarm/ With a jam of striped fighters'. The choice, as the poet sees it, is between assassination and genocide: either to despatch the queen now, or face having to burn the entire brood next summer in 'their dug-out hangers'. It is a no-brainer: the queen must die, but the decision has uncomfortable echoes of the larger reality pursued in Macbeth's spy thrillers: 'the responsible man/ With a cold nose, who knew he must kill,/ Coming to no sure conclusion, nor anxious to come'.[14]

Wasp, a short but gritty drama about a woman living near the bread line on a run-down housing estate, won an Oscar in 2003 for film director Andrea Arnold. Zoe bumps into Dave, a bloke she used to fancy. When he asks her out, she decides to leave her four kids outside the pub. Ominously, wasps buzz around the rubbish bins. In a surreal image that sparked the title of the film, one of them crawls into the baby's mouth.[15] The wasp becomes a metaphor for the dangers of growing up in this kind of environment.

Hornets, *Vespa crabro*

vn: Harnet, hornicle

Hornets are huge wasps of legendary strength and fury. In the Far East, they are even eaten, mixed with honey, in the hope of imbibing some of their energy and vigour. Yet, despite appearances, a hornet is a gentler insect than other social wasps. It rarely stings except *in extremis*. I have watched birds from a hide in which an active hornet nest hung from the roof like a Christmas decoration and been tolerated by the residents. My friend Ted Green once found a fully occupied hornet's nest inside a bird box. Deciding to move it somewhere safer, he stuffed the hole up with a rag, and placed it on the back seat of his car. In mid-journey he heard an ominous noise. The hornets, making short work of the rag, had chewed their way out and were now swarming inside the car. The indignities they endured would have taxed the patience of humankind, but, characteristically, they did no more than buzz.

Nonetheless it is a bad idea to kill a hornet near its home. Its dying body releases pheromones that may arouse the whole nest. Hornet stings are comparable with bee stings in intensity. Being larger than wasps, they inject more venom, though it is venom of exactly the same kind. Yet, despite their increase in the southern half of England and Wales in recent years, hornet stings seem to be much rarer than wasp stings.

Hornet is an old name dating back to Saxon times (when it was spelt *hyrnet*). It probably comes from horn, either invoking the insect's powerful sting (its 'horner') or its loud buzz (horn-blower). In local dialects the name is still pronounced 'harnet', or, in south-east England, 'hornicle'. Because they buzz and sting, hornets have been traditionally seen as angry insects; to be very angry is to be as 'mad as a hornet'. In his *Divine Comedy*, Dante punished those feeble souls who in life had been neither good nor bad with hellish swarms of hornets and wasps. That, he would have reckoned, would teach them to make their minds up.

Moth-trappers in the southern half of Britain regularly come on face-to-face terms with hornets, especially on warm evenings in late summer. Hornets are attracted to light, and if a nest is nearby, they may arrive in large numbers. A couple of dozen hornets among the chewed-up remains of the night's catch can be intimidating, as well as annoying. They rarely attack, even after being confined under a powerful light all night. But one 'moth-er' had a near-death experience when a hornet became stuck in his T-shirt and finally stung him on the neck, setting off an allergic reaction that affected his breathing.

Another group who see a lot of hornets are beetle-collectors, especially those searching avidly for a large, fabulously rare rove beetle, *Velleius dilatatus*, which lives only inside hornet nests. The late Eric Gardner once disturbed hornets nesting inside a hollow tree while hunting for *Velleius*. He was stung so many times on his bald head that he ended up in the casualty ward. But once his wounds had been treated, he was back again at the same hollow tree and eventually bagged his beetle.[16]

How intelligent are hornets? 'I watched a hornet mining its way into a ripe apple,' says Lawrence Trowbridge. 'Having dug out a tunnel about the length and width of the hornet's body, it flew to a perch about a metre away. After a short while, flies began to be attracted to the hole in the apple. The hornet waited patiently until several flies were inside feeding on the sweet juice. Then it suddenly darted out, perched on the apple and killed one fly after another as they tried to escape. Soon afterwards it returned to the apple and carried off the corpses, one at a time, presumably to its nest to feed its brood.'[17] Whether or not 'intelligence' is the right word, hornets are quick to spot an opportunity and exploit it.

Left: *The Hornet, a powerful but non-aggressive social wasp.*

Bees in general *Apidae*

Beehives in a Buckinghamshire meadow.

By bee, we usually mean honeybee, the 'tame' bee of beekeeping, honey and beeswax. The honeybee is a wholly domesticated insect bred from extinct wild ancestors, like a cow or a horse. But in Britain, we also have 250 species of wild bees, some of them social with organised societies and elaborate honeycombs (the bumblebees) and others, the majority, which are solitary – that is, consist of only an adult pair and its brood. But wild or domesticated, social or solitary, they all gather nectar and pollen from flowers and manufacture honey to feed their offspring. Bees are fundamental to plant life – and to the pleasures of a quiet summer's afternoon in the garden. We like bees: there are more place names, brand names and pubs named after bees than any other insect.

There were probably even more bee names at the time of the Domesday Book. Honey was of crucial importance as a sweetener before cane sugar became available. Ancient names incorporating the Old English word *beo* include Beausale, Warwickshire (hill of bees), Beoley, Worcestershire (bee meadow), Beckett, Berkshire (bee cot), and Bickerstaffe, Lancashire (bee-farmer), as well as several Beestons (bee farm). Equally, in Wales and Ireland, there are places named after the Gaelic word for bee: *be-ach*, or *beach* (pronounced 'bah'). Places noted for the excellence of their honey include Honington, Suffolk (honey farm), Honiley, Warwickshire (honey meadow) and Honeydon, Bedfordshire (honey town), as well as Honeyborne, Gloucestershire, which is perhaps best translated as 'hives by the stream'. Deborah and Melissa are human bee names, based on the respective Hebrew and Latin words for honey.

Bee words and phrases

Bee is an old word. The Old English collective name for bees was, rather charmingly, a *beogang*, while a beekeeper was a *beo ceorl*. What 'beo' actually meant is uncertain. Possibly it was drawn from a lost prehistoric language and meant something like 'the buzzer'. But though its origins are lost in prehistory, bee is an economic word, and it sounds right.

There are at least eight collective names for bees. The one heard most often is a hive of bees, while a swarm is usually reserved for the mass movement of bees intent on forming a new colony. Another, older word for a swarm is a drift, derived from the word drove. Large numbers of cattle on the way to market were called droves (hence drove roads) and so, it seems, were bees as they were herded from one hive to another. When the swarm coalesces around the queen bee, the drift becomes, naturally enough, a cluster of bees.

The term 'a grist of bees' seems to be fairly modern, first surfacing in print around 1930. The familiar meaning of grist is corn ready for grinding, now most often used proverbially as 'grist to the mill'. In America, the word also meant a portion or quantity, and this seems to be the sense in which it was applied to bees. We might regard grist as a relatively small number of bees ready to make a portion of honey or wax.

In Scotland the name for a swarm of bees is a bike or byke. The same word is used for a beehive or the nest of wild bees or wasps. Less often, Scots speak of a cast of bees. The first swarm of the beekeeper's year is known as a top or tap.

Bee sayings are more numerous than for any other kind of insect. It would be impossible to include them all, but here is a selection.

Bees that have honey in their mouths have stings in their tails. For hundreds of years, writers moralised over this paradox of nature. 'Under sweet honey, deadly poisons lurk,' warned Ovid, meaning that you can do little without taking risks or, as the SAS might put it, 'Who Dares Wins'. The pithiest expression of all was John Bunyan's: 'The bee goes out and honey doth bring/ And some who seek that honey find a sting.'[18]

To have *a bee in your bonnet* is to drone on and on about something no one else cares about. 'To have a head full of bees' was the earlier version, though in Scotland, the phrase was also used of someone who had drunk too much. Evidently the phrase was first used in the early nineteenth century by the poet Thomas de Quincy, who noted that a gifted but somewhat obsessive surgeon, John Hunter, 'notwithstanding he had a bee in his bonnet, was really a great man.'[19]

To be *the bee's knees* means to be outstandingly good at something, the very height of excellence. The phrase was originally jazz-age New York slang and survived while others, such as 'the caterpillar's kimono' or 'the snake's hips' did not. Bees have knees of a sort, on the back of which hang their pollen-baskets (called blobs in Scotland), and given that bees are such excellent pollen-gatherers, the phrase retains a modicum of sense. Some insist that the original bee's knees belonged to Bee Jackson, a well-known dancer in New York who specialised in the Charleston.

To make a beeline is to go directly towards your goal, like a bee to a flower. Honeybees have a body language of waggles and buzzes. A bee that has spotted a good source of nectar returns to the hive and performs a special waggle dance, which informs its fellow workers of the direction of the flowers and roughly how far away they are. Like 'bee's knees', the expression is American and dates from the early nineteenth century.

As busy as a bee. The eternal business of the bee was seen as one of their great moral virtues, along with diligence and order. In addition to gathering the 'dew' from the flowers, the bee kept its wings bright and, it was thought, carried a piece of earth in its feet as ballast. Hence, explained the medieval homilist, Richard Rolle, wise men, like bees, are never idle; they remember their vile earthliness and engage in charitable acts. An early example of the phrase appears in Chaucer's *Canterbury Tales* at the point when the host, having heard a tale about the infidelity of wives, offers his opinion:

Eh, Goddes mercy
Now such a wyf I pray God keep me from.
Lo suche sleights and subtiltees
In womman be; for ay as busy as bees
Be thay us seely men for to desceyve.[20]

The word bee is also used, especially in America, for any social gathering that performs a concerted, beneficial task. Hence a spelling bee is a spelling contest, a game played in pioneer America to encourage literacy. The word has obvious analogies with concerted activity within a hive, though it is also said to derive from the Middle English word *bene*, of which the modern successor is 'benefit', from the Latin *benefactum*, meaning good deed.

Telling the Bees, *by Charles Napier Hemy (1841–1917).*

The birds and the bees. Sooner or later comes the dreaded moment to explain the facts of life to a child, who probably knows already. The phrase is emblematic of the lengths to which parents used to go to avoid speaking openly about sex and pregnancy. It was all done by analogy to insect pollination and stork nests.

The drone bee dies soon after the wedding night. Whatever their other virtues, bees are not romantic. The drone is the male bee that mates once and is then thrown out of the hive. The queen bee thinks of nothing but herself and her brood, and her sterile workers have never heard of sex.

Beehive hair. The fashion for 'big hair' in the shape of an old-fashioned bee skip began in America in the late 1950s (where it was also known as the B-52 after the bulbous nose of a nuclear bomber). Among those led astray were the early Dusty Springfield, Audrey Hepburn in *Breakfast at Tiffany's*, and Bet Lynch of *Coronation Street*. Patsy, the Joanna Lumley character in *Absolutely*

Fabulous, wore a retrospective beehive, as did the singer, Amy Winehouse. The tallest beehive of all must be Marge Simpson's in *The Simpsons*, around two feet high and bright blue.

Like spiders and beetles, the behaviour of bees could foretell a change in the weather. When bees journey far from the hives, it was held to be a sign of settled, fine weather. Gaelic Scotland had another saying: *Tha an seillean fo dhoin; thig gailleann is sian* – if the bee keeps close, a storm is coming. Another Gaelic bee proverb recalls the Victorian notion of bees as diligent entrepreneurs: *Bheireadh seillean math mil a sin* – that is, a good bee could get honey out of that.[21]

According to the medieval *Book of the Mysteries of Women*, if a woman swallows a live bee, she will never conceive.

Bee stings

Bees sting once and then die. Unlike many proverbial expressions, this is true: bees sting only in defence, and their weapons are designed to deal with other insects, not mammals with thick hides. The barbs get stuck in human skin, and in a bee's haste to withdraw the sting, it is torn from the body, along with its internal apparatus. The wounded bee dies soon afterwards.

Most bee stings are the result of accidentally crushing a bee, for example by sitting on it, or by approaching a hive in such a way that the bee thinks its home is under attack and so acts instinctively. Single bee stings are not dangerous except to those with allergies (roughly 2 per cent of us). But the stinging bee may release alarm pheromones that prompt other bees to join in the attack, and so it is a good idea to go indoors if stung. The comic-book way of escaping a swarm of bees, to jump into the nearest pond, is not a good idea, since the pheromones do not wash off easily, and when you emerge, the bees may be waiting.

Bee venom is at its most potent in the summer when the bee has been feeding on protein-rich pollen. It is a good idea to remove the sting as quickly as possible, for it can continue to pump out venom after being parted from the bee. The sting should be flicked off (a credit card is handy for swiping off bee stings) rather than pulled out with tweezers, which might squeeze and empty the poison gland. An ice cube or a cold compress helps to reduce the swelling and pain. Some swear by home-made remedies, which include tobacco, meat tenderiser or baking powder (as the old saying goes, 'vinegar for wasps, but bicarb for bees'); more dubious are remedies that smear mud, urine or toothpaste on the sting or use garlic or a copper coin to rub it. Since the venom is injected subcutaneously, none of these remedies are likely to contribute more than a slight soothing (though you should never underrate the power of faith; if you believe something works, then it probably will). Rubbing with a dock leaf seems to help, but commercial antihistamine creams are the surest remedy. The pain of a bee stings wears off naturally after a few hours. Bee stings (and wasp stings) are rarely fatal; in an average year, only four people succumb, usually those with serious allergies or who have had the misfortune to be stung repeatedly.

Bee venom is rich in enzymes and other active ingredients, some of which have pharmaceutical properties. Hence, venom has long been used in alternative medicine, especially in China, where live bees are used to sting the sufferer in the appropriate part. Apitherapy works by modifying our immune system and increasing cortisol production, thus helping wounds to heal and soothing arthritic or rheumatic pains. Though it seems rather drastic, it is still used as a traditional folk-cure, especially in rural communities that may not be able to afford industrial pharmaceutical products.

Solitary bees *Apidae*

vn: yirdie bee (Scot.)

Big bees, notably bumblebees and the honeybee, live socially and raise their brood in honeycombs. Smaller bees, by contrast, nest in pencil-thin holes and crannies in banks, walls and decaying wood, as did John Clare's 'white-nosed bee' that 'bores its little hole/ In mortared walls'.[22] They are known as solitary bees because their family unit is simply a pair, not a queen serviced by legions of drones and workers. Though much less well-known, solitary bees are very numerous – there are more than 200 species of them in Britain – and, like honeybees, they pollinate flowers and feed their young on a mixture of pollen and nectar. Solitary can be a misnomer: in favoured locations, the small bees can swarm in large numbers. But each one is a loner, going about its separate business and simply sharing the same home turf.

Solitary bees include mason bees, which collect mud as a building material, leaf-cutting bees, which cut neat half-moons out of garden roses for their nests, and mining or digger bees, which excavate tunnels in the soil. Some species will exploit any ready-made holes that come to hand, such as aeration holes in brick walls or drainage holes in window frames. But fascinating as they are, small bees look very similar to a non-expert, and only a few are sufficiently common and distinctive to have long-established common names. One is the Wool-carder Bee, which strips the hair from plants to weave into its nest. If you plant lamb's ears in a sunny border, you stand a good chance of attracting them to the garden. The Long-horned Bee, much

The Long-horned Bee, one of the few solitary bees with a familiar name.

Glass tubes of a bee-box containing cells of the Red Mason Bee.

rarer nowadays, is easily spotted by its outsize antennae, like a butterfly's.

By far the largest species is the Violet Carpenter Bee. It is familiar in southern Europe (and increasingly so in northern Europe, too), a big, dark buzzing bee with electric-blue wings. It may be on the verge of colonising Britain, with the help of warm southerly winds and increasingly mild winters. It nested and hibernated successfully in dead apple trees in a garden in a Leicestershire and another in Kent – both during the warm summer of 2006. Reports of huge black bees, sometimes buzzing over flowers or, even more loudly, inside plastic polytunnels, are piling up.[23] The bee has already acquired a nickname, perhaps as the result of a felicitous typo: the 'violent' carpenter bee. But, though large and certainly capable of stinging, it is not aggressive.

One of the commonest garden bees is the Red Mason Bee (often known by its scientific name, *Osmia rufa*), which builds nests in hollow plant stems or beetle-bored cavities in dead wood. It has been marketed as a safe and supposedly stingless bee (like all bees, the female can, in fact, sting but rarely does and is, in any case, less potent than the honeybee). It is easy to keep and, in a world increasingly without honeybees, can act as a substitute pollinator. The Red Mason Bee is also usefully active in the spring, before bumblebees have built up their colonies, and so good for early flowers. Bee-boxes can be bought for this and other wild bees at garden centres, though it is easy enough to make your own by tying hollow plant stems, such as dry hogweed or elder, into a bundle and attaching them to a wooden framework.

The fancier boxes have detachable lids and use glass tubes so that you can watch the bee constructing her cells and, later on, see the developing grubs.

Solitary bees are in need of such help. They tend to live in small, circumscribed patches of warm bare ground, such as the banks of pits and quarries, which in today's safety-conscious (and landfill-demanding) environment are likely, sooner or later, to be filled in. Some of the best sites are on urban brownfield land ripe for development. Fortunately, habitat management for snakes and lizards, such as the sandy strips maintained for the benefit of sand lizards, is virtually tailor-made for small bees. They also feed eagerly on the nectar and pollen of cottage flowers such as lavender, catmint and Canterbury bells, as well as apple blossom in the spring. In gardens, they appreciate a wild, sunny corner with native flowers, such as umbellifers and speedwells. Most are normally casual visitors to small gardens, but they can be persuaded to stay with well-placed bee-boxes or by stripping the topsoil from a patch of bare ground in the sun.

Solitary bees are useful, attractive and interesting. Unfortunately, they are also fiendishly difficult to identify. Many species are very similar, and the situation is complicated by look-alike cuckoo bees – cleptoparasites that masquerade as their hosts. The recently published *Bees of Surrey* will go some way to popularising the group, at least among the most entomologically determined (Surrey has 90 per cent of British bee species).[24] A new handbook for the whole of Britain is in preparation; it is much needed – the last such work on British solitary bees was published in the reign of Queen Victoria.

The Red-tailed Bumblebee, otherwise known as bummie-bee, dumbledore, red arsie.

Bumblebees *Bombus*

VN: bumbard (Scot.), bummie, bummie-bee (Scot.), bummle (Scot.), bumbee, bummler or bummlor (Durham), canny nanny or canny annie (Scot.), droner, drumbee, drummel-drain or drammel-drain (Devon), dumbledore, dumbledory (Cornwall), dumbledrane, dusty miller, foggie, foggie-bummer (Scot.), foggie-toddler (NE Scot.), gairy-bee (Scot.), humbledore (Glos.), humbler (Kent), hummobee (Lancs.), hymie (Scot.), red arsie (Scot.), sunny sodger

Gaelic: *seillean-mor*

Bumblebees have large, furry bottoms, but their name refers to their hum, not their bum. To bumble used to mean to drone or buzz, the familiar sound of bees gathering nectar and pollen on a summer's day or, as John Clare expressed it, 'piping rustic ballads upon busy wings.'[25] Transferred to the human race, bumble came to mean bustling about in a stupid, blundering way. The older name humblebee catches

the same meaning; the bees were never humble, modest or inferior, they simply hum or humble about.

Another country name, especially in the west, is 'dumbledore' or 'drumbledory' (there are variations on the name, such as 'drumble-do' and 'drumbee'). A dor is any roundish insect that buzzes loudly (and so a common name for certain large beetles), while dumble, like bumble, indicates a droning sound. Bumblebees were said to be among the familiars of witches and might have given J. K. Rowling the name of her wizard, Dumbledore. Dickens also made good use of a bee name in the pompous Mr Bumble in *Oliver Twist*.

The hum of bees also lies behind their scientific name *Bombus*, which means booming. The similar-looking cuckoo bumblebees, which invade the nests of ordinary bumblebees and rob them of their honey, are necessarily quieter on the wing, and until recently they were placed in a separate genus, *Psithyrus*, meaning 'murmuring'. They had a saying in the West Midlands – 'he's like a humblebee in a pitcher' – he has something to say but no one can

First brood bumblebee
(watercolour), by Carol Mullin.

hear him. On the Isle of Man, the saying was 'he sings like a bumbee in a barrel', meaning he is all noise and no tune.

Though some dialect names are common to all bumblebees, others are more appropriate to particular species or groups of similar species. As late as the 1950s, 'bummlers' were divided in north-eastern English dialect into 'red arsties', 'white arsties' and 'sandies'.[26] 'Arsties' is probably a polite name for 'arsies', as red-tailed bumblebees are known north of the border. They were also called 'sunny sodgers', that is, soldiers, from the days when military men wore scarlet. Some bumblebees could be kept in a wooden 'bummler box' and, by extension, the name came to be used in the north-east for a notably small and poky house.

'Canny nanny' or 'canny annie' is a name still used in parts of the north for a stingless male, or drone, bumblebee ('canny' is a Geordie word for anything good, gentle or kind). Such bees could be distinguished by their 'yellow noses', and, according to Dallas Seawright of Fife, catching them in your bare hands was a good trick to impress onlookers:

My father, who grew up in Lanarkshire in the 1930s, knew such bees as canny nanny or 'hymies'. He would take great pleasure in catching them in his hands and then daring

me to take them from him. I still catch canny nannies on the cotoneaster outside the park where I work, and the trick still amazes people, and sparks off conservations about bumblebees and their importance.

The name 'gairy bee' is reserved for those with brown-and-yellow striped bodies, such as the Garden Bumblebee. A 'foggie toddler', or moss bee, is another name for the Common Carder-bee, which weaves together a nest from moss and grass; foggie comes from fog, the old word for moss or grass, while toddling is yet another way of referring to the bumblebee's uncertain, meandering flight, like a two-year-old taking its first steps round a room. Babbitty Bumble in Beatrix Potter's *The Tale of Miss Tittlemouse* is an accurately drawn queen bumblebee, whose mossy lair is characteristic of a carder bee.

One of the few bumblebees to have a long-established name is the Common Carder-bee, so called because it weaves a nest in the manner of one who cards wool by combing different strands together. It is a spring bee, clearly John Clare's 'bumble' in 'livery dress half sable and half red/ Who laps a moss ball in the meadow grass/ And hoards her stores when April showers have fled'.[27] (Coincidentally, if appropriately, some of Clare's early work was published in his local paper, called the *Stamford Bee*).

Until recently, most bumblebees were known only by their scientific names. Though some of them are garden insects, they are too similar to identify easily. Even today many experts prefer to stick to the scientific names on the grounds that the English ones are too new and untried. It helps that all bumbles are called *Bombus*, so that there is only one name to learn.

A taste of honey

A Hebridean crofter remembered how they used to raid the wild bee nests during haymaking to find a little honey to spread on their bread. The combs could be found by watching the bees intently to see where they disappeared into the ground, generally into a crack between the soil and a projecting rock or along the crumbling banks of drainage ditches. The trick was to flap your hat hard against the entrance hole to stun any bees inside before digging out the honeycomb. It made a good, sweet mouthful, he said, redolent of wild clover and the scents of the *machair*. With bumblebees so much less common today, the crofter now felt sorry for having robbed the bees.[28]

Wild honey was the all-consuming passion of the bee-boy of Selborne, whose story was told by Gilbert White in one of the letters making up *The Natural History of Selborne*. To the 'idiot boy', bees were 'his food, his amusement, his sole object' on which he exerted all his faculties. 'Honey-bees, bumble-bees and wasps were his prey wherever he found them', marveled White. 'He had no apprehension from their stings, but would seize them *nudis manibus*, and at once disarm them of their weapons, and suck their bodies for the sake of their honey-bags . . . He was a very *merops apiaster*, or bee-bird, and very injurious to men that kept bees; for he would slide into their bee-gardens, and, sitting down before the stools, would rap with his fingers on the hives, and so take the bees as they came out . . . As he ran about he used to make a humming noise with his lips, resembling the buzzing of bees.' Had he the intellectual capacity to equal his energy and single-mindedness, mused White, the bee-boy might have surpassed the men of science.[29]

Though very little, if any, commercial honey comes from bumblebees, theirs is the image by which bee products are generally labelled. Being plump and banded in yellow and brown, they make a more attractive symbol than the comparatively thin and dull-coloured honeybee, and so it is the non-commercial bumblebee that appears on honey jars, beer bottles, co-operative societies and the like. Children love to draw bumblebees, finding their portly forms friendly and, for an insect, even cuddlesome – though the results, often with big stings attached, do tend to look more like hornets.

'When I was very small', writes our contributor Rachel Costigan, 'I managed to get hold of a bumblebee and stuff it into my mouth. What with the stripes, the shape and the name, I momentarily associated it with humbugs and thought it would taste nice. I don't remember my mum trying to pull the sting out of my tongue with tweezers – but she does!'

Bees and their buzzing have also inspired musicians. The famous 'Flight of the Bumblebee' by Nikolai Rimsky-Korsakov originated as an orchestral interlude in the opera *The Tale of Tsar Saltan*, about a swan princess and her two jealous sisters. In it the strings imitate the buzzing, circling flight of the magical bumblebee as it appears to the princess before going on to sting the sisters, blind the villain and generally sort things out. The music has been scored for numerous instruments including flute (James Galway), electric guitar (Troy Stettina), trombone (Spike Hughes) and kazoo (Barry Manilow). It was also borrowed for *The Muppet Show*'s Gonzo, who ate a rubber tyre to the tune, and *The Simpsons* in the episode where Homer slips on a peanut, and the 20 dollar bill he is flourishing slips out of his hand, twirls around the room and out of the window.

Bees in decline

There are 24 species of bumblebee in Britain, plus three that are no longer with us (an extinction rate as high as any group of British insects, with the possible exception of oil beetles). Between a third and a half of our species are in serious decline. A century ago, when Frederick Sladen was studying bees in his Kentish garden, he would spy up to 15 species pollinating his flowers. Today anyone would be lucky to have six, and many urban gardens have only two or three. The earliest is the large fat queen of the Buff-tailed Bumblebee, John Clare's 'black and yellow bumble first on wing/ To buzz among the sallow's early flowers'.[30] Queen bees need to replenish their food reserves before starting to house-hunt, and this one is attracted to gardens with winter blooms such as jasmine and heathers. Thanks to gardens and global warming, it now nests throughout the winter in the south. It is much more likely to be noticed than the misnamed Garden Bumblebee, which has a longer tongue and is more interested in tubular flowers, including weeds such as ground ivy or dead-nettles, though it does visit borders, plant pots and hanging baskets where aubrietia or pansies are grown.

Bumblebees need large areas of flower-rich grassland to forage the large amounts of nectar and pollen needed to feed and sustain a colony. Such places are fewer than they were, and in consequence, there are fewer bumblebees. Of the long-tongued bees, so important for pollinating crops such as field beans, as well as many wild flowers, only the Garden Bumblebee and the Common Carder Bumblebee are still widespread, and the former seems to be in steep decline. On the positive side, we have recently gained a new species, *Bombus hypnorum*, dubbed the New Garden Bumblebee; it is the commonest bumblebee on the European mainland and may be on the way to becoming equally common here, at least in the south. It was first spotted visiting gardens in Southampton in 2001 and now abounds on the university campus. Soon afterwards, the bee also turned up around London and in the Midlands, and by 2008 it had reached Northumberland.

An academic paper in the journal *Science* made the news headlines in 2006 by drawing attention to the parlous state of bumblebees and, by extension, of bees generally. An international team of researchers from Britain, Germany and the Netherlands had compiled biodiversity records from hundreds of sites, and by comparing the results with past records, concluded that we have lost up to 80 per cent of our bee population since 1980. The results were consistent across all three countries, with only minor differences. Interestingly it seems that the rare ones are getting rarer while a few of the common ones have actually increased; 'even in insects, the rich get richer and the poor get poorer,' commented Stuart Roberts of Reading University.[31] This means that a small number of generalist pollinators are gradually taking over from a larger number of rarer specialist ones. Unfortunately many plants depend on the specialists.

In an afterthought, the team decided to monitor the flowers, too, and was surprised to discover that wild flowers had declined at almost the same rate as the bees. 'The parallel declines of wild flowers and their pollinators seem too strong to be a coincidence,' commented Dr Ralf Ohlemüller of the University of York. Wild flowers and their insect pollinators seem to be locked into a vicious spiral: as the bees decline, fewer flowers are being pollinated, and less pollination means fewer flowers for the bees.[32]

In the circumstances it is important to draw attention to the plight of our bees and to enlist as many people as possible in a concerted effort to help them. In what passed for a summer in 2007, the charity Buglife organised the Big Bumblebee Hunt in London and the Thames Gateway.[33] Some 22 bumblebee events were held, as well as school workshops and, to help them, Buglife produced a stripped-down list of bumblebees that can be spotted and named by the colour of their bottoms: white, yellow or red. An unexpected discovery was the rare Brown-banded Carder-bee, which found a substitute habitat in derelict industrial land near the Millennium Dome and upstream as far as Mile End.

In 2006, a new UK charity, the Bumblebee Conservation Trust, sprang up to 'promote public awareness and involvement' in protecting our beleaguered bees. The one thing we can all do to help, it says, is to create a bee-friendly garden.[34] We are also seeing the beginnings of bee-consciousness among the mainstream conservation charities. The RSPB, for example, has established a bee meadow at its Vane Farm nature reserve by Loch Leven in Perth and Kinross, billed as Britain's first bumblebee sanctuary.

The most extraordinary bumblebee project, however, must be the unlikely tale of the Short-haired Bumblebee. The bee, which was once fairly common in parts of East Anglia and the South-east, was last seen at Dungeness in 1998 and now seems to be nationally extinct. By chance, it was one of four bumblebee species that was exported to New Zealand (in one of the first refrigerated lamb boats) as a pollinator for red clover. Ironically it has survived, if not thrived, half a world away. Now the Bumblebee Trust, in partnership with Natural England, has come up with a plan to bring back 100 of the settlers to Britain for a captive breeding-programme. If all goes well, the bees will be released close to where they were last seen. It would be nice if they returned to Britain in the opposite direction to complete their journey around the world.

Worker Honeybees unload their honey into their waxen cells.

Honeybees *Apis mellifera*

VN: bees: hive bee, skeppie-bee (Scot.)
hives: bee-butt, bee lippen (Devon), bee-pot (Sussex), bees'-cap (Cumbria), bee-skep (NE Eng.), beeves, bike or byke (Scot. and N Eng.), skep

Aristotle knew a lot about bees. Though he wrongly assumed that the ruler of the hive to be a king, he described the birth of bees, the grades of society within the hive and the way bees collect honey all more or less accurately. Every ancient civilisation valued honey as a sweetener. Honey, said Pliny, is 'the sweat of heaven', 'the saliva of stars'. Virgil described it as the 'essence divine', 'air-born honey, a gift of heaven'. By extension, the insects that created it were also semi-divine. Bees were seen as a gift from Bacchus, the bountiful, goat-footed god of wine and pleasure. Some went so far as to claim that bees were blessed with a divine intelligence superior to all earthly insects.

The early entomologists were equally transfixed.

One of the first to peer at a honeybee through a microscope discovered an inner world just as beautiful and compelling. The leg of a bee, enthused the Dutch entomologist Jan Swammerdam, 'is more lovely than a peacock's feather, and their guts are prettier than a rose.'

The beehive and the social order

Like all social insects, bees depend on one another: *Una apis, nulla apis*, so the proverb goes – one bee is no bee. The honeybee can do nothing except through co-operation and self-denial. Alone it can look forward to nothing but a short, careless life, as male bees expelled from the hive quickly find out. But as part of a society, a bee can do what eludes nearly every other animal on earth: it can manufacture products.

The beehive has long been used as a metaphor for

human society, with its stratified social ranks and organised work, each member with its own part to play. Few have put it as succinctly and poetically as William Shakespeare, conveyed through the mouth of the Archbishop of Canterbury in *Henry V* (Act I, Scene ii), though he, too, erred in believing the ruler of the hive to be a king:

> . . . for so work the honey bees;
> Creatures, that, by a rule in nature, teach
> The act of order to a peopled kingdom.
> They have a king, and officers of sorts:
> Where some, like magistrates, correct at home;
> Others, like merchants, venture trade abroad;
> Others, like soldiers, armed in their stings,
> Make boot upon the summer's velvet buds;
> Which pillage they with merry march bring
>   home
> To the tent-royal of their emperor;
> Who, busied in his majesty, surveys
> The singing masons building roofs of gold;
> The civil citizens kneading up the honey;
> The poor mechanic porters crowding in
> Their heavy burdens at his narrow gate;
> The sad-eyed justice, with his surly hum,
> Delivering o'er to executioners pale
> The lazy yawning drone.[35]

The apparent state of order and rule inside a beehive offered a kind of blueprint to an ideal society. For social conservatives, the way in which all bees knew their place and obeyed orders without question became a justification for monarchy and degree. To the Elizabethan Charles Butler, for example, bees were a 'pattern unto men', abhorring 'polyarchy or anarchy' while living content 'under the government of one Monarch'.[36] Sir Walter Raleigh used the same analogy to compare the tyranny of Henry VIII with bad beekeeping: 'To how many gave he abundant flowers from whence to gather honey and in the end of the harvest burnt them in the hive.'[37]

Victorian Britain also saw the hive as a place of harmonious industry – hence the expression, 'a hive of activity'. It was an apt symbol for the new industrial age, and the hive was often used by cartoonists as an emblem of British society, with the Queen at the top, the lords chief justices below her, and arranged in their various tiers, the panoply of doctors, lawyers and professional men, down to the labourers with their picks, shovels and mops, propping up the whole edifice. The Great Exhibition of 1951 was compared to 'a great gathering of industrious bees', while a contemporary article spoke of 'two thousand little

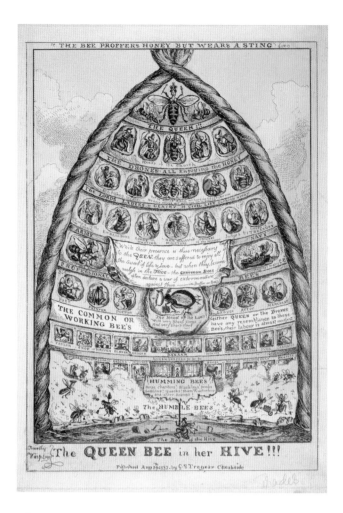

The Queen Bee in her Hive, *an allegory of British social hierarchy, published by G.S. Tregear (1837).*

labourers . . . diligently engaged in their various daily duties, while their reigning sovereign reposes quietly in her regal apartments.'[38]

As the nineteenth century drew on, little labouring bees appeared carved in stone on the porticos and entrance halls of town halls, especially in northern manufacturing cities such as Manchester and Sheffield. The lace manufacturers, Birkins of Nottingham, for example, chose a bee for its figurehead and placed stone bees above the door of its warehouse (which still stands in the city's lace market). The most famous image of all is that of the Co-operative Movement, whose original stores all contained beehives chiselled in relief over the entrance. The message was that unity is strength; as in that other iconic symbol, the wheatsheaf, we create profit by co-operative work. One ear of cut corn cannot stand, but a sheaf will defy the wind and ripen in the sun.

Republicans, by contrast, were impressed by the

apparent equality within beehives as much as by the bees' shared prosperity. The French Republic adopted as symbols both the hive and its hexagonal honeycomb cell, which by happy coincidence echoed the six-cornered boundary of France (the hexagonal shape, in fact, produces the greatest structural strength with the smallest circumference). When Napoleon made himself Emperor of the French in 1805, he chose the golden imperial bee as his personal symbol. Social radicals went further, arguing that the queen bee did not, in fact, have sovereignty over the hive, and as for the drones, they were no more than idlers and parasites, like the rich capitalists who grew fat on the toil of the workers. The first trades-union-sponsored newspaper, launched in 1862, was naturally called *The Bee-Hive*.

Yet Karl Marx himself took a more jaundiced and perhaps more realistic view of bee society. Since bees lack human consciousness, what they achieve, he thought, is in fact very limited. They are mere automatons, without aspiration:

> A spider conducts operations that resemble those of a weaver, and a bee puts to shame many an architect in the construction of her cells. But what distinguishes the worst architect from the best of bees is this, that the architect builds the cell in his mind before he constructs it in wax.[39]

Charles Dickens seems to have been another sceptic. In *Our Mutual Friend*, the devotedly idle Eugene Wrayburn takes issue with Mr Boffin's bland assertion that 'there's nothing like work. Look at the bees.' '"Conceding for a moment that there is an analogy between a bee and a man"', drawls Wrayburn in his lawyerly way, '"and that it is settled that the man is to learn from the bee . . . the question remains, what is he to learn? To imitate? Or to avoid? . . . They work so much more than they need – they make so much more than they can eat – they are so incessantly boring and buzzing at their one idea till Death comes upon them – that don't you think they overdo it?"'[40]

Christianity was able to hold up the bee as a moral exemplar from Solomon's injunction to 'go to the bee' and learn how diligent she is. 'What a noble work she produces, whose labour kings and private men use for their health. She is desired and honoured by all, and though weak in strength, yet since she values wisdom she prevails' (Proverbs, 6:8). Isaac Watts, the hymn writer, managed to put this fabled business of bees into a didactic rhyme that any Christian child could understand:

> How doth the little busy Bee
> Improve each shining hour
> And gather Honey all the day
> From every opening Flower![41]

For Watts, the honeybees' proverbial busyness and diligence were moral qualities that made them better than other insects. It is the idle, not the industrious, that are tempted to sin. The busy bees were God's small messengers or winged servants. Being such virtuous insects, some said that they would never deliberately sting godly folk but deliberately target swearers, adulterers and philanderers. Even today, it is generally agreed that to kill a honeybee is to invite bad luck or retribution. Bees, it is said, have special access to heaven (a privilege they share only with eagles). Some imagined Paradise as a great garden humming with bees. The bee was the only creature in the whole of the Garden of Eden to escape from the consequences of Adam's fall. One story has the bees voluntarily accompanying Adam and Eve as they fled Eden, without incurring any divine censure for doing so. On the contrary, a Welsh legend insists, when the bees left Paradise because of man's sin, God blessed them.

These prelapsarian bees, all honey and no sting, must have been in Wordsworth's mind when he penned these lines from his 'Vernal Ode':

> Humming Bee!
> Thy sting was needless then, perchance unknown,
> The seeds of malice were not sown;
> All creatures met in peace, from fierceness free,
> And no pride blended with their dignity.[42]

The divinity of wax

The proof, as it were, of the honeybee's privileged status lay in the special quality of candles made from beeswax. Wax made from the glands of honeybees is exceptionally hard and strong (the cells of the hive have walls only 0.07 millimetres in width). It has a relatively high melting point, producing a steady, smokeless flame with a pleasant aroma. Theologians explained that the reason for this 'heavenly' glow is that the wax represented the spotless body of Christ, the wick his soul and the pure flame his divinity. Tallow candles, by contrast, being tainted by fleshliness, are earthly and lack spiritual quality.

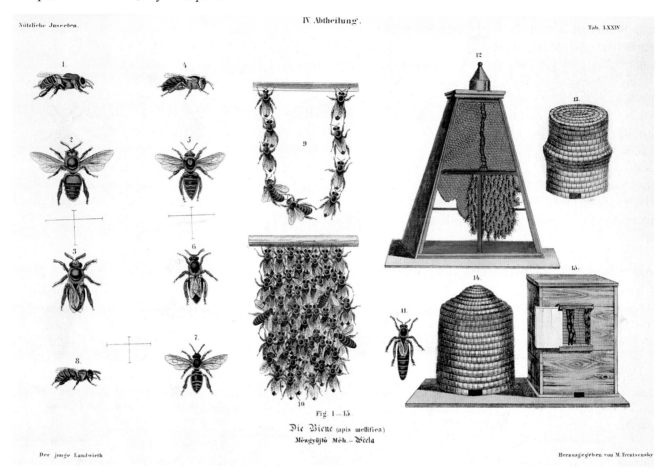

Bees and bee-keeping, *hand-coloured plate from* The Young Landsman, *published in Vienna, 1845.*

In consequence, Mass is never to be said without candles made from beeswax.

Beeswax, however, is expensive. For every pound of wax, the bees must consume about six pounds (2.7 kg) of honey, the equivalent of millions of foraging bees and thousands of bee-miles. Beeswax was originally traded by one of London's medieval livery companies, the Worshipful Company of Wax Chandlers, established in 1358. It had a monopoly on wax candles for churches and monastic communities and for the nobility (no one else could afford them: the poor got by on tallow). The company survives today as a charitable institution, patrons of the Royal Honey Show and the British Beekeeping Association. It also awards an annual wax prize of £5000 to support innovation in the design or use of wax.

The divinity of honey

The Virgin Mary had a special care of bees. All beekeepers knew that worker bees were themselves virgins and that only the queen was fertile. This led to the belief that bees exercised free will and, like the angels, had chosen chastity. Moreover, just as the Virgin lived on 'the heavenly dew of divine grace', so bees fed on the 'dew' of flowers. In accordance with such beliefs, an intercessionary icon of the Virgin Mary was sometimes hung from old beehives, both as protection for the bees and as an inducement to provide a plentiful supply of sweet honey.

Honeybees also appear in Christian iconography as symbols of Christ's forgiveness and goodwill towards humankind. In still-life paintings, they are often associated with sugared loaves or dishes of honey. Georg Flegel's *Still Life with Bread and Sweets*, for example, rubs in the message through a crosswise configuration of loaves with a hugely enlarged bee sitting on top. The cross was, of course, a reminder of Christ the Redeemer, while the bee's sting was a reminder that He will one day sit in judgement over sinners.

Mellifluous is a rarely used word nowadays. It means to sound as sweet as honey: 'A mellifluous voice, as I am true knight', murmured the foolish knight Sir Andrew Aguecheek, as he listened to Feste's sweet-flowing song in Shakespeare's *Twelfth Night*.[43] The word of God was compared with the taste of honey in the mouth. In St Luke's gospel, the risen Christ chose a piece of honeycomb to prove to his disciples that he had risen in body as well as spirit.

Divine honey was also associated with St Ambrose, one of the four great Latin 'doctors' of the early Christian church. When Ambrose was a baby in his cradle, a swarm of bees flew into his mouth and out again and thence ascended skywards to heaven (either these were very small bees or baby Ambrose had an unusually large mouth). They signified that Ambrose would grow up to be an unusually eloquent man and that words as sweet as honey would flow from his mouth. His symbol is a swarm of bees around a hive.

Another saint whose mouth flowed with verbal honey was St Bernard, the abbot and theologian, who soon after his death at Clairvaux in 1153 was accorded the title Doctor Mellifluus – the honey-sweet teacher. Among the abbeys founded in consequence of St Bernard's teaching was Mellifont – the honey-fountain – in Ireland. His symbol, too, is a beehive.

Before the Reformation, monasteries were great centres of beekeeping. The hives provided honey and wax for candles. But beyond their strictly utilitarian role, the bees were a constant example to the brothers of activity, vigilance and order. Thomas of Cantimpre, a thirteenth-century French Dominican monk, wrote a lengthy and influential allegory comparing the hive and its organisation with the clergy, likening the stingless 'king' bee to the bishop and the drones to the lay-members of the order. He compared the foraging of the bees to the scholarship of religious orders, gathering the 'sweet nectar' of the ancient philosophers and fathers of the Church.

The corruption of bees

Against the image of heavenly bees was an opposing belief based on an equally imaginary view of their biology. This was that bees were corrupt, in that they originated in putrid and filthy matter. Wild bees were said to emerge spontaneously from mud or rotting corpses, and such a birth meant that they were imperfect and, in a theological sense, earthly and fallen. Hence Noah was said to have excluded bees from the Ark. And because bee grubs look so different from the adult insects, bees were also seen as equivocal. All in all, they were a paradox, both earthly and divine, makers of honey, with stings in their tails.

Every keeper of bees from Aristotle onwards knew perfectly well that bees were born in waxy cells from eggs laid by the queen bee, and yet the theory of corrupted, mud-born bees held equal force. It seems to have originated in ancient Egypt, where swarms of 'bees' (more likely bee-like hoverflies) were seen emerging from the mud of the Nile. Bees were also said to emerge from rotting carcasses; the more noble the carcass, the better quality the

'Out of the strong came forth sweetness'. Samson's riddle has adorned tins of golden syrup for a century.

401

The home apiary at Buckfast Abbey, Devon, where the placid, disease-resistant Buckfast Bee was bred.

bee. Hence the best honey would come from bees buzzing from a dead lion or prize bull. Beekeepers would sometimes, in all seriousness, bury a dead calf near the hives to ensure a supply of top-quality bees. The association of bees with cattle linked them to the ancient Egyptian's sacred bull Apis, the legend behind its scientific name, *Apis mellifera* – Apis the honey-maker – while the formal name for beekeeping is apiculture.

The best-known corpse-born bees live on the splendidly Edwardian tins of Lyle's Golden Syrup. The image is based on a Biblical story in the Book of Judges, when Samson sets the Philistines a riddle: 'Out of the eater came forth meat, and out of the strong came forth sweetness'.[44] The answer, which the dull-witted Philistines failed to guess, is a swarm of bees and a cache of honey inside the carcass of the lion.

Breeding the perfect bee

Ever since its re-foundation in 1862, Buckfast Abbey on the edge of Dartmoor has been famous for its bees. Early in the twentieth century, the abbey's hives, populated as most hives then were by the native British 'black bee', were all but wiped out by mites. The only survivors were bees imported from Italy. Brother Adam (born Karl Kehrle) made it his life's work to breed a new variety of bee that was both disease-resistant and gentler in nature than the hardy but somewhat ill-tempered black bee. It took him a long time, but the eventual result was that triumph of apiculture, the Buckfast super-bee, a calm-natured insect that sits quietly on the comb when the hive is opened and stings only in the most provocative circumstances. Moreover, it is resistant to disease and its honey is both abundant

A 'bee house' with panels of baked mud for mining bees – a European conservation measure that has not yet caught on in Britain.

and delicious. The Buckfast bee is now recognised as one of the most important varieties in the world. Brother Adam was awarded an OBE for his work and retired from monastic beekeeping in 1990, aged 93. Together with the other great British luminary of beekeeping, Eva Crane, he founded the International Bee Research Association. Someone once asked Eva Crane how many beekeepers there were in Britain. 'I only know about two,' she replied, 'Adam and Eve.'

Hives, booze and honey

Honeybees have long been dependent on hives. The word hive is very old; spelt in Old English as *hyf*, it may be based on the Latin equivalent *alvus*, and if so, it suggests we have been using the same word for the home of a bee for the past 2000 years. Old-fashioned beehives, basket-shaped and built of wickerwork or coiled straw or rope, were known as 'skeps' (from an Old Norse word for a basket; skip, in the sense of a receptacle for rubbish, comes from the same source). Skeps were placed in gardens and orchards on low wooden stands or, in some areas, in niches in an outside wall known as bee boles (it comes from the Scots word for a recess), set either in pairs or rows at about two feet above the ground. The International Bee Research Association has recorded 855 of them, many of them in northern England or Devon. They are also known locally as bee niches, bee shells, bee walls, bee houses, bee holes, bee boxes or bee garths.[45] The skep had one serious disadvantage. It was impossible to harvest its honey without destroying the colony. By the nineteenth century, this had come to be regarded as cruel. With the Victorian's thirst for invention came new designs that resulted in the modern hives, with each honeycomb held in detachable frames that can be withdrawn without damage to the rest of the hive.

The shape of old-fashioned hives has been borrowed by chemists for the beehive shelf used for collecting gases produced by a reaction. The name beehive has also been used by archaeologists for the quaint stone huts traditionally occupied by monks and hermits, especially in Ireland. In parts of Wales, Scotland and south-west England, where suitable stone is plentiful, you also find such beehive huts as adjuncts to the farm and used as tool-sheds, henhouses or simply as shelters from the wind and rain. Their shape comes from the ingenious corbelling technique used for their construction; the resemblance to a beehive is coincidence.

The purpose of a hive, whether ancient or modern, is to make honey. Though the bees do most of the work, the nature of the honey is associated, like fine wine, with the nature of the land around it. Different flowers produce honey with distinct textures and flavours. Heather honey is considered by many to be among the best, with a highly prized, jelly-like texture, a strong taste and a heavenly fragrance. Keepers have long taken their hives to the moors and fells in late summer to take advantage of the flowering heather.

Clover honey is the most popular lowland honey, with a rich, buttery taste and a hint of caramel. In Kent and other fruit-growing areas, bees from hives placed in orchards provided a double function, as honey-producers and as pollinators (though the pesticides used in some orchards now make life difficult for the bees). Opinions differ on the merits of honey made from oil-seed rape; though pleasanter than the rape's eye-watering reek would lead one to expect, some find it weak and prone to crystallise. Borage or 'starflower' grown as a crop produces a pleasant but runny honey that is ideal for pouring or as a sweetener.

A major use of honey in the past was as a sweetener, not least in alcoholic drinks. Tastes have changed over the years, and in the Middle Ages, drinkers seem to have had a sweet tooth, putting honey into everything from ale to wine. Mead, a honey-ale popular in Saxon times, is possibly the world's oldest alcoholic drink. Because of secondary fermentation, it is stronger than most kinds of ale or beer, and it is said that when Wellington made

the mistake of serving it to his soldiers, they became too drunk or hung-over to fight properly. The word honeymoon comes from the old Germanic practice of drinking mead at weddings.

Honey is the key ingredient in a whole range of forgotten alcoholic delights. A medieval pub might have served the following:

Metheglin – a spiced mead
Pyment – fermented grape juice and honey
Melomel – a fruit and honey wine
Hippocras – wine enhanced with herbs and
    honey

Bees and their hives make a perfect metaphor for a pub – convivial buzzing allied to sweet and boozy delights. The Beehive Inn at Abingdon, Oxfordshire, for example, bears the following inscription:

Within this hive, we're all alive,
Good liquor makes us funny;
If you are dry, step in and try
The flavour of our honey.

There are more Beehive Inns at Deanshanger, Northants, Lilliput in Dorset, Riverhead in Kent and Wallingford in Berkshire, as well as in many city centres. There is a Bee Vaults Inn at Southam, Warwicks, The Bee's in the Wall at Whittlesford near Cambridge, and Busy Bee Inns at Bradford and Wallasey. The Beehive Inn at Grantham has produced its own honey since 1830 from hives perched in a lime tree.

Some beers, too, feature either a honeybee or a hive. Young's Waggledance is a honey-flavoured ale named after the flight-language of a bee that has fed well on pollen; its label bears the image of a hive. A bumblebee (a more satisfactory image than a honeybee) adorns many of the beers of Brakspear's ales, among them Bee Sting (a 'honey lager') and Oxford Gold, which bears the readily recognisable image of a Garden Bumblebee.

Talking to the bees

Can bees recognise human faces? There is no particular advantage to them in doing so, but in experiments, bees that were rewarded with nectar when shown some photographs of faces and not rewarded when shown photographs of others, soon learned to tell the difference. Perhaps they saw the faces as rather odd-looking flowers. Literary bees generally behave much like real ones, though often with a much enhanced empathy with their keeper, whom they instinctively recognise and even communicate with.

Talking to one's bees is an age-old practice. It was traditional among some beekeepers to share with the bees the small joys and tragedies of domestic life. When someone died, the news could be conveyed to the bees by striking the hive with an iron door-key, followed by the solemn pronouncement. The bees could then be 'put into mourning' by tying a ribbon of black crepe to the hive. They might even serve the bees with sweet titbits from the funeral table. Some claimed that, when their owner died, the bees, too, will die, or at least swarm away somewhere else. A swarm that settles on a dead tree is a warning, for it signifies that a member of the family is about to die.

Happier news was also shared with the bees. A newly engaged young woman could increase her chances of a long and happy marriage by whispering the news to the hives: 'Little Brownies, Little Brownies, your mistress is to be wed.' On the wedding day itself, it was prudent to leave a piece of the cake out for the bees. Some held that bee swarms should never be bought with money. A swarm could be bartered or borrowed, and a swarm that settled on your property was yours by right, since the bees had chosen it.

Of course, certain steps could be taken by the wily beekeeper to ensure the bees made the right choice. This was the reason for tanging – beating a pan with a metal spoon or house-key to persuade the bees to settle. A great practitioner of this art was Queenie, the wise old cottager in Flora Thompson's

book of rural life a century ago, *Lark Rise*. On warm, sunny days, Queenie would be found sitting on a low stool close to her hives with a bit of lace in her lap and her lilac sunbonnet drawn down over her face, watching the bees intently:

> If they swarmed, she was making sure of not losing the swarm; and if they did not, it was still, as she said, a 'trate' to sit there, feeling the warmth of the sun, smelling the flowers, and watching 'the craturs' go in and out of the hives.
>
> When, at last, the long-looked-for swarm rose into the air, Queenie would seize her coal shovel and iron spoon and follow it over cabbage beds and down pea-stick alleys, her own or, if necessary, other people's, tanging the spoon on her shovel: Tang-tang-tangety-tang!
>
> She said it was the law that, if they were not tanged, and they settled beyond her garden bounds, she would have no further claim on them. Where they settled, they belonged. That would be a serious loss, especially in early summer, for, as she reminded the children:

> *A swarm in May's worth a rick of hay;*
> *And a swarm in June's worth a silver spoon;*

While:

> *A swarm in July isn't worth a fly.*[46]

Opinions differ as to whether the bees were frightened by or encouraged by the tanging. Experts hold that they would be unable to hear it, though recent evidence suggests they can detect vibrations in the air.

Up front and personal: the face of a worker honeybee.

The honeybee in peril

These are hard times for beekeepers. Beehives are failing across the whole of the United States and, increasingly, in Britain and Europe, too. A name has been coined for the mysterious phenomenon that is emptying the hives: Colony Collapse Disorder. The cause of CCD is disputed. John Chapple, who chairs the London Beekeepers' Association, calls it the Marie Celeste syndrome.[47] It is not a disease or something that can be attributed to a single cause, yet CCD killed around 1.8 billion bees – one in five hives – in the winter of 2007/08 alone, according to the British Beekeeping Association.

There are many reasons why life could be getting difficult for honeybees: the Varroa mite, the industrialisation of agriculture, pesticides (which seem to be less discriminatory than it says on the tin), the loss of nectar-rich flowers such as heather and clover, the increasingly unpredictable weather, the catastrophically wet summers of 2007 and 2008. Possibly the bees themselves have become 'over-industrialised'; modern ways of high-intensity apiculture may be producing bees that are less adaptable than wild populations. In 2007, the farming minister Jeff Rooker warned that 'frankly, if nothing is done about it, the honeybee population could be wiped out in 10 years.'[48] Yet his government spent just £200,000 on bee-health research in 2008. More and more people are giving up beekeeping. The hives are becoming mausoleums.

'If the bee disappeared off the surface of the globe, then man would have only four years of time left. No more pollination, no more plants, no more animals, no more man.' This oft-quoted remark is attributed to Albert Einstein, though almost certainly, since he was never noted for his knowledge of bees, he said no such thing.[49] His name seems to have been drafted in for publicity reasons possibly by the French Beekeepers Association in the early 1990s, 40 years after his death. Yet it is true enough. Bees, and honeybees in particular, are by far the most important pollinators on the planet. Many plants depend on them, and many animals and other insects depend on those plants. And so, in the end, do we.

Ants *Formicidae*

VN: ammet or ammut, eemock (Scot.), emmet or emmit, emmerteen, horse emmet (Kent), immick, meryan (Cornwall), morrow, myroo (Orkney), pismire or pishmire, pish-minnie (Scot.), pish-mither, pish-mool (Scot.), pissmire (Essex), pissmote (Lancs.), yammet

VN: anthills: ammet-casts, ammut-casties (Sussex), anty-tumps, casties, emmetbuts (Dorset), emmet batches (Somerset)

Ants attract hyperbole. Their most ardent admirers have claimed them as the cleverest, most organised, hardest-working, most numerous, most fecund, most dominant insects in the world. Ants are also supposed to be the most bellicose, competitive and communicative of insects. Some say that if they were of human size it would be they and not us who would rule the earth (though a human-sized ant would immediately collapse and die from asphyxiation). It is all too easy to see human aspirations in the ant-heap. 'Look at the ants,' exclaimed the nineteenth-century entomologist John Lubbock. 'They build houses, they keep domestic animals [aphids], and they make slaves . . . [they] cannot speak but they evidently communicate by means of their antennae, just like certain North American Indians who cannot understand one another's language, but who can yet converse together with ease and fluency by a code of signs.'[50]

Whatever their merits as social beings and role models, ants are certainly numerous. An estimated 10,000 trillion ants walk the earth at any given moment, with a joint weight equal to all other insects put together. Termites alone are thought to make up one tenth of the weight of all living things in the tropics. Three large termite colonies equal the entire human population of Britain. Yet a single field may contain dozens of colonies.

We tend to admire bugs with an independent spirit. Unlike honeybees, ants are not, in the main, dependent on humans, nor do we have much direct need of them. They are unusual among familiar insects in having few medical uses. Ants do, on the other hand, invite speculation about their inner lives and even a certain amount of envy. More than 2000 years ago, Plato marvelled that ants could lead such diligent social lives without any need

A Wood Ant nest in old pine forest at Abernethy Forest, Scotland.

of the kind of philosophy that Plato considered fundamental to human discourse. The American biologist E. O. Wilson found them superior to chimpanzees in their social interactions; chimps are mere individuals, considered Wilson, but ants are a society. 'And which of us builds the most impressive nests – ants or humans? Scaled up, I would maintain it would be a Wood Ant's nest or a termite's earthen skyscraper.'

Ant names

A common country name for an ant, especially a biting ant, was 'pismire' (though more usually spelt as plural, since ants rarely come singly). Mire is from an Old Norse word, *myro* or *morrow*, and ants are still sometimes known by that name in Orkney and the Faeroes. As for 'pis-', ants, and wood ants in particular, squirt quantities of formic acid when annoyed, and its sharp, sour smell is reminiscent of urine. The name turns up in Scots dialect as 'pish-minnie' or 'pish-mither' and in old manuscripts as 'pissemyre'. Shakespeare knew ants by that name: 'Why, look you, I am whipped and scourged with rods,/ Nettled and stung with pismires,' exclaimed Hotspur in *Henry IV Part 1*.

Formic acid from ants provided the chemical cue for formica, the laminated plastic shelf-covering. The Wood Ant's generic name, *Formica*, also provides the word for a captive ant colony, a formicary or formicarium, kept between panes of glass. The obsolete verb to formicate meant to crawl around on all fours like an ant. To test the acidic power of a Wood Ant nest, you need only to rest a blue flower, such as a forget-me-not, on the mound. Very quickly it turns pink, like floral litmus paper.

Another ant name, 'emmet', is still used, especially in the north and the south-west. The name is variously spelt as ammets, eemits, yammits and the like, while in Scotland it is rendered in dialect as eemocks, immicks and emmerteen. In Cornwall, the name has become attached to tourists who swarm into the county during the summer holidays. The collective name for ants is colony, swarm or army. Those who study ants are myrmecologists, a term first used in 1906.

The names of anthills appear in a few place names, such as Ampthill (ammet-hill) in Bedfordshire and Antley (ant glade) in Lancashire. The kind of anthill most likely to impress itself on the scenery and so become part of a place name, is that of the Yellow Meadow Ant, which often dot the hillsides with grassed-over hummocks. Large nests may be at least a century old, the product of as many generations of ants, and they are good evidence that the soil has not been ploughed or otherwise disturbed. Someone once counted the anthills at Parsonage Down in Wiltshire, an area of 275 hectares: it came to more than 3 million, made by perhaps 35 billion ants. The nests are usually angled east–west to catch as much sunshine as possible – so reliably that European shepherds are said to have used them as a compass.

Anthills, which often start as molehills, add significantly to biodiversity, for bumpy swards have more plant species than flat ones, and the soil is kept sufficiently open for annual flowers by the constant activity of the ants. On one typical down, some 68 kinds of wild flowers were found on Yellow Meadow Ant nests, including uncommon ones such as Bastard Toadflax and Dwarf Mouse-ear. Moreover, many species of insects and woodlice live in the nests of ants, especially (despite their fierceness) those of Wood Ants.

A colony of the Black, or Garden, Ant. The 'flying ants' are the short-lived winged males, which take their nuptial flights on warm, still days in late summer. The ant 'eggs' are, in fact, cocoons.

Ants and people

The 36 species of ant that live in Britain are all social, living in nests ruled over by a queen with her attendant workers (wingless, sexually undeveloped females). Flying ants are the short-lived winged males (the wings soon drop off) and the newly hatched queens, which are noticed mainly on their mass flights on still, warm, humid days in summer. Ants have long had a small but devoted following, which has included many leading animal behaviourists and ecologists, notably Horace Donisthorpe, Julian Huxley, M. V. Brian, Barry Bolton and Cedric Collingwood, as well as E. O. Wilson in America. Wilson in particular sees the ant colony as a super-organism, a tightly knit colony formed by altruistic co-operation, with interior networks, caste systems and even a kind of chemical language.

Ants and humans normally live well apart, but a few species of ant sometimes enter our living spaces, especially in hot weather. An age-old superstition held that ants in the living room, along with wild bees and black beetles, were harbingers of bad luck. Outside, ants were, if anything, a good sign. A nest near the front door was a sign of financial security. Agitation among ants was seen as a sign of approaching bad weather, and stepping on an ant very quickly brought a shower of rain.

Indoor ants normally leave of their own accord and seldom become a nuisance (ants in hot countries can be far more persistent). Though ant traps laced with insecticide are available, if you are more kindly disposed to ants (and aware of the good they do in the garden), use deterrents. Ants seem allergic to many pleasant-scented things, notably cucumber, cloves or mint leaves (peppermint tea-bags are said to make effective deterrents). Other anti-ant substances include baby powder, cayenne pepper, lemon juice, cinnamon or coffee. Dipping cotton wool in lemon juice or strong coffee and leaving it at the entrance to the ant trail is said to be a good way of sending them the other way. 'My grandmother put out pepper to get rid of ants, saying it made them sneeze and bump their heads.'[51]

The only real nuisance among British ants is the cosmopolitan Pharaoh Ant, a tiny, pale brown, almost translucent ant that cannot live for long out of doors. It is a problem in some hospitals and care homes, where it finds its way into drip-lines and monitors, and is capable of spreading germs on its scurrying little legs. It is also small enough to wriggle under bandages. It is said to have been the ant sent by God as one of the plagues of Egypt (on the grounds that He would have sent the worst kind of ant available), hence its name Pharaoh Ant. What makes the ant difficult to deal with is its extremely rapid rate of reproduction. There is no inter-nest aggression between Pharaoh Ants, which means that a single queen can populate a whole hospital in six months. The ants breed all year round and eat everything we eat, plus dead insects, shoe polish and rubber goods. Once established, they are very difficult to eradicate.

Ants and their image

Since Biblical times, ants have enjoyed the status of role models. The ant symbolises frugality and provision. One of the best-known Biblical adages, Proverbs 6:6, urges us to 'Go to the ant, thou sluggard; consider her ways and be wise: Which having no guide, overseer, or ruler . . .' yet gathers food at times of plenty and stores it against the lean times to come. Others down the years, from Aesop to Walt Disney, have echoed these words. The Biblical ant was probably the common Harvester Ant of the Middle East, a species not found in Britain, but it was important to some of the early British naturalists to prove that our ants are just as prudent and sagacious. Perhaps it was no accident that our first authorities on ants tended to be country vicars. In 1747, the Rev. William Gould published a moralising tract, *An Account of English Ants*, which held up ants as exemplars of a wise and just society. In his view, ants are affectionate towards their young, while their constant labouring should 'shame the lazy part of mankind.' In the same spirit, the Rev. William Kirby devoted several pages in his *Introduction to Entomology* (1815–26) to demonstrating the God-given devotion and far-sightedness of the always-busy British ant.

For Aesop, the central fact about the ant was its prudence in providing for its extended family during the winter when food was scarce. His famous fable of the Grasshopper and the Ant contrasts the industriousness of the ant with the idleness of the grasshopper (in another version of the fable, the idle one was a dung beetle). The ant lives on its hard-won investment in grain, while the spendthrift grasshopper puts nothing by and so eventually perishes for want. The fable represents the triumph of the apparent underdog over an adversary that takes its superiority for granted.

From another point of view, the grasshopper's life seems more endearing as well as more fun. The clash between hard, puritanical work and pleasurable frivolity must have seemed particularly pointed during the English Civil War, when it seemed to sum up the essential difference between Roundheads and Cavaliers. In 'The Ant', the Cavalier poet Richard Lovelace turns the moral lesson on its head by presenting the ant as an unattractive character, cold, joyless, parsimonious and mean. 'Forbear, thou great good husband, little ant', says Lovelace. Stop a while, 'and teach thy frowns a seasonable smile . . . not one hour t'allow/ To lose with pleasure, what thou got'st with pain'. All work and no play, he implies, makes you a dull ant. Gently at first but with gathering severity, the poet satirises the ant's dour virtues, and by the end, he imagines with clear relish the magpies and jackdaws gathering over the ant's stored-up wealth and cheerless underground lair. 'The Ant' turns on its head the Aesopian moral lesson:

Thus we unthrifty thrive within earth's tomb
For some more rav'nous and ambitious jaw:
The grain in th' ants, the ant in the pie's womb,
The pie in th' hawk's, the hawk i'th' eagle's maw.
So scattering to hord 'gainst a long day,
Thinking to save all, we cast all away.[52]

Lovelace contrasts two value-systems. His grasshopper is the cavalier, warmed in defeat by friendship and the cup that cheers. As in the Civil War, the puritan-ant is the winner, but who would want to live in its miserable, mirth-free world? Not Lovelace, for one.

A Bug's Life (1998) is an imaginative modern take of Aesop's fable, with a bit of *The Seven Samurai* thrown in. In this Pixar/Disney animated film, the grasshoppers are the bad guys, operating a mafia-style protection racket in which the hard-working ants are milked of their hard-earned grain in return for protection from bigger bugs. The blundering ant-hero Flik is an oddball inventor who, by attempting to raise yields with a special harvesting machine, accidentally destroys the entire year's grain supply. The ants decide to fight back with the help of a circus troupe of insect desperadoes living in a junk heap nearby. The Samurai bugs include a stick insect, a praying mantis, a gypsy moth, an aggressive ladybird, a pair of pill-bug twins – who speak Russian for some reason – and an impressionable rhinoceros beetle called Dim. In the end, the baddest of the grasshoppers, one Hopper (voiced by Kevin Spacey), is fed to the chicks and everyone else lives happily ever after.

It is easy to be impressed by the ability of ants to organise themselves as a society, to build large and impressive structures and even, apparently, to plan ahead. Their ability to work co-operatively without leaders has led to their portrayal as exemplars of a socialist Utopia. Thomas Muffet, for example, saw strong echoes of human society in the microcosm of the ant nest:

> Every one, yet without any Commander, follows some honest labour, and for the good of their democratical state, each one mutually employs his pains by turn. For they all, like those that labour in the Mines, do stoutly exercise themselves in digging of trenches, some serve to repair their houses, to adorn them and to keep them clean, others with great assemblies and funeral solemnities bury their dead in the place of burial adjacent, others again visit the sick, and out of their Granary they fetch some Physical [i.e. medicinal] grain (for they have Corn and grain almost of all plants) and prepare that and carry it to them. They have Offices of all sorts, as Purveyors for Corn, Gleaners, Storers, Yeomen of the Larder, Householders, Carpenters, Masons, Arch-workers, Pioneers; for such is the virtue and skill of every one, that each Ant knows what is needful to be done, and willingly doth his best to keep the Common-wealth.[53]

Inevitably there came a backlash when entomologists looked a little further into the behaviour of real ants and found that the Biblical stereotype was not universal nor even typical. Some ants keep other kinds of ants in a permanent state of submission, which in a human society would be called slavery. Scientists prefer to avoid such loaded words, opting instead for terms like brood parasites or auxiliaries. But it is hard to ignore the parallels from human history when studying the behaviour of an ant such as *Formica sanguinea*. This ferocious insect raids a colony of another species, killing some of their workers and then pillaging the nest. They return to their own nest with looted larvae and pupae in their jaws, and the emergent slaves are set to work. The dark colour of their main victim, *Formica fusca*, brought forth its nineteenth-century name of the Negro Ant. The parallel with our own unfortunate history is deepened by the colour of the ant slavers, red, the colour of blood – traditionally associated with anger and hence with tyranny (in Dante's Hell, tyrants are punished by immersion in a boiling river of blood).

Abraham Lincoln himself used an ant analogy in what today reads like a patronising reference to slaves but which was intended to suggest that human morality should rise above that of the ant:

> The ant who has toiled and dragged a crumb to his nest will furiously defend the product of his labour, against whatever robber assails him. So plain, that the most dumb and stupid slave that ever toiled for a master, does constantly know that he is wronged.[54]

With the rise of the dictatorships in the twentieth century, the Biblical model of an ideal co-operative society was replaced by one of a terrifying ant-heap state. In T. H. White's *The Sword in the Stone*, written at the outbreak of the Second World War, the young Arthur, with the help of the wizard Merlin, learns the secrets of kingship from the animals. His most terrifying experience is his descent underground to join a colony of ants known as Thisnest. White's ants are clearly Nazis – their national anthem is 'Antland, Antland Over All' – and they live in a totalitarian state that prefigures George Orwell's *Nineteen Eighty-Four* in which 'everything that is not compulsory is forbidden'. The ants, which are known only by numbers, obey each order unhesitatingly, and their language allows only orders and instructions. Its aggressive political philosophy dooms the ant state to perpetual war: 'We are a mighty race and have a natural right to subjugate their puny one ... We must attack them in self-defence.' The ants have no opinion about this: 'They did not look at [the laws] as good or bad,

Black Ants tending aphids.

exciting, rational or terrible. They did not look at them at all, but accepted them as "Done".'[55]

One reason why ant society works is that every individual seems willing at all times to sacrifice itself for the greater good. There is no such thing as a cowardly ant. Each springs to arms when the nest is threatened, and all seem willing to fight to the death. Such qualities impressed the ancient writers. In Homer's *Iliad*, the elite troops, companions of the great warrior Achilles, are the Myrmidons, so named from the Greek word for ants, *myrmex*. Like ants, they were fearless and unquestioningly loyal. They even cultivated ant-like characteristics, wearing black armour, carrying black shields and moving in a tight-packed formation like a trail of soldier ants, 'shield to shield, helmet to helmet, man to man, that when they moved their heads the glittering peaks of their plumed helmets met.'

The film *Troy* (2004) took its cue from this passage to present the Myrmidons, led by Brad Pitt, moving forward with interlocked shields in the form of a Roman *testudo*, in effect, a human tank, wiping out the opposition and establishing a beach-head for the Greek ships. In Shakespeare's cynical, anti-war play *Troilus and Cressida*, the Myrmidons appear in a less heroic light, taking the Trojan hero Hector unawares and bludgeoning him to death. In one version of the myth, the Myrmidons had been born as ants but had been turned into human automatons by Zeus. In another they were the progeny of a princess seduced by a son of Zeus in the unlikely form of an ant. Either way, it was the retention of ant-like qualities such as robotic discipline, persistence and organisation that made them such formidable fighters.

The Myrmidons were mythical prototypes for the Spartans, and in his novel *The Ant People* (1927), Hans Ewers found another sinister parallel between ourselves and the ants: they, like Spartans, killed their sick and injured. 'Those whose death is imminent are thrown out of the nest', he wrote. 'Just so the Spartans exposed their sickly or crippled children on rocky Taygetus.' Shockingly, to a modern ear, Ewers seems to approve of this: 'It seems to me more humane to give over the hopelessly ill or incurably insane to speedy death, rather than to prolong the agony of their lives as much as possible, as we men do; it is a much sounder sentiment for the general good of the people.'[56] As it happened, ants were highly regarded in Nazi Germany, not only because of their totalitarian tendencies but also because they were seen as beneficial to forest ecology and so a shaper of the true German landscape. Hitler passed a law forbidding the collection of ants' eggs.

Ant robotics

The monotony of modern society is satirised in the song 'Ants Marching' by the American Dave Matthews Band. Just like the trundling ants, each one of us trundles off to work and comes back home at night, day in day out, month after month. The message is reinforced by the music's monotonous tramping beat.[57]

Ants are not quite automatons. They appraise their environment and communicate by chemical signals. They perform simple and repetitive tasks with efficiency. Individually they are no more intelligent than other insects, yet without orders or leadership (queen ants are simply brood mares), they form a self-regulating colony capable of constructing sophisticated tunnels and nests and solving comparatively complex problems. How do they do it?

The answer seems to be a system of communication that takes on the attributes of a super-organism. It is the product of 'a collective intelligence constructed out of a multitude of separate and simple minds' known by specialists as 'swarm intelligence'.[58] It is the order emerging from the apparently random, chaotic actions of individual ants that has long fascinated behaviourists, and now mathematicians. Using simple experiments allied to the power of modern computers, it has been possible to explore aspects of ant behaviour mathematically and to create conceptual models showing how the tiny units coalesce to perform a collective task. For example, 'gravedigger' parties of ants are driven to make neat ant cemeteries not by appraisal and calculation but by instinctively adding to big piles and taking away from smaller ones. Ant behaviour can now be turned into predictive computer models that can do much the same thing, but using mechanical signals rather than chemical scents.

Ant bio-technology is still confined mainly to the lab but has great potential to produce order in our own complex world. The way ants find the shortest way between A and B despite long mathematical odds against them has applications in telephone systems and traffic management. Ants are also the cue for a new generation of miniature robots which co-operate to perform tasks that they are individually incapable of. As in the ant-heap, it seems to be smarter to let the group self-regulate than to impose authority from above – in other words, to leave the robot to act in accordance with simple behavioural rules, according to its own appraisal of its environment. One day, perhaps, such artificial ants will be exploring the surfaces of other planets on our behalf.

Ant stars

The film world has traditionally held a negative view of ants, regarding them as malign and sinister and even homicidal. This image of them as flesh-eating swarms began with nineteenth-century travellers' tales of army ants. In the 1840s, a medical missionary, T. S. Savage, reported finding vast swarms of ants in West Africa that would kill and strip the corpse of any animal unable to get out of the way. A few years later, Thomas Belt, a geological surveyor in Nicaragua, was told about army ants that streamed along in moving carpets, similarly devouring everything in their path, living or dead. There were rumours of even more terrifying species, such as the *siafu* of West Africa, which made a memorable appearance in *Indiana Jones and the Kingdom of the Crystal Skull*, or the *buni* of Bolivia, whose ferocious 'stings' would drive barefoot peasants from their corn patches.

What made such stories so deliciously gruesome was the contrast in size between the tiny ants and their large prey, including jaguars and pythons. The insects seem to have bypassed the normal rule by which animals tend to grow larger as they progress up the food-chain. Paradoxically, had driver ants been an everyday sight in Britain, they might have had a less powerful hold on our imaginations, since real ant columns move quite slowly and are a danger only to tethered livestock. Some farmers welcome them on the grounds that they drive real crop pests, such as cane rats, out of the fields. But for the writers of horror stories and films, there is something

Wood Ants communicate by touching antennae.

especially unpleasant about the piecemeal way an animal could be nipped to shreds by thousands of remorseless little jaws. We also appreciate their invulnerability. Weapons are useless against ants: stamp on one and another twenty run over your boot.

The archetype of fictional ant tales is H. G. Wells' short story 'Empire of the Ants' (1905), about an engineer, Holroyd, whose mission is to investigate reports of giant ants at a settlement in South America. His mission fails through cowardice and incompetence, and he leaves the ants to their mastery of the land. The sting in the tale is that these ants rival humans as imperialists: 'Suppose', wonders Holroyd, 'the ants began to use weapons, form great empires, sustain a planned and organised war? And why should they stop at tropical South America?'[59] In 1977, a film of the same title, loosely based on Wells' story, transferred the ants to the Everglades, with an arrogant Joan Collins in the place of the engineer.

1954 was the peak year for ant films. In *The Naked Jungle* (1954), Charlton Heston's cocoa plantation is threatened by a freak ant army 20 miles long and 2 miles wide. These ants are more or less realistic and are powerful only in their numbers. By contrast, the ants in the film *Them!* are billed as 'a horror horde of crawl-and-crush giants clawing out of the earth from mile-deep catacombs' (the title comes from their terrified, wild-eyed victims who can only scream, 'It's them! It's them!'). The film is a cold-war fantasy in which the malign but wickedly intelligent giant ants are red in every sense, products of a militaristic society deep underground and set on the domination of the United States. Ironically, the ants turn out to be mutants, the ecological fall-out of America's atomic-bomb tests in the desert.

The British-directed 1970s film *Phase IV* used real ants in its special effects. Scientists led by Nigel Davenport set up an isolated research base in the Arizona desert to study the creatures, and predictable mayhem follows. This time the ants

413

draw their victims screaming into the loose sand. We have all long forgotten the foolish plot, but the film is still remembered by its tag-lines, 'adapt or die', and 'when you can't scream any more'.

Infinitely more subtle is *Angels and Insects* (1995), an adaptation of A. S. Byatt's novella *Morpho Eugenia*. Largely filmed on location in Warwickshire, it is a Gothic fable about a penniless entomologist, William Adams, who is taken in by a wealthy Victorian clergyman to organise his natural history collection. Out of his depth socially, Adamson and the governess create an artificial ant nest to amuse the children. As the story unfolds, he finds increasingly disturbing parallels between the world of the formicarium and the dysfunctional, incestuous family around him, especially the delicious Eugenia herself, played in the film by Patsy Kensit. For a change, the ants are perfectly normal ones, but for Adams, their behaviour suggests disturbing truths about religion, science, gender and family. In the end, humans without discipline and responsibility are no better than the ants. All that separates us is aspiration, and that is a quality of individuals, not of society.

Though we have long been fascinated by ant lives, their impact on the arts has been relatively low-key. Ants, it seems, have more to offer to mechanics and computer designers than creative artists. Yet Tessa Farmer's minuscule sculptures of skeletal ant-like creatures strike an authentic chill. Close inspection reveals them as tiny winged human skeletons behaving just like ants as they swarm over dead insects or torment live ones. Watching these skeletal ant-devils enjoying themselves, one can almost sense the pattering feet on one's own skin. Farmer describes her work as 'a tool to realize imaginative possibilities that might otherwise linger unseen, just below the surface.'[60]

Ant words and phrases

Ant eggs are, in fact, cocoons, or pupae. Real ant eggs are, of course, too small to be noticed by anything except another ant.

What's the matter, got ants in your pants? Apart from the Pharaoh Ant, ants are unlikely to be found inside pants (though the expression would spring vividly to life if anyone sat on a Wood Ant's nest). The expression, which indicates a state of restless impatience, probably owes its origin to nothing more than the word-rhyme.

Stirring up an ant's nest means to provoke a furious, even violent response, usually unwittingly. In Britain, the commoner expression is to stir up a hornet's nest. Perhaps, compared with most countries, we have calmer, relatively non-violent ants.

A teenager who overzealously protects his girlfriend from the attention of other, perhaps more attractive, boys, is known as *an ant guarding a mango*.

Misheard: 'The ants are my friends; they're blowing in the wind'.

SHELLED LIFE
Mollusca

Molluscs (shelled life) is the collective name for invertebrates with soft, fleshy bodies enclosed by hard shells. Instead of moving around rapidly on legs or wings, they glide slowly using the muscular action of a single 'foot'. Shelled life divides broadly into those with a single, usually coiled, shell – the gastropods (meaning 'belly-foot') – and those sandwiched between a pair of shells linked on one side like book-bindings – the bivalves. Slugs and their marine counterparts, the sea-slugs, are molluscs without a shell or with only a small one hidden away in the folds of the mantle. Octopus, squid and cuttlefish are also ranked as molluscs, though instead of a 'foot' they have tentacles.

All molluscs except for the slugs and land snails are aquatic. Altogether the Mollusca is the largest phylum of invertebrates after the arthropods, with around 80,000 species worldwide and about 743 species in Britain and its inshore waters (219 land and freshwater species and 524 marine). Those who study molluscs are known as malacologists. The older word, generally meaning someone who collects shells, is a conchologist. The parent society is the Conchological Society of Great Britain and Ireland, founded in 1876.

Right: *A shell-craft vase of flowers composed entirely of seashells.*

Left: *Unimaginable numbers: a tribe of wood-ants shift a fallen leaf.*

415

Land snails *Gastropoda*

VN: box-snail, bull-gog (Lincs), bulgrannick, bull-jig, buljinks or bulorn (Cornwall), cattle, chucks or chuckies, cock, cockle-shell, cogger (Midlands), conker, crammag (Isle of Man), diamond or 'dimey', doddiman (Norfolk), dodman, drutheen (Ireland), earthy-horse, goggle-shell, guggle (Midlands), hodmandod, hollyman-dod, horn-top (Northumb.), hornywink or orniwink, horse-snails, jan jeaks (Cornwall), jin-jorn, John Jacks, malorn, oddie-doddie, oddy, packman, pooty-shell, snag or snaig, snail-hausen, snarl-gugs, snarly-gig, snarly-'orn, snegge, sniggles, wallfish sneel-haisen (Cheshire)

For centuries we have regarded the humble snail with a mixture of puzzlement and admiration. Unlike other land animals, it carries its home on its back (2700 years ago, Hesiod dubbed the snail *phereoikos*, or 'house-bearer'). Lugging this heavy burden wherever it goes suggested to the medieval mind qualities of thrift and modesty. It also, necessarily, makes the snail a slow animal, indeed a byword for leisurely travel. Meanwhile the snail's 'horns', suggested a kind of extrasensory sensitivity, and its slime hinted at a kind of built-in cure-all medication. Altogether the snail was an unusual creature with a lot going for it.

Our unusual regard for snails is suggested by their numerous folk-names. Snails – above all, the commonest species, the Garden Snail – were often known as 'packmen' or 'dodmen'. The original dodman was a poor, vagrant cloth-seller, like Autolycus in Shakespeare's *The Winter's Tale*, who would plod slowly along in his ragged clothes with a round, well-stuffed sack on his back. The name was still sufficiently well-known in Victorian times for Charles Dickens to put it into the mouth of Peggotty in *David Copperfield*: 'I'm a regular dodman, I am.'[1] That was what the reader needed to fix in his mind about Mr Peggotty: he was a slow man, simple and honest. In eastern England, where Peggoty lived, dodman was also the name of the slowest horse in a team. We still say doddery and doddering, which were no doubt also characteristics of the poor dodman, as were the 'duds' he carried.

The word was also rendered as 'hodmandod', a nickname the snail shared with scarecrows or tramps. The 'dod' seems to be a child's word, like 'gog', for a roughly globular object, as in 'goose-gog' for gooseberries. In different parts, snails have been called 'bull-gogs' (from their horns), 'bull-jigs' or 'John-jogs'. Roundness is also inferred by names such as 'cockle-shell', 'goggle-shell' or 'conker'. Another snail name, 'snarligigs', suggests a twisted as well as a round shape, as in 'snarled up'.[2]

Shouldering your home on your back like a knapsack implied qualities of thrift and independence. In his poem simply entitled 'The Snail' (1803), William Cowper seems almost to envy the snail's secure, self-reliant life:

> Where'er he dwells, he dwells alone,
> Except himself has chattels none,
> Well-satisfied to be his own
> Whole treasure.
>
> Thus, hermit-like, his life he leads,
> Nor partner of his banquet needs,
> And if he meets one, only feeds
> The faster.[3]

With the snail, the home is always where the heart is. An early Christian tradition used the snail as an unlikely symbol for Christ. It originated in the belief that snails buried themselves in the earth during the winter, to emerge resurrected when the sun returned to warm the ground. There was a visual sign in the snail's domed shell, similar to the vaulted tomb in which Christ had been buried.

The poet John Donne drew on the snail when exhorting his fellow bard, Sir Henry Wotton, to consider the metaphysical merits of a self-fulfilling soul:

> And seeing the snail, which everywhere doth
>   roam,
> Carrying his own house still, still is at home,
> Follow (for he is easy-paced) this snail,
> Be thine own palace, or the world's thy gaol.[4]

In less serious vein, Sabine Baring-Gould, author of 'Onward Christian Soldiers', pointed up the physical limitations of a fragile, shelly home:

> The snail crawls out with his house on his back,
> You may know whence he comes by his slimy
>   track.
> Creep, creep, how slowly he goes,
> And you'd do the same if you carried your
>   house.
>
> The snail crawls out with his house on his back,
> But a blackbird is watching him on his track.
> Tack, tack! On the roof of his house,
> And gobbles him up as a cat does a mouse.[5]

The snail in Christian iconography: a knight praying, from the early fourteenth-century Gorleston Psalter. *The same document also shows a knight in combat with another snail. The snail may have been both an emblem of sloth and also a representation of Christ risen from the empty tomb.*

Medieval emblem books associated animals such as snails and tortoises with privacy – their tag-line was *secret est a louer* (privacy is praiseworthy).[6] The hard shell contrasted with the tenderness and vulnerability of the body inside it, especially the snail's mysterious 'horns', which emerge from the depths of the soft slime and retreat back into it at any sign of danger. Such notions long survived as nursery rhymes and country lore, in which the snail is always being coaxed to show us its horn. Since snails normally put forth their horns in wet weather, their help was invoked in times of drought, as in the old Somerset rhyme:

Snail, snail, put out your horn,
We want some rain to grow our corn.
Out, horn, out.[7]

In Scotland the wise snail was a weather prophet:

Snailie, snailie, shoot out your horn,
And tell us if it will be a bonnie day, the morn.

In other versions, the snail is coaxed forth to bring news of theft or disaster, as in: 'Here comes a thief to steal your corn' or 'Here comes an old beggar to cut off your corns'. In Cornwall, where the snail was a 'bulorn' (bull-horn), it could be made to open its door to hear some bad news:

Bulorn, Bulorn, put out your long horn
Your father and mother is dead;
Your sister and brother is to the back-door,
A-begging of barley bread.[8]

Snails could also predict your future love. You placed a garden snail or a small slug on a surface dusted with flour or fine ash from the grate and covered it with a bowl. Minutes later the snail would invariably trace the initial of a name as it wandered about looking for the exit. John Gay tried it out in his poem, 'The Shepherd's Week':

Last May-day fair I search'd to find a snail
That might my secret lover's name reveal;
Upon a gooseberry bush a snail I found,
For always snails near sweetest fruit abound.
I seized the vermin, home I quickly sped,
And on the hearth the milk-white embers
    spread,
In the soft ashes mark'd a curious L:
Oh, may this wond'rous omen lucky prove,
For L is found in Lubberkin and Love.[9]

This game is still played. Naturalist Brett Westwood remembers placing slugs on the underside of a dustbin lid coated in ash. As they did for John Gay, so they continue to spell out the initials of the partner you will marry. In North America, and perhaps here, too, the snail has other amorous uses. On the first day of May, a girl should take care to find a snail with a shell and not a slug, for the first indicates a prosperous marriage ('a man with a house') and the other, a homeless and presumably poor man. Another saying goes, 'see a slug, marry a bachelor, see a snail, marry a widower.'

The slowness of snails

Snails are, of course, proverbially slow. In *As You Like It*, Shakespeare's whining boy creeps 'like a snail unwillingly to school'. In Christian iconography, the snail represents a kind of spiritual sloth; it stands for those who are content with material gains in this world and never get far on their spiritual journey. Yet, though snails are slow, they get there in the end. In *The River at the Centre of the World*, about the great Yangtze River in the heart of China, Simon Winchester suggests that the slowness of the snail hides a certain duplicity:

> I had never been much of an admirer of the Chinese worker; he seemed always to work at half speed, sleeping whenever he seemed not to be needed. And yet look away, and where he once was, a bridge has risen! A trench has been dug! A building has advanced a floor! The Chinese worker is in this respect just like a snail: you rarely see him in the actual act of moving, but look away for a second, and then look back, and he is somewhere else from where you last remember him, a small trail shows where it was that he went.[10]

Snail-mail is the derogatory word for postal mail, which operates at sedate Victorian speed compared with the instant communication of email and text messaging. There is, however, another connection: snails eat and digest paper if there is nothing better (one pet snail ate a large, neat hole through a pile of flat Ordnance Survey maps) and they do, on occasion, nibble letters in damp postboxes, especially those set into their favourite habitat, a damp wall. In Devon, the problem became bad enough for the Royal Mail to attach anti-snail strips of bristles on certain postboxes. It's said that local post offices even have a special cancellation ready saying: 'Eaten by snails'. In Terry Pratchett's Discworld, they go one better. When snails were attracted by stamps bearing the typographed image of a cabbage field, the postal authorities introduced toads to the boxes to get rid of them. When the toads, too, became a problem, they added snakes, and then mongooses.[11]

Snail cough syrup, an advertisement from c. 1860.

Snail slime

Snails lay down trails of slime, custom-built runways, to slither along on the minimum of energy. The quantities of slime produced by snails and slugs suggested to some that the animal was turning from solid to liquid. This strange 'melting' is the subject of one of the best-known Biblical proverbs: 'As a snail which melteth, let every one of them pass away: like the untimely birth of a woman, that they may not see the sun.' (Psalm 58) 'They', of course, are the wicked.

Pre-scientific generations used the 'doctrine of signatures' to find remedies in the natural world. There is a well-known, but apparently apocryphal, story that snails were gathered to treat the wounded after the Battle of Crecy in 1346. The 'clue' lay in the resemblance of the snail's slime to diseases such as consumption that produce a lot of mucus. It was also used to treat gout.

The slime was normally extracted from the snail and then boiled. The snail was easily parted from its slime by what the conchologist John W. Taylor called 'the barbaric practices of the village dames of Sussex', who would prepare a kind of snail-syrup 'by passing a stout thread through the shell and body of any number of snails, and suspending them over a dish of coarse brown sugar, upon which their mucilaginous exudations are allowed to drip'.[12] There was also a hot drink infused with slug or snail slime used to sooth sore throats and coughs.[13]

As so often, there is a scientific basis to the lore. Snail slime has antibacterial properties, and it makes an effective skin lotion. It is also effective in repairing

Breasting the tape at the snail races.

skin blemishes, whether caused by acne, burns, stretch-marks or scar tissue. The bio-chemicals that make all this possible include allantonin, which stimulates skin regeneration, and elastine, a protein that bonds the skin tissue and helps to give it a smooth, pleasing appearance. In 2007, a product based on snail slime was launched by Holland & Barrett, which claim that, used regularly, it will support elasticity, ease out the wrinkles, and 'leave you with silky soft and smooth skin'.

Happily, slime can be extracted without causing the animal serious damage by placing it on muslin-covered wooden planks to encourage it to produce as much slime as possible. Snail farmers in Chile, who supplied the raw materials to Holland & Barrett, have tried to persuade the world that only their snails possess this useful quality. But the snail in question is the universal Garden Snail, and we suspect backyard British ones would work just as well.

Snail fun

After its modesty, homeliness and want of speed, the other quality associated with snails is more surprising: lust. It has a biological basis to the extent that snails are often found mated together (they are hermaphrodites) and have intriguing sex lives involving firing 'love darts' at each other. An Italian malacologist made a film of the courtship patterns of snails, which he called 'the slowest blue movie in existence'.[14] For some, the snail's shell became a fetish object. For example, by carrying a snail shell in her pocket or purse and presenting it to a man, a girl was making a coded declaration of love.[15]

We have also played games with the unfortunate snail. Folk-names like 'cocks' or 'conkers' remind us of the fate of snails of the right size, threaded on strings for schoolboy duels. The latter name comes from a dialect word for conch, which in turn derives from the French word *conquer*: hence the original conkers game was called 'conquerors' and played with snail-shells. Stripy shells like those of the banded snails (*Cepaea* species) were preferred. Sometimes, instead of taking it in turns to whack the rival conker on a string, the shells were simply held in a certain way between your finger joints and pressed together until the weaker one smashed. Clearly, horse chestnuts made better conkers, and when the tree became fashionable in Victorian times, the snail-shell origins of the game were forgotten.

The poet John Clare played the original, molluscan version of the game as a boy in rural Northamptonshire, where the conkers were called 'cocks' and were kept threaded on a string ready for use. For the cock-fight, they chose a day in spring and searched for the 'painted pooty shells' on the sides of a particular bridge that spanned a meadow brook. The champion cock, perhaps the only survivor, was judged 'the hero of the day'. Clare's admiration for the girdled pooty shells survived into adulthood, and he described many varieties of banded snail in his notebook.[16]

In north-east England, shells are known collectively as 'chucks' or 'chuckies' and used to play the game of 'chuckie-stones' (i.e., throwing stones). In the usual form of the game, four shells are spread out and a fifth tossed into the air. To win, all four shells must be grabbed and the falling one caught in the same hand. In another version of the game the chuckies are snatched up one at a time, and the player has to take all four to win. Another trick with chuckies is to place one on the palm, flick it into the air and catch it on the back of the same hand. In Scotland they play the same game but normally use small pebbles.

Today the favoured sport is snail-racing. At the backyard level this is a basic slow-motion race around a plate or an old tyre. Bob Powley's children played an even simpler game by collecting snails from the garden, making piles of them and seeing who had most. The moment of delight comes when the snails 'awake' and the pile gradually breaks down and wanders off.[17]

At the other extreme, snail-racing is a recognised competitive sport. As a wet country with abundant snails, England takes pride in its pole position in world snail-racing. The sport took off in the 1960s when the late Tom Elwes inaugurated the World Snail Racing Championships held every year, weather permitting, at Congham in Norfolk. Congham, the organisers point out, is the ideal breeding ground for racing snails, being flat with plenty of ponds. The race is held over a damp cloth or chicken wire on a table with more than 200 snails slugging it out for the coveted trophy, a silver tankard stuffed with lettuce. With distinguishing

stickers or racing numbers painted on their shells, the snails are herded together in a circle in the middle. By tradition, the race begins with 'Ready, Steady, Slow!' and the first to cross the line 14 inches (35 cm) away is the winner. 'It doesn't take long', commented one organiser. 'Some go off fast, but then do a turn-about just before the line'. Heats are held throughout the day, culminating in a grand finale at the end, accompanied by deafening cheers as each owner wills his or her snail to reach the line without changing its mind and direction. The current record is held by a snail called Archie, who broke the tape in an impressive two minutes at an estimated average speed of 0.03 miles per hour (or 0.013 metres per second). The championship had to be cancelled in 2007 due to wet weather; not that the snails would have minded, but the organisers feared no one would turn up.[18]

A rival Grand Championship Snail Race is held at the appropriately named Snailwell in Cambridgeshire, attracting up to 400 racing fans and temporarily doubling the population of the village. Other recent venues include Brighton, in which the racers run in lanes, attracted by a succulent piece of lettuce by the finishing post. Among the most successful racing-snail owners are children; for example, in the 2005 world champion, a snail called Thiery, was owned by six-year-old Liam Ellis from Grimston near Kings Lynn. A good relationship between owner and snail is essential in this sport – though, as racing pundit John McCririck points out, 'It's always difficult to study the form, since they hide inside their shells.' There is, at least, plenty of time to commentate on the race. Guinness sponsored the first competitive snail race in London in 1999, and the following year featured extracts from the race in its advertisements, which included the tag-line 'Good things come to those who wait'. They certainly do; the advert won the silver award at the Cannes Advertising Festival.

With such activities, and the prominent place of snails in country lore, you might expect there to be many snail-based place names, but they are in fact rare. Snail Down, on the eastern edge of Salisbury Plain near Tidworth, is named after the abundance of snail shells found there in former times. Snailwell in Cambridgeshire takes its name from a stream or a spring frequented by snails. A Snailing Lane connects the Hampshire villages of Selborne and Liss, and a famous lead mine in Shropshire is called Snailbeach (snail valley).

Snails have occasionally inspired music and

dance. The Snail Creep dance is an old Cornish folk-dance enjoyed by young people. It takes place in a large meadow to a simple but lively marching tune struck up by the village band. Each villager grips the shoulders of the person in front and follows the band as a line, keeping time with a lively step. The band forms the head of a long human serpent, which coils in an ever narrowing circle, turning about at the centre and back on itself in a counter-movement, with one line of dancers passing another in the opposite direction. The dancers are directed with almost military precision by young men holding long leafy branches. Two or three hundred people may join in, not counting the band. In another version, the dancers are led by two people holding leafy branches aloft to represent the horns of the snail. There is also a novelty song that is still trotted out occasionally on Radio 3: Sir Frederick Bridge's 'Two Snails', an argument between the slimy antagonists, one English, the other French.

Though normally silent, a land snail can make its own sound, which is half squeal, half whistle. It happens when the snail retracts rapidly into its shell. To force its body into the confined space, the snail compresses its lung, forcing the air out through a breathing pore. If the pressure and pore size are right, this makes the high-pitched sound.

Collecting shells was very popular in the eighteenth and nineteenth centuries, when 'conchology' rivaled entomology as a pursuit. It was one of the things that drew naturalists to the seashore. Marine shells are much more decorative, but collections of land snails became part of many school nature tables and, being easy to mount and preserve, could be put on permanent display. Sea and land shells are abundant in Britain – so much so that we take them for granted, though in most parts of the world, including North America, you have to search much harder to find land snails. Partly for that reason, perhaps, Britain's molluscs are among the best studied in the world, and for the past 200 years, there has usually been at least one excellent identification work in print. The forerunner was George Montagu's *Testacea Britannica*, published in 1803, followed by a series of ever more elaborate tomes culminating in the sumptuous *Monograph of the land and freshwater Mollusca* by J. W. Taylor, published by instalments from 1894. For much of the twentieth century, the standard work was A. E. Ellis's *British Snails* (1921), while today, enthusiasts have an excellent *Field Guide to the Land Snails* by Michael Kerney and Robert Cameron (1979). In

1999, an *Atlas of the Land and Freshwater Molluscs of Britain and Ireland* was published, the end-product of years of assiduous recording by several hundred amateur malacologists.

Mating Garden Snails, the archetypal 'dodman' snails of country lore.

The Garden Snail, *Helix aspera*

The largest common land snail is the Garden Snail, with a heavy, coiled shell about the size of a 50p coin. In dry weather, they are often found in clusters, like large, brown winkles, on the damp underhang of walls, in flowerpots or in drains or hollow trees, their openings sealed with a crust of dried mucus. We also see their handiwork in the vegetable plot, especially on lettuces. As a relatively large snail, it is capable of consuming surprising foods. One lady in Wolverhampton found them attacking the putty around a newly installed window.[19] The Garden Snail is the only snail (as distinct from slugs) that really is a pest. The others eat mainly decaying vegetation or graze films of algae.

In Britain, snails were never eaten with the enthusiasm that the French reserve for *les escargots*, but Garden Snails were nonetheless a useful diet supplement to poor families, especially in the West Country. In a nice description of their climbing habit, they were called 'wallfish', and 'Mendip wallfish' were still being eaten in Somerset in the 1960s, using cider and herb butter (but never garlic) to bring out their flavour. Until recently, wallfish were served at The Miner's Arms in the village of Priddy.

The Garden Snail is intolerant of long periods of cold weather and, until recently, was absent from northern England and most of Scotland except near

Brown-lipped banded garden snails, or 'pooty shells'. No two ever seem the same.

the sea. The combination of warmer winters and less pollution in cities has created a population explosion of Garden Snails in places such as Manchester, where they were once absent. Britain's loss of polluting heavy industry is the Garden Snail's gain.

The Roman Snail, *Helix pomatia*

AN: apple snail, burgundy snail, edible snail, vine snail

Roman Snail is the largest land snail in north-west Europe, easily recognised by its coarsely grooved, creamy shell with its narrow entrance. Though it is sometimes known as the 'apple snail', its species name *pomatia* translates not as apple but as 'pot-lid'. The snail is an ancient introduction to Britain, brought in quite possibly by the Romans, as its name indicates.

In 2008, the Roman Snail was given protected status after the British Conchological Society submitted evidence of its decline (unfortunately, Roman Snails are difficult to farm and so most are gathered from the wild). Though the snail is rarely gathered for domestic consumption in Britain, it is being targeted by collectors in some parts for sale to the restaurant trade or overseas. Investigation revealed that restaurant *escargots* are often not Roman Snails but a large, domesticated form of the Garden Snail. Some kitchens keep a supply of empty

Roman Snail shells in which to serve the garlic-butter baked bodies of their humbler brethren.[20]

Banded Snails, *Cepaea* species

AN: banded wood snail, grove snail, humbug snails

The Brown-lipped Snail and its close relative the White-lipped Snail, also known as banded snails, are among the most easily recognised British snails. With their candy colours of yellow, brown or pink, dark bands and round shape they have been called 'humbug snails' from their resemblance to old-fashioned mint humbugs. Banded snails are common in gardens and, since they feed mainly on decaying vegetation, do little harm, while being a favourite food of song thrushes, hedgehogs and other desirable animals. In America, by contrast, where they were introduced by a well-meaning but misguided shell collector, they have become a minor horticultural pest.

These snails are highly variable – no two ever seem alike – and their genetics have been studied intensively for the light they shed on natural selection and evolution, not least in 2008 as part of Darwin Year. The two *Cepaea* snails have a genetic database second only in size to that of *Homo sapiens*.

The minute Desmoulin's Snail, briefly famous in the 1990s for standing in the way of the Newbury Bypass.

Desmoulin's Snail *Vertigo moulinsiana*

Though few would be able to recognise it, Desmoulin's Snail, or Desmoulin's Whorl-snail, is among the best-known British snails, thanks to the publicity surrounding the building of the Newbury Bypass in the 1990s. No larger than a matchhead, the snail had been protected under EU law, being scarce over much of Europe – though, as it happens, quite widespread in marshy river valleys in southern England. This meant that the UK government had to make extravagant attempts to save it during the 'Battle of Newbury', since the bypass would pass over two of its colonies on the Rivers Lambourn and Kennet. Locating and removing the little snails to a supposedly safe site proved difficult and a complete waste of time, as they soon died out in their new home. However the absurdity of the exercise ensured the snail plenty of media play and gave the protestors a legal loophole in which to appeal to the European legislature. The bypass went ahead, and in Newbury, a gallery-cum-café was renamed Desmoulin's in honour of the snail. Since then, the snail has been found in places as far apart as Kent, Cornwall and North Wales. It seems, in fact, to be fairly adaptable. In 2008, the snail was found living happily in the centre of Maidstone between a flyover and a supermarket.

Other land snails

Other familiar garden snails include the neatly whorled Strawberry Snail, which has a taste for tender plants and not just strawberries. The Garlic Snail gives off a surprisingly powerful whiff of garlic when handled. The name of another ancient introduction, the Kentish Snail, is a misnomer. Though it contains the word Kent in both its English name and its scientific name (*cantiana* is from Cantia, the ancient name for Kent), it is common in verges, hedgerows and waste ground all over southern and eastern England, though not especially so in Kent.

The Cheese Snail, so named because of its resemblance to a tiny flat Cheshire cheese, is a woodland species found especially in the 'hanger' woods of the South Downs. The mollusc specialist Martin Willing suggested that it would make the perfect symbol for the newly formed South Downs National Park (and perhaps an allusion to the bureaucratic slowness of the park's designation).

In 2008, a small but elegant snail with a spiral pattern was found on the brickwork of Cliveden House in Buckinghamshire, now looked after by the National Trust. This is *Papillifera papillaris*, known as the Italian Snail (or at least *an* Italian snail) but which the Trust now prefers to call the Cliveden Snail. It was probably introduced around 1898, when antique marble was imported from the Villa Borghese to build a showpiece balustrade, and must have been living quietly among the brickwork and statuary ever since. No fewer than four invertebrates new to Britain have been found on National Trust property in the past few years – a paper wasp, a mistletoe bug, a small fly and now this pretty Italian snail.[21]

Another snail to hit the news is the Girdled Snail, whose modestly sized coiled shell was once considered a rarity but has, over the past 20 years, spread with increasing speed throughout the southern half of England. It reached Sheffield just in time for the millennium, and Leeds and York a few years later. It seems to be one of nature's hitchhikers, a testimony to the brisk trade between garden centres and homes.

Freshwater snails

Pond snails keep a low profile and are of interest mainly for those who have a garden pond or the declining number of people who keep a freshwater aquarium. The species in greatest demand are the Great Pond-snail with its large and graceful spire-shell, and those with tight-coiled shells known as rams-horns or trumpet-shells. Both are available commercially, though they will often turn up for free in the pond on the feet of visiting waterbirds.

Only a few freshwater snails are sufficiently well known to have long-established English names. The

Wandering Snail is our commonest species and, being seemingly always on the move, in water and out of it, is usually one of the first snails to find a newly dug pond. It feeds on decaying matter of all kinds, including its own kind (especially in overcrowded tanks). Edward Step once observed it 'industriously assisting in the dissolution of a superfluous dog that has been consigned to the waters attached to a brick.'[22] This is not a snail to keep in an aquarium, as it produces a defensive toxin that can cause convulsions in fish.

The two native and two introduced bladder snails are named after their thin, fragile shells, which give the impression of having been partly inflated like blown glass. The Freshwater Nerite, by contrast, has a thick, heavy shell with a half-moon-shaped opening and attractive mottled markings. It is our only representative of a largely marine group of colourful shells, popular as craft shells; the name 'nerite' means sea-rock.

Spire-shells have tall, pointed shells reminiscent of church spires. The tiny Jenkin's Spire-shell can be abundant enough to form what look at first like beds of dark gravel in streams. Originally introduced here from New Zealand, possibly in shipboard barrels of drinking water, and aided by sex-free reproduction (parthenogenesis) and a mild tolerance to pollution, it made itself at home in both fresh and brackish water throughout the country. In some reservoirs it has become abundant enough to block the outflow pipes.

A rare freshwater snail, the Shining Ram's-horn Snail, was included in a set of six stamps on Endangered Species released by the Post Office in 1998. Apparently a victim of falling water quality and overzealous ditch management, it is now chiefly confined to the Norfolk Broads and marsh ditches near the coast. Sometimes living with it is the tiny Little Whirlpool Rams-horn Snail, which was legally protected under the EU Habitats Directive in 2008, the only British mollusc so honoured.

The Shining Ram's-horn, one of a set of six stamps of Endangered Species issued by the Post Office in January 1998.

Slugs *Limacidae*

VN: dew-snail, marly-sarly, mollscroll (Devon), musicel, sligs, slimeys, snaig (Kent), snail (Scot.), snake (Scot.)

Slug is an old word meaning slow or slothful. Before the eighteenth century, any slow-moving animal could be described as a slug, but the name gradually attached itself to a group of shell-less molluscs that commonly made a nuisance of themselves in the garden. The name's sound suggests sliminess as well as slowness. Perhaps it is only coincidence that they resemble the shape, if not the speed, of that other kind of slug, a bullet.

Slugs were also sometimes known as snails or 'dew-snails' (a Cornish expression is 'as slippery as a dew-snail'). Gilbert White referred to slugs as 'naked snails', which is still their name in most other European languages.[23] In the north, where slugs are often much commoner than snails, they tended to call the smaller ones slugs and the large black ones as 'black snails' or 'snakes'. A dialect name used mainly in south-west England was 'mollscroll' or 'marly-sarly', which might also be used for any creepy-crawly. It probably comes from a Middle English word, 'malshawe', meaning caterpillar.[24]

Slugs are bywords for slowness (though some of them can move with surprising speed). To call someone a slug is to emphasise his or her incorrigible laziness. In times gone by, slug could be used as a verb, as in 'the idle old codger is slugging in bed when he ought to be out there mucking out the chickens.' 'Fie, what a slug is Hastings', said someone of Lord Hastings in Shakespeare's *Richard III*, to which the affable Buckingham replies, 'And, in good time, here comes the sweating lord.'[25]

Slugs are drawn to a remarkably wide range of foods, which they detect with an impressive acuteness. Edward Step noted that 'apples and bean-pods dropped in the road will draw slugs from hedges on either side. They are also able to locate a dish of milk in a dairy and proceed to drink from it.' He found that the black garden slugs will feed on almost anything sufficiently soft and moist: 'seasonal fruit and vegetables, wild plants, a dead mouse or bird, its own kith and kin, or their slime.'[26] When very hungry, they have even been known to eat damp newspapers. One slug kept by Step ate 'the dead bodies of five other slugs, a

A Leopard Slug, or Great Grey Slug. Its acrobatic mating habits, pivoting at the end of a rope of slime, were voted one of the top-ten sights of the invertebrate world in a BBC survey.

dead freshwater mussel, some insects and finally a little Pears soap.' The ever-curious Step went on to offer it poisonous berries, which it nibbled with reluctance, leathery leaves, lichens, which it chewed happily, and peppery fungi.

Being dense repositories of succulent produce, gardens are favourite places for slugs, and they regularly come near the top of the poll of worst garden pests. A bare half dozen species live in our backyards, of which the most familiar are the Large Black Slug, the smaller Garden Slug and the Field, or Netted, Slug. As every gardener knows, slugs are fond of fruit, vegetables and tender plants, especially, for some reason, hostas. Different species have their own tastes: the introduced Budapest Slug, for example, likes potatoes.

British gardeners spend about £30 million a year battling slugs. Their traditional weapon is the slug pellet. These contain metal compounds, such as copper, which repel the slug by generating something akin to an electric shock. Any slug that ignores this and feeds on the toxic pellet will soon be in its death throes, spewing out mucus as its energy reserves are depleted, after which its cell membranes burst and it dies horribly. Unfortunately, the toxic ingredients of slug pellets, such as methiocarb, are harmful not only to them but to birds, hedgehogs, honeybees and dogs. This particular chemical has now been withdrawn, but in 1998, a slightly less toxic one based on metaldehyde still managed to kill a dog that had eaten some of the interesting blue pellets.[27]

Many gardeners choose less environmentally damaging forms of slug warfare. Some say that porridge will attract every slug in the vicinity and so save the lettuces. Slugs are also attracted to beer, which can be used as bait to trap and drown them, like the Duke of Clarence in the malmsey butt. Others interplant garlic among the vegetables; experiments at Newcastle University have shown that garlic oil is fatal to slugs and snails, though, of course, harmless to man. Many gardeners simply go out after dark with a torch and pick off the slugs by hand. An effective bio-control in the form of a nematode worm is now available; these are simply mixed with water and poured into the soil. Having located their slug, the worms drill into the slug's head and cause its eventual death. Some wildlife-friendly gardeners are nervous about this form of alternative, as the same worms kill harmless snails, and no one can predict the wider effect of large numbers of nematode worms in the soil.

Taken as a whole, slugs are much maligned. Of nearly 30 British species, only a few cause a nuisance and, like snails, they are significant recyclers of decaying plant material (significant in the sense that, if they disappeared, we would all rue it). Several species, including the Ash-black Slug, are environmentally sensitive and confined to undisturbed old woodland. A few are rather elegant and attractive. The Leopard Slug, otherwise known as the Great Grey Slug, is our largest slug, measuring up to 20 centimetres at full stretch, and is attractively marked and spotted. Its nocturnal mating routine, twisting like a double helix on a self-made mucus rope, has been described by the

BBC as one of the great sights of the natural world (and good enough to star in David Attenborough's *Life in the Undergrowth* series). The rare Kerry Slug is even more beautiful, spotted and marbled with yellow and white on a greeny grey background, a bold pattern that serves as an effective camouflage on a lichen-covered rock.

Moreover, slugs have had their uses. Though they are seldom eaten nowadays, there are nineteenth-century reports of poor villagers in the West Country collecting them. Two spinster sisters who lived at the now ruined Snaily House on Dartmoor enjoyed turning the tables on black garden slugs by salting and bottling them, and eating their pickled remains with garden vegetables. On a Channel 4 cookery programme in 2009, Hugh Fearnley-Whittingstall tried out some slug fritters, having first rinsed off their slime with hot water and vinegar. The chopped-up slugs, mixed with egg, breadcrumbs and tomato sauce, looked fairly appetising, but the consensus was that the fritters would taste even better without the slugs.

Slugs were also used for medicinal purposes. The small Field Slug was boiled in milk as a country cure for consumption. Slugs could also help to remove warts. One of the more bizarre exhibits in the Pitt Rivers Museum in Oxford is a glass jar containing a slug impaled on a thorn. The label reads: 'Charm for Warts. Go out alone & find a large black slug. Secretly rub the underside on the warts and impale the slug on the thorn. As the slug dies the warts will go.'[28] The cure was based on transference: as the animal shrivelled and died, so would the wart, being 'impregnated with its matter'. Others tied a slug or a Garden Snail to the wart with a bandage or pierced it with a pin for as many times as you have warts or, after wiping the wart with slug-slime, pointed the slug at the new moon (a cure which has its origins in ancient Rome).

Slugs (1987) was a low-budget horror film based on a novel by Shaun Hutson. In typical shock-horror fashion, the citizens of a small town are terrorised by parasitic man-eating slugs warped by toxic chemicals leaking into the environment. Even their slime devours human flesh, as someone finds out to his cost when he slips on a glove in which a slug has been sleeping. A rubbishy film even by schlock standards, it was nonetheless successful enough to spawn a sequel, *The Breeding Ground*. *Slugs* was a late-comer in a line of 1970s monster-movies which include *Squirm* (worms), *Bug* (cockroaches), *The Swarm* (Bees) and *Phase IV* (ants), as well as a 1993 offering, *Ticks*.

Chitons *Polyplacophora*

AN: butterfly shells, coat-of-mail shells, sea cradles

Chitons are primitive molluscs which look like a cross between a limpet and a woodlouse. Like limpets, they live on rocks (usually on the lower surface) on the lower shore. When we find them at low tide, they are normally motionless but, like limpets, they feed by moving slowly and methodically over their rocky territory between the tides, always returning to the same place afterwards. Unlike limpets, their overlapping plates allow them to curl into a tight ball when displaced. These plates, eight in number, provide their alternate name of 'coat-of-mail shells' (the scientific name, *Polyplacophora* means 'bearing many tablets'). When the animal dies, the tiny plates detach and sometimes wash up on the beach, and because they are slightly bow-shaped with a dip in the middle, they have been called 'butterfly shells' (though that name has also been applied to various other, unrelated shells).

Chitons are an ancient group that does not seem to have changed much in 500 million years. The British species are all small and easily overlooked, but in America there are much larger and more colourful chitons called sea cradles from their curved shape. The word chiton is Greek and refers to a form of military tunic in which strips of metal were intersown. It seems that the Greeks borrowed it from the Middle Eastern word *kittan*, meaning a tunic of linen or wool. Scholars think that even that word may have been borrowed from still older word-forms preserved on clay tablets from ancient Mesopotamia. The moral seems to be: why invent a new word when an old one will do?

Tusk-shells *Scaphopoda*

Tusk-shells are ivory-white and gently curved, like the tusks of a miniature elephant. They sometimes wash ashore in great numbers after a storm, especially on the south-west coast where, because of their unique shape, they are in much demand for shell-crafts. In North America they were even used as currency by native tribes.

Left: *The chiton, or coat-of-mail shell,* Acanthochitona fascicularis, *a relatively large species of the south-west coast.*

Limpets *Patellidae*

VN: baarnagh, barnagh (Isle of Man), bonnet-shell, croggan (Cornwall), flithers (Yorks.), flitters (Isle of Man), lampet or lempot (Cornwall), lampit (Scot.), limpin, spiko (Orkney)

Gaelic: *bairneach*

Limpets are wonderfully hardy molluscs that withstand the pounding waves and the hot midday sun with equal indifference. Their tent-like shells are adapted to a life of clinging; essentially a shelled sucker, the limpet clamps immovably to the rock almost as though it had become stone itself. What we do not see is what the limpet does when the tide is in. For a few relatively manic hours, it wanders off, grazing algae from the rock's surface before returning to its home base, a hollow in the rock worn away by its fidgeting, and eases itself back into the exact same space. These food-seeking journeys were first reported by Aristotle. More than 2000 years later, Edward Step wrote of the rasping sound of an army of limpets on the move as they drag their shells over the rough barnacles.[29]

Limpet comes from the Old English word *lempedu*, meaning rock-licker. The name shares the same origin as lamprey, an eel-like fish that can fasten itself to a rock by a sucker. Limpets are the most important foreshore grazers. On occasions when they have been wiped out by an oil slick (or, rather, by the detergents used to remove the slick), the rocks soon become covered by an unsightly green slime. Limpets are numerous enough to maintain the balance of bare rock and weed – there can be up to 180 per square metre – but because they need space to graze, they do not completely crowd the surface as do filter feeders such as barnacles. Each full-grown limpet needs about 484 square centimetres of encrusting weed to scrape a living.

Most if not all of the limpets of the upper shore, with their strong, ribbed, tent-like shells, will be the same species, the Common Limpet (whose generic name *Patella* means a small dish, a word the limpet shares with our knee-caps). On some western and northern shores it is joined by two superficially similar species, the China Limpet and the Black-footed Limpet, which are most easily distinguished when you turn them over. The Black-footed Limpet has a beautifully rayed margin and, as its name implies, a dark or blackish foot; that of the Common Limpet is normally coloured dirty yellow

427

Common Limpets and impressions left by their departed neighbours.

or greenish-yellow. The China Limpet is flatter and has a white, polished inner lining like porcelain, together with an orange 'sucker', or foot. Unlike the other two, it is confined to the lower shore.

Limpets are edible but tough; John Wright aptly describes the experience as like 'pencil rubbers dipped in fish paste'.[30] To judge from the middens of limpet shells preserved under ancient coastal settlements, including the ancient ruins of Skara Brae in Orkney, they were nonetheless gathered in quantity as a kind of rugged Stone Age fish supper.

Limpets are a humble form of sustenance, but there is an inexhaustible supply of them on rocky shores. Collected by slipping a blade under the side of the shell and giving it a sharp sideways flick, they can be eaten like cockles, soaked in their shells overnight, boiled or parboiled and then fried. They are still regularly eaten on the Isle of Man, in a traditional Easter meal, as 'flitters', served with bread and butter for breakfast or with fish and eggs for supper. For those wishing to extend the limpet experience further, there is a special Flitter Dance accompanied by an Irish harp. Nineteenth-century Irish labourers would satisfy their hunter-gatherer instincts by knocking limpets off the rocks with their knives and swallowing them raw. Immigrant Cornishmen in nineteenth-century Chicago so longed for the taste of home-cooked limpets that a local shopkeeper arranged for a supply of them, pickled in vinegar and then canned, to be shipped

across the Atlantic (or so he claimed). Limpets also make handy fishing bait and are especially attractive to flatfish and wrasse.

Children play with limpet shells as tiny scoops or to decorate sand castles. Few however would envy the fate of Jan Tregeagle, a legendary Cornishman who made a pact with the Devil and was punished in the hereafter by being made to empty Dozmary Pool with a leaky limpet shell. Dozmary Pool, a dark lake in the middle of Bodmin Moor, is said to be bottomless. You can still hear Tregeagle's despairing wail on a windy night, especially in autumn.

Limpets lend their name to a naval mine that was developed in 1939, just in time for the Second World War. Designed to be attached to the hulls of warships by divers, the prototype was an English invention reportedly based on materials bought from Woolworth's – a large tin bowl and a packet of aniseed balls (apparently, aniseed balls dissolve in acid at just the right rate to set off a timed detonation). Britain made half a million of them, but the joke was on us as limpet mines were used by Italian divers to blow up two of our battleships in their own dockyard.

Smaller, more exquisite limpets occur in rock pools on the lower shore, and some have familiar names based on a distinctive feature. The Tortoiseshell Limpet has a smooth, oval shell prettily marbled in brown and white. A cold-water species, it is fast retreating northwards through global warming and is now reasonably common only on the far north

Blue-rayed Limpets grazing on kelp. They have shivers of electric blue radiating like fireworks across their shells.

coast of Scotland; it may be facing extinction in British waters.

The Keyhole Limpet has a finely grooved shell with ribs and cross-ribs and a distinctive 'keyhole' at the apex. By contrast, slit limpet species have an equally distinctive notch in front of the shell. In both cases, the hole functions as a siphon for sea water: the limpet sucks water in from its sides, pours it over the gills and then expels it through the hole or slit. Both forms feed on (and are usually found among) sponges in rockpools and so are technically carnivorous, if grazing on sponge counts as carnivory.

The prettiest of the common shore limpets is the jewel-like Blue-rayed Limpet, which has shivers of startling electric blue radiating like fireworks across its translucent, amber-like shell. It can be found by searching the fronds and stipes of kelp, in which the animal is often half buried. Sometimes the limpet destroys its own home base by burrowing too far and causing the kelp to snap. Hence those strands of kelp on the tideline may be the result of a little limpet that failed to place limits on its appetite.

There are two freshwater limpets, the River Limpet and the Lake Limpet, both of which are common on rocks or water plants in shallow water, though they are small and drab and so easily overlooked (but people, especially children, are often surprised and amused to be shown a limpet living in a stream). They have recently been joined by a third, even smaller, North African species that probably 'escaped' from greenhouse tanks.

Ormers *Haliotidae*

VN: abalone, green ormer, sea-ear

The name Ormer is a local twist on the French *oreille de mer*, or sea-ear. There is a faint resemblance to a human ear in the flattened oval shell, which has a curl at one end representing the lobe and a curving line of holes along the margin, perhaps standing in for an enthusiastic set of piercings. When alive, the shell is normally mottled dirty green or reddish brown, but the colours start to fade once the animal inside is dead, and shells found on beaches are usually bleached. Ormer shells are hard and difficult to break, but their allure lies not only in their attractive shape but their lining of mother-of-pearl, which has iridescence greater than that of mussels or oysters (though, strangely enough, Ormers rarely produce natural pearls). They belong to a family of warm-water shells known as abalones, and the sole British species, the European Abalone (or *the* Ormer), is confined to the Channel Islands.

In times past, Ormer shells were in demand by the furniture trade for mother-of-pearl inlay. Slivers of iridescent Ormer are also found in jewellery and on electric guitars, while the shells themselves are standard souvenirs of the Channel Islands. A more humble use of them was to scare birds. Several shells threaded together on a stick (the holes are ready-

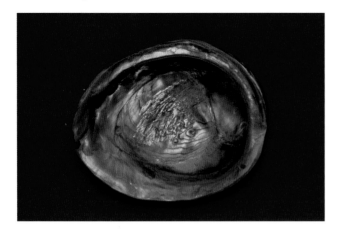

An Ormer, or abalone shell, revealing its deep mother-of-pearl lustre.

made) clatter together in the wind like castanets. As a nod to the place of the Ormer in the cultural life of Jersey, a special gold coin with an image of the shell was minted for the Queen's Silver Jubilee in 1977.

Ormer meat is a great delicacy and is traditionally collected in the early spring for a traditional seafood stew. The flesh is naturally tough and has to be beaten to tenderise it before cooking, but well-stewed Ormer has a sweetness of flavour all of its own. Ormer fishing is a social occasion joined in by many islanders and takes place between January and April at 'ormer tides', exceptionally low tides that expose the kelp-covered rocks where the Ormers live. To safeguard the fishery, the rules are strict. Fishers are allowed neither to wear wetsuits nor to put their heads underwater. And only full-sized specimens can be taken. Diving for Ormers is strictly forbidden, and one Guernsey man who broke the law became reputedly the first subject of an underwater arrest when, doubtless to his great surprise, he felt a grip on his shoulder by a policeman in full diving gear.

Despite the care taken to preserve stocks, Ormers are scarcer than they were. In the nineteenth century, some ten to twenty tonnes a year were harvested on Jersey alone, but in recent times, one would be lucky to find a dozen. In the late 1980s, Jersey's Ormers were further decimated by a fatal infection transmitted by toxic marine algae, and divers reported large numbers of shells on the seabed with lobsters gorging themselves on the dead and dying contents. By 1999, they had become so scarce that a temporary ban on ormer fishing was imposed to conserve what stocks remain. So far, the Ormers of Guernsey and Sark remain free of the disease.

Slipper limpets *Calyptraeidae*

vn: bonnet-limpet, bonnet-shell

The American Slipper Limpet arrived by accident. When American blue-point oysters were introduced into Britain in the 1920s to replace the failing stocks of native oysters, the limpet came along as a hitchhiker. Unfortunately, the hitchhiker has hijacked the vehicle. Along the south and south-east coast, there are now dozens of failed oyster beds where slipper limpets carpet the sea floor, representing yet another object lesson in the dangers of introducing foreign species without the natural systems that control their numbers.

The slipper limpet has a unique and attractive shape, coiled at one end with a concave shelf halfway across the wide mouth. Some see them as shelly slippers, others as little boats with rounded hulls and a single deck. Their shape accommodates the limpet's picturesque breeding behaviour, to which its scientific name *fornicata* seems to allude. Adult slipper limpets live one on top of another in chains of up to 20 or 30 shells, the bottom of each one corresponding with the shelf of the individual below. The oldest and largest limpet lies right at the bottom, clinging tightly to a stone. Those near the bottom of the chain are the mother limpets, which release clouds of tiny eggs, while the younger ones further up the chain are all males, a less demanding role in limpet sexuality. As they grow older, these males will, in turn, change sex to assume maternal duties. Perhaps some arcane sexual allusion lies behind the accepted collective name: a *bungalow* of slipper limpets.

A short sequence of slipper limpets, with the female at the bottom.

Slipper limpets can occur in enormous profusion, not only because of their efficient reproduction but because they also filter-feed the tides like mussels and cockles. Limitless food, few serious predators and a strategy of passive aggression are a recipe for runaway success. Twenty tonnes of slipper limpet have been dredged from a single acre of former oyster bed, while their empty shells, driven ashore by storms, pile up into shell-banks as high as the waves can dump them. In places, they are not only the commonest seashell but in some danger of becoming the only ones.

At West Mersea in Essex, slipper limpets were so numerous that two limpet factories were set up in the 1940s to pulverise their shells for chicken feed and road grit. They were also, ironically, used to form a shelly layer known as 'culch' in oyster beds for the baby oysters (spat) to settle on. During the war, some people, driven to desperate measures by food rationing, gathered slipper limpets as food. According to Rick Stein, when cooked like snails with garlic, parsley and a little wine, and presented in their attractive shells, they are quite palatable and fill the kitchen with a rich savoury smell. Anglers use them all the time as general-purpose bait.

Our only native slipper limpet is the harmless little Chinaman's Hat Limpet. It can be found at low tide on the rocks of northern and western shores and is distinguished by a neat, white, symmetrical shell reminiscent of the conical hats worn by peasant labourers in the Far East. It is also known as the cup-and-saucer limpet.

Winkles *Littorinidae*

VN: chequers (NE Eng.), corvin (N Eng.), easter-shell (NE Eng.), gwean or gweggan (Cornwall), horse-winkle (N Ireland), jack (Isle of Man), pennywilk (Northumb.), pinpatch, sea snail (Kent), trig, whillicks, winks, wrinkle

Big winkles, *by Anna Kirk-Smith. 'I don't know what it is about this wonderful little mollusc that appeals so directly to me. It is ubiquitous, drab, chewy, and stuck to a rock with sticky mucus. But just sit and watch – it is also industrious, determined, sexually voracious and just plain cute.'*

The satisfaction of eating winkles lies not so much in their taste or nutritional value as in the ritual of extracting each match-head of flesh from its shell. Winkling is a fiddly business. The morsel of boiled snail must be winkled from its shell with a deft twist of a stout pin or customised winkle pick. And before that, you must first remove the tiny, hard, mica-like lid that seals the shell. Hence the winkler sits with a bowl of winkles in his or her lap, picking them out one at a time and fishing out the meat, totally absorbed by the process and at peace with the world. As a veteran winkler remarked, 'they do pass the time along very pleasantly.'[31]

Winkle or periwinkle is an old word of uncertain origin but probably combines the Latin *pina*, meaning a mussel, with the Old English *wincel*, meaning snail shell. The full periwinkle is usually reserved for the Common, or Edible, Periwinkle, while related but less sought-after species are mere winkles. In north-east England and Northern Ireland, winkles sold as food are 'whillicks', while in Cornwall, the empty shells left stranded by the tide are called 'trigs', from a Cornish dialect word for the ebb-tide. In nineteenth-century London, where an extraordinary 3 million pints of winkles were sold each year as street food, they were 'winks'. Wink sellers had their own 'speeches' or songs; one of them, not perhaps of the best, was recorded by Henry Mayhew in his 1851 *London Labour and London Poor* and went as follows:

> Winketty-winketty, wink-wink-wink,
> Wink, wink,
> Wicketty-wicketty-wink,
> Fine fresh winketty-winks, wink-wink.[32]

Winkles are grazers, living on the film of algae on intertidal rocks or on seaweeds. Unlike oysters or mussels, there is no obvious mechanical way of stripping winkles from the rocks, and so they have never been farmed. You must therefore 'pick' your own, gathering them from the rocks and pools on the middle shore. You can also still buy them from seafood sellers on the beach or the pier, though the taste, or perhaps the required patience, for fresh winkles seems to be declining. In *A Poor Man's House*, the author Stephen Reynolds shared the life of a fisherman and his family in Sidmouth, Devon, hunter-gathering among the rocks and pools for seafood, including winkles:

> Underneath the stone, clinging to it and lying on the bed of the pool, were so many large winkles

Sea-worn colour forms of the Common Periwinkle.

that instead of picking them out, I found it quicker to sweep up handfuls of loose stuff and then to pick out the refuse from the winkles. When Uncle Jake came across an unusually good pocket he would call me to it and hop on somewhere else. There was an element of sport in catching the dull-looking gobbets so many together. I soon got to know the likely stones – heavy ones that wanted coaxing over – and discovered also that the winkles hide themselves in a green, rather gelatinous weed, fuzzy like kale tops, from which they can be combed with the fingers. They love, too, a shadowed pool which is tainted, but not too much, by decaying vegetable matter. Uncle Jake likes the stones turned back and replaced 'as you finds 'em'.[33]

The winkles were brought home in a covered bucket (otherwise they are apt to break loose and make a kind of slow-motion run for it) and soaked in fresh water to get rid of the sand and grit, before boiling.

Though abundant around the coast, the Common Periwinkle is largely confined to the north-west Atlantic coast of Europe. More than most seafood, winkles truly are the taste of Britain. Around 2000 tonnes of British winkles are sold each year, much of them exported to France, where demand exceeds supply. Unlike other commercially important molluscs, there is no statutory control or close season.

Such was the allure of fresh seafood to Londoners that the old railway from Canterbury to Whitstable on the north Kent coast became known as the Crab and Winkle Line. The first regular passenger railway service in the world, it opened in 1830 and was the making of Whitstable as a resort, synonymous with fresh-caught crabs, oysters and periwinkles. The historic line closed in 1952, but in 1997 the Crab and Winkle Line Trust was set up as a charity to reopen it as a footpath and cycle-way. The Crab and Winkle is still a common name for pubs and restaurants specialising in seafood.

When sharp-pointed shoes came briefly into fashion in the early sixties, they became known as winklepickers. There was a brief revival in the late seventies, and old pairs with battered turned-up toes once worn by Dad or even Granddad are still in vogue in Goth and punk circles. Winkle is also a nursery word for a boy's penis.

Three more species of winkle are common on different parts of the shore, though they are rarely gathered for food. The hardiest, the Small Winkle, has a dark little shell with a sharp spire and lives on the upper shore in the 'splash zone'. Further down it is joined by the Rough Winkle, with its plump shell of many colours and distinctive spiral grooves. Lower down still is the Flat Winkle, also with numerous colour forms, which is usually found among seaweeds. Their confinement to particular zones of the foreshore makes them a popular group on field courses.

Topshells *Trochidae*

VN: jack-a-dandy (Isle of Man)

Like winkles, topshells are among the most numerous snails of the rocky seashore. Their neat shells have a flat bottom and a pointed apex, rather like an old-fashioned wooden spinning top. Some have prettily mottled or striped patterns. Topshells graze seaweeds and detritus from the rocks, and since food is not therefore a limiting factor, they are often present in large numbers. They are not gathered as food in Britain, though larger species are eaten in China and the West Indies, but their empty shells are collected as they are sometimes lined with mother-of-pearl. The silver lining of the Grey Topshell in particular lends a sea-worn topshell its name of 'silver willie' in Scotland or 'silver tommy' in England.

Topshells inhabit different parts of the shore and so endear themselves to beachcombers and field courses. The upper zone belongs to the Thick Topshell, also called the Toothed Topshell, which has a thick shell to cope with crashing waves on western headlands and cliffs. It often occupies a tight band only a metre or so wide near the high-water mark of neap tides.

Next comes the Common, or Flat, Topshell, which is confined to the Atlantic and Channel coasts but occupies almost the entire intertidal zone. Further down is the Grey Topshell, while the lowest shore is the place to look for the most attractive species, the Painted Topshell, with its neat, perfectly conical shells and attractively grooved whorls. The Pearly Topshell is a deeper-water species of northern shores that is seldom seen alive, but its delicate, polished shell with orange or brownish tints and pearly luster is sometimes found washed up on the beach. In general, topshells are less hardy than limpets or winkles and are more common in clean rockpools than exposed on the rocks.

The related Pheasant Shell has a high natural polish and a reddish striped or zigzag pattern, both of which attract shell collectors. It can be found grazing on red seaweeds in rockpools on the Atlantic coast, while its empty shell is a popular home for young hermit crabs. The richly coloured blotches on some shells are reminiscent of the red wattles and plumage of pheasants.

Other marine shells

Cowries *Triviidae*

VN: ginnamoney (Cornwall), gowry, groatie-buckie (Scot.), John o' Grot's buckie (Scot.), maidenhead (Isle of Man), the nun, porcelain shell, stick-farthing

It takes a sharp eye to spot a British cowrie shell on a beach – a pale pinkish speck the size of a chickpea. Nonetheless, few shells are more eagerly sought after. Though small, cowries are exquisitely shaped; Michael Viney likened their lemon-shaped, characteristically grooved shells to 'rolled up fingerprints'. They carry in their tiny shells a sense of the exotic, and they are said to bring good luck. The commonest kind is the Spotted Cowrie, which has a glossy shell and three diagnostic brown spots (hence its Latin name, *Trivia*, meaning not 'commonplace' but 'three-way'). On the seldom-seen live cowrie, the shell is almost hidden inside the folds of its blackish, lace-like flesh.

Searching for cowries is an island passion. In Orkney 'there is hardly a house without a jar of these little shells.'[34] On the Isles of Scilly, they are known as 'ginamoney' or, perhaps in more genteel

A lone cowrie washed up on a Cornish beach.

circles, 'guineamoney'. There is a Ginamoney Carn on the island of St Agnes – a group of granite rocks above a shell beach noted for cowrie shells. Here, every Easter before the Second World War, the island's children would picnic by the beach and search among the wet, gritty sand for ginamoney, as well as amber beads from a shipwreck and small fish in the rock pools.

The Poached-egg Shell is a translucent, china-white relative of the cowrie with a flared shell reminiscent of the cooked white of an egg. The live snail lives below the tideline, feeding on sea-fans and hydroids, but empty shells are occasionally found cast up on western shores (though you need all the good luck a cowrie can bring to find one).

Raft shells *Janthinidae*

The best-known British species of these ocean-wandering, floating shells is the Violet Snail. A whorl of delicate purple, it is borne along on the currents on a self-made raft of mucus, hardened into something resembling bubble-wrap, and occasionally washes ashore on the Atlantic-facing coast. Finding one is every shell-collector's dream; Rachel Carson walked the East Atlantic shore for years before finally spotting one, 'light as thistledown, resting in a depression in the coral rock of Key Largo, where some gentle tide had laid it.'[35] Michael Viney, still more fortunate, 'felt the beachcomber's sense of uplift' on finding two of them, side by side, just yards from his home by the tide line in County Mayo.[36]

The Violet Snail feeds almost exclusively on a fellow floater, the By-the-wind-sailor, a relative of jellyfish. In Viney's words, predator and prey must 'bob together like toy boats on a park pond'. So close is their association that some, having witnessed the jellyfish apparently emerging from the mouth of the snail, assumed the latter was giving birth to

a different organism. Live Violet Snails defensively release clouds of purple ink when touched and so are not ideal for aquariums. The animal is functionally eyeless, hence its former name of 'blind-snail-of-the-sea'.

Auger shells *Turritellidae*

The name auger shell was coined by Thomas Pennant in the eighteenth century, but this elegant, screw-like shell is also called the turret shell or, in Northern Ireland, the cockspur. Auger shells are up to five centimetres long and end in a sharp point. Such a long, narrow shell is ill-designed for wandering, and a live auger shell lives in the sediment, where it filter-feeds detritus. Auger shells are living fossils, and their genus, *Turritella*, is one of the oldest among molluscs: very similar ones have been found preserved in mudstones 135 million years old. Well-preserved auger shells are in demand for shell-craft. Unfortunately, by the time we find them, they are often sun-bleached with their points broken off.

The similarly shaped Common Wentletrap (sometimes spelt 'wendletrap') is among the prettiest of seashells. Its name is borrowed from the German word for a winding staircase, a very apt analogy to the thick ribs that coil round the shell like steps. Wentletraps were highly prized by shell collectors. At the height of an eighteenth-century craze for shells, as much as 40 guineas changed hands for a good one, but the price eventually fell to half that, and later still to a few shillings. The fall was known in the shell trade as 'the wentletrap slump'.[37] Craftsmen in the Far East are said to have resorted to manufacturing fake wentletraps out of ivory or hardened rice-flour paste.

Pelican's-foot shells *Aporrhaiidae*

The unmistakable fan-like projection on the Common Pelican's-foot Shell makes it a favourite with collectors. The live snail moves in a unique way by raising up its shell and then letting it fall a few millimetres forward; the projections prevent the snail from sinking as it lurches its way onwards through the silt. It normally lives below the tideline and so is rarely seen except by divers, but the empty shells are frequent on some beaches. A second, rarer species, De Serre's Pelican's-Foot, has even longer 'toes'.

Necklace shells *Naticidae*

AN: moon shells

Necklace shells are roughly globular with a small flat spire (hence their alternative name of moon shells) and a characteristic glossy sheen. They live in the sand on the lower shore, feeding on sand-dwelling bivalves such as tellins and cockles by drilling into their shells. Empty shells found on the beach with a neat round hole are likely victims of necklace shells. Though they are as good as any other for a shell necklace, the name comes from the collar-shape of their egg-masses, commonly found in wet sand. The distinctive bubble-shaped shells have been found in Celtic burials, either scattered over the body, placed on the hands and feet or arranged in a pattern above the head. Possibly their shape suggested the shape of the sun and moon, as symbols of the afterlife.

Whelks *Buccinidae*

VN: boockie (NE Eng.), buckie, mutlag (Isle of Man), mwatlag-buckee (Isle of Man), sea snail, slavvery buckie, wilk or wulk (Scot.)

Gaelic: *mudliogh*, *mutlyag*
Egg masses: sea wash-balls

Whelks are the standard large seashells of art and advertising. Their handsome, spired shells with wide, flaring mouths are among the largest shells on the beach, and when you blow away the loose sand and hold the shell to your ear, you hear the sound of surf. Whelks are often called 'buckies', a generic name for any big, coiled shell. On the North Sea coast of Northumberland they distinguish between a 'slavvery buckie', with the live whelk inside, and a 'craalin buckie', an empty shell occupied

The Violet Snail clinging to its raft of bubbles.

Neptune's antique: empty shell of the Red Whelk.

by a hermit crab. There are several Buckie place-names in Scotland, the largest of which was the county town of Banff (before local government reorganisation marooned it inside an enlarged Moray). Appropriately, Buckie has a fine harbour and a fish market at which whelks are often on sale.

Like jellied eels, tripe, pig's head and other robust dishes of yesteryear, whelks are falling out of fashion. Traditionally, they were eaten by the poor and generally bought doused in malt vinegar from a stall on the pier. The remark 'he's not fit to run a whelk stall' supposes that selling whelks is an undemanding activity within the capability of almost anyone. It seems to have been coined by Winston Churchill when drawing attention to the shortcomings of the opposition.

In the more expensive restaurants, whelks are extracted from their shells, cooked and then popped back again with a dressing to disguise or mollify the presence of naked, boiled whelk. The trouble with whelks is that, unless they are served fresh, they tend to be rubbery and often rank. There used to be a separate demand for them as cod bait, but that, too, has declined, along with the cod.

The centre of the whelk trade was the north Norfolk coast, where Brancaster and Wells-next-the-Sea were to whelks what Colchester and Whitstable are to oysters. Bridlington, Grimsby, Whitstable and Selsey are other ports associated with the whelk trade. In former times, fleets of small boats caught them in baited buckets. Along the harbour stood lines of sheds, where the whelks were cleaned and boiled before being sent by train to market –

a journey which, alas, is no longer possible, as the station has closed. Today, if they have not been sold for offices, whelk sheds are more likely to be used for processing mussels and oysters.

The whelk trade now finds its main market in South Korea, where whelks are thought to be aphrodisiacs. A large processing plant at Fleetwood in Lancashire pressure-cooks, processes and freezes the whelks prior to their flight halfway around the world. Unfortunately, the crash of the 'Tiger' economies in the mid-nineties and the consequent fall in prices forced many former whelk-fishers to re-equip and switch to crabs or whitefish or face going out of business.

Some people catch their own sea-fresh whelks by lowering baited pots and buckets from the pier. Whelks feed on carrion and are considered a nuisance by crab- and lobster-fishers because they frequently get to the bait first. Another traditional method of catching them is to bury a bucket of bait under stones at low-water and dig it up again on the ebb tide when, with luck, it should be swarming with whelks. In nineteenth-century Cheshire, according to Richard Jefferies, they used a dead dog as bait.

Blowing over the mouth of a big Red Whelk makes a low, booming sound and gives the shell its nickname of 'roaring buckie'. At one time, buckies were used by crofters to call cattle and sheep. Smaller whelks make a whistling noise. A large buckie could also be fashioned into an oil lamp, the wick protruding from the opening. When kept horizontal, the lamps work well enough but tend to reek of fish. Red Whelks have very strong shells; some of those that wash ashore may be tens or even hundreds of years old. The discovery of their great age lay behind the whelk's name *Neptunea antiqua*, 'Neptune's own antique'.

The classical proportions of the whelk shell are perfect for heraldry and design. They adorn the coat-of-arms of, among others, the Storey, Joce and Wilkinson families. The appropriately named Shelleys have a particularly interesting set: 'Sable, on a fesse engrailed between three whelks, [with] as many maiden's heads proper, of the second.'

The egg capsules of whelks look like the nests of bumblebees or punctured bits of bubblewrap. They say sailors used them as makeshift sponges, hence their folk-name 'sea wash-balls'.

Dog Whelks *Muricidae*

VN: cattie buckie (Orkney), dog-winkle, horse-winkle, jack (Isle of Man), purple, purple-shell

The Dog Whelk has a thick, strong shell; its scientific name, *lapillus*, means little stone. It is a multicoloured species, with forms varying from off-white, pinkish or yellow to dark or banded. The prefix 'dog' is an indication of inferiority; though shaped roughly like a whelk and technically edible they are not worth eating (though large ones in other parts of the world certainly are). Dog Whelks are easily confused with winkles, and so are also called 'dog-winkles' or 'horse-winkles'. Ever going their own way, the folk of Orkney insist on calling them 'cattie buckies' or 'cat whelks'.

Dog Whelks do have other potentially useful attributes. As members of the murex family, their body fluids turn purple when exposed to the light and so can be used to make a permanent purple dye. The stripe on the togas of the senators of ancient Rome was coloured with this dye, and the emperor himself wore 'the purple'. By processing Dog Whelks gathered from the shore, poor cottagers on the west coast of Ireland could wear the colour of aristocrats. The chemical that produces the colour, purpurin, is believed to help the whelk break open the shells of barnacles and other well-armoured prey.

Dog Whelks must be among the world's most abundant carnivores. They feed mainly on barnacles and mussels by boring a hole in the shell and sucking out the innards. It takes a whelk up to three days to gain entry to a mussel, for which it employs a double method of attack: rasping with its chainsaw-like 'tongue' while secreting acidic chemicals to soften the shell. After digesting the mussel, the Dog Whelk rests for about a week. It's a leisurely life that can go on in this way for years.

Though it feeds on economically important shellfish, the Dog Whelk is not considered to be a pest. In fact, it would hardly come to notice at all had it not been for an impending ecological meltdown in which it served mankind as a miner's canary. In the 1960s, a new paint was developed to prevent seaweeds and barnacles from fouling the hulls of pleasure craft and so reducing their speed. This was tri-butyl tin (TBT), which used the toxic strength of a heavy metal to render the hull biologically inert. Unfortunately, not all the paint stays attached to the hull, and some slowly leaches into the water. TBT is toxic to most forms of marine life, and filter-feeding organisms such as mussels and barnacles trap and absorb the chemical. It concentrates further in the tissues of their predators, and in the case of Dog Whelks, sub-lethal doses caused them to change from females to males and so cease to reproduce.

In many harbours and marinas, Dog Whelks were effectively wiped out by TBT and, by the 1990s, this once-abundant sea-snail had become a 'species of conservation concern'. It was partly the scientific studies of the impact of TBT on Dog Whelks that led to the eventual withdrawal of the use of the paint on small craft and to the manufacture of less damaging substitutes. Dog Whelks are now moving back into their former territory at an observed rate of about two metres a year.

Confusingly, a snail from an unrelated family shares the name dog whelk. This is the Netted Dog Whelk, a common shell on the lower shore, where it burrows in pockets of soft sediment between the rocks, feeding on dead shellfish and other organic debris. It is an attractive shell, easily recognised from the block-like pattern of its shell, as though built with tiny bricks.

Sting-winkles

VN: drill, hedgehog murex, oyster-drill, rough tingle, tingle, whelk-tingle

Sting-winkles are not, in fact, winkles but relatives of the Dog Whelk, and they share similar carnivorous habits. The 'sting' is the mollusc's proboscis, a customised drill, with which it bores a neat round hole in the shell of its prey, before injecting a toxic muscle-relaxant that simultaneously kills the prey and relaxes the muscle that closes the shell. The European Sting-winkle looks like a small whelk with bold ribs and warty projections that gave it the name 'hedgehog murex'. Found mainly on southern rocky shores, it is a predator of tubeworms and barnacles.

A much more harmful species is the non-native American Sting-winkle, or oyster-drill, which specialises in oysters. It attacks chiefly young 'spat' oysters, killing up to 20 or more every day, and once established, it is difficult to get rid of. Oyster-bed owners have little alternative but to weed out the sting-winkles by hand. The American Sting-winkle was one of the unwelcome aliens that arrived with Blue Point oysters from the US in the 1920s (the other was the Slipper Limpet).

The Sea Hare, our most familiar naked marine mollusc, named after its large 'ears' (they are in fact 'noses' which detect scents in the water).

Sea-slugs *Nudibranchia*

Sea-slugs, like land slugs, either lack a shell or carry only a small one half-hidden in the body folds. Some crawl on the seabed while others, such as the 'sea butterflies' and 'sea angels', have wing-like flaps for swimming. Sea-slugs are among the most colourful animals in the sea; T. E. Thompson suggested that 'they are to the molluscs what the butterflies are to the arthropods or the orchids to other flowering plants'.[38] Unfortunately most of our 80 or so British species live offshore and, despite their colourful livery, they blend in well among weed, sponges and hydroids.

One of the largest and most common sea-slugs is known as the Sea-hare from the long 'ears' at its head end. When alarmed, like a squid, it releases a toxic violet ink, which makes the Sea-hare an uncomfortable neighbour in an aquarium. It has a much larger relative, *Aplysia fasciata*, that can weigh a couple of kilograms and always creates a sensation when caught up in a fishing net, as one was in a catch of Dover sole in October 2008.

Sea-hares have greatly enlarged nerve cells, which have been used by neurologists to study the chemical processes of nerve transmission. The compound they use to attract a mate seems to work on humans, too. Described by the *Independent* as 'a cross between Chanel No. 5 and Viagra', it is an ingredient in performance-enhancing pills sold in the Far East. Sea-slugs are also eaten in Far Eastern cuisine, served as fresh as possible (which unfortunately means they are sometimes chopped up and fried while still alive); they are said to taste clean and salty, while being simultaneously crunchy and chewy.

Few sea-slugs have English names. The beautifully coloured Sea Shawl is confined to warmer waters, but deep rock pools sometimes contain the Sea Lemon, also known as 'warty Doris', whose colour and tough skin is reminiscent of lemon rind (and, still more, of the Mediterranean citron). Though common, it can be hard to spot among the coloured sponges on which it grazes. A related species, described unkindly as 'a dirty white thing with dirty white lumps' by Simon Barnes in *The Times*, has acquired the nickname 'dirty Doris'.

The beauty of sea-slugs caught the attention of Newcastle naturalist Albany Hancock, whose paintings adorn the standard Victorian work on the group, named, in the portentous style of the day, *A Monograph of the British Nudibranchiate Mollusca, with Figures of the Species*. His paintings and extensive collections are now housed in the Hancock Museum in Newcastle, named after Albany and his brother. A whole family of sea-slugs, the Hancockiacae, was also named in his honour.

Cockles *Cardiidae*

Cockles are among the cheapest and most popular forms of seafood, sold from barrows and booths and, at one time, by women street vendors, with their enticing calls of 'alive, alive-oh'. The real live cockle lives buried in the sand between the tides, often in vast numbers. A good cockle bed, such as Burry Inlet in South Wales or parts of Morecambe Bay, can contain upwards of a million of them per acre. Like other seafood, cockles go off rapidly and, before refrigeration, were normally boiled on the spot and sold locally or pickled in vinegar. Their attractive ribbed shells are also a mainstay of shellcraft, and they have been used to decorate house fronts and walls in a form of shelly pebbledash. They are also crushed for use as road hardcore or chicken grit.

The main centres of the cockle trade lie on the soft, flat shores in the Wash, the Thames estuary, the inlets of South Wales, Morecambe Bay and the Solway Firth. They are at their plumpest and best during autumn and are harvested right up to Christmas. Cockle sands are famously dangerous and shifting; the flood tide comes rushing in, it's said, with the speed of a fine horse. Apart from the danger, cockle-picking is back-breaking work, with the keen wind searching for holes in your oilskin and the salt and sun flaying your skin. As a fisherman from the Cumbrian village of Flookburgh put it, cockling is 'like being married. The first 20 years are bloody hard, but thou gets used to it.'[39]

Seasoned cocklers expect to lose a tractor or two in an unlucky tide, but their knowledge of the sea and its hazards mitigates the risks of the trade. The mostly Chinese immigrants exploited by gangmasters and ignorant of the shifting winds and tides are much more at risk. On 5 February 2004, a band of Chinese cockle-pickers out on the distant sands after dark were cornered by the tide, and 23 of them drowned in Britain's worst cockling disaster. The gangmaster responsible was later jailed for 14 years. The 2006 film *Ghosts* was based on the incident.

Commercial cockle-picking needs a licence, and the beds are periodically closed to allow stocks to recover. But some have stayed closed for much longer through pollution incidents that have devastated the beds (they presumably devastated other species, too). Cockles are filter-feeders and are sensitive to changes in the water quality. In 2008, one of the best cockle grounds in the Burry Inlet was struck by a mystery bug that undermined the cockle's immune system; the result was a seabed carpeted with the rotting innards and empty shells. Some linked the incident to a nearby sewage works, which was undergoing repairs. The Towy estuary, where in 1993 rival gangs clashed in what were known locally as the Cockle Wars, was closed for health reasons for four years in 2001 after another mysterious mass-mortality.

Cockling has its own language and hardware. The wooden cockle rakes are custom-designed and, like farm gates, vary in detail from place to place. To operate them, the cockler first 'rocks his jumbo' – that is, puts down a special wooden plank with a handle on either end which, when rocked, softens the sand and sucks the cockles to the surface. The shells are gathered up with the rake and 'riddled' to sort the larger saleable ones from the small fry. Sometimes the cockler uses a claw-like iron fork, known in Lancashire as a cockle-cram, to scoop them out of loose sand but more often the sorting is done with a wooden griddle or sieve. In the days when cockles were sold in the streets, they were kept in wickerwork baskets known as tiernals.

Less romantically, most of today's cockles are shovelled into 25-kilo nylon-mesh bags destined for the white refrigerated vans waiting by the shore. Hand-gathering is still the rule in South Wales, but elsewhere most commercial cocklers use hydraulic dredgers, an all-too-efficient method that needs careful regulation to avoid overfishing the beds. Cockle beds are deemed to be temporarily exhausted when the density has fallen to below a hundred per square metre.

The cockle fishery is worth around £20 million a year and, in Wales, is larger than the whitefish and other shellfish fisheries put together. The most expensive cockles come from Stiffkey (pronounced 'stookey') in Norfolk, whose 'Stewkey blues' or 'blue stones' owe their beguiling colour (ranging from lavender to grayish-blue) to the dark-coloured sediment in which they live. Their main rivals are those from Leigh-on-Sea in Essex, which claims to be 'the epicentre of the world cockling trade' and whose pretty harbour is still lined with sheds selling prime seafood.

Fresh-boiled cockles were traditionally eaten in the open air with vinegar and a little pepper. But the taste for downing them on a windy pier is declining, and today most British cockles are exported to West European countries that have overfished their own

Empty cockle shells, useful for shellcrafts, or for decorating walls and houses, or for children's gardens.

beds. They are still a popular pub snack in some city bars, and cockles are now sold in supermarkets in sealed packets complete with plastic cockle prongs.

It is perhaps the Welsh who love cockles the most, to judge from the wide range of recipes including cockles and eggs (*Cocos ac wyau*) or, best of all, cooked for breakfast with bacon and home-made laver bread. Perhaps cockles have an image problem; might sales pick up after an image makeover and a new, more alluring, name such as the French *vongulet*? The name cockle may come from the Latin *corculum*, meaning a small heart, related to its roughly heart-shaped shell. It has other, negative connotations in English: cockle is the name of a once-notorious weed and was a dialect word meaning to tangle or to pucker. 'Cockle-bred' means foolish.

The commercial cockle, known as the Common, or Edible, Cockle, is one of a dozen species found in British waters. Others, such as the Prickly Cockle, Spiny Cockle and Norway Cockle, are familiar to collectors but have more value for shellcraft than the food industry (though they are all perfectly edible). The Egg, or Smooth, Cockle has a fishery in some countries, though not in Britain, where we perhaps have a surfeit of the common kind. The Dog Cockle, as its name betrays, is regarded as too

tough to eat, though experiments are under way to try to tenderise its meat with polyphosphates.

One of the most famous commando raids of the Second World War involved the use of the collapsible 'cockle' canoe, so named because its ribbed plywood deck and bottom were reminiscent of a ribbed cockle-shell. The commandos were to be dropped by submarine off the French coast with orders to penetrate the harbour of Bordeaux and blow up as many ships as possible, after which they would skedaddle. Ten brave men paddled their cockle canoes along the River Gironde for 70 miles before sinking one ship and damaging four others. Most were either caught and shot or drowned in the icy waters. Just two escaped and made it back to Britain. The event inspired a book and then a classic war film, *The Cockleshell Heroes* (1955), starring Trevor Howard and Jose Ferrer. It is strange how many aspects of this raid involved the names of invertebrates. Apart from the cockleshell canoes, the heroes used limpet mines, and two of their canoes were named 'Cuttlefish' and 'Crayfish'.

'To warm the cockles of our heart' is an old saying, famously used by Winston Churchill when congratulating the sea captains for cornering the German battleship, the *Graf Spee*.

Mussels *Myrtilidae*

VN: gobaloo (Isle of Man), krane (Orkney), mushel (NE Eng.)

Mussel-beds represent one of the densest accumulations of animal life on earth. The marine biologist Maurice Yonge calculated that an acre of dense mussel-bed will produce 40,000 pounds (17,144kg) of mussels, which once stripped of their shells, yield about 10,000 pounds (4,536 kg) of meat.[40] Moreover, they are fast growing and easy to harvest. An acre of grass, by comparison would yield a mere 100 pounds of beef, in the 1950s at least, and require a much greater investment in fertiliser and animal feed. No known system of livestock farming can approach the food-production value of a good mussel-bed.

Unfortunately, good mussel-beds are not as plentiful as grass fields. Mussels aggregate wherever there is a suitably solid surface, whether rocks, breakwaters, wooden jetties or piers, but only exceptionally favoured locations produce the large, plump mussels needed for the market. Mussels clinging to intertidal rocks are no use at all: since the mussels cannot feed when the tide is out, they never fatten up sufficiently. Good-quality mussels grow only on or below low-water in sheltered harbours and estuaries. Such places generally have other uses and often become polluted. Though the mussels themselves might welcome a bonus of warm, soupy sewage in their seawater, it rules them out as potential food, especially because, in times past, mussels were notorious transmitters of typhoid. The need for clean water in mussel-friendly habitats in practice limits commercial mussel-gathering to certain parts of the coast, most notably the Wash and north Norfolk, North Wales between Bangor and Conway, Morecambe Bay and, rather more widely, in Scotland and Ireland. In Scotland, all the wild mussels (and oysters) are legally owned by the Crown, and though foraging for personal consumption is tolerated nowadays, larger-scale gathering requires a licence.

Today, about half the annual production now comes from farmed mussels. Some are dredged as year-old mussels from the seafloor and transferred to sheltered bays called 'lays', where they are harvested every couple of years. Others, especially in Scotland, are grown on ropes suspended from

A crowded group of Common Mussels exposed by the tide.

lines or floats. Some of the most prized mussels come from Brancaster Saithe in Norfolk, where they have been cultivated for more than a hundred years in mussel-beds.

Mussels have been a popular food since the Middle Ages, when they were traditionally eaten at Shrovetide (the modern Pancake Tuesday) and at other times when flesh was forbidden. Today we eat more mussels than all the cockles, scallops, winkles and whelks put together. In 2004, the total UK production was 26,600 tonnes and worth £22.7 million. Our native mussel has, however, faced stiff competition from the larger and juicier green-lipped mussel from Australia and New Zealand. The interloper has a pretty green-fringed shell, and sales were boosted by its reputation as a health food; the mussels contain glucosamine, which maintains supple joints and perhaps also helps to ward off cancer. Now that glucosamine extract is available, the green mussel is going out of favour, and sales of the native blue have revived. Some Sainsbury's stores now sell them live in running seawater.

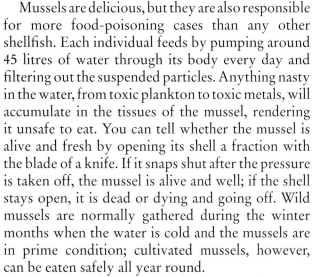

Hand-grading mussels on a Norfolk salt-marsh.

Mytilus Edulis (2007), *a mussel sculpture by Graeme Mitchison on Conwy Quay, North Wales.*

Mussels are delicious, but they are also responsible for more food-poisoning cases than any other shellfish. Each individual feeds by pumping around 45 litres of water through its body every day and filtering out the suspended particles. Anything nasty in the water, from toxic plankton to toxic metals, will accumulate in the tissues of the mussel, rendering it unsafe to eat. You can tell whether the mussel is alive and fresh by opening its shell a fraction with the blade of a knife. If it snaps shut after the pressure is taken off, the mussel is alive and well; if the shell stays open, it is dead or dying and going off. Wild mussels are normally gathered during the winter months when the water is cold and the mussels are in prime condition; cultivated mussels, however, can be eaten safely all year round.

Mussels are traditionally eaten the French way as *moules marinière*, flavoured with parsley and a splash of white wine, though some Scots like to make a mussel broth by thickening the brew with oatmeal. In coastal parts of western Scotland and Ireland, mussels are traditionally cooked very simply by boiling and then seasoning lightly with vinegar. The brewings, or 'bray', make a supplementary hot drink. Like oysters, mussels were considered to be an aphrodisiac and so sometimes portrayed by artists as a symbol of carnality and lust. In *The Garden of Earthly Delights*, Hieronymus Bosch shows two lovers actually carrying on *within* a giant mussel.

The word mussel derives from the Latin *musculus*, meaning a little mouse and, until around 1870, was spelt 'muscle'. The analogy lies in the shape; the shells are convex, and narrow to a point at both ends, rather as a mouse appears as it scuttles across the floor.

The one we normally eat is the Common Mussel, though it is only one of 40 species of marine mussels. But it lives in conveniently dense aggregations, and so to everyone except a marine biologist it is *the* mussel.

Adult mussels live a sedentary life, anchored to the rocks by a mass of fibres known as the byssus, or 'beard'. The fibres act like guy ropes on a tent, so that however the sea strikes it, some of the threads will be able to take the strain. They are incredibly tough, as anyone who has tried to remove a mussel from its rocky home ground will know. They have even been used as a kind of natural mortar on bridges and piers. The ancient bridge at Bideford in Devon was actually held together by byssal fibres. The tidal flow was too rapid to allow masons to repair this bridge in the usual way, so instead, handfuls of mussels were pushed into the gaps. Stripping mussels from the bridge was strictly forbidden.

Perhaps the largest British town named after an invertebrate is Musselburgh, which claims to be the oldest town in Scotland. Its residents used to say that 'Musselburgh was a burgh when Edinburgh was nane/ An' Musselburgh will be a burgh when Edinburgh's gane.' The civic coat-of-arms proudly incorporates three mussels, along with three anchors, and mussels are still harvested from along this part of the coast, though environmental considerations are currently casting doubt on their future. Other mussel place names include Mussel Point, near Zennor in Cornwall, and Musselwick Sands in Pembrokeshire.

Horse mussels

VN: clabbydoo or clappy doo (Scot.), corduroy mussels (Cornwall), yarn or yug (Orkney)

Horse mussel is another way of saying 'coarse mussel'. It is larger than the Common Mussel but is equally gregarious and often forms small reefs of densely packed shells. It is therefore a keystone species in a rich community of marine animals and plants. Unfortunately, the mussel often shares its sheltered waters with scallops, whose high price encourages trawlermen to dredge the seafloor, smashing the mussel reefs to splinters in the process. Large Horse Mussel-beds are very old, perhaps even a relic of ancient times when the water was colder and clearer, and they are now listed in the UK Biodiversity Action Plan as a conservation priority. Those of Strangford Lough in Northern Ireland have been severely damaged by fishing vessels, but since trawling and dredging were banned from the remaining mussel-beds in 2003, a restoration plan is in progress.

In the Glasgow area, where there was a small Horse Mussel fishery based on the Clyde, they were sold at fish markets and in fish-and-chip shops as 'clabbidoos', from the Gaelic *claba-dubh*, or 'big wide mouth'. Big, black mussels are still generally called 'clappy doos' in parts of Scotland.

Freshwater mussels

Six native species of large freshwater mussels occur in Britain, five of which live in lowland waters, while the sixth, the Pearl Mussel, is restricted to fast-flowing upland streams. Though they can be abundant (but hard to spot unless the water is clear), they are becoming rarer through habitat loss. In the Middle Ages, freshwater mussels were sometimes cultivated in fish ponds, partly because their filter-feeding kept the water clean but also for gathering as food on fast days, though they are rather tough and tasteless. Today they are used mostly as angling bait.

Mussels have sometimes been used as natural filtering agents in garden ponds and even as a water purifier in aquariums. A large one can filter up to 40 litres of water per day and so help to keep a tank clear of algae and bacteria. Unfortunately, they also have a habit of ploughing their way along the bottom, tearing up the substrate and uprooting any water plants. Moreover they are prone to die suddenly and without warning and so pollute the water. Even so, Swan Mussels are in demand by fish breeders, for they are the host of a popular aquarium fish, the bitterling, which lays its eggs inside the mussel's siphons.

The Swan Mussel and the commoner Duck Mussel are large but thin-shelled molluscs that live embedded in the clay and gravel at the bottom of lakes and canals. In ancient times it was believed that the Swan Mussel was a resting stage, like an egg, that would eventually hatch out into a beautiful swan, in much the same way that geese were supposed to come from barnacles. The clue lay in the body shape: Swan Mussels are vaguely similar to the shape of a swan's body, while its siphons could be seen, with due imagination, as rudimentary wings. The Duck Mussel, being smaller, was considered to produce mallards. A fully grown, 12-year-old Swan Mussel can measure 15 centimetres long or more, though the empty thin oval shells one sometimes sees washed up by a canal towpath are usually much smaller. The Duck Mussel has a thicker, somewhat darker shell and is found in slow rivers as well as lakes and canals.

Bitterlings inspecting a Swan Mussel. The fish inserts its eggs into the shells's gill cavity using its unique worm-like ovipositor.

Right: *Freshwater Pearl Mussels in the bed of the Ballinderry River in County Tyrone.*

A third, much rarer species is the deliciously named Depressed River Mussel. It has cause for depression, since it has supposedly declined throughout Europe, and though it is still locally frequent in a few British rivers, the European Habitats Directive require us to take good care of it. David Aldridge and his colleagues at Cambridge University have discovered that this mussel often lives in localised hotspots in the lowest reaches of large rivers. It is fairly tolerant of poor-quality water but vulnerable to dredging, which can wipe out whole populations of the mussel at a stroke. Aldridge is hopeful that more mussel-friendly ways of removing mud and waterweeds can be introduced in the stretches of river inhabited by Depressed Mussels.[41] In the meantime, his research team is promoting it and its fellow mussels as a friend to mankind – as nature's way of filtering clean, chemical-free drinking water.

Two smaller species of freshwater mussel are known as river mussels, and they can be abundant in quiet, clean stretches of rivers, canals and sometimes lakes. The commonest is known as the Painter's Mussel, since its roughly oblong shells were once used by artists to hold their pigments and also as containers for the gold and silver foil used for illuminating.

The small, attractively striped Zebra Mussel was accidentally introduced to Britain via the London Docks in the 1820s, probably on imported timber. It spread rapidly through the canal network, and being gregarious as well as lacking natural enemies, forms dense mussel-beds on submerged power-station intake pipes, the masonry of locks and bridges and the hulls of boats. The mussel is currently spreading in the Thames and Great Ouse catchments, where it is encrusting practically every available solid surface. The steady filtering of millions of these mussels causes ecological change, including the growth of marginal weeds (at the expense of spawning grounds for trout and grayling) and reduced numbers of native mussels and freshwater fish. In 2004, the Zebra Mussel appeared in Ireland for the first time and is already causing problems at waterworks that are costing around £100,000 a year to put right.

Traditionally Zebra Mussels were controlled by chlorinating the water, but this has environmental drawbacks, and the mussel can fight back by snapping shut its shell for up to three weeks. David Aldridge and his team at Cambridge have pioneered an alternative, an environmentally safer 'bio-bullet' that, when imbibed by the mussel, releases a lethal chemical (it breaks down quickly and is harmless to ducks and other animals).[42] Zebra Mussels have had at least one positive impact. They are a favourite food for duck, especially the tufted duck. A sudden and almost unlimited supply of them was the spur behind the spectacular increase in this once-rare duck in the nineteenth century.

Common in ponds and rivers are six tiny species of orb mussel (or 'orb shells', known as 'fingernail clams' in North America) and sixteen species of pea mussel, but it needs an expert eye to distinguish them. The Witham Orb Mussel and the Fine-lined Pea Mussel are listed on the UK Biodiversity Action Plan as priority species.

Pearl Mussel, *Margaritifera margaritifera*

Britain has long been famous for its freshwater pearls. According to Suetonius, they were the reason why Julius Caesar invaded Britain in 55BC. Caesar was a pearl connoisseur and 'would sometimes weigh them in the palm of his hand to judge their value'. At one time, Pearl Mussels were found in fast-flowing streams throughout Britain and Ireland. Conwy in North Wales was famed for its freshwater pearls, and Cornwall and Devon once contained thriving pearl fisheries. It is Scotland, however, that has produced the majority of home-grown pearls. The twelfth-century Scots King Alexander I is said to have acquired the finest collection of pearls of any man living, while the Kelly Pearl, an exceptionally large and fine specimen fished from the River Ythan 400 years ago, is among the Scottish crown jewels. At one time, the River Tay alone produced around £8000 worth of pearls each year.

Most pearls produced by mussels are brown and valueless. Jewellers are only interested in the exceptional pearl, with a subtle smoky lustre and in shades of pink, grey or pale brown. These are produced by perhaps one mussel in several hundred, often from a large, scarred old veteran. A perfect pearl – pea-sized, regular in shape and clear in colour – was worth £3–£4 at the height of the trade in the mid-nineteenth century (that is around £4000–£5000 at today's prices). The prospect of finding such a pearl was enough to send many poor crofters down to the riverbank to try their luck during the quiet time before the harvest. The crunch time for Scottish freshwater pearls arrived in 1861 in the form of a German merchant, Moritz Unger, who offered to buy every pearl that could be found. This seems to have encouraged over-fishing, for the industry went into decline soon afterwards.

The Pearl Mussel's scientific name *Margaritifera* means 'pearl-bearing', and its pearl – produced in response to a bit of irritant grit or a parasite inside the shell – was its undoing. A mussel lives for up to a century and matures only after about 15 years, and so it is doomed to decline in the face of fierce demand and worsening habitat conditions. Today it lives in localised populations of aging adults.

The first sign of the Pearl Mussel's presence in a river is often a pile of gaping shells on the bank where a fisher has been searching for pearls. Breaking open a mussel shell almost invariably tears the animal's muscle tissues, resulting in death. Special tongs were available for examining the mussel without harm, but only a few bothered to use them. In 1998, Peter Cosgrove counted 800 parted shells lying on the river bank in a heap that represented, at his estimate, around 64,000 years of mussel growth.[43] This kind of exploitation is unsustainable. Pearl Mussels have declined to the point when fewer than 70 colonies are known, many of them seemingly on their last legs, with no young shells, and hence no recruitment.

The decline is not only due to fishing. The fundamental cause seems to be falling water quality and, above all, the increased loads of sediment carried by most rivers, even in the Highlands. Pearl Mussels feed by drawing in river water and sieving out the fine organic debris. But too much silt clogs up the spaces between the stones on the riverbed and so prevents oxygenated water from reaching the smaller, younger mussels. Concern for the mussel's future is not confined to conservationists: it is regarded as a keystone species, since it helps to keep the river clean for salmon and trout. It is the endless filtering of mussels half buried in the gravel that helped to create the crystal-clear water so admired by tourists and so necessary for fly-fishing. It is this that is now threatened by our neglect of the mussels.

In 1998, after sufficient evidence had been collected to satisfy the government, the Pearl Mussel was given the status of a protected species, making it an offence to 'intentionally or recklessly kill, injure or disturb' it or to damage its habitat. Effectively, this outlawed what is left of the pearl trade (in the 1990s, most Scottish pearls were sold to a single jeweller in Perth), though it does not seem to have made much difference in practice, for illegal fishing goes on regardless.

The battle is on to safeguard the Pearl Mussel's best remaining sites from silt and eutrophication. On Harris, where a colony was becoming clogged up with gravel and peat, the only available solution was to dig the mussels up and move them somewhere else. The same tactic was used to preserve the last colony on the River Torridge in Devon. In some rivers, such as the Wye and the Dee, all the remaining stock has been taken into captivity in order to breed baby mussels that can later be introduced into depleted rivers – desperate measures indeed.

Fan shells *Pinnidae*

AN: fan mussel

VN: caper longer (Devon), pen-shell, Spanish oyster

The Fan Shell is the largest bivalve in Britain, expanding upwards and outwards at a steady three centimetres a year to the size of a dinner plate. The shells become correspondingly wedge-shaped and sit half-buried in the seabed, with the broad end projecting into the ocean. While we liken them to fans, the French see these shells as hams and call them *jambons*. The Italians find a resemblance to cloaks, or *cappa lunga*, which name was repeated by Plymouth fishermen as 'caper longer'.

The 'cutlet' from a single one of these molluscs could feed a hungry man, and they appear, expensively, on seafood menus in the Mediterranean and Far East (where a related species is cultured artificially in aqua-farms). The Fan Shell was once famous for an even more valuable product, a fine silk known as pinna-silk or pinna-wool. It comes from the tough fibres that anchor the shell to the seabed and lent it the ancient name of 'silkworm of the sea'. When washed and processed the silk looks like fine threads of gold and is incredibly supple and durable. They say you can roll a scarf woven from pinna-silk into a ball no bigger than a walnut. In the Great Exhibition of 1851, there was even a pinna-

silk muff made in Cornwall, presumably from local Fan Shells. The craft was kept alive in nineteenth-century Italy by the nuns of Tarentino, who used it to make embroidered gloves and other small cloths. Pinna-silk is still used on a small scale in Italian coastal towns to make special cloth for polishing delicate jewellery and also for small articles for the tourist trade.

Today the Fan Shell is better known as an example of endangered sealife, and it is one of only five marine organisms listed as a protected species on the Wildlife and Countryside Act (and one of only four listed as a priority species on the UK Biodiversity Action Plan). As a result, Fan Shells are now legally protected from 'killing and injuring, possession or sale', though not necessarily from accidental damage by trawling. Its scientific name, *Atrina fragilis*, is well-merited, for the shells are brittle, especially at their growing margin. When hit by a drag-net or scallop dredge, they snap. A century ago, Fan Shells occurred in multitudes in sheltered waters off the south-west coast. Fishermen used to avoid grounds where they were for fear of damaging their nets on their sharp edges. Today, this is no longer a problem because Fan Shells are now rare and seen mainly in ones and twos (marine biologists became quite excited when 20 were spotted at the bottom of Plymouth Sound in 2006). Conservationists are currently considering the rather desperate expedient of transplanting them out of harm's way.[44]

A Fan Shell, or fan mussel, its formerly exposed part encrusted with barnacles.

Scallops *Pectinidae*

VN: clam or clam-shell, gimmer shell (Orkney), harpo (Orkney), pecten, queens or quins, raugan (Isle of Man), sea butterfly, squins (Dorset)

Scallop is an honest English rendition of an older French word, *escalop*, simply meaning shell (an *escalop* of beef is a bit of meat cut into a shell shape). It is the archetypal seashell and one of nature's loveliest shapes, though it is, of course, strictly functional – the stabilising 'fins' on the shell enable the mollusc to swim for short distances, hence their folk-name of 'sea butterflies'. The shell has influenced human architects and designers since classical times. Roman funerary monuments often use a scallop-like ornament to radiate behind the head of a statue to indicate life in the hereafter, a style that was taken up again in Christian iconography. Scallops were also used as shells in heraldry, probably for no other reason than that they looked good. We talk of scalloped edges, meaning a scooped or frilly design based on the outline of a scallop shell. And we still use the empty shells of King Scallops (or as ersatz pottery copies) for soap dishes, ashtrays or containers for seafood.

Perhaps most famously, the Shell petrol company adopted the scallop as the symbol for its garages and petrol pumps, and through various forms, it remains the company logo to this day. The corporate word Shell first appeared in 1891 as the trademark of Marcus Samuel & Co, which imported oriental seashells as well as kerosene for lamps. The word was elevated in status six years later when the Shell Transport and Trading Company was formed. The first shell symbol was a sunset, or sun-rayed, tellin shell, and it was only in 1904 that the more familiar scallop was introduced – the idea coming from a company director, Mr Graham, whose family arms included a 'St James's shell' adopted by a distant ancestor after a pilgrimage to Compostela in Spain (*see below*). To celebrate its sixtieth anniversary in 1957, the company published an illustrated book, *The Scallop*, as a momento. Over the years, the original shell design has seen numerous stylistic changes until, in 1971, Raymond Loewy designed the simple red and yellow version still in use – one of the world's most recognised symbols.

No doubt the company directors of Shell were well aware that the scallop shell is an ancient

Scallop-surfing: The Birth of Venus *by Sandro Botticelli (1485). The scallop shell is beautifully painted.*

symbol of immortality. One of the great foundation myths of the world is the birth of Venus, the goddess of beauty, in the surf of the ocean. She was conveyed to the shore on a giant shell, riding it like a surfboard. This story appealed to the imagination of Renaissance artists, particularly as Venus – the most beautiful woman on earth – was surfing naked. The most famous *Birth of Venus* is Botticelli's picture in the Uffizi in Florence, which includes a beautifully painted scallop shell. The symbolism is multi-layered. The Middle Ages imagined life as emerging from the water, and hence the water world was associated with fertility. And from its general shape, the scallop shell was associated with the womb (scallop possibly originates from *skalpr*, the Old Norse word for vagina). It is the moment when, in the pagan imagination, beauty and desire came into the world.

Christians borrowed the scallop as a symbol for pilgrimage, one of many animals drafted into the great cosmic saga of rebirth and resurrection. The shell is associated above all with the apostle St James, who is traditionally shown wearing one in his hat or embroidered on his tunic. They are an allusion to the legend where, after the apostle's relics were taken by ship from Jerusalem to Spain, a mysterious rider approached and plunged into the waves. Both horse and rider sank into the sea and re-emerged covered in shells as a sign of Christian baptism and rebirth. Hence churches dedicated to St James tend to lie close to the sea and feature scallop or cockle-shell imagery. The one at Cooling, by the Thames estuary, for example, has a vestry lined with thousands of cockle-shells picked from the nearby beach. The arms of Poole incorporate three scallop shells, a reference to the original parish church dedicated to St James. On his feast day, 25 July, it is customary to serve shellfish.

Pilgrims to the shell-decorated shrine of St James at Compostela in Spain wore metal badges of scallop shells, while real ones decorated with a red cross are sold today to pilgrims and tourists alike. In former times, pilgrims to other shrines carried the scallop shell as a kind of food token, which they would present at a church or abbey and be allowed as much food as they could pick up with a single scoop. The Swedish name for scallop translates as 'pilgrim shell'.

A four-metre-high, stainless-steel sculpture of two

interlocked scallop shells stands on the shingle beach at Aldeburgh, both as an image of ocean mysteries and a fitting monument to the composer Benjamin Britten. Designed in 2003 by Maggi Hambling, it is intended to provoke thoughts about the wonders of the deep, with the help of a line from Britten's opera *Peter Grimes* pierced along the edge of the shell: 'I hear those voices that will not be drowned.' The community is divided about its merits, and the monument has been repeatedly vandalised.

The most valuable commercial scallop is the Great, or King, Scallop. The smaller Queen Scallop, known in the trade as 'queens', is equally good, but its delicate meat decays more quickly and does not travel so well, and so it is usually sold frozen. The UK scallop industry lands around 20,000 tonnes of kings and 5000 of queens, worth £40 million per year. Most scallops are obtained by dredging or trawling, using special shovels or weighted nets to lift them from the seabed. Environmentalists object that such methods can cause severe damage to fragile seabed communities; in 2009, Helen Phillips, chief executive of Natural England – memorably, if a little tactlessly – described the recent activities of scallop vessels in Lyme Bay as 'rape and pillage.'[45] They are increasingly being farmed by being collected when young and grown on in mesh bags known as lanterns. Some chefs rely on especially large and fine (and expensive) scallops, cherry-picked by divers.

Scallops are delicious, but they are all too often past their best by the time they reach our plates. They are best cooked quickly (seared) to retain the

The monument to Benjamin Britten by Maggi Hambling on Aldeburgh beach, Suffolk, taking the form of a weatherbeaten scallop shell.

succulent interior. Some people prefer to remove the orange 'coral' first – the 'foot' of the scallop – the white meat being the muscle that closes the shell.

Vast quantities of empty scallop shells are produced by the shellfish industry, some of which are turned into decorative pieces, while, in south-west Scotland, the Forestry Commission has used the ground-up shells as a top-dressing on forest tracks. They are also used as a source of lime in kilns. The shells are too brittle to be much use as tools, but gardeners sometimes use them as a small trowel and, in Orkney, they once used them for scooping out hard-packed oatmeal. Such a scoop was known as a 'harpo'.[46]

The evolution of the scallop-inspired Shell 'Pecten' over the past century.

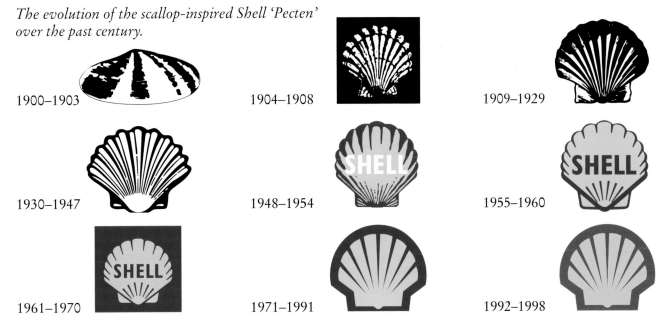

1900–1903   1904–1908   1909–1929

1930–1947   1948–1954   1955–1960

1961–1970   1971–1991   1992–1998

Razorshells *Solenidae*

AN: razor-clam, razorfish

VN: solen or soten, spoots (Orkney), spoutfish (Scot.)

The long, squared-off shell of the 'razorfish', so similar to an old-fashioned cut-throat razor, is unmistakable. The animal that inhabits the razor is less easy to find. It lives inside a vertical burrow near the low-tide mark and, using its shell as a spade, can bury itself in the wet sand with the rapidity of a mole. It takes an experienced eye (preferably with the aid of polarising sunglasses) to spot the dimple in the sand that marks the razorshell's burrow, though the mollusc sometimes gives away its presence with a little squirt of seawater.

Digging out a razorshell, too, takes some skill and determination since the shell is smooth and slippery as well as sharp, and easily slips through the fingers. One method is to squirt a little salt into the hole. Upset by this sudden, unbearable salinity, the razorshell will dart to the surface leaving you just time to nimbly draw it from the burrow like a cork from a bottle. Other people prefer the harpoon method, jabbing a makeshift spear or a bit of barbed wire down the hole until it connects with the shell, then twisting it to jam the barbs against the side before pulling out the unfortunate animal. A more laborious, but perhaps surer, method is to cut off the shell's retreat by digging down with a spade and then under the shell and lifting it out. But nimble fingers are still needed to catch the razorshell before it dives down again.

Razorshells are one of the best-kept culinary secrets. Steamed like a clam or mussel with a little wine and garlic, or fried in butter, they are sweet and chewy with a slight peppery taste. Perhaps the only reason they lag behind scallops and mussels in popularity is the peculiar, alien shape of their shells. But razorshells are now being fished commercially, and potentially unsustainably, using suction dredgers. They also make excellent all-purpose angling bait, though it seems a waste, like giving caviar to a cat.

The shells are sometimes known as solens, or sotens (from the Greek word *solen*, meaning pipe or tube and referring to the animal's long siphon). The shell's resemblance to a guttering spout also provides the Orkney name of 'spoots'. Low spring

Pod-razor, a common razor-shell of sandy beaches.

tides when the shells can be dug up in quantity are known there as 'spoot tides'.

There are four common species of razorshell, and they all share the same delicious taste. The American Jack-knife Clam is a New World razorshell that has spread rapidly along the European coast. The first British record was as recent as 1989, but it has since colonised the whole east coast from Kent to the Humber. It is a deep-burrowing species, which seems to have found a vacant ecological niche for itself in bare, slightly muddy sand. In this unpromising sea desert, the Jack-knife Clam shows no sign of competing with native shellfish and so could be considered a benign if not a welcome new species. The live 'clam' has a narrow, curved shell with a long 'foot' analogous to the blade of a penknife.

Other razorfish include the Grooved Razorshell, which has a constriction in its shell as though it had been tied with string while in a soft state. Those with broader shells and rounded ends are known as Pod-razors, while the smaller, still more rounded *Pharus legumen* (the species name means legume or pea-pod) is known as the Bean Solen. Small Pod-razors and Bean Solens are among the favourite food of scoter ducks.

Other marine bivalves

Coin-shells *Leptonidae*

Coin-shells have a flat, round shape, like a little coin; *Lepton*, their generic name, was also the name of a small-denomination coin in Greece. Also known as a mite, it was worth a fraction of a farthing. But even that was bigger than certain coin-shells; one species is no more than a millimetre across. The somewhat larger Montagu's Shell hitches a ride on the backs of burrowing sea urchins and lives off their scraps.

Hatchet-shells *Lucinidae*

The Minute Kelly-shell (a direct translation of its scientific name, *Kellia minuta*) is sometimes called the mullet shell, for it is a favourite food of the grey mullet, a common inshore and harbour fish. Someone once counted 35,000 of the tiny shells in one mullet's stomach, which 'certainly showed praiseworthy industry on the part of the fish' – and to the counter, too, perhaps.[47]

'Clams'

A clam is a seashell that lives in the sand or mud and breathes by way of a tube or siphon. Various groups of molluscs have adopted such a lifestyle, though by convergence rather than by common origin, and 'clam' is not an exact scientific term; it refers only to twin-shelled (bivalve) molluscs with a similar rounded, thick-shelled appearance, whether or not they are related. The word comes from the Old English, for which the associated verb is 'clamp'. Some clams *clamp* themselves to a rock and, when disturbed, they clamp their shell together. Most are oval- or wedge-shaped, and they vary in size from delicate tellins the size of a fingernail to robust old gapers and Quahogs at the bottom of the sea that may exceed the size of a plate. Clams are good to eat but, in Britain, are usually found as a bycatch while raking for cockles. In America, by contrast, they are eagerly sought after and even cultivated.

Quahogs and carpet-shells *Veneridae*

The most popular thick-shelled clam in America is the Quahog, pronounced 'koh-hog' or 'kwa-hog', according to taste, and named after a Native American word meaning horse-fish. It is also known as 'mahogany-clam' or 'hard-shell clam'. In New England, Quahogs are almost as popular as mussels in Britain, either dredged from the seabed or farmed, with their centre of production in Rhode Island. Young Quahogs, known as 'littlenecks', are often eaten raw with a piquant sauce or lightly steamed and served with melted butter. Older ones, known as chowder clams, need slow stewing to make that signature east-coast dish, clam chowder. Middle-sized ones are known as 'cherrystones'. The shells themselves have an attractive deep-purple edge and were traded by the Native Americans; the scientific name *mercenaria*, meaning wages or reward, is a reference to their use by tribes as *wampum*, or money tokens.

Since the early sixties, would-be clam fisheries have introduced Quahogs to inlets on the British south coast and the Humber, but all seem to have failed. A self-sustaining colony in Southampton Water, originating either from the kitchen throw-outs of transatlantic liners or from dumped ship's ballast loaded on the eastern seaboard of the US, has since spread all along the south-east and east coast. They are now quite common on the beach, alive or dead, for they are picked up and dropped onto rocks by gulls in an attempt to break open the tough shells and extract the animals inside.

The nearest native species we have to the Quahog is a dark, thick-shelled clam known as the Icelandic Cyprine or, increasingly, by its American name of Ocean Quahog. It is a northern mollusc, best known in Orkney, where it is called the 'koo-shell' (cow-shell), apparently because it traditionally represented the cow in parlour games in which seashells are used to represent different farm animals. They are dug out at low tide and, after cleaning, steamed up in a seafood stew. Opinions differ as to their quality. Their dark meat makes Ocean Quahogs unsuitable for New England-style chowder, and in America they are normally used for minced-clam products. We are advised to remove the liver from wild-caught specimens to avoid a taste of iodine or seaweed (though, some must have wondered, which bit is the liver?).

Ocean Quahogs are among the longest-lived animals on earth. A large one dredged up from the coast of Iceland was estimated by its growth rings to be around 400 years old.[48] It was nicknamed Ming after the ruling Chinese dynasty of its birth. Like rings on an ancient oak, the layers of shell also provide a record of changes in the seawater and food supply over the centuries.

Venus shells, or Venus clams, are attractive and sweet-tasting molluscs found on sandy shores just below the low-tide mark. They are also known as Artemis shells, after the name of the hunting goddess associated with wild places and wild animals. Among them are the carpet-shells, which have attractive patterns reminiscent of tapestries or carpet designs and are popular with shell collectors. The tessellations of the Pullet Carpet-shell also suggest hens, and the shells are often called 'pullets' for short. The Speckled, or Chequered, Carpet-shell, known in France as *palourde*, has the sweetest flavour and is the most sought-after and expensive of the group.

Gapers *Myidae*

VN: brallions, clam, gaper, grice (Orkney), nannynose or nanny's nose, old maids, piss clam, smirlin (Orkney), soft clam, soft-shelled clam, steamer clam

The Sand Gaper is one of the largest British shelled molluscs; a full-grown one can be 15 centimetres long and 8 centimetres broad. Its name is misleading for it is usually found in muddy creeks and estuaries, where it filters suspended particles with the help of a thick, muscular siphon shaped like an elephant's trunk – the only part worth eating. It is the permanent bulge and gape left between the shells by this siphon that gives it its common name of 'gaper'. In America, where there is an important gaper fishery on the north-east Atlantic coast, gapers are better known as soft-shelled clams. They are common in Britain, sometimes forming 'clam cities' in the muddy sand, their burrows only centimetres apart, and are often found when digging for cockles. An attempt in the early 1960s to farm Sand Gapers failed after the entire stock (imported from America rather than using what nature provides) was killed off by low water temperatures in the frozen winter of 1963.

Wild gapers are sometimes gathered for food in Ireland, where they are known as 'brallions'. In the Hebrides and Northern Isles, too, this and a related species, the Blunt Gaper, known in Shetland

as 'smurslin', are a traditional wild food. Dug from the beach early in the morning, they are first rinsed and then scalded in boiling water, after which the rather watery meat is scooped from the shell. In a New England clambake, the shells are traditionally cooked in layers of seaweed over a fire pit on flat stones gathered from the shore, as in the clambake scene in Roger and Hammerstein's Broadway hit, *Carousel*.[49] Our neglect of all this fun and local colour can only be put down to British conservatism.

Admittedly, digging for gapers is a hard and messy business. A gaper can be detected at low tide by the little depression, about the size of a five-pence coin, left by its siphon. It can be dug for with a fork, after which you plunge an arm into the hole and feel about for the shell, trying to avoid its sharp edges. Gapers can be kept alive and fresh for some days by daily dunkings in seawater or by wrapping them in layers of seawater-wet newspaper at the bottom of the fridge. Most British gapers so gathered are destined to be angling bait – perfect for flounders and other estuarine flatfish, they will also attract dogfish, bass or cod. Smaller gapers are eaten by oystercatchers, sea ducks and other shorebirds, as well as crabs, flatfish and ragworms.

Trough-shells *Mactridae*

AN: surf clams

VN: aitkens (Scot.), lady cockles (N Ireland)

Trough-shells have very hard shells – the commonest of them, the Thick Trough-shell, also known as the surf clam, may last for decades after being washed up on shore. Several surf-clam fisheries exist in Ireland, the largest of which is in Waterford Harbour, but the catch-rate is unpredictable, with up to 400 tonnes one year followed by next to none the following year. In Britain, a small fishery has recently been established in the Exe estuary. The Cut Trough-shell used to be sold at market in Northern Ireland, where it was known as 'lady cockle', and in Glasgow, where it was called 'aitkens'. Trough-shells are often found by fishermen digging for lugworms.

The largest trough-shell, *Mactra glauca*, can be 10 centimetres across when well-grown. It is found mainly in the Channel Islands, where the shells were once in demand by collectors, who were willing to pay up to two half-crowns for a perfect specimen – hence its local name (probably used with a sly wink) of 'the five-shilling shell'.

Trough-shells are extremely sensitive to marine pollutants. After the *Sea Empress* ran aground on the Pembrokeshire coast in 1996, large numbers of Rayed Trough-shells were washed up on the Gower coast more than 80 kilometres from the site of the spill. Analysis showed they had been killed by hydrocarbons, ingested by feeding in contaminated seawater.

Otter shells

vn: clumps, duickies

an: otter-shell clam, otter-shell gaper, soft-shelled gaper

The Otter Shell, *Lutraria lutraria*, acquired its intriguing name through the similarity of its Latin name to *Lutra lutra*, the European otter. Linnaeus must have intended to call it *lutaria*, meaning 'in the mud', but either he or his printer made a mistake and the name ended up as *lutraria*. Mistake or not, under the rules, *lutraria* it had to remain. The misnamed Otter Shell does indeed live in the mud, along foreshores and in estuaries. It has similar habits to the gaper but has a thinner shell that gapes at both ends. Being fragile, Otter Shells tend to be washed up in fragments rather than whole. Piles of their shattered shells have been found in prehistoric kitchen-middens near the coast, especially in Ireland. Some of the shells were shaped into blades, suggesting that, having consumed the contents, our thrifty forebears then turned the shells into cutting tools. Otter Shells are still eaten in the northern and western isles, as well dug up for angling bait. In Scotland, smooth shells like this were often called 'duickies'. On Herm in the Channel Islands, where Otter Shells were also eaten, they were known as 'clumps'.

Tellins and furrow-shells

Tellins (Tellinidae) have thin, flattened, paired shells and are common on sandy shores, where their delicate, soft colours – pink, orange, buff, yellow or white – ensure they attract the eye of shell-gatherers. In Scotland, shells like this would be threaded together to make shell bracelets or necklaces known as 'motheries'. The live tellin burrows in the sand near the low-water mark, where it filters seawater with the help of a siphon. Though too small to be worth eating by themselves, tellins are used in steamed seafood dishes such as paella or as drink snacks. Anglers dig them up as bait, searching for the telltale lumps of sand that mark buried tellin. Tellins with pink rays are known as sunset-shells.

A related group of clams with pale, fragile shells is the genus *Abra*, otherwise known as furrow shells (Scrobiculariidae). In 1957, a new warm-water species was discovered and happily named *Abra cadabra*. Alas, the magic failed, for just a few years later, the mollusc was renamed *Theora cadabra*, which, as others have pointed out, is no fun at all.

Piddocks *Pholadidae*

We are told that piddocks are boring molluscs. They drill into peat, clay or even solid rock, while two species specialise in submerged wood. A piddock slowly grinds out a passage with the filed blade of its deceptively thin shell, effectively a one-way journey, for since its shell is broadest at the front, retreat is impossible. The toughest piddock is the Rock-borer, which can grind its way into stone like a power tool (albeit on the slowest of speeds) and is responsible for those mysterious holes you sometimes find in limestone pebbles on the beach.

Piddocks contain an enzyme, pholasin, that emits an eerie blue-green glow at night. It transfers to the human skin when piddocks are handled, and if the raw flesh is chewed, it is said to create luminous, flame-like breath. The bioluminescent chemical has been isolated from farmed piddocks and used to test athletes for signs of infection. The over-hectic activity of white blood corpuscles that comes as a result of training too hard creates a piddock-like

Piddock shells.

glow when combined with pholasin and indicates that it is time to take a rest. The British sailing team took the piddock test with them to the Beijing Olympics in 2008.[50]

Shipworms *Teredinidae*

At one time it was thought that shipworms really were worms. Not until 1733 did someone spot two small shells clinging to the rear end of a 'worm' and realised that it was, in fact, an odd-looking mollusc. Shipworms are wood-boring piddocks that have taken the next logical step and become long and tubular, reducing the shell to minute proportions in the process. Most of the animal consists of a fleshy siphon ten times the length of the shell, with grinding gear consisting of two sharp plates known as pallets. As the shipworm chews through the wood, it lines its tunnel with a layer of warm and insulating lime.

When the hulls of large ships were made of wood, shipworms could be a disaster. Linnaeus called them 'calamitas navium'. Shipworms are the main reason why the Royal Navy went to the immense expense of copper-bottoming its warships. In 1730, shipworms threatened the very existence of the Netherlands when they honeycombed that country's protective dykes, and in the 1920s, they caused millions of dollars of damage to San Francisco harbour. Yet the animals that do the damage are rarely seen. Like piddocks, shipworms are one-way diggers, leaving only a small exterior hole but a progressively larger tunnel as they eat their way into the wood. A shipworm's tunnel serves as a refuge rather than a larder, for instead of digesting wood cellulose, it filter-feeds small algae and other particles from the water. Now that boats are made of metal or fibreglass, shipworms are no longer feared and have, for the most part, returned to their ancestral habitat of floating logs.

A shipworm's distinctive grinding plates are said to have given the engineer Marc Brunel (father of the better-known Isambard) the idea for a patent tunnelling shield, with which he proposed to dig the first tunnel beneath the Thames in London. After various mishaps, and twice being abandoned after the river broke in, the tunnel was completed in 1843 and later accommodated the East London railway.

Oysters *Ostreidae*

VN: ooastyn (Isle of Man), pan-door (E. Scot.)

British 'native oysters' have long been famous for their flavour and quality. Though smaller and flatter than those from the Mediterranean, they taste better. An export trade began in Roman times, when naturally occurring oysters were pickled in barrels and transported by sea and land all the way to gourmet establishments in Rome. Even then, the best oysters came from the south-east coast, around Richborough and Whitstable Bay in Kent, or from the Pyefleet Channel near the old British capital of Colchester.

Oyster-beds are found in warm, clear inlets, sheltered from rough seas but scoured twice a day by the tide. An oyster cements itself to the seabed and feeds by endlessly pumping water past a filter in its gill-chamber that collects diatoms and other tiny algae for digesting. On such a diet, it grows slowly: native oysters take three years to breed and four to reach a marketable size.

Nature compensates the oyster for a dull, sedentary existence with an interesting sex life. The same oysters can be male or female at different times. Those whose turn it is to be female spawn together at the full moon in high summer when the water is at its warmest. Each oyster produces thousands of tiny free-living larvae known as 'spat' (the process is called 'spatting'), which live in the plankton for a couple of weeks before settling down on the seafloor, often on the shells of their ancestors, so that successive generations of oysters build up into a reef. By ancient custom, oysters are left alone to replenish their numbers between Easter and Lammas, that is, between the first full moons of May and August (the months without an 'r'). This close season is no loss since oysters lose condition when spatting, becoming stringy and tasteless. They are traditionally fattened up or 'greened' when the September tides bring in plenty of algae. Clean water is essential for the process, since the spat cannot establish when a film of mud covers the shells.

Native oysters were dredged by shallow-drafted oyster smacks, custom-designed for sailing in shallow waters. They were also farmed by collecting spat or young shells and fattening them up in special oyster pits. Those found around Mersea on the Essex coast were renowned for the green lining to their shells, which they acquire from a diet rich in green algae and which gave them a special flavour. As the demand for oysters soared in the nineteenth century, many were farmed by suspending oyster baskets or trays above specially levelled and harrowed beds. Predators such as crabs, starfish and sting-winkles, as well as any other sealife that might compete with the oysters for food and space, were weeded out as far as possible. Until around 1900, this system seemed to be sustainable, and railways supplied vast quantities of fresh oysters to Billingsgate in London. At the height of the trade, 7 million oysters were produced each year from the River Colne alone.

Then it all started to go wrong. One reason was that sewage and industrial pollution affected the rivers close to the oyster-beds. When those in Langstone Harbour were polluted by a sewage outfall, the oyster-loving Dean of Winchester died of typhoid. Another growing problem was a protozoan parasite, *Bonamia ostreae*, which devastated neglected oyster-beds during and after the First World War. In an attempt to increase supply, some farmers introduced the larger American Blue-point Oyster, which was set in the beds as 'seed oysters' and left to grow to marketable size. In the long run this was another disaster, for it unwittingly introduced a predator, the American Sting-winkle, and a competitor for space, the Slipper Limpet, which, between them, ruined many long-established beds on the south coast. The *coup de grâce* was the frozen winters of 1947 and 1963, which between them killed off most of the stock. More recently, floods and chemical pollution from anti-fouling paint on boats have added to the pressure on the native oyster. The government has now placed them on the UK Biodiversity Action Plan with the aim of trying to secure a recovery and a sustainable fishery in the few places where they are still collected.

The fall of the British oyster has to some extent been made good by the success of cultivated foreign oysters. The first to be introduced was the Portuguese, or Rock, oyster, which was used to boost the failing beds in the River Blackwater in 1926. The strain eventually died out and survives today only as government brood stock in the Menai Strait. But since the 1960s, the Pacific form, known as the Japanese Oyster, has met with more success, and it has been established at more than 300 oyster farms around the British coast, as well as in Ireland. Japanese oysters are larger and narrower than natives, and stocks need constant replenishment, as the species does not breed well in British waters

Japanese, or Pacific, Oysters, the most widely cultivated oyster today.

(where it nonetheless has the capacity to escape into the wild). Most oysters swallowed by the British are now this species. To the connoisseur, it lacks the sharp, tangy taste of the native as well as the subtle regional differences in taste – some sweet, others salty or with a mineral flavour that told an expert exactly where it had originated from. Natives, much interbred with European stock, are still grown in select beds, especially in the inlets of the Essex coast, though many of those on the market are not produced in Britain but Ireland or France. Colchester is currently lobbying the European Union for special protected status for 'Colchester Natives'.

Swallowing the oyster

'He was a bold man,' remarked Jonathan Swift, 'that first ate an oyster.' His contemporary, the playwright John Gay, agreed that, whoever he was, he must have had a death-wish:

> The man had sure a palate covered o'er
> With brass or steel, that on the rocky shore
> First broke the cozy oyster's pearly coat,
> And risked the living morsel down his throat.[51]

The merits of swallowing cold, raw oysters have been hotly debated. 'If you don't love life,' suggested Eleanor Clark, 'you can't enjoy an oyster; there is a shock of freshness to it; some piercing intuition of the sea and all its weeds and breezes. They shiver you up for a split second.'[52] Ambrose Bierce was less enthusiastic: 'A slimy, gobby shellfish which civilization gives man the harditude to eat . . . The shells are often given to the poor.'[53]

Oysters, like snails, are traditionally served by the dozen. Opening a live oyster is a skill, as the rough, tightly clamped shells offer little purchase for a blade; the operation has long been known as 'shucking' an oyster. Oyster knives have a large handle, a short, strong blade and a hilt to guard against slips. Shucking an oyster is really just a matter of deciding which end is which, and then using brute force. The oyster is held wrapped in a teatowel in one hand and the knife shoved in at the hinge end. The blade is twisted to break the hinge and then slid along the length of the shell to the other end, where the flesh is attached to the shell by a muscle. Once that is cut, the top shell comes away, leaving the flesh in the bottom one in which the oyster is served. Dead oysters reveal themselves by their partly open, gaping shells. Occasionally one is sealed shut by gluey sand but makes a distinctive sound when tapped. Such oysters are called 'clackers' and should not be eaten.

Swallowing live oysters is a relatively modern fad. Before the increased population of industrial Britain forced up their price, oysters were cheap at three a penny and were eaten by the poor as well as the rich (in Britain, few places were more than 50 miles (80km) from the nearest oyster-bed). They were so popular that buried oyster shells often turn up in the back garden of any cottage over 150 years old. As the streetwise Cockney Sam Weller remarked to Mr Pickwick, 'poverty and oysters seems to go together. The poorer a place is, the greater call there seems to be for oysters.'[54] In Sam's view, if a poor man was reduced to his last few pennies and didn't know which way to turn, he would probably rush out to the nearest stall and drown his sorrows in oysters. On fish days, oysters made a welcome change from salt herrings and could be served in a variety of ways, sometimes raw but more often stewed, fried, roasted or grilled. They could be made into sauces, stuffed into capons and geese or added to soup. There were even oyster sausages. A steak-and-kidney pudding into which a few oysters have been thoughtfully inserted is still known as a Pickwick Pie. Today a still more common way to serve cooked oysters is to wrap them inside strips of streaky bacon, to be served at parties as 'angels on horseback'.

Oyster guzzling is one of the more bizarre competitive sports and seems to have a long pedigree. Perhaps the champion of all time was the Roman Emperor Vitellius, who is said to have downed a thousand at a sitting. More recent contenders include the German statesman Bismarck and the England cricket captain A. P. F. 'Percy' Chapman, who once consumed 208 oysters 'before witnesses'. Competitive swallowing is indulged at the annual festival at Hillsborough in County Down, where in 2003, Rune Naeri from Norway downed 187 in three minutes, seeing off the hotly fancied local man Jim Glackin. 'Oysters are supposed to be an aphrodisiac,' noted another contestant, 'but I think that's only true for the first three dozen.'[55]

Those who prefer to consume oysters in more sedate circumstances can frequent an oyster bar. The world's most famous oyster bar, Wiltons, began in 1742 as a street stall selling oysters, shrimps and cockles to passers-by. It received a Royal Warrant as 'Purveyor of Oysters' from Queen Victoria in 1884 and moved to its present premises at Jermyn Street exactly a hundred years later. The other top London bar, Bentley's, opened in 1916 with its own oyster-beds at West Mersea near Colchester. Wheelers in Whitstable is a rare survivor of the smaller local oyster bar and has not greatly changed since the days when it purveyed local seafood to the first arrivals from the Crab and Winkle railway line.

The town of Colchester has owned the exclusive fishing rights to its oyster-beds since the Middle Ages. The fishery is opened in style each September, when the Mayor, the Town Sergeant and the chief of the Colchester Oyster Company set off in a sailing barge with 40 guests from Brightlingsea to visit the ancient beds in the Pyefleet Channel near Mersea

Island. Once there, the proclamation of 1256 affirming the town's fishing rights is read out and the fishery declared open. The Mayor then drinks a loyal toast to the Queen, traditionally a nip of gin, followed by a serving of gingerbread. Back in town, everyone sits down to an oyster lunch. A month later, on the eve of St Denis's Day (21 October), a grander feast is held in Colchester's Moot Hall with 400 honoured guests, numerous toasts and speeches and selections from the classics playing in the background. More recently, the town has run a medieval-themed summer oyster 'fayre' (jousts, jugglers, bric-a-brac), while the local Labour Party, not to be outdone, hosts an alternative festival, a 'hearty and entertaining meal' for the town's pensioners.[56]

At Falmouth, where oysters are dredged by what is said to be the last sail-powered fishing fleet in the industrial world, the festival is in October, when boat races are held in the harbour and seafood served on the shore. Whitstable hosts another ancient festival coinciding with St James's Day on 25 July (they say that whoever eats oysters on St James's Day will want for nothing). The first catch of the season is blessed and presented to the Mayor and then drawn through the town by shire horses, followed by the civic party and the town band. The fun includes a regatta, boat rides and a carnival, and the festive week ends with a solemn blessing of the waters and a fireworks display. In the olden days, a boat was blown up, but that has been deemed unacceptable in our more safety-conscious times.[57]

The grandest festival of them all is the Galway Oyster Festival ('International' was recently added to the title to stress its world status), which celebrates the mystic union of oysters and Guinness. Among the highlights is a great oyster-opening, in which contestants are given 30 shells each to open as speedily as they may. The contestant rings a hand-bell when finished and presents the result to the judges on a tray. Points are awarded for neatness and good appearance and deducted for cut oysters and damaged shells. This is not a lengthy contest: in 2007, the winner, from Sweden, opened all his in 2 minutes 40 seconds.[58]

Along the Thames estuary there used to be piles of oyster shells left by the dredgers. Around St James's Day, children would cash in by building 'grotters' – piles of sand decorated with oyster shells. The trick was to cover the sand with the shells so that the grotter looked as though it was built entirely of shells. The custom is said to have its origin in makeshift shelly shrines to St James, but grotter-making was a competitive schoolboy enterprise done in the same spirit as 'a penny for the guy'. Raising a few pennies for a well-built grotter might seem harmless enough, but the local authorities thought otherwise and did their best to stamp it out. The tradition still survives in the more liberal-minded Whitstable as part of its St James's Day fun.

Literary oysters

The word oyster comes from the ancient Greek word for bone, *osteon*, by way of the Norman-French *oistre*. Surprisingly few places are named after oysters, but there is an Oysterfleet on Canvey Island in Essex and an Oyster Ness near the Humber in Yorkshire. To be 'as close as a Kentish oyster' is more complimentary than it sounds. It originally meant 'all sorted out', in the sense of 'all sealed tight'. 'The world's your oyster' is another old phrase, reminding us that the world is full of opportunities, spread out before us like a living buffet. Shakespeare gave the phrase to Pistol in *The Merry Wives of Windsor*: 'Why then, the world's mine oyster which I with sword will open.'[59]

Oysters can sum up a man's character. P. G. Wodehouse's Mosley-like character Roderick Spode, the leader of the British Blackshorts, had 'the sort of eye that can open an oyster at sixty paces'.[60] 'The first man gets the oyster, the second man gets the shell' was the philosophy of the American plutocrat Andrew Carnegie. Towards the end of his life, Oscar Wilde reflected: 'The world was my oyster, but I used the wrong fork.'[61]

In *The Walrus and the Carpenter*, Lewis Carroll's masterpiece of nonsense, oysters are the victims of a mean trick: summoned from the sea for a promised treat, they end up as lunch. Carroll's illustrator John Tenniel was faced with the problem of how to portray oysters (shown as true British 'natives') wearing shoes, which, in the rhyme, 'were clean and neat –/ And this was odd, because, you know,/ They hadn't any feet'.[62] He compromised by showing them with thread-like legs, like the byssus threads of mussels, ending in tiny shoes. The picnic ends with a picture of a pile of empty shells, a sadly prescient premonition of the fate of native oysters in the twentieth century – not from greedy walruses, though, but from disease.

'But wait a bit . . . ' (engraving), by John Tenniel for Lewis Carroll's Through the Looking Glass. *The soon-to-be-devoured oysters are the native British kind.*

The poem inspired John Lennon to write, 'I am the Walrus', though he forgot that the walrus was, in fact, the villain of the piece. His friend Donovan set the actual poem to music in his 1971 album *HMS Donovan*. Presumably it also inspired the young Bill Oddie to write, 'Taking my Oyster for Walkies', which first appeared on the BBC Radio 4 show *I'm Sorry, I'll Read That Again* in 1964 and described Bill's helpless and unexplained attraction for various molluscs.

Mock oysters

Various groups of marine bivalves are called oysters from a general family resemblance, though they are not necessarily close relatives of true oysters. Those with backwardly projecting spines called thorny, or spiny, oysters are closer to scallops. They are not eaten but are sought after by shell collectors and are also sometimes introduced into saltwater aquariums as living ornaments.

Saddle oysters (Anomiidae) have a deep notch on the larger shell, with projecting wings like the pommel and cantle of a saddle. The thin, brittle shells are lined with mother-of-pearl and are sold as seaside knick-knacks, known as jingle-shells from the sound they make when threaded together on a string.

Pearl oysters

True pearl oysters belong to a non-British family, the non-edible Pterridae, or feathered oysters. But pearl oysters were imported to Britain, generally from the Far East, in large numbers and can be considered part of our cultural invertebrate legacy. The pearl was always more than a mere freak of nature. With its pale iridescence, it seemed to be made from the fused light of the moon and other celestial bodies. Like the moon, a pearl was an emblem of femininity as well as purity and virginity (which is why the Virgin Queen, the ageing Elizabeth I, was generally shown festooned with them). An ancient legend held that pearls were 'born' when an oyster crept out of the sea just before dawn to drink the heavenly dew and light from the moon, stars and rising sun. Christianity glossed the story in the following way: the sea is the world and its pearls are the doctors of the church. Sinners secrete the pearls away, but the wise person is 'a pearl of great price'. All Bible-reading Christians would also have known Christ's words on the subject in St Matthew's gospel: 'The kingdom of heaven is like unto a merchant man, seeking goodly pearls, who, when he had found one of great price, went and sold all that he had, and bought it.'

Pearls take between three and six years to develop, and all but the most expensive are now made from cultured oysters. British oysters secrete mother-of-pearl concretions that can turn into pearls but they are of a distinctive lumpy type known as 'baroque and blind' and unsuitable for necklaces (though several were incorporated into a gold ring on display in Colchester's Town Hall). Historically, our own pearl fishery came from the land, not the sea, and not from oysters but freshwater mussels.

Devil's toenails

VN: crouching shell or crouching stone, cuckoo shell, milner's thumb

Fossil oysters have thick, curved shells. They are so common in some limestone rocks that people collected them as 'Devil's toenails'. In ground-up form they were said to have medical powers. In Lincolnshire, where they were known as 'milner's thumbs', powdered fossil could cure the sore back of a sick horse in two to three days. In Scotland, where they were *clach crubain*, or 'crouching shells', the crushed stone could cure pain in the joints, a power suggested by the contorted shape of the 'toenail'. Crushed fossil oyster is still an ingredient of Chinese folk medicine, where it is known as *long gu*, or 'dragon bone'.

Cephalopods *Cephalopoda*

Cephalopod means head-footed – a reference to the topsy-turvy shape of octopus and squid, which seem to bear 'legs' on their heads. They are familiar as images and as food – the octopus often appears as a seaside icon on children's buckets and spades, and many people nowadays enjoy squid or calamari – but less so as living organisms, at least in British waters. The name of one group of warm-water cuttlefish – nautilus – has launched numerous submarines, from the fictional one in Jules Verne's *Twenty Thousand Leagues Under the Sea* to the world's first atomic powered ship.

Squid *Loliginidae*

VN: barr'l-arse or baa'ld-arse (NE Eng.), calamari, inkfish, paddylincum, padelenca (Cornwall)

Irish: *Iair bhan*
Eggs: sea-mops

Squid is one of those obscure names that sounds right without having any understood meaning. Of all counties, Cornwall seems to have the closest cultural affinity with squid and cuttlefish, where fishermen knew the big ones by the dialect word 'padelenica' and small, 'boneless' ones as 'paddylincums'. Yet until its post-war entry into mainstream cuisine as calamari, the British used squid mainly as bait. They can be caught easily enough by fastening a pilchard to a line and pulling in when a tug is felt. Yet fishing for live squid has its hazards. The consequence of carelessly gaffing a large squid is likely to be a tremendous outpouring of water and ink as the animal struggles for its life. Getting drenched in squid ink is best avoided for it can be difficult to wash off.

The black concealing ink released by cuttlefish and squid has become a powerful metaphor for obscuration, for example in the burying of bad news or unpalatable facts by a cloak of lies. In his famous essay on 'Politics and the English Language', George Orwell noted that 'the great enemy of clear language is insincerity. When there is a gap between one's real and one's declared aims, one turns as it were instinctively to lying words and exhausted idioms, like a cuttlefish squirting out ink.'[63]

The one that most haunts our imaginations is the giant squid, a legendary beast that would supposedly attack large ships without hesitation (most notably Captain Nemo's submarine *Nautilus*). Giant squids do exist, though they are not as large and nowhere near as ferocious as they are portrayed in fiction, while the largest are deep-sea animals out of the normal range of divers (though their sucker marks are often seen on whales). There have been only 15 recorded strandings and nine captures of giant squid in British waters – the first off the Dingle in Ireland in 1673 and the most recent in a trawler's net off the Hebrides in January 2002. Our giant is *Architeuthis dux*, the Atlantic Giant Squid, which measures a relatively modest three to ten metres long (the largest ever giant squid, dragged up off New Zealand in 1880, supposedly measured 18.5 metres when fully unrolled).

The giant squid now on display in the Natural History Museum has won more sympathy for the erstwhile terror of the deep. Called Archie (short for *Architeuthis* – despite its name, it is probably a female), it was captured alive off the Falkland Islands in 2004 and measures 8.6 metres. For its acrylic tank, the Museum hired the same people that made tanks for Damien Hurst, where Archie now swims forever in a mixture of formaline and saltwater. A more modest, only half-grown, three-metre squid caught in 2002 is now a star feature at the National Maritime Museum Aquarium in Plymouth. Preserved in its own tank as a 'Creature of the Deep', it lacks the usual long pair of feeding tentacles (lost when the creature was caught by a trawler), which would have taken it to about five and a half metres.

Tall tales of huge squids inspired the legend of the Kraken, a gigantic sea monster so malignant and powerful it could drag sailing ships down into the depths. Tennyson borrowed a bit of that and a bit of the Biblical whale Leviathan for his sonnet where 'far, far beneath in the abysmal sea/ His ancient dreamless, unintended sleep/ The Kraken sleepeth'.[64] Tennyson's squid lies motionless at the bottom of the sea, like the wreck of the *Titanic*, but on Judgement Day he will awake and 'in roaring he shall rise and on the surface die', which is indeed what giant squids generally do when dragged out of the depths.

The science-fiction writer John Wyndham took Tennyson's slumbering squid as the title of his 1953 novel *The Kraken Wakes*. Wyndham's Krakens are aliens, seeded in the deep sea by invaders from outer space. In true sea-monster fashion they attack shipping and eventually appear on land, sending out betentacled sea-tanks to capture hapless humans at the seaside ports. The aliens also melt the icecaps, causing sea levels to rise, with attendant mayhem and social collapse. By the time the skids are on the squids, four fifths of the human race has been wiped out.

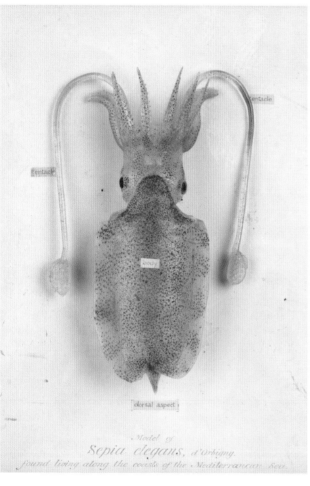

Cuttlefish *Sepiidae*

VN: cuddle (Cornwall), diaklum (Isle of Man), footho (Orkney), hosack (Scot.), hose-fish (Scot.), inkfish, inkspewer (Kent), man-sucker (Kent), musk or musk-shell (NE Eng.), pen, skeeto (Orkney), squib (Kent)

Though few of us might relish being cuddled by a cuttlefish, Edward Step reasoned that the old Cornish fisherman's name of 'cuddle' referred to 'the embracing action of its arms.'[65] Cuttlefish are best known from their internal 'bone' known as a cuttle or cuttlebone. (In squid, the corresponding, thinner bone is known as a pen.) The light and porous cuttlebone acts as a buoyancy tank so that, by pumping air in and out, the animal can rise and fall in the water with the ease of a submarine. Its best-known use is as a source of calcium-rich seafood for cage birds (it doubles as a beak-sharpener). Cuttlebone is sold in pet shops and can also be gathered fresh from the sea (though, unless thoroughly dried, it soon smells of rotting crab). Another sign of cuttlefish offshore is their black egg-masses, or 'sea grapes', which wash up in rough weather; the corresponding egg-masses of squid are 'sea mops'.

In the days before blotting-paper, cuttlebone was also used to make 'pounce', a fine powder for sprinkling over wet ink to hasten the drying. Another literary cuttlefish product was a fine ink used for sketching and drawing. Initially black, it dries to sepia, the brownish colour named after the cuttlefish's scientific name *Sepia officinalis*. Sepia ink is extracted from the animal's ink sacs, dried and ground and then mixed with another invertebrate product, shellac (made from scale aphids). Though long replaced by cheaper alternatives, sepia ink is still available from specialised outlets. A more frequent use of cuttlefish ink today is as food flavouring (*nero di sepia*), bringing that authentic whiff of the sea to pasta and risotto dishes. Powdered cuttlebone was also once used as a dentrifice, or toothpowder.

Above left: *Glass model of a cuttlefish by Leopold and Rudolf Blaschka.*

Left: *Cuttlefish 'bones', one of the lightest yet strongest substances in the natural world.*

We have not yet exhausted the potential of cuttlebones to aid mankind. They combine incredible lightness – a cubic centimetre weighs only 0.06 grams – with great internal strength obtained through a latticework of calcium carbonate resembling the metal skeleton of a high-rise building. Strengthened further by a dip in metal-solution, cuttlebone shows potential as a feather-light superconductor for devices ranging from space satellites to mobile phones.

A mini-cuttlefish occasionally found in rockpools in the south-west is the Little Cuttlefish. Being only two centimetres long, with large eyes, it is small enough to catch with a shrimp net (though it shoots backwards when alarmed) and cute enough for children to want to take home. This is a pity, for they are impossible to keep and rarely even survive the journey back. Irish trawlermen, who catch and discard such diminutive cuttlefish by the thousand, call them 'Mickey Mouse squids'.

LE POULPE COLOSSAL

Octopuses *Octopodidae*

The seafarers of ancient Greece held the octopus in high regard, painting its image on their vases and wearing octopus medallions as security. The octopus is too rare in British waters to form part of native folk culture, and we seem to lack nicknames for them such as the American 'devilfish'. The two British species live mainly offshore and are rarely seen in rockpools. The plural, incidentally, is octopuses. Octopus is a Latinised Greek word (meaning, of course, eight legs) and so 'octopi', strictly speaking, is non-grammatical.

Octopuses are sometimes kept in aquariums, though they are formidable escape artists, capable of lifting heavy lids off tanks, squeezing along narrow inlet pipes or slithering through surprisingly narrow cracks. In November 2008, an octopus called Otto, annoyed by a bright light shining into its eyes, clambered laboriously out and squirted water at the offending object, thus short-circuiting the entire aquarium. 'Once we saw him juggling hermit crabs,' recalled the director of the Sea Star Aquarium in Coburg. 'Another time he threw stones against the glass. And from time to time he completely rearranges his tank to make it suit his own taste better – much to the distress of the other inhabitants.'[66]

Those who have studied octopus behaviour invariably conclude that the animal is concealing a formidable intelligence inside its alien form. J. Z. Young, who set captive octopuses all kinds of memory tests and puzzles, considered them as intelligent as dogs. They have learning skills and are capable of solving simple problems and of recognising their keepers. Octopuses are certainly sentient enough to become bored and depressed in captivity. Duly impressed with their abilities, the government included them as honorary vertebrates in its sinisterly named Animals (Scientific Procedures) Act 1986 and also in anti-cruelty legislation. The octopus would probably impress us more had it not been for three blows of fate. First, we associate intelligence with animals like us, with only four appendages, and so eat octopuses without

Left: *The mythical giant octopus as imagined by Count Georges de Buffon in his* Natural History of Molluscs *(1805).*

461

a qualm (in science fiction, aliens are routinely given octopus-like eyes and tentacles). Second, they are abandoned almost immediately by their parents and so never acquire their experience and must rely purely on instinct to survive. Third, octopuses do not live long enough to acquire the accumulated life experience of an elephant or a dolphin. They are imprisoned by their biology.

The spreading tentacles of the octopus are a potent metaphor for reaching out. The name is used by a communications company, a travel agency, an investment company and a publishing group.

Belemnites

VN: bat stones, bullets, devil's fingers, ghostly candles, St Peter's fingers, thunder arrows, thunderbolts, thunder stones

Before the science of geology, people were mystified by inexplicable blackish, dart-like objects found sticking out from chalk-faces or rocks by the sea shore. What made the darts doubly strange was that they were black, smooth and sharp-ended, as if manufactured. Some held that they were the burnt remains of missiles discharged by the God of thunder and sent hurling down to earth in bolts of lightning. Others believed that they were darts shot at men and their animals by mischievous elves or possibly the spurs worn by secret goblins of the night. They were known in different parts as dart-stones or thunder-stones or, alternatively, elf-arrows or elf-stones. In western Scotland they were thought to have something to do with bats and were so were called bat stones. Since magic operated by cancelling like with like, possession of the stones could guard against being struck by lightning or shot at by elves.

'Terrible apprehensions are raised of Fayrie stones and elves' spurs', wrote Sir Thomas Browne in the mid-seventeenth century. That the stones might be useful in medicine was suggested by their sharp, dart-like points, which by analogy could alleviate sharp, rheumatic pains (the divine benevolence revealed in such shapes gave them yet another folk name: St Peter's fingers). In due course, they were identified as the protective guards of an extinct squid-like sea creature, but they kept the older name

of belemnites, named from the Greek *belemnites*, a spear-point or arrowhead. The other parts of the living animal were soft and so, as in living cuttlefish, they rotted away leaving only the tougher guard or cuttlebone to join the fossil record.

Ammonites

VN: conger eels (Dorset), crampstones (W Scot.), Horns of Ammon, hymenanny (Isle of Man), snakestones, snail guggles (Glos.)

Ammonites are archetypal British fossils. Their elegant, coiled shells, which vary from the size of a small coin to that of a cartwheel, are often displayed in rock shops and used to decorate walls and fireplaces. The shell is all that remains of extinct nautilus-like animals that teemed in the world's seas at the time of the dinosaurs (and perished with them). Long before their true nature was discovered, they were known as ammonites, after the curly horns of the Greek god Ammon, who was traditionally shown with a pair of them sprouting from his head. Small ammonites were carried as good luck charms or tucked under the pillow at night to bring sweet (or possibly horny) dreams.

Some said that ammonites were the remains of wicked fairies punished by being turned into snakes and then into stone. At Whitby in Yorkshire, where they were known as snakestones, they were thought to be the remains of snakes banished by St Hilda, the founder of Whitby Abbey. Local entrepreneurs collected them and, after carving a little snake's head on the shell, sold them as relics. Today, three ammonites stand guard on Whitby's coat-of-arms, and St Hilda's public-spirited action was commemorated in a genus of ammonites called *Hildoceras*, or 'Hilda's head'. Keynsham, Bristol, has a similar tradition involving its own holy woman, St Keyne.

By the law of analogies, snakestones could be helpful in treating snakebites and, more generally, were reputed to guard against impotence, blindness and infertility. In the Western Isles, where they were known as 'crampstones', farm animals with cramped muscles were washed in water in which the stones had been steeped.

The shape of ammonites, so similar to the scrolled

A classic ammonite (Asteroseras) on the beach at Lyme Regis, Dorset. The fossilised shell is all that remains of a sea animal that flourished at the time of the dinosaurs.

capitals of Ionic columns, inspired a kind of rustic counterpoint to classical architecture known as the Ammonite Order. Its main practitioner was the London architect George Dance, who first used it on the since-abolished Shakespeare Gallery on Pall Mall. Duly impressed by his work, a Lewes builder and amateur geologist, felicitously named Amon Wilds, began to carve his own rustic ammonites as a kind of trademark, a style continued by his son, who helped to build the Regency terraces in Brighton, cutting the odd ammonite wherever he could. Ammonites still decorate Amon Wilds' home on Lewes High Street – later, by another happy coincidence, to become the home of Gideon Mantell, the Sussex physician who discovered the first dinosaur.

SPINY-SKINS
Echinodermata

The Common Brittlestar can cover the bed of sheltered waters in a gorgon's nest of serpentine arms.

The spiny-skins, or echinoderms, are a group of entirely marine organisms, of which the most familiar are the starfish and the sea urchins. They are an ancient phylum, which has been producing fossils of various kinds since the Cambrian period, more than 550 million years ago. While most life from worms onwards has a bilateral symmetry, with one half of the body mirroring the other, echinoderms have gone out on a limb with their pentameral, or five-fold, geometry. This is most obvious with the starfish, which looks like a child's drawing of a star, with five triangular 'arms' radiating from the central point. Some echinoderms hardly look like animals at all (at least until they move), more like cast-away toys: starfish resembling stuffed cushions or the shiner on top of the Christmas tree, and spineless sea urchins like hard pink balls (or transformed into maritime-flavoured lamp shades). Others reminded us more of vegetables: sea cucumbers and sea potatoes. Some sea urchins even look vaguely like minerals.

Starfish *Asteroidea*

VN: asteroids, badger or badges (NE Eng.), cashlings (Norfolk), cassock-cats, cleavers (Yorks), cramps, crossfish, crossfit (Scot.), Devil's hand, five-fingered jack, fivefingers, fiveleg, fivetoes, frones or frawns (NE Eng.), hornheads (Norfolk), keelfraw (North Eng.), krossick (Orkney), miller's thumb (NE Eng.), old five-fingers, red-caps (Yorks), scoukie (Scot.), sea star, seathorn (Yorks), thornhead, thorns

The starfish has long been seen as a kind of living star, an emblem of hope and compassion. According to one story, starfish were born at the bottom of the ocean as reflections of the stars twinkling in the heavens above. In Catholic Europe, they became associated with the Virgin Mary as *Stella Maris*, or stars of the sea, a sign of salvation in troubled waters

Dried-out starfish stranded on a Norfolk beach.

Spandel for Galla Placidia *(paint on canvas, using dried starfish), at Salthouse Church on the Norfolk coast, by Margie Britz and Liz McGowan, inspired by mosaics in the Mausoleum of Galla Placidia in Ravenna.*

or, more broadly, as a talisman for troubled times. In a modern extension of the legend, gold starfish pins have been marketed as an anti-bullying symbol in schools.

The ancients were impressed by the ease in which the starfish grew a new limb or managed to regenerate after being cut in half, seeing in this an echo of the regeneration of the soul after death. A fisherman in Jersey brutally combined both images when he ripped off a leg of a starfish to make the sign of a cross.[1] Strangely, given its prominence in Christian symbolism, the starfish is not mentioned in the Bible even once.

Another aspect of the starfish that intrigues us is the ability of its five limbs to work together as a team; in a two- or four-legged creature, we might take this for granted, but the starfish seems somehow more robotic, with satellite organs radiating inwards to a central control point. The way each limb works for the common benefit makes the starfish a potent

image of political co-operation. The European Union used it in 1992 as a symbol of the single market, portraying the organisation as an eager yellow starfish rushing forward with outstretched limbs and a smile on its silly little face.

The name starfish is very old, dating back in print to the sixteenth century. Most of the many dialect- or folk-names focus on a starfish's tough, prickly skin (thornhead, cleavers), its five-limbed shape, resembling fingers or toes (five-fingers, fivetoes) or a warty hand (devil's hand) or, ignoring the fifth limb, as a cross (crossfish).[2] Most of these names are appropriate to the archetypal Common Starfish. The one often portrayed cast ashore on the sand in posters of the seaside is more likely to be the Sand Star, which has a stiff, angular shape like the stars awarded at primary school for good behaviour. The cushion stars (Asterinidae) are stubbier and well-padded and are also known as starlets. The sunstars (Solasteridae), by contrast, have up to a dozen radiating limbs, like the dials of a clock or a child's drawing of a smiling sun.

Some claim that large starfish can bite or sting, but though they are powerful enough to prise open mussels and clams, there is no evidence of them harming humans. Fishermen dislike them for what Sue Clifford calls 'their light-fingered prowess in decimating shellfish.'[3] An enormous gathering of starfish in Cornwall in 2004 was judged to have cleared about 4000 tonnes of young mussels over four months.

Occasionally, large numbers of starfish, especially

A Common Sunstar on a bed of brittlestars at St Abbs, Berwickshire.

Sand Stars, are washed ashore in mass strandings. These are often gathered and sold as seaside souvenirs. The Norfolk-based artists Margie Britz and Liz McGowan also use their dried bodies to create designs and images inspired by the East Anglian landscape.[4] One of their starfish sculptures links their stiff, stellate arms into a sphere, like a giant dandelion clock (it currently hangs in the hallway of BBC East in Norwich). Others have been raised into heavenly objects, such as sun, moon and stars, in beautiful patterns reminiscent of the ceilings of Byzantine churches. It is an imaginative idea, though even admirers say that starfish art, when viewed close up, is apt to be a bit smelly.

Brittlestars *Ophiuroidea*

VN: basket-stars, ophiuroids, serpent stars, tyed-legs (NE Eng.)

Brittlestars are fragile-looking starfish relatives with round button bodies and five long, serpentine limbs bristling with tube-like false feet. They use their limbs to move about the seabed and also to sweep food into their mouths. The limbs detach readily, hence the name brittlestar, and can be shed like a lizard's tail to confuse predators. Brittle-stars can be extremely abundant in clean, sheltered waters, such as some of the Scottish sea-lochs.

Hundreds can be found on a single square metre of shallow seabed (a submerged mountain off New Zealand inhabited by tens of millions of the creatures was dubbed Brittlestar City).

Brittlestars are not gathered for food, and their impact on our lives is slight. In an allusion to the fickleness of fame, they have lent their name to a literary magazine specialising in short stories and poems, especially of new writers.

Feather-stars, or sea lilies *Crinoidea*

VN: Cuddy's Beads, fairy money, St Cuthbert's Beads, screwstones, star stones

The Feather-star is like a brittlestar that has grown a stalk to anchor it to one spot and whose arms have sprouted feathery projections to form a kind of collecting basket for passing titbits. It is occasionally found in deep rockpools but is more familiar to divers, and related kinds are common in the deep sea.

The animal is a living example of a group of echinoderms once known only as fossils. With their long stalks and outspread heads, they were easily mistaken for plants and were called sea-lilies. Often the rest of the animal has disappeared leaving only the hollow segments of the stalk washed up on the beach. In northern England, they became known as St Cuthbert's Beads or, less formally, Cuddy's Beads, said to be the beads from the rosaries of the great holy man of Lindisfarne. In his poem 'Marmion', Sir Walter Scott referred to the legend where 'St Cuthbert sits, and toils to frame/ The sea-born beads that bear his name.'

In other parts, the beads were picked up as 'fairy money', while pentagonal forms were known as 'star stones'. The impressions they left behind in the rocks were 'screwstones'.

Sea urchins *Echinoidea*

VN: burr (Scot.), echinus, fairy loaves, hairy burr, ivegar or uivigar (Orkney), Manx-cat's-head (Isle of Man), piper-urchin, scadman's heids (Orkney), sea-egg, sea-hedgehog or sea-hog, sea-potato, skates's eggs (NE Eng.)

Gaelic: *conan-mara* (sea-dog), *cragan* or *crogan* (pot), *cragan-feannaig* (pot-stick), *cragan-traghad* (beach-pot), *garbhan* (roughie or burr)

At low tide, spiky sea urchins seem inanimate, sitting passively like mines for the unwary to tread on. Once the tide rolls in, however, they come to life. Hundreds of alien tube feet protrude through perforations in the creature's shell and explore their environment. The animal uses them to breathe, feed and grip the surface, slowly shifting the bulky shell along the sea floor; the spines are used for moving on a flat surface and the tube feet for climbing. At the bottom of the shell around the animal's mouth lies an organ unique to sea urchins called the Aristotle's lantern, named in honour of the great philosopher, who made a minute and scientifically accurate description of it in his *History of Animals*. Analogous to a pair of jaws, the lantern houses the animal's feeding gear, a ring of abrasive teeth adapted for rasping and scraping edible matter from the rocks. The rattle inside the shell of a preserved sea urchin is the broken-off Aristotle's lantern clattering about like a pea in a drum. The only danger a sea urchin presents to us is when we unwittingly tread on one. The spines are brittle and easily snap leaving the points embedded in the skin, and the wound can go septic if not treated.

Our largest and most familiar species is the pinkish, grapefruit-sized Edible Sea Urchin. Its spines fall off after death, leaving an attractive scored pattern, and it is in this state that the empty shells are sold as seaside souvenirs and lampshades. It is also collected for food. Sea urchins are generally harvested during spring tides in winter, when they are held to be at their best, though only one shell in three has anything worth eating, as the animals are killed for a mere mouthful of expensive reddish roe known as coral. It has a clean, tangy taste that, like oysters, is held by aficionados to be the very distillation of the sea. 'There is no sea-food that better synthesises the sea so perfectly as the urchin,' wrote the Catalan gourmand, Julio Cambo. '[It is]

Sea urchin shells from Cornwall – shore life turned to holiday knick-knacks.

an extract of the sea, a breath of a storm, an essence of tempests.'[5]

In Japan, sea urchin roe, known as *uni*, is eaten raw in sushi dishes. Urchins are also gathered in quantity in the West Indies, where they are known as sea-eggs. The taste in France and Spain is for the smaller species such as the Purple Sea Urchin, and all too many of them have been looted unsustainably from rockpools in western Ireland. Known in France as *garotes*, the urchin roe is scooped out in communal feasts known as *garotades*, and some restaurants have got in on the act, inventing ever more elaborate ways of serving them, thus encouraging high prices and overcollection. One of the best-known urchin-eaters was Salvador Dalí who, perhaps drawn by their surreal shape, ate quantities of them at his Catalan hideaway and even designed a handbag based on their spherical and radial symmetries.

The answer to overcollection may be farming. At Hillswick Bay in Shetland, a local entrepreneur has obtained planning permission for a moored pair of experimental cages in which to 'grow' sea urchins for the export trade. Since the prices for prime urchin roe are high, other sea-farmers, eager to diversify, are watching the experiment intently. For home consumption, however, the demand is not for the coral so much as the shells. In the Isles of Scilly, local children used to earn pocket-money by gathering Edible Sea Urchins and selling them to souvenir stalls and shops for drying and varnishing. Many more sea urchins were collected by local divers: around 40,000 in 1984/85 alone.[6] Mercifully, the craze for sea-urchin souvenirs has waned, but the trade has resulted in a serious reduction in sea-urchin populations along the south-west coast, with all kinds of likely knock-on effects on marine ecology.

Sea urchins and hedgehogs share a common name; indeed one of the alternative names for sea urchins is 'sea hedgehog'. Urchin comes from the Norman French word *herichon*, which the English rendered as 'hurcheon' and thence urchin, a word still used in northern dialects for a hedgehog. In Shakespeare's day, an urchin was also a mischievous imp who could transform itself at will into a round, prickly object. The hedgehog analogy extends to scientific names. The Greek word for a hedgehog was *echinos*, and *Echinus* is the generic name of the

Common, or Edible, Sea Urchin. The Irish language takes a slightly different line, calling them *garbhan*, or 'the little rough one'. The ancient Greeks named them after chestnut burrs.

Perhaps the commonest sea urchin is the Shore Urchin, a small species whose green, purple-tipped spines provide the alternative name of purple-tipped urchin. They are easily overlooked, as the urchin camouflages its shell with pebbles, other shells and bits of seaweed. Visitors to the limestone coast of western Ireland will also find vast numbers of Purple Sea Urchins inside self-drilled cavities in the rock, deep purple against white. There seems to be little to feed on in its bare, rocky pools, but the urchins get by from filter-feeding suspended particles brought in from the ocean on each tide. A similar but smaller greenish sea urchin is chiefly memorable for its outsize name: *Strongylocentrotus drobrachiensis*. A deep-sea species with immense spines has been dubbed the Pencil Urchin, also likened to a ball of wool with stuck-in knitting needles.

Heart urchins *Spatangoidea*

AN: sea biscuit, sea potato

Heart urchins are a distinctive type of urchin with flattened, heart-shaped shells and backward-pointing bristles instead of hedgehog-like spines. One roundish species is known as the Sea Potato, while a related order with more flattened shells is known as sand dollars. A heart urchin burrows into sand on the lower shore, leaving a small hole at the surface as the only sign of its existence. It feeds on whatever detritus and small invertebrates it comes across as it tunnels through the wet sand a safe distance below the surface. Beachcombers know heart urchins mainly from the smooth empty shells cast up on the beach.

Fossil sea urchins

VN: chalk eggs, fairy hearts, fairy loaves, fairy stones, jewstones, pundstones or pundibs, quoitstones, shepherd's crowns, shepherd's mitres, shepherd's purses, snake-eggs, sugarloaves

Animals similar to modern sea urchins and sea potatoes were common in the ancient seas when the chalk was being formed a hundred million years ago.

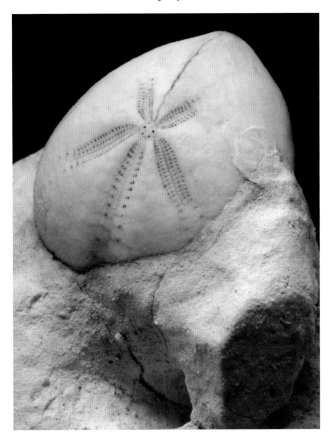

A fossil sea urchin in chalk (Upper Cretaceous). Known as shepherd's crowns or snake eggs, stone sea urchin were believed to have magic properties.

Their fossils turn up as chalk-coated, flint objects in chalk pits and where the underlying chalk has been disturbed by the plough. They have long intrigued country folk and have been given various fanciful names. A bun-shaped form, known as pundstone or quoitstone, was kept by women to use as kitchen weights. Some said they represented the little balls of dough shaped by the Christ-child while his mother baked the bread, an echo of the mystery of the Eucharist, when bread is miraculously transformed into flesh.

A different legend held that the mysterious stone balls were the petrified remains of snakes' eggs. The proof, as it were, lay in the indentations in the surface, which looked like tooth marks. Stone snake eggs could be used as talismans to help patients with heart or liver complaints. They were also said to protect their owner from poisons and deadly vapours, as well as from injury in battle. These were clearly useful objects to have around. Snake eggs were not laid in the usual way but were formed magically from balls of foam produced when snakes congregate together at midsummer. Their powers could be preserved by keeping the balls inside a special piece of cloth. Stealing the magic eggs from the snakes was said to be risky. Would-be foam-ball thieves were recommended to swim across a river so that the angry snakes pursuing behind would be unable to follow.

Snake eggs are commonest on chalk downs on which sheep are pastured, where they were known as 'shepherd's crowns', 'shepherd's purses' or 'shepherd's mitres', depending on the shape. Flatter forms were called 'fairy hearts' or 'fairy loaves'. People of a mathematical bent were intrigued to find that the markings of snake eggs resembled the Pentagram of Pythagoras and hence suggested a secret and mystic code. By the 'law of signatures', such magical stones were held to be useful in alleviating the pain of gallstones. Perhaps because the stones were also round, like eyeballs, their chalky dust was used to clear the eyes of horses. Another fossil urchin shaped like a bladder was used to treat diseases of the urinary tract.

The stones were also used to ward off seasickness. In this case, at least, there was some substance in the tale. Fossil urchins trap fine-grained chalk within the hollow of their mineralised shells that is nearly pure calcium carbonate, the active principle of most stomach-settlers. The pioneer geologist John Woodward considered urchin powder to be 'one of the finest remedies for subduing acrid humours of the stomach'.[7] It also helped those at sea who, unable 'to vomit at their first setting, fall frequently into loosenesses, which are sometimes long, troublesome and dangerous.' No landsman, he concluded, should consider venturing on board without a quantity of finest Kentish chalk eggs in his pocket.

Sea cucumbers *Holothurioidea*

VN: *beche de mer*, cukes, sea slugs

Sea cucumbers (a small species is known as the sea gherkin) are found in our cold waters, but they are much scarcer than in tropical seas and rarely found in rockpools. They are lethargic, sausage-shaped animals, often with a warty or spiny skin, which passively sift whatever organic detritus they can extract from the sediment. One group has tentacles allowing them to sieve plankton from the seawater. When conditions are unfavourable, sea cucumbers simply stop feeding and slowly shrink, surviving in a state of effective hibernation for up to six months. Their bodies are made from a connective tissue known as 'catch collagen', which can change from solid to a rubbery fluid in an instant, giving the creature the useful ability, when menaced, to blow itself up like a party balloon or to expel water from its body until it has shrunk to the size of a pebble.

Sea cucumbers are best-known for their habit of squirting water out of their rear ends. One species, the Cotton Spinner, adds a host of sticky white threads to the mix, a habit which inspired the eccentric French composer Erik Satie to pen a piano composition in its honour, adding to the score the observation that 'this sea animal purrs like a cat; also it produces disgusting silky threads.'[8] The most popular sea cucumbers in aquariums are the warm-water group known as sea apples, which are multicoloured and resemble giant sea anemones. Unfortunately, their beauty comes at a risk. If injured, the sea apple reacts by blowing its guts out of its rear end to flood the water with a toxic soup known in the trade as a 'cuke nuke'. An angry blast from a sea apple is said to be capable of wiping out every fish in a small aquarium before the sea apple itself succumbs. In Japan, the wonderful properties of sea cucumbers have inspired an entire subset of verses in their honour, based on the haiku form; but in Britain, it seems, we have not a single rhyme, song or poem of note.

Sea cucumbers are prized as *beches de mer* in oriental cuisine, said to combine healing properties with a possibly exaggerated repute as an aphrodisiac. This has led to massive overexploitation. There is some biochemical support for the claims. Scientists have isolated a protein, lectin, which the animal synthesises to discourage parasites. Bioengineered into the guts of mosquitoes, it is hoped to create a race of malaria-free mosquitoes that could, in due course, take over from the harmful kind, though the idea is still very much at the vision stage. Sea cucumber skin-moisturiser, on the other hand, is available on the High Street, but it has nothing to do with echinoderms; it is, rather, extract of vegetable cucumbers with an injection of algae and sea salt.

NOT-QUITE-BUGS
AND NEARLY-VERTEBRATES

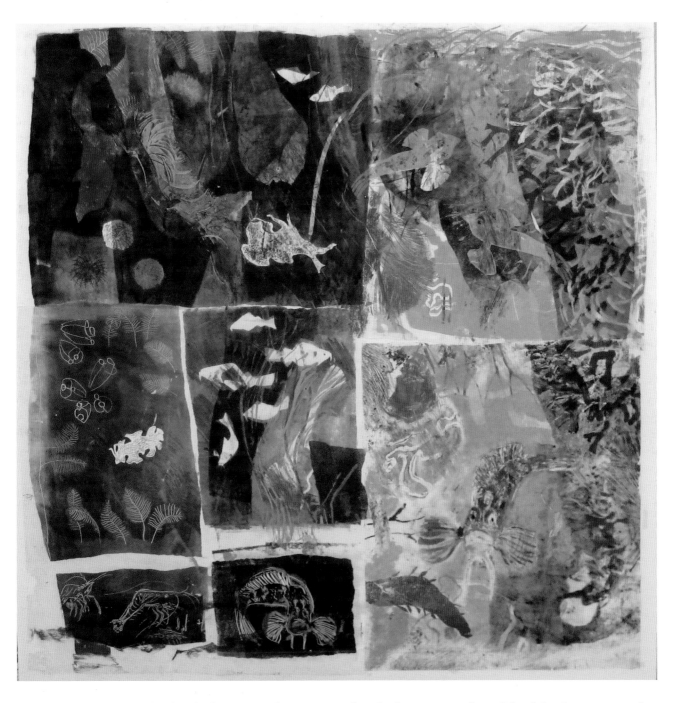

Sea Life *with prawns, hydroids, limpets and sea squirts sketched on perspex from life of the Dorset coast, by Kim Atkinson.*

For the most part, evolution has made a clear distinction between 'bugs' and backboned animals. All the latter, from fish to humans, possess a set of spinal bones running from head to tail (or, in our case, top to bottom) to protect the vital chord that connects the brain with the rest of the body. Animals with a spine, whether made of bone or cartilage, are vertebrates. Those possessing a spinal chord, with or without a bony spine, are also known as chordates, and it is here that the distinction starts to blur slightly. There are species that look like invertebrates which, at least at some stage in their lives, possess a spinal chord. One group, the Hemichordates (half-chords), look like worms, a second, the sea squirts, or Urochordates (tail-chords), resemble sponges, while the third, the Cephalochordates (head-chords), look vaguely like fish. With these strange forms, not quite bugs – invertebrates – but not quite vertebrates either, we take leave of this tour of the colliding worlds of invertebrate life and the human imagination.

Acorn worms *Hemichordata*

AN: tongue worms

Acorn worms have a plump and distinctive proboscis that sits on a fleshy collar, resembling a long, ripe acorn swelling from its cup. Others see a closer resemblance to a lolling tongue, hence the alternate name, tongue worms. The worm's body is divided into three parts: the proboscis, a trunk and finally a long, flaccid wormy body. Some acorn worms have a medicinal smell that probably helps to fend off bacteria and predators. They do not come to the attention very often since they inhabit U-shaped burrows in the sand or mud, usually offshore, with only the tip of the proboscis poking out.

Biology students know them mainly as faded specimens pickled in a jar, for acorn worms are on the A-level biology syllabus because of their

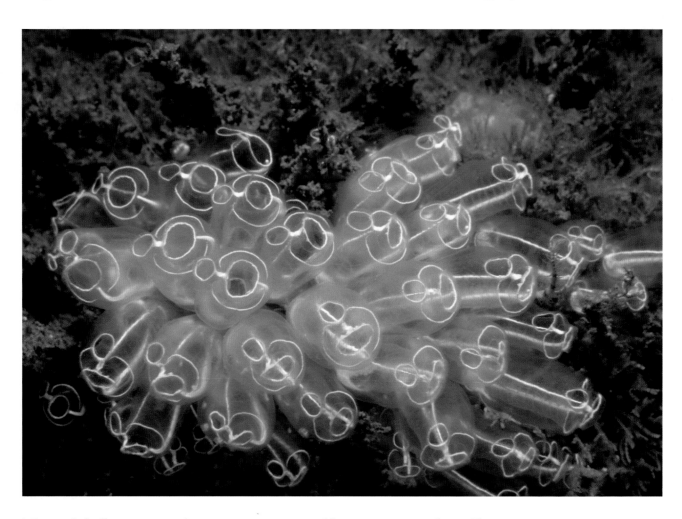

The Lightbulb Sea-squirt shows an uncanny resemblance to tungsten lamp filaments.

evolutionary significance. But though they look thoroughly worm-like from the outside, their innards are in some ways more like those of fish. The worms have gill-slits, a heart (which thriftily doubles as a kidney) and blood vessels, as well as an interesting set of nerve tubes that have points of similarity with a vertebrate brain. Yet their larvae are more like starfish, and acorn worms do suggest distant and unlikely seeming links between echinoderms and vertebrates.

The alternate name, tongue worm, is reflected in the scientific names of acorn worms, most of which contain the Latin word for a tongue, *glossus*. *Saccoglossus* (sack-tongue) is the genus most often used in research; *Balanoglossus* (acorn-tongue) is the biggest genus, ranging up to half a metre long in British waters (though a tropical species, *Balanoglossus gigas*, ranges up to two metres long – a python among acorn worms).

Sea squirts *Urochordata*

AN: ascidians, tunicates

VN: haddock bags (NE Eng.), sea pork

Sea squirts appear to be very simple animals, more like sponges than anything, consisting of little more than a stout bag equipped with a pair of openings or siphons. Their bag-like nature is underlined by their alternate name of tunicates (tunic animals). With this simple arrangement they take in seawater from one siphon, filter out anything edible, and then blow the clean water back into the environment. When taken away from the water and gently squeezed, a sea squirt lives up to its name by spurting a thin jet of water like a water pistol, a trick that always goes down well with that other kind of sea squirt, a small child on a beach.

The Star Ascidian, or Star Sea-squirt . Each 'ray' of a star is a separate individual, a zooid.

Sea squirts, *Urochordata*

Sea squirts live permanently attached to a hard surface, sometimes singly, sometimes in colonies. Their lifestyle has much in common with sponges, yet they lie at opposite ends of this book. Strange as it appears, they are much more closely related to us than to sponges, clams or insects. While no one would suspect it from the passive adult sea squirt, its larva is an agile little creature the shape of a tadpole, whose tail is stiffened by a chord – a distinct, if primitive, spine. If a sea squirt was a sentient being, it might seem a disappointing destiny to be so close to a vertebrate as a baby only to grow up into a sedentary, squirting sack.

can also be found encrusting piers and wharves. Large ones have been known to foul ship's hulls and intake pipes. One of the commonest is the star ascidian (from another sea squirt name, meaning wineskin), which encrusts rocks in a variety of pretty colours, all with star-shaped patterns like the petals of a flower. Other species include the 'baked-bean sea squirt', the 'gooseberry sea squirt' and the transparent 'lightbulb sea squirt' (complete with 'filaments'), all named after their similarity to those commodities. A thick, rubbery kind is known as sea pork.

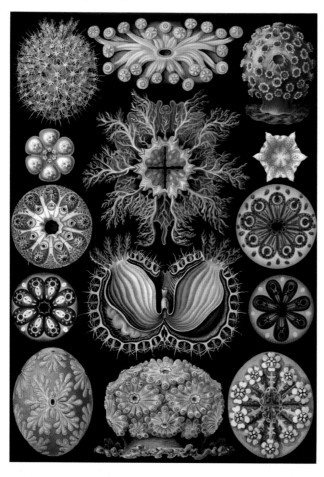

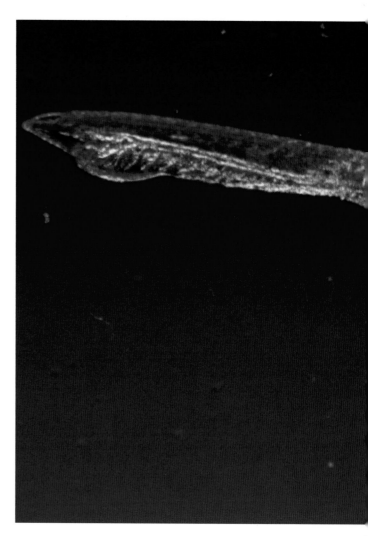

'Various species of sea squirts', from Ernst Haeckel's Kunstformen der Natur *('Nature's Patterns'), first published in 1904.*

Sea squirts are also set apart by their peculiar body chemistry (for inscrutable reasons, they concentrate the rare element vanadium from sea water), which includes compounds that are of interest in cancer therapy.

Sea squirts are common in clean rockpools and

Lancelets *Cephalochordata*

Lancelets, also known as amphioxus, are famous among evolutionary biologists as living fossils, as an apparent link between invertebrate and vertebrate life. They are shaped like a fish (*amphioxus* means 'pointed at both ends'), have gill slits and fins along the back and tail and, most significantly, a nerve chord running the length of the spine, similar to those of lampreys and hagfish. Anyone spotting the narrow, pale outline of an amphioxus swimming about at night might well assume it is a fish. On the other hand, an amphioxus has no eyes or, indeed, any of the paired sense organs possessed by vertebrates. Instead of a mouth, it has a cluster of feathery cirri like a barnacle. And, more fundamentally, an amphioxus has no bones.

Branchiostoma lanceolatum is a worldwide species that occurs in British waters but is rarely seen, since by day it is usually hiding in the sand, with only the eyeless, pointed head poking out. In East Asia, a related species is trawled and marketed as amphioxus fish-paste.

At one time, an amphioxus was presumed to be our ultimate ancestor, a kind of proto-fish that lay at the bottom of the vast Darwinian tree of vertebrate life. In the 1920s, a New England marine biologist, Philip H. Pope, composed a witty ditty sung to the tune of 'It's a Long Way to Tipperary', whose chorus line runs:

> It's a long way from Amphioxus,
> It's a long way to us,
> It's a long way from Amphioxus
> To the meanest human cuss.
> It's good-bye, fins and gill slits,
> Welcome, lungs and hair!
> It's a long, long way from Amphioxus,
> But we all came from there.[1]

The genome of *Branchiostoma lanceolatum* was recently investigated, and the results suggest that it is an even longer way to amphioxus than we thought. Though it shares many vertebrate genes, scientists now believe the animal to be an early offshoot from the vertebrate line rather than a genuine ancestor. Even so, one has only to look at an amphioxus to feel a faint thrill of distant paternity. It is hard to regard it as an invertebrate. Long ago, somewhere around 520 million years ago at the latest estimate, streamlined creatures looking something like this began to swim like fish, transferring orders from the brain to the tail via a strengthened rod of nerve cells. They thrived and multiplied. They took off into the world's oceans and explored wonderful new possibilities of life. They turned into more advanced animals, including the ancestors of modern fish.

And the rest, one might say, is Beasts Britannica.

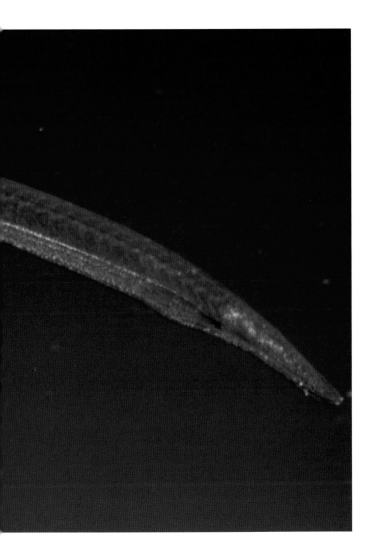

The larval form of an amphioxus, or lancelet – our distant ancestor?

APPENDIX I:
Scientific names of species in the text

We have followed the nomenclature of recently published fieldguides (augmented by more specialised publications where necessary) of which the following were particularly useful:

Richard Lewington (2008) *Guide to Garden Wildlife*; British Wildlife Publishing.

Michael Chinery (2007) *Collins Guide to the Insects of Britain and Western Europe;* A & C Black.

Malcolm Greenhalgh & Denys Ovenden (2007) *Freshwater Life;* Collins Pocket Guide.

Peter Hayward, Tony Nelson-Smith & Chris Shields (1996) *Sea Shore of Britain & Europe;* Collins Pocket Guide.

Paul Waring & Martin Townsend (2003) *Field Guide to the Moths of Great Britain*; British Wildlife Publishing.

Simple Life

Barrel Jellyfish *Rhizostoma octopus*
Bath Sponge *Spongia officinalis*
Beadlet Anemone *Actinia equina*
Birdbath Rotifer *Philodina roseola*
Bluefire Jellyfish *Cyanea lamarckii*
Boring Sponge *Cliona celata*
Breadcrumb Sponge *Halichondria panicea*
Brown Hydra *Hydra oligactis*
By-the-wind-sailor *Velella velella*
Compass Jellyfish *Chrysaora hyposcella*
Dahlia Anemone *Urticinia felina*
Daisy Anemone *Cereus pedunculatus*
Dead Man's Fingers *Alcyonium digitatum*
Devonshire Cup Coral *Caryophyllia smithii*
Elephant's-hide Sponge *Pachymatisma johnstonia*
Freshwater Jellyfish *Craspedacusta sowerbyi*
Green/Common Hydra *Hydra viridissima*
Hornwrack *Flustra foliacea*
Jewel Anemone *Corynactis viridis*
Lion's Mane Jellyfish *Cyanea capillata*
Mauve Stinge *Pelagia nocticula*
Mermaid's Glove *Haliclona oculata*
Moon Jellyfish *Aurelia aurita*
Oaten Pipes Hydroid *Tubularia indivisa*
Pink Sea Fan *Eunicella cavolini verrucosa*
Plumose Anemone *Metridium senile*
Pond Sponge *Spongilla lacustris*
Portuguese Man-o'-War *Physalia physalia*
Purse Sponge *Scypha compressa*
Queen of the Pond rotifer *Stephanoceros* species
River Sponge *Ephydatia fluviatilis*
Scarlet-and-gold Cup Coral *Balanophyllia regia*
Sea Fir *Sertularia cupressina*
Sea Gooseberry *Pleurobrachia pileus*
Sea Walnut *Mnemiopsis gardeni*
Snakelocks Anemone *Anemonia viridis*
Strawberry Beadlet *Actinia fragacea*
Venus's Girdle *Cestus veneris*
Walled Corklet *Phellia murocincta*

Worms

Australian Flatworm *Australoplana sanguinea*
Bird Leech *Theromyzon tessulatum*
Bootlace Worm *Lineus longissimum*
Brandling Worm *Eisenia fetida*
Cockspur Worm *Dendrodrilus rubidus*
Estuary Ragworm *Nereis diversicola*
Green Spoon Worm *Bonellia viridis*
Feather-duster Worm *Sabella spallanzanii*
Fish Leech *Piscicola geometra*
Honeycomb Worm *Sabellaria alveolata*
Horse Leech *Haemopsis sanguisuga*
King Rag *Nereis virens*
Lobworm *Lumbricus terrestris*
Longworm *Aporrectodea (=Allobophora) longa*
Lugworm *Arenicola marina*
Medicinal Leech *Hirudo medicinalis*
New Zealand Flatworm *Arthurdendylus triangulatum*
Paddleworm *Phyllodoce lamelligera*
Peacock Worm *Sabella pavonia*
Sand Mason *Lanice conchilega*
Sea Mouse *Aphrodita aculeata*
Sheep/Common Liver Fluke *Fasciola hepatica*

Crustaceans

Acorn Barnacle *Chthamalus stellatus*
Blunt-tailed Snake Millipede *Cylindroiulus punctatus*
Boring Millipede *Polyzonium germanicum*
Brine Shrimp *Artemia salina*
Brown/Common Shrimp *Crangon crangon*
Buoy Barnacle *Dosima fascicularis*
Chinese Mitten Crab *Eriocheir sinensis*
Common Flat-back Millipede *Polydesmus angustus*
Common Hermit Crab *Eupagurus Pagurus bernhardus*
Common Pill Woodlouse *Armadillidium vulgare*
Common Prawn *Palaemon serratus*
Common Spider Crab *Maja squinado*
Common Squat Lobster *Galathea strigosa*
Common/Rough Woodlouse *Porcellio scaber*
Crawfish *Palinurus elephas*
Edible/Brown Crab *Cancer pagurus*
Fairy Shrimp *Chirocephalus diaphanous*
Four-spotted Orb-weaver *Araneus quadratus*

Freshwater/White-clawed/Atlantic Stream Crayfish *Austropotamobius pallipes*
Freshwater Shrimp *Gammarus pulex*
Goose Barnacle *Lepas anatifera*
Goose-neck Barnacle *Pollicipes pollicipes*
Greenhouse Millipede *Oxidus gracilis*
Gribble *Limnoria lignicola*
House Centipede *Scutigera coleoptrata*
Lawn Shrimp/Common Land-hopper *Arcitalitrus dorrieni*
Lobster *Homaris gammarus*
Masked Crab *Corytes cassivellaunus*
Norway Lobster *Nephrops norwegicus*
Pill Millipede *Glomoris marginata*
Pink Shrimp *Pandalus montagui*
Red King Crab *Paralithodea camtschaticus*
Red-spotted/Snake Millipede *Blaniculus guttatus*
Salmon/Sea Louse *Lepeophtheirus salmonis*
Sea Slater *Ligea oceanica*
Shore Crab *Carcinus maenas*
Signal Crayfish *Pacifastacus leniusculus*
Sponge Crab *Dromia personata*
Spotted Snake Millipede *Blaniulus guttatus*
Tadpole Shrimp *Triops cancriformis*
Velvet Swimming Crab *Necora puber*
Water Hoglouse *Asellus aquaticus*
Water Springtail *Podura aquatica*

Arachnids

Black Lace Weaver Spider *Amaurobius ferox*
Cardinal Spider *Tegenaria parietina*
Cave Spider *Meta menardi*
Cellar Spider *Steatoda grossa*
Cheese Mite *Tyroglyphus casei* and other species
Common House Spider *Tegenaria domestica*
Daddy-longlegs Spider *Pholcus phalangioides*
Distinguished Jumping Spider *Sitticus distinguendus*
Dust Mite *Dermatophagoides pteronyssinus* and other species
False Widow *Steatoda nobilis*
Fen Raft Spider *Dolomedes plantarius*
Flour Mite *Acarus siro*
Flower Crab Spider *Misumenia vatia*
Garden Centre Spider *Uloborus plumipes*
Garden Spider *Araneus diadematus*

Scientific names of species in the text

Giant House Spider *Tegenaria gigantea*
Harvest Mite *Neotrombicula autumnalis*
Hobo/Yard Spider *Tegenaria agrestis*
Lace Weaver Spider *Amaurobius similis*
Ladybird Spider *Eresus cinnabarinus*
Purse-web Spider *Atypus affinis*
Raft Spider *Dolomedes fimbriatus*
Red Spider Mite *Tetranychus urticae*
Scabies Mite *Sarcoptes scabiei*
Sheep Tick *Ixodes ricinus*
Tube-web Spider *Segestria florentina*
Varroa Mite *Varroa destructor*
Velvet Mite *Eutrombidium rostratus*
Walnut Orb-weaver *Nuctenea umbratica*
Wasp Spider *Argiope bruennichi*
Water Spider *Argyroneta aquatica*
Woodlouse Spider *Dysdera crocata*
Zebra Spider *Salticus scenicus*

Small insect orders

Alderfly *Sialis lutaria*
Angler's Curse *Caenis horaria*
Antlion *Euroleon nostras*
Azure Damselfly *Coenagrion puella*
Banded Demoiselle *Calopteryx splendens*
Beautiful Demoiselle *Calopteryx virgo*
Broad-bodied Chaser *Libellula depressa*
Cat Flea *Ctenocephalides felis*
Cinnamon Sedge *Limnephilus lunatus*
Common/Green Lacewing *Chrysoperla carnea*
Common Mayfly/Greendrake *Ephemera danica*
Crab Louse *Phthirus pubis*
Emperor Dragonfly *Anax imperator*
Firebrat *Thermobia domestica*
Giant Lacewing *Osmylus fulvicephalus*
Golden-ringed Dragonfly *Cordulegaster boltonii*
Grannon *Brachycentrus subnubilis*
Large Stonefly *Perlodes microcephala*
Hairy Dragonfly *Brachytron pratense*
Head Louse *Pediculus humanus capitis*
Human Flea *Pulex irritans*
Land Caddis *Enoicyla pusilla*
March Brown *Ecdyonurus venosus*
Rabbit Flea *Spilopsyllus cuniculi*
Rat Flea *Xenopsylla cheopsis*
Scorpionfly *Panorpa communis*
Silverfish *Lepisma saccharina*
Snow Flea *Boreus hyemalis*
Southern Hawker *Aeshna cyanea*
Yellow Sally *Isoperla grammatica*

Grasshoppers and crickets

American/Ship Cockroach *Periplaneta americana*
Australian Cockroach *Periplaneta australasiae*
Bone-house Earwig *Marava arachnidis*
Dark Bush-cricket *Pholidoptera griseoaptera*
Earwig/Common Earwig *Forficula auricularia*
Field Cricket *Gryllus campestris*
Field Grasshopper *Chorthippus brunneus*
German Cockroach *Blatella germanica*
Giant/Tawny Earwig *Labidura riparia*
Great Green Bush-cricket *Tettigonia viridissima*
Greenhouse Camel Cricket *Tachycines asynamorus*
Heath Grasshopper *Chorthippus vegans*

Hissing Cockroach *Gromphadorhina portentosa*
Hop-garden Earwig *Apterygia media*
House Cricket *Acheta domesticus*
Laboratory/Indian Stick Insect *Carausius morosus*
Large Marsh Grasshopper *Stethophyma grossum*
Lesser Earwig *Labia minor*
Long-winged Conehead *Conocephalus discolor*
Migratory Locust *Locusta migratoria*
Mole Cricket *Gryllotalpa gryllotalpa*
Mottled Grasshopper *Myrmeleotettix maculates*
Oak Bush-cricket *Meconema thalissinum*
Oriental Cockroach *Blatta orientalis*
Rousel's Bush-cricket *Metrioptera roeselii*
Rufous Grasshopper *Gomphocerippus rufus*
Scaly Cricket *Pseudomogoplistes squamiger*
Southern Field/Black Cricket *Gryllus bimaculatus*
Speckled Bush-cricket *Leptophyes punctatissima*
Stripe-winged Grasshopper *Stenobothrus lineatus*
Unarmed Stick Insect *Acanthoxyla inermis*
Wart-biter Bush-cricket *Decticus verrucivorus*
Wood Cricket *Nemobius sylvestris*
Woodland Grasshopper *Omocestes rufipes*

True bugs

Apple Capsid *Plesiocoris rugicollis*
Apple Sucker/Apple Psyllid *Psylla mali*
Bay Sucker *Trioza alacris*
Bedbug *Cimex lectularius*
Birch Shieldbug *Elasmostethus interstinctus*
Bishop's Mitre *Aelia acuminata*
Blackfly/Black Bean Aphid *Aphis fabae*
Box Bug *Gonoceris acuteangulatus*
Cabbage Aphid *Brevicoryne brassicae*
Cabbage Whitefly *Aleyrodes proletella*
Common Backswimmer/Water Boatman *Notonecta glauca*
Common Green Capsid *Lygocoris pabulinus*
Common Froghopper *Philaenus spumarius*
Common Pond Skater *Gerris lacustris*
Cushion Scale *Chloropulvinula floccifera*
Firebug *Pyrrhocoris apterus*
Flybug *Reduvius personatus*
Forest Bug *Pentatoma rufipes*
Green Shieldbug *Palomena prasina*
Green Spruce Aphid *Elatobium abietinum*
Green Vegetable Bug/Southern Shieldbug *Nezara viridula*
Greenfly/Rose Aphid *Macrosiphum rosae*
Greenhouse Whitefly *Trialeurodes vaporariorum*
Horse Chestnut Scale *Pulvinaria regalis*
Lupin Aphid *Macrosiphum albifrons*
Martin Bug *Oeciacus hirundinis*
Negro Bug *Thyreocoris scarabaeoides*
New Forest Cicada *Cicadetta montana*
Parent Bug *Elasmucha grisea*
Peach-potato Aphid *Myzus persicae*
Phylloxera *Daktulosphaira vitifoliae*
Pigeon Bug *Cimex columbarius*
River Saucer Bug *Aphelocheirus aestivalis*
Saucer Bug *Ilyocoris cimicoides*
Sloe/Hairy Bug *Dolycoris baccarum*
Soft Scale/Brown Soft Scale *Coccus hesperidium*
Tarnished Plant Bug *Lygus rugulipennis*

Tortoise Bug *Euryaster maura*
Turtle Bug *Podops inuncta*
Water Measurer *Hydrometra stagnorum*
Water Scorpion *Nepa cinerea*
Water Stick Insect *Ranatra linearis*
Wheel Bug *Arilis cristatus*
Woolly Aphid *Eriosoma lanigerum*
Woundwort Shieldbug *Eysarcoris fabricii*

Butterflies

Scientific names of all the British species are in the main text.

Moths

Angle-shades *Phlogophora meticulosa*
The Anomalous *Stilbia anomala*
Argent-and-Sable *Rheumaptera hastata*
August Thorn *Ennomos quercinaria*
Bee Moth *Aphomia sociella*
Bird-cherry Ermine *Yponomeuta evonymella*
Blair's Shoulder-knot *Lithophane leautieri*
Blomer's Rivulet *Discoloxia blomeri*
Broad-bordered Bee Hawkmoth *Hemaris fuciformis*
Brown China-mark *Elophila nymphaeata*
Brown House-moth *Hofmannophila pseudospretella*
Brown-tail *Euproctis chrysorrhoea*
Buff Arches *Habrosyne pyritoides*
Buff-tip *Phalera bucephala*
Burnished Brass *Diachrysia chrysitis*
Cabbage Moth *Mamestria brassicae*
Case-bearing Clothes Moth *Tinea pellionella*
Cinnabar *Tyria jacobaeae*
Clifden Nonpareil *Catocala fraxini*
Cocoa Moth *Ephestia elutella*
Codlin Moth *Cydia pomonella*
Common/Case-bearing Clothes Moth *Tineola bisselliella*
Common Swift *Hepialis lupulinus*
The Confused *Apamea furva*
Convolvulus Hawkmoth *Agrias convolvuli*
Corn Moth *Nemapogon granella*
Coxcomb Prominent *Ptilodon capucina*
Currant Clearwing *Synanthedon tipuliformis*
Dark Crimson Underwing *Catocala sponsa*
Death's-head Hawkmoth *Acherontia atropos*
December Moth *Poecilocampa populi*
Dingy Shears *Parastichtis ypsillon*
Dried Currant Moth *Ephestia cautella*
Drinker Moth *Euthrix potatoria*
Early Moth *Therla primaria*
Elephant Hawkmoth *Deilephila elpenor*
Emperor Moth *Saturnia pavonia*
Ermine Moth *Yponomeuta evonymella* and related species
Eyed Hawkmoth *Smerinthus ocellata*
Figure of Eighty *Tethea ocularis*
Forester Moth *Adscita statices*
Fox Moth *Macrothylacia rubi*
Garden Pebble *Evergestis forficalis*
Garden Tiger *Arctia caja*
Green Oak Tortrix *Tortrix viridana*
Grey Dagger *Acronicta psi*
Ghost Moth *Hepialis humuli*
Goat Moth *Cossus cossus*
Gypsy Moth *Lymantria dispar*
Haworth's Minor *Celaena haworthii*
Heart Moth *Dicycla oo*
Hebrew Character *Orthosia gothica*
Horse Chestnut Leaf Miner *Cameraria ohridella*

Hummingbird Hawkmoth *Macroglossum stellatarum*
Iron Prominent *Notodonta dromedarius*
Jersey Tiger *Euplagia quadripunctaria*
July Belle *Scotopteryx luridata*
Kentish Glory *Endromis versicolora*
Lackey Moth *Malacosoma neustria*
Lappet Moth *Gastropacha quercifolia*
Large Tabby *Aglossa pinguinalis*
Large/Common Yellow Underwing *Noctua pronuba*
Leopard Moth *Zeuzera pyrina*
Lesser Swallow Prominent *Pheosia gnoma*
Lesser Wax Moth *Achroia grisella*
Light Crimson Underwing *Catocala promissa*
Lime Hawkmoth *Mimas tiliae*
Lobster Moth *Stauropus fagi*
Lunar Hornet Moth *Sesia bembeciformis*
Magpie Moth *Abraxas grossulariata*
Many-plumed/Twenty-plume Moth *Alucita hexadactyla*
March Moth *Alsophila aescularia*
Mediterranean Flour Moth *Ephestia kuehniella*
Merveille du Jour *Dichonia aprilina*
The Miller *Acronicta leporina*
Mint Moth *Pyrausta aurata*
Mother Shipton *Callistege mi*
Mother-of-Pearl Moth *Pleuroptya ruralis*
Mottled Umber *Erannis defoliaria*
Narrow-bordered Bee Hawkmoth *Hemaris tityus*
New Forest Burnet *Zygaena viciae*
Ni Moth *Trichoplusia ni*
November Moth *Epirrita dilutata*
Oak Eggar *Lasiocampa quercus*
Oak Nycteoline *Nycteola revayana*
Orange Underwing *Archiearis parthenias*
Orange Upperwing *Jodia croceago*
Pale Prominent *Pterosoma palpina*
Pale Tussock *Calliteara pudibunda*
Peach Blossom *Thyatira batis*
Pebble Prominent *Notodonta ziczac*
Peppered Moth *Biston betularia*
Phoenix Moth *Eulithis prunata*
Pine Beauty *Panolis flammea*
Pine Hawkmoth *Hyloicus pinastri*
Pine Processionary *Thaumetopoea pityocampa*
Pine-tree Lappet *Dendrolimus pini*
Plumed Prominent *Ptilophora plumigera*
Poplar Grey *Acronicta megacephala*
Poplar Hawkmoth *Laothoe populi*
Poplar Lutestring *Tethea or*
Portland Moth *Actebia praecox*
Privet Hawkmoth *Sphinx ligustri*
Puss Moth *Cerura vinula*
Ragwort Plume *Platyptilia isodactylus*
Raisin Moth *Ephestia figulilella*
Raspberry Clearwing *Pennisetia hyaleiformis*
Red Underwing *Catocala nupta*
Satin Lutestring *Tetheella fluctuosa*
Scarce Bordered Straw *Helicoverpa armigera*
Scarlet Tiger *Callimorpha dominula*
Scotch/Mountain Burnet *Zygaena exulans*
September Thorn *Ennomos erosaria*
Seraphim *Lobophora halterata*
Silver Y *Autographa gamma*
Six-spot Burnet *Zygaena filipendulae*
Skin Moth *Monopis laevigella*
Small Elephant Hawkmoth *Deilephila porcellus*
Small Magpie *Eurrhypara hortulata*
Spectacle *Abrostola triplasia*

Spinach Moth *Eulithis mellinata*
Sprawler *Asteroscopus sphinx*
Spring Usher *Agriopis leucophaearia*
Spurge Hawkmoth *Hyles euphorbiae*
The Suspected *Parastichtis suspecta*
Swallow Prominent *Pheosia tremula*
Swallow-tailed Moth *Ourapteryx sambucaria*
Sycamore Moth *Acronicta aceris*
Tapestry Moth *Trichophaga tapetzella*
True Lover's Knot *Lycophotia porphyrea*
Turnip Moth *Agrotis segetum*
The Uncertain *Hoplodrina alsines*
V-Moth *Macaria wauaria*
Vapourer Moth *Orgyia antiqua*
Water Veneer *Acentria ephemerella*
Wax Moth *Galleria mellonella*
White Plume Moth *Pterophorus pentadactyla*
Winter Moth *Operophtera brumata*
Yellow-tail *Euproctis similis*

Flies

Banded General Soldierfly *Stratiomys potamida*
Banded Mosquito *Aedes punctor* and *Culiseta annulata*
Barred Green Colonel Soldierfly *Odontomyia hydroleon*
Common/Dark-edged Bee-fly *Bombylius major*
Common Mosquito *Culex pipiens*
Black Dump Fly *Hydrotaea aenescens*
Black Soldierfly *Hermetia illucens*
Blandford Fly *Simulium posticatum*
Bluebottle *Calliphora vomitoria*
Cheese Fly *Piophila casei*
Common Banded Hoverfly *Syrphus ribesii*
Common Cleg *Haematopota pluvialis*
Common Orange Legionnaire *Beris vallata*
Cluster Fly *Pollenia rudis*
Daddy-longlegs *Tipula oleracea* and related species
Dark Giant Horsefly *Tabanus sudeticus*
Dead Donkey Fly *Centrophlebomyia furcata*
Deer Botfly *Cephenomyia pratti*
Delicate Soldier *Oxycera nigricornis*
Dronefly *Eristalis tenex* and other species
Fever Fly *Dilophus fibrilis*
Fleshfly *Sarcophaga carnaria*
Fruitfly *Drosophila melanogaster*
Garden Midge *Culicoides obsoletus*
Greater Bulbfly/Narcissus Fly *Merodon equestris*
Greenbottle (commonest) *Lucilia caesar*
Highland Midge *Culicoides impunctatus*
Horn Fly *Haematobia irritans*
Hornet Cranefly *Ctenophora dorsalis*
Hornet Robberfly *Asilus craboniformis*
Horse Botfly *Gasterophilus intestinalis*
Housefly *Musca domestica*
Large Cranefly *Tipula maxima*
Lesser Bulbfly (commonest) *Eumerus funeralis*
Lesser Housefly *Fannia canicularis*
Marmalade Hoverfly *Episyrphus balteatus*
Pygmy Soldier *Oxycera pygmaea*
St Mark's Fly *Bibio marci*
Sheep Ked *Melophagus ovinus*
Sheep Nostril-fly *Oestrus ovis*
Snipefly/Downlooker Fly *Rhagio scolopacea*
Sweat Fly *Hydrotaea irritans*
Truffle Fly *Sullia gigantiae*
Warble-fly (Common) *Hypoderma bovis*
Western Bee-fly *Bombylius canescens*
White-footed Ghost *Dolichopeza albipes*

Yellow Dung Fly *Scathophaga stercoraria*

Beetles

Bacon/Larder Beetle *Dermestes lardarius*
Beaulieu Dung Beetle *Aphodius niger*
Bee Beetle *Trichius fasciatus*
Biscuit Beetle *Stegobium paniceum*
'Black Belly' Diving Beetle *Dytiscus semisulcatus*
Bloody-nose Beetle *Timarcha tenebricosa*
Bombardier Beetle *Brachinus crepitans*
Bryony Ladybird *Epilachna argus*
Burying/Sexton Beetle *Nicrophorus vespillo*
Capricorn Beetle *Cerambyx cerdo*
Cardinal Click Beetle *Ampedus cardinalis*
Carpet/Museum (Varied) Beetle *Anthrenus verbasci*
Cherrystone Beetle *Hyphydrus ovatus*
Churchyard/Cellar Beetle *Blaps mortisaga*
Cockchafer *Melolontha melolontha*
Colorado Beetle *Leptinotarsa decemlineata*
Common Malachite Beetle *Malachius bipustulatus*
Common Whirligig *Gyrinus substriatus*
Death-watch Beetle *Xestobium rufovillosum*
Devil's Coach-horse *Ocypus olens*
Dor Beetle *Geotrupes stercorarius*
Elm Bark Beetle *Scolytus scolytus*
Engraver Beetle *Ips typographica*
'Enigma' Diving Beetle *Dytiscus circumcinctus*
Firefly *Luciola lusitanica*
Flour Beetle *Tribolium confusum*
Fur/Two-spotted Carpet Beetle *Attagenus pellio*
Furniture Beetle/Woodworm *Anobium punctatum*
Garden Chafer *Phyllopertha horticola*
Glow-worm *Lampyris noctiluca*
Golden Buprestid *Buprestis aurulenta*
Grain Weevil *Sitophilus granarius*
Great Diving Beetle *Dytiscus marginalis*
Great Silver Beetle *Hydrophilus piceus*
Great Spruce Bark Weevil *Dendroctonus micans*
Green Tiger Beetle *Cicindela campestris*
Harlequin Ladybird *Harmonia axyridis*
Hazel Weevil *Curclio nucum*
House Longhorn *Hylotrupes bajulus*
Khapra Beetle *Trogoderma granarium*
Lesser Stag Beetle *Dorcus parallelipipedus*
Lily Beetle *Liloceris lilii*
Lundy Flea Beetle *Psyllioides luridipennis*
Mealworm Beetle *Tenebrio molitor*
Minotaur Beetle *Typhaeus typhoeus*
Mint Beetle *Chrysolina herbacea*
Musk Beetle *Aromia moschata*
Oil Beetle (commonest) *Meloe proscarabaeus*
Pine Ladybird *Exochomus quadripustulatus*
Powderpost Beetle *Lyctus brunneus*
Red Soldier Beetle *Rhagonycha fulva*
Rhinoceros Beetle *Sinodendron cylindricum*
Rosemary Leaf Beetle *Chrysolina americana*
Scarce Seven-spot Ladybird *Coccinella magnifica*
Scarlet/Welsh Oak Longhorn *Pyrrhidium sanguineum*
Scarlet Malachite Beetle *Malachius aeneus*
Screech Beetle *Hygrobia hermanni*
Seven-spot Ladybird *Coccinella 7-punctata*
Short-necked Oil Beetle *Melow brevicollis*
Spangled Water Beetle *Graphoderus zonatus*
Spanish Fly *Lytta versicatoria*
Stag Beetle *Lucanus cervus*

Scientific names of species in the text

Streaked Bombardier Beetle *Brachinus sclopeta*
Summer Chafer *Amphimallon solstitialis*
Tansy Beetle *Chrysolina graminis*
Timberman *Acanthocinus aedilus*
Tobacco/Cigarette Beetle *Lasioderma serricorne*
Two-spot Ladybird *Adalia 2-punctata*
Vine Weevil *Otiorhynchus sulcatus*
Violet Click Beetle *Limoniscus violaceus*
Violet Ground Beetle *Carabus violaceus*
Wasp Beetle *Clytus arietis*
'The Wasp' Diving Beetle *Dytiscus circumflexus*

Wasps, bees and ants

Alder Wood-wasp *Xihydria camelus*
Apple Sawfly *Hoplocampa testudinea*
Artichoke Gall Wasp *Andricus fecundator*
Bedeguar Gall Wasp *Diplolepis rosae*
Bee-wolf *Philanthes triangulum*
Black/Garden Ant *Lasius niger*
Brown-banded Bumblebee *Bombus humilis*
Buff-tailed Bumblebee *Bombus terrestris*
Cherry Gall Wasp *Cynips quercusifolia*
Common Carder-bee *Bombus pascuorum*
Common Sand-wasp *Ammophila sabulosa*
Common Wasp *Vespula vulgaris*
Garden Bumblebee *Bombus hortorum*
German Wasp *Paravespula (Vespula) germanica*
Giant Wood-wasp *Urocerus gigas*
Gooseberry Sawfly *Nematus ribesii*
Great Yellow Bumblebee *Bombus distinguendus*
Honeybee *Apis mellifera*
Hornet *Vespa crabro*
Knopper Gall Wasp *Andricus quercuscalinus*
Long-horned Bee *Eucera longicornis*
Marble Gall Wasp *Andricus kollari*
Mason Wasp (Wall) *Ancistrocerus parietum*
Median Wasp *Dolichovespula media*
Negro/Ash-coloured Ant *Formica fusca*
Oak Apple Gall Wasp *Biorhiza pallida*
Ophion Wasp *Ophion luteus*
Pharaoh Ant *Monomorium pharaonis*
Potter Wasp *Eumenis coarcticus*
Red Mason Bee *Osmia rufa*
Red-tailed Bumblebee *Bombus lapidarius*
Ruby-tailed Wasp *Chrysis viridula* and other species
Sand Digger Wasp *Ammophila sabulosa* and other species
Saxon Wasp *Dolichovespula saxsonica*
Short-haired Bumblebee *Bombus subterraneus*
Sirex Wood-wasp *Sirex noctilio*
Solomon's-seal Sawfly *Phymatocera aterrima*
Turnip Sawfly *Athalia rosae*
Violet Carpenter Bee *Xylocopa violacea*
Wood Ant *Formica rufa*
Wool Carder-bee *Anthidium manicatum*
Yellow Ant *Lasius flavus*

Shelled life

American/Blue Point Oyster *Crassostrea virginica*
American Sting Winkle *Urosalpinx cinerea*
Ark Shell *Arca tetragona*
Ash-black Slug *Limax cinereoniger*

Atlantic Giant Squid *Architeuthis dux*
Augur Shell *Turritella communis*
Black-footed Limpet *Patella depressa*
Blue-rayed Limpet *Helcion pellucidum*
Blunt Gaper *Mya truncata*
Brown-lipped Banded Snail *Cepaea nemoralis*
Budapest Slug *Tandonia budapestensis*
China Limpet *Patella ulyssiponensis*
Chinaman's Hat Limpet *Calyptraea chinensis*
Common Bladder Snail *Physa fontinalis*
Common/Edible Cockle *Cerastoderma edule*
Common/Spotted Cowrie *Trivia monacha*
Common Cuttlefish *Sepia officinalis*
Common Limpet *Patella vulgate*
Common/Edible Mussel *Myrtilus edulis*
Common/Edible Periwinkle *Littorina littorea*
Common Razorshell *Ensis ensis*
Common/Flat Topshell *Gibbula umbilicaris*
Common/Edible Whelk *Buccinum undatum*
Cut Trough-shell *Spisula subtruncata*
Depressed River Mussel *Pseudanodonta complanata*
Desmoulin's Snail *Vertigo moulinsiana*
Dog Cockle *Glycymeris glycymeris*
Dog Whelk *Nucella lapillus*
Duck Mussel *Anodonta anatina*
Egg Cockle *Laevicardium laevigatum*
Fan Shell *Atrina fragilis*
Field/Netted Slug *Deroceras reticulatum*
Flat Winkle *Littorina obtusata*
Freshwater/River Nerite *Theodoxus fluviatilis*
Garden Slug *Arion hortensis*
Garden Snail *Helix aspera*
Garlic Snail *Oxychilus alliarius*
Girdled Snail *Hygromia cinctella*
Great Pond Snail *Lymnaea stagnalis*
Great/King Scallop *Pecten maximus*
Grey Topshell *Gibbula cineraria*
Grooved Razorshell *Solen marginatus*
Horse Mussel *Modiolus modiolus*
Icelandic Cyprine/Ocean Quahog *Arctia islandica*
Italian Snail *Papillifera papillaria*
Jack-knife Clam *Ensis directus*
Japanese/Pacific Oyster *Crassostrea gigas*
Jenkin's Spire-shell *Potamopyrgus antipodarum*
Kentish Snail *Monacha cantiana*
Kerry Slug *Geomalacus maculosus*
Keyhole Limpet *Diodora graeca*
Lake Limpet *Acroloxus lacustris*
Large Black Slug *Arion ater*
Leopard Slug/Great Grey Slug *Limax maximus*
Little Cuttlefish *Sepiola atlantica*
Little Whirlpool *Ramshorn Snail*
Marsh/Common Pond Snail *Lymnaea palustris*
Minute Kelly-shell *Kellia minuta*
Mussel (Common) *Myrtilus edulis*
Necklace Shell *Polinices catenus*
Netted Dog Whelk *Hinia reticulata*
Noah's Ark *Arca noae*
Norway Cockle *Laevicardium crassum*
Octopus (Common) *Octopus vulgaris*
Ormer/European Abalone *Haliotis tuberculata*
Otter Shell (Common) *Lutraria lutraria*

Oyster (Common/Flat) *Ostrea edularis*
Painted Topshell *Callistoma zizyphinum*
Painter's Mussel *Unio pictorum*
Pearl Mussel *Margaritifera margaritifera*
Pearly Topshell *Margarites helicinus*
Pelican's-foot Shell (Common) *Aporrhais pespelecani*
Pheasant Shell *Tricolia pullus*
Piddock (Common) *Pholas dactylus*
Poached-egg Shell *Simnia patula*
Pod Razor/Bean Solen *Ensis siliqua*
Portugese Oyster *Crassostrea gigas*
Prickly Cockle *Acanthocardia echinata*
Pullet Carpet-shell *Venerupis senegalensis*
Quahog *Mercenaria mercenaria*
Queen Scallop *Aequipecten opercularis*
Rayed Trough-shell *Mactra stultorum*
Red Whelk/Buckie *Neptunea antiqua*
River Limpet *Ancylus fluviatilis*
Roman Snail *Helix pomatia*
Rough Winkle *Littorina saxatilis*
Sand Gaper *Mya arenaria*
Sea Hare *Aplysia punctata*
Sea Lemon *Archidoris pseudargus*
Shining Ramshorn Snail *Segmentina nitida*
Shipworm *Teredo navalis*
Slipper Limpet *Crepidula fornicata*
Slit Limpet *Emarginula fissura*
Small Winkle *Littorina neritoides*
Speckled/Chequered Carpet-shell *Tapes decussatus*
Spiny Cockle *Acanthocardia aculeata*
Sting Winkle *Ocenabra erinacea*
Strawberry Snail *Trichia striolata*
Swan Mussel *Anodonta cygnea*
Thick Trough-shell *Spisula solida*
Tortoiseshell Limpet *Tectura tessulata*
Violet Snail *Janthina janthina*
Wandering Snail *Lymnaea peregra*
Wentletrap (Common) *Epitonium clathrus*
Whirlpool Ramshorn *Anisus vortex*
White-lipped Banded Snail *Cepaea hortensis*
Zebra Mussel *Dreissena polymorpha*

Spiny-skins and nearly-vertebrates

Amphioxus/Lancelet *Branchiostoma lanceolatum*
'Baked bean' Sea Squirt *Dendrodoa grossularia*
Common Brittlestar *Ophiothrix fragilis*
Common/Edible Sea Urchin *Echinus esculentus*
Common Starfish *Asterias rubens*
Common Sunstar *Crossaster papposus*
Cotton Spinner *Holothuria forskali*
Cushion Star *Asterina gibbosa*
Featherstar *Antedon bifida*
Gooseberry Sea Squirt *Distomus variolosus*
'Lightbulb' Sea Squirt *Clavelina lepadiformis*
Purple Sea Urchin *Paracentrotus lividus*
Sand Star *Astropecten spinulosus*
Sea Apple *Pseudocholochirus violaceus*
Sea Gherkin *Pawsonia saxicola*
Sea Pork *Amaroucium stellaris*
Sea Potato *Echinocardium cordatum*
Shore Urchin *Psammechinus miliaris*
Spiny Starfish *Marthasterias glacialis*
Star Ascidian *Botryllus schlosseri*

REFERENCES AND SOURCE NOTES

Simple life

1. H. S. Jennings (1906) A much quoted remark made originally in: *Behaviour of the Lower Organisms*. Indiana University Press, p336.
2. From online biography **www.euronet.n/users/warner/leeuwenhoek**
3. Henry Baker (1742) *The Microscope Made Easy*. London. p298.
4. Bland J. Finlay (2001) 'Protozoa'. In: David Hawksworth (ed) *The Changing Wildlife of Great Britain and Ireland*, Systematics Association Special vol. 62. Taylor & Francis, London, pp175–187.
5. Douglas Botting (1999) *Gerald Durrell. The Authorised Biography*. HarperCollins, p219.
6. Online advertisement, 2006.
7. Anne Reid (2007) 'Neptune plant – 2'. *BSBI News*, 105, p16.
8. Alister Hardy (1957) *The Open Sea: The World of Plankton*. Collins, London, p118.
9. L. P. Hartley (1944) *The Shrimp and the Sea Anemone*. Putnam, pp1–2.
10. Amy Mae King (2005) 'Reorienting the Scientific Frontier: Victorian Tide Pools and Literary Realism'. *Victorian Studies*, 47 (2), pp153–163.
11. Philip Gosse (1860) *Actinologia Britannica. A History of the British Sea-Anemones and Corals*. Van Voorst, London.
12. Edmund Gosse (1907) *Father and Son. A Study of Two Temperaments*. William Heinemann, London, p124.
13. P. Gosse, op. cit.
14. Charles Kingsley (new edn. 1904) *Glaucus; or The Wonders of the Shore*.
15. Philip Gosse (1852) *Devonshire Coast*.
16. 'Jellyfish attack wipes out salmon farm.' *Daily Telegraph*, 22 November 2007.
17. Colin Howes (2003) 'The amazing Amazonian Freshwater Jellyfish in Yorkshire'. *British Wildlife*, 14 (3), pp169–170.
18. David Wright (2009) 'Glowing ghosts of the sea'. *Natur Cymru*, 30, Spring 2009, pp29–32; Rachel Carson (1955) *The Edge of the Sea*. Mariner Books.
19. Josef Donner (1966) *Rotifers*. Warne, London, p71.
20. F. J. W. Plaskitt (1926) *Microscopic Fresh Water Life*. Chapman & Hall, p186.
21. Baker, op. cit.
22. Richard Fitter & R. Manuel (1986) *Freshwater Life*. Collins Field Guide, p156.
23. Plaskitt, op. cit. p269.
24. **www.micrographia.com**

Worms

1. **www.planarian.org**
2. Hugh Jones (2005) 'British land flatworms'. *British Wildlife*, 16 (3), pp189–194.
3. Miriam Rothschild & Theresa Clay (1952) *Fleas, Flukes and Cuckoos. A Study of Bird Parasites*. Collins, p199.
4. Adam Watson & Robert Moss (2008) *Grouse: The Natural History of British and Irish Species*. Collins, p334.
5. Lucy Middleton (2007) 'The discreet charm of nematode worms' (interview with Eileen Harris). *New Scientist*, December 2007, pp70–71.
6. Irvine Welsh (1998). *Filth*. Vintage Press.
7. Charles Kingsley (1855) *Glaucus or the Wonders of the Sea-Shore*. Routledge.
8. Professor Janet Moore, Swavesey, Cambridgeshire.
9. Nathaniel Cobb (1914) *Yearbook of the United States Department of Agriculture*, 1914. The quotation became famous through repetition in biology textbooks, notably *Animals without Backbones* by Ralph Buchsbaum.
10. Gilbert White, *The Natural History of Selborne*, Letter XXXV, 20 May 1777.
11. Buglife. **www.buglife.org.uk**
12. Mary Beith (1995) *Healing Threads: Traditional medicines of the Highlands and Islands*. Polygon, Edinburgh.
13. **www.wormcharming.com**
14. Leonard New.
15. William Wordsworth 'Resolution and Independence'. *The Complete Poetical Works*. **www.bartleby.com**
16. Romney Marsh Countryside Project. **www.rmcp.co.uk**
17. Owen Leyshon, East Sussex. See also: Malcolm Ausden et al. (2002) 'The status, conservation and use of the Medicinal Leech'. *British Wildlife*, 13 (4), pp229–238.
18. **www.biopharm-leeches.com**
19. **www.seabait.com**
20. **www.teara.govt.nz/en/marine-animals-without-backbones/3**

Crustaceans

1. Charles Darwin's two-volume barnacle books: *Living Cirripedia* (1851) and *Fossil Cirripedia of Great Britain* (1854); Rebecca Stott (2003) *Darwin and the Barnacle: The story of one tiny creature and history's most spectacular scientific breakthrough*.
2. Gerald of Wales (1188) *Topography of Ireland*, v.47.
3. John Gerard (1597) *Gerard's Herbal: The History of Plants*. 'Of the Goose-tree, Barnacle tree, or the tree bearing goose', chapter 188.
4. F. J. W. Plaskitt, *Microscopic Fresh Water Life*. Chapman & Hall, London, p265.
5. **www.tardigradesinspace.blogspot.com**
6. Anthony Flemming (2008) 'Bears in Britain'. *British Wildlife*, 19 (6), pp393–398.
7. **http://en.wikipedia.org/wiki/Notostraca** citing a German academic paper.
8. More entertaining detail on *Triops* rearing at **www.mytriops.com**
9. **http://en.wikipedia.org/wiki/Sea-Monkeys**
10. Tony Harwood, Maidstone, Kent.
11. **www.baxterspottedshrimps.co.uk**
12. 'Scientists film "jogging" shrimp on a treadmill.' *Daily Telegraph*, 4 November 2008.
13. 'Environmental impact of prawn trawling.' *Daily Mail*, 11 March 2009.
14. Rachel Costigan.
15. **http://news.bbc.co.uk/1/hi/uk/1514630.stm**
16. **www.nationallobsterhatchery.co.uk**
17. 'High hopes for Scottish fish ranch.' *Observer*, 2 February 2003.
18. 'Claws for concern? Scientists suggest prawns and lobsters feel pain just like humans.' *Daily Mail*, 9 November 2007.
19. Peter Marren (1986) 'The lethal harvest of crayfish plague'. *New Scientist*, 30 January 1986.
20. David Holdich, Peter Sibley & Stephanie Peay (2004) 'The White-clawed Crayfish – a decade on'. *British Wildlife*, 15 (3), pp153–164.
21. **www.newbury-manor-hotel.co.uk**
22. 'Crab'. In: Hope B. Werness (2006) *Animal Symbolism in Art*. Continuum International Publishing Group, New York, p113.
23. **www.gerrycambridge.com**
24. Andrew Young 'The Dead Crab'. In: D. J. Enright (ed) (1987) *The Oxford Book of Death*, OUP.
25. Robert Burton (2008) 'Through a naturalist's eyes'. *British Wildlife*, 19 (4), p240.
26. 'Norway fears giant crab invasion.' *BBC News*, 9 August 2006.
27. 'Pincer Darkness; John says crab is Mandelson.' *Daily Mirror*, 19 August 1997.
28. J. B. Smith (2008) 'Granfer-Grig to Tiddly-Tope: A look at names

for representatives of the natural world in the Laver corpus'. *Transactions of the Devonshire Association*, 140, 157–164.
29. Dr Ray Barnett.
30. Thomas Muffet 'Of Chisleps'. In: *Theatre of Insects*. Facsimile edn (as vol. 3 of *The History of Four-footed Beasts and Serpents and Insects*, arranged by Edward Topsell), Da Capo Press, New York, 1967, book II, chapter IX.
31. Nicholas Culpepper, *A physicall directory, or, A translation of the London dispensatory code*, made by the Colledge of Physicians of London. **www.med.yale.edu/library**
32. Anna Pavord (2005) *The Naming of Names*. Bloomsbury, p386.
33. Jonathan Swift 'A Serious Poem upon William Wood, Brasier, Tinker, Hard-Ware-Man, Coiner, Founder, and Esquire'. **www. nls.uk/broadsides**
34. A. O. Chater (1988) 'Woodlice in the Cultural Consciousness of Modern Europe'. *Isopoda*, 2, pp21–39.
35. Chater, op. cit.
36. Algernon Charles Swinburne, 'The Poet and the Woodlouse' **www.pseudopodium.org/repress/parody/poet-and-woodlouse. html.**
37. Alfred Lord Tennyson, 'Winter'. **www.humanitiesweb.org/ human**
38. Jean Kenward, poem in *The Countryman*, 1978, cited by Chater, op. cit.
39. Tony Harwood.
40. Steve Hopkin (2003) 'Woodlice, chiselbobs and sow-bugs'. *British Wildlife*, 14 (6), pp381–387.
41. Tony Harwood.
42. Richard Lord.
43. Tony Harwood.
44. Thomas Muffet 'Concerning the Scolopendrae and Juli'. In: *Theatre of Insects* (op. cit.), chapter VIII, p1045.
45. Muffet, op. cit., p1047.
46. P. Lee & P. Harding (2006) *Atlas of the millipedes (Diplopoda) of Britain and Ireland*. Biological Records Centre, Huntingdon.
47. Steve Hopkin (2004) 'Millipedes'. *British Wildlife*, 16 (2), pp77–84.
48. 'British Myriapod', *The Isopod Newsletter*, 15, autumn 2007.
49. Trevor Lorne Campbell (2006) *Strange Things: Father Allan, Ada Goodrich-Freer and the Second Sight*. Birlinn.
50. Cited in: Gerald Waldbauer (2003) *What Good are Bugs? Insects in the web of life*. Harvard University Press.
51. **www.kirkcudbright.co.uk/club/centipede.htm**
52. Muffet, op. cit., p1046.
53. Muffet, op. cit., p1047.
54. **www.lyricsmode.com**
55. Michael Viney (2003) *Ireland*. The Blackstaff Press, Belfast, p116.
56. Geoff Frampton & Steve Hopkin (2001) 'Springtails – in search of Britain's most abundant insects'. *British Wildlife*, 12 (6), pp402–410.

Arachnids

1. W. S. Bristowe (1958) *The World of Spiders*. Collins New Naturalist, pp3–4.
2. Frank Gibson (2003) *Superstitions about Animals*. Kessenger Publishing, New York. Originally published in 1903.
3. Paul Hillyard (1994) *The Book of the Spider*. Hutchinson, London, pp18–19.
4. Robert Southey 'To a Spider' (1799).
5. Bristowe, op. cit., p4.
6. Thomas Hardy, *Far from the Madding Crowd*, chapter XXXVI.
7. Bristowe, op. cit., p8.
8. Charles Kingsley, **www.fullbooks.com/Gluacus-or-The-Wonders-of-the-Shore2**
9. Stephen Dalton (2008) *Spiders: The Ultimate Predators*. Firefly Books, p199.
10. Hillyard, op. cit., p4.
11. John Byrne Leicester Warren 'The Study of a Spider'. Set to music at **http://recmusic.org/lieder**
12. Cited in: Hillyard, op. cit., p28.
13. William Shakespeare *The Winter's Tale*, Act II, scene i.

14. Primo Levi (1989) 'The Fear of Spiders'. In: *Other People's Trades*, pp141–45. Abacus, London.
15. **www.songmeanings.net/songs/view/3530822107858643 881/**
16. **www.circletimekids.com**
17. Muffet, op. cit. A part-summary of chapter XV, 'Of the generation, copulation, and use of Spiders'.
18. Ken Thompson (2006) *No Nettles Required. The reassuring truth about wildlife gardening*. Eden Project Books.
19. 'Venomous spiders nest near Queen's house.' *BBC News*, 19 June 2001.
20. **www.urbanlegends.about.com/library**
21. 'Louise Bourgeois's giant spider returns to Tate Modern.' Tate online, 28 April 2004.
22. 'Revealed: The secrets of the 50ft robo-spider.' *Daily Mail*, 6 September 2008.
23. The masterpieces: *The Biology of Spiders* by T.H. Savory (1928); *The World of Spiders* by W.S.Bristowe (1958); *The Book of the Spider* (1994) by Paul Hillyard.
24. Bristowe, op. cit., pp257–258.
25. Hannah Rigden.
26. Bristowe, op. cit., p109.
27. Urban legends **www.snopes.com/critters/wild/longlegs.asp**
28. Hillyard, *Book of Spiders*, p19.
29. Robert Burton, personal comment.
30. Hillyard, op. cit., pp18–19.
31. Francis Kilvert *Diary, 1870–1879*. Jonathan Cape.
32. Geoffrey Chaucer *The Canterbury Tales*. 'The Squire's Tale.'
33. Gilbert White. *The Natural History of Selborne*.
34. William Shakespeare *A Midsummer Night's Dream*, Act III, scene i.
35. Bristowe, op. cit., p230.
36. Chris Packham (1989) *Collins Wild Habitats. Heathlands*. Collins, London.
37. Gerald Durrell (1978) *The Garden of the Gods*.
38. Ian Hughes & others (2008) 'The Ladybird Spider in Britain – its history, ecology and conservation'. *British Wildlife*, 20 (3), pp153-159.
39. Muffet, op. cit. 'Of the Water Spider', p1021.
40. Tony Harwood.
41. Ayesha Chouglay.
42. 'Watch out, the black widow's sister is ready to bite you.' *Daily Telegraph*, 17 November 2006.
43. UK Spider Bites. **www.naturalhistorymuseum.org.uk/nature-online/life/insects-spiders**
44. Gregor Lamb (1988) *Orkney Wordbook. A dictionary of the dialect of Orkney*. Birsay. **www.orkneyjar.com**
45. George Adams (1771) *Essays in the Microscope*.
46. William Kirby & William Spence (1815) *An Introduction to Entomology: or elements of the natural history of insects*. Longman, London.
47. Cited in: Jolyon Medlock & others (2009) 'British Ticks'. *British Wildlife*, 20 (5).
48. **http://wikipedia.org/wiki/The_Tick**
49. Muffet, op. cit. 'Of Tikes, and Sheeps Lice', p1098.
50. Rachel Costigan.
51. Colin McLeod.
52. John Cameron (1993) 'Ticks and Lyme Disease'. *British Wildlife*, 4 (5), pp280–282.
53. Robert Hooke (1665) *Micrografia: or some physiological descriptions of minute bodies made by magnifying glasses with observations and inquiries thereupon*.
54. 'Cheese mites and other wonders.' *BBC online news magazine*, 29 May 2008.
55. White, op. cit. Letter to Thomas Pennant, XLIII.
56. Jon Balaam.

Small insect orders

1. P. B. Shelley 'Adonais: An elegy on the death of John Keats', verse XXIX.
2. Dominic Couzens (2008) *Secret Lives of Garden Wildlife*, Helm, p70.

3. Izaak Walton, *The Compleat Angler: or, The Contemplative Man's Recreation*. Full text at: **www.fullbooks.com**
4. Jan Swammerdam (1685) *Histoire Generale des Insectes*.
5. J. W. Dunne (1924) *Sunshine and the Dry Fly*. A & C Black, London.
6. Roger Deakin (1999) *Waterlog: A swimmer's journey through Britain*. Chatto & Windus, London, p23.
7. Mayfly Marketing. **www.mayflymarketing.co.uk**
8. In: *The Golden Legend: or, The Lives of the Saints*. First printed by William Caxton in 1483.
9. Francis Bacon (1626) *Sylva Sylvarum: or a Naturall Historie in Ten Centuries, Century VIII*.
10. M. Jill Lucas (2002) *Spinning Jenny and Devil's Darning Needle*. Privately published, Huddersfield.
11. Jill Lucas, op. cit., p14.
12. Muffet, op. cit. 'Of the divers kindes of Flies', chapter XI.
13. Mary Webb (1924) *Precious Bane*, 'Dragon-flies', book 3, chapter 5.
14. Frances Brown (1990) *A Harefoot Legacy*. In: Lucas, op. cit., p23.
15. A. L. Carvalho (2007) 'On some paintings of Odonata from the late Middle Ages'. *Odonatologica*, 36(3), pp243–253.
16. Charles Kingsley (1863) *The Water Babies: A fairy-tale for a land baby*. From chapter 3.
17. Webb, op. cit.
18. **www.lyricsmode.com**
19. **www.imdb.com**
20. Cynthia Longfield (1937) *Dragonflies of the British Isles*. Warne, London.
21. Cyril O. Hammond (1977) *The Dragonflies of Great Britain and Ireland*. Curwen Books, London.
22. Philip Corbet & Stephen Brooks (2008) *Dragonflies*. Collins New Naturalist 106, Collins, London.
23. Jonathan Bye.
24. Gregor Lamb (2004), *Orkney Wordbook*.
25. George Coppard. **www.spartacus.schoolnet.co.uk**
26. Tony Harwood.
27. William Shakespeare *The Taming of the Shrew*, Act IV, scene iii, 118.
28. Robert Hooke. *Micrographia*, p412. **http://books.google.co.uk**
29. Robert Burns 'To a Louse. On Seeing One on a Lady's Bonnet at Church'. In: *Robert Burns: Selected Poems*. Penguin Classics, pp85–86.
30. Miriam Rothschild & Theresa Clay (1952) *Fleas, Flukes and Cuckoos*. Collins, London, p118.
31. Muffet, op. cit. 'Of the Flea', chapter XXVIII.
32. R. S. George (2008) *Atlas of the Fleas (Siphonaptera) of Britain and Ireland*. Biological Records Centre, Huntingdon.
33. Muffet's, op. cit. 'Of the Flea', p1102.
34. M. Rothschild & B. Ford (1964) 'Breeding of the rabbit flea controlled by the reproductive hormones of the host'. *Nature*, 201, pp103–104.
35. Adoration of fleas in poetic rendering. **www.agriculture.purdue.edu/agcomm**
36. John Obadiah Westwood. In: Michael Salmon (2001) *The Aurelian Legacy*, Harley Books, p150.
37. William Shakespeare *Henry V*, Act III, scene vii, 141–42.
38. Kevin Page.
39. Alice Starmore.
40. **www.roberthooke.org.uk**
41. G. K. Chesterton (1910) 'William Blake'. In: Chesterton's *Monographies*, p155.
42. John Donne 'The Flea'. **Lardcave.net/hsc/2eng-donne-flea-comments**
43. L. Bertoletto *The History of the Flea, with Notes and Observations*. **www.fleacircus.co.uk**
44. Colin Plant (1999) 'The Suffolk Ant-lion *Euroleon nostras*'. *British Wildlife*, 10 (5), pp303–309.
45. Izaak Walton *The Compleat Angler* (in chapter 11 he recommends 'cod-worm' as bait for tench).
46. William Shakespeare *The Winter's Tale*, Act IV, scene iv, 202.
47. David Harding.
48. G. H. Green & Brett Westwood (2005) 'In search of the Land Caddis'. *British Wildlife*, 17 (1), pp21–26.

Grasshoppers and crickets

1. John Clare 'Summer Evening' ('fretting song'), 'Summer Images' ('treble pipe' and 'chickering crickets tremulous and long').
2. Judith Marshall & E. C. M. Haes (1988) *Grasshoppers and Allied Insects of Great Britain and Ireland*. Harley Books, Colchester.
3. **www.urbandictionary.com**
4. **www.luminarium.org/sevenlit/marvell/appleton.htm**
5. Richard Lovelace *Aubrey's Brief Lives*, Penguin Classics edn, pp264–65.
6. Richard Lovelace 'The Grass-hopper', *The poems of Richard Lovelace*. **www.luminarium.org**
7. *BBC News*, 19 September 2008.
8. Marshall & Haes, op. cit.
9. E. C. M. Haes & P. T. Harding (1997) *Atlas of grasshoppers, crickets and allied insects in Britain and Ireland*. ITE/JNCC, Huntingdon.
10. W. H. Hudson (1903) *Hampshire Days*. Oxford University Press edn, p108.
11. David W. Baldock (1999) *Grasshoppers and Crickets of Surrey*. Surrey Wildlife Trust.
12. Gary Farmer.
13. M. D. Burr (1936) *British Grasshoppers and their Allies*. Allan & Co, London.
14. Charles Dickens *The Cricket on the Hearth: A fairy tale of home*. 'Chirp the first'.
15. **www.dartmouth.edu/~milton/reading.../penseroso/index.shtml**
16. Bob Powley, Conwy, North Wales.
17. Tony Harwood.
18. Gilbert White, *The Garden Kalendar*, 20 May 1761.
19. Muffet, op. cit. 'Of Grashoppers (sic) and Krickets', p995.
20. White, op. cit. Letter XXXVIII to Daines Barrington.
21. 'Field-Cricket'. *John Clare: Selected Poems*, Penguin Classics.
22. David Sheppard, Peterborough.
23. White, op. cit. Letter XLVIII to Daines Barrington.
24. Marshall & Haes, op. cit. p99.
25. **www.nhm.ac.uk/about-us/news/2005/sept/news_6328.html**
26. Peter Sutton (1999) 'The Scaly Cricket in Britain: A complete history from discovery to citizenship'. *British Wildlife*, 10 (3), pp145–151.
27. Marshall & Haes, op. cit. pp141–44.
28. Richard Schweid (1999) *The Cockroach Papers: A compendium of history and lore*. Four Walls, Four Windows, New York.
29. Gwen Walker.
30. John Crompton (1955) *The Hunting Wasp*, New York.
31. Gerald & Lee Durrell (1982) *The Amateur Naturalist*, p26.
32. Blattodea Culture Group. **www.blattodea-culture-group.org**
33. Cited in: Marion Copeland (2003) *Cockroach*. Reaktion Books, London, p154.
34. Janell Cannon (2000) *Crickwing*. Harcourt Children's Books.
35. Marion Copeland, op. cit.
36. **www.planetark.com/dailynewsstory.cfm/newsid/38449/story.htm**
37. Dave Freeman (1999) *100 Things To Do Before You Die: Travel events you just can't miss*. Taylor Publishing.
38. David George Gordon (1996) *The Compleat Cockroach: A Comprehensive Guide to the Most Despised (and least Understood) Creature on Earth*. New York, p37.
39. Copeland, op. cit. p106.
40. Copeland, op. cit.
41. Bob Powley.
42. MS copied to author by Margaret Hansen.
43. Traditional children's rhyme. **www.mamalisa.com**
44. Muffet, op. cit. 'Of the Forficula, or Earwig'.
45. Marshall & Haes, op. cit. p139.
46. Copeland, op. cit. (2003).

True bugs

1. T. R. E. Southwood & Dennis Leston (1959) *Land and Water Bugs of the British Isles*. Warne, London (still the standard work).
2. Bob Cowley.
3. Alexander Pope (1735) *An Epistle to Dr Arbuthnot*. Lines

309–312 (the preceding line is his famous 'Who breaks a butterfly on a wheel?').

4. Roger D. Hawkins (2003) *Shieldbugs of Surrey*. Surrey Wildlife Trust, pp51–52.
5. Michele Kirsch 'Infested Britain'. *The Times Magazine*, 8 September 2007.
6. John Southall (1730) *A Treatise of Buggs: Shewing When and How they were first brought into England*. Printed as a pamphlet costing one shilling. **http://books.google.co.uk**
7. Jonty Denton (2007) *Water Bugs and Water Beetles of Surrey*. Surrey Wildlife Trust, Woking, p40.
8. Muffet, op. cit. 'Of the Locust, Scorpion, Notonectum, the Grasshopper, the Wasp, the forked claw, the Newt, the little Heart, and the Lowse, all Water-Insects', chapter XXXVIII.
9. Tony Harwood.
10. John Arthur Power (1810-1886). In: Michael Salmon (2000) *The Aurelian Legacy*, Harley Books, Colchester, pp153–54.
11. Muffet. 'Of the Locust etc' op. cit.
12. Denton, op. cit., p61.
13. Brian Hamdwerk 'How hairy legs help bugs walk on water'. *National Geographic*, 3 November 2003.
14. **http://wikipedia.org/wiki/Charles_Darwin's_illness**
15. W. H. Hudson (1903) *Hampshire Days*. OUP edition, pp105–107.
16. Bryan Pinchen & Lena Ward (2002) 'The history, ecology and conservation of the New Forest Cicada'. *British Wildlife*, 13 (4), pp258–266.
17. Sir Thomas Browne (1646) *Pseudodoxia Epidemica. Enquiries into Very Many Received Tenentes, and Commonly Presumed Truths* (often simplified as *Vulgar and Common Errors*.) 'Of the picture of a grasshopper', chapter 3.
18. John Clare, letter to John Taylor, March 1820. **http://books.google.co.uk**
19. Eric Carle (1997) *The Very Quiet Cricket*. Puffin Books.
20. Sheila Somerville.
21. White, op. cit. Letter XCVII to Daines Barrington.
22. **www.metrolyrics.com**
23. Leonard New.
24. 'How aphids become suicide bombers.' *Daily Telegraph*, 11 July 2007.
25. **http://wikipedia.org/wiki/Antz**
26. White, op. cit., letter CVIII.
27. 'Insect army called up to fight knotweed.' *Daily Telegraph*, 4 May 2008.
28. Stefan Buczacki (2007) *Garden Natural History*. Collins New Naturalist, 102, p233.

Butterflies

1. Miriam Rothschild (1991) *Butterfly Cooing Like a Dove*. Doubleday, London, p23.
2. e.g.: 'Swich talking is nat worth a boterflye/ For therinne is ther no desport ne game.' Geoffrey Chaucer, *The Canterbury Tales*, prologue to 'The Nun's Priest's Tale'.
3. Michael Chinery, note in *The Entomologist*, early 1960s.
4. Anatoly Liberman, comment, 22 August 2007, 'Wilhelm Oehl and the Butterfly'. **http://blog.oup.com/2007/08/butterfly**
5. Liberman, ibid.
6. Rothschild, op. cit. p26.
7. Edward Thomas 'The Brook'. **www.richmondreview.co.uk/library/thomas02.html**
8. Paul Weller 'Amongst Butterflies.' **www.metrolyrics.com**
9. **www.asklyrics.com**
10. **www.butterfly-conservation.org**
11. John Moore (1961) *You English Words*.
12. Walton, op. cit.
13. Charles Kingsley 'The Oubit' (1850) *Andromeda and other Poems* **www.fullbooks.com**
14. Ian Wallace.
15. Andrew Bissitt, Salford.
16. Eric Carle (1969) **http://wikipedia.org/wiki/The_Very_Hungry_Caterpillar**
17. 'Caterpillar Girl' **www.metrolyrics.com**; Roy Campi 'Caterpillar' **www.rockabilly.nl/lyrics**

18. **http://wikipedia.org/wiki/Little_Arabella_Miller**
19. Brian Boyd & Robert Michael Pyle (2000) *Nabokov's Butterflies*. Allen Lane, London.
20. Moore, op. cit.
21. Michael Salmon (2000) *The Aurelian Legacy*, pp241–42.
22. C.W. Mackworth-Pread (1942) 'Carterocephalus palaemon in Western Inverness-shire'. *Entomologist*, 75, p216.
23. Arthur Conan Doyle (1902) *The Hound of the Baskervilles*, chapter 7.
24. Jeremy Thomas & Richard Lewington (1991) *The Butterflies of Britain and Ireland*. National Trust, p24.
25. A. Maitland Emmet (1991) *The Scientific Names of the British Lepidoptera: Their history and meaning*. Harley Books, Colchester, p145.
26. Muffet, op. cit. 'Of Butterflies', chapter 14.
27. Vladimir Nabokov (1951) *Speak, Memory*, p94.
28. Frederic Prokosch (1983) 'Voices: A Memoir'. In: Rothschild, p95.
29. Ian Wallace, Liverpool.
30. 'BB' (Denys Watkins-Pickford) (1944) *Brendon Chase*. Methuen.
31. David Corke (2002) 'The affair of the "Long-willied" (Reals's) Wood White'. *British Wildlife*, 13 (4), pp240–243.
32. William Shakespeare *King Lear*, Act V, scene iii, 11–13.
33. William Shakespeare *Coriolanus*, Act I, scene iii, 60–66.
34. Irving L. Finkelstein (1985) 'Death, Damnation and Resurrection: Butterflies as symbols in western art'. *Bulletin, Amateur Entomologists' Society*, 44, pp123–32.
35. Thomas & Lewington, op. cit., p37.
36. 'The man who caught 800 Pale Clouded Yellows.' In: Michael A. Salmon & Peter J. Edwards (2005) *The Aurelian's Fireside Companion: An Entomological Anthology*. Paphia Publishing, pp31–32.
37. L. Hugh Newman (1967) *Living with Butterflies*, pp199–201.
38. Rothschild, op. cit.; 'among the wortes on a boterflye', Chaucer 'The Nun's Priest's Tale'.
39. Stefan Buczacki (2002) *Fauna Britannica*. Hamlyn, p78.
40. John Feltwell (1986) *The Natural History of Butterflies*. Croom Helm, London.
41. L. Hugh Newman *Living with Butterflies*, p63.
42. Philip Norman (1984) *The Stones*. Elm Tree Books, London, p271.
43. Cited in: *Butterfly*, 97, spring 2008.
44. E. B. Ford (1945) *Butterflies*. Collins New Naturalist 1, plate 1.
45. John Masefield (1921) *King Cole*. Macmillan, London.
46. Vladimir Nabokov *Speak, Memory* (1951). In: Patrick Matthews (1957) *The Pursuit of Moths and Butterflies: An Anthology*, Chatto & Windus, p21.
47. *The Observer's Book of Butterflies* (1938), p139. The Wagstaff passage was removed from later editions.
48. Mark Webb & Andrew Pullin (1997) 'The Orange Argus: A history of the Large Copper butterfly in Britain'. *British Wildlife*, 9 (1), pp29-37.
49. P. B. M. Allan (1943) *Talking of Moths*, p23.
50. Tim Bernhard.
51. Michael A. Salmon (2000) *The Aurelian Legacy*, p297; Salmon & Edwards, op. cit. *Aurelian's Fireside Companion*, p32.
52. Gary Farmer.
53. Andy Horton, Shoreham, Sussex.
54. Robert Frost (1923) 'Blue-Butterfly Day'. **www.love-poems.com**
55. Rothschild, op. cit. p30.
56. Heinrich Heine. Cited in: Rothschild, op. cit. p28.
57. Richard Fox & others (2006) *The State of Butterflies in Britain and Ireland*. Pisces Publications, Newbury, p46.
58. Charles Dickens (ed 1838). *The Memoirs of Joseph Grimaldi*.
59. Salmon (2000), op. cit. pp308–309.
60. Stuart Blackman (2005) 'The singing blues'. *BBC Wildlife*, November 2005, pp32–37.
61. A. Maitland Emmet & John Heath (eds 1989) *The Moths and Butterflies of Great Britain and Ireland*, vol. 7 (1), p179.
62. George Crabbe (1810) 'The Borough'.
63. Joseph Dandridge (1664–1746). In: Salmon, op. cit., p106.
64. Francis Orpen Morris. Cited in: Thomas & Lewington (1991), p115.
65. Mathew Oates (2005) 'Extreme butterfly-collecting: A biography of I. R. P. Heslop'. *British Wildlife*, 16 (3), pp164–171.

66. Matthew Oates (2006) 'Extreme butterflying: The 2006 Purple Emperor Season'. Circulated report.
67. Salmon, op. cit., p311.
68. Emmet & Heath, op. cit. vol. (1), pp192–193.
69. Stefan Buczacki *Fauna Britannica*, p82.
70. Finkelstein, op.cit.
71. Buczacki, op. cit., p82.
72. Moses Harris (1766) *The Aurelian, or The Natural History of English Insects*, Plate XI.
73. Muffet, op. cit. 'Of Butterflyes'.
74. Paul Waring, Blackburn, Lancashire.
75. Lynn Fomison.
76. Finkelstein, op. cit.
77. Ken Thompson (2006) *No Nettles Required. The reassuring truth about wildlife gardening*. Eden Project Books, pp86–87.
78. Harris (1766), op. cit., Plate XII.
79. W. S. Coleman (1860) *British Butterflies*.
80. Siegfried Sassoon (1938) *The Old Century and Seven More Years*, p279.
81. Muffet, op. cit. 'Of Butterflyes', chapter XIV, p968.
82. Karl Goswell, Birmingham.
83. C. E. Raven (1942) *John Ray: naturalist*, p411.
84. Moses Harris (1775) *The English Lepidopterist: or The Aurelian's Pocket Companion*.
85. Philip Bertram & Murray Alla (1943) *Talking of Moths*. 'The Canterbury Buccaneers in Allan'.
86. Martin Warren, Butterfly Conservation.
87. Thomas & Lewington, op. cit., p149.
88. F. W. Frohawk (1934), *The Complete Book of British Butterflies*. Ward Lock, London, p119.
89. Thomas & Lewington, op. cit, p152.
90. Harris (1766), op. cit., Plate XVI.
91. Eleanor Glanville (c.1654–1709). In: Salmon (2000) op. cit.
92. Roger Deakin (2008) *Notes from Walnut Tree Farm*. Hamish Hamilton, 1 September, p214.
93. Jim Asher & others (2001) *The Millennium Atlas of Butterflies in Britain and Ireland*. Oxford University Press, pp250–51.
94. Harris (1766), op. cit., Plate XXVII.
95. Raven (1942), op. cit., p413.
96. Finkelstein, op. cit.
97. Ford (1945), op. cit. pp159–60.

Moths

1. Deakin (2008), op. cit. pp176–77.
2. Roger Deakin (2007) *Wildwood: A Journey Through Trees*. Hamish Hamilton. 'The Moth Wood', p59.
3. Sir Arthur Quiller-Couch (1895) 'The White Moth'. **www.poemhunter.com**
4. John Byrne Warren (1895) 'The Study of a Spider', line 12.
5. Brett Westwood, Worcester.
6. John Keats (1819) 'Ode to Psyche'. **www.bartleby.com**
7. Robert Gittings 'The Great Moth'. In: *The Oxford Book of Twentieth-Century English Verse*, p446.
8. Virginia Woolf (1942) *The Death of a Moth, and other essays*. Hogarth Press.
9. Frances Cooke.
10. John Gay (1728) *The Beggar's Opera*, Act I.
11. William Shakespeare *The Merchant of Venice*, Act II, scene ix.
12. W. H. Hudson (1904) *Green Mansions. A romance of the tropical forest*, chapter 20.
13. Don Marquis 'Archy and Mehitobel'. In: Miriam Rothschild, op. cit. 'Candles', chapter 8.
14. P. B. Shelley (1824) 'One Word is Too Often Profaned', verse 2. **www.classicalauthors.net**
15. Vladimir Nabokov (1951) *Speak, Memory*.
16. Peter Marren (1998) 'The English names of moths'. *British Wildlife*, 10 (1), pp29–38.
17. Eleazar Albin (1720) *A Natural History of English Insects*.
18. James Petiver (1702–06) *Gazophylacium Naturae et Artis*.
19. Harris, op. cit.
20. Adrian Hardy Haworth. In: Salmon, op. cit., p128.
21. Albin, op. cit.
22. Walton, op. cit.
23. Muffet, op. cit. 'Of Butterflies'.
24. Benjamin Wilkes (1749) *The English Moths and Butterflies*.
25. Revd. John Hellins (1886) 'Superstition regarding the Death's-head Hawk-moth'. In: Salmon & Edwards, op. cit., pp346–47.
26. Annie Dows (1881) 'Vitality of the Death's-head Hawk-moth'. In: Salmon & Edwards, op. cit., pp345–46.
27. Thomas Hardy (1878) *The Return of the Native*, chapter 8.
28. Martin Looker.
29. Virginia Woolf, *The Common Reader*, chapter 13.
30. Annabelle Tipper.
31. Allan, op. cit., (1943) pp229–231.
32. Salmon & Edwards, op. cit., caption, p323.
33. P. B. M. Allan (1937) *A Moth Hunter's Gossip*. Watkins & Doncaster, p91.
34. Diane Redfield Massie (1985) *Lobster Moths*. Granite Impex Ltd.
35. Muffet, op. cit. 'Concerning Caterpillers and their several kindes, and namely of Silk-spinners, and Silk-worms', book II.
36. Walton, op. cit.
37. Harris (1766), op. cit., plate XXXVIII.
38. L. Hugh Newman (1967) *Living with Butterflies*. John Barker, p84.
39. William Curtis (1782) *A Short History of the Brown-tail Moth*. Curwen Press facsimile, 1969.
40. Allan (1937), op. cit., p248.
41. Jan Goedart (1662–67) *Metamorphosis et Historia Naturalis* 'History of Insects'.
42. Deakin (2008), op. cit., pp176–77.
43. Harris (1766), op. cit., plate XVII.
44. Harris (1766), op. cit., pXXV.
45. Wilkes (1749), op. cit.
46. John Keats (1820) *The Eve of St Agnes*.
47. Emmet, op. cit., p224
48. Harris (1766), op. cit., plate XXXI.
49. Allan Shepherd (2005) *Curious Incidents in the Garden at Night-time: The fantastic story of disappearing night*. Centre for Alternative Technology publications.
50. From the 1952 film *Hans Christian Anderson*.
51. John Ray (1710) *The History of Insects*. In: C. E. Raven (1942) *John Ray: Naturalist*, pp394–95.
52. John Whiscombe, Thatcham, Berks.
53. Philip Smith, Ainsdale, Lancashire.
54. In: Deakin (2007), op. cit., p65.
55. Roger Key, North Lincs.
56. Pieter Lyonnet (1760) *Traite anatomique de la Chenille, qui ronge le bois de Saule*.
57. 'Ghosts – and Cossus'. In: P. B. M. Allan (1948) *Moths and Memories*. Watkins & Doncaster.
58. 'Tree in web of horror.' *Diss Mercury*, 7 June 2007.
59. Amanda Callaghan, Reading, Berks.
60. Kenneth Blair (1922) 'The Ghost Moth' and a 'Will-o-the-Wisp'. In: Salmon & Edwards, op. cit., pp329–34.
61. C. G. Barrett (1892-1904) *The Lepidoptera of the British Islands*.
62. Emmet (1991), op. cit., p83.

Flies

1. Steven Connor (2006) *Fly*. Reaktion Books, Singapore, p54.
2. Conner, ibid., p15.
3. William Shakespeare *King Lear*, Act IV, scene vi, 115–17.
4. Edward Halford Ross (1913) *The Reduction of Domestic Flies*; John Ruskin 'The Queen of the Air'. In: Conner, op. cit., p25.
5. Ogden Nash, 'The Fly'. In: *Collected Verse from 1929 on*, London, 1961.
6. Muffet, op. cit. 'Of the use of Flyes', book I, chapter XII.
7. **www.hno.harvard.edu/gazette/1996/04.11/SandFly SalivaMa.html**
8. P. B. Shelley (1819) 'The Witch of Atlas', line 364; John Keats (1817) 'Endymion', line 852.
9. Samuel Wesley (1685) *Maggots; or, 'Poems on Several Subjects Never Before Handled'*. In: Connor, op. cit., p169.
10. William Golding *The Lord of the Flies*, chapter 8.
11. Irvine Welsh (1994) 'The Granton Star Cause'. In: *The Acid House*, Secker & Warburg, London.
12. **http://ebooks.adelaide.edu.au/y/yeats/william_butler/y4c/part113.html**

13. www.julialohmann.co.uk
14. Laurence Sterne (1759) *The Life and Opinions of Tristram Shandy, Gentleman.* Chapter 1, XXXVII.
15. William Blake (1794). In: 'The Fly'. *Songs of Experience.*
16. William Shakespeare *Titus Andronicus*, Act IV, scene i, 60–65.
17. Poems of Charles Tennyson Turner, **www.poemhunter.com**
18. Iona & Peter Opie (1997) *The Oxford Dictionary of Nursery Rhymes.* Oxford University Press.
19. Craig Brown 'Daddy, I hardly knew you'. *Daily Telegraph*, 23 September 2006.
20. www.nottinghamshirewildlife.org.uk
21. Louise Searle.
22. Hannah Rigden.
23. Steve Palin.
24. Andrew Eames.
25. Tony Harwood, Kent.
26. D. H. Lawrence 'The Mosquito Knows'; 'The Mosquito'. In: *Birds, Beasts and Flowers* (1923), Secker, London.
27. Alice Starmore, Outer Hebrides.
28. Roger Deakin (1999) *Waterlog.* Chatto & Windus, p49.
29. Alan Stubbs & Martin Drake (2001) *British Soldierflies and their Allies.* British Entomological Society, London.
30. Stubbs & Drake, ibid, p335.
31. www.scottisharts.org
32. Muffet, op. cit. 'Of the divers kindes of flies', book I, chapter XI.
33. Gwen Walker, Isle of Man.
34. Stubbs & Drake, op. cit., p374.
35. Muffet, op. cit. 'Of the divers kindes of flies', book I, chapter XI.
36. Stubbs & Drake, op. cit., p374.
37. Tony Harwood.
38. Miriam Rothschild & Theresa Clay (1952) *Fleas, Flukes and Cuckoos.* Collins, London.
39. Stubbs & Drake, op. cit., p185. Based on: Alan Stubbs (1997) 'British Bee-flies'. *British Wildlife*, 8 (3), pp175–179; D. K. Clements (1997) 'The enemy within: Conopid flies as parasitoids of bees and wasps in Britain'. *British Wildlife*, 8 (5), pp310–315.
40. Stubbs & Drake, ibid, p194.
41. Alan Stubbs 'Flies'. In: David Hawksworth (ed) (2001) *The Changing Wildlife of Great Britain and Ireland.* Taylor & Francis, London, p246.
42. Alan Stubbs & Steven Falk (2nd edn. 2002) *British Hoverflies.* British Entomological Society, London.
43. Stubbs & Falk, ibid, p32.
44. Tony Harwood, Kent.
45. *The Rat-tailed Maggot and other poems* (1998) **www. attilathestockbroker.com**
46. Muffet, op. cit. 'Of Flyes', book I, chapter X.
47. Andre Bay (1979) *Des mouches et des hommes.* In: Connor, op. cit.
48. John Clare 'House or Window Flies'. In: Eric Robinson & David Powell (eds 1984) *The Later Poems of John Clare: 1837–1864*, vol. II, Oxford.
49. Connor, op. cit., p32.
50. Edward Hanford Ross (1913) *The Reduction of Domestic Flies.* London, p8;
    J. F. M. Clark (2009) *Bugs and the Victorians.* Yale University Press, p232.
51. Steven Connor, op. cit., p111.
52. J. R. Harris (1952) *An Angler's Entomology.* Collins, London, p171.
53. Richard Conniff (1997) *Spineless Wonders: The joys of formication.* Souvenir Press, London, p9.
54. Steven Connor, op. cit., p144.
55. Raymond Queneau (1944) 'Fantasies'. In: Connor, op. cit., p28.
56. *The Goon Show* (1953), 3rd series, 'The man who never was'.
57. William Cowper (1782) 'The Progress of Error'. In: Robert Southey (ed) (1835-37) *The Works of William Cowper*, vol. VIII, p155; Ben Jonson (1606) *Volpone*, Act V, scene v.
58. Frank Balfour-Browne (1925) *Concerning the habits of insects.* Cambridge.
59. 'Bugs in the head – fly larvae living on man's skull.' *Daily Mail*, 18 July 2007.
60. http://wikipedia.org/wiki/Deer_botfly

Beetles

1. Francis Darwin (1887) *The Life and Letters of Charles Darwin.* John Murray, London.
2. Arthur V. Evans & Charles L. Bellamy (1996) *An Inordinate Fondness for Beetles.* Henry Holt, New York.
3. http://wikipedia.org/wiki/Terry_Erwin
4. A. A. Gill (2007) *Previous Convictions: assignments from here and there.* Weidenfield & Nicolson.
5. Thomas Gray (1750) 'Elegy written in a Country Churchyard', verse 2.
6. Gregor Lamb (1988) op. cit.
7. www.poetryfoundation.org/archive/poem.html?id =174638
8. Dave Persails (1996) 'The Beatles: What's in a Name?' http://abbeyrd.best.vwh.net
9. Paul Shipton (2003) *Bug Muldoon and the Garden of Fear.* OUP Oxford.
10. Gavin Maxwell (1965) *The House of Elrig.* Longmans.
11. Alex Ramsay.
12. Roger Key, N. Lincolnshire.
13. A. A. Milne (1926) *Winnie the Pooh.* Methuen, chapter 7. Also in A. A. Milne (1927) *Now We Are Six.*
14. Tony Harwood.
15. 'Extinction looms for Britain's rarest beetle.' Buglife, October 2007. www.buglife.org.uk
16. Jonathan Spencer, Newbury, Berks.
17. Ann Kelly (2005) *The Burying Beetle.* Luath Press.
18. David Streeter.
19. www.greatstaghunt.org
20. Colin Hawes, Suffolk
21. In: Jane Campbell Hutchison (1990) *Albrecht Dürer: A Biography.* Princeton University Press, p. 69.
22. 'Sex education with Bill Oddie.' *Daily Telegraph*, 31 May 2008.
23. John South, Wallingford, Berks.
24. Roger Key, Nature Conservancy Council, Peterborough.
25. W. H. Hudson (1903) *Hampshire Days.* Longman, p98.
26. William Shakespeare *Hamlet*, Act I, scene v; John Webster, *The Duchess of Malfi*, Act IV, scene ii;
27. Edmund Gosse (ed) (1894) *Letters of Thomas Lovell Beddoes.*
28. William Blake (1794) 'A Dream'. In: *Songs of Innocence and of Experience.*
29. John Clare (1820) 'To a Glow-worm'. Glow-worm Quotes www.worldofquotes.com
30. Muffet, op. cit. 'Of the Glow-worm', book I, chapter XV.
31. Hudson (1903), op. cit.
32. Gilbert White (1766) *Flora Selborniensis*, 14 June.
33. Robin Scagell. www.galaxypix.com/glowworms
34. Graham Bathe.
35. Thomas Hardy (1978) *The Return of the Native*, book 3, chapter VIII, 'A New Force Disturbs the Current'.
36. Winston Churchill quotes at www.brainyquotes.com
37. William Shakespeare *Romeo and Juliet*, Act III, scene i.
38. A. W. Exell (1991) *The History of the Ladybird: With some diversions on this and that.* Privately printed, Blockley Antiquarian Society.
39. John Clare, 'Clock-a-Clay', *Selected Poems.* Geoffrey Summerfield (ed), Penguin Classics, p343; Robert Southey, 'The Burnie Bee'. In: Exell, op. cit.
40. Exell, ibid.
41. Exell, ibid.
42. John Gay, from 'The Shepherd's Week: Thursday; or, The Spell.'
43. Exell, op. cit.
44. Exell, op. cit.
45. 'Disaster Warning?' In: Chris Roberts (2004) *Heavy Words Lightly Thrown: The Reason behind the Rhyme*, Granta Books, p53.
46. Bob Powley, Conwy, N. Wales.
47. Roger D. Hawkins (2000) *Ladybirds of Surrey.* Surrey Wildlife Trust.
48. Hannah Rigden.
49. www.ladybird-survey.org
50. Tony Harwood, Maidstone, Kent.
51. 'Invasion of the Harlequins and a Threat to the Survival of British Ladybirds.' *Independent*, 13 July 2007.

52. Jonathan Swift (1726) 'Wood An Insect'. In: *The Select Works of Jonathan Swift*, vol. IV, p179. **http://books.google.co.uk**

53. Oliver Goldsmith 'Citizen of the World', 17 December, 1760. In: Arthur Friedman (ed) (1966) *The Collected Works of Oliver Goldsmith*. Clarendon Press, Oxford, vol. 2, p367.

54. 'Forlorn' (1899). In: *Poetical Works of Alfred Lord Tennyson*. **http://books.google.co.uk**

55. Edgar Allan Poe (1843) 'The Tell-tale Heart'. **http://books.google.co.uk**; John E. Reilly (1969) 'The Lesser Death-Watch' and 'The Tell-Tale Heart', *The American Transcendental Quarterly*, II, pp3–9.

56. Julian Barnes (1989) *A History of the World in 10½ Chapters*. Jonathan Cape.

57. Muffet, op. cit. 'Of Beetles', book I, chapter XXI.

58. Henri Fabre (1919) *The Glow-worm and other beetles*.

59. **www.buglife.org.uk/getinvolved/surveys/oilbeetle** survey; Alex Ramsay (2002) 'British oil beetles'. *British Wildlife*, 14 (1), pp27–30.

60. Muffet, op. cit. 'Of the Cantharides, or Spanish Fly', book I, chapter XX.

61. Muffet, ibid.

62. Muffet, ibid.

63. Amanda Callaghan (2002) 'Spanish Fly Undone'. *Antenna*, Bulletin of the Royal Entomological Society, 26 (3), pp164–67.

64. 'Alien giant that crept out of the woodwork.' *The Times*, 29 June 2006.

65. Brett Westwood, Worcester.

66. Geoff Oxford & others (2003) 'The jewel of York – ecology and conservation of the Tansy Beetle'. *British Wildlife*, 14 (5), pp333-337.

67. Michael Shannon, York.

68. J. Clark (2009) *Bugs and the Victorians*, p152.

69. Roger Key, North Lincs.

70. Jonty Denton (2007) *Water Bugs and Water Beetles of Surrey*. Surrey Wildlife Trust, p1.

71. Peter Sutton (2008) *The larger water beetles of the British Isles*. Amateur Entomologists' Society, p48.

72. Paul O'Neil & Trevor Beebee (2005) 'The Great Silver Water Beetle in Britain – a cry for help'. *British Wildlife*, 16 (4), pp265–269.

73. E. F. Linssen (1959) *Beetles of the British Isles*. Warne.

74. Garth Foster (2008) 'Whirligigs in Britain and Ireland'. *British Wildlife*, 20 (1), pp28–35.

75. Hilaire Belloc (1899) *A Moral Alphabet: W for Waterbeetle*. **www.mainlesson.com**

Wasps, bees and ants

1. Charles Darwin. Cited in Stephen Jay Gould (1982) 'Nonmoral Nature', *Hen's Teeth and Horses Toes: Further Reflections in Natural History*. Norton, New York, pp32–44.

2. Jim Porter, *Atropos* magazine.

3. Jennifer Owen (1991) *The Ecology of a Garden: The first fifteen years*. Cambridge University Press.

4. Ken Thompson (2006) *No Nettles Required: The reassuring truth about wildlife gardening*. Eden Project Books.

5. David Baldock.

6. Graham Bathe.

7. Leonard New.

8. Gilbert White, *The Natural History of Selborne*, letter LXIV to Daines Barrington.

9. Miles O'Hare (2005) *Does Anything Eat Wasps? (and 101 other questions)*. Profile Books.

10. Tony Harwood, Kent.

11. William Shakespeare *The Taming of the Shrew*, Act II, scene i, 209; *Julius Caesar*, Act IV, scene iii, pp49–50.

12. **www.staylace.com**

13. **www.poemhunter.com**

14. George Macbeth (2002) 'The Wasp's Nest'. In: *Selected Poems* (2002), Enitharmon Press.

15. **www.imdb.com/title/tt0388534**

16. Jonathan Cooter (1991) *A Coleopterist's Handbook*. Amateur Entomologist's Society, p12.

17. Lawrence Trowbridge.

18. John Bunyan (1701) *A Book for Boys and Girls or Temporal Things Spiritualized*.

19. **www.phrases.org.uk/meanings**

20. Geoffrey Chaucer 'The Merchant's Tale', epilogue. In: *The Canterbury Tales*.

21. Alice Starmore, Outer Hebrides.

22. John Clare, 'Wild Bees'. In: Geoffrey Summerfield (ed) (2000) *John Clare: Selected Poems*. Penguin Classics, pp114–115.

23. 'The Honey Monster.' *Independent*, 17 March 2007.

24. David Baldock (2008) *Bees of Surrey*, Surrey Wildlife Trust.

25. John Clare 'Wild Bees' op. cit.

26. Bill Griffiths (2005) *A Dictionary of North Eastern Dialect* (2nd edition). Northumbria University Press, Newcastle.

27. John Clare 'Wild Bees' op. cit.

28. *Bumblebees*. Scottish Natural Heritage, Naturally Scottish series, 2004.

29. White, op. cit., letter XXVII to Daines Barrington.

30. John Clare, 'Wild Bees' op. cit.

31. David Goulson (2006) 'The demise of the bumblebee in Britain'. *Biologist*, 53(6), pp294–99;

32. J. C. Biesmeijer *et al.* (2006) 'Parallel declines in pollinators and insect-pollinated plants in Britain and the Netherlands'. *Science*, 21 July 2006, pp351–54.

33. **www.buglife.org.uk**

34. **www.bumblebeeconservationtrust.co.uk**

35. William Shakespeare *Henry V*, Act I, scene ii, pp187–204.

36. Charles Butler (1609) *The Feminine Monarchie: or The History of Bees*.

37. Walter Raleigh (1829) 'The History of the World'. In: *The Works of Sir Walter Raleigh*, II, xvi.

38. Alison Benjamin & Brian McCallum (2008) *A World Without Bees*. Guardian Books, p9.

39. Karl Marx, *Das Kapital*, vol.1, chapter 7.

40. Charles Dickens (1865) *Our Mutual Friend*, part 1, chapter 8.

41. Isaac Watts (1715) 'How doth the Little Bee'.

42. William Wordsworth (1817) 'Vernal Ode'. In: *Complete Works*, **www.everypoet.com**

43. *William Shakespeare Twelfth Night*, Act II, scene iii, 754.

44. Samson's riddle: Judges, 14:14.

45. Sue Clifford & Angela King (2006) *England in Particular. A celebration of the commonplace, the local, the vernacular and distinctive*. Common Ground, Hodder & Staughton, 'Bee Boles', p35.

46. Flora Thompson (1939) *Lark Rise*. Oxford University Press, chapter 5, pp80–82.

47. Benjamin & McCallum, op. cit.

48. He goes on: 'In terms of the worth to the horticultural industry, our best estimate is that the bee population contributes something like £165 million extra in yields'. Lords Hansard, 27 November 2007.

49. 'Famous Einstein Bee Quote is Bogus.' **www.thedailygreen.com**

50. J. Clark, op. cit., p89.

51. Graham Bathe.

52. **www.poemhunter.com**

53. Muffet, op. cit., book II, chapter XVI, 'The Commendation of Pismires; Wherein We Shall Describe Their Differences, Nature, Ingenuity and Use'.

54. Abraham Lincoln (1990) *Collected Works*, vol. II. In: Charlotte Sleigh (2003) *Ant*. Reaktion Books, London, p19.

55. T. H. White (1958) *The Once and Future King*, part I, 'The Sword in the Stone', chapter XIII.

56. Hans Ewers (1927) *The Ant People*. In: Sleigh, op. cit., p85.

57. **www.antsmarching.org**

58. Laurent Keller & Elisabeth Gordon (2009) *The Lives of Ants*. Oxford University Press, part VIII, 'High-tech Ants'.

59. H. G. Wells (1905) *Empire of the Ants*. In: Sleigh, op. cit., pp99–104.

60. **www.tessafarmer.com**

Shelled life

1. Charles Dickens, *David Copperfield*, chapter VII.

References and source notes

2. J. B. Smith (2008) 'From Granfer-grigs to Tiddly-topes: A look at names for representatives of the natural world in the Laver corpus'. *Transactions Devonshire Association*, 140, pp157–64.
3. William Cowper (1803) 'The Snail'. In: Arthur E. Ellis (1975) 'The snail in nineteenth century verse'. *Conchologist's Newsletter*, 55, pp464–466.
4. John Donne 'To Sir Henry Wotton'. **www.luminarium.org/sevenlit/donne/wotton.htm**
5. Sabine Baring-Gould (1895) 'The Snail'. In: Ellis (1975), op.cit.
6. Hope B. Werness (2006) *Animal Symbolism in Art*. Continuum, London, p376.
7. A. E. Ellis (1973) 'Cochlea Liberum: The snail in old nursery rhymes'. *Conchologist's Newsletter*, 47, pp346–48.
8. Ellis (1973), ibid.
9. John Gay (1714) 'The Shepherd's Week', 4th 'pastoral'. In: Ellis (1975) op. cit.
10. Simon Winchester (1996) *The River at the Centre of the World*. Penguin Books.
11. **http://wikipedia.org/wiki/Discworld**
12. J. W. Taylor (1894–1921) *Monograph of the Land and Freshwater Mollusca of the British Isles*. Taylor Brothers, Leeds.
13. Sara Bellis.
14. Robert Cameron.
15. Charles Godfrey Leland (2002) 'Gypsy sorcery and fortune-telling'. In: *The Faber Book of Exploration*, Benedict Allan (ed), Faber & Faber, London.
16. e.g.: 'Stepping Stones' Geoffrey Summerfield (ed) (1990). In: *John Clare, Selected Poems*. Penguin Classics, p87.
17. Bob Powley, Conwy, N. Wales.
18. **www.snailracing.net**
19. Robert Cameron, Wolverhampton.
20. Martin Willing (2008) 'Wildlife Reports'. *British Wildlife* 19 (4), pp287–88.
21. 'Snails pace discovery reveals amazing find.' National Trust website.
22. Edward Step (2nd edn 1945) *Shell Life – An Introduction To The British Mollusca*. Warne, London, p318.
23. Gilbert White, *Journal*, 31 March 1775.
24. Smith, op. cit.
25. William Shakespeare Richard III, Act III, scene i, 22, 24.
26. Step, op. cit., p345.
27. Stefan Buczacki (2007) *Garden Natural History*. Collins New Naturalist, p67.
28. **http://england.prm.ox.ac.uk/englishness-slug-on-a-thorn**
29. Step, op. cit., p192.
30. John Wright (2009) *Edible Seashore*, River Cottage Handbook No.5, p157.
31. Dorothy Hartley (1954) *Food in England*. Brown Book group
32. John Wright, op. cit., p134.
33. Stephen Reynolds (1909) *A Poor Man's House*.
34. **www.buyorkney.com** guide book.
35. Rachel Carson (1955) *The Edge of the Sea*. Houghton Mifflin, Boston.
36. Michael Viney (2001) 'Edge of the tide: a natural history of beachcombing'. *British Wildlife*, 12 (6), pp381–87.
37. Step, op. cit., p212.
38. Michael and Ethna Viney (2008) *Ireland's Oceans: A natural history*. Collins Press, Cork, p64.
39. Rachel Cooke 'The secret life of cockles'. *Observer*, 14 March 2004.
40. C. M. Yonge (1949) *The Sea Shore*. Collins New Naturalist, 12, p283.
41. 'Mussel bound.' *Independent*, 10 December 2003.
42. 'Toxic pill attacks zebra mussels.' *BBC News*, 2 February 2006.
43. Peter Cosgrove, Lee Hastie & Mark Young (2000) 'Freshwater Pearl Mussels in peril'. *British Wildlife*, 11 (5), pp340–347.
44. Jean-Luc Solandt (2003) 'The fan shell *Atrina fragilis* – a species of conservation concern'. *British Wildlife*, 14 (6), pp423–427.
45. **www.worldfishing.net**
46. Gregor Lamb, op. cit.
47. Step, op. cit., p102.
48. BBC Science online news, 28 October 2007.
49. **www.lyricsondemand.com**
50. 'Luminous mollusc can tell when you're going to be ill.' *Daily Telegraph*, 4 August 2008.
51. John Gay (1714) 'Trivia'.
52. Eleanor Clark (2006) *The Oysters of Locmariaquer*. Harper-Collins.
53. Ernest Hopkins (ed) (1967). *The Enlarged Devil's Dictionary* Penguin, p239.
54. Charles Dickens *The Pickwick Papers*, chapter VIII.
55. 'Oyster world record smashed.' BBC online news, 6 September 2003.
56. **www.colchesteroysterfishery.com**
57. **www.falmouthoysters.co.uk**
58. **www.galwayoysterfest.com**
59. William Shakespeare *The Merry Wives of Windsor*, Act II, scene 2, 797.
60. P. G. Wodehouse (1938) *The Code of the Woosters*, chapter 2.
61. Oscar Wilde, **www.thinkexist.com**
62. Lewis Carroll (1871) *Alice through the Looking Glass,* 'The Walrus and the Carpenter'.
63. George Orwell, 'Politics and the English Language'. In: Sonia Orwell & Ian Angus (eds) (1968) *The Collected Essays, Journalism and Letters of George Orwell*, vol. 4, 'In Front of Your Nose', p156.
64. Alfred Tennyson, 'The Kraken Wakes'. **www.jojaffa.com/guides/callouts/kraken.htm**
65. Step, op. cit., p390.
66. 'Otto the octopus wreaks havoc.' *Daily Telegraph*, 3 November 2008.

Spiny-skins

1. Buczacki (2002), op. cit., p21.
2. Willy Elmer (1973) 'English Dialect – The Terminology of Fishing: a survey of English and Welsh inshore fishing things and words'. *Cooper Monographs*, 19, English Dialect Series, Franke Verlag. In: Sue Clifford & Angela King (2006) *England in Particular*. Common Ground and Hodder & Stoughton, p386.
3. Elmer, ibid.
4. **www.lizmcgowan.com**
5. **www.iberianature.com**
6. Rosemary Parslow (2007) *The Isles of Scilly*. Collins New Naturalist 103, London.
7. John Woodward (1695) 'An Essay towards a Natural History of the Earth . . . an Account of the Universal'.
8. Erik Satie 'The desiccated embryo of a Holothurian'. In: '*Embryons desséchés*' for piano solo.

Not-quite-bugs and-nearly-vertebrates

1. 'It's a long way to Amphioxus'. **www.flounder.com/amphioxus**

ACKNOWLEDGEMENTS

Bugs Britannica could not have been written without the help of contributors, who responded generously to our appeals for stories, anecdotes and snippets of bug-lore from their personal experience. We thank the following for sharing these with us:

Phil Ackery, David Agassiz, John Balaam, Brian Banks, Tony Barber, Simon Barker, Ray Barnett, Margaret Bateman, Graham Bathe, James Bell, Sara Bellis, Anthony Bennett, Tim Bernhard, Anne Beverton, Carrie Bewick, Johnny Birks, Andrew Bissitt, Val Bourne, Alison Brackenbury, John Bradbeer, Fleure Bradnock, Allan and Gloria Brandon, Andrew Branson, Loraine Bridge, Margaret Bristow, Henri Brocklebank, Ruth Brompton-Charlesworth, Liz Brownlee, Victoria Burge, John F. Burton, Roger Butterfield, Jonathan Bye, Dr Amanda Callaghan, Professor Rob Cameron, Richard Chadd, Arthur Chater, Lynette Choppin, Ayesha Chouglay, Dr David Clarke, Sylvia Coates, Anna Coburn, Frances Cooke, Rachel Costigan, Jerry Cotter, Terry Coult, Karen Cox, Hana Cree, Alasdair Cross, Sally Cryer, John Davis, John Dellow, Graham Dixon, Jeremy Doe, Jo Dunn, Michael Easterbrook, Rosemary Eaton, Peter Eeles, Rachelle Evans, Sue Everett, Gary Farmer, Clive Farrell, Lynn Fomison, Dr Garth Foster, Richard Fox, Terry Franklin, Brian Gardiner, Tim Gardiner, Karl Goswell, Penny Green, Suzanne Gyseman, Robin Hamilton, Margaret Hansen, David Harding, Basil and Annette Harley, Dr Eileen Harris, Elizabeth Harris, Debbie Harrison, Jack Harrison, Lorraine Harrison, Miles Harrison, Neil Harvey, Adam Harwood, Tony Harwood, Colin Hawes, Trevor Hiorns, Penelope Hoare, John Hodgkin, Jo Hodgkins, Paul Holt, Pat Honeybone, Andy Horton, Jon Hudson, Libby Ingels, Julia Jacs, Professor Ed Jarzembowski, Dee Jarvis, Janet Jarvis, Judith Jones, Nigel Jones, Rosy Jones, Farmer Jonesy, Roger Key, Jane Kiely, Adrian Knowles, Richard Lewington, Owen Leyshon, Julia Lohmann, Tom Long, Martin Looker, Richard Lord, M. Jill Lucas, Dr Caroline Macafee, Mrs B. McGlen, Colin McLeod, Sam Maddocks, Quentin Mair, Jan Miller, Janet Moore, Paul Morgan, Geoff Morries, John Morris, Leonard New, Patricia L. Orr, Dr Geoff Oxford, Kevin Page, Steve Palin, Mark Parsons, John Pellat, Neil Pinder, Julia Plumptre, Colin Pope, Tom Prescott, Dr Roger Prior, Alex Ramsay, Sara Reading, Ivor Rees, Debbie Rendall, Professor Chris Richardson, Hannah Rigden, Jamie Roberts, James Robertson, Liz Robertson, Roger Robinson, Charlie Routh, John Rowe, Mike Savage, Dick Seamons, Louise Searl, Caroline Searle, Dallas Seawright, Michael Shannon, Matt Shardlow, Allan Shepherd, David Sheppard, Paul Shipton, David Shirt, John Showers, Alan Showler, Helen Shute, Lorna Sokolowski, Philip H. Smith, Rebecca Smith, Terry Smith, Peter Smithers, Sheila Somerville, Alice Starmore, C. R. Stevenson, Dr Alan Stewart, Malcolm Storey, Professor David Streeter, Angela Thompson, Annabelle Tipper, Sini Tipper, Tony Tipper, Lawrence Trowbridge, Judy Vickery, Gwen Walker, Ian Wallace, Paul Waring, Martin Warren, Giles Watson, Will Watson, Brett Westwood, Andrew Whitehouse, Matthew Wilde, Dominica Williams, Martin Willing, John Wiscombe, John Wright, Dr Mark Young.

I particularly thank my old friend James Robertson for putting out feelers for insect encounters in Wales. Sincere thanks, too, to Malcolm Scoble at the Natural History Museum, Peter Smithers at Plymouth University and Roger Key, formerly at Natural England, for their close and constructive interest in our project.

Our text was very kindly expert-checked by the following: David Baldock (Hymenoptera), Max Barclay and Andrew Duff (beetles), Professor Robert Cameron (slugs and snails), Stephen Cham (dragonflies), Garth Foster (water beetles), Eileen Harris (parasitic worms), Dr Andrew Cabrinovic (echinoderms), Helen Read (woodlice, centipedes and millipedes), Peter Smithers (spiders), Alan Stubbs (flies), Martin Warren (butterflies), Paul Waring (moths), Martin Willing and John Llewellyn-Jones (sea shells), Dr Mark Young (freshwater mussels). The responsibility for any remaining mistakes in the text is of course our own.

There would have been few public contributions without friends to help spread the message. We thank first Matt Shardlow and Buglife for supporting the project from the outset. *Bugs Britannica* was the lead item in the first of the new series of the 'Shared Earth' on Radio 4 in May 2007, courtesy of Brett Westwood and Dylan Winters, and we got a mention in dispatches on *Springwatch*. Mike McCarthy gave us a splendid two-page launch in the *Independent*, and *BBC Wildlife* gave us a whole article in August 2007. Simon Barnes gave us an encouraging boost in *The Times,* and Andrew Branson allowed me space to run a couple of long articles and many reminders in *British Wildlife*. The Royal Entomological Society hosted a lecture on the project at their annual conference in 2008. The following journals ran articles or newslines about the project: *Atropos* (journal for Lepidoptera and dragonflies), *Bulletin* of the Amateur Entomological Society, *Butterfly* (journal of Butterfly Conservation), *Ecos*, *Isopoda* (newsletter of the British Woodlouse Study Group), *Latissimus* (newsletter of the Balfour-Browne Club), *Newsletter* of the British Arachnological Society, *Newsletter* of the Dipterist's Forum, *Mollusc World* (Journal of the British Conchological Society). We thank Stella Brecknell, librarian of the Hope Department, Oxford, for her assistance in running down obscure journals, and Claudine Fontana, librarian at the Natural History Museum, for various services including images of the new 'cocoon' wing at the museum.

I thank my old friends Bob Gibbons and Roger Key for generously allowing us to make use of their vast collections of insect images.

At Chatto & Windus, we thank Penny Hoare and her assistant Parisa Ebrahimi for their constant support and understanding during the lifetime of the project, and Paul Herbert who created the *Bugs Britannica* blog site. As page designer, we were lucky to have Peter Ward, who previously designed *Birds Britannica.* Rosamund Kidman Cox edited the text with her customary skill and expertise, and we owe an enormous debt to Penny for her many comments and excellent suggestions on the text. And finally I thank Sue, partly for putting up with my droning on about bugs for what must have seemed many years but also for her constant suggestions and encouragement.

Peter Marren,
December 2009

CREDITS

We would like to thank the following for the use of the pictures listed below according to page number. Every effort has been made to trace the holders of copyright in text and illustrations. Should there be inadvertent omissions or errors, the publishers will be pleased to correct them in future editions.

TOM ADAMS 215

STEVE ALTON AND THE CASTLE ROCK BREWERY 301

KIM ATKINSON 471

BARCLAY'S GROUP ARCHIVES 33/875 162

AMY BARTLETT WRIGHT 173

GRAHAM BATHE 136t, 236

ANTHONY BENNETT 307

TIM BERNHARD 226, 227

BRIDGEMAN ART LIBRARY ix, 35tl, 42, 46, 78, 79, 98, 100, 102, 105br, 129, 142, 159, 160, 199, 203, 206, 211, 256, 266, 298, 351tr, 390, 398, 400, 415, 417, 418, 448, 458

BUCKFAST ABBEY HOME APIARY 402

ANDREW DUNN 449tr

SUE EVERETT 73

NANCY FARMER 258

ROBIN FORD/WATKINS AND DONCASTER 212

GETTY IMAGES/HULTON ARCHIVE 241 GETTY IMAGES/ROGER VIOLLET 219 GETTY IMAGES/PHOTODISC 414

JENNIE HALE 340

HALL AND WOODHOUSE 309

ANNABEL HARRIS 67bl, 300

INSECTCIRCUS. CO.UK 332

ROGER KEY 30, 43, 87tl, 90, 107br, 117, 123, 153, 154br, 167tl, 186, 187, 188, 189, 192, 204, 205, 207, 221, 239, 242, 263bl, 275tl, 287tr, 299, 310tl, 310b, 314, 326, 364tr, 364br, 365, 368, 379, 380bl, 381, 392tl, 423, 434

ANNA KIRK-SMITH 57, 431

JONATHAN LATIMER 289

RICHARD LEWINGTON 272, 280

LIVERPOOL CITY MUSEUMS AND GALLERIES 162tl

JULIA LOHMANN 297

JILL LUCAS 70, 85, 92, 191, 278, 294

HARRIET MEAD 118, 137

GRAEME MITCHISON 442tr

JILL MOGER 275tr

CHARLOTTE MORETON 138

CLAIRE MOYNIHAN 282–3

CAROL MULLIN 323, 360, 394

NATIONAL GALLERIES OF SCOTLAND 149tr

NATIONAL GALLERY, LONDON 276

NATURAL HISTORY MUSEUM i, 4, 6t, 6br, 15tr, 22, 33tl, 33r, 54, 64, 95, 97, 120, 122, 124, 143, 144, 148, 150tr, 150br, 201, 216, 229tl, 237, 249, 261, 265, 319, 321, 330, 336, 356, 460tl, 461

NATURAL IMAGE David Element 232b, 380br, Bob Gibbons 16, 93, 130tl, 134, 136b, 165, 179, 181, 202, 209, 217, 219tl, 254, 260, 262, 269, 313, 334, 337, 349, 374br, 376tr, 377, 393, 446–7, 473, Alec C. Harmer, 222–3, Peter Wilson 1, 316, 317, 335, 366, 367, 372, 373, 421, 422

NATUREPL.COM John Cancalosi 463, Phillipe Clements 358, 453, Simon Colmer 430br, Andrew Cooper 346tr, Christophe Courteau 426, 438, Sue Daly 12, 15tl, 17, 21, Damschen/ARCO 305, Adrian Davies 253, 287tl, Geoff Dore 94, Paul Hobson 274, Ross Hoddinott 244, 247, 468, Alan James 19, Christophe Keppel 233, Willem Kolvoort 11, 24, Thomas Lazar 255, Bengt Lundberg 286, Conrad Maufe 44, Meul/ARCO 127, 132, 351tl, 353, Andy Sands 73t, Gary K. Smith 210, 440, 442tl, Sinclair Stammers 49, 469, Kim Taylor 14, 141, 229tr, 342, 392tr, 405, 444, David Watts 41

NHPA 107tr, 324–5, 378, 384, 435, 460bl, 474–5, Jim Bain 74, 75, Anthony Bannister 59, 154t, 355, 380tl, George Bernard 62, 430tl, Simon Booth 183, Mark Bowler 77tr, John Brackenbury 155, 386, N. A. Callow 51, 83, 88–9, 91, 116, 119, 194, 411, Gerry Cambridge 185, 428, Laurie Campbell 376tl, 436, 441, Bill Carter 263br, Stephen Dalton vi, vii, 43tl, 47tl, 101, 109, 110, 112, 113tl, 114, 115, 128, 130–1, 133tl, 147, 152, 156, 169, 176, 182, 190, 214, 264, 281, 292, 302, 315, 339, 343, 346tl, 350, 354, 362, 369, 374bl, 382, 397, 408, 413, 425, Martin Garwood 108, David Hueclin 170, 363, 455, Ernie Janes iv, v, 76tl, 76–7, 172, 388, 450, 465tl, Yves Lanceau 69, 80, Jean-Louis Le Moigne 184, Lutra 67br, 87br, Trevor MacDonald 52, 464, David Maitland 385, Linda Pitkin 72, 466, Dr Eckert Pott 113tr, Mark Smit 56, Robert Thompson 267, 271, 279, 423, 445, David Tipling 407, Roy Waller 429, 472, Daniel Zupanc 359

PHOTOSHOT Charles Hood 71, Richard Revels 285, 383, David Woodfall ii–iii, 196

JAMES ROBERTSON 403

ROYAL MAIL GROUP 164, 232tl, 424

MARK SCASE/TONY SCASE NEWS SERVICE LTD. 419

SHELL INTERNATIONAL LIMITED 449b

ERIC SMEE 465tr

PETER SMITHERS 133tr, with Lydford School 126

MALCOLM STOREY 291

TATE & LYLE 401

RICHARD TRATT 246

WIM VAN EGMOND 3, 7, 8, 9tl, 9tr, 13, 25, 26, 27, 28, 29, 38, 61, 63, 65, 66

JOHN WALTERS 158, 284

WELLCOME COLLECTION 47tr, 304, 328

WIKIPEDIA COMMONS 35tr, 37, 39, 53, 105tl, 149tl, 162tr, 195tl, 195tr, 268, 344, 474

CHRIS WILSON, HALLSON GARDENS 167

We also thank the following for permission to quote from copyright material: The Society of Authors (Virginia Woolf, *The Death of the Moth*), Attila the Stockbroker at attilathestockbroker.com (*The Rat-tailed Maggot*), Jonathan Cape (Julian Barnes, *A Short History of the World*), Faber & Faber (L.P. Hartley, *The Shrimp and the Anemone*), Enitharmon Press (George Macbeth, *The Wasps' Nest*), Rob MacFarlane (published works by Roger Deakin), the Flanders & Swann Estates (*The Spider in the Bath*).

INDEX